# Contemporary Human Behavior Theory

## A CRITICAL PERSPECTIVE FOR SOCIAL WORK

Third Edition

# Contemporary Human Behavior Theory

## A CRITICAL PERSPECTIVE FOR SOCIAL WORK

### Susan P. Robbins
*University of Houston*

### Pranab Chatterjee
*Case Western Reserve University, Emeritus*

### Edward R. Canda
*University of Kansas*

**Allyn & Bacon**

Boston   Columbus   Indianapolis   New York   San Francisco   Upper Saddle River
Amsterdam   Cape Town   Dubai   London   Madrid   Milan   Munich   Paris   Montreal   Toronto
Delhi   Mexico City   São Paulo   Sydney   Hong Kong   Seoul   Singapore   Taipei   Tokyo

**Editorial Director:** Craig Campanella
**Editor in Chief:** Dickson Musslewhite
**Executive Editor:** Ashley Dodge
**Editorial Product Manager:** Carly Czech
**Director of Marketing:** Brandy Dawson
**Executive Marketing Manager:** Jeanette Koskinas
**Senior Marketing Manager:** Wendy Albert
**Production Manager:** Meghan DeMaio
**Editorial Production and Composition Service:** Kalpana Venkatramani / PreMediaGlobal
**Printer/Binder/Cover Printer:** R. R. Donnelley & Sons
**Creative Director:** Jayne Conte
**Cover Designer:** Suzanne Behnke
**Cover Image:** Vetta Stock photo/Istockphoto

Credits appear on appropriate pages, which constitutes an extension of the copyright page.

**Library of Congress Cataloging-in-Publication Data**

Robbins, Susan P.
  Contemporary human behavior theory : a critical perspective for social work / Susan P. Robbins, Pranab Chatterjee, Edward R. Canda.—3rd ed.
    p. cm.
  Includes bibliographical references and index.
  ISBN-13: 978-0-205-03312-6 (alk. paper)
  ISBN-10: 0-205-03312-1 (alk. paper)
  1. Social service.  2. Human behavior.  3. Social ecology.  I. Chatterjee, Pranab, 1936–  II. Canda, Edward R.  III. Title.
  HV40.R575 2012
  361—dc22

                                                                2010053558

12  16

**Allyn & Bacon**
**is an imprint of**

www.pearsonhighered.com

ISBN-10: 0-205-03312-1
ISBN-13: 978-0-205-03312-6

*There is nothing so practical as a good theory.*
—Kurt Lewin

*There is no theory that is not beset with problems.*
—Karl Popper

*There is nothing as harmful as a bad theory.*
—Bruce Thyer

# CHAPTER CO-AUTHORS
# AND CONTRIBUTORS

**Barbara Becker, MPH**
late

**Brené Brown, PhD**
Research Professor
*University of Houston*
*Graduate College of Social Work*

**Thomas M. Brown, PsyD**
Psychologist
*Orem, Utah*

**David Lawson Burton, MSW, PhD**
Associate Professor
*Smith College*
*School for Social Work*

**Graciela Couchonnal, PhD**
Program Officer
*Health Care Foundation of Greater*
*Kansas City*

**Cynthia Franklin,**
**PhD, LCSW, LMFT**
Professor
*University of Texas at Austin*
*School of Social Work*

**Fernando J. Galan, PhD,**
**LMSW-ACP**
late

**David Hussey, PhD**
Clinical Director
*Beech Brook of Cleveland*

**James McDonnell, PhD**
Associate Professor
*University of Tennessee at Chattanooga*

**Beverly McPhail, PhD**
Director
*University of Houston*
*Women's Resource Center*

**Fred Richardson, PhD**
Professor Emeritus
*University of Texas at Austin*
*Department of Educational Psychology*

**Mende Snodgress, JD, LCSW**
MHMRA of Harris County
*Houston, TX*

**Kimberly Strom-Gottfried, PhD**
Professor
*University of North Carolina at Chapel Hill*
*School of Social Work*

**Joanne Yaffe, PhD**
Associate Professor
*University of Utah*
*College of Social Work*

# CONTENTS

# FOREWORD

Theories of human behavior have been one of the foundational elements of professional knowledge for social work throughout its 100-year history. The profession rose out of twin impulses: helping people constructively surmount the problems of daily living and trying to understand why this goal often proves difficult to achieve. Theories about human development and human motivation became a lifeline in trying to make sense of this mysterious and extremely complex area of study.

The typical route to helping students learn about human behavior has been the presentation of a small array of theories, the choice influenced by the historical period, and the intellectual preferences of a school and its faculty. In some cases, students of a particular period might study in great depth only one theory as the theoretical basis for their practice. In a more common approach, students are introduced to a variety of theories, each presented as having equal footing with its peers. Students are then left to weave together bits of this and that to serve as a theoretical orientation to their practice. The first instance may lead to dogmatism—a belief that one particular theory is sufficient to inform practice. The second instance may lead to relativism—that every theory is equally useful in shaping a view of how human beings grow and change.

In social work education, it is rare to find a text that consciously sets out to present theory from a critical perspective. To do so, it is necessary to create a context larger than the theory to be studied. If the only issue guiding investigation is to understand what authors intend, then students learn to describe, analyze, and apply each theory, but they do not learn the art of critique. What this book presents in a comprehensive way is the art and discipline of critique.

The basis for critique is a framework of concerns against which any theory can be judged. As the authors so well present, the context of theory is filled with large preoccupations: ideological positions, beliefs about what is normal and what is good, and constructions about how people grow and change. This context is stretched to become even larger by adding the social, political, and economic environments within which theory develops and is put to use. By bringing this level of analysis to the study of human behavior theory, students not only learn the substance of a theory in a straightforward way, they also learn how to stand apart from a theory and systematically compare it with other theories. The act of creating a set of concerns by which to evaluate theory gives students a different standpoint. They are no longer passive consumers of what is put before them. Instead, they become active knowers, whose critique of theory gives them the power to assign their own judgments to the results. In this way, the study of human behavior theory can help achieve the sophisticated, complex, and independent thinking required of good social work practitioners.

The authors have developed an impressively comprehensive presentation of theories for faculty teaching human behavior. Their inclusion of theories of empowerment, phenomenology, social constructionism, hermeneutics, and transpersonal theory is particularly notable because it brings needed attention to points of view not typically presented in such full and careful fashion. Also in contrast with existing texts, the array of theories focusing on broader cultural, political, and economic perspectives offers a useful antidote to the insistent attention given to individual and family functioning. In every case, students are asked to consider each theory in light of its value roots and consequences, its inclusiveness, and its essential view of who people are and what makes them tick.

In this text, Robbins, Chatterjee, and Canda have taken the study of human behavior theories to a new level. In both substance and approach, they have established a new ground from which students can view and interact with theory and its consequences. Theirs is an ambitious and intellectually challenging approach, couched in a readable and reflective style. It is also a courageous book. They have consciously chosen to focus on the issues surrounding the study of theory and, in doing so, will assuredly raise the consciousness (and conscience) of readers. A critical perspective is ultimately a value-based approach, in which professional values become an explicit, rather than submerged, element of focus. Calling theory to task for its assumptions about human development and its consequences for practice inserts a level of analysis and reflection essential to competent practice. This process is demanding, but it promises to more surely guide social work toward its roots as a value-based profession. The authors deserve special recognition for accomplishing this very significant task.

*Ann Weick, PhD*
*Professor Emerita and Former Dean*
*University of Kansas*
*School of Social Welfare*

# PREFACE

In revising this textbook for the third edition, we retained the overall structure of the first two editions and added new theory content that we believe is critical for social work practice at the beginning of the 21st century. In addition to many chapter updates, exciting new additions to the theory base are:

- A full chapter on feminist theory
- Wilber's full integral theory, which includes and transcends transpersonal experience
- Knowledge about normal childhood sexuality
- Expanded content on successful aging and geotranscendence
- Expanded content on lesbian, gay, bisexual, transgender, queer, questioning and intersexed (LGBTQI) persons

There is no question that human behavior is complex. It is this very complexity that makes it difficult to design a single textbook that adequately covers the knowledge base necessary for courses in the Human Behavior in the Social Environment (HBSE) curricular area. Most textbooks are based on either a social-systems perspective or a life-span development approach, although some have now attempted to incorporate a slightly broader range of theory while retaining an overall systemic or life-span approach. Books utilizing a social-systems perspective typically have been organized according to systems levels; thus, content on individuals, groups, families, organizations, institutions, and communities has been divided into separate chapters. In contrast, those texts utilizing a life-span approach have been organized the same way as life-span textbooks found in psychology, with each chapter reflecting a different stage of the life span.

Although systems theory and developmental theory are important components of human behavior knowledge, we believe that by themselves, they reflect a rather narrow and individualistic definition of human behavior and an underlying ideology that is, at its heart, politically conservative.

We wrote this textbook with several purposes in mind. First, we hope to broaden the scope of our social-work knowledge base about human behavior. Rather than relying on the largely psychological (and traditional) approach to human behavior that utilizes a person-in-environment framework, we have adopted a broader definition of human behavior that focuses on the person *and* the environment, giving equal focus to each.

Second, we hope to expand our theoretical base in understanding human behavior. We have chosen a multidisciplinary theoretical approach that incorporates relevant theory from a variety of social and human science disciplines that have traditionally been omitted from HBSE textbooks.

Third, we hope to illuminate the fact that *all* knowledge about human behavior is socially constructed and thus is inherently value-laden and ideological. As such, our knowledge base reflects the values, concerns, and ideologies of not only the authors constructing theories and studies but also the prevalent values, concerns, and ideologies of the existing social order (historical or contemporary).

Finally, and perhaps most importantly, we hope to encourage critical thinking about the knowledge and theories that we choose for practice. To accomplish this, we believe that it is important to use consistent standards to evaluate each theory and to provide a discussion and critique of alternative views and an analysis of the social, ideological, and economic structures of society that impact individual problems. Most often, critical thought and analysis of this nature have been omitted from human behavior textbooks in social work.

Above all, we hope that this book will be intellectually challenging to BSW, MSW, and PhD students alike and that it will encourage you, the reader, to question some of your most deeply held assumptions about why people behave the way they do and to better understand the role of various influences on human behavior.

# ACKNOWLEDGMENTS

This book would not have become a reality without the support and assistance of many people. First and foremost, we thank Carolyn Brooks, who provided consistent secretarial support and encouragement throughout this entire first edition of this project. In addition, we would like to thank Darlyne Bailey, Hwi-Ja Canda, Manjirnath Chatterjee, Marian Chatterjee, Jim Daniel, Richard L. Edwards, Bob Fisher, Howard Goldstein (in memorium), Karen S. Haynes, Karen A. Holmes, Darlene Hurt, Joe Kotarba, Daniel B. Lee, Walter Lee, Elizabeth Loftus, Carole Marmell, Holly Nelson-Becker, Joe Paull (in memorium), Bill Simon (in memorium), Jack Taylor, Terri Thomason, and Ann Weick. Thanks to Sachiko Gomi for assistance with literature search and to Heather Larkin for a careful review of Chapter 12. We are also indebted to our many students and colleagues who gave us feedback on the early drafts of these chapters.

We also acknowledge our chapter coauthors and contributors Barbara Becker (in memorium), Brené Brown, Thomas M. Brown, David Lawson Burton, Graciela Couchonnal, Cynthia Franklin, Fernando Javier Galan (in memorium), David Hussey, James McDonnell, Beverly McPhail, Fred Richardson, Mende Snodgress, Kimberly Strom-Gottfried, and Joanne Yaffe.

In addition, we express our gratitude to the songwriters who contributed their lyrics to the book chapters: Rick Beresford, Bobby Bridger, Chris Chandler, Allen Damron (in memorium), Jim Daniel, Tom Dundee, Michael Elwood, Anne Feeney, Rex Foster, Tim Henderson, Anne Hills, Rod MacDonald, Susan Martin, Bill Muse, Phil Rockstroh, David Roth, Hans Theessink, and Bill Ward. Special thanks also go to Lendell Braud, Blair Powell (in memorium), and the Conroe Association of Live Music, and to Rod Kennedy, Nancylee Kennedy, Dalis Allen, and the Kerrville Folk Festival.

Thanks to reviewers Steve Applewhite, University of Houston; Sharon Moore, University of Louisville; Melanie Otis, University of Kentucky; Dana Sullivan, University of Louisville. We also express our thanks to the initial reviewers Paul Abels (California State University Long Beach), Beverly Black (Wayne State University), Eugene Jackson (Purdue University), Betty J. Kramer (University of Wisconsin-Madison), Ferol E. Mennen (University of Southern California), Georgianna Shepard (State University of New York, Brockport), and Elizabeth L. Torre (Tulane University) for their time and input.

Finally, we thank Ashley Dodge at Pearson and Beth Kluckhohn at PreMediaGlobal for their infinite patience and continued encouragement and assistance with this book.

# Contemporary Human Behavior Theory

## A CRITICAL PERSPECTIVE FOR SOCIAL WORK

# The Nature of Theories

## THEORIES

- explain and predict human behavior from micro to macro levels
- explain and predict the impact of larger social structures on human behavior
- explain and predict social problems
- guide social work practice
- inform social policy
- direct social work research
- give credibility to a profession
- are socially constructed and ideological

During the past few decades, the social work profession has witnessed the proliferation of textbooks on human behavior in the social environment. Although there is variation in both substance and design, these texts have all demonstrated a growing commitment to systematically integrating content about the social environment into our core knowledge of human behavior. With a few exceptions, most attempts to address linkages between the person and the environment have relied heavily on functionalist systems and ecological theories. We believe that although this is an important theoretical perspective, it has led to a rather narrow view of both the environment and human behavior. With this text, we hope to offer a more expansive view of both.

The task of covering essential human behavior content for social work practice is a formidable one at best. As Brooks (1986, p. 18) observed:

> If you are expected to be an expert on the biological, psychological, social, economic, and cultural dimensions of human behavior . . . you are undoubtedly a teacher of Human Behavior and the Social Environment.

Given that a single textbook cannot adequately cover comprehensive content from six or seven disciplines, we have made deliberate choices in our design of this text. We have chosen a comparative theoretical approach in which we critically compare and contrast the dominant human behavior theories primarily from the disciplines of social work, psychology, social psychology, sociology, and anthropology.

We believe that this contribution is necessary because studies on the human behavior curriculum have found social work courses and previous textbooks to be dominated by a systems or ecological perspective and a focus on individual life span development (Brooks, 1986; Fiene, 1987; Gibbs, 1986). In her analysis of course and text content, Fiene (1987, p. 17) concluded that "the addition of systems theory has not altered the continued dominance of the Neo-Freudian, life stages orientation." Although several recent textbooks have attempted to introduce a somewhat broader scope of theory and have included frameworks such as feminist theory, symbolic interactionism, and social constructionism, among others (R. R. Greene, 1999; Longres, 2000; Saleebey, 2001; Schriver, 2010), the overall orientation in social work has not changed significantly. An overriding psychological orientation to human behavior continues to persist, we believe, because of our failure to systematically incorporate substantive interdisciplinary theories into the human behavior curriculum. We hope that the theories presented in this text lead to a broader understanding of many of the complex forces that shape people's lives.

Recent and historical social work publications have discussed and debated the role and definition of theory and its utility for social work practice (Forte, 2006; Gomory, 2001; Simon, 1994b; Thyer, 1994, 2001). Although there are clearly different and contradictory viewpoints on this topic, we believe that a sound knowledge and understanding of theory is essential for social work practice. We discuss the reasons for this in this chapter.

## ORGANIZATION OF THE BOOK AND RATIONALE FOR SELECTION OF THEORIES

Chapter 1 presents a detailed discussion about the nature of theory, its social construction, the role of ideology in theory and practice, and the issues we believe need to be considered in a critical assessment of theory.

Chapters 2 through 6 draw from sociological, anthropological, feminist, empowerment, and social psychological theories as well as theories of political economy that teach us about various sociocultural contexts, structures, processes, and the dynamics of social life. These theories assist us in understanding persistent social conditions and problems such as oppression, poverty, homelessness, violence, and others that are particularly relevant to social work practice. They also aid us in our quest to more fully understand and appreciate human diversity, resiliency, and empowerment.

Chapters 7 through 13 draw from psychoanalytic, psychological, social psychological, and transpersonal theories that teach us about human growth, development, and functioning in various contexts. Although we do not include a separate chapter on biological theory, we do present discussion on the ongoing debate about nature versus nurture and explicit content on physical, biological, and motor changes over the life span. We also present findings of contemporary research about prenatal, neonatal, early childhood, and older age development, normal sexual development in children, and the nature and development of memory.

Finally, Chapter 14 summarizes the previous chapters, compares and contrasts the various theories, provides an application of the theories to a case situation, and outlines some challenges for achieving theory-based practice in social work.

To allow for critical comparison among and between theories, every theory chapter is organized to reflect the following common content:

- a brief overview of the theory
- a discussion of the theory's historical context
- an overview of the theory's key concepts
- a discussion of the theory and its variants
- a discussion of contemporary issues related to the theory
- a discussion of the theory's application to social work practice
- a critical analysis of the theory (which we discuss in more detail later in this chapter)
- a summary

The theories contained in this book represent a wide range of historical and contemporary thought that we believe to be essential in understanding human behavior. We also include some insights from time-tested philosophical and cultural traditions that help stretch understanding beyond conventional Eurocentric thinking. Human behavior is complex; the numerous internal and external forces that interact and shape our personalities, preferences, ideas, beliefs, and actions cannot be explained by any one theory or discipline. With great deliberation we have chosen theories that help us understand the relationship of the individual to society and the relationship of society to the individual. In addition, these theories should help us to achieve a fuller understanding of the complex biological, psychological, social, cultural, spiritual, economic, political, and historical forces that shape our behavior as human beings.

However, this book's organization according to theories rather than levels of social systems (as is common in many human behavior and social environment texts) may present a challenge to readers who are accustomed to analyzing human behavior in terms of its relationship to discrete and separate systems levels. As a profession, we have become so reliant on systemic approaches to human behavior content that it is sometimes difficult to see or appreciate other possibilities. In choosing a comparative theory approach that includes but is not limited to systemic thinking, we hope to open up new possibilities that include a critical approach to studying human behavior. Although this is currently being debated in the literature (Gibbs & Tallent, 1997), we concur with Gibbs that this is an area in which critical thinking is necessary.

To help the reader identify content relevant to individuals, groups, families, organizations, institutions, and communities, Table 1.1 indicates the chapters containing relevant content on each of these systems levels. In addition, in our critical analysis at the end of each chapter we evaluate how applicable each theory is to these varying levels of systems.

**TABLE 1.1**  Chapter Content on System Levels

| System Level | Chapter |
| --- | --- |
| Individuals | 2, 3, 4, 5, 6, 7, 8, 9, 10, 11, 12, 13 |
| Groups | 2, 3, 4, 5, 6, 10, 12, 13 |
| Families | 2, 5, 6, 8, 10 |
| Organizations | 1, 2, 3, 4 |
| Institutions | 2, 3, 4, 5, 6, 8, 10, 12, 13 |
| Communities | 2, 3, 4, 6, 10, 13 |

In addition, it is important to understand how the content of this book fits with the new Council on Social Work Education Educational Policy and Accreditation Standards (Council on Social Work Education, 2008) that mandate competency-based education. Table 1.2 identifies where the competencies are addressed in each chapter.

## WHY STUDY THEORIES OF HUMAN BEHAVIOR?

The knowledge explosion that has accompanied the technological advances of the 20th century has generated a wealth of information about people, their behavior, and the various contexts in which they interact and live. Theories, first and foremost, help us organize this vast information.

The term *human behavior* has classically been used in social work to refer to behavior of the individual with rather limited attention to contexts of larger social and natural environments (Besthorn & Canda, 2002; Coates, 2003a, 2003b). The concept of person-in-environment provides a good example of this individualistic focus. Other disciplines, however, use a broader definition of human behavior to include the behavior of groups, families, communities, organizations, cultures, and societies within global and earth ecological contexts. Because the focus of this text is on interdisciplinary theories, we have adopted the broader of the two definitions.

Theories help us conceptualize how and why people behave the way they do, and help us understand the contextual nature of behavior. The term *context* refers to the settings and social groups in which human behavior takes place; these contexts may be biological, physical, psychological, sociocultural, spiritual, economic, political, historical, and natural environmental. Whereas some theories focus on the individual, the family, or the small group, other theories teach us about the larger social contexts or structures in which people operate (Bloom, 1985). The term *environment* is commonly used in the social work literature to describe these contexts, groups, and structures. Because all human behavior is contextual, an understanding of people must also include an understanding of these contexts.

Theories also help us focus our attention on the intrapsychic dynamics of psychological processes as well as the interpersonal and transpersonal dynamics of social life. Knowledge of each is critical to an understanding of human behavior. The pervasive psychological orientation in social work has provided us with substantial expertise in the former while neglecting the latter. Theories that emphasize power, ideology, spirituality, political and economic differences, and the natural environment are an often excluded but necessary part of the interdisciplinary knowledge base that is essential for professional practice.

Finally, and perhaps most importantly, the theories we use as social workers shape the way in which we view our clients. They shape the questions we ask, the assessments we make, and ultimately the interventions we choose. We believe, therefore, that it is important for social workers to expand their theoretical knowledge base and to develop a broader understanding of human behavior.

### The Macro–Micro Continuum

The wide variety of theories covered in this book represents not only different disciplines but also different levels of abstraction and explanation about contexts and social groups. Macro-level theories are usually highly abstract and general and attempt to explain the structure and functioning of large entities such as societies, cultures, and communities. Meso- (or mid-) level theories are less abstract, are more testable, and explain "smaller components of social reality" (Chafetz, 1987). Meso-level

**TABLE 1.2** Connecting Core Competencies Chapter-by-Chapter Matrix

| Chapter | Professional Identity | Ethical Practice | Critical Thinking | Diversity in Practice | Human Rights & Justice | Research Based Practice | Human Behavior | Policy Practice | Practice Contexts | Engage, Assess, Intervene, Evaluate |
|---|---|---|---|---|---|---|---|---|---|---|
| 1 | X | X | X | | | X | X | | | |
| 2 | | X | X | X | X | X | X | X | X | X |
| 3 | | X | X | X | X | X | X | X | X | X |
| 4 | | X | X | X | X | X | X | X | X | X |
| 5 | | X | X | X | X | X | X | X | X | X |
| 6 | | X | X | X | X | X | X | X | X | X |
| 7 | | X | X | | | X | X | | X | X |
| 8 | | X | X | | | X | X | | X | X |
| 9 | | X | X | | | X | X | | X | X |
| 10 | | X | X | | | X | X | | X | X |
| 11 | | X | X | | | X | X | | X | X |
| 12 | | X | X | | | X | X | | X | X |
| 13 | | X | X | X | X | X | X | X | X | X |
| 14 | X | X | X | X | X | X | X | X | X | X |
| Total Chapters | 2 | 14 | 14 | 7 | 7 | 14 | 14 | 7 | 13 | 13 |

theories often focus on interactions between people, groups, and organizations. Micro-level theories are generally more concrete and specific and are therefore more testable. They are primarily used to explain individuals, small groups, and families.

We recognize, however, that not all theories are clearly placed on this continuum; in some cases there is overlap. Macro-focused theories are sometimes applied to individuals just as micro-focused theories are sometimes applied to societies. Meso theories are often applied to both.

We believe that broadening our theoretical knowledge allows us to become more flexible in moving back and forth along this continuum. The relevance of macro theory to clinical practice and micro theory to community practice becomes apparent as we discuss the applicability of each theory to all social system levels.

## THEORIES: WHAT ARE THEY?

The terms commonly used in discussions of theories are *theory, paradigm, model,* and *perspective*. Of these words, *paradigm* and *model* are often used interchangeably and usually represent a visual arrangement of two or more variables in graphic, tabular, or other pictorial form. *Paradigm* may also refer to a philosophical framework, such as positivist or postmodern paradigms. The word *perspective*, in contrast, simply translates as emphasis or view. We distinguish these from the term *theory*, with the acknowledgment that although we use them interchangeably, they are not in fact equivalent.

Theories, according to Chafetz (1987, p. 25):

> . . . consist of a series of relatively abstract and general statements which collectively purport to explain (answer the question "why?") some aspect of the empirical world (the "reality" known to us directly or indirectly through our senses).

Theories are constructed through a systematic process of inductive and deductive reasoning in our attempts to answer "why?" Dubin (1969, p. 9) suggested that theories are used for the pursuit of two distinct goals in the scientific study of human behavior: explanation and prediction. To understand theory construction, *explanation*, and *prediction*, it is important to understand the differences between empirical structures and theoretical structures. Empirical structures are those that we experience through our senses, in our environment. Theoretical structures are those that we "*construct in our mind's eye* [italics added] to model the empirical system" (Dubin, 1969, p. 9). In addition, theories prescribe ideal goals for human functioning and offer guidelines for therapeutic and social action designed to help people achieve their goals.

Thus, a theoretical structure is an abstraction; it is both a description and a generalization that stems from our experiences. As a result, the constructs, or concepts, of a theory become the tools with which we study human behavior and attempt to influence it in social work practice.

Most scholars believe that theories are important because few scientific ventures are possible without them. In Figure 1.1, we show how abstractions develop over a period of time. Without theoretical structures, it is difficult to understand and order information about the world around us; without empirical structures, we have no basis for theory.

Further, many theories are cumulative. Initially, a theorist may make an abstraction from one observation. Subsequent observations may lead to more abstractions, and these, in turn, may lead to controlled observations and scientific studies for the purpose of confirming these abstractions.

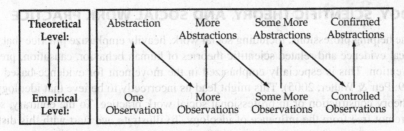

| Theoretical Level: | Abstraction | More Abstractions | Some More Abstractions | Confirmed Abstractions |
| Empirical Level: | One Observation | More Observations | Some More Observations | Controlled Observations |

**FIGURE 1.1.** The interdependence between theoretical and empirical structures.

The cumulative nature of theory may be based on one person's lifelong pursuit, or the collective pursuit of knowledge undertaken by several generations of scholars. Not all theories, however, are built cumulatively. As Chafetz (1987) pointed out, luck or serendipity often plays a role in theory development, as scholars sometimes experience a flash of insight from events or experiences unrelated to their research. Even when this is the case, the theorist must return to the process of description and generalization to build and refine the theory.

## THE SOCIAL CONSTRUCTION OF THEORIES

We can see from the preceding description that theories are based on constructs that arise from cognitive and experiential processes of individuals. They arise from social processes as well. All knowledge—including theoretical knowledge—is developed within a specific social, cultural, and historical context. These contexts, in turn, influence the content of theory.

In their classic book, *The Social Construction of Reality*, Berger and Luckmann (1966) argued that all knowledge, including our knowledge of what is "real," is socially constructed. By this they were referring to the fact that we are all born into an already existing society, and thus, "a given social order precedes any individual organismic development" (1966, p. 51). Predefined patterns of conduct and group definitions of what is real are socially transmitted and reinforced by social sanctions. We learn these group definitions through the process of socialization, and this knowledge becomes part of our worldview and ideology. We rarely stop to question these group definitions and, unless challenged, we take it more or less for granted that we see the world in the same way as everyone else does.

Theorists often operate under the same assumptions. Consequently, they bring their own cultural, class, and gender biases (to name a few) into their work. Not surprisingly, theories are often extensions of the theorists themselves. They reflect their concerns, values, and overall worldviews. Although this is not unusual, it becomes problematic when a theory claims to apply to all people.

Postmodern-oriented social work theorists draw on this awareness of the social construction of any theory (Witkin & Saleebey, 2007). They encourage critical and creative reflection about the underlying assumptions of particular theories, the personal and cultural vantages they represent, and who is advantaged or disadvantaged when the theories are applied to practice. This requires a process of dialogue between people who hold different theories, between people of different social locations and levels of power, and between and among theorists, practitioners, and clients. Through such a process, theories can be continuously refined, rejected when necessary, and applied in ways to fit the values of our profession and the goals of our clients and their communities.

## IDEOLOGY, SCIENTIFIC THEORY, AND SOCIAL WORK PRACTICE

Most of the helping professions, including social work, heavily emphasize practice that is based on empirical evidence and related scientific theories of human behavior, causation, prevention, and intervention. This is especially emphasized in the movement for evidence-based practice (Petr, 2009; Petr & Walter, 2005). This might lead us incorrectly to believe that ideology has no place in theory construction or in professional social work practice. To the contrary, scientific theories are not free from the influence of ideology. To illustrate, we start with this distinction: *Ideology* is a set of prescriptions, or "thou-shalt" and "thou-shalt-not" statements, whereas scientific *theory* is a set of abstractions derived from empirical observation that becomes subject to verification through the testing of predictions (called hypotheses).

Despite the veil of scientific objectivity, theories of human behavior are ideological in nature because they cannot be "free of material interests and uncompromised by moral and cultural commitments" (Brown & Martin, 1991, p. 11). Thus, their underlying assumptions are often associated with different political positions. As Campbell has noted (1981, p. 22):

> . . . theories are ideological in that even the most neutral-looking factual claims about social phenomena can be taken up and used in the competition between social groups for positions of power, wealth, and influence . . .

Further, theories of human behavior can become self-fulfilling or self-refuting based on our beliefs. Our beliefs about ourselves, our relationships, and our societies, for example, influence our actions, which, in turn, may serve to validate (or refute) a certain theoretical perspective (Campbell, 1981). A person who believes that early childhood experiences are the root cause of problems in adulthood tends to look for previously undiscovered traumatic experiences in her or his family of origin. This may intensify, create, or bring to the surface unpleasant memories that may have been less pronounced if she or he had believed that the source of the problem was rooted in present-day stressors. Similarly, theories that promote individuation as a developmental goal lead their adherents to seek independence rather than interdependence, thus validating one developmental path while refuting the other. Theories of human behavior are "in the complicated position of being a part of the reality they purport to analyze" (Campbell, 1981, p. 22). It is important, therefore, to understand not only the content of theories but also their practical and political implications. To accomplish this, we must be aware of the ideological underpinnings that are inherent in each theory so that we can subject each theory to thoughtful and critical analysis. The literature is replete with debates about value-free social science. It is our firm position that value-free social science is simply not possible.

Ideology is also present in all professional social work settings. It prescribes, for example, how a client should behave; the respective status of the client and the social worker; and whether, how, and how much the social worker should be paid.

For example, various views of evidence-based practice reflect different ideologies. A positivist approach to theory in social work, strongly influenced by the traditional medical model, says that practice should only be based on information about the effectiveness of interventions as determined by a narrow range of research methods, such as experimental and quasi-experimental designs, surveys, and statistical analysis (Witkin & Saleebey, 2007). This approach derives from European philosophers of science in the so-called Age of Rational Enlightenment. They counterposed the medieval emphasis on faith and religious authority with a commitment to rational thinking and physical observation as bases for knowledge. It reflects an ideology of objectivity and power to control research and practice vested in experts. While this type of evidence is useful, it is limited to questions and answers about human behavior framed in terms of physical observations, causality, and mechanistic interactions as determined by people who are outsiders to the situation. Hence, the understanding tends to be reductionistic and inapplicable to many real situations in practice settings.

More broad approaches, some of which are postmodern (and reacting against positivism), recognize the importance of understanding complex and dynamic behaviors and transactions in context and from the vantage point of those who actually live in the situations studied and of participants in research studies. They go beyond the previous kinds of research to also include ethical and professional value issues, client/consumer voices, culture-specific understandings, and evidence from qualitative research methods such as ethnography, grounded theory, and in-depth interviews (Petr, 2009). The understanding tends to be more situation-specific, contextual, and grounded in direct experience of clients, their communities, and human service practitioners. Indeed, various theories emphasize positivist and/or more context-sensitive types of research.

Flowchart 1.1 demonstrates how ideology directly influences the helping situation and indirectly influences both scientific theory and its related intervention strategies. Each society has its

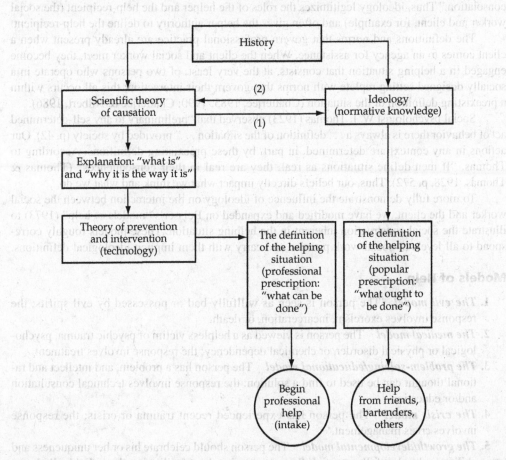

**FLOWCHART 1.1.** The interplay between scientific theory and ideology.  © 1998, S. P. Robbins, P. Chatterjee, & E. R. Canda

own unique history within which certain ideological traditions and scientific theories emerge. These, in turn, define the nature of the helping situation, be it medical, legal, psychological, or social.

Flowchart 1.1 illustrates that there are at least two ways to define a helping situation: (1) a professional definition, which emerges from the application of scientific theory but under the influence (often unknown) of existing ideologies; and (2) a popular definition, which develops from existing ideologies of society (or normative knowledge) and, often, a rather inadequate knowledge of scientific theory. Because there are many types of ideologies and, similarly, many types of scientific theories, we can understand why there are numerous professional definitions of the helping situation (variations of the pathway to the left) as well as many popular definitions (variations of the pathway to the right). These are not totally independent, however (as indicated by the two-way arrows between the two), and may at times influence each other directly or indirectly.

## The Definition of the Helping Situation: The Historical Context

According to Choi, Martin, Chatterjee, and Holland (1978, p. 157), ideology is an important factor in social work because it "(a) prescribes care-giving systems; (b) justifies and legitimizes who shall receive and what they shall receive; and (c) serves as a means of giving people hope and consolation." Thus, ideology legitimizes the roles of the helper and the help-recipient (the social worker and client, for example) and often gives the helper authority to define the help-recipient.

The definitions and norms that govern professional practice are already present when a client comes to an agency for assistance. When the client and social worker meet, they become engaged in a helping situation that consists, at the very least, of two persons who operate in a socially designed setting replete with norms that govern their interaction; this all occurs within a preexisting definition of the situation (Chatterjee, 1985, 1990; Chatterjee & Hilbert, 1986).

Social psychologist W. I. Thomas (1923) observed that "preliminary to any self-determined act of behavior there is always a . . . definition of the situation . . ." provided by society (p. 42). Our actions in any context are determined, in part, by these preexisting definitions. According to Thomas, "If men define situations as real, they are real in their consequences" (Thomas & Thomas, 1928, p. 572). Thus, our beliefs directly impact what we think and what we do.

To more fully demonstrate the influence of ideology on the interaction between the social worker and the client, we have modified and expanded on Beisser's "models of help" (1973) to illustrate the social construction inherent in the helping situation. These models roughly correspond to all levels of social work practice and carry with them implicit ideological definitions.

## Models of Help

1. *The evil model*    The person is seen as willfully bad or possessed by evil spirits; the response involves exorcism, incarceration, or death.
2. *The medical model*    The person is viewed as a helpless victim of psychic trauma, psychological or physical disorder, or chemical dependency; the response involves treatment.
3. *The problem-solving/educational model*    The person has a problem, and intellect and rational thought can be used to find a solution; the response involves technical consultation and/or education.
4. *The crisis model*    The person has experienced recent trauma or crisis; the response involves crisis management.
5. *The growth/developmental model*    The person should celebrate his or her uniqueness and ability to develop full potential; the response involves facilitating the individual's latent capacities.

6. ***The social issues/advocacy model***   The person is a victim of social forces or structural features of society; the response involves community organization or social advocacy.

7. ***The personal responsibility model***   The person is seen as unproductive, irresponsible, and dependent on society; the response involves minimal help with maximal policing.

8. ***The entitlement model***   The person has a right to a certain kind of help because she or he is a member of society; the response involves provision of services.

9. ***The deviance model***   The person is deviant and may also be sick; the response involves correction of deviant behavior and may also involve incarceration.

10. ***The self-help model***   The person is a victim of heredity, a dysfunctional family, external substances, or control by others; the response involves support and solidarity from like-sufferers. When guided by religious ideology, this often resembles the Twelve Step program developed by Alcoholics Anonymous.

Table 1.3 summarizes these models and their attendant ideology. Of particular importance is the second column in Table 1.3. Ideology circumscribes the roles of the helper and help-recipient by defining (1) who or what is to be blamed or held accountable for the situation, (2) what the help-recipient deserves, and (3) what the helper deserves. Ideology is also embedded in the helping situation itself because it both defines and sustains the context of helping as well as the interactions between the parties involved.

In addition to the historical context of ideological definitions, the helping situation is influenced by its organizational and professional contexts. All three are extremely important because together they encourage the use of some theories in the helping process, discourage others, and exclude yet even others.

## The Organizational Context

Although different types of organizational structures have been identified in the literature, all organizations are structured in such a way as to facilitate the processing of cases (or individuals) through the system. The specific model that any one agency uses is largely dependent upon its historical context, the professions involved in service delivery, and the service(s) being offered. In any case, all agencies are faced with a common problem of people management. To ensure that the services offered are correctly matched with the clients seeking the services, agencies must, of necessity, devise categories of clients that the agency is prepared to serve. Thus, an out-patient mental health facility is structured so as to serve only clients who seek mental health services that fall within the predetermined categories.

Implicit in the categorization of clients is an ideology about which model(s) of help the agency is based upon. This, in turn, defines the roles of the helper and help-recipient. As Pfuhl (1980, p. 166) noted, the organizational context of services is based on

> . . . a relatively clear definition of the nature of the problem and the clientele to be dealt with. Logically, this definition precedes assigning such responsibilities since, in the absence of a definition, no rational course of action is likely. For example, assigning responsibilities for a given problem to the police, medical, social welfare, or some other specialized agency requires a prior definition of that problem.

For example, an inpatient psychiatric hospital serves categories of patients based on specific diagnoses and utilizes the illness model, in which the professional helper is a therapist and the client is a patient. In contrast, a legal advocacy agency serves only categories of clients based on

| TABLE 1.3 | The Helping Situation | | | |
|---|---|---|---|---|
| **Definition of the Situation** | **Ideology** | **Helper** | **Help-Recipient** | **Disciplinary Custodian** |
| Evil | Blame a demon or the recipient. Recipient does not deserve sympathy. Helper deserves sacred status and payment from society | Exorciser | Possessed | Medieval clergy |
| Personal responsibility | Blame recipient who deserves minimal help. Helper deserves low policing status and payment by society | Policing | Chiseling | Early social work |
| Medical | Blame a disease. Recipient deserves sympathy. Helper deserves direct or third-party payment and high status. | Treatment agent | Patient | Medicine Nursing Social work Psychology Psychiatry |
| Problem | Blame malfunction. Recipient deserves knowledge. Helper, direct, or third-party payment, and somewhat high status. | Technical consultant | Client | Education Law Psychology Social work Psychiatry |
| Deviance | Blame recipient's behavior. He or she deserves to be corrected. Helper paid by society, deserves low status. | Correctional agent | Deviant | Law Medicine Psychology Psychiatry |
| Entitlement | Blame no one. Recipient deserves help without stigma and helper, paid by society | Clearing agent | Receiving agent | No disciplinary custodian |
| Crisis | Blame source of crisis. Recipient deserves sympathy and understanding. Helper deserves pay by either recipient or society, and varying status. | Crisis manager | Crisis victim | Clergy Medicine Psychology Social work Psychiatry |
| Growth | Blame the developmental phase. Recipient deserves education. Helper deserves direct or third-party payment and varied status | Facilitator | Responsible individual | Education Psychology Social work |
| Social issues | Blame society. Recipient needs restitution. Helper deserves some limited pay from third-party and varied status. | Advocate | Victim | Clergy Law Social work |
| Self-help | Blame outsiders (either people or substance). Recipient deserves solidarity. Helper deserves no pay, elder status. | In-group elder | In-group member | No disciplinary custodian |

*Source:* Adapted from P. Chatterjee and D. Bailey, 1993.

specific legal problems and utilizes the social issues model, in which the professional helper is an advocate and the client is a victim. Some agencies may be based on more than one model (such as a family service center) and may use, for example, a problem model, crisis model, and growth model. Direct service agencies may also utilize a social issues model if, for example, they are providing services to persons who have been the victims of elder abuse. Thus, the organizational context has a direct influence on the models and theories used in practice.

## The Professional Context

A final element that substantially influences the definition of the situation is the professionalization of the helper role. In the quest for professional status, social work's early adoption of psychoanalytic and psychodynamic theory led to an individual and intrapsychic view of people and ushered in a medical model of treating the sick. The quest for knowledge about neurosis, psychosis, and other emotional problems "helped facilitate the social workers' shift from a socio-economic to an individual-psychological base" (Trattner, 1984, p. 245).

Although our professional theory base has expanded greatly since the 1920s, psychodynamic thought, ego psychology, and psychological perspectives on the life span still dominate much of social work practice. The relatively recent addition of systems theory and the ecosystems perspective has led to a largely uncritical acceptance of these theories as the predominant paradigms used in most human behavior textbooks. An emphasis on family systems is also reflected in the contemporary literature and in the proliferation of books on that topic. To its credit, the focus on systems and ecosystems not only expanded our perspective of the environment but also shifted the definitions of the helping situation from illness to that of problem and growth. Despite this change, it is important to recognize that the current use of systems-based theories has largely retained a micro- and meso-level focus for direct practice rather than a broader focus for social action.

Perhaps not surprisingly, given the reliance of the profession on social approval, the theories that the profession has adopted and defined as central to our knowledge base tend to be politically conservative. We discuss and critique this in greater detail in Chapters 2 and 3. Clearly, in the struggle for increased professionalization, social work selected some theories of human behavior and omitted others—some by accident and others by design.

## DETERMINISM AND REDUCTIONISM: A PROBLEM OF SOCIAL CONSTRUCTION

When ideology, theory, and professional practice interact, a variety of problems emerge. Two important ones that we discuss here are determinism and reductionism. These, however, are not mutually exclusive and overlap at times. Together, they pose a very old dilemma in the philosophy of science and create a barrier to our understanding of the complexity of human behavior.

*Determinism* refers to the position that one phenomenon is caused (determined) solely by another phenomenon such as genetics, neurotransmission, biology, culture, or economy. Since human experience is affected by many different kinds of biopsychosocial, spiritual, and natural environmental factors, it is unlikely that any single deterministic view will provide an adequate understanding. Ideological biases sometimes establish the type of determinism involved. Take, for example, theoretical explanations of why children from poor families more often do poorly at school. Some may insist that poor performance is due to biological or genetic inferiority. Proponents of this position may even produce empirical evidence with impressive statistical armor. Others may explain the same situation by insisting that it is due to economic hardship;

they too may produce equally statistical armor. Here we have examples of biological determinism on one side and economic determinism on the other. When people are at war they often justify killing each other by insisting that they have God on their side; in controversial arguments they might denigrate each other by insisting that they have science on their side.

Differences in history and ideology lead to two basic forms of determinism: biological (including biogenetic and psychological) and environmental (including social, cultural, economic, etc.). As a consequence, we often see prescriptions and actions that claim their legitimation in scientific theory but, in reality, originate in ideology.

*Reductionism*, in contrast, is the problem posed by the claim that a certain phenomenon can be explained only by one specific discipline such as sociology, psychology, or economics. Not surprisingly, a person trained in a given discipline develops a great deal of loyalty to it. Loyalty to a discipline, occupational group, or a profession is often similar to that given to religion, politics, or even a football team. Reductionism also occurs when a holistic human phenomenon is reduced to simplistic explanation in terms of its component parts. For example, reductionism occurs when human consciousness is analyzed only in terms of biochemical and anatomical aspects of brain function. Thus, the human being is reduced to a machine. Of course, neurology is relevant to consciousness, but consciousness cannot be reduced to it.

To some extent, all theories are reductionist in the sense that they help us make sense of the world or some aspect of human behavior by identifying the most salient factors involved. It is literally impossible to take into account everything in the universe to understand a given topic. This is not a problem if a theory is clear in the way it is simplifying and is also clear about the usefulness and limitations of the simplification. Then, the theory is simplified but not simplistic. Unfortunately, theories and their proponents too often portray simplifications as the whole picture, which is, in actuality, an incomplete or false picture.

As we begin to better understand the role of theory in social work practice, we can expect to face ongoing problems caused by determinism and reductionism. Ideological bias, disciplinary loyalties, and simplistic analyses lead to these problems and they, in turn, shape the definition of the professional relationship.

For the most part, problems of determinism originate in various forms of ideology, whereas problems of reductionism originate from a scientific discipline that develops a given theory of causation. The two, however, may be closely related and often overlap. As we look back at Flowchart 1.1, we can see that most issues regarding determinism develop from the right pathway, whereas those of reductionism develop from the left pathway. Both have their own influences on the definition of the helping situation.

## THEORIES: APPLICATION TO PRACTICE

As discussed earlier, two of the main functions of theory are to explain and predict. In addition, theories are used to inform policy, guide practice, and direct research (Table 1.4).

Because of their explanatory and predictive nature, theories can inform us about social policies that are necessary to change the conditions of target groups or vulnerable populations. Macrolevel theories illuminate why some problems, such as oppression, homelessness, poverty, crime, and substance abuse, occur or persist. We can then use this knowledge in our attempts to change problematic conditions through policy design and implementation, class advocacy, and social action.

Theories further guide practice by providing social workers with conceptual frameworks that can be used to examine the "presenting problem" or aspirations of an individual, family,

**TABLE 1.4** Applications of Human Behavior Theories to Social Work Practice

| Functions | Macro-Level Theories | Micro- and Meso-Level Theories |
|---|---|---|
| Problem analysis | Social problem analysis | Personal, family, small group, or organization problem analysis |
| Identify vulnerability | Identify vulnerable populations | Identify vulnerable persons, families, and small groups |
| Develop assessments | Assess conditions of target groups and populations | Assess conditions of persons, families, small groups, and organizations |
| Guide practice | Guide community practice<br>Guide social action<br>Guide client advocacy | Guide clinical practice<br>Guide class advocacy<br>Guide administration practice |
| Inform policy | Inform social policy | Inform agency policy |
| Direct research | Sociological, cross-cultural, historical, political economy, and program evaluation research | Biological, psychological, clinical, historical, and organizational research |

group, organization, or community. They provide conceptual tools for describing what occurs in the lives of our clients and in the wider world. They are valuable tools for use in assessment of clients and client groups and of their situations and their environments. Theories also guide us in developing treatment or intervention plans to alleviate problems and enhance client functioning. They help us anticipate the likely outcomes of specific helping practices. Thus, theories are an important tool in guiding all levels of professional social work practice.

Theories also have an important role in directing research. Without a theoretical base, it is difficult to coherently interpret our observations. Basic research guides us in our attempts to learn the cause(s) of individual and group conditions and behaviors and thus adds to our cumulative knowledge of why certain things occur. In addition, applied research can help us determine, for example, whether our programs are effective or if specific interventions are successful.

Theories provide languages for professional discourse about human behavior and social work practice. Their key concepts encapsulate complex ideas concisely. Once we understand the theory's terminology, we can discuss a situation using a shorthand, but in a deep and insightful manner. When we discuss with colleagues who share understanding of the theory, we can communicate efficiently. The challenge is that each theory may have distinctive terms used in specific ways. Those unfamiliar with the theory may not understand the terms and perspective involved. So once we understand the languages of multiple theories, we become able to communicate with other professionals who work from those points of view and we can help to mediate between the theoretical perspectives. For example, as we will see, the term *ego* has different meanings for Freudians, ego psychologists, and transpersonal theorists. The well-educated social worker can understand, compare, and contrast the various meanings and their implications for practice.

Finally, the use of theories is necessary for professional credibility. Historically, it was proposed that social work did not merit the status of an established profession because it did not have a theoretical knowledge base (Flexner, 1915). Social work has since borrowed human behavior theories, primarily from the disciplines of psychology and medicine. The theoretical knowledge from sociology, anthropology, social psychology, and transpersonal psychology has been used to a lesser extent but has never been an integrated or central part of the human development curriculum (Coyle, 1988; Fiene, 1987). Although the ecological perspective is widely used as a framework for understanding human behavior, it offers little guidance in analyzing macro-level social problems that have an impact on people's lives. Its primary focus is on the interface between people and their environments, which is a meso-level interaction. However, its attention to the harmful effects of power disparities (Germain & Gitterman, 1995) may increase its usefulness for macro-level analysis in the future. Consequently, we believe that sophistication in the analysis of both social dynamics and human behavior is essential for our knowledge base and adds credibility to the social work profession. In addition, we hope that an expanded theory base helps us gain a more holistic view of people and helps to reintegrate our profession's original concern for social justice.

## CRITICAL ANALYSIS OF THEORY: THE MISSING DIMENSION

In our attempt to compare and contrast a variety of interdisciplinary theories, we believe that it is also important to add an element that is often absent in the social work literature—an analysis of each theory based on critical thinking. Given the inherently ideological nature of human behavior theory, it is crucial that theories be held open to intellectual analysis, criticism, and evaluation. We believe this must go further than a simple analysis of a theory's strengths and weaknesses, which are often presented as having equal merit. According to L. Gibbs and Gambrill (1996), critical thinking is a necessary component of professional practice that goes beyond an appraisal of the claims and arguments that may be embodied in a theory. It involves, for example, the use of specific standards in evaluating evidence and requires a fair and thorough critique of alternative views. Critical thinkers "question what others take for granted" (Gambrill, 2004, p. 3).

Further, due to the individualistic and psychological orientation to human behavior discussed earlier, we believe that it is especially relevant for social work that critical thinking also draws on the assumptions of critical theory to analyze the social, ideological, and economic structures of society and their impact on individual problems. According to critical theory, "Most individual problems are in fact social problems, caused by an inequitable social structure" (Findley, 1978, p. 55). Given the politically conservative theory base that has predominated social work (i.e., functionalist systems/ecological and psychosocial life span theory), we believe that the addition of this perspective is long overdue. We agree with Witkin and Gottschalk (1988, p. 218) that theories for social work practice should include "a reflexive element concerning its historical, cultural, and political/economic significance." It is only through analysis of this kind that we can demystify issues of power and truth and begin to examine alternative conceptualizations (Longres, 1995; Witkin & Gottschalk, 1988).

As we examine each theory presented in this book, we use the following questions as standards for a *critical analysis* of issues that are often taken for granted in most human behavior textbooks:

**1.** *What specific aspects of human development and human relations does the theory address and emphasize?*    (a) To what extent does the theory account for biological, psychological, and spiritual factors? (b) To what extent does the theory account for social, cultural, and economic forces?

Because theorists hold a variety of personal beliefs, interests, assumptions, and worldviews, it is not surprising that they are often interested in different aspects of human behavior.

This is reflected in the theories they construct and, consequently, in the dimensions of behavior that are included (and excluded) in their theories. Some theorists may focus on only one dimension (such as psychological processes), while others focus on several (such as social processes, physical growth, spiritual development, and the cultural context). It is important to analyze the dimensions that are addressed and to be aware of those that are excluded. Theories that appear to be at odds with one another may, in fact, simply be asking different questions and addressing different aspects of development (R. M. Thomas, 1985).

In addition, theorists give different emphasis to the dimensions they cover. A theorist may acknowledge biological, psychological, and social aspects of behavior but place primary emphasis on only one of these aspects. Theories that appear to be holistic because they include several dimensions may, in fact, be reductionistic or deterministic if only one aspect is seen as primary. It is not uncommon for a theory that appears, at first glance, to be holistic to place its emphasis on nature (biology) over nurture (environment) or vice versa.

Critical analysis of theory should help us recognize problems of determinism and reductionism as we examine the dimensions of behavior that are covered and emphasized in a given theory.

**2.** *What is the theory's relevance and application to individuals, families, groups, organizations, institutions, and communities?*    The contextual nature of human behavior may also vary from theory to theory. While some theories simultaneously focus on a variety of contexts or levels of social relationships and factors related to the larger environment, others do not. Previously, we referred to the level of abstraction and variety of contexts as the macro–micro continuum. Theories that start with the individual as the focal point may include either a narrow or broad range of contexts, social relationships, and environments in their attempt to explain the behavior of the individual; the same is true for theories that start with the group (such as a family, a culture, or a society) as the focal point. Similarly, some theories address a variety of contexts but place primary emphasis on only one. Analysis of theory should ideally entail an examination of the contexts and structural relationships that are included and excluded in the theory. It is especially important to know where in the micro–macro continuum the theory is most relevant and applicable.

This is extremely relevant because social work has for some time sought a meta- (or grand) theory that is applicable to all contexts and levels of social work practice. Although it has been claimed that certain theories have equal relevance and applicability to all levels of practice, critical thinking suggests that we cannot take these claims for granted.

**3.** *How consistent is the theory with social work values and ethics?*    As a helping profession, social work has embodied a set of values and ethics that are uniquely expressed in the design of our professional curriculum. These values include, for example, specific emphasis on helping people achieve optimal health and well-being, promoting respect for human diversity, and working toward the goal of empowerment for individuals and groups. Ethical practice mandates adherence to the profession's values.

Our psychodynamic/life span theory base has placed great emphasis on psychological and physical well-being. The addition of systems/ecological theory has also made us more aware of the issue of goodness of fit between people and their environments—especially social and physical. To more fully address issues related to oppression and discrimination we must expand this focus to explicitly include economic well-being. Similarly, if we are to see people more holistically, it is critical to address issues of spirituality as well.

In the social work literature (Bullis, 1996; Canda & Furman, 2010; Sheridan & Bullis, 1991; Sheridan, Bullis, Adcock, Berlin, & Miller, 1992), *spirituality* most often refers to a search for meaning, purpose, and moral standards for relationships between oneself, other people, the universe, and the ground of reality, understood in theistic, atheistic, animistic, or other terms.

Spiritual development may result in expansions of consciousness beyond the personal ego boundary into a profound sense of connection and union with others, the divine, or the fundamental nature of reality. It may also lead to a sense of personal wholeness, involving integration and balance between the biological, mental, and social aspects of our experience. Spirituality can also motivate action toward social justice as well as conflicting views of morality and justice. A person may or may not express *spirituality through religion*, which refers to formalized and organized patterns of belief, ritual, and mutual support shared by a community and developed over time.

Given these definitions, it is clear that there are numerous, diverse, and even conflicting religious and nonreligious spiritual perspectives that shape the lives of ourselves, our clients, our institutions, and social policies that surround us. Spirituality and religion pervade all social work settings in some way, so it is imperative that we consider the degree to which human behavior theories address these issues. The Council on Social Work Education's most recent statements of educational policies (1992, 2002, 2008) reincluded the topics of religious diversity and spiritual development after a gap of more than 20 years. Accordingly, we examine the issues of spirituality in each chapter and give this special consideration in the chapters on systems theories, moral development, and transpersonal theories.

Further, respect for human diversity is central to our value base. This is an important area for theory analysis because most theories claim to be universal; few are. This presents a very specific set of problems when considering human behavior in general and human diversity in particular. Because most theorists write from their personal and cultural frame of reference, attempts to generalize are often problematic, to say the least. Given that the vast majority of commonly used human behavior theories have been classically authored by white, middle-to-upper-class, Western European and American men (most of whom are now dead), it is not surprising to find biases of race, gender, culture, religion, sexual orientation, and social class inherent in most of them. Although there have been corrective tendencies in recent years (many of which contain their own—albeit different—biases), human behavior theory continues to be dominated by the ideas of dead white European American men and their protégés.

Admittedly, we use the term *dead white men* both seriously and tongue-in-cheek to make a point. The issue here is not who authors a given theory, but rather, to whom the theory is applied—and the consequences of that application. People are often seen as deficient when they do not fit a theory's constructs (Gilligan, 1982; Howard & Scott, 1981; Robbins, 1984). And because we rarely question the validity of a well-accepted theory, we come to question the validity and worth of the person instead. The ideological nature of theory often creates serious constraints on our ability to appreciate differences that do not conform to our mainstream social norms.

In contrast to other helping professions, social work has a specific commitment to understanding empowerment and human strength at both the personal and political levels (L. M. Gutierrez & Ortega, 1991; Hartman, 1993; J. Lee, 2001; Saleebey, 2009; Simon, 1994b; Weick & Saleebey, 1995). Empowerment is a proactive response to personal and societal forces that oppress and restrict human potential and well-being. In social work, we are especially concerned about ways to assist people who experience systematic forms of discrimination, harassment, and oppression. Therefore, it is imperative to examine the implications of theories for political consciousness-raising, enhancing self-efficacy, and supporting collective action. This is closely related to the *strengths perspective,* which guides social work practice to build on clients' personal and community talents, strengths, and resources to achieve their aspirations.

The strengths perspective emphasizes the human capacity for resiliency, courage, strength in the face of adversity, ingenuity in accessing and creating resources, and the right of individuals to form their own aspirations and definitions of their situations. As a value orientation, the strengths perspective rejects models of pathology that are widely used in social science to describe oppressed groups. Pathologizing oppressed populations results in a focus on deficit, illness, and problems. The strengths perspective is based on the assumption that people are most likely able to grow and develop when their strengths are recognized and supported (Rapp & Wintersteen, 1989; Saleebey, 2009; Weick, Rapp, Sullivan, & Kisthardt, 1989). Even when people identify challenges, troubles, and obstacles, social workers should not diminish them and their situations merely to diagnostic labels, problem preoccupations, or hopeless cases (Saleebey, 1996, 2009).The strengths perspective views all individuals and groups, regardless of their histories, as having value, capabilities, resources, skills, motivations, and dreams that must be considered when working with them such that they gain more control over their lives. This perspective offers a basis from which helpers become agents of the focus group or individual, and from which the group or individual is treated with dignity and respect and is regarded as having special expertise (Weick & Saleebey, 1995, p. 148).

Empowerment and strengths perspectives not only caution us to beware of theories that pathologize or blame the victim but also challenge us to cull the insights from theories that are conducive to self-actualization and social justice. Therefore, throughout this book we examine the implications of theories as they relate to people of color, gender issues, sexual orientation, dynamics of class and poverty, religious and spiritual diversity, and other forms of human diversity.

Thus, in evaluating a theory's consistency with social work values we must pay specific attention to the way in which it addresses—or fails to address—issues related to health, well-being, diversity, empowerment, strengths, and resiliency.

**4. *What are the theory's philosophical underpinnings?*** All theories in the social sciences contain certain assumptions that are philosophical in nature and cannot be studied scientifically. According to Haworth (1984), any scientific venture in theory construction includes assumptions that are often implicit. We have already discussed that theories contain underlying values and ideological preferences. In philosophical terms, this is the *axiology* of the theory. Two other important philosophical components are: (1) *ontology,* pertaining to assumptions about the nature of human nature, and (2) *epistemology,* pertaining to assumptions about how knowledge is or should be generated. These philosophical foundations then guide methods for research and social work practice.

Ontological statements pertain to a philosophical position or belief about the basic nature of humans and human interaction. Prior to the advent of formalized theory, philosophers throughout the centuries engaged in endless discourse and debates about subjects such as the nature of truth, the nature of people, and the nature of society. According to Durant (1961, xxvi), "Philosophy is a hypothetical interpretation of the unknown (as in metaphysics), or of the inexactly known (as in ethics or political philosophy) . . . ." As scientific reasoning replaced philosophical reasoning as the primary means for understanding human behavior, theorists (either consciously or unconsciously) incorporated philosophical assumptions, usually consistent with their personal beliefs, into their work. Thus, differences in theories are often a reflection of different philosophical assumptions or underpinnings.

For example, British philosopher Thomas Hobbes depicted human nature as basically self-serving and selfish; people were brutish loners in a primeval jungle. The popular phrase "looking out for number one" typifies this view. Because people were not innately cooperative, he believed that political coercion was necessary to prevent anarchy. By contrast, German philosopher Karl Marx believed human nature to be essentially altruistic. He saw people as basically giving beings who became corrupt when separated from the fruits of their labor (Israel, 1971). It is clear that the ontological assumptions of Marx are opposite to those of Hobbes. As we evaluate and compare theories, it is important to examine each theory's underlying ontological assumptions. The following are some questions that you might ask yourself as you read each chapter:

1. Are people assumed to be basically good or bad? Moral, immoral, or amoral? Are they born that way? Is it possible to change from this condition? How?
2. Is behavior believed to be based primarily on biology and genetics (nature) or the environment (nurture)? Is one seen as more primary than the other?
3. Do people have free will? Or is their behavior believed to be determined by internal or external forces outside their control?
4. Are people seen as ill or deviant and in need of medical, psychological, and social intervention? Or are they seen as healthy and adaptive?
5. Are social relations portrayed as being basically competitive or cooperative? Is the "glue" of society and social life based on consensus or conflict?
6. Can society and social organization be explained through an understanding of individual behavior? Or can individual behavior be explained through an understanding of society? Which takes primacy?
7. What behaviors are assumed to be inherently desirable or undesirable? Normal or abnormal? Sick or healthy? Functional or dysfunctional?
8. Is the human being portrayed only as a material creature, composed and governed by biomechanical and environmental forces? Or is the human being understood in terms of transcendent, holistic, or even sacred qualities?

As we can see, the answers to most of these questions are largely value based and cannot be determined by controlled observation and scientific study. While most theories do not address all of these questions, all theories are embedded with at least some type of ontological assumptions. It is especially important that we recognize this because philosophical assumptions are often at the root of both theories and their attendant ideology.

**5. *What are the methodological issues and evidence of empirical support?*** Numerous methodological assumptions and issues underlie every theory. *Epistemology,* which refers to the content and basis of knowledge and standards for knowing, is at the core of these assumptions. Two contrasting methodological assumptions, positivism and constructionism, have been the issue of numerous debates in the social and behavioral sciences.

*Positivism,* a term originally proposed by Auguste Comte, one of the founders of modern social science, stemmed from the ideas of Claude Henri de Rouvroy Saint-Simon, who believed that every social order had a corresponding ideology; Saint-Simon proposed that science was the basic ideology of industrial societies. Comte differentiated between phenomena that are knowable (such as the laws of physics, chemistry, and sociology) and unknowable (the existence of God, afterlife, and reincarnation). Phenomena that are knowable by humans can be understood by the method of positivism, which involves a scientific sequence of observation, formation of hypotheses, and experimentation. According to the positivistic approach, all human behavior can be understood and explained by this process.

Disputing this, proponents of constructionism argued that many human experiences (such as love, grief, perception, ideological orientations) are unique and subjective and consequently cannot be understood by objective observation and measurement. Edmund Husserl (1970), the first major author in this tradition, emphasized that human behavior could be described only by detailed observation to discover the structures of different types of human experiences.

From this debate between positivism and constructionism, two schools have emerged: One emphasizes rigorous measurement and experimentation, and the other calls for detailed description of subjective experiences. The positivists argue that any scientific venture must eventually come to terms with the problem of measurement and its use as a basis of comparison between study subjects. The constructionists (sometimes called constructivists) counter this by suggesting that it is the context and uniqueness of behavior that must be understood and that an emphasis on measurement leads to a loss of too much information.

At this point we must note that problems in epistemology are not just those of objective measurement versus detailed description. They also relate to who is conducting the study, from what interest and perspective it is being done, with what mind-set the subject is being observed, and why one subject is chosen over another. Why, for example, do most social scientists study colonized or oppressed peoples, their customs, and their institutions rather than the coercive and oppressive behaviors and policies of the colonizers? The choice of a subject is an epistemological concern, because choices are often based on cultural, social, economic, and political factors.

Further, there is a relationship between any given theory and the methodology it employs. It is sometimes difficult, however, to determine whether the theory's structure defines the methods to be used or if the methods used define the theory. When analyzing a theory, one must know what methods of investigation are implicit or explicit. Despite ongoing historical debate about the superiority of one method over the other, most social scientists now acknowledge that many ways of knowing are important in our study of human behavior (Thomas, 1979; Tyson, 1995). Although social work research has been largely rooted in the positivist paradigm, the constructionist perspective is now becoming evident in the social work literature (Payne, 2005; Rodwell, 1998; Witkin & Gottschalk, 1988).

In addition, it is extremely important to know the degree to which a given theory has received empirical validation. Theories, by their very nature, are part of a scientific venture and thus are more than mere opinions, ideology notwithstanding. Further, according to B. P. Cohen (1989, p. 22), "evaluating theories requires evidence, and the evaluation of evidence demands an evaluation of the methods by which the evidence was obtained." A critical analysis of theory, then, must also include both an empirical evaluation of the central concepts and an evaluation of the adequacy of the methods used.

Empirical evidence derives from direct experience gained through systematic inquiry, including qualitative, quantitative, historical, and phenomenological types of research. Theories are not only evaluated by research, they also offer suggestions for which types of research are most useful for the phenomena under consideration. For example, behaviorist theories are both derived from and advocates of experimental and quantitative research, in keeping with their materialist and causality-based philosophical assumptions.

Because a primary purpose of human behavior theory is to explain or predict behavior, we must also examine how good the theory actually is at explanation or prediction. There is a common misconception that in the natural (or hard) sciences, behavior can be explained or predicted 100% of the time. While this may be true of certain biological or physical structures, it is rarely true of human beings. When explanation or prediction is accurate 100% of the time, it is referred to as *deterministic*. In contrast, when accurate less than 100% of the time, it is known as *probabilistic*.

There are two reasons that probabilistic explanation exists. First, it is sometimes not possible to specify all of the variables involved, and consequently, a certain amount of information is missing. Second, certain entities (such as a pair of rolling dice or humans in social contexts) tend to behave in a probabilistic manner—or ways that we can never fully predict or understand. Thus, to better understand human behavior, researchers often choose nonconforming (or deviant) cases for special study to learn why they behave differently.

Related to this, a basic question we must consider is whether the theory is applicable to all of the people being studied or to only some of them. Because probabilistic explanation applies less than 100% of the time, it generally applies only to properties of groups and is not necessarily generalizable to all individuals within that group. Properties of specific individuals, on the other hand, may or may not apply to other group members. However, there are some situations in which there are no observable differences between properties of individuals and properties of groups. In other words, there are no deviant or conforming cases. Given a specific group, all members of that group may share a certain behavior or trait; the behavior or trait of the individual is found in all group members. In this case, deterministic explanation applies because no differences exist.

Many human behavior theories are *heuristic*, meaning they are provisional but useful guides for understanding human behavior and for opening up avenues for exploration in research and practice. In this sense, even theories with concepts that cannot be tested empirically can still be useful. For example, the concept of the unconscious cannot be verified empirically. The unconscious cannot be directly observed or measured. Yet it is a very useful metaphorical construct for understanding certain aspects of psychodynamics. Likewise, the concept of human potential in humanistic theories is similar. Potential cannot be measured because it refers to a future possibility, not a present condition. However, the metaphor of human potential offers an optimistic, growth-oriented, strengths-based view of human behavior. So theories and concepts can also be evaluated for their heuristic value for research and practice. A theory's heuristic value relates to its ability to generate new lines of inquiry and knowledge.

We have presented some basic considerations for criteria that are necessary to empirically evaluate a theory. To determine whether a theory's central concepts and main hypotheses are scientifically well grounded, it is also necessary to evaluate the adequacy of the proposed methods, the degree to which it is supported by evidence, and the theory's explanatory and predictive power. If science is to inform practice, it is critical to be able to distinguish between what a theorist has claimed and what has actually been empirically demonstrated.

**6. *On what grounds does the theory base its appeal for acceptance?*** As we summarize each theory, an important consideration is the theory's appeal for acceptance. What leads us to choose one theory over another? What type of evidence do we need to convince us of a theory's worth? Theorists use different approaches in their appeal for acceptance of their theories. Their ideas about what constitutes a good explanation affect their selection of facts and words. Ultimately, whether a theory appeals to any individual is a personal matter. It is largely determined by its match or mismatch with the individual's convictions about the type of evidence that should be accepted as proof (Campbell, 1981; Thomas, 1985).

A person who believes that the subjective nature of experience is more important than quantifiable observations is not likely to accept behavioral theory. Likewise, a person who insists on quantifiable observation is not likely to accept humanistic or existential theory. Thus, our choice of theories is a subjective process and is largely determined by our beliefs. Not surprisingly, we are much more likely to accept a theory that fits with our life experiences and worldview. It is important, therefore, to understand the basis of any theory's appeal.

## AN AFTERTHOUGHT: PATHS TO HUMAN KNOWLEDGE

The establishment of knowledge through the use of scientific theory, as we have described, is derived primarily from Western European thought. By contrast, a sentiment often credited to Albert Einstein proposes: "At times, imagination provides a superior form of knowing than hypotheses-testing science." In social science, this matter was called to attention by conflict theorist C. Wright Mills and others. As we examine Buddhist, Hindu, or Islamic ways of knowing, we find that not all paths to human knowing are empirically based. Our discussion of transpersonal theory and Buddhist thought in Chapter 13 attests to this as does our discussion of social constructionism in Chapter 11. As we will see, an understanding of the self based on Eastern thought or on transcendental philosophy presents a very different approach from that of the Western empirical social scientists.

## Summary

Theories are a basic tool in social work practice. They help us organize our thoughts, evaluate and interpret the world around us, and explain and predict human behavior. Theories, however, develop in a social, cultural, and historical context. Despite the fact that they are scientific in nature, theories are a product of social construction and consequently contain ideological underpinnings. The underlying assumptions and biases inherent in theories often lead to explanations of human behavior that are reductionistic and deterministic.

We believe it is essential to recognize that social work theory and practice are ideologically based. Our choice of theories (with their inherent ideologies) influences our definition of our clients, their situations, and the interventions we choose. Ideology also constructs the definition of the helping situation as it defines the parameters of the professional relationship, its legitimacy, and the role and status of both the social worker and the client.

As we begin to analyze the assumptions underlying our theories, we must be cognizant of these potential ideological biases. We must also understand the relationship between the power of theory to define reality and the impact this has on persons who do not share in this reality. Quite simply, this often leads to negative stereotyping and labeling of persons who operate from a different framework. Their inability or reticence to act or develop appropriately (according to our theories) is often seen as problematic or pathological.

Finally, the biases that may be the most difficult for us to detect are those that relate to our taken-for-granted cultural norms. Most theory, by its very nature as a scientific endeavor, is permeated with Western value assumptions that we rarely think to

question. Western values of individuality, mastery, capitalistic democracy, logic and rationality, self-development, a future time orientation, and the primacy (if not superiority) of the nuclear family structure are ingrained in us throughout childhood and later life socialization. Because these values play a significant role in our overall worldview, it is often difficult for us even to detect these cultural biases when they are incorporated into theories of human behavior (Howard & Scott, 1981; Triandis, 1990). It is our firm position that we must become aware of these biases if we are to serve our clients in ways that can lead to empowerment.

The cultural anthropologist Gregory Bateson popularized the expression that "the map is not the territory." Each theory is a map of human behavior that suggests possible routes and goals of development and the life terrain through which we must pass. Like a road map, "there is nothing so practical as a good theory," as Kurt Lewin said, for helping social workers consider how to get from here to there in working with clients. But when we mistake the map for the territory, we make a grave error. A road map is not much use for a cross-mountain hike. For that, one needs a trail map, showing topography and water availability. Even when a car is guided by a satellite's global positioning system, the driver is not forewarned of an impending traffic accident. As Karl Popper said, "There is no theory that is not beset with problems." And perhaps more problematic, as Thyer warned, "There is nothing as harmful as a bad theory." We hope that this book helps readers to identify the insights revealed by each theory as well as the important aspects of human behavior that are concealed or omitted. Although we firmly believe that one must be open to a variety of

ways of knowing, it is equally important to not harm
clients with theories that may be novel or popular, but
repeatedly fail to hold up to scientific scrutiny.

In the chapters that follow, we present a broad
base of human behavior theories from the social and
behavioral sciences that includes a discussion of their

historical context, key concepts, primary authors, and
application to social work practice as well as a critical
analysis as previously outlined. One of our primary
goals is to encourage you, the reader, to engage in
critical thinking about the theories you will use in
practice.

# Systems Theory

*And it's all such a delicate balance*
*It takes away just as much as it gives*
*And to live it is real*
*And to love it is to feel*
*That you're a part of what everything is*

© Thomas Dundee
1991, Jack of Hearts Music (BMI)

## SYSTEMS-BASED THEORIES

- assist us in developing a holistic and relational view of people and their environments
- help us understand the interactions between individuals, groups, organizations, communities, larger social systems, and their environments
- enhance our understanding of the contextual nature of human behavior
- are useful in formulating assessments at all levels of practice

In this chapter, we discuss five interrelated theories: structural functionalism, the ecological perspective, dynamic systems theory (often known as general systems theory), deep ecology, and ecofeminism. This group of theories is based on the idea that human systems, from the micro to the macro, are intricately connected to one another and to the natural environment; therefore they must be viewed holistically. Despite variation among the five theories presented here, all are based on a model of society, social life, and human behavior that focuses on the interrelatedness of people and their environments as well as their interactions with and adaptations to each other. Dynamic systems theory, deep ecology, and ecofeminism provide an additional focus on the processes of change and development that lead to dynamic system transformation, creativity, and harmony.

## HISTORICAL CONTEXT

What is loosely called "systems theory" today has its intellectual origins both in sociology and in biology. By the end of the 19th century, several pioneer macro sociologists were identifying major differences in societies. Ferdinand Tönnies, for example, identified two types of social organizations: the *gemeinschaft* and *gesellschaft. Gemeinschaft* referred to agrarian communal societies in which human relationships were ends in themselves (rather than means to ends) and were typified by tradition, unity, and a high degree of intimacy. *Gesellschaft* referred to larger industrialized and urbanized societies in which relationships were a means to an end and were typified by bureaucracy, differentiation, self-interest, and a high degree of impersonality. Using another typology, Emile Durkheim differentiated between organic and mechanical societies. Sir Henry Maine also proposed two basic types of societies: those in which social action is governed by the status of its actors and those in which it is governed by contract between its actors. All three of these theories were macro-sociologically oriented and portrayed social behavior as primarily influenced by one or the other type of social system. Although they did not use the term *system*, their thought very closely corresponds to our current concept of a system.

Working in this tradition, German sociologist Max Weber looked at two dimensions of social reality. One related to the "subjective meanings of actions" and the other to the "emergent regularities of social institutions" (Turner, 1986, pp. 52–53). His work analyzed the actions of individuals in relation to social institutions. It is Weber's work, along with that of several British anthropologists, that contributed to the modern structural-functionalism of American scholars Talcott Parsons and Robert Merton. Also contributing to the development of systems theory was sociologist George Homans, who applied systems concepts to the study of the small group. His later work on exchange theory is discussed in Chapter 12. The work of both Parsons and Merton is discussed in this chapter.

Analogies between biological organisms and social systems (called organicism) laid the groundwork for the development of functionalist thought. Social systems are considered to perform functions that protect and maintain their survival, just as biological systems do. This influence can be seen in the disciplines of psychology and anthropology as well as sociology and is sometimes referred to as the *order paradigm* because of its focus on cohesion, consensus, and integration. According to Martindale (1988), "The fundamental explanatory model of functionalism is that of the organic system" (p. 447). As Kingsley Davis noted, functionalism does two things: "to relate the parts of society to the whole, and to relate one part to another" (1959, p. 758).

Although the roots of organicism were apparent in early anthropological writings, the evolution of functional thought has been credited to sociologist Emile Durkheim's functionalist analysis of ethnographic reports on Australia. As Radcliffe-Brown acknowledged (1952, p. 178), Durkheim offered "the first systematic formulation of the concept as applying it to the strictly scientific study of society." Sociologist Vilfredo Pareto has also been recognized as an early pioneer in social systems analysis (Martindale, 1988).

Most prominent in the later development of functionalism in ethnology (the anthropological approach to social knowledge) were A. R. Radcliffe-Brown, Bronislaw Malinowski, and Ruth Benedict. In particular, Malinowski, a Polish-born English anthropologist, is widely regarded as the founding father of functionalism. He began doing fieldwork studying the institutions of the various cultures in Oceania, and one of his purposes was to compare those institutions with the two cultures (Polish and English) he had known as a part of his childhood experience. He believed that the human experience and existence were basically the same everywhere, but that the social structure that develops in each locale was somewhat unique. His basic axiom was that functions are universal, but structures that develop to perform these functions vary from locality to locality. For example, death in human families is a universal event (or function), but giving meaning to it and giving it a social foundation (such as whether or what kind of funeral should take place, how the deceased person's property should be distributed, etc.) require giving it a social structure that may vary. In Malinowski's vision, birth, death, marriage, reproduction, governance, formation of voluntary networks, economic activity, and rules of exchange were universal functions in all human groups; it is the structures that emerge to perform these functions that vary from location to location. In the footsteps of Malinowski, sociologists Talcott Parsons and Robert Merton continued their studies of systematic orientation in sociology over a thirty-year span between the 1930s and 1960s.

Canadian biologist Ludwig von Bertalanffy began developing general systems theory as early as the 1920s. We use the term *dynamic systems theory* to refer to the contemporary perspective that developed from Bertalanffy's work and its many refinements. As Bertalanffy (1968; 1981) applied his theory to human systems, he was especially interested in avoiding the overemphasis on conservative system maintenance that existed within behaviorism and functionalism. He clarified that living systems, and especially human systems, are characterized by development, creativity, and transformation. In contrast, cybernetic theory, developed by Norbert Wiener (1948), is based on closed systems of information exchange that are self-regulated by feedback loops. Although the cybernetic model has broad application to human behavior (Bateson, 1972; Haley, 1971; Watzlawick & Weakland, 1977), it is not adequate to fully explain human systems that, unlike machines, have the capacity for self-generated activity (C. G. Hudson, 2010). The capacity for symbolic activity (the ability to think and create symbols, attribute meaning to them, and act on those meanings) distinguishes humans from both machines and other forms of life (Bertalanffy, 1967; Duhl, 1983; J. G. Miller, 1978). Thus, general dynamic systems theory includes cybernetic theory but does not see it as a complete or inclusive theory of human behavior (Duhl, 1983, p. 63). *Deep ecology* and *ecofeminism* complement and expand dynamic systems concepts with ideas from philosophical, social critical, and spiritual perspectives, especially from Asian traditions, indigenous North American cultures, and European American holistic thinking. They focus attention on the interrelationship between human beings and the planetary ecology, including the moral responsibility that results from this relationship.

Dynamic systems theory was introduced to social workers in the late 1950s by Gordon Hearn (1958), under the name general systems theory, but it was not widely adopted until an ecosystems approach evolved in social work in the late 1970s. As Lloyd (1983) pointed out, "Hearn and others had sensitized the profession to both the need, and a (partial) explanation for holistic understanding of people and interactions" (p. 4). This theory has now cut across the dimensions of micro and macro perspectives, as well as across the disciplinary boundaries of sociology, biology, physics, engineering, social work, psychology, and others. The comprehensive and holistic perspective of dynamic systems theory and deep ecology enables them to encompass and integrate insights from numerous disciplines. Insights similar to dynamic systems theory can be found in a variety of family systems theories that are widely used in social work practice. Although not yet prominent in the social work literature, deep ecology and ecofeminism have been introduced to the profession through scholarship on transpersonal theory and environmentalism (Besthorn, 2001; Besthorn &

Canda, 2002; Besthorn & Pearson McMillen, 2002; Coates, 2003a, 2003b, 2007; Cowley, 1993; Hoff & McNutt, 1994).

## KEY CONCEPTS

The theories discussed in this chapter share several concepts about human behavior and are based on the idea that human social systems are analogous to biological systems in certain respects. As such, social systems attempt to protect their survival through *adaptation* and *self-preservation* and are interrelated and *interdependent*; human systems and their environments are intricately connected to one another. Thus, *people* and their *environments* are involved in a process of continual adaptation to one another and must be viewed holistically.

There is considerable variation among theories that adopt a systems perspective, however. Some focus primarily on the *individual*, some on the *interpersonal*, some on the *societal*, and some on the *earth ecological* (Abrahamson, 1990; Coates, 2003b). Also, some focus more on social system maintenance (e.g., functionalism) while others focus more on creative development (e.g., dynamic systems theory) and ecojustice (e.g., deep ecology and ecofeminism). Because of this variation, a fuller description of the key concepts is covered separately in our discussion of each theory.

Variation in their focus also leads to variation in their levels of application. Dynamic systems and the ecological approach are usually seen as having applicability to all systems, from the individual system to larger sociocultural systems. In contrast, structural functionalism is generally applied to macro social systems such as organizations, communities, and societies and is based on the study of large systems and their impact on groups and individuals. Dynamic systems theory, deep ecology, and ecofeminism have the broadest scope, from the smallest sub-atomic systems to the entire universe. For our purposes, we concentrate on the aspects of these theories that are directly relevant to human behavior. Because dynamic systems theory, deep ecology, and ecofeminism are broadest in scope, they are presented last. Table 2.1 summarizes the levels of application of these theories.

## STRUCTURAL FUNCTIONALISM

Sociologist Talcott Parsons introduced structural functionalism as a major paradigm or "grand theory" in his book *The Social System* (1951). This theory, also known as the "general theory of action," examines how social systems survive and why institutionalized patterns of interaction persist. Parsons was primarily concerned with the *structure* and *function* of social systems. According to Parsons, social action is structured in three ways: through the social system, the personality system of individuals, and the cultural system. Inasmuch as social systems are self-maintaining and enduring, Parsons tried to explain how biological systems, personality systems, and cultural systems become integrated into the social system in ways that ensure the normative behavior on the part of individuals that is necessary to maintain the system's equilibrium and survival. He elaborated on how the mechanisms of socialization and social control operate to structure personality systems in ways that are compatible with the social structure. The biological plasticity and sensitivity of people, he believed, gives them the capacity to learn and be influenced by the attitudes of others. This provides motivation for the personality system that becomes socialized to societal norms and values through interaction with others. The cultural system maintains symbolic resources as well as values and beliefs that legitimize the prevailing normative social order (Abraham, 1988; Turner, 1986).

| TABLE 2.1 | Levels of Application of Systems Theories |
|---|---|
| **Level** | **Examples of Application** |
| **Interaction between and among:** | |
| Individual | Biological, emotional, cognitive, and spiritual systems of individuals |
| | Individuals and other individuals, groups, organizations, communities, and the planetary ecosystem |
| Family | Family members |
| | Families and individuals, other families, groups, organizations, communities, and the planetary ecosystem |
| Other small groups | Group members, individuals, other small groups, organizations, communities, and the planetary ecosystem |
| Organizations | Organizational members |
| | Organizations and other individuals, groups, organizations, communities, larger social structures, and the planetary ecosystem |
| Communities | Community groups and organizations |
| | Community groups and larger social structures |
| Societies and larger social structures | Societal members |
| | Majority and minority cultures |
| | National and state governments |
| | Societies and cultures |
| | Societies and other societies, micro and meso systems, and the planetary ecosystem |

In discussing the latter point, he noted that the structural stability of a social system at any given time also depends on the extent to which all elements of the system can share the same value orientation. "Value-orientations," wrote Parsons, "constitute definitions of the situation in terms of directions of solutions of action-dilemmas." Ideology, therefore, serves as one of the primary bases of the cognitive legitimation of patterns of value orientation (Parsons, 1951, pp. 350–351). Thus, in Parson's formulation, the notion of value consensus, or shared values within a society, was central. It is through the shared values that the larger social structure maintains the cultural patterns necessary to preserve the stability of the social order.

In later collaborations with Robert Bales, Edward Shills, and then with Neil Smelser, Parsons concretized the notions of *functional prerequisites* and delineated four systems *requisites*. He theorized that any social system (e.g., a family, an organization, a society) must perform four functions to maintain its equilibrium (T. Parsons & Bales, 1954; T. Parsons & Smelser, 1956). The four systems' functions, or functional prerequisites, that Parsons delineated are adaptation, goal attainment, integration, and latency (or pattern maintenance and tension management, as it is alternatively called). This is sometimes known by its acronym, the AGIL model.

*Adaptation* is the process by which a system copes with external demands by securing the necessary resources from the environment. Because systems are interactive and make reciprocal demands upon one another, the system simultaneously seeks changes in the environment and adapts to the environment in ways that protect the system's own survival. *Goal attainment* is the process by which the system prioritizes goals and mobilizes the necessary resources to attain them. *Integration* is the internal process by which the system coordinates the interrelationships of the various units of the system. *Latency* is the process by which a system maintains motivation and deals with internal tensions. This corresponds closely to Parsons' earlier notions of socialization and social control (R. E. Anderson & Carter, 1990; Martindale, 1988; Perdue, 1986; Ritzer, 1992; Turner, 1986).

All of these functions are interrelated. For example, consider the hypothetical case of the multiservice community agency. The executive director decides to recruit and hire more staff in order to respond to increasing caseloads. This is an adaptation function in which a change in the environment requires obtaining additional resources from outside the agency. To accomplish this, she sends publicity materials and recruiters to the nearby social work education program. This is a goal attainment function, in which resources are applied to the environment to shape it toward agency goals. Once new staff are hired and trained, she assigns them to different types of clients based on a match between staff expertise and client needs. This is an integration function in which internal staff resources are organized and distributed. After six months on the job, the new workers have a job performance review. The more efficient and effective workers are given commendations and a pay raise. This is a pattern maintenance (latency) function, in which conformity of staff behavior to agency goals is enforced.

Robert Merton, a protégé of Talcott Parsons, revised traditional structural functionalist thought by focusing on the differential social consequences of existing social structures and on their manifest and latent functions (Merton, 1968). In his reformulation of functionalism, Merton argued that not all social arrangements within a system contribute to the system's unity. Rather, he noted that specific practices may be *functional*, *dysfunctional*, or *nonfunctional*. In one of his early works he attempted to explain the deviant behavior of individuals from the societal level. The typology he devised (commonly known as Merton's paradigm) looked at the discrepancy between the cultural goals in a society that define success, and the means available to individuals to achieve those goals.

Merton posited five types of responses relating to the match or mismatch of goals and means that can lead to either conformity or deviance (Merton, 1938). People who internalize cultural goals and have access to socially approved means (such as good paying jobs and opportunity for upward mobility) can be seen in terms of *conformity*. In contrast, when there is a mismatch between goals and means, the adaptation may be one of four types of deviance. *Innovation* (the most common type), results from having internalized the goals for success but not having access to (or rejecting) socially sanctioned means. Thus, alternative means of gaining success are sought—often through criminal activity that can yield monetary rewards that are not otherwise attainable. *Ritualism* is typified by those who have access to the means but have rejected or lost sight of the goals. This results in inflexible and obsessive behavior, such as those found in bureaucracies. *Retreatism* refers to people who accept neither the goals nor the means, such as hermits or societal dropouts like hard-core drug addicts. In contrast, rebellion represents those who not only reject both the goals and the means but also envision new goals and means that can be achieved through nonconformist behavior that may involve violence or other antisocial acts. Importantly, Merton did not see these deviant adaptations as forms of psychopathology but rather as role responses that were a result of a breakdown between expectations for success and the means to achieve it (Perdue, 1986).

Merton's paradigm pointed to the fact that not all of society's practices contribute to the adaptation or integration of the system. In fact, the *manifest* (or intended) functions of cultural ideals and norms aimed at integrating individuals into the social order may have *latent* (or unintended) functions and consequences in creating unexpected or deviant modes of adaptation. Merton's reformulations, unlike those of his predecessors, were directed toward specific empirically based social phenomena rather than abstract notions of societies as social systems. His paradigm could be used to explain, for example, why the illegal drug trade has proliferated in poor urban areas. Lacking the ability to make substantial money in jobs typically available to inner-city teenagers, his concept of innovation might explain why some youths are willing to take the risks associated with selling drugs. He would argue that they have internalized society's values, or "cultural goals," that equate success with money. However, unable to attain financial success in conventional ways through socially approved jobs (i.e., blocked means), they turn to illegal means such as selling drugs to meet cultural expectation of success.

One of the first organized efforts to apply Merton's paradigm came from Cloward and Ohlin (1960), who suggested that delinquency could be seen as a mode of adaptation by working-class youth who aspire to the same cultural goals as those in the middle class (i.e., decent housing, automobiles, jobs with appropriate salaries, consumer goods) but who lack the means (appropriate schooling and other such resources) to pursue the culturally defined goals. It is this lack of means that Merton, and later Cloward and Ohlin, called lack of opportunity.

The application of structural-functionalist theory can best be seen in Herbert Gans' 1972 essay titled "The Positive Functions of Poverty," in which he pointed out the conservative bias inherent in the theory. Keep in mind that structural functionalists see all social practices serving the purpose of maintaining the social system, and thus they seek to explain the "positive functions" of such practices. Gans (1972, p. 278) noted that poverty served numerous economic, social, political, and cultural functions for society. For example, maintaining an underclass provides laborers who will perform menial, dangerous, and undesirable work; subsidizes the wealthy; provides jobs in loan sharking, running numbers, and social welfare; reinforces the work ethic and dominant values by defining poverty as deviant; and gives the wealthy an outlet for charitable contributions.

As we can see, functionalist analysis attempts to describe social systems by delineating the interrelationships among the system's components that function to maintain the system. Although activity within the system may be functional for some system components and dysfunctional for others, it is the maintenance and ongoing stability of the overall system that is primary. Despite the numerous criticisms that have been leveled against structural functionalism (which we discuss later in this chapter), it remains one of the major paradigms in sociological thought today and has given rise to a contemporary neofunctionalist revival in Europe and in the United States (J. C. Alexander, 1985, 1998; Turner, 1986).

American sociologist Jeffrey C. Alexander, who coined the term *neofunctionalism*, has become one of the most influential authors carrying on the tradition of Parsons while bridging classical and modern theory (1985, 1998). Examining the process of social change, cultural politics, and postmodernism, he attempted to synthesize functionalism with other theories. Contemporary neofunctionalism can also be seen in the work of German sociologist Niklus Luhmann (1986, 2000), who suggested that the structure of a modern society cannot be understood without a comprehension of the communications media (TV, radio, major newspapers and magazines, etc.). What Parsons referred to as the *goal-setting function* is now greatly affected by the communications media and can be seen in the media's influence on the political behavior of the voting public. Further, the integration function of societies as envisioned by Parsons is also greatly influenced by the media. Hence, political behavior in relation to welfare, immigration, labor, and foreign policy are all highly influenced by the media.

## THE ECOLOGICAL PERSPECTIVE

The ecological perspective has become an increasingly popular framework for social work practice and is derived from earlier ecological theories that were popular in the fields of anthropology, sociology, and psychology. In sociology, ecological theory is derived primarily from social Darwinism and Robert E. Park's work on human ecology. Psychologist Kurt Lewin, strongly influenced by Gestalt psychology, was one of the earliest theorists to promote a holistic view of the individual within the environment through his development of field theory. In the field of anthropology, Colin Turnbull, drawing on the earlier tradition of Radcliffe-Brown and Malinowski, focused on ecology and culture. The current use of ecological concepts in social work is influenced by its earlier use in these social science disciplines. The idea of adaptation is an essential concept.

According to Y. Cohen (1971, pp. 2–4), "Adaptation in man is the process by which he makes effective use for productive ends of the energy potential in his habitat. . . . Adaptation in man refers to fitness for reproduction and survival. A population's adaptation is its relationship to its habitat."

The emphasis here is on adaptation of a *population or a group*. Adaptation is related to differences in cultural styles and their corresponding technologies such as hunting and gathering, agricultural, or industrial. These technocultural styles form the macro-level ecosystem in which individuals and families operate. This macro-level ecosystem greatly influences the adaptation of the individual in the environment. The term *ecosystem*, coined by botanist A. G. Tansley, refers to the *reciprocal relationships* between organisms and their environments.

An important distinction is made between the natural and the social environment. The *natural environment* is the geophysical environment, whereas the *social environment* is the network of relationships of the individuals and groups. This network of relationships has two elements: habit-forming predictability, which P. L. Berger and Luckmann (1967) called *institutionalization*, and *interdependence*, which may take several forms. Sociologist Robert Ezra Park of the Chicago Ecological School referred to two types of interdependence in society: *symbiotic* (hostile or competitive interdependence) and *commensalistic* (communicative and consensual interdependence). Park also introduced two concepts that are now popular in ecological theory: *dominance* (of one group over another due to different resources) and *succession* (the orderly sequence of changes through which a community passes from a relatively unstable to a relatively stable stage). As Elgin (1985) noted in his discussion of literary fantasy and ecological comedy, "ecology itself underscores three features of natural life: interdependence, diversity, and vulnerability" (p. 27).

Ernest Burgess, a colleague of Parks, believed all types of social events to be adaptive responses (Bogue, 1974). Burgess (1925) introduced the concept of *zones* in urban structures, which refers to a series of concentric circles in which the innermost circle represents the central business district of a city. The second circle is the zone of transition; the third circle is the zone of working people's homes; the fourth, the residential zone; and the outermost circle is the commuter's zone. This concept became important in epidemiology in public health and sociology as a predictor of social problems (Theodorson, 1961). Burgess later traced the distribution of multiproblem families in relation to these zones (Burgess & Wallin, 1953).

Both Burgess (1926, 1927) and Harvey Zorbaugh (1926) introduced the concept of the *natural area*, a "geographical area characterized both by physical individuality and by the cultural characteristics of the people who live in it" (Zorbaugh, 1926, p. 190). Examples of natural areas are Little Italy or Chinatown. Both Burgess and Zorbaugh argued that these natural areas were the proper way to define a community and were useful for neighborhood-based community organization (Burgess, 1926). Rene Dubos (1963, 1968a, 1968b, 1978) was intellectually close to this school of thought and believed that many modern cultures have forced people to separate from their roots in nature. Consequently, problems of adaptation exist because of the splits between human nature and human culture. This insight is also reflected in deep ecology, which we discuss later in this chapter.

The classic Chicago School of ecological theory has also led to a more contemporary version of ecological analysis with the writings of William Julius Wilson, whose work on the declining significance of race (1980) became prominent despite its being extremely controversial. Since then, his books on the ecological distribution of the underclass, poor, and disadvantaged populations in the inner city (1987, 1996) have emerged from the tradition of the Chicago School. More recently, the works of Mirowsky and Ross on social causes of psychological distress (2003a) and education, social status, and health (2003b) can also be counted as emerging from the new Chicago Ecological School.

Although there have been a variety of ecological theories (see, for example, Barker, 1968; Duncan, 1972; Lewin, 1951), we primarily focus on the way in which the ecological concepts previously discussed have been adapted for use in social work theory and practice today through adoption of the ecosystems and ecological perspectives.

First introduced to social work by Carel B. Germain (1973), the ecological perspective has been proposed as a unifying paradigm that can apply to the numerous and diverse models of social work practice (Allen-Meares & Lane, 1987; Greif, 1986). In her early work, Germain proposed an ecosystems theory for social work practice that was based on ecological concepts. Ecosystems theory was an offshoot of functionalism, ecological theory, dynamic systems theory, and many other psychological and developmental theories (Greene & Ephross, 1991). It is also known as the *ecological perspective* and the *life model*.

In *The Life Model of Social Work Practice* (1980), Germain, in collaboration with Alex Gitterman, elaborated on her earlier work in this area. Ecosystems theory focuses on transactions between people and their environments. Thus, the ecological notion of interface, or common boundaries between systems, is an important component of this theory. Interface, according to Germain (1978, p. 545), "takes into account the fluidity in the arena of social functioning in which both the person and environment are involved." "Goodness of fit" between people and their environments enables people and their environments to reciprocally adapt to one another. A basic assumption here is that people strive for a goodness of fit with their environments because of the interdependence between them, and in doing so, people and their environments constantly change and shape one another. This adaptation process, which is biological, psychological, social, and cultural, is both reciprocal and continuous.

Because transactions between people and their environments are often complex processes, it is not uncommon to find problems or upsets in the goodness of fit. As Germain noted, "When inputs or stimuli are insufficient, excessive, or missing altogether, an upset occurs in the adaptive balance which is conceptualized as stress; the usual 'fit' between the person and environment has broken down" (1978, p. 542). Stress is conceptualized here as a transactional concept rather than an individual or situational one. More specifically, stress is "a psychosocial condition, generated by discrepancies between needs and capacities and environmental qualities . . . it arises in three interrelated areas of living: life transition, environmental pressures, and interpersonal processes" (Germain & Gitterman, 1980, p. 7). Germain and Gitterman also noted that poor adaptation or a lack of fit between people and their environments can be damaging to both.

Unlike psychoanalytic theory, which assumes psychic determinism, or behavioral theory, which assumes environmental determinism, the ecosystems perspective views humans as purposive and goal seeking. As such, people make choices and decisions and are seen as being relatively free from deterministic forces outside of their control. Given this philosophical stance, this perspective focuses on growth, development, and potentialities (Germain, 1979).

The evolutionary, adaptive view of people proposed in this model sees the adaptive achievements of individuals as the outcome of interaction between inherited genetic traits and environmental circumstances. The environment, which is physical and social and further characterized by time and space, can either support or fail to support the adaptive achievements of autonomy, competence, identity formation, and relatedness to others. As a life model, the ecosystems perspective focuses on life transitions such as developmental stages and changes, external stressors such as unresponsive social and physical environments, and interpersonal stressors such as communication and relationship problems. Ecosystems theory came under sharp attack, however, due to its portrayal of oppression, for example, as a transaction between people and their environments (Gould, 1987).

In a subsequent book, *Human Behavior in the Social Environment: An Ecological View*, Germain (1991) elaborated on her earlier perspective. In this updated view, she identified ecological concepts to discuss life course development within various contexts such as the family, formal organizations, community, and society. Although power and oppression, as well as pollution, were still seen as person/environment relationships, they were now described as negative "conditions of life" that "threaten health and social well-being" and "impose enormous adaptive burdens" on people (pp. 24–25). In addition to discussing the impact of social stressors, transitional life event stressors, and subjective stress, Germain included concepts from anthropology that have previously received little attention in the social work literature.

Human behavior, for example, is guided by biological clocks (temporal behavior varying by day, month, season, and year) and culture. Culture shapes both the physical and the social environment, and these, in combination with the biological clock, influence spatial behavior. Both interpersonal spacing and territoriality are a function of spatial behavior. Successful spatial behavior leads to a desirable level of social interaction, whereas unsuccessful spatial behavior leads to an *undesirable level*. The term *undesirable level* refers to crowding or isolation, both of which are often dysfunctional for human life.

The human quest for identity, competence, self-direction, and self-esteem has an impact on one form of universal spatial behavior—the search for a *community*, which is both a social and a physical setting. Both settings, in addition, have two components, habitat and niche. *Habitat* refers to housing arrangements, and some arrangements, such as high-rise public housing, can add to stress. *Niche* refers to "a special place" attributed to humans either because of their special competence or ability (thus a constructive niche) or because of discrimination based on factors such as race, gender, disability, or sexual orientation (a destructive niche).

Germain pointed out that many forms of social work deal with either (a) spatial behavior of persons or groups that led to undesirable forms of social interaction or (b) issues and problems arising as a result of a person or a group's destructive niche. As in her earlier work, the primary emphasis of social work practice is on improving transactions between people and their environments. She also suggested that social workers assist people to improve their habitats and reshape destructive niches. Despite the switch in focus from her original ecosystems theory to a broader ecological model, the destructive effects of inequality and oppression were not adequately addressed.

In a more recent work, however, Germain and Gitterman (1995, 2008) further refined their ecological perspective and explicitly addressed the concepts of coercive power and exploitative power. Proposed as "newly added ecological concepts," they defined coercive power as "the withholding of power from vulnerable groups," which results in the "oppression of vulnerable populations that leaves them powerless" (p. 819). They also linked *coercive power* to "social pollutions" such as poverty, sexism, and homophobia, to name a few. *Exploitative power* involves the infliction of injustice and suffering on powerless groups by those in power and leads to conditions such as environmental pollution. In addition, they expanded their life model of practice to incorporate empowerment-based practice.

## DYNAMIC SYSTEMS THEORY

Dynamic systems theory is more commonly known in the social work literature as general systems theory or, simply, systems theory (R. E. Anderson & Carter, 1990; Greene & Ephross, 1991; Hearn, 1979). Often, concepts from general systems theory are mixed with social functionalism, creating a more conservative understanding of social systems. Although Parson's model and dynamic systems theory are both concerned with functions that maintain system survival, structural functionalism does not go as far as dynamic systems theory in addressing creative system transformation. Also, contemporary theory derived from dynamic systems theory embraces many different disciplines and systems terminology beyond the original formulation by Bertalanffy. To include contemporary developments and to emphasize the distinctive focus on system creativity, we use the term *dynamic systems theory* to encompass general systems theory and its closely related varieties such as cybernetics, nonequilibrium thermodynamics, catastrophe theory, dynamic systems theory, and chaos theory.

Hall and Fagan (1956, pp. 18–21) provided a classic definition of systems, using two basic concepts: object and environment.

> A system is a *set of objects* together with *relationships* between the objects and between their *attributes.* . . . For a given system, the *environment* is the set of all objects, a change in whose attributes affects the system and also those objects whose attributes are changed by the behavior of the system [*emphasis added*].

However, in the case of human systems, it is more accurate to refer to system members as *subjects*, because they are characterized by mind and subjectivity (Laszlo, 1972). This avoids the dehumanizing implications of applying mechanical system terms to human beings. In fact, Bertalanffy extended general systems theory from biology to psychology and sociology specifically to counter the reductionist and mechanical assumptions inherent in behaviorism and functionalism (Bertalanffy, 1968, 1981).

A family of four, for example, can be thought of as a system in which (a) each person is a subject, (b) all family members together are mutually influencing, (c) family relationships are woven together into patterns and developmental processes, (d) the family as a whole encompasses subsystems (e.g., parent and sibling subsystems), and (e) the family transacts with external suprasystems (e.g., neighborhood or social service agency).

Each system has a certain degree of autonomy and is distinguished from the environment by a boundary. Yet each system is also interdependent with all other systems to some degree. Transactions may be with smaller subsystems, such as a family system (as a whole) in relation to each of its individual members; with collateral (nonencompassing) suprasystems, such as a family in relation to a social service agency; and with larger more encompassing systems, such as a family in relation to its societal context. The mutually interdependent relationship between different levels of systems is expressed in the concept of holon (Koestler, 1967). Every system is a *holon*, which means that every system is simultaneously a whole with its own distinctive qualities, a part of larger systems, and a container of smaller systems. This may be most easily visualized by thinking about Chinese boxes or Russian wooden dolls that contain smaller and smaller forms inside.

Systems, therefore, have a horizontal relationship with other collateral systems and a nested relationship with more encompassing systems. In evolutionary terms, systems tend to develop toward greater complexity and comprehensiveness, with larger holons including smaller holons; these sometimes develop characteristics that transcend the limits of holons that evolved earlier. For example, human beings and social systems exhibit greater complexity than cells and organ systems, not only by virtue of size but also by virtue of having self-awareness and complex symbolic cultural patterns (Jantsch & Waddington, 1976; Wilber, 1995).

This ordered relationship between successively more encompassing and complex systems is named a *holarchy* (an order of wholes). This can be represented by a set of concentric circles, each larger circle including and transcending the previous circles (Wilber, 2000, 2006). Wilber emphasizes that holarchies should not be considered merely as scales of physical systems, as some reductionist systems theories do. Rather, especially when considering human experience, holarchies involve scales of increasingly sophisticated, complex, and inclusive modes of consciousness (e.g., global awareness and ecojustice values including but transcending ethnic, cultural, or nation-centered awareness and values).

Sometimes scales of systems are referred to as a *hierarchy,* represented in a linear fashion, as shown in Boulding's hierarchy of systems (Table 2.2). For example, in Boulding's hierarchy, relatively closed static systems are listed at the top and more dynamic and self-aware systems are listed at the bottom.

**TABLE 2.2**  Boulding's Hierarchy of Systems

| Type of System | Level of System | Function of System | Example | Disciplines Studying This System |
|---|---|---|---|---|
| Closed static system | Framework | To give structure | A skeleton | The physical sciences |
| Closed dynamic system | Clockwork | To give structured motion | A clock | The physical sciences |
| Closed self-regulating dynamic system | Thermostat | To regulate with structured motion | A thermostat | The physical sciences |
| Open self-maintaining system | The cell | To maintain self with regulation | A cell | The biological sciences |
| Open self-maintaining and self-reproducing system | The plant | To maintain and reproduce with regulation | A tree | The biological sciences |
| Open self-maintaining, self-reproducing, and self-aware system | The animal | All of the above, plus self-awareness | An animal | The biological sciences |
| All of the above, plus using symbols | The human | All of the above, plus communicating | A human | The behavioral sciences |
| All of the above, plus using culture | The human groups | All of the above, plus a network of values | A group (small to large) | The social sciences |
| Unknown | Transcendent | Unknown | The universe | The metaphysical sciences |

Although the first three levels depict relatively closed systems, levels four through eight are open systems that are biological and social. The ninth level is cosmological and metaphysical, and, at this time, limited conventional scientific knowledge is available about this system level. However, contemporary theories such as transpersonal theory and deep ecology have evolved to address this. Social workers are usually most interested in the systems from levels six through eight, although during the past 15 years the ninth level (which encompasses matters pertaining to philosophy, cosmology, religious beliefs, and spiritual experiences) has been increasingly recognized as being important (Canda, 1989, 1991; Canda & Furman, 2010; Derezotes, 2006).

As we have noted, a system is simultaneously a part and a whole. Take, for example, a family system that is made up of a mother (Marge), father (Jack), and two children, a brother and sister (Peter and Joan); each individual is also a system. As we examine the key concepts of systems theory, we refer to this hypothetical family to help us illustrate the basic applications to human systems.

Three concepts that help us understand the interrelatedness of systems are (a) the focal system, (b) subsystems, and (c) suprasystems. Quite simply, the focal system is the system on which you are focusing at any given point in time; it is your primary system of attention or focus. It is the focal system that defines the sub- and suprasystems.

The focal system is determined by the observer and, as such, may be changed during the course of systems assessment. Using the individual as the focal system (here we designate Jack as our focal system), a *subsystem* is a part of the focal system, which is smaller than and internal to the focal system (Figure 2.1). Examples of Jack's subsystems shown here are his biological

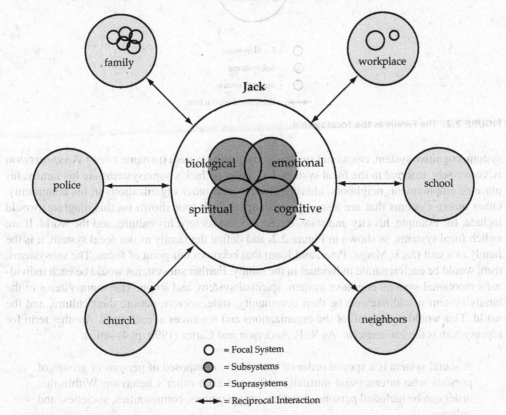

**FIGURE 2.1.** Jack as the focal system.

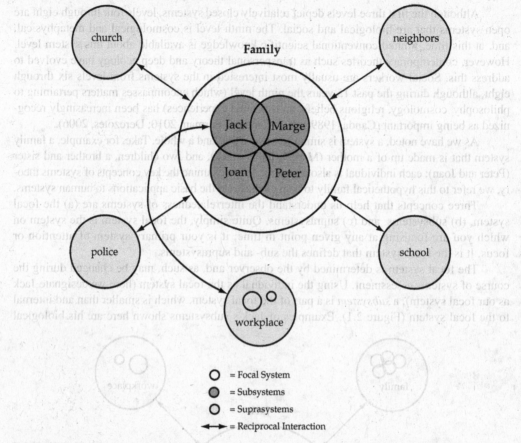

**FIGURE 2.2.** The Family as the focal system.

system, cognitive system, emotional system, and spiritual system (to name a few). A *suprasystem* is, conversely, external to the focal system. Examples of Jack's suprasystems are his family, his place of employment, neighbors, church, schools, and other organizations in his community. Other macro systems that are also suprasystems to Jack (not shown on this diagram) would include, for example, his city and state, the nation and society, his culture, and the world. If we switch focal systems, as shown in Figure 2.2, and define the family as our focal system, it is the family as a unit (Jack, Marge, Peter, and Joan) that becomes our point of focus. The subsystems, then, would be each separate individual in the family. Further subsystems would be each individual's emotional system, cognitive system, spiritual system, and so on. The suprasystems to the family system would likewise be their community, state, society, nation, their culture, and the world. This would include all of the organizations and resources at each level. Another term for suprasystem is the *environment*. As R. E. Anderson and Carter (1990, p. 4) stated:

> A social system is a special order of systems . . . composed of persons or groups of persons who interact and mutually influence each other's behavior. Within this order can be included persons, families, organizations, communities, societies, and cultures.

As we can see from the two previous examples, each system is a system unto itself, contains smaller systems within it, and at the same time is part of larger systems. Thus, we say that systems are interrelated and interdependent. Interrelatedness and interdependence are important in understanding how systems function.

A system is distinguished from its environment by its boundaries. A *boundary* helps us determine what is part of the system and what is not. Some boundaries are easy to determine, while others are more difficult. For example, the physical boundary of any individual is his or her skin. Boundaries of larger social systems such as groups, families, organizations, and communities are social rather than biological and may not be as clear. Boundaries may be determined by the interaction among the system's components. As noted by Rodway (1986), it is the observer who sets the criteria for defining boundaries. A boundary demarcates a system so that there is relatively more intense interaction and interdependency within the boundary (as within a family) than between the system and its environment (as between a family and its neighbors).

In living systems, boundaries must be semipermeable to allow energy and resources to transfer between themselves, their environments, and their subsystems. A system with cross-boundary exchange is termed an *open system*. While a living system must be somewhat self-contained for protection from the environment, it must also be somewhat open for exchange. The exchanges of energy and resources between systems that promote growth and transformation are termed *negative entropy* or *negentropy*. Transactions within or between human systems (and other kinds of systems) that lead to enhanced creativity and fulfillment are termed *synergy*, as when students who work together on a project stimulate insights and enthusiasm in each other, leading to enhanced productivity and enjoyment. A closed social system would become increasingly disorganized and stagnant, using up or dispersing its available energy, and die, just as when a person is cut off from food and air. This condition is termed *entropy*. An extremely closed political system, for example, would be totalitarian, impervious to external influences, and intolerant of internal dissent. In contrast, a chaotically open political system would be a society collapsing in confusion and anarchy. Therefore, dynamic social systems must have a reasonable degree of openness as well as organization.

A distinctive feature of open dynamic systems is that they are both self-maintaining and self-transforming. To survive, a human system must protect itself from excessive, destructive disruptions. To grow, a human system must adapt in response to environmental changes and internal drives for creativity and development. The self-maintaining property of dynamic systems is termed *morphostasis* (form maintaining). This is similar to the concept of homeostasis in functionalism. The self-transforming property is termed *morphogenesis* (form changing). This is similar to the concept of dialectical change in conflict theory, as described in Chapter 3. Both of these properties are complementary within the constant change and development of systems. Together, these properties keep dynamic systems in a process of constant flow and change that is called a dynamic steady state, kinetic homeostasis, or *homeokinesis* (R. E. Anderson & Carter, 1990; Capra, 1982; Koestler, 1976). Homeokinesis literally means continuity with change. To avoid confusion with the conservative and relatively static connotations of homeostasis and steady state, we prefer the term *homeokinesis*.

Because there is always change, relevant areas for social systems analysis would involve a determination of the rate of change, the degree of intensity, and the direction of change (i.e., retrogression or progression). Relatively gradual, incremental change commonly occurs, such as during the hardly perceptible growth of the hair, moment by moment. But dramatic and radical changes can also occur that propel a system into chaos or significant growth (Imbrogno & Canda, 1988). For example, a person in crisis may initially feel overwhelmed by disorientation and shock. But if the person is able to use the disruption of the usual psychosocial status quo as an opportunity for growth, then a dramatic transformation and enhanced functioning and fulfillment are possible (Canda, 1988, 2009). Thus, the application of dynamic systems theory to human systems emphasizes the importance of creativity.

Dynamic systems theory also gives insight into a phase of development that is often very troubling to people—death. As Capra (1982, pp. 282–283) noted:

> We have seen that self-renewal—the breaking down and building up of structures in continual cycles—is an essential aspect of living systems. But the structures that are continually being replaced are themselves living organisms. From their point of view the self-renewal of the larger system is their own cycle of birth and death. Birth and death, therefore, now appear as a central aspect of self-organization, the very essence of life. . . . Death, then, is not the opposite of life but an essential aspect of it.

It is important to recognize that human systems are much more complex and creative than mechanical systems. As an illustration, consider the thermostat on an air conditioner. It can sense environmental temperature changes, and in response it can modulate temperature; but it cannot consciously make itself change the temperature setting. In contrast, self-reflective consciousness allows human beings to creatively alter their own programs as well as their environments (Wilber, 1995).

Within the homeokinetic process, dynamic systems must perform four functions: input, throughput, output, and goal direction. All systems must be goal directed; all systems must have goals that they are actively pursuing. For people, goal direction involves the setting of priorities, values, and morals. To attain the goals of the system, the system must obtain from the environment the resources that are necessary to accomplish the goals. This is called *input*. In a general sense, all input that a system uses can be called *energy*. The specific type of energy a system uses is related to and dependent on the goal(s) to be accomplished. The family, for example, has numerous goals as a family unit. In addition to the physiological goals of being fed and having adequate shelter for the family, the family may also strive for better communication, a better standard of living, and a stronger emotional bond between family members. The types of energy that might be used by the system to meet these goals might include, for example, food, water, information about housing, money, and counseling.

Once the system has taken the energic input into the system, it must integrate that energy into the system in such a way that it can be used by the system to accomplish its goal(s). This is called *throughput*. The system here transforms the energic input as part of the cycle.

The fourth part of the energic cycle is called *output*. This is the product that the system exports to the environment. Because of the interrelatedness of systems, the output of one system becomes the input of another system, and thus, the cycle continues. An easy example of this can be seen in the oxygen–carbon dioxide transfer between humans and plants. The output of plants' photosynthesis (oxygen) becomes an input sustaining our lives. Plants then absorb and assimilate the carbon dioxide that we exhale.

For the energic cycle to be complete, the system must also be open to feedback. Feedback is information that a suprasystem gives to the system about the system's output. In a sense, it tells the system how well it is doing. Feedback becomes a type of input for the system as it continues its energic cycle. Feedback is critical in assisting the system in maintaining a dynamic steady state. Importantly, this process of goal attainment, input, throughput, output, and feedback is continuous and cyclical, rather than linear. Each open system is exchanging with all other systems, thereby producing the web of life. A change in any one system produces changes to some degree in other related systems, as when a pebble is dropped into a pond, causing ripples throughout the water.

Another related concept is *equifinality*, which means "arriving at the same end from different beginnings." This tells us that systems can achieve similar end states or outcomes by using different paths or by beginning from different points. Rather than there being only one correct way or path to achieve a certain outcome, there are many. This concept draws our attention to the fact that a variety of interventions with clients and intervention at different levels may produce a specific desired outcome. Because systems theory focuses our attention simultaneously on the individual and the environment, it helps us identify the different levels at which intervention can take place.

The idea of nonlinearity and nonlinear thinking in dynamic systems theory is sometimes difficult to grasp, because conventional European American culture and science tend to emphasize linear logic (deduction and induction) and dichomoties (either/or thinking). Because English language is based on linear concepts (for example, north to south, here to there, past to present), it may be difficult for English speakers to perceive the world in a nonlinear fashion. Systems thinking, however, mandates that we focus on the interrelatedness and interaction between and among systems and systems components in a nonlinear fashion. When using systems theory, we must abandon the linear notion of cause and effect and instead substitute the idea of omnidirectional cause–effect spirals or loops. Because systems are interrelated and interdependent, a change in any one system has an impact on numerous other systems in a variety of ways. Thus, a linear cause-effect relationship cannot accurately describe the mutual interaction that occurs in human systems. Linear cause-effect models may be useful for describing simple and static systems, but not complex and dynamic systems. For this reason, many dynamic systems thinkers are turning to contemporary quantum physics and ancient Asian philosophies for holistic metaphors (Capra, 1982; Imbrogno & Canda, 1988; Lee, Ng, Leung, & Chan, 2009).

One such metaphor is the T'ai Chi symbol (Figure 2.3), which looks like a circle divided by an S-shaped curve. This symbol is used in Chinese Taoism and Confucianism as a metaphor for the nature of reality (Imbrogno & Canda, 1988; Lee, Ng, Leung, & Chan, 2009) and fits well with the dynamic systems view of the world. Each side of the S curve represents a complementary opposite, called *yin* (literally meaning *shadow*, implying receptivity) and *yang* (meaning *light*, implying activity). Light and shadow depend on each other. There can only be both

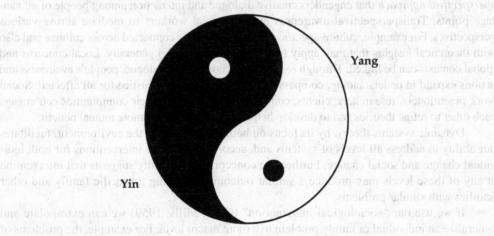

**FIGURE 2.3.** T'ai Chi (The Great Ultimate): Chinese symbol of holism and unity.

light and shadow, not one or the other alone. Yin (like morphostasis) interacts with yang (like morphogenesis) to produce dynamically all things in the universe (like homeokinesis). Further, the encompassing circle refers to ultimate reality, without separation or duality. This is the metaphysical aspect of the universe to which various religions and spiritual systems point. This ultimate level of reality cannot be captured in the limitations of words or images. Although dynamic systems theory does not pretend to give a definitive statement about what this ultimate reality is, it has generated many metaphysical questions from its inception to the present (Bertalanffy, 1968; Capra, 1982; Churchman, 1971; Koestler, 1976; Imbrogno & Canda, 1988). From a dynamic systems view, reality is complex and creative. There are an infinite number of holons of infinite gradations of size, from the subatomic to the cosmic, all interpenetrating and shaping each other. As this might seem rather far removed from social work, it is helpful for our purposes to remember the importance of determining a focal system to help us establish which other systems are most directly relevant to our work with clients (Hearn, 1979). This creates a useful simplification that supports social work practice.

On the other hand, dynamic systems theory reminds us not to be deceived by this artificial simplification. Like a magnifying glass, when we put something into sharp focus, everything else goes out of focus. For example, when focusing on a family, it is appropriate to concentrate our efforts on family system dynamics, perhaps using family systems theories. However, a member's unusual behavior may be due to a biophysical subsystem (such as a possible neurochemical imbalance in the brain as in Tourette's disorder or autism) rather than to family dynamics, per se. Medical assistance, along with family and community support and advocacy for accommodations and social justice for people with disabilities, would be important for this person. Likewise, family stress may be related to the experience of institutional racism, which would require appropriate political antiracist action, rather than anxiety symptom control or family therapy alone. Dynamic systems theory reminds us to be flexible, transdisciplinary, and creative.

This requires an understanding that reality is *perspectivistic* (R. E. Anderson & Carter, 1990), which means remembering that every understanding about reality is relative to the observer's personal history, cultural context, ideology, theoretical framework, choice of focal system, gender, and other personal factors as well as a host of environmental and contextual factors. Comprehensive understanding requires the ability to take the perspectives of others and to engage in mutual learning (Checkland, 1981). Canda and Furman (2010) take this further to a *transperspectival approach* that engenders creative dialogue and interaction among people of all vantage points. Transperspectival awareness enables social workers to mediate across various perspectives. For example, culture-specific perspectives can be connected across cultures and also with theoretical insights that may apply (or are claimed to apply) generally. Local concerns and global contexts can be linked. Through respectful encounter and dialogue, people's awareness and actions expand in understanding, compassion, and commitment to justice for all affected. Social work practitioners, researchers, clients, consumer advocates, and their communities can engage each other to refine theories and to develop helping practices that promote mutual benefit.

Dynamic systems theory, by its focus on both the person and the environment, facilitates our ability to address all levels of systems and, accordingly, devise interventions for both individual change and social change. Further, the concept of equifinality suggests that intervention at any of these levels may produce a similar outcome—assisting a specific family and other families with similar problems.

If we use our "sociological imagination" (C. W. Mills, 1959) we can extrapolate and generalize an individual or family problem to a more macro level. For example, the problems of adjustment in blended families are commonly felt by many and are not unique to only one family. By generalizing from the individual to the community and national levels, we can reconceptualize (in the words of C. Wright Mills) a private trouble as being a public issue. Private troubles, according to Mills, occur within individuals, their characters, and their immediate relationships with others. People are generally aware of the troubles in their immediate environments. Public issues, in contrast, are related to structural arrangements of society and its institutions. They transcend the immediate environments of individuals and cannot be defined in individual terms (C. W. Mills, 1959).

We have noted that problem analysis can take place at any level of the social system—from individual to societal to global. An important feature of this model is that assessment and intervention can simultaneously address the individual, the family, organizations, communities, and so on. In working with a family we are not forced to dichotomize between working with the individual on the micro level or, on the other hand, creating social change on the macro level. Dynamic systems theory allows us to simultaneously address all levels or focus on particular levels as the need dictates. It is also important to note that dynamic systems theory does not restrict social work practice to any specific form or level of intervention. It is best used as a model for an understanding that can be further elaborated with the use of other theories and a wide variety of intervention strategies.

Following the lead of Wilber (1995), Theobald (1987), and Lee et al. (2009), we can summarize the major insights of dynamic systems theory in the following principles: Reality is not composed of mere things or processes but of interrelated and interconnected systems, each system being a holon. Each holon is a whole that includes and transcends its component systems. All systems are changing at all times in various directions and degrees of intensity and speed. Dynamic systems engage in four complementary activities: self-preservation, self-adaptation, self-transcendence, and self-dissolution. There is a general evolutionary trend for dynamic systems to evolve toward greater complexity, comprehensiveness, and self-awareness. All systems develop through mutual influence. Diversity of human beings, life forms, and ecological niches is natural; it contributes to the overall health, creativity, and development of dynamic systems. Human beings, as organisms aware of themselves and the environment, have a moral responsibility to consider carefully the consequences of their change activity. Intentional personal and social change activity should seek the mutual benefit of all systems, human and nonhuman, that are impacted significantly by the change. This brings us to the topics of deep ecology and ecofeminism.

## DEEP ECOLOGY

*Cease fire 'cause the seas are on fire*
*The atmosphere's a burning up with acid rain*
*There's a hole in the ozone*
*Must have holes in our head*
*We must protect this good earth*
*For generations ahead.*

© Susan Martin, Jim Daniel, Bill Ward,
and Allen Damron, 1991 (BMI)

The term *deep ecology* was coined by the Norwegian ecological philosopher Arne Naess in 1972 (Sessions, 1995). He developed this term to distinguish between two major approaches to environmental protection that emerged during the 1960s. One approach, called *shallow ecology*, is technocratic and anthropocentric (human centered); it emphasizes natural resource management for the benefit of human beings. The other approach is *ecocentric* (earth ecology centered). It emphasizes the moral responsibility of human beings to engage in nonviolent, sustainable lifestyles and social behavior, based on a respect and spiritual awareness of the inherent worth of the entire planet, that support the survival and growth of the entire life web.

Deep ecology sharpens the focus of dynamic systems theory on the interdependency between human beings and the total planetary ecology (Coates, 2003a, 2003b, 2007). It refines the metaphysical speculations of dynamic systems theory by drawing on transpersonal theory (which we discuss in Chapter 13; Besthorn, 2001), ecopsychology (Roszak, Gomes, & Kanner, 1995), spiritual perspectives of Buddhism (Badiner, 1990; Halifax, 1993; Macy, 1991; Pyles, 2005), Christian-rooted creation or nature-honoring spirituality (Canda, Ketchell, Dybicz, Pyles, & Nelson-Becker, 2006; Fox, 1979), Indigenous cultures (Coates, Gray, & Hetherington, 2006; Glendinning, 1994; Halifax, 1993; Snyder, 1995), and many other traditions and philosophies. It also has a strong connection with the social activism of the international Green political movement (Capra & Spretnak, 1984; Poguntke, 1993). Deep ecology brings the dimension of value commitment in social theorizing to the fore. Like dynamic systems theory, it points out that all theorizing is linked to particular values and perspectives. It advocates the value of mutual benefit (win/win solutions) in the arena of human relations with all other forms of life. According to deep ecologists, clear personal awareness of the interconnectedness of all gives rise to moral imperatives for nonviolence and compassion toward all beings (Macy, 1991).

For example, Macy (1985) used Buddhist concepts from the Sarvodaya Shramadana movement of Sri Lanka to suggest how social action should be conducted. *Sarvodaya* means "the awakening of all," that is, a process of helping that seeks maximum participation at the grassroots level and that seeks the well-being of all. Shramadana means generous "giving of human energy." Similar to the spiritually attuned social action approaches of Mahatma Gandhi and Hindu karma yoga, this approach emphasizes proactive nonviolent efforts for justice and local action within awareness of the global context (Pandey, 1996; Patel, 1987; Walz & Ritchie, 2000). In the deep ecology context, this means that the welfare of all beings, human and nonhuman, should be considered within planning and implementation of personal and social change.

Naess (1988) described the link between human self-awareness and natural compassion. When a human being deeply and vividly realizes that he or she does not exist apart from the larger ecological holon of the earth system, the sense of self-identity expands from an ego-centered self-concept to an earth ecosystem–centered self-concept. This is called the *ecological self*. Some deep ecologists extend this self-awareness to the total universe, cosmic, or divine level to realize the *True Self,* which can be defined as one's experience of identity when all artificial or self-limiting, ego-related boundaries of the mind are completely open and transcended. This results in an experience of oneness or intimate communion with the True Nature of the Cosmos. In this case, compassion arises because one recognizes not only interrelationship but also unity. From this metaphysical perspective, compassion toward others is also compassion toward self. Thus, deep ecology and transpersonal theory (see Chapter 13) are interrelated perspectives (Besthorn, 2001).

To reach a holistic and deep ecological awareness, it is necessary to study self and other systems through means that not only include conventional science but also go beyond it. For example, empirical observation and rational analysis need to be converged with deep emotional sensitivity, empathetic intuition, and contemplative wisdom (Imbrogno & Canda, 1988; Wilber, 1995). To learn about the world, then, practices of meditation, ritual celebration, and profound personal experiential immersion in nature are encouraged (Badiner, 1990; Halifax, 1993; Seed, Macy, Fleming, & Naess, 1988).

The basic principles of deep ecology are well summarized in the Platform of Deep Ecology as described by LaChapelle (1988). The tenets of this platform indicate that there is intrinsic value in all life; diversity, interdependence, and complexity reflect the nature of life. Further, humanity is a part of nature with extraordinary power, which puts us in a position of great responsibility toward all species. We have created a false sense of estrangement from nature that has led to personal, social, and global problems, and we need to change the basic structures and policies of society that perpetuate this estrangement. Within ourselves, we must seek a high quality of self-realization rather than a high quantity of material consumption. Finally, deep ecology emphasizes that we need to develop new kinds of communication that encourage identification with nature.

## ECOFEMINISM

Ecofeminism shares many of the conceptual insights and social justice concerns of dynamic systems theory and deep ecology. It shares deep ecology's rejection of human-centeredness and a form of rationalism that prioritizes abstract thought and decontextual understanding of the world. It values feeling, intuition, empathy, and contextual understanding along with rationality. It also shares deep ecology's critique of Eurocentric perspectives that place humans separate from and over nature (Spretnak, 1990).

Ecofeminist philosophers, however, have criticized some deep ecologists for analyses that do not clarify the links between the oppression of nature and the oppression of women, both of which are linked to patriarchal social structures and worldviews. In ecofeminist analysis, modern societies (and many traditional societies that are patriarchal) give privilege to humans over nature and men over women. Concomitantly, men are the politically predominant shapers of worldview, social norms, and environmental relations in these societies. Ecofeminists also express concern about some interpretations of Arne Naess' concept of the ecological self that imply obliteration of the individual particular self, because women have struggled against patriarchal pressures to subjugate themselves to the needs and goals of husbands and children.

The French writer Francoise d'Eubonne coined the term *ecofeminism*. Ecofeminist thought has been influenced by postmodern feminist theory, Marxian critiques of political domination, nature-based religions and spirituality, and grassroots involvement in the Green political movement (Besthorn & Pearson McMillen, 2002). Essentially, ecofeminism focuses feminist concerns on the human–nature relationship. It debunks the interconnected oppressions of nature and women (Gomes & Kanner, 1995). Ecofeminists extend feminist critiques of all types of social domination to critique of the social domination of nature. Within this critique they highlight the importance of challenging hierarchy and oppressive power structures, especially those linking misogyny with hatred or condescension toward nature. Ecofeminism also highlights the importance of interconnectedness, relationality, and wholeness within, among, and between humans and nature.

Ecofeminism has been subject to its own internal debates and sometimes polarized thinking in relation to other environmental perspectives, such as deep ecology. For example, while some ecofeminists have criticized deep ecologists for ignoring gender politics, some deep ecologists have criticized ecofeminists for falling into a type of human-centered thinking (i.e., women centered). However, as we have discussed, there are many shared interests and insights between deep ecologists and ecofeminists. In practice, people who are guided by ecofeminism and deep ecology often work together or do not make rigid distinctions between themselves and others who share a sincere desire to heal the human–nature split and to overcome the social injustices that are interwoven with environmental destruction.

Common concerns among many environmentally conscious social activists are expressed in the Earth Charter (see http://www.earthcharterinaction.org/content/pages/Read-the-Charter.html). The Earth Charter includes four principles and many points that can be summarized as follows: (a) Respecting the interdependent community of life through caring for all beings, responsible use of resources, building of sustainable democratic societies, and supporting a flourishing world for future generations; (b) Protecting the integrity of earth's ecological systems through precautions and protections of environment in production, consumption, and reproduction patterns; (c) Ensuring social and economic justice by eradicating poverty, promoting equitable and sustainable social development, assuring gender equity and equality, upholding the rights of all to a supportive natural and social environment with special attention to rights of Indigenous peoples and minorities; (d) Strengthening democratic and socially just institutions at all social system levels through nonviolent political action, education, prevention of cruelty to animals and humans, and promoting tolerance, nonviolence, and peace.

## CONTEMPORARY ISSUES

Many of the issues discussed here as being contemporary have long been debated in sociology and anthropology. They are, nonetheless, contemporary issues for social work practice because they have received little attention in the social work literature in general and even less attention in human behavior textbooks.

One pervasive problem of systemic theories relates to tautological reasoning. The system is explained in terms of its adaptation while evidence of adaptation is explained by the existence of the system (Perdue, 1986; Turner, 1986). Another central concern was well reflected by Dahrendorf and Moore (1958) in their critique of the conservative utopian view of society that functionalism presents. With its emphasis on integration and the assumption of consensual values, functional analysis only describes the mechanisms that support the status quo. This model does not adequately account for power and does not account for revolutionary social change. Inasmuch as deviance and social change threaten the stability of the system, they can only be seen as undesirable or dysfunctional (Martindale, 1988; Perdue, 1986; Turner, 1986). Further, because functionalism fails to treat power as a central feature of social life, functionalism ignores the mechanisms that preserve inequality.

Although the conservative nature of the ecosystems perspective has been given some attention in the social work literature (Gould, 1987; McDowell, 1994; Rodway, 1986), it is rarely mentioned in human behavior textbooks. This perspective, in particular, has been criticized for promoting a "classless model in a rigid class society" by assuming that the needs of the individual and the needs of society can be simultaneously met (R. M. Berger, 1986, p. 51). As Gould suggested, "An implicit belief in a positive outcome (goodness of fit) of the person–environment relationship might not only falsify the social reality of alienation, but precipitate it by promoting unrealistic expectations" (1987, p. 348). McDowell (1994) has criticized not only the deterministic underpinnings of the ecosystems perspective but has pointed out that this deterministic view "serves social work's conception of professionalism . . . by delimiting the boundaries of self-determinism by virtue of superior theoretical and technical knowledge" (p. 53). Other problems with the life model that have been cited are the absence of context when considering adaptation or failures of adaptation, the forcing of all phenomena into an overarching plan, the meso-level focus that slights the larger societal focus, an "optimistic determinism" that undergirds the model, and a lack of clarity caused by borrowing terminology from other professions (R. M. Berger, 1986; Gould, 1987; Leighninger, 1977). As R. M. Berger (1986, p. 51) pointed out, the statistical concept of "goodness of fit" is used in the life model, but what constitutes "fit" is not specified nor is how it is assessed. Thus, it is the social worker's subjective perception that defines this fit. Additionally, Leighninger (1977) suggested that social workers too easily assume similarities between systems without analyzing structural points of difference. Wakefield (1996a, 1996b) examined the clinical and conceptual utility of the ecosystems perspective and concluded not only that arguments for its clinical usefulness are invalid but also that "The ecosystems perspective must be considered to be a vague and unsupported theory masquerading as a perspective" (1996b, p. 207).

Further, contemporary work in biology and thermodynamics (Nicolis & Prigogine, 1989; Prigogine, 1989) has suggested that nonequilibrium conditions can lead to self-organizing change in systems. Instability is problematic for professionals (such as social workers) who depend on relative stability for the purpose of control (McDowell, 1994; Prigogine, 1989).

Numerous authors have noted that contemporary society is characterized by instability and rapid technological and social change. Thus, the concept of system equilibrium must give way to the reality of nonequilibrium and dynamic conditions. Schon (1971) suggested that during unstable times, people resist change through a "dynamic conservativism" and retreat to traditional values in an effort to stay the same. It is increasingly clear, however, that previous patterns of adaptation can no longer adequately absorb the pace of change. Our major social institutions are faced with the task of major transformation. Accordingly, C. G. Hudson (2010) advocates that social workers should pay greater attention to systems complexity, dynamic change, and diversity than is captured in traditional systems theories.

As indicated by the Earth Charter mentioned previously, these are precisely the concerns that motivate deep ecologists, ecofeminists, and contemporary dynamic systems theorists to engage in advocacy for a dramatic change in our worldview and in our way of relating within the global community and planetary ecology. Our pace of sociocultural and technological change is unprecedented in human history (L. Brown, Lenssen, & Kane, 1995). For example, in the past 110 years there has been more human population growth than in the entire preceding four million years. The average world temperature is increasing, due in part to human-generated atmospheric pollution. World consumption of grain continues to increase more than production, resulting in lowering world grain stocks. In some African countries, the incidence of AIDS is expected to cut life expectancy by 25 years. U.S. residents continue a trend of disproportionately high consumption of world resources as well as production of pollution and weapons (Walz & Canda, 1988). To many it has become increasingly obvious that local social welfare issues cannot be separated from global human welfare and the well-being of the planetary ecosystem. Dynamic systems theory, deep ecology, and ecofeminism provide a theoretical structure and challenge for the profession to address these issues in both theory and practice.

The very notion of a meta theory, however, has been questioned by those in social work who are wary of overgeneralization and the vagueness of broad concepts (DeHoyos & Jensen, 1985). C. Wright Mills had earlier attacked Parsons for "advancing an empty, pretentious form of 'grand theory'" (Martindale, 1988). More recently, Nagel (1988) suggested that "a unified theory for social work practice not only is undesirable, if not impossible, but also perhaps no monochromatic model is all-encompassing or capable of unifying theory" (p. 369).

## APPLICATION TO SOCIAL WORK PRACTICE

Over the past three decades, systems theories have become widely used in social work practice. As discussed in Chapter 1, the systems perspective is extremely prominent in the human behavior curriculum in social work courses and textbooks (Brooks, 1986; Fiene, 1987; Gibbs, 1986) and, as noted, both systems theory and the ecosystems perspective have been proposed as meta theories for social work practice (Broderick, 1971; Siporin, 1980). More recently, Netting, Kettner, and McMurtry (2004) have used systems theory as the primary theory for planned change in macro social work practice.

Systems theories have supported the refinement of social work's person-in-environment perspective by embedding it within a comprehensive, multidisciplinary, and holistic conceptual framework. However, social work has often failed to make careful distinctions between functionalist, ecological, and dynamic systems ideas. Consequently, in most textbooks the prevailing version of systems theory implicitly overemphasizes the functionalist concepts of adaptation and system maintenance, leaving it vulnerable to criticisms of political conservatism.

Structural functionalism has received little explicit attention in the social work literature despite wide borrowing of its ideas such as homeostasis. DeHoyos and Jensen have suggested, however, that Parsons' structural functionalism may be the only systems approach that provides new ways of working with social problems (1985, p. 496).

Further, contemporary insights of dynamic systems theory, deep ecology, and ecofeminism on system transformation, mutuality, and global ecological well-being are not widely addressed in the social work literature. Nonetheless, the ecological model of practice has the potential to further expand to include these insights. Recent attempts to bring concerns about geopolitics and planetary ecology into social work practice may encourage this (R. M. Berger & Kelly, 1993; Besthorn, 2002; Coates, 2003a, 2003b, 2007; Coates, Gray, & Hetherington, 2006; Hoff & McNutt, 1994; Muldoon, 2006; Ramanathan & Link, 1999; Ungar, 2002). For this potential to be fully realized, it is important that systems theory focus equally on the structural features of society that necessitate dynamic transformation toward justice for all people and harmony with local and global natural ecological systems. This is a critical point because there is nothing inherent in systems theory that addresses either the structural features or power relationships in society. Deep ecology, ecofeminism, and recent efforts to link holistic systems perspectives with traditional cultural insights about holism are helping to correct this.

For example, Lee et al. (2009) have developed an Integrative Body–Mind–Spirit Model of social work practice by integrating concepts from Taoism, Buddhism, and Chinese yin/yang theory with dynamic systems theory and contemporary Eastern and Western holistic perspectives on evidence-based practice. Indigenous cultures have long upheld many holistic ways of representing human life in harmony with nature, such as Medicine Wheels of the North American First Nations peoples (Coggins, 1990; Dumbrill & Green, 2008; Gilgun, 2002; Nabigon & Mawhiney, 1996; Verniest, 2006). Although there are many variations of Medicine Wheels, they typically portray an ideal of developing harmony with all aspects of oneself (e.g., physical, emotional, intellectual, spiritual) and all aspects of the world (e.g., rotation of the four seasons and relationships with all beings in the four cardinal directions, sky, and earth) as we move through the life cycle of birth to youth, old age, and death. Medicine Wheels are increasingly being incorporated into culturally appropriate social work with Indigenous people and are also enhancing the holistic outlook of our profession in general. Such holistic approaches can be joined with local and culturally relevant efforts to overcome oppressions, colonialism, genocide, earth environmental degradation, and ongoing effects of trauma (Gray, Coates, & Yellow Bird, 2008).

## Definition of the Helping Situation

The five interrelated theories discussed here create the following four definitions of the helping situation: problem, crisis, growth, and social issues. Dynamic systems, the ecosystems perspective, deep ecology, and ecofeminism suggest that when there is an imbalance or lack of harmonious operation within or between systems, a problem results. Problems may occur at any system level. When they occur at the societal level, they are defined as social problems or social issues. Frequent repetition of a problem situation may also lead to a crisis situation. In contrast, structural functionalism applies a more macro-level perspective and typically defines dysfunction in terms of social problems or social issues. All systems theories also recognize the potential for growth to stem from resolution of a problem, crisis, or social issue. Flowcharts 2.1 and 2.2 illustrate application of the definitions discussed here.

## Assessment, Practice Strategies, and Methods

The theories discussed here are used primarily for assessment and forming practice strategies. They require that information be collected about multiple systems levels. A complete systems assessment of a family would include, for example, information about each family member's cognitive, emotional, spiritual, behavioral, cultural, and biological attributes; information about the home, school, and work environments, and interaction between family members and significant others; structural and sociocultural aspects of the larger social system; the availability and use of appropriate information about community resources; and the family's relationship with the natural environment. It is through a comprehensive assessment that the social worker is able to accurately identify problems relating to adaptation, goodness of fit, and sociocultural dislocation (Allen-Meares & Lane, 1987; DeHoyos & Jensen, 1985; Germain & Gitterman, 1980, 2008; Greif, 1986).

Systems-based theories lend themselves to a wide variety of practice methods. Dynamic systems and ecosystems theories suggest that intervention may be focused at any or all systems levels, and intervention strategies must be diverse enough to encompass a broad range of individual and environmental change. Germain and Gitterman (1980) suggested that the life model be directed toward supporting the adaptive capacities of people, their environments, and their interaction. More recently (1995) they added empowerment to their model. As Greif (1986) pointed out, the ecosystems perspective, through its multiple foci, can accommodate all models of social work practice.

Structural functionalism is best suited for macro-level practice methods such as community organizing, community development, or legislative advocacy. Macro-level practice methods that stem from a functionalist framework likely promote incremental rather than radical change. The concept of homeostasis mandates that policies and programs preserve stability while, at the same time, they promote change that can be absorbed by the system.

Although dynamic systems theory does not directly prohibit or prescribe specific interventions, it does offer guiding principles (Capra & Spretnak, 1984; Imbrogno & Canda, 1988; Theobald, 1987; Wilber, 1995). Because dynamic systems have an inherent developmental potential, there is a preference for solutions that remove environmental obstacles to potential (such as institutional racism as a barrier to people of color) and that nurture growth within the system (such as cooperating with African American community supports like churches or the Kwanzaa movement that celebrates African heritage and spirituality). Exchange of energy and resources stimulates social system creativity. Therefore, it is also desirable to encourage creative exchanges between diverse groups. Because all systems are interdependent, the benefit of one can benefit others; likewise, the harm of one can harm others. This leads to an ethic of helping based on mutuality, that is, seeking solutions that optimize the benefit of all parties involved. This is often referred to as *win/win problem solving.* Because the extremes of social system maintenance or social system chaos can be destructive, solutions that maintain system integrity while encouraging creative change should usually be sought. However, when a given social order

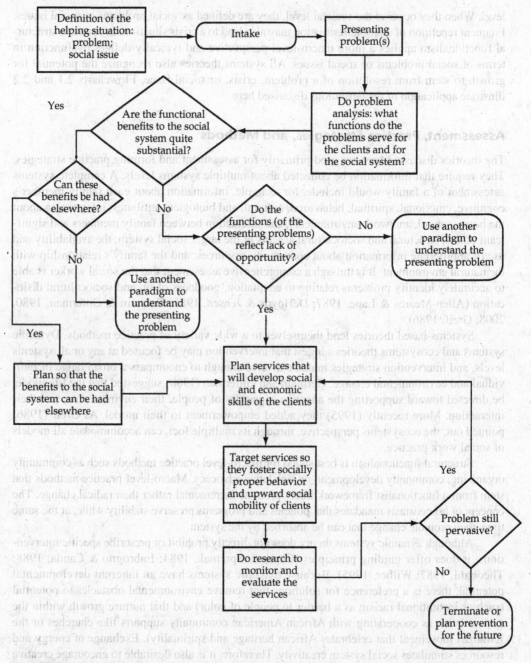

**FLOWCHART 2.1.** One example of applying structural functionalism. © 1998, S. P. Robbins, P. Chatterjee, & E. R. Canda.

or psychosocial condition has become obsolete, constrictive, or oppressive and unyielding, then dramatic transformative change is natural and necessary. When these principles are taken together, dynamic systems theory suggests that creative social change is best promoted by nonviolent means that support the development of everyone's fullest potential.

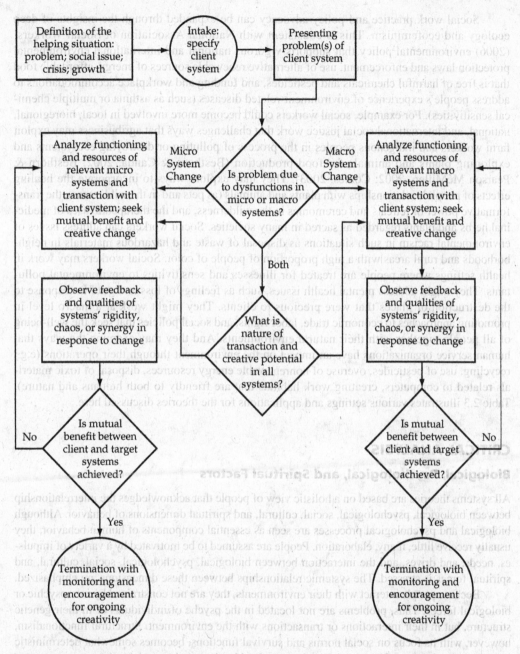

**FLOWCHART 2.2.** A possible application of dynamic systems theory with individuals, families, groups, organizations, and communities. © 1998, S. P. Robbins, P. Chatterjee, & E. R. Canda.

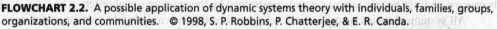

Further, dynamic systems theory supports a transdisciplinary and transprofessional approach to helping, because it is impossible for any single social worker, agency, or helping profession to deal with this complexity alone (Imbrogno & Canda, 1988). Therefore, interagency collaboration and linkage between formal and informal support systems is encouraged (Egan & Cowan, 1979).

Social work practice and policy advocacy can be expanded through the insights of deep ecology and ecofeminism. This is consistent with National Association of Social Workers' (2006) environmental policy that supports vigorous national and international environmental protection laws and enforcement, use of alternative renewable sources of energy, affordable food that is free of harmful chemicals and pesticides, and funding and workplace accommodations to address people's experience of environment-related diseases (such as asthma or multiple chemical sensitivities). For example, social workers could become more involved in local, bioregional, national, and international social justice work that challenges ways that agribusiness may exploit farm workers and indigenous peoples in the process of polluting or destroying ecosystems and exploiting plants and animals for food production (Besthorn & Canda, 2002; Besthorn & Pearson McMillen, 2002; Coates, 2003). They may explore ways to incorporate the healing effects of people's relationships with plants and animals (as pets and in the wilderness), the transformative power of retreats and ceremonies in the wilderness, and the therapeutic uses of medicinal herbs and plants regarded as sacred in many societies. Social workers can address issues of environmental racism in such situations as disposal of waste and hazardous materials in neighborhoods and rural areas with a high proportion of people of color. Social workers may work in health settings where people are treated for illnesses and sensitivities to environmental pollutants. They might address mental health issues, such as feelings of loss and grief in response to the destruction of places that were precious to clients. They might work at a macro level in promoting approaches to economic trade, labor rights, and social policies that seek the well-being of all people together with their natural environments. And they may examine the ways that human service organizations have an impact on the environment through their operations (e.g., recycling, use of pesticides, overuse of nonrenewable energy resources, disposal of toxic materials related to computers, creating work habitats that are friendly to both humans and nature). Table 2.3 illustrates various settings and applications for the theories discussed here.

## CRITICAL ANALYSIS

### Biological, Psychological, and Spiritual Factors

All systems theories are based on a holistic view of people that acknowledges the interrelationship between biological, psychological, social, cultural, and spiritual dimensions of behavior. Although biological and psychological processes are seen as essential components of human behavior, they usually receive little, if any, elaboration. People are assumed to be motivated by a variety of impulses, needs, and drives, and the interaction between biological, psychological, social, cultural, and spiritual forces is stressed. The systemic relationships between these dimensions are emphasized.

Because people interact with their environments, they are not constrained by intrapsychic or biological forces. Thus, problems are not located in the psyche of individuals or in their genetic structure, but in their interactions or transactions with the environment. Structural functionalism, however, with its focus on social norms and survival functions, becomes somewhat deterministic because it portrays people as passive and constrained by the existing social order.

All systems theories recognize that religious institutions can provide a structure for community as well as beliefs and psychosocial support for many people. They also point out that religious institutions often play a major role in determining and enforcing social norms that may be helpful or harmful to different groups. Understanding the particular role of religion and religious institutions for clients is an important aspect of systemic analysis.

Deep ecology and ecofeminism most directly emphasize spiritual issues in a nonsectarian manner. They raise questions about the moral implications of human interdependence with the

| TABLE 2.3 | Various Settings and Possible Applications of System Theories |
|-----------|--------------------------------------------------------------|

| Type of Agency | Type of Presenting Problems | Method | Definition(s) of the Helping Situation | Type of Focus |
|---|---|---|---|---|
| **Structural Functionalism** | | | | |
| Community center | Behavior problem of groups | Purposive group work | Problem Social issues | Explore how lack of opportunities has created the presenting problem |
| Community center or community agency | Behavior problem of communities | Purposive community work | Problem Social issues | Create opportunities and explore latent functions of the problem and alternative to that |
| **Ecological Perspective** | | | | |
| Family service agency | Problems of interpersonal adjustment | Direct service counseling | Problem | Provide individual counsel—focus on personality and interpersonal systems |
| Family service agency | Problems of marital adjustment | Direct service counseling | Problem Crisis | Provide marital counsel—focus on individual, family, and community systems |
| Community center | Problems due to inequality and lack of resources | Purposive community work | Problem Social issues | Begin community effort toward problem solving; may need advocacy |
| **Dynamic Systems Theory** | | | | |
| Community center | Social isolation | Advocacy group work | Problem | Help individuals network and access resources |
| Community center | Industrial pollution of neighborhood | Community organizing | Problem Social issues | Help groups develop solidarity for collective action |
| Family service agency | Behavior problem of family members | Family counseling | Problem | Help family members deal with problems of communication and boundary confusion in the family system |
| Family service agency | Impact of inequalities on family system | Family counseling and advocacy | Problem Crisis Social issues | Help family members access resources in community and overcome institutional barriers |

*(Continued)*

| TABLE 2.3 | Various Settings and Possible Applications of System Theories (*Continued*) | | | | |
|---|---|---|---|---|---|
| **Type of Agency** | **Type of Presenting Problems** | **Method** | **Definition(s) of the Helping Situation** | **Type of Focus** |
| **Deep Ecology** | | | | |
| Grassroots community movement | Trafficway construction through wetlands and low-income neighborhood | Community organizing | Problem Social issues | Raise public awareness and collective action about vulnerable people and the natural ecosystem |
| **Ecofeminism** | | | | |
| Political campaign | Public official who opposes women's and animals' rights | Public education Purposive community work | Social issues | Raise public awareness of link between patriarchy and oppression of nonhumans; mobilize votes |

natural world. They advocate for a developmental shift in personal and societal worldview from egocentrism, anthropocentrism (human-centeredness), and androcentrism (male-centeredness) to ecocentrism and cosmocentrism. While social workers differ and disagree about these issues, deep ecology and ecofeminism challenge the profession to take seriously the interconnectedness between personal well-being, social justice, and ecojustice. This suggests a commitment to compassion and action on behalf of all life, not only that of human beings. Whereas it is appropriate for the profession to concentrate its efforts on biological, psychological, and social factors, deep ecology and ecofeminism point out that it is dangerous to divorce these from the full planetary and cosmic ecology.

## Social, Cultural, and Economic Forces

Systems theories portray social processes as essential and emphasize the impact of larger social structures on individual and group functioning. Nonetheless, cultural, economic, and structural conditions that produce inequality are largely ignored or minimized in functionalism.

Although the social environment in ecosystems theory includes macro-level systems, Germain (1991) and Germain and Gitterman (1980) originally placed heavier emphasis on interpersonal and organizational environments. In her critique of the life model, Gould (1987) noted that "societal factors such as poverty, racism, sexism, and ageism are interpreted within the transactional framework as processes that are created by human beings as they strive to reach a goodness-of-fit with their environment" (p. 347). However, Germain and Gitterman (1995) have now more clearly defined macro-level processes involving coercive and exploitative power as stressors that have harmful effects on the lives of people in general and on vulnerable groups in particular.

Deep ecology and ecofeminism provide a strong focus on social, cultural, and economic forces and have produced a strong critique of the prevailing social order. They trace links between individual distress and psychopathology, urban alienation and crime, racism, sexism, and other forms of oppression, neocolonialist destruction of Indigenous peoples, and global ecological damage (Roszak, Gomes, & Kanner, 1995; Sessions, 1995). The underlying theme to this pattern of harm is that the creation of a false split between human beings and nature generates other false splits within the psyche and between people. This splitting has become widespread with the emergence of industrial and postindustrial forms of capitalism and socialism. These conventional political systems view people and nature as resources to be exploited by an ever-expanding cycle of production and consumption (Walz & Canda, 1988). The solution to this global threat is believed to require a fundamental revisioning of worldview and social relations. This theme is captured well in the tongue-in-cheek title of the book *My Name is Chellis and I'm in Recovery from Western Civilization* by the ecopsychologist Chellis Glendinning (1994).

### Relevance to Individuals, Groups, Families, Organizations, Institutions, and Communities

All theories discussed here address the full range of human system levels including the individual, family, small groups, organizations, institutions, communities, and larger sociocultural systems. Related theories that focus on particular system levels have branched off from these broad-scale system theories. For example, family social work and family therapy frequently use a variety of family systems theories pertaining to family development, communication patterns, structure, and therapeutic strategies (Longres, 1995). These also reflect a range of conservative and proactive assumptions regarding the capacity for family system change. Likewise, organizational theories apply systems analysis to agency function, structure, and development (R. E. Anderson & Carter, 1990). For example, the potential for innovation in social work agency administration has been illustrated by the principles for organizational *humanocracy*, in contrast to bureaucracy (M. J. Aldridge, Macy, & Walz, n.d.). Humanocratic principles are consistent with dynamic systems and deep ecology concepts. For example, humanocracy (and more generally, humanistic and spiritually sensitive approaches to administration) proposes that agency systems be based on principles such as maximum participation in decision making, human fulfillment, flexible rules and policies, comfort and aesthetic enjoyment, compatibility with the social and natural environment, and shared leadership (Benefiel, 2005; Damianakis, 2006; Doe, 2004; Mitroff & Denton, 1999; Moss, 2005, Svare, Hylton, & Albers, 2007). Although some may see this as a utopian or unrealistic concept, it underscores the tranformational potential that dynamic systems theory can bring to analyses and proposals for proactive intervention at the organizational level. Recently, organizational behavior research has shown that organizations that promote the well-being of their employees actually enhance productivity, decrease worker stress, and decrease employee turnover. This is significant for human service organizations because social workers are especially at risk for job related stress. Therefore, Canda and Furman (2010) have developed a detailed set of principles and activities to promote spiritually sensitive human service organizational culture that fosters mutual benefit and fulfillment of administrators, staff, clients, their communities, and the local natural environment. Clearly, the ability of systems theories to address all levels of systems is one of their most significant strengths.

## CONSISTENCY WITH SOCIAL WORK VALUES

Systems theories contain implicit assumptions about the nature of people, their environments, and change as they relate to health and well-being. In functionalist theory, stability is necessary for the well-being of the system. Homeostasis is necessary to maintain a healthy adaptive balance, and incremental and gradual change is seen as the norm for well-being. Radical change is disruptive to the system and antithetical to well-being. The ecosystem perspective defines adaptation as the norm for health and well-being. Dynamic systems theory, deep ecology, and ecofeminism suggest that social change and development be based on the pursuit of peaceful win/win solutions that take into account the developmental potential inherent within client systems and simultaneously respect the integrity of the contextual social and natural environment. Well-being is based on both system maintenance and dynamic transformational change.

One must recognize that functionalist theories do not adequately address human diversity. Although cultural differences are acknowledged, structural conditions such as racism, sexism, class inequality, homophobia, and other forms of institutionalized prejudice are reduced to systemic transactions or societal values that are consensual or system-maintaining in function. In contrast, dynamic systems theories, deep ecology, and ecofeminism point out that human diversity, like biodiversity, is natural, inevitable, and desirable. Human diversity within and between societies means that there are many different resources and perspectives that can be creatively converged to enhance synergy and creativity in social development. However, as we have discussed, some ecofeminists have criticized deep ecology because they believe the focus on anthropocentrism (human-centeredness) obscures the primary problem of androcentrism (i.e., male-centeredness). In other words, patriarchy and male domination of worldview and political processes are seen by some as the root cause of alienation from the natural world (Fox, 1995).

Greene and Frankel (1994) indicated some ways that systems theories can be applied to working with families that are diverse in terms of ethnicity, sexual orientation, structure, and other characteristics. Systems theories highlight the importance of cultural context and cultural variability among families. They can help practitioners understand the link between internal family patterns and environmental issues of oppression or lack of resources. They suggest possible target systems for change to enhance resource utilization and maximize families' natural community support systems. Application of functionalist based family system theories, on the other hand, can be used to support an oppressive status quo. Sexist, racist, homophobic, and other oppressive practices are seen as functional for some and dysfunctional for others; the primary concern is that they contribute to the stability of the overall system. Also problematic is the tendency of ecosystems theory to view racism and sexism as transactional processes. The reinterpretation of macro-level stressors (such as racism and sexism) that are involuntarily imposed on people as being cultural processes that are created by people striving for a goodness of fit, appears to be a new form of "blaming the victim." As Gould (1987, p. 348) so aptly noted, this position "ignores the institutional, structural explanations, the roles of power and wealth in maintaining social stratification, and the lack of available resources for oppressed groups to overcome their victimization on an individual basis." However, the recent reformulation of the ecological perspective appears to have addressed some of these issues. What is not clear yet, however, is the degree of attention that will be accorded to power relationships within the ecological framework.

We believe that the conservative bias in functionalism and in the earlier ecological models presents a substantial limitation to their application in contemporary practice. This is especially compounded when they are the primary or sole framework that is used to analyze interactions between people and their environments. However, incorporation of insights from dynamic systems theory, deep ecology, ecofeminism, and conflict theory (discussed in Chapter 3) could lead to important innovations in social work practice that will encompass both personal and social advocacy and a broader vision of social justice. Indeed, the principles of the Earth Charter are highly consistent with NASW's policy on environmental protection as well as the Global Standards for the Education and Training of the Social Work Profession (http://www.ifsw.org/cm_data/GlobalSocialWorkStandards2005.pdf).

## PHILOSOPHICAL UNDERPINNINGS

Systems theories are based on a paradigm that assumes a holistic view of people and of human behavior; both must be viewed within their social and physical contexts. Functionalist systems theories contain additional implicit assumptions about the nature of people, their environments, and change. First and foremost is the assumption that stability is necessary for the smooth functioning of society. Given that the steady state is critical in maintaining the system's ability to function and be self-correcting, incremental and evolutionary change are seen as the norm. Radical change is viewed as being dysfunctional and disruptive. In contrast, although dynamic systems theory allows for more radical transformative change, this has received little attention in the social work literature. Deep ecology and ecofeminism further rest on the assumption that transformative change is based on moral imperatives of self-awareness, nonviolence, and compassion as well as recognition of the unity of all life and our interconnectedness with and responsibility to the natural ecosystem.

Although dynamic systems theory posits only the interrelatedness and interdependence of systems, structural functionalism adds to this the notion of value consensus. The cultural patterns necessary to preserve stability are assumed to be dependent upon shared values of individuals in a society. Each of these assumptions is normative, inasmuch as they describe how society *should* function. Gould (1987) pointed out that the ecosystem perspective also contains implicit assumptions of a normative nature. As a meso (or middle) level rather than macro theory, the life model approach assumes a goodness of fit toward which all forms of life strive. Growth and change are seen entirely within the context of this fit, and adaptation is defined as the norm. In addition, the life model holds an inherent conviction and visionary view that social work practice be aimed simultaneously at the individual and the environment (Gould, 1987).

## METHODOLOGICAL ISSUES AND EMPIRICAL SUPPORT

Although systems theories originated from the positivist paradigm, they departed from it in emphasizing the organic and holistic nature of systems. Dynamic systems theory, deep ecology, and ecofeminism have drawn on contemporary postmodern developments in physics, biology, psychology, and philosophy. This adds an appreciation for qualitative, phenomenological, and naturalistic methods to our traditional quantitative and experimental methods (Lincoln & Guba, 1985). Within social work research, the heuristic paradigm (Tyson, 1995), Petr's (2009) multidimensional evidence-based practice approach, and the Integrative Body–Mind–Spirit Model (Lee, et al. 2009) are perhaps most consistent with dynamic systems thinking, because they recognize the need for many perspectives and ways of knowing to be brought together to develop more realistic understandings of human behavior.

However, numerous methodological problems and limitations relating to systems theories have been cited in the literature. The overarching theme of these criticisms involves the methodological and philosophical dilemmas arising from grand or meta theory (R. M. Berger, 1986; Blauberg, Sadovsky, & Yudin, 1977; DeHoyos & Jensen, 1985; Gould, 1987; Nagel, 1988; Perdue, 1986; Turner, 1986). Structural functionalism, in particular, has been accused of an absence of clarity, because many of the central concepts are poorly or ambiguously defined (Perdue, 1986). Related to this are problems of measurement. Poorly defined core concepts based on a high level of abstraction become impossible to operationalize, and the lack of empirical referents leave the theory unverifiable (Perdue, 1986; Turner, 1986).

Although Merton's mid-range functionalist theories were more empirically based, they did not achieve as much prominence. Functionalists have been criticized for not separating cause and function, and thus functional analysis does not give us adequate information about causal processes (Turner, 1986). This criticism has also been leveled at general systems theory (Rodway, 1986).

Early ecological theory in sociology and anthropology established a long tradition of empirical research on the distribution of social problems (Dunbar, 1972; Galaskiewicz, 1979; Lenski & Nolan, 1984). This tradition, in turn, has influenced newer disciplines such as urban studies and epidemiology. Attempts by Norton (1993) to use an ecological framework in the study of early childhood socialization are discussed in Chapter 6. Although the ecosystems perspective seems adept at analyzing problems at multiple systems levels, there have been few empirical studies (Austin, 1981; Rose, 1981; Vosler, 1990). As a mid-range theory, it holds great potential for future empirical elaboration.

When used in the social sciences to describe social systems, all systems theories are better at description and explanation than at prediction and are better at a probabilistic level of explanation than at a deterministic level. They are adequately suited for explaining properties of both individuals and groups. Although all systems theories do address the impact of different levels of systems on one another, dynamic systems, deep ecology, ecofeminism, and the ecosystems perspective are used most often to explain behavior at both micro and macro levels. This is not necessarily due to the nature of the theories themselves but to the micro orientation of most social work practitioners. Structural functionalism, on the other hand, is used primarily to explain behavior at the organizational and societal levels.

## Summary

Systems theories have made an enormous contribution to social work practice. Historical and professional elements previously led us to embrace a psychoanalytic and psychodynamic view of people that prevailed for more than half a century. Systems theory and the ecosystems perspective can be credited with bringing the environment solidly back into the concept of person-in-environment. Used as a framework for assessment, these theories guide the social work practitioner to focus on the environmental context in which people function. Further, they bring to our attention the complex nature of interaction between individuals and their environments. The ecological perspective has, to date, held the greatest appeal for contemporary social work practice. This is not surprising as it is generated solely by social workers for use in practice.

Although structural functionalism has not had widespread appeal in social work, DeHoyos, DeHoyos, and Anderson (1986) have suggested that it is a useful theory base for working with cultural minorities suffering from sociocultural dislocation. They proposed a three-stage process that includes sociocultural intervention aimed at the larger social system.

Even though we do not believe that any of these theories can be used as a conclusive unifying or meta theory, the fact that they address all levels of social systems makes them particularly appealing and relevant for social work practice in two ways. First, they can be used by practitioners working in direct service, administration and organizational development, and community organization and by those in organizations focusing on larger societal change. Second, the systems concept of equifinality allows workers at any level to focus on multiple paths for intervention. In this limited sense they can encompass all fields of practice. We must be mindful, however, of the failure of functionalist and adaptation-oriented systems theories to adequately address power and social inequality. The emphasis on system transformation within dynamic systems theory, deep ecology, ecofeminism, and more recent versions of the ecological perspective, makes them more suitable for a proactive approach to social work.

Last, and perhaps most important, they free us from the medical model of practice and the accompanying assumption of pathology as we work with clients. The move away from the illness model allows us to see people in a healthy light, free of the deterministic forces of their psyches. The ecological life model, in particular, through its focus on the various stages of the life span, draws attention to the expectable transitional issues of growth for clients of all ages. In addition, systems theories allow for a wide variety of interventive techniques as we work with clients to increase their problem-solving skills and assist them in their quest for growth and self-knowledge.

# Conflict Theories

*The company keeps telling us that we want too much*
*I see most of them still got that midas touch*
*Now all we ever wanted was a home of our own*
*Instead we're gonna bail out some savings and loan*
*Whatever happened to the eight-hour day*
*Can't feed a family now on one person's pay*
*I can't take much more, I just got one thing to say*
*Whatever happened to the eight-hour day?*

© ANNE FEENEY
1992 (BMI)

## CONFLICT THEORIES

- help us understand conflict and inequality between persons, ideas, groups, social classes, communities, and larger social structures
- enhance our understanding of power structures and the way in which power disparities impact people's lives
- are useful in formulating assessments involving oppression and client vulnerability
- may be used to inform policy and guide macro-level practice

Theories of conflict stand in direct contrast to functionalist systems theories. Whereas functionalist systems theories assume that value consensus, intended or unintended cooperation, and stability are at the heart of social interactions, conflict theorists see stability as a temporary and unusual state. For the latter, conflict rather than consensus is assumed to be the norm, and coercion rather than cooperation is considered the primary force in social life. Conflict theorists are primarily interested in two phenomena—power and change. More specifically, they are interested in the ways that people use power to resist or create change (Abraham, 1988; Federico, 1979).

## HISTORICAL CONTEXT

The idea of conflict as a central feature of society can be found in early writings of Eastern and Western philosophers. Martindale (1988) traced historical theories of conflict from the fifth century B.C. in classical Indian, Chinese, and Greek philosophy. Concepts of power relations, social instability, revolution, social solidarity, and pluralist influence are apparent in these early writings.

Western conflict theory found its voice in the writings of Niccolo Machiavelli, Jean Bodin, and Thomas Hobbes. These early political philosophers provided the theoretical bases for the British, Scottish, and French conflict theorists who were to follow. Although 17th- and 18th-century conflict theory primarily reflected political concerns and formulations, many of the central propositions were adapted for use in classical economics. Applications of conflict theory later became the foundation to explain biological phenomena as well (Martindale, 1988).

A wide variety of theorists have used conflict as a central concept in their formulations of individuals, interpersonal relationships, and group relations. Conflict, for example, plays a central role in the psychodynamic theories of Freud and Erikson and, while less central, it is an important concept in role theory, cognitive theory, and behavioral theory. We discuss these in greater detail in later chapters.

An early pioneer on interpersonal and intragroup conflict, German sociologist Georg Simmel gained attention for his work on *forms* of interaction and *types* of interactants. Unlike the structural functionalists of his day, Simmel saw conflict as pervasive and healthy. His work on social conflict focused on groups and the size of groups. Studies on dyads (two-person groups) led him to observe that extreme fluctuation between intense intimacy and intense conflict was characteristic of two-person groups. Dyadic conflict had a tendency to be cyclical, with ongoing movement between these two extremes. The addition of a third person alters the dyadic structure and brings new dynamics to the group. In a triad, "two may form alliances against the one, or the third may mediate differences between the others or seek to divide them" (Perdue, 1986, p. 190). In a foursome, conflict may arise between two dyads or between a dyad, an individual, and another individual. These dynamics influenced the group work tradition in social work and are known as social geometry. In addition, Simmel studied specific outcomes of human interactions such as the emergence of fashion, in which certain human preferences win out over other preferences and become, at least for a short period, the dominant style of fashion. He was perhaps the first social scientist to posit that money management by human beings is a result of often several types of intrapersonal and interpersonal conflict. These group dynamics on the micro and meso levels are paralleled in larger society and represent a pluralist image of society, which we discuss later in this chapter.

According to Abraham (1988), classical conflict theory reflects two distinct traditions: power relations in political philosophy and competitive struggle in classical economics.

Contemporary social theory represents a synthesis of the two. With Karl Marx as its "leading architect," conflict theory has been furthered by later writers such as C. Wright Mills, Ralf Dahrendorf, Lewis Coser, Randall Collins, Herbert Marcuse, Georg Lukacs, and Jurgen Habermas, to name a few. Although conflict theory has never been as popular as structural functionalism and other systems theories, it adds an important dimension to sociological analysis. As Abraham noted, "conflict and consensus, harmony and constraint, are two faces of the same social reality" (p. 140).

## KEY CONCEPTS

*Conflict theory* is a broad term encompassing several theories that share underlying assumptions about the nature of social phenomena. Despite the fact that certain concepts may be particular to a specific theorist, there are basic propositions that are common to this group of theories. First and foremost, conflict is seen as a fact of social life and as a natural process in society. Change, rather than stability, is the norm. In contrast to functionalist systems theorists who believe that value consensus is the "glue" that holds society together, conflict theorists point to the role of coercion, constraint, and domination.

Abraham (1988) identified two categories of conflict literature. *Endogenous conflict* refers to conflict that occurs within a system or a society. It includes conflict about change, values, the distribution of desired resources, and authority. It may also include conflict between the individual and society. *Exogenous conflict* refers to conflict that occurs between systems or from the external environment and is generally based on wars, cultural invasion, and ideology.

Denisoff and Wahrman (1979, p. 22) have summarized the central propositions in conflict theory:

1. Interests are basic elements of social life.
2. Social life involves coercion.
3. Social life involves groups with different interests.
4. Social life generates opposition, exclusion, and hostility.
5. Social life generates conflict.
6. Social differences involve power.
7. Social systems are not united or harmonious.
8. Social systems tend to change.

To this we add Dahrendorf's (1973, p. 105) ideas:

1. Every element in society contributes to its change.
2. Every society rests on constraint of some of its members by others.

These propositions indicate that conflict generates social change. For social justice–oriented theorists, such as Karl Marx, conflict is seen as desirable because it propels social action against oppression. This is in direct contrast to the functionalist systems theorists who emphasize system maintenance activities and regard conflict as in threat to system survival.

As we examine the different varieties of conflict theory and the ideas of specific theorists, we find both commonalities and differences in their theoretical concepts. Concepts that are central to conflict theory such as power, conflict, interests, coercion, and change often have diverse meanings for different theorists. Conflict, for example, is defined by some authors as an "extreme form of competition," while others use the terms *conflict* and *competition* interchangeably. Still others deliberately separate the two concepts (Blalock, 1989).

We offer some general definitions of the following terms, with the understanding that these may vary by author: *conflict*, *power*, *minority*, and *change*. *Conflict* is a clash or struggle between opposing forces or interests. *Power* is the ability to control and influence collective decisions and actions. *Minority* refers to groups that have limited access to power even when they represent a numerical majority. Change is a transition or transformation from one condition or state to another. *Change* can be either rapid or slow, radical or conservative, evolutionary or revolutionary. Some conflict theories perceive change as rapid and radical while others see slow, incremental change as the norm. Change, however, is seen as normative and healthy and the central propositions listed above are at the core of most conflict formulations.

Conflict theory encompasses two major schools of thought on group conflict, one based on class conflict and the other on interest group conflict. Although theories of class conflict relate most directly to macro-level phenomena, interest group theories are used at either a macro or a meso level. Most conflict theories, however, are somewhat restrictive in nature and limit their analyses to specific conditions (such as racial conflict, ideological conflict, labor-management conflict). Several notable scholars have attempted to formulate more comprehensive theories that address conflict and change at the societal level.

## CLASS CONFLICT

Sociological theories of class conflict originate with the writings of Karl Marx. As Martindale (1988, p. 149) noted, "Conflict theory tends to be only a step away from *ideology*," so it is not surprising that many sociologists embracing the scientific method deliberately distanced themselves from Marx's view of society and social relations. Marx's work, however, has had an important impact on sociological theory worldwide, and most would now agree that "although Marx was not simply a sociologist, there is a sociology in Marx's work" (Lefebvre, cited in Ritzer, 1992, p. 42).

### Karl Marx: Class Struggle

Marx's theory is based on the premise that inevitable and continual conflict is caused by inequality that results from social class differences. A basic feature of Marxist thought is the use of the dialectic method to analyze social relations in the material world. Influenced by the philosophical writings of 18th-century German idealists Immanuel Kant and Georg Wilhelm Friedrich Hegel, Marx adopted the dialectical method that sought to uncover "truth" through revealing internal contradictions in opposing historical social forces. The philosophical use of the dialectic focused on contradictions in thoughts and ideas; Marx refocused the dialectic to address contradictions in the material world. Its application to the material world suggests, for example, that although "the social world influences and perhaps oppresses them (people), they may also influence it." Thus, "individuals create history, as well as being made by it" (Payne, 1991, pp. 207–208).

Marx saw his contemporary society as a polarization between two dominant classes: the workers and the capitalists, which he referred to as the *proletariat* and the *bourgeoisie*. For Marx, most of history was a history of class struggle. In his historical analysis of the development of society, Marx held that class antagonism and struggle over resources have always been central features of society. As capitalism rose from the ruins of feudalism, a new class system and new forms of oppression became established. Although workers were legally "free" to sell their labor, they were "existentially constrained to do so" (Coser, cited in Abraham, 1988, p. 115). Thus, capitalist society created a form of exploitation that is unique to capitalism, historically specific, and cannot be directly compared to earlier periods.

Capitalist society, according to Marx, is marked by distinctive features that are specific to industrial economies. Perhaps the most important of these is the ownership of the means and tools of production, which determines one's social class. As this "property" is concentrated in the hands of a few (the bourgeoisie), the others (the proletariat) are forced to sell their labor to the privileged owners. Marx saw several problems with this arrangement.

First is the problem of exploitation. Because capitalist owners seek to maximize their own profits, wages paid to the laborers do not reflect the full value of the wealth (product) created by their work. The profit that the owners accrue represents *surplus value*, which he defined as the difference between the selling price of the item and the cost of the labor to produce it. Marx saw this as exploitation that was further compounded when the same items were later sold back to the workers at inflated costs (Perdue, 1986).

Poverty in society is an extension of the principle of surplus value. As the exploitation of the worker grows, so does the pauperization of the working class. According to Marx, "Accumulation of wealth at one pole is, therefore, at the same time the accumulation of misery, agony of toil, slavery, ignorance, brutality, mental degradation, at the opposite pole" (Marx & Engels, cited in Beer, 1955, p. 93).

The exploitation of workers leads not only to pauperization but also to alienation. In his earliest writings, *The Economic and Philosophic Manuscripts of 1844* (1932/1964), Marx examined three types of alienation: political, religious, and economic. Alienation is a process by which people become estranged, demeaned, and depersonalized. He believed that the competition and exploitation inherent in the capitalist system cause people to become alienated from their productive activity, from the products they produce, from other workers, and from their own human potential (Perdue, 1986; Ritzer, 1988; Rius, 1976). Thus, alienation results in "self-estrangement and powerlessness" (Abraham, 1988).

Because a small privileged group owns the means of production and exploits others for their profit, a class struggle becomes inevitable as people struggle against exploitation. During this struggle, the owners and the laborers become increasingly polarized and antagonistic toward each other. A class consciousness—an awareness of class position—develops among the bourgeoisie, who consolidate their common interests based on their need to exploit others for profit. Their economic monopoly, however, manifests itself not only in the work arena but also in the political arena. Through their consolidation of interests, they transform their economic power into political power and dominate the political institutions that then become subservient to them (Abraham, 1988; Rius, 1976).

In addition to controlling the economic and political institutions, Marx believed that the bourgeoisie also controlled the ideas by which the masses understood the world around them. In collaboration with Frederick Engels (1845–1846/1970, p. 64), he wrote:

> The ideas of the ruling class are in every epoch the ruling ideas, i.e., the class which is the ruling material force of society, is at the same time its ruling intellectual force. The class, which has the means of material production at its disposal, has control at the same time over the means of mental production, so that . . . those who lack the means . . . are subject to it.

In controlling ideas, the wealthy control the dominant ideologies that manifest themselves as religion and nationalism, for example. Ideology is used by the ruling classes to disguise conflicting class interests and subdue class conflict; it becomes a form of social control. The relationship between ideological control and alienation is inherent in this social arrangement.

Marx believed that "consciousness is influenced by social conditions" (Israel, 1971, p. 91). He saw the conditions of capitalistic exploitation and alienation as being intricately interwoven with those of ideological domination. A false consciousness prevails when people accept definitions of reality that further their own oppression.

Religion, according to Marx, "is the sign of the oppressed creature, the sentiment of a heartless world, and the soul of soulless conditions. It is the *opium* of the people" (as quoted in Israel, 1971, p. 32). With its emphasis on rewards in the afterlife, religion focuses attention away from earthly inequality and oppression. It also serves the interests of the capitalists when it proclaims that existing class arrangements are natural or divinely ordained. Such doctrines can become a form of social control when oppressed people internalize them, because acceptance of one's lot in life prevents people from becoming rebellious. For the privileged, life's happiness is here and now; for the less privileged, it is in some other promised land. Marx saw this as a central feature of *religious alienation*.

Political ideology and *political alienation* function in a similar manner. The ideology of "nationalism" disguises the inequalities inherent in a capitalist system. The working classes surrender their labor and life (in the case of war) to serve the interests of the elite. They do so under the guise of serving their country and mistakenly believe that the system is equal for all.

Marx passionately believed that through the use of labor, humanity could transform the world. However, certain socioeconomic conditions, legitimized by accompanying ideologies (e.g., capitalism), transform this most basic human attribute, labor, into a commodity to be sold in the marketplace. Selling one's labor without being creatively and affectively attached to its fruits is like selling one's body without being emotionally attached to the buyer. The human need to find meaning and creativity in one's work, when coupled with an economic ideology that converts that work into a purely economic exchange, results in *alienated labor*.

Thus, the religious, political, and economic ideologies of the wealthy legitimize and reinforce the status quo, which favors their interests. Marx believed that the struggle for *both* the proletariat and the bourgeoisie was to free themselves from the stranglehold of ideologies that produce false consciousness for both groups. Although the wealthy elite may have developed a class consciousness, it is a false consciousness according to Marx. They accept the existing social order uncritically, believe the ideologies that legitimate their self-interest, and thus cannot see the inherent contradictions of capitalism. The laborers, on the other hand, are kept from seeing their common plight by their acceptance of repressive ideology and by the competition that capitalism creates. Marx believed that laborers would eventually shed this false consciousness and develop class consciousness because class tensions would continue to become increasingly strained under the weight of capitalism. Their material position (being relatively propertyless) put them in a position to unite and organize a revolutionary movement in which they would be able to break the chains of their bondage (Perdue, 1986).

In addition to the bourgeoisie and proletariat, Marx acknowledged the existence of two other classes, the *petty* (or petit) *bourgeoisie* and the *lumpenproletariat*. The petty bourgeoisie were the shopkeepers and professionals, for example, who aspired to bourgeois status, while the lumpenproletariat were the "dangerous class" who preyed on society. Marx believed that the crisis of capitalism and its growth of monopolies would pull the petty bourgeoisie downward into the ranks of the proletariat.

In *The Communist Manifesto* (1848/1955), Marx and Engels advocated that "workers of the world, unite" in their struggle against the ruling class. They believed that people must become politicized in an organized struggle to bring about the revolution that would lead to the violent overthrow of capitalist exploitation. In their utopian vision, the political and economic order that would follow this revolution was that of socialism, whereby private property and private ownership would be abolished through planning government that would represent the needs of the workers. This would then be followed by communism, a stage in which private property and social classes would cease to exist. As defined in his philosophical writings, communism is an ideal future social arrangement in which all forms of antagonism between human beings and nature would be overcome (Fromm, 1961).

We note here that many of Marx's concepts can be used to understand the existing conditions of a society, or "what is." Much of his work represents his sociological and economic analysis of society. Schumpeter (1950) suggested that we separate Marx the Sociologist and Marx the Economist from Marx the Prophet. In his forecast of "what will be," Marx the Prophet recommended revolution; he believed that violent change may be necessary when polarization between oppressors and oppressed is extreme and oppressors refuse to accept fundamental change. These three sides of Marx are discussed in more detail in C. Wright Mills's (1963) *The Marxists.*

Revolution has not yet led to the demise of capitalism, as Marx predicted. As Abraham noted, "Marx's classless and stateless society is an utopia" (1988, p. 119). In Marcuse's reexamination of revolution, he argued that the "Marxian concept of a revolution . . . is 'overtaken' by historical development" (1974, p. 304). Marx's assumption that capitalist relations would limit the growth of productive forces failed to anticipate the impact that technology would have in perpetuating and creating new forms of capitalism. Further, worker and oppressed group protests in capitalist countries have led to social policy compromises improving working conditions and protecting human rights. This has defused potential for revolution. Because these compromises have not resulted in the abolition of oppression, however, Marxian analysis would view such incremental change as co-optation.

In answer to these criticisms, theorists writing in the Marxian tradition have refined his work and addressed many of these concerns.

## ROADS FROM MARX

The works of Marx have led to several generations of scholars on Marxism. They can be divided into two groups: the interpreters and the reformulators.

The interpreters are similar to biblical or Talmudic scholars who examine chapters, verses, and footnotes to interpret what Marx meant; they then recommend specific action. Prominent among such interpreters are Vladimir Lenin, Mao Tse-tung, Georges Sorel, and Leon Trotsky. They are admirers of Marx the Prophet.

In contrast, the reformulators are scholars who update the works of Marx the Sociologist and Marx the Economist. Prominent among this group are Ralf Dahrendorf, Richard Bernstein, Karl Mannheim, Theda Skocpol, and Georg Lukacs, to name a few. The reformulators can be further divided into two traditions or schools of thought: those who extend and refine Marx's original formulation of class conflict and elite control and those who reject the notion of elite control and point to the role of interest group conflict in shaping society. Our focus is on the works of the reformulators, with the caveat that the summaries offered here by no means include the full array of theory or theoretical writings in the conflict tradition.

### Ideology and Class Consciousness: Neo-Marxian Formulations

Four of the theorists who build on Marx's work on ideology and its impact on collective cognition are Karl Mannheim, Georg Lukacs, Herbert Marcuse, and Jurgen Habermas. We briefly review the aspects of their work that are particularly relevant to our understanding of the relationship between ideology and oppression of vulnerable groups.

In his extension of Marx and Engels, Mannheim (1936) expanded on the idea that one's mode of cognition, or the way a person thinks (and acts), is systematic and determined by class origin. Mannheim argued that the *ideologies* or idea systems of the ruling class are "the fictions which are used to stabilize the social order"; their legitimacy is based on myths from the past. *Utopias* are idea systems that are created by the oppressed to legitimize their challenging the existing order; their legitimacy is based on promises of the future. When the oppressed (e.g., Black slaves) embrace an ideology taught by their oppressors (Christians), they endorse the instrument of their own oppression. Those who subscribe to ruling-class ideologies instead of utopian visions live an existence with a false consciousness.

Although Mannheim saw ideological, economic, and class structures as interrelated, he diverged from Marx in his belief that some people in capitalist societies belong to a special stratum based on their education. Those in this intellectual stratum have the potential ability to understand the hidden nature of class relations and the true conflict in society (Perdue, 1986). He believed that a science of politics would emerge in the course of dialectical debate, which would eventually reveal the true nature of power.

For Georg Lukacs, the ideological nature of oppression was central to his understanding of class relations. He agreed with Marx about the class divisions inherent in capitalism but believed that the structural powerlessness of the underclass was prevalent in *all* social institutions—not just the workplace. He proposed the existence of a *universal commodity structure* in capitalistic societies in which personal relationships are commodified and gain a "phantom objectivity" (1971, p. 83). In other words, people in a commodified society are unable to clearly see the social forces that shape their lives. Instead, they see society, its economic organizations, and its social institutions as structures that have a life of their own, and they "surrender" to a supposed "objective reality" that includes oppression. Denial of and surrender to these external forces results in *reification* (treating these false ideas as if they had an actual material existence). Reification, in turn, leads to continued oppression, and it is only the development of a true class-based consciousness that can lead to revolutionary change (Perdue, 1986; Ritzer, 1992).

Many scholars from the Frankfurt School in Germany provided additional insights on ideology and cognition. Critical thinkers such as Theodor Adorno, Max Horkheimer, Franz Neumann, Erich Fromm, and Jessica Benjamin, to name a few, were associated with the Frankfurt School. The Frankfurt School, founded in 1923 as the Institute of Social Research in Germany, was established by a group of neo-Marxists who blended the German idealist tradition of Hegel with Marx's theory of political economy. In addition to their Marxist roots, they tied together the works of Max Weber, Karl Mannheim, and Sigmund Freud in their development of "critical theory." We discuss two of these theorists here: Herbert Marcuse and Jurgen Habermas.

In his reconstruction of Marxism, Marcuse focused on the cultural rather than economic structure of society. Marcuse (1964) argued that legitimation of prevailing ideology in capitalist societies happens tacitly because mass technology and mass production have distorted the personal and the public sides of "self." In *One-Dimensional Man*, he proposed that people have two dimensions, the private and the public. Technological advances, however, were accompanied by new forms of oppression and domination, one of which was the loss of the private self. The one-dimensional person is unable to critically evaluate one's circumstances and thus accepts definitions of reality that are promoted by the ruling elites and the mass media. In essence, people not only come to accept limited aspirations but become oversatisfied by them as well. He believed that liberation from materialistic, competitive conditioning was possible through a radical restructuring of the social-economic institutions that foster competitive values.

In a similar vein, Habermas focused on the "irrationality" of culture in capitalist societies. According to Habermas, the technocratic consciousness of capitalism is a "form of ideology that makes a 'fetish of science'" (Perdue, 1986, p. 382). As technocratic consciousness becomes pervasive, people become compliant, depoliticized, and unable to use "reason," which is necessary to see the contradictions in the existing power structure. However, Habermas also pointed to an increasing crisis in legitimation of the status quo in late capitalism and held that through the basic human reliance on communication, people may come to develop a universal morality that would transcend private and state interests (Perdue, 1986).

## Neo-Marxian Theory: Structural, Historical, and Economic

Contemporary Marxian theory reflects several themes in addition to the Hegelian focus of the Frankfurt School and the development of critical theory. We offer a brief comparison of some of their basic ideas and focus on a few theorists whose writing is particularly pertinent to our understanding of power and oppression in contemporary society.

Structural Marxism stems from the works of French thinkers such as Nicos Poulantzas (1975) and Louis Althusser (1969) who analyze, for example, the hidden structures of modern capitalism (such as the economy, the state, and ideology) that underlie social life. They contend that the main concern of theorists should be an understanding of the basic structures of contemporary society that foster inequality (Ritzer, 1992). In contrast, historical Marxists such as Immanuel Wallerstein (1974, 1979) and Theda Skocpol (1979) believe that Marxist research must include his concern for the historical context of social change. Wallerstein's work gives us an excellent insight into the nature of global exploitation and oppression.

Wallerstein (1974, 1979) focused on international inequality in the capitalist world system. He traced the genesis of the world system to the 16th century with the beginning of European expansion and colonial exploitation. Arguing that colonial expansion brought with it a significant shift from political and military domination to domination based on economic subjugation, Wallerstein proposed that the capitalist world economy is made up of a *core* of nations that change over time and dominate the world economy while exploiting other nations and international labor. The *periphery* is composed of regions with cheap raw materials, resources, and labor that are exploited by the core. The *semiperiphery* is composed of the regions in between that may, at some point, ascend to the core or descend to the periphery. Although Wallerstein's broader focus provides us with a good analytical tool for examining economic inequality and exploitation between nations, he has been criticized for ignoring class inequality within societies (Perdue, 1986; Ritzer, 1992). World systems theory, however, forces us to examine the context of events in relation to the capitalist world economy and, according to M. S. Kimmel (1991), provides the most comprehensive methods for this type of analysis.

Contemporary economic Marxists provide us with insightful and provocative ideas about the nature of power in contemporary capitalist society. According to Morell (1997, p. 1), the effects of economic globalization and global capitalism are "at the root of many of the challenges that social workers and their clients face." Thus, it is important to gain a better understanding of the ways in which the political economy shapes our lives, our consciousness, and our opportunities.

Authors such as Paul Baran, Paul Sweezy, and Harry Braverman have argued that the competitive capitalism of Marx's era no longer exists. A new form of capitalism, *monopoly capitalism*, has taken its place. By monopoly capitalism, they are referring to the rise of multinational megacorporations with their interlocking boards of directors. The competition that characterized the early stages of capitalism has been supplanted by capitalism based on monopolistic pricing.

Baran and Sweezy (1966) argued that despite this significant change, the ideology of competitive capitalism is alive and well and institutional practices reflect the new monopolistic reality. The government, they contended, now absorbs the economic surplus produced by these new monopolies. The "narrowly circumscribed" uses of this surplus go to support a growing military machine and a civilian government with expanded roles and functions. These expenditures, however, are "based on the production and absorption of waste" (Perdue, 1986, p. 336).

In a similar vein, H. Braverman (1974) analyzed the new universal market in which services have become the primary industry and service jobs the new working-class occupations. Monopoly capitalism, he believes, has led to the degradation of work as clerical, retail, and service workers receive low pay in low skill jobs with little chance for advancement and high paying careers (Perdue, 1986). Braverman is also concerned about the use of "scientific management" in controlling workers and dictating to them "the precise manner in which work is to be performed" (p. 90). Braverman argued that managerial control of this sort is dehumanizing and adds to the degradation of work.

The nature and structure of contemporary capitalism is also the concern of M. D. Pohlman and Charles Hamilton, who believe that in modern society class conflict and class antagonisms are disguised. In their concept of *conduit capitalism*, they proposed that private corporate profits flow to the upper class due to the labor of the middle and the working classes (Figure 3.1). Personal taxes paid by the middle and working classes flow to the government, but corporate subsidies flow from the government to the upper class. Although the government provides public assistance to the lower class, various proportions of the governmentally funded purchases also flow back to the upper class (Pohlman, 1990). Thus, through conduit capitalism, the poor, the working class, the middle class, and the government all contribute to the wealth of the upper class.

As we have seen, contemporary neo-Marxian theories cover a broad array of concepts and perspectives. Ritzer (1992) suggested that "because Marx's theory is encyclopedic, a variety of different theorists can all claim to be working within the guidelines set down in his original work" despite the "many irreconcilable differences between them" (p. 274). We turn now to theories of elite control that are not specifically Marxist in origin but build on the concept of a governing elite and coercive politics.

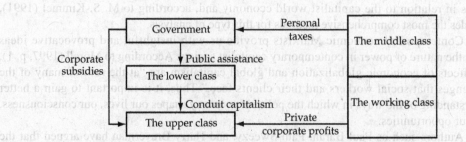

**FIGURE 3.1.** Conduit capitalism. *Source:* Adaptation of fig. 5.6, p. 82, from *Black Politics in Conservative America* by Marcus D. Pohlman. Copyright 1990 by Longman. Reprinted by permission of Pearson Education, Inc.

## The Governing Elite: Early Formulations

Early theories of elite dominance can be found in the works of social scientists Gaetano Mosca, Vilfredo Pareto, and Robert Michels, who were writing around the turn of the 20th century. In contrast to Marx, Mosca (1896/1939) believed that the ruling class was political rather than economic and his "law" of constancy held that all political systems were controlled by a ruling class. Pareto (1968), on the other hand, concurred with Marx about the relationship between economic interests and political power but disagreed with Marx's analysis of the role of the masses in social change and economic revolution. Pareto believed that the masses lacked the national capacity to be a revolutionary force (Ritzer, 1992). Mosca and Pareto each wrote about the cyclical nature of elite dominance. In their formulations, the elites in power are eventually replaced by new elites who overthrow the old order. This process is continuous and reflects, in Pareto's theory, a "circulation of elites."

Michels examined the organizational processes of trade unions and political parties and found them to be governed by small elites, referred to as "oligarchy." He proposed an *iron law of oligarchy* in which elite dominance is an inevitable outcome of organizational life.

Despite the fact that these early theorists wrote about ruling elites, their views of society reflect the assumptions of the consensus paradigm that underlies organicism and functionalism. In contrast to Marx, who believed that human nature was essentially good but constrained by the environment and social setting, these theories share a Machiavellian view of human nature (greed and selfishness) and "mandates for the domination of society by an elite of command" (Perdue, 1986, p. 91).

## C. Wright Mills: The Power Elite

American sociologist C. Wright Mills extended the theories of Max Weber in his analysis of political institutions and class structure. His work also expanded on Marx's notion of a ruling elite. Although he rejected Marx's economic determinism, he was not writing specifically in answer to Marx. His work, however, kept a "Marxian tradition alive in sociology," which was otherwise predominated by structural functionalism (Martindale, 1988; Ritzer, 1992). In *The Power Elite* (1956), Mills outlined a historical analysis of power relations in the United States and proposed a model of elite rule comprising three interlocking bases of power: industrial, political, and military.

According to Mills, preindustrial society in the United States was characterized by competing interest groups rather than an elite. The technological advances that ushered in industrialization also created a shift in the balance of power that now became concentrated in the hands of the wealthy industrialists. Corporate power was further consolidated by congressional elections and a Supreme Court decision in 1866 that extended constitutional protection to corporations. Two important circumstances eventually led to the diversification of corporate power. First, the New Deal of the 1930s gave rise to a greatly expanded role for government and government officials. Next, the Cold War strategy of the 1950s gave rise to the military–industrial complex and an expanded role for the military. Thus, he concluded that by the mid-1950s, the American power elite consisted of a few men from these interlocking hierarchies. This new power elite controlled not only economic power but also political and social power.

In his formulation, Mill proposed three levels of society—the power elite, the government planners (middle level of power), and the masses (Figure 3.2). At the top of the social structure are the elite, "a triumvirate consisting of the top men in economic, political, and military positions who coalesce to form a unified hierarchy" (Abraham, 1988, p. 123). At the middle level are

**FIGURE 3.2.** The power elite. *Source:* Adapted from *Understanding Public Policy*, 11th ed., by Thomas R. Dye, p. 23. Copyright 1995. Reprinted by permission of Pearson Education, Inc.

the government planners and functionaries (such as the legislature, interest groups, and the Supreme Court), who *appear* to formulate and enact policy. In reality, according to Mills, this middle level simply "rubber stamps" the will of the elite. The bottom level, which is the largest, comprises the masses or, simply, the rest of us. Mills believed that the media plays a large role in disguising the true nature of this power structure. Inasmuch as the elite own and control the media, they are able to manipulate the masses into believing that the democratic process still exists. They can sway our opinions about issues or even "create" issues to distract us because they control what we read, see, and hear; therefore, they control what we believe (Parenti, 1993).

According to Mills, the illusion that policy is formulated through our traditional democratic processes and institutions is just that—an illusion. In his rejection of the pluralist model of power upon which our assumptions of democracy are built, he was responding directly to David Riesman's concept of "veto groups" (discussed later in this chapter). Mills (1956) argued that "undue attention to the middle levels of power obscures the structure of power as a whole, especially at the top and bottom" (p. 245).

The elite, who give the orders and enact policy in their own interest, do so behind the scenes with little, if any, accountability to the masses. Mills, however, did not see this as a conspiracy, per se, but rather as a coincidence of interests. Their similarities in social class, religion, education, and lifestyle lead to commonalities among them in their social, civic, and business circles. Much of the "business" that they conduct (i.e., policy formulation) takes place as they mingle, for example, in gentlemen's clubs, on the golf course, and on transcontinental flights (Mills, 1956). Mills noted that "nowhere in America is there as great a 'class consciousness' as among the elite." It is their structural coincidence of interests that allows them to say of one another, "He is, of course, one of us" (p. 283).

Although the elite may have internal conflicts of interests, Mills believed that their "community of interests" binds them together in a way that transcends internal divisions. Thus, with a "maze of public relations" that they control, they have disguised the real issues, and Americans have come to mindlessly accept the "utopian image of capitalism" that they project.

The image of society that Mills portrayed is an unsettling one, and it is the radical nature of his theory that put him on the periphery of sociological thought during his lifetime (Ritzer, 1992). His writings have since made an important contribution to conflict theory.

## Interest Group Conflict

Although some theorists believe that political, economic, and social power resides in the hands of a small elite, others contend that no one group has total control (Perdue, 1986; Ritzer, 1992). Rather, people with diverse interests join together to form coalitions. These theorists agree that conflict is a permanent feature of society but believe that conflict exists between interest groups rather than between classes. Interest groups, unlike elites, undergo constant change as people coalesce around specific interests and issues. If any one group becomes too powerful, a veto group forms in opposition to restore the balance of power. As such, groups with divergent interests act as watchdogs in a democratic system.

The image of society that is portrayed in interest group theory is one of pluralism. Society is seen as heterogeneous; therefore, the clashes that occur between cultures and interest groups are seen as inevitable. However, interest group theorists believe that both consensus and conflict guide social interaction. Although there may be consensus *within* groups and conflict *between* groups, there may also be consensus *between* groups and conflict *within* groups. Despite their acceptance of consensus, interest group theorists share with the neo-Marxists a focus on change rather than equilibrium.

Ralf Dahrendorf has been one of the foremost proponents of interest group theory. Other social theorists writing in the pluralist tradition are David Riesman, Daniel Bell, and Lewis Coser. In addition, Randall Collins integrated Marxist and pluralist theory with a variety of other theories. We briefly review their works here.

## Ralf Dahrendorf: Struggle for Authority

German sociologist Ralf Dahrendorf, writing in the pluralist tradition, rejected Marx's theory of class conflict and offered a reformulation based on interest groups and the struggle for authority. According to Dahrendorf, both conflict theorists and functionalists create a theoretical utopia: The functionalists do so by claiming that society rests on consensus, and the conflict theorists by claiming that continued conflict is the norm. Building on the meso-conflict theory of Simmel, Dahrendorf argued that domination and subordination are inherent in all structures of authority. Authority, rather than property, is the structural determinant of conflict and change.

Dahrendorf and Moore (1958) suggested that the distribution of authority in social organizations leads to a conflict of interest groups, which he refers to as classes. He does not, however, mean social class in the Marxian sense, but rather contradictory interests involving domination and subordination. He pointed to the fact that conflict in society involves more than simply conflict of social class; it involves conflict that arises out of incompatible interests of "those who give orders and those who take orders" (Abraham, 1988, p. 125). Thus, conflict emanates from roles in a dynamic industrial society due to *role interests.*

When people become aware of their common interests, they begin to organize themselves into interest groups. Once organized, interest groups clash with each other in their efforts to maintain or change the status quo. Changes that occur in society, then, are changes in the system of authority. However, as Perdue noted, "structural change in this theory does not refer to society as a whole"; rather it only refers to the associations within which it occurs (1986, p. 204).

## The American Pluralist Tradition

Two American sociologists who have made significant contributions to interest group theory are David Riesman and Daniel Bell. In contrast to Mills, both D. Riesman (1950/1961) and Bell (1960) argued that power was not controlled by a small elite. Criticizing "neo-Marxist theories" as being inapplicable to American society, Bell pointed to group interests and Riesman to veto groups as the source of political power in the United States. Both subscribed to economist John Kenneth Galbraith's notion of countervailing power. Although groups do form and organize to further their own interests and causes, others who oppose those efforts form veto groups to block their actions (Figure 3.3). Thus, groups such as environmentalists and energy lobbies or pro-choice and pro-life coalitions act as countervailing powers to keep any one group from having total control. Policy, in this model, is not mandated by an elite, but is formulated and enacted through the legislative process in which interest or veto groups play a major role.

## Randall Collins: A Micro Foundation for Macro Conflict

The conflict theory of Randall Collins drew on the works of Marx but also incorporated the functionalism of Durkheim and the pluralism of Weber with symbolic interactionism and phenomenology. In his attempt at an integrated theory of conflict, he approached his topic with a focus on radical microsociology, which is essentially an individual-level theory (Ritzer, 1992). He criticized the structural functionalists for their focus on structure and norms and the conflict theorists for their focus on property and authority as objective phenomena. His theory was based, instead, on interaction patterns that emanate from internalized subjective definitions arising from conflicts over control.

Collins (1975) argued that people's experiences in "giving and taking orders" lead them to internalize their experiences with dominance and subservience. Their ensuing subjective definitions result in specific outlooks and behaviors that guide their future interactions. In addition to their subjective orientations, they bring to these interactions the material resources that they

**FIGURE 3.3.** Competing interest groups. *Source:* Adapted from T. R. Dye, 1975.

possess. Those who possess fewer resources are likely to be controlled by others, both materially and ideologically.

Although he addressed external conditions relating to the unequal distribution of resources, Collins's focus remained on the individual who seeks to maximize his or her status and share of resources. In this process, those with greater resources and status "consolidate their position, maximize their interests, and dominate the structural arrangements" (Abraham, 1988, pp. 134–135). This results in ongoing interpersonal conflict that is reflected in the macro structures of society. We can see some similarities here between Collins and Dahrendorf, as both recognized the role of dominance and subordination in the creation of conflicting interest groups. Collins, however, reduced "all macrophenomena . . . into combinations of micro events" (1981, p. 985).

## Lewis Coser: The Functions of Conflict

Lewis Coser's work on conflict was an attempt to expand on Simmel's earlier formulations. Although he rejected Parsons's theory that characterized conflict as a dysfunction of the system, Coser's metaphors were taken directly from structural functionalism. His work focused on the functions of conflict, with specific attention to its positive functions. In his analysis of conflict, Coser distinguished conflict from hostile sentiments, which he saw as a predisposition. Conflict, he argued, is a "transaction" between people.

Coser noted that conflict serves an integrative or "binding" function, as conflict with others unifies the group and sharpens "identity and boundary lines." In addition, conflict provides a "safety valve" to "drain off hostile and oppressive sentiments" (1956, p. 48). Conflict also helps to define the nature and structure of relationships between conflicting parties. The causes of conflict are many and may include closeness of relationships, a need for group cohesion, or a need to define the group structure. These needs may, at times, lead to a "search for enemies" to strengthen social cohesion.

Coser further distinguished between realistic and nonrealistic conflict. Realistic conflict arises from "specific demands" and "estimate of gains," and are "means toward a specific result" (p. 49). Nonrealistic conflict is based on the "need for tension release" and not toward a specific result. According to Coser, realistic conflict usually results in a less violent confrontation than nonrealistic conflict. In addition, if there is no built-in "safety valve" for channeling hostility, and inequality is simultaneously fostered, the potential for violence is great.

As we can see, Coser's concept of conflict is one that assumes a "balance of opposing forces" and a "process whereby a succession of new equilibriums is created" (Perdue, 1986, pp. 222–223). This constant rearrangement and accommodation between groups reflects the pluralist paradigm of Dahrendorf, Riesman, and Bell. Coser refocused his theory, however, so that the function of conflict is catharsis rather than that of social structural change (Perdue, 1986). His work did, however, bring conflict theory into empirically testable ground at the meso level.

## CONTEMPORARY ISSUES

Pluralist theories in American sociology developed, in part, as a reaction to structural functionalism (Ritzer, 1992). Not surprisingly, with their simultaneous focus on consensus and conflict, they have been criticized for remaining embedded in the structural-functional tradition. This conservative bias has limited their view of conflict and the scope of their analysis (Ritzer, 1992; Turner, 1986).

Related to this are the ongoing attempts by theorists to integrate conflict theory with structural functionalism. The functionalist conflict theory of Coser is a case in point; the functionalist bias distorts and overshadows the focus on conflict. As Andre Gunder Frank (1974) has pointed

**FIGURE 3.4.** The elite and interest groups combined. © 1998, S. P. Robbins.

out, conflict theorists and systems theorists not only ask very different questions but also start with very different assumptions about the nature of society. Frank believed that the Marxian dialectic was best suited for integration of the two perspectives. To date, this integration has not occurred.

Another issue relates to the different views of policy suggested by the pluralist model of Riesman and Bell and the power elite model of Mills. We believe that these are not incompatible but rather different aspects of the same reality. The existence of elites does not *necessarily* negate the impact of interest groups as Mills has suggested. An alternate view would suggest that policy is made at both levels (Figure 3.4). The specific policy issues decided at each level are likely determined by elites as they seek to protect their interests. Not all policy, however, is of direct concern to them, and this is where interest groups may make a significant impact on policy decisions.

Importantly, both Marxian conflict theory and non-Marxian notions of conflict have influenced five overlapping modern, and mostly European, forms of critical theory: social constructionism, social reproduction theory, cultural capital theory, poststructuralism, and postmodernism (Baudrillard, 1983, 1988; Bourdieu, 1977a, 1977b, 1990; Chambon, Irving, & Epstein, 1999; Derrida, 1978, 1981, 1994; Eco, 1989; Foucault, 1965, 1974, 1975, 1979; Laird, 1993; Lyotard, 1984; MacLeod, 1995; M. Mann, 1970; McNamee & Gergen, 1992; Searle, 1995; Swift, 1995).

Finally, some important questions about social work practice emerge from theories presented in this chapter: Are social workers primarily agents of the elites, in charge of managing the poor, the underprivileged, and the marginal populations? How does the source of our income influence the definition and performance of our social work functions? Are we part of a repressive system that exerts ideological control over the masses? To what extent are we, in fact, agents of control? These questions are inherent in the tension between the two poles of social work professional mandates: social change and social control. This tension inevitably involves the profession in moral and ethical dilemmas. For example, if practice is designed to improve client coping or adaptation, is this merely a way of preventing conflict and diffusing action toward social justice?

Although these questions and, perhaps, the answers may be disquieting, they stem from Marxian critical analysis and force us to confront both the nature of power in society and our role in supporting the existing power structure.

# APPLICATION TO SOCIAL WORK PRACTICE

In contrast to systems theories that are best used as models for assessment, conflict theories provide us with models for both assessment and intervention. Conflict theories, unfortunately, have not received widespread recognition in social work in the United States. The models of social activism that they promote are sometimes seen as detrimental to "professional" practice (Haynes & Mickelson, 2009) and social workers using these approaches have been accused of being too political and unrealistic in their quest for structural change (Finn & Jacobson, 2003, 2007). Activism, however, is seen by many as essential in addressing issues of social and economic injustice and plays a central role in the concept of radical social work (Abramovitz, 1993; Fisher, 1995; Galper, 1980; Morell, 1997; Payne, 1991, 2005; Rees, 1991; Reeser & Leighninger, 1990; Specht & Courtney, 1994). At the least, conflict theories, both classic and current European versions, can be used to understand *alienation* of individuals, groups, and communities.

Conflict theory is conspicuously absent in the social work literature pertaining to human behavior theory. Although several authors have noted the importance of emphasizing the economic, political, and ideological aspects of human behavior (Forte, 2006; Longres, 2000; Payne, 2005; Queralt, 1996; Schriver, 2010; Witkin & Gottschalk, 1988), conflict theory is covered in a cursory fashion, if at all, in most leading textbooks. Inasmuch as issues of power and inequality are central to social life and human existence, conflict theory in all of its varieties is an important theoretical base for social work practice.

A relatively recent development in social work has been increasing interest in antioppressive practice that draws on a variety of theories closely related to conflict theory. Although this includes a diverse body of literature, the main emphasis is on power, privilege, and domination and the way in which structural inequality affects the personal, interpersonal, structural, and cultural aspects of people's lives. Due to this, there is a considerable amount of overlap with stratification theory, social justice theory, critical theory, feminist theory, empowerment theory, and theories of racial oppression. It is likely that antioppressive practice is seen as a better "fit" with social work, given the diverse interests that it encompasses. Despite the emerging literature on antioppressive practice (see, for example, Appleby, Colon, & Hamilton, 2007; Baines, 2008; Clifford & Burke, 2009; Dominelli, 2002; Fook, 2002; Marsiglia & Kulis, 2009; Mullaly, 2002, 2007; Sinclair & Albert, 2008; van Wormer, 2004), much of this work is highly derivative and no unique theories have emerged in the field of social work.

According to Finn and Jacobson (2003), because "the logic of late capitalism and the forces of globalization have profoundly altered social conditions, social welfare policies and social work practice . . . social justice workers need the theoretical and political capacity to grapple with questions of discourse, domination and globalization in order to be effective players on this challenging terrain" (p. 169). We agree and believe that conflict theory and contemporary critical theory can assist us in becoming more effective in this domain.

## Definition of the Helping Situation

Conflict theories lend themselves to two definitions of the helping situation—"problem" for the small group level and "social issues" for larger groups. The *problem* definition may arise when power imbalances in small groups result from external conditions (such as unequal resources) or from the development of internal coalitions that leave a dissatisfied minority. The social issues definition emanates from institutional policies that deny access of resources to specific groups (based on factors such as class, race, gender, sexual orientation, religious or political conflict) or situations that involve exploitation or domination. Flowcharts 3.1 and 3.2 demonstrate applications of conflict theories derived from these definitions.

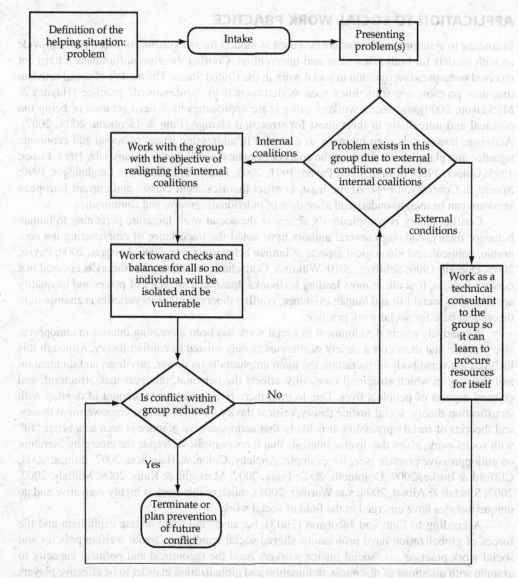

**FLOWCHART 3.1.** An example of applying conflict theory at the small group level. © 1998, S. P. Robbins, P. Chatterjee, & E. R. Canda.

## Assessment, Practice Strategies, and Methods

Conflict theories lend themselves to a variety of practice applications at the group, community, organizational, and societal levels. In working with small groups, social work assessment can employ theoretical concepts from Simmel and Coser pertaining to intra- or intergroup conflict involving the analysis of dyads, triads, and coalitions. Assessment of power differences between and among group members may be one area of focus and would include an assessment of

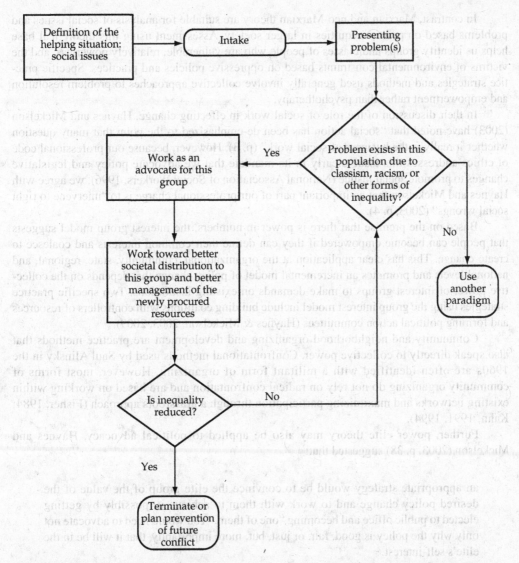

**FLOWCHART 3.2.** An example of applying conflict theory at an oppressed group level. © 1998, S. P. Robbins, P. Chatterjee, & E. R. Canda.

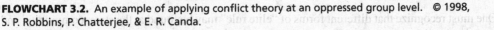

factors that leads to power differentials such as inequality in status or resources. Additionally, assessment may include factors that contribute to group stability. The group work method developed in the settlement house tradition, for example, has been used for work in inner-city neighborhoods with rival groups (such as youth groups or racial and ethnic groups). Conflict management within and between groups is another model of practice stemming from these theories.

In contrast, Marxian and neo-Marxian theory are suitable for analysis of social issues and problems based on power inequities in larger society. Assessment using this theoretical base helps us identify groups and classes of people who are vulnerable, relatively powerless, and the victims of environmental constraints based on oppressive policies and practices. Specific practice strategies and methods used generally involve collective approaches to problem resolution and empowerment rather than psychotherapy.

In their discussion of the role of social work in effecting change, Haynes and Mickelson (2003) have noted that "social action has been de-emphasized to the point that many question whether it really is the business of social work" (p. 3). However, because our professional code of ethics addresses this issue clearly in its mandate that we advocate policy and legislative changes to promote social justice (National Association of Social Workers, 1996), we agree with Haynes and Mickelson that an important part of our professional charge is to "intervene to right social wrongs" (2003, p. 4).

Based on the premise that there is power in numbers, the interest group model suggests that people can become empowered if they can define their common interests and coalesce to create change. This has clear application at the organizational, community, state, regional, and national levels and promotes an incremental model of policy change that depends on the collective power of interest groups to make demands on existing institutions. Two specific practice strategies using the group interest model include building coalitions with controllers of resources and forming political action committees (Haynes & Mickelson, 2003, 2009).

Community and neighborhood organizing and development are practice methods that also speak directly to collective power. Confrontational methods used by Saul Alinsky in the 1960s are often identified with a militant form of organizing. However, most forms of community organizing do not rely on radical confrontation and are based on working within existing networks and maximizing participation through a grassroots approach (Fisher, 1984; Kahn, 1991, 1994).

Further, power elite theory may also be applied to political advocacy. Haynes and Mickelson (2003, p. 38) suggested that:

> an appropriate strategy would be to convince the elite group of the value of the desired policy change and to work with them to achieve it, possibly by getting elected to public office and becoming "one of them." You would need to advocate not only why the policy is good, fair, or just, but, more importantly, that it will be in the elite's self-interest.

One must recognize that different forms of "elite rule" may be found at the state, community, and organizational levels as well. The strategies outlined by Haynes and Mickelson can be adapted for use at these various levels.

Social work in the United States is, for the most part, committed to achieving social and economic justice through reform of existing institutions rather than through Marxist revolution. Inasmuch as our code of ethics mandates a professional responsibility not only to our clients but also to our colleagues, employing organizations, the profession, and society as a whole, tactics involving violent, revolutionary change will likely conflict with our professional mandate. We point out, however, that the Latin American social work model of *conscientization* fits well with Marxist thought. Writing in the Marxist tradition, Paolo Freire (1970) suggested that when people are provided with the proper tools, they can become conscious of the inherent contradictions in personal and social reality and deal with this in a critical fashion. Freire referred to this new

## TABLE 3.1    Various Settings and Applications of Conflict Theories

| Type of Agency | Type of Presenting Problems | Method | Definition(s) of Helping Situation | Type of Focus |
|---|---|---|---|---|
| **Micro-Level Conflict Theories (Simmel, etc.)** | | | | |
| Community center | Conflict within neighborhood groups (or gangs) | Purposive group work | Problem | Help groups attain mutually satisfactory coalitions |
| Community center | Conflict within neighborhood groups (or gangs) | Purposive group work | Problem | Help groups attain acceptable levels of coexistence |
| **Macro-Level Conflict Theories (Marx, neo-Marxians, etc.)** | | | | |
| Community center | Conflict between this community and greater society | Purposive community work | Social issues | Help this community demand a better share of distribution |
| Special issue-oriented community agency | Conflict between this population and greater society | Purposive community work | Social issues | Help this population demand a better share of distribution |
| Collective bargaining agency | Conflict between this group and a group with resources | Purposive group and community work | Social issues | Help this group attain a better return for themselves |

consciousness as *conscientizacao,* or an awareness of these conflicts coupled with an action plan. The first step, of course, is education. Burstow (1991) has recently applied Freire's work for use in classroom settings. Although conscientization is not now widely used in the United States, its basic tenets of educating and organizing people for collective action have long been accepted practice methods (Payne, 2005).

Finally, conflict theory provides an excellent framework for analyzing the policy-making process (Domhoff, 1990; Dye, 1975; Lindblom, 1968) and has application for analysis at all levels in which policy is formulated and enacted. Table 3.1 illustrates a variety of settings and applications of conflict theories.

# CRITICAL ANALYSIS

## Biological, Psychological, and Spiritual Factors

Conflict theories do not address biological or psychological processes directly. Although psychological processes are not directly addressed, the impact of ideology and inequality on the human psyche and human behavior are at the heart of these formulations. Religion is portrayed in Marxist theory as an ideological tool that serves the interests of those in power. Interest group theory, in contrast, points to the constantly shifting power relations within and between religions as groups vie for dominance over one another. Not surprisingly, due to their primarily macro focus, conflict theories have been criticized for being reductionistic in their attempt to attribute human behavior to economic and social processes alone. Although Karl Marx adamantly opposed institutional religions' tendency to support an oppressive social order, his ideals for communism have a distinctly spiritual tone, in the sense of the word commonly used in social work (Canda & Furman, 2010). That is, Marx sought the transcendence of all forms of oppression and the full humanization of all people. This involves a search for authentic, humanizing ways of relating that allow everyone to achieve full potential. Fromm (1961, p. 64) put this forcefully:

> Marx's atheism is the most advanced form of rational mysticism, closer to Meister Eckhart or to Zen Buddhism than are most of those fighters for God and religion who accuse him of "godlessness."

It should not be surprising that some contemporary activist movements have converged Marxian thought with their religious frameworks. For example, liberation theology explicitly links Marxian analysis with Christian advocacy for the poor and oppressed, even against the forces of both state and church if necessary (Breton, 1989).

## Social, Cultural, and Economic Forces

Conflict theories analyze the social, political, economic, and historical bases of human behavior. Some theorists emphasize the interrelationship between various contexts (economic, social, and political), while others retain a more narrow focus and emphasize one of these over the others. In addition, dimensions of culture that do not directly relate to power disparities and inequality receive little attention.

However, a particular strength of conflict theory is in its explicit focus on the social, political, and economic forces that impact people's lives. Analysis of power disparities that result in group conflict, inequality, and oppression assists us in understanding historical and contextual elements that have previously received little attention in human behavior textbooks. The focus on political economy adds an important dimension of theory that helps us understand the larger context of personal and social life. The issue of social class, in particular, has received almost no attention in human behavior theory for social work practice. Conflict theory helps us refocus our attention on factors related to social class and class consciousness.

## Relevance to Individuals, Groups, Families, Organizations, Institutions, and Communities

The theories discussed here primarily focus on membership in groups and social classes. It is the institutions of society (social, political, economic) and their structural arrangements that are believed to influence individual, family, group, and community life. Human behavior is seen as a product of the larger contexts that define the roles, rules, and expectations of a society.

Although conflict theories are most often used to describe and explain power disparities and conflict between large groups or classes, they may also be applied to families, small groups, and organizations. Their application to individuals is limited to conditions of inequality that affect people because of their membership in a specific group or class. Table 3.2 shows the application of conflict theory to these various levels.

| TABLE 3.2 | Levels of Application of Conflict Theories |
|---|---|
| **Level** | **Examples of Applications** |
| Individual | Intrapsychic, cognitive, or philosophical conflict |
| | Conflict due to membership in oppressed group |
| Family | Interpersonal conflict |
| | Conflict between family members |
| | Conflict in role expectations |
| | Conflicts in roles |
| Other small groups | Intragroup conflict |
| | Conflicts for leadership |
| | Conflicts due to contradictory roles or role expectations |
| | Conflicts due to different socialization |
| | Intergroup conflict |
| Organizations | Conflict within organizations (includes interpersonal, intragroup, and intergroup and conflict of roles and role expectations) |
| | Conflict between organizations |
| Communities | Conflict within and between communities due to social class, ethnicity, race, religion, ideology, and other forms of human diversity |
| Larger social structures | Conflict between larger groups due to social class, ethnicity, race, gender, religion, ideology, and other forms of human diversity |
| | Conflict between occupational and professional interests |
| | Conflict between nations |

## CONSISTENCY WITH SOCIAL WORK VALUES AND ETHICS

Conflict theories suggest that optimal health and well-being are related to environmental and contextual factors rather than personal ones. Power disparities that lead to inequality, exploitation, and oppression are seen as the primary factors that thwart the realization of full potential. It is a well-established fact that health is related to both income and access to health care, and several authors have suggested that life satisfaction results from better health, which in turn is affected by increased income (Chatfield, 1977; Fengler, Little, & Danigelis, 1983; Mancini, 1981; Marson & Della Fave, 1994).

Further, in both Marxian and elite theory formulations, ideological control prevents people from gaining true knowledge of the extent of their exploitation, and thus they come to expect and accept a lesser standard of health and well-being than do those in power. Optimal health and well-being are thus preserved for those with money, power, and influence in capitalist societies. By contrast, in pluralist theory, health and well-being for individuals and societies are achieved through a balance of being both sociable and self-assertive, cooperative, and competitive.

A pitfall of conflict theory may be the risk of overemphasis on polarization and antagonism. Social workers who analyze situations only in conflict terms may be prone, ironically, to dehumanize clients as victims and opponents as oppressors. Solutions may be sought that seek victory for one interest group at the expense of another, thus creating a new act of oppression.

Conflict theories deal directly with concepts of inequality, oppression, exploitation, and coercion. Few conflict theorists, however, write specifically about women, racial and ethnic minorities, or gays and lesbians. The concept of *minority* is assumed to be implicit in discussions of power and inequality. This can be misleading because the dichotomies of bourgeoisie/proletariat and elites/masses do not recognize the varying degrees of inequality within these groups, nor do they recognize other bases of oppression. Thus, only certain aspects of diversity are explicitly addressed.

Marx, not surprisingly, was one of the first theorists to speak out against the exploitation of women and children. In *The Communist Manifesto* (1848/1955), he, along with Engels, held that the modern individual family is based on the open or disguised enslavement of both women and children. In capitalist society, he contended, women were "mere instruments of production" and their children were transformed into "simple articles of commerce and instruments of labor" (p. 28). The demise of capitalism, he believed, would bring an end to domestic enslavement.

Conflict theory, with its emphasis on empowerment and change (either revolutionary or incremental), rejects the status quo and the "equilibrium" that maintains inequality. In this group of theories, discriminatory and oppressive policies and practices become a clear target for change. They are not accepted as "functional" for the system but are seen as "dysfunctional" for people who are victims of coercive exploitation.

## PHILOSOPHICAL UNDERPINNINGS

The broad array of theories presented here shares some common assumptions about conflict and change. Conflict is seen as natural and normal, and change is assumed to be the norm. In addition, both the Marxist and the pluralist paradigms assume rationality on the part of individuals, but diverge otherwise on their views of human nature. The Marxian formulation assumes people to be basically good and sociable but constrained by their environment. For human nature to flourish, it must be placed in an environment of "collective enrichment" that is antithetical to capitalistic exploitation and coercion. Although it assumes a coercive present, a utopian society is believed to be attainable through the voluntaristic overthrow of repressive political and economic systems. Ideology is paradoxically assumed to be a tool of oppression and the means to liberation.

Pluralist theory, in contrast, assumes a dualistic view of both human nature and society. People are both sociable and self-assertive, cooperative, and competitive. Society reflects this same dualism with consensus and conflict both being features of social life. According to Perdue (1986), the pluralist paradigm reflects the philosophical views of German idealist Immanuel Kant and French philosopher Jean-Jacques Rousseau.

Abraham (1988) pointed out several fallacies inherent in these assumptions. The assumption of incessant flux, he argued, negates the historical reality of stability in traditional societies. Additionally, both change and stability are natural characteristics of society. Another problem is equating conflict with change, given that some changes occur without conflict. The failure of conflict theorists to "distinguish between positive and negative conflicts" tells us little about the consequences, and, he asserted, "conflict can contribute as much to social integration and stability as to disintegration and change" (p. 139).

## METHODOLOGICAL ISSUES AND EMPIRICAL SUPPORT

Conflict theories are grounded in both the positivist and the phenomenological traditions in that they examine the relation between material and social conditions and the production of false or authentic consciousness. In addition, some call for historical analysis. We see, however, a near absence of the scientific method, precise measurement, and use of statistical induction. Although lawlike propositions appear in many of these theories, the constructs do not easily lend themselves to quantitative measurement. Measurement of this sort is, of course, possible. As Martindale noted, "Conflict theory was more empirically positivistic than even organismic positivism" (1988, p. 203).

Methodological problems, however, abound. Turner (1986) has criticized pluralist conflict theory for its vagueness, as there is rarely a clear definition of conflict. Mills's elite theory presents us with a different type of methodological dilemma. If the elite are largely unknown to anyone but themselves, and if they formulate policy informally in their coincidence of interests, empirical verification of their existence and their impact on policy becomes difficult, if not impossible. One notable attempt to study a community elite (Hunter, 1957) has been challenged by scholars who suggest that it only documented *perceptions* of political power; however, they did not address the way in which it was exercised. This illustrates the very dilemma posed by Mills's theory. Numerous studies on community power have focused on either the institutional bases of influence or specific interpersonal relationships and roles (Agger, Goldrich, & Swanson, 1964; Clelland & Form, 1964; Dahl, 1961; Presthus, 1964; Sayre & Kaufman, 1960; Vidich & Bensman, 1958; Wildavsky, 1964). Although some studies support an elite model of power, others support the pluralist model. Hawley and Wirt (1968) noted that both methodological and theoretical issues present continuing problems in the study of community power, not the least of which is the difficulty in measuring power.

Contemporary world systems theorists have noted that there is still controversy over the measurement and conceptualization of *core* and *periphery* (Arrighi & Drangel, 1986; Chase-Dunn, 1989; Chase-Dunn & Hall, 1993) and have noted the increasing complexity in studying and comparing intersocietal hierarchies in different world systems (Chase-Dunn & Hall, 1993).

In addition to lack of conceptual clarity and problems in measurement are the problems of determinism and reductionism. Marxist thought has been criticized for its economic determinism. Perdue pointed out that there are many variables that Marx "appeared to ignore, preferring instead to examine those particular dimensions with clear implications for social change" (1986, p. 328). Marx has also been accused of reifying the "state," and Mills, likewise, has been accused of reifying power.

Reductionism is a problem that can be clearly seen in Collins's theory. In his translation of macrophenomena into micro events, he reduced conflict to "interactions" between people. In the same manner as Coser and social work theorists Germain and Gitterman, he reinterpreted conditions that are imposed on people as being cultural processes that they create.

Methodological arguments have developed between the various schools of thought that constitute neo-Marxism. Structural Marxists have criticized the others for their lack of attention to structure. They, in turn, have been criticized for their ahistorical analyses and lack of quantification. Critical theorists, on the other hand, have criticized the empiricists for "losing sight of the actor." Clearly, there is little if any consensus about proper methodology in neo-Marxist thought.

Although Marxist conflict theory has generally relied on historical analyses rather than empirical studies, Abraham pointed out that there is an abundance of data about conflict on the meso level. Narrow formulations that study specific types of conflict (i.e., role conflict, value conflict, political conflict) have yielded a wealth of data. Quoting Duke, he asserted that "any methodology may be adopted for use . . . and no methodology is unusable" (1988, p. 140).

The conflict theories discussed here are better at explanation than prediction and are better at a probabilistic level than at a deterministic level. These theories are adequately suited for explaining properties of groups but have limited utility for use with individuals. Attempts to reduce conflict to a micro level and explain it through the motivations and internalizations of the individual have been widely criticized.

# Summary

The broad array of theories presented here offers important concepts to aid us in our understanding of the historical, social, political, and economic factors that have an impact on people's lives. The diversity in conflict theories and their applicability at a variety of levels provide a sound theoretical base in political economy for an activist model of practice. Because pluralist interest group theories contain implicit functionalism, they should appeal to those who also find appeal in systems theory. Additionally, their mandate for incremental change within existing channels fits well with established practice principles.

Marxist theory and its neo-Marxist variants may hold broad appeal for the disenfranchised or oppressed or those with a particular interest in political advocacy. We have seen acceptance of Marxist thought in third world countries, for example, and this approach may gain in popularity in the United States if income disparity and economic insecurity continue to be salient factors in people's lives. The current attempts to dismantle public social services may hasten this process. The Marxist dialectic and critical thought may also appeal to intellectuals who may find a dialectic of ideas more appealing than Marx's material application. One does not have to accept Marx's revolutionary vision to accept his sociological analysis.

Martindale (1988, p. 203) pointed out that the sociological gains in moving from organicism to conflict theory are immense due to its reformulation of problems related to social class, attention to the interrelationships between political and other institutions, and shift to the analysis of group relations and factors that disrupt stability. He also noted that the ideological formula of conflict theory reflects "the paradox of maturity: 'If you know enough to carry out a revolution, you know better.'"

# Theories of Empowerment

Hard times in my homeland, trouble in my town
Seen oppression—I've seen torture
Seen blood upon the ground.
Had to run for my life to escape from captivity
Now you tell me that the boat is full
And there ain't no room for me.
Rock the boat—don't let me down
Rock the boat—don't let me down.

© HANS THEESINK
1993, MARVIDIC MUSIC (BMI)

## THEORIES OF EMPOWERMENT

- provide conceptualizations of social stratification and oppression
- identify the personal and political barriers and dynamics that maintain oppression
- offer value frameworks for promoting human empowerment and liberation
- identify practical strategies for overcoming oppression and achieving social justice
- build on people's strengths, resiliency, and resources

This chapter was coauthored with Graciela Couchonnal, PhD; Mende Snodgress, JD, LCSW; and Barbara Becker, MPH.

Theories of empowerment address the dynamics of discrimination and oppression. They are theories for social action and have a pragmatic, social justice orientation. In contrast to many theories of human behavior, empowerment theories are more concerned with application and practice than description and prediction. They are designed to promote both awareness of real-life circumstances and actions that produce change rather than "blaming the victims" for their experiences of oppression and discrimination (Adams, 2008; Freire, 1973; Gutierrez & Ortega, 1991). They can be used to help people realize their own highest aspirations and strengths and to engage in actions that support both personal well-being and social justice. In addition, they facilitate the process by which clients and communities can learn to recognize conditions of inequality and injustice and take action to increase their power and to regain control of their destinies (Gutierrez, Glenmaye, & DeLois, 1995; Mullaly, 2007).

In this chapter, we examine the sociopolitical context of empowerment theories and discuss two specific empowerment traditions: theories of lesbian, gay, bisexual, transgender, queer, questioning, and intersexed empowerment, and social work empowerment theories.

## HISTORICAL CONTEXT

Historically, empowerment theories have reflected a wide range of ideas and themes drawn from sociology, economic and political theory, liberation theology, and the social work tradition. As theories that promote social activism, they have been grounded in a conflict model based on Marxist thought and a mandate for social action and consciousness raising derived from the work of Paulo Freire. In the United States, the Marxist and socialist elements of social work empowerment theories have been de-emphasized, whereas in Canada and the United Kingdom, they remain influential.

Although social work began as a movement to ameliorate poverty and injustice, through the years its purpose has broadened to include social action, advocacy, and client empowerment. The development of empowerment as a central purpose of social work practice grew out of the early social reform efforts (Simon, 1994a). Seeking to address discriminatory practices, social workers such as Jane Addams and Bertha Capen Reynolds worked to eliminate oppression of minorities, immigrants, women, and children. Social work leadership in the social reform issues of the time included the peace movement, efforts to reduce poverty, the role of economic oppression, the need for racial justice, and the movement to protect women's and children's rights.

The social reform mission of social work led to the development of a particular view of the role of social workers, the nature of clients, and the process of change. These early perceptions of practice, workers, and clients contained elements that are characteristic of empowerment-oriented practice. These include the worker–client relationship as an "alliance," the worker–client relationship as a reciprocal exchange of learning, an emphasis on the value of client self-determination, and efforts to change the social structural and policy bases of oppression (Adams, 2008; Addams, 1893; Reynolds, 1951).

Since that time, group work has continued to be an important arena for empowerment-oriented social work, growing out of the collective living experience of settlers who worked and engaged in dialogue, mutual aid, and collective action to find solutions to common problems (J. Lee, 2001; Simon, 1994a). More recently, civil rights activities and community organizing and development have been important empowerment approaches in social work. Feminist social workers have addressed the link between patriarchy, sexism, homophobia, racism, and poverty and have challenged conventional male-centered developmental theories and research strategies (L. V. Davis, 1985; Van Den Bergh & Cooper, 1986). The works of Solomon, Lee, Gutierrez,

Adams, and Mullaly reviewed in this chapter demonstrate that empowerment theories have been receiving significant attention in social work for at least 20 years.

## KEY CONCEPTS

Central to all empowerment theories is the concept of empowerment. *Empowerment* refers to the process by which individuals and groups gain power to access resources and to control the circumstances of their lives (Adams, 2008). In doing so, they gain the ability to achieve their highest personal and collective aspirations and goals. Empowerment theories explicitly focus on the structural barriers that prevent people from accessing resources necessary for health and well-being. These barriers include, for example, the unequal distribution of wealth and power inherent in postindustrial economies as well as the effects of prolonged powerlessness on oppressed and marginalized individuals and groups. Empowerment theories are concerned both with the process of empowerment and with results that produce greater access to resources and power for disenfranchised individuals and groups.

*Power*, in the context of these theories, refers to the ability to access and control resources and people. A related concept, *stratification*, refers to the way in which human groups in society are differentiated from each other and placed in hierarchical order of relative privilege and oppression. Empowerment theorists contend that stratification and hierarchy automatically exclude some individuals and groups from access to valuable resources, power, and control over their own lives. *Powerlessness* is "the inability to manage emotions, skills, knowledge, and/ or material resources in a way that effective performance of valued social roles will lead to personal gratification" (Solomon, 1976, p. 16). Powerlessness is thought to arise from the negative valuations that develop among those who are considered to be marginalized and less valued groups.

Empowerment theories propose that empowerment requires linking a sense of self-efficacy with critical consciousness and effective action. Developing a *critical consciousness*, or consciousness raising, is the process of increasing awareness of how political structures, personal assumptions, and unequal distribution of power affect individual and group experience and contribute to personal or group powerlessness (Freire, 1973; Sakamoto & Pitner, 2005). L. M. Gutierrez (1990a, 1990b) suggested that critical consciousness involves three cognitive components: identification with similar others, reducing self-blame for past events, and developing a sense of personal freedom.

## STRATIFICATION, OPPRESSION, AND INEQUALITY: THE SOCIOPOLITICAL CONTEXT OF EMPOWERMENT THEORIES

Empowerment theories are based on the idea that society consists of stratified groups possessing different and unequal levels of power and control over resources.

Social stratification is the process by which people are grouped hierarchically based on inequalities in wealth, power, prestige, access to resources, and life opportunities. Although inequality exists in all societies, some have minimal and flexible patterns of stratification, whereas others have more complicated and rigid forms. Stratification is commonly based on differences in gender, age, race, ethnicity, religion, linguistic groups, sexual orientation, disability, caste, and class. Issues relating specifically to race, ethnicity, and culture are discussed in more detail in Chapter 6. In this chapter, we focus on inequality based on the *combined* factors of social class, race, gender, age, and sexual orientation.

Social classes are groups that share similar and unequal amounts of wealth, prestige, or power. Despite efforts at precise measurement, most researchers admit that class boundaries are often arbitrary and difficult to define. In the past, social class distinctions were based on long-standing and clearly understood cultural traditions. In industrial and postindustrial societies, class distinctions are usually based on some combination of four factors: income, education, occupation, and wealth. However, contemporary theories propose a model that includes class distinctions based on access to political power (Beeghley, 1989). Class stratification, however, is a contributory factor in race, gender, and age stratification as well as in the stratification of individuals based on sexual orientation. As L. E. Davis and Proctor noted, "combinations of race and gender, and gender and socioeconomic status, place many individuals in triple jeopardy" (1989, p. 125).

Although American society promotes the ideal that upward mobility (moving to a higher social class) can be attained by anyone, most studies have shown that this is rarely true. Although there is some upward mobility in the United States, it has historically occurred for people who receive higher education (Beeghley, 1989; Blau & Duncan, 1967; Gilbert & Kahl, 1987; Hauser & Featherman, 1977; Lipset & Bendix, 1961; Vanfossen, 1979). Persons of color, women, and those with less education and less access to education have less opportunity, as a group, to become upwardly mobile.

When upward mobility is systematically denied to identifiable groups over prolonged periods of time, it results in *oppression* that, according to Turner, Singleton, and Musick (1987, pp. 1–2), prevents people from "attaining access to the scarce and valued resources of that system." Many authors have noted that class-based oppression has resulted in a "caste-like" structure in the United States (O. C. Cox, 1970; Dollard, 1937; Turner et al., 1987; Verba, 1978; Willie, 1979). According to Turner et al. (1987, p. 3):

> Black-white relations in America have historically involved relegation and confine-
> ment of Blacks to the lowest rank in the stratification system, thereby denying them
> access to material well-being, power, and prestige. As long as we recognize the
> limitations involved, we can term the plight of Blacks caste-like.

The contemporary caste-like system in the United States has been vividly described by folk-rap artist Chris Chandler and reflects a resurgence of music dealing with contemporary social and political issues:

> *Now somebody told me that slavery had been abolished*
> *Seems to me that the rules were only polished*
> *Yeah, polished like the Formica and chrome*
> *At the Ronald McDonald plantation burger home. . .*
> *In the indentured service industry*
> *There's a new slave ship conspiracy*
> *It's a fast food confederacy.*
> *They've been plottin' something rotten*
> *Yeah, burgers are the new cotton*
> *In the fast food confederacy.*

> © Chris Chandler and Phil Rockstroh
> The Only People That Would (BMI)

The caste-like structure can be seen most clearly in the continuing overrepresentation of racial and ethnic minorities among the poor. As Harrington (1987, pp. 14–15) observed, this leads to the "increasing alienation of the poor people of color in communities of highest unemployment and deepest poverty" and leads to an "utter hopelessness that often comes with being Black or Hispanic and poor." According to Freire (1970, p. 32), the dehumanizing effects of oppression are damaging to both oppressor and oppressed. The oppressed, however, "have adapted to the structure of domination in which they are immersed, and have become resigned to it." Thus, they come to believe that they are incapable of fighting against oppression.

Another pervasive problem has been the "glass ceiling," or invisible barrier, that keeps women and minorities from attaining top jobs. While the ideal of equal opportunity is espoused, it is far from a reality. Women and minorities continue to "peak out" at a low level of management (Kelborn, 1995). Minorities hit this peak even more quickly than women.

Many factors contribute to this disparity in occupational opportunity, not the least of which are discriminatory practices such as stereotyping women and minorities into dead-end career paths. In addition, the exclusion of women and minorities from established professional networks compounds the disadvantage. Many women are, in effect, forced to choose pink-collar jobs because these jobs are readily available. The failure of companies to devise flexible policies to accommodate the needs of working parents—especially mothers who are still expected to be the primary caretakers—continues to impede occupational advancement for all except those with the most resources. As Jean Baker Miller (1986b) has astutely pointed out, issues of dominance and subordination that produce gender stratification often govern the distribution of limited resources.

Discrimination based on age has also become a growing reality, and the current trend of corporate downsizing has forced many older workers out of the job market. Policies such as forced retirement also contribute to ageism. Ageism, according to R. N. Butler (1975, p. 12), "is manifested in a wide range of phenomena, both on individual and institutional levels—stereotypes and myths, outright disdain and dislike . . . (and) discriminatory policies in housing, employment and services of all kinds."

In American culture, sexual orientation has also served as a basis for discrimination and oppression across cultures, socioeconomic strata, and gender lines. According to Foucault (1978), it is likely that heterosexism can be traced to economic theory that seeks to restrict and limit sexual behavior, thus preserving the economic power of the nuclear family as the primary economic unit in capitalistic society. Other scholars place heterosexism in the context of sexism and gender-role identification. Suzanne Pharr (1988, p. 8) has suggested that women suffer most from gender roles, restrictions, and expectations and that gender roles are maintained, in part, by homophobia.

Despite our egalitarian ideal, interpersonal and structural forms of discrimination and oppression remain prevalent in our society. For example, inequality of health, wealth, and opportunity are related to race, social class, age, and gender (Chesler, 1976; Gilbert & Kahl, 1987; Hollingshead & Redlich, 1953; Spitzer & Denzin, 1968; U.S. Department of Commerce, 1989). One must recognize, however, that not all oppressed groups are equally oppressed. Only some groups are placed in the lowest rank and denied access to all resources (power, property, prestige). As Turner et al. (1986, p. 3) noted, "oppressive acts can be selective with respect to only scarce resources." Some oppressed people are allowed access to material well-being but are denied access to power or prestige. Others are allowed some prestige and wealth but not power.

For these reasons, some have suggested that use of empowerment techniques should be limited to populations that are stigmatized or otherwise powerless, oppressed, and marginalized (J. Lee, 2001). The empowerment tradition can be seen in several schools of thought that embrace activism for the purpose of eliminating oppression: feminist theory; theories of lesbian, gay, bisexual, transgender, queer, questioning, and intersexed empowerment; and social work empowerment theories. As discussed in Chapter 3, a recent addition to the social work literature is an emerging interest in antioppressive practice that includes diverse interests and literature that overlaps with and is derived from a number of theories that are also concerned with structural inequality and oppression. Feminist theories are discussed in more detail in Chapter 5.

## LESBIAN, GAY, BISEXUAL, TRANSGENDER, QUEER, QUESTIONING, AND INTERSEXED EMPOWERMENT THEORIES

The lesbian and gay liberation movement is the beginning point of any discussion of empowerment theory as it relates to sexual orientation. The "Stonewall riots" of June 27, 1969, mark the formal beginnings of the gay and lesbian liberation movement (D'Augelli & Garnets, 1995). This was one of the first occasions on which gay men publicly fought back against police force exerted in a raid on a gay bar, the Stonewall Inn in Greenwich Village, New York. Following Stonewall, a large number of gay and lesbian political and social organizations formed and became visible in major cities throughout the United States. Recognizing, as did feminists, that the personal is political, gays and lesbians became a more viable force in local and national politics. Coming out and openly revealing one's sexual orientation was the moving force behind the gay and lesbian liberation movement, fueled by the understanding that invisibility both permits and invites oppression (D'Augelli & Garnets, 1995). Central to the gay and lesbian liberation movement was the feminist movement's challenge of patriarchy and gender-role stratification. The centrality of the feminist movement must be acknowledged despite the fact that, until relatively recently, there was painfully little feminist support for concerns of lesbians and gays (Kanuha, 1990). To date, there remain ambivalent feelings on all sides of this issue.

Although the gay and lesbian liberation movement has had a dramatic impact on the visibility of some lesbians and gay men in American culture, overt oppression is still pervasive. The continued existence of such oppression may be a testament to the fact that gays and lesbians have gained some personal freedoms in a diligent struggle for acceptance, but such freedoms ring somewhat hollow in a system that is based on fundamental power inequalities. Within this paradigm, white gay men have more power than white lesbians, but not as much power as white heterosexual men. Gays and lesbians of color and poor gays and lesbians have less power than heterosexuals of color or those who live in poverty. Recognition of continued oppression and relative powerlessness is, however, a necessary and unavoidable component of empowerment.

Empowerment in the lesbian and gay population has taken many forms that include the following: coming out; the outing of prominent public figures; grassroots community organizing; political organizing within traditional politics; the gay and lesbian liberation movement; separatism; civil disobedience; rioting, demonstrating, and marching; and the queer movement.

*Coming out* is the process by which lesbian and gay individuals disclose their sexual orientations to themselves and others. This represents a form of personal liberation in which the individual comes to accept himself or herself, not as "less than" heterosexuals but as equal to them. The theory that drives public disclosure of sexual orientation is that oppression of invisible populations is much more easily accomplished than oppression of highly visible populations.

*Outing* others is the process by which public figures, such as politicians who have not disclosed their sexual orientations, are publicly identified as being lesbian or gay. The theoretical basis for outing is the idea that as more public figures who are known to be lesbian or gay are publicly revealed, increasing power will be held by lesbian and gay people; this, it is believed, will lower the risk of oppression. Outing is used with special vehemence in identifying political figures whose voting records oppose civil rights for gays and lesbians.

Gays and lesbians have *organized at grassroots levels* to provide a variety of social services at the local, state, and national levels. Gay and lesbian community centers have been established in many large cities, as have been a host of specific services and referral programs. The AIDS pandemic, in particular, galvanized lesbians and gays in many communities to establish case management services, medical care, and direct aid for people living with HIV.

The gauntlet has now been taken up by lesbian groups who are forming service provider organizations to deal with issues such as breast cancer and other chronic illnesses. This is part of the community's response to heterosexist health care services that effectively limit access by lesbians and gay men. People of color have also established grassroots organizations to deal with the issues of multiple oppression faced by lesbians and gays within these racial and ethnic groups. These organizing efforts represent a fundamental way in which lesbians and gays have empowered themselves to care for one another within their specific communities. These activities are a direct response to oppression that excludes lesbians and gays from access to a host of economic, social, and political resources.

*Separatism* has also been promoted as one form of empowerment in the lesbian community. There currently exist several women's communities that operate on the principle that the only way to eradicate the effects of patriarchal domination and heterosexism is to separate entirely from the male-dominated social sphere. Although utopian in theory, separatism is difficult to maintain in practice, particularly because of the danger of intrusion by external forces such as governmental entities and hatemongers. Few separatist communities have reported long-term success, but efforts to achieve separatism continue. Separatism is a practice that appears to have little appeal to lesbians of color who often have strong ties to family and culture. In addition, separatism is virtually inaccessible to poor lesbians because it requires money and access to a means of maintaining financial independence.

*Civil disobedience* has been a popular tool of empowerment used by many lesbians and gay men. Most notable for its civil disobedience efforts is the AIDS Coalition to Unleash Power (ActUP). Although ActUP is primarily an AIDS organization, many of its members are lesbians and gays. Members of ActUP have participated in taking over radio broadcasts and staging "die-ins" at political gatherings. Other forms of civil disobedience have involved gays and lesbians chaining themselves to the banisters in front of the U.S. Supreme Court building to protest Supreme Court decisions adverse to the interests of gays and lesbians.

Gays and lesbians are a growing *political force* and are credited with the success of several candidates at local and state levels. In addition, lesbians and gays represented a powerful political presence in the 1992 presidential election and were considered crucial to Bill Clinton's successful bid for the presidency.

A more recent liberation movement in the lesbian and gay population is the self-described *queer movement*. The conceptual underpinnings of the queer movement are expressed in the rhetoric of Queer Nation, a nationwide political and social organization that rejects the goal of gay and lesbian assimilation into heterosexual culture and advances a social constructionist view of sex-role identification. The queer movement advocates that instead of being accepted for how alike they are to heterosexuals, lesbians and gays should be accepted and celebrated for their differences. The queer movement argues that the mere use of terms such as *lesbian, gay, or any other terms to describe sexual and gender identity* is limiting and role constricting.

Subsequently, queer theory emerged in the 1990s as an outgrowth of the queer movement; lesbian, gay, bisexual, and transgender (LGBT) studies; and feminist studies. Although queer theory and the queer movement overlap with similar interests, they are not the same. Queer theory suggests that identities are fluid, culture dependent, and due to social conditioning. Influenced by the writings of Michel Foucault, theorists such as Eve Kosofsky Sedgwick, Judith Butler, Michael Warner, and David Halperin, among others, examine identity politics and the way in which sexual acts and gender identities are socially constructed (Butler, 1990; Halperin, 2003; Sedgwick, 1990; Warner, 1993).

The logical extension of queer theory is to recognize that the interests of lesbians and gays and other sexual minorities are best served by ending oppression of all people and by honoring sexual and gender diversity in all of its forms. The emphasis on diversity and political action appealed to other sexual minorities who saw common interests in the nonassimilation stance of the queer movement. The contemporary Lesbian, Gay, Bisexual, Transgender, Queer, Questioning, and Intersexed (LGBTQI) Movement was formed as bisexuals, transgenders, and other sexual minorities joined forces with gays and lesbians to effect change. The terms that sexual minorities use to describe themselves are discussed in more detail in Chapter 8.

In today's climate, it is especially important for LGBTQI empowerment efforts to remain active on several fronts. The LGBTQI community must continue to work within traditional legislative systems to prevent discrimination in housing, in employment, and in other areas of institutional heterosexism, such as the institution of marriage. Controversy continues over the moral acceptability of outing public figures who have chosen not to disclose their sexual orientations. The Supreme Court's decision in *Romer v. Evans* (1996) prohibited the wholesale exclusion of gays and lesbians from local ordinances and executive orders in Colorado designed to ensure nondiscrimination in areas such as public employment, housing, medical benefits, and health care. The effects of this decision, however, have not been widespread, and attempts to end workplace discrimination have been met with resistance.

Some significant gains, however, have been made in other areas. The December, 2010 repeal of the "Don't Ask, Don't Tell" policy paves the way for gay, lesbian, and bisexual service members to serve openly in the military and not be forced to hide their sexual orientation. In November 2003, the U.S. Supreme Court struck down a Texas state law banning private consensual sexual acts between adults of the same sex. This historic decision enshrined a broader constitutional right to sexual privacy. In February 2004, Massachusetts's highest court ruled that full marriage rights for gay couples, rather than civil unions, would be legally necessary to conform to the state's constitution. Immediate backlash occurred as the U.S. Congress attempted to pass the Federal Marriage Amendment, which legally defines marriage as the union between a man and a woman only. This failed to pass the House vote but is likely to reemerge in the future. In several states, such as California, the local and state laws regarding same-sex marriage and LGBTQI rights are currently in the courts. Currently, in 2010, gays and lesbians can legally marry in New Hampshire, Massachusetts, Connecticut, Iowa, Vermont, and Washington, DC. A handful of other states recognize same-sex marriages that are performed legally in other jurisdictions and yet others recognize civil unions. However, a number of states have approved constitutional amendments to ban same-sex marriage, and many have voted to ban civil unions as well. LGBTQI activists continue to pursue marriage-rights lawsuits in states where they believe the high courts might eventually rule in their favor. LGBTQI rights are in the legal forefront now more than they have ever been before, and the laws at the local, state, and federal level are in flux. The American Civil Liberties Union and many LGBTQI groups are using the Internet, as well as traditional methods, to rally widespread support to gain equal human rights.

Despite concerted efforts at activism, one must recognize that recent critics of the LGBTQI liberation movement have described it as a movement that has accomplished little more than assimilation for the lesbian and gay population. According to this critique, assimilation renders lesbians and gays more tolerable to the heterosexual majority so long as they mirror the values of heterosexual consumers and "traditional" (patriarchal) views in support of families and relational commitment (Brookey, 1996). Perhaps the most significant reason why white middle- and upper-class lesbians and gays experience growing acceptance is because they also represent a growing consumer market.

The LGBTQI liberation movement has done little to promote the interests of LGBTQI persons of color or to take into account those whose socioeconomic status does not permit them to assimilate. Even among the population of those who have been favorably affected by the LGBTQI liberation movement, some complain that, far from liberating them, the very use of the terms *gay*, *lesbian*, *bisexual*, *transgender*, *queer*, and *intersexed* limits and compartmentalizes sexual behavior and makes sexual behavior the central focus of the movement. Compelling arguments have been made by some LGBTQI leaders that the single-issue orientation of the LGBTQI liberation movement falls far short of meeting the needs of all (or even most) of the LGBTQI population. Because the movement now encompasses a broader population with diverse needs, this becomes a more difficult issue to address. Whereas there have been changes for LGBTQI persons within an oppressive system, some critics argue that the system itself must be changed. This goal can only begin to be accomplished if the LGBTQI liberation movement broadens its vision to include "human rights, sexual and gender equality, social and economic justice, and faith in a multiracial society" (Vaid, 1995, p. 305). The LGBTQI movement must be seen as a human rights movement.

## SOCIAL WORK EMPOWERMENT THEORIES

Given the commitment of the social work profession to work on behalf of oppressed populations, several social work theorists have developed varieties of practice-oriented empowerment theories that include analysis of oppressive structures as well as empowerment strategies. These go under names such as empowerment, structural, antiracist, antioppressive, and participatory approaches. S. M. Rose (1990, p. 41) has pointed out ironically that the profession of social work is, itself, "embedded in a structural and ideological contradiction" arising from the fact that its professional legitimation and primary funding come from the very "capitalist state . . . (and) structural base that creates the poverty and abuses of its clients." Several notable authors, such as Barbara Solomon, Judith Lee, Lorraine Gutierrez, Stephen M. Rose, Bob Mullaly, and Robert Adams, have written about the power dynamics and social structures that give rise to and sustain oppression and empowering social work practices at micro and macro levels.

Barbara Solomon's (1976, 1987) work on Black empowerment was a pioneering effort in this area of theory development. Building on Solomon's work, Judith Lee (2001) presents a broad "multifocal vision" of empowerment that includes (a) a historical perspective on particular groups' experience of oppression; (b) an ecological view, especially drawing on the ecological/life model (see Chapter 2), stress and coping concepts, and ego psychology; (c) an ethclass perspective on connections between ethnicity, culture, racism, classism, and the importance of cultural competence; (d) a cultural/multicultural perspective that fosters knowledge of and appreciation for cultural diversity; (e) a feminist perspective on women's experience of oppression, connection between personal and political dimensions of life, and holistic ways of relating in the world; (f) a global perspective on the worldwide interconnections and ramifications of social and economic injustice; and (g) a critical perspective that critiques various types of power and links individual and social change. L. M. Gutierrez and colleagues' work (Gutierrez, 1990a, 1990b, 1994, 1995; Gutierrez & Lewis, 1999) focused more specifically on the empowerment of women of color. In contrast, S. M. Rose (1981, 1990, 1992, 1994) is more concerned with the political economy and the structural features of social service provision that restrict both human potential and options for service. Mullaly (2007), writing from a Canadian context, critiqued the contemporary neoconservative and neoliberal paradigms that pervade much social work in North America (including much empowerment practice) because they serve to maintain the overall social system while working within it for social control of clients or gradual reform. He emphasizes a revitalized and reconstructed socialist perspective that encompasses critique of all forms of discrimination and oppression, rather than prioritizing class conflict. His approach to empowerment includes reform efforts, but goes beyond them to challenge fundamental social structures and policies. He describes ways of working against the dominant system from within social work institutions and from outside them (such as in alternative organizations and social movements, progressive unionism, and electoral politics). Adams (2008), writing from a United Kingdom context, integrated insights from various conflict theories and social activist traditions to present frameworks for empowerment practice with individuals, groups, organizations, communities, political systems, and social work research. All of these authors emphasize the importance of empowerment to promote well-being and justice for marginalized and oppressed groups in the context of all forms of human diversity. These theories, because of their general applicability to all forms of stratification and oppression, are synthesized in the following section.

In Barbara Solomon's (1976, p. 29) formulation, empowerment is defined as "a process whereby the social worker engages in a set of activities with the client or client system that aim to reduce the powerlessness that has been created by negative valuations based on membership in a stigmatized group." Empowerment involves identification of power blocks that contribute to powerlessness as well as the development and implementation of specific strategies to overcome these blocks.

When working with people who have been stigmatized and marginalized, however, one must recognize that empowerment has both objective and subjective dimensions. Self-efficacy, a subjective aspect of empowerment, refers to the belief that one has "the ability to produce and to regulate events in life" (Bandura, 1982b, p. 122). R. White (1959) proposed that the development of the ego is based on a growing sense of competence, and the ability to feel competent is based on the ability to experience competence. Ultimately, to the extent that we are able to meet or get our needs met, we experience feelings of competence and a sense of well-being. A sense of self-efficacy lends initiative and confidence to empowering actions; becoming empowered increases self-efficacy and enables the empowered individual or group to experience personal power or strength (Adams, 2008; Cowen, 1991; L. M. Gutierrez, 1990a, 1990b; J. Lee, 2001; R. J. Parsons, 1991; Staples, 1990). Self-efficacy, however, must then be linked to the development of individuals' and groups' critical consciousness that helps identify oppressive power structures and leads to actions aimed at changing oppressive or disempowering social conditions.

Working to change oppression, even within one's immediate social environment, is usually perceived as too overwhelming for any one individual, and thus, solidarity and involvement with similar others in collective action is crucial. This may involve, for example, developing support groups among individuals who share a common status or situation. Such support systems attempt to enhance emotional or concrete assistance as well as to organize large groups of people for common action. Another important aspect of empowerment practice is working with clients to reduce the powerlessness created by negative valuations based on membership in a stigmatized group (Adams, 2008; Solomon, 1976). In this process, social workers need to engage in their own consciousness raising about their biases and complicity in oppression so that they can engage in effective collaborations with clients that reflect clients' own goals. This includes a realistic appraisal of the role of power difference within the helping relationship and finding ways to engage and catalyze the capacities of clients and communities, rather than imposing the oppressive or culturally inappropriate expectations of governments, elites, human service organizations, and social work practitioners (Adams, 2008; Finn & Jacobson, 2003; Mullaly, 2007; Sakamoto & Pitner, 2005; Sheppard, 2006).

Solomon emphasized that before individuals can begin to develop and increase skills to gain power and control over their lives, they must first identify the direct and indirect power blocks that contribute to the problems they are facing. Power blocks include "any act, event or condition which disrupts the process whereby individuals develop effective personal and social skills" (1987, p. 80). Indirect and direct power blocks operate at primary, secondary, and tertiary levels.

*Indirect power blocks* occur throughout the person's developmental process and are mediated by significant others. At the primary level, negative valuations or stigmas generated by oppression may be incorporated into family processes and interfere with optimum development of personal resources such as self-respect or cognitive skills. At the secondary level, indirect power blocks occur when personal resources, limited by blocks at the primary level, inhibit the development of interpersonal and technical skills. Tertiary-level indirect power blocks occur when limited personal resources and interpersonal and technical skills limit effectiveness in performing valued social roles.

*Direct power blocks* occur when negative valuations are applied directly by agents of our major social institutions. For example, at the primary level, direct power blocks occur when oppressed populations are devalued and receive inferior health services. This leads to poor health conditions for both individuals and the community as a whole, and constitutes a direct block to the development of good health. At the secondary level, direct power blocks occur when African Americans, as individuals, are denied the chance to develop interpersonal or technical skills through limitations placed on their educational opportunities, staff development, or technical training within organizations. Although individuals may have the personal resources required to develop interpersonal or technical skills, they are not permitted to do so. At the tertiary level, they are denied either valued social roles or material resources necessary for effective performance (Solomon, 1976, p. 17).

In sum, Solomon's model of empowerment practice with oppressed populations requires an analysis of power issues, with special attention placed on identifying power deficiencies. Solomon emphasized that powerlessness contributes to a person's inability to use resources to achieve individual or collective goals. Empowerment is the method for overcoming power blocks that are experienced by negatively valued individuals and groups.

J. Lee's work builds on Solomon's model to encompass all people who experience oppression. She identified three components of empowerment: (a) development of a more positive and potent self (self-efficacy), (b) development of knowledge and a capacity for critical comprehension of the social and political realities of one's environment (critical consciousness), and (c) development and cultivation of resources and strategies or more functional competence to facilitate achieving personal and collective goals (2001).

To address these three components of development, empowerment theorists emphasize that empowerment practice must address the personal, interpersonal, and institutional or political dimensions. At the personal level, the social worker assists individuals in identifying the sources of powerlessness and helps them to redefine themselves in a more positive, self-determined manner, using a strengths perspective. This process involves awareness of negative valuations experienced in life and identification of indirect and direct power blocks that interfere with personal and social growth. Through self-reflection and dialogue with others, these negative valuations and power blocks are culled out so that the person's positive, resilient, and powerful dimensions can grow (Greene, Lee, & Hoffpauir, 2005).

At the interpersonal level, social workers use their knowledge about how families, groups, and communities develop strengths and access or create resources to help people overcome oppression. Recognizing that isolation intensifies powerlessness, social workers must assist in the affiliation of people who share common obstacles; solidarity and mutual help are critical to the empowerment process.

Finally, at the institutional or political level, the task for social workers is to help individuals and groups develop the knowledge and skills needed to recognize and affect political processes. Empowerment-oriented social work includes collaborative activity with individuals, families, and groups to help them achieve their goals by increasing personal and interpersonal competence and by learning how to challenge social structural obstacles and inadequate resources. It may also extend to community development, community organizing, social policy analysis, and political advocacy, reaching to national and international levels as necessary (J. Lee, 2001). Further, social service agencies themselves need to be scrutinized for the ways their policies and practices might intentionally or inadvertently sustain oppression and discrimination (Adams, 2008; Mullaly, 2007).

S. M. Rose (1990) focuses on the oppressive nature of traditional social work practice and the adoption of individual deficit models that fail to address the capitalist structures that shape one's objective circumstances and subjective consciousness. To engage in advocacy/empowerment practice, social workers must first become aware of the way in which distribution of power within their agencies (and their roles in these agencies) reproduces and legitimizes the prevailing social order. Without a recognition of power imbalances, opportunities for empowerment get co-opted by provider-driven practice. Rather than participating in defining their own needs and goals, clients are forced to "choose" from limited options (1990, 1992).

According to S. M. Rose (1990), three principles underlie the advocacy/empowerment approach: contextualization, empowerment, and collectivity. *Contextualization* means "acknowledging the social being of the client" and being open to the idea that "clients know themselves better than we do" (1990, p. 46). We must be open to the ways in which clients define themselves, their circumstances, and their needs and be committed to an open dialogue rather than to problem solving or contracting. *Empowerment* is essentially a shared process of dialogue that provides the client with an opportunity to produce a range of possibilities to meet needs. It is client centered and not based on a predetermined "menu" of services. Central to this dialogue is the "externalization and critical questioning about contextual experience" to facilitate the client's social development and produce the client's desired outcomes. Finally, the principle of *collectivity* refers to bringing people together to "mutually externalize and reflect upon previous or present feeling," the origins of these feelings, and their relation to existing social structures such as family and schooling (1990, pp. 49–50). It is through collective consciousness raising that Rose believes people can achieve individual and social transformation.

Mullaly (2007) and Adams (2008) carry the analysis of power blocks further than most of the U.S.-based theorists by dealing with issues of colonialism, neocolonialism, globalized capitalism, and the interactions between local and national issues and worldwide dynamics of social injustice and power stratification. They draw more heavily on a wide range of research and empowerment practice approaches from around the world.

## CONTEMPORARY ISSUES

Unfortunately, inequality, discrimination, and oppression continue to operate in American society. When diversity is negatively valued by people and groups that hold power, those with less power face compounded structural disadvantages.

Since the Reagan era of supply-side economics and the current prominence of neoconservative and neoliberal politics, the old adage that "the rich get richer and the poor get poorer" has become an ever-growing reality, both in the United States and around the world. Supply-side economics funnels more wealth to the wealthy and assumes that the poor will be able to pull themselves out of poverty by individual effort. This, however, ignores the reality of structural oppression and discrimination. The need for empowerment-oriented social action has become even greater in the current political and economic environment.

As many scholars have cautioned, however, the term empowerment has become pervasive in social work, so much so that it is often used as a vague platitude or as a guise for another way to maintain and enforce the social status quo (Adams, 2008; Bartle, Couchonnal, Canda, & Staker, 2002; Mullaly, 2007; S. M. Rose, 1994; Sakamoto & Pitner, 2005). Social workers may, out of a sense of "political correctness," be led to promote the concept of empowerment without thinking carefully about the serious implications for justice and macro-social action (Zippay, 1995). It is especially critical not to allow the term *empowerment* to be co-opted by socially conservative policy makers seeking to maintain the status quo. Such co-opting can foster the illusion that oppressed groups' life chances can be significantly improved without addressing the macro-social structural issues and policies that prevent genuine equality. A subtle concern is the way that social workers' or agencies' own standards for what is socially just, morally correct, or culturally appropriate can be forced on clients and their communities, distorting empowerment from a mode of "power with" and "power for" to "power over."

Perhaps the most hotly contested issue on LGBTQI empowerment is the question of whether achieving assimilation within heterosexual culture extends any real power to this population in the absence of changes in the political and social structure of our society. As other cultural groups have recognized in their efforts to achieve equality, an equal slice of vastly unequal resources does not go a long way toward the attainment of any real power. At best, LGBTQI assimilation seems to represent an achievement of capitalism, which extends certain limited recognition to LGBTQI persons because of their power as consumers. Recognition based on consumption results in the exclusion of many members of the LGBTQI population who are not able to consume anything other than that which meets their basic human needs. In such a system, it is difficult to determine whether the LGBTQI liberation movement has produced any liberation at all or whether the status quo has merely been perpetuated, with some tangential recognition extended to LGBTQI persons as "window dressing."

## APPLICATION TO SOCIAL WORK PRACTICE

Social work is directed toward helping people overcome personal and environmental obstacles that inhibit growth, development, and adaptive functioning (Germain & Gitterman, 1995). Given this professional commitment, empowerment has often been described as a central goal and process of social work practice (DuBois & Miley, 1992; Gutierrez & Ortega, 1991; Hartman, 1993; R. J. Parsons, 1991; E. B. Pinderhughes, 1983; Solomon, 1976; Weick & Saleebey, 1995). However, as we have seen, empowerment may too often be more a matter of platitude and lip service than real consciousness raising and social action. The authors cited here give detailed conceptual and practical guidelines for practice that can be truly empowering.

Although the concept of empowerment is central to social work practice, empowerment theories have not yet received much empirical research support as theories relevant to an understanding of human behavior. Due to their strong attention to macro issues and strong practice orientation, they are sometimes mistakenly seen only as prescriptions for a form of macro activist practice (Adams, 2008; Mullaly, 2007). On the contrary, empowerment theories help practitioners to understand and act upon the intersections of micro and macro levels of human behavior and social structures. We are committed to the position that an understanding of the dynamics and effects of stratification, discrimination, and oppression is central to the knowledge of human behavior.

## Definition of the Helping Situation

The helping situation is one in which structural barriers are identified, power dynamics are explored, personal and collective strengths and resources are maximized, and effective actions for social change are taken. Whether the presenting concerns of the clients focus on micro, meso, or macro levels of social systems, the helping situation of empowerment requires that the personal and the political are linked. These theories primarily lend themselves to defining situations in terms of *social problems* and *social issues*. In addition, attempts to help clients enhance their self-efficacy, strengths, capacities, and resources can be defined in terms of *growth*. Flowchart 4.1 demonstrates an application of empowerment theories derived from these definitions.

## Assessment, Practice Strategies, and Methods

Empowerment theories include several principles that set the context for understanding assessment, practice strategies, and methods. (a) All oppression is considered to be destructive of life and should be challenged by social workers and clients. (b) Social workers should maintain a holistic, systemic, and comprehensive vision of oppression. (c) People have the inherent capacity to empower themselves. Social workers should assist clients rather than assume power themselves in determining helping goals and strategies. (d) People who share common ground need each other to attain empowerment. (e) Social workers should establish an "I and I" relationship of mutual respect and collaboration with clients. (f) Social workers should encourage the client to tell his or her own story and define his or her own aspirations and life meaning. (g) Social workers should maintain a focus on the person as victor, not victim. (h) Social workers should maintain a focus on social change rather than simply on the amelioration of symptoms or encouragement of conformist adaptation. (i) Social workers should include in their assessment critical analysis of ways in which their own behaviors and the procedures and policies of their agencies may overtly or subtly contribute to disempowerment of clients and then work to overcome these social work profession-based problems. (j) Empowerment practice may engage micro-, meso-, and macro-focused practices in the context of linkages between local, national, and global patterns of oppression and movements for worldwide social and economic justice (Adams, 2008; Gutierrez, Parsons, & Cox, 1998; J. Lee, 2001; Mullaly, 2007; O'Melia & Krogsrud Miley, 2002).

Empowerment theories focus assessment on the personal, interpersonal, and political power blocks that restrict people from achieving their aspirations. Assessment should also identify the personal goals, strengths, and talents of clients as well as the resources and support systems available in their communities.

Much social work practice that goes by the name of empowerment focuses primarily at the micro level, such as helping the so-called high-risk or low-income families to achieve aspirations and become more self-sufficient (Bartle et al., 2002; Dembo & Schmeidler, 2002; Hewitt, Crane, & Mooney, 2010; Palmer-House, 2008). This can be appropriate and helpful. Yet social workers must be cautious that such efforts are more than merely helping clients to adapt or conform to existing structural conditions of oppression.

An empowerment approach requires that practitioners engage in empowering roles; empowerment involves not only the desired outcomes but also the process of helping itself.

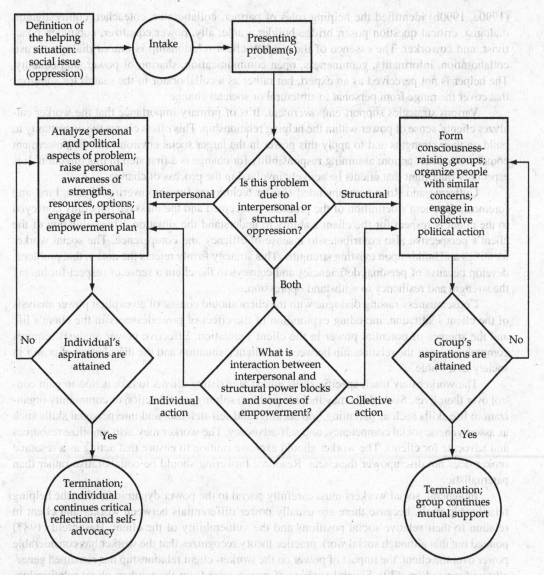

**FLOWCHART 4.1.** A possible practice application of empowerment theory with individuals, families, groups, or communities. © 1998, S. P. Robbins, P. Chatterjee, & E. R. Canda.

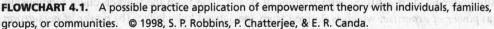

Solomon identified these roles as the following: (a) the *resource-consultant role*, which emphasizes the importance of linking clients to resources in a manner that enhances their self-esteem and their problem-solving capacities; (b) the *sensitizer role*, which involves helping clients gain the knowledge necessary to take control of their lives; (c) the *teacher-trainer role*, which places the practitioner as the manager of the learning process aimed at helping clients find solutions for their situations; and (d) the *cooperator role*, in which the worker understands the client as the one who is self-determining in achieving self-efficacy and empowerment. Similarly, L. M. Gutierrez

(1990a, 1990b) identified the helping roles of partner, collaborator, coteacher, coinvestigator, dialogist, critical question poser, bridge builder, guide, ally, power equalizer, cobuilder, coactivist, and coworker. The essence of the worker–client relationship is one of dialogue, trust, collaboration, informality, genuineness, open communication, sharing of power, and equality. The helper is not perceived as an expert, but rather as a collaborator in the search for solutions that cover the range from personal to structural or societal change.

Various strategies support empowerment. It is of primary importance that the worker catalyzes clients' sense of power within the helping relationship. This offers clients the opportunity to build on their strengths and to apply this power in the larger social environment. Empowerment comes from direct action; assuming responsibility for change is a first step in this direction. It is especially important that clients be actively involved in the process of change.

Gutierrez and Rose recommended similar techniques for empowering clients. First and foremost, the client's definition of the problem is accepted and the message hopefully conveyed to the client is respect for the client's ability to understand the situation. This validation of the client's perspective also contributes to a sense of efficacy and competence. The social worker identifies and builds upon existing strengths. This strategy firmly rejects the notion that problems develop because of personal deficiencies and conveys to the client a sense of respect for having the strength and resiliency to withstand oppression.

Consciousness-raising dialogue with the client should consist of an explicit power analysis of the client's situation, including exploration of the effect of powerlessness in the client's life and the sources of potential power in the client's situation. Effective power analysis requires comprehension of the relationship between the client's situation and the distribution of power in society as a whole.

The worker may teach specific skills aimed at assisting clients to take action to gain control over their lives. Such skills may include problem solving; social action or community organization; life skills such as parenting, job seeking, and self-defense; and interpersonal skills such as assertiveness, social competency, and self-advocacy. The worker may also mobilize resources and advocate for clients. The worker should exercise caution to ensure that acting as a resource broker does not disempower the client. Resource brokering should be collaborative rather than paternalistic.

In general, social workers must carefully attend to the power dynamics within the helping relationship itself, because there are usually power differentials between worker and client in relation to their relative social positions and the vulnerability of the client. Hasenfeld (1987) pointed out that although social work practice theory recognizes that the worker has considerable power over the client, the impact of power on the worker–client relationship has remained generally understated (p. 470). Several sources of power arise from the worker–client relationship: (a) *power of expertise*, which is derived from specialized knowledge; (b) *power of persuasion*, which is derived from interpersonal skills, including the ability to develop empathy, trust, and rapport with the client; (c) *power of agency resources and services*, which they control; and (d) *legitimate power*, which is derived from the dominant cultural values and authoritative norms (Hartman, 1993; Hasenfeld, 1987).

According to E. B. Pinderhughes (1983), the ultimate goal of social work practice should be helping clients to exert their own power and to obtain needed resources. Within this framework, understanding of power dynamics and the process by which negative societal valuations and structural barriers entrap clients becomes essential. According to Pinderhughes, workers should become aware of issues of power at three levels: (a) knowledge of themselves as participants in the societal projection process, (b) skill in using power on behalf of clients in teaching them to understand and use it, and (c) a readiness to share power with clients. In sharing power with clients, social workers empower both their clients and themselves (p. 338). Adams (2008) and Mullaly (2007) emphasize that this goal should be set within a larger goal of advancing well-being and justice for everyone through challenges to oppressive and discriminatory social structures and policies.

Because of the necessity for solidarity and mutual support in empowerment practice, group work is one of the preferred modalities (Dodd & Gutierrez, 1990; J. Lee, 1989; R. J. Parsons, 1991; Pernell, 1985). Group work helps people speak about common experiences, receive social support, and see the connections between the personal and the political (Gutierrez & Ortega, 1991). Within groups, individuals may be more likely to reject self-blame and with others develop an awareness of shared oppression and to critique systemic power blocks. Groups also promote the identification of a wider range of effective action strategies.

Special consideration should be given to the role of the social worker in the LGBTQI community. It is an especially difficult one and requires walking the balance between assisting in empowerment and enabling clients to maintain personal safety. For example, without the benefit of legal protection, clients who choose to empower themselves by coming out may place themselves at risk of losing their jobs, their homes, their families, and other members of their support systems. Clients who choose to engage in community organizing may become victims of hate crimes. Clients who work toward the overthrow of a cultural system that is oppressive may face a host of legal and social dangers. These may be risks inherent in efforts to achieve liberation, but the existence of such risk factors vastly complicates the role of the social worker. These risk factors may also limit the empowerment of the client to areas in which successful coping strategies can be applied—coping within an oppressive system rather than changing it.

The generic guidelines for empowerment practice discussed here must be further tailored to the specific situations of each client, considering whether the primary dynamics of oppression relate to issues of gender, race, ethnicity, religion, class, sexual orientation, disability, and the intersection between these (Gutierrez & Lewis, 1999; J. Lee, 2001). Some possible settings and applications of empowerment theories are shown in Table 4.1.

## CRITICAL ANALYSIS

### Biological, Psychological, and Spiritual Factors

With their primary focus on structural conditions of oppression, empowerment theories largely ignore the importance of biological factors in human development. Such factors would be considered relevant only to the extent that they constitute additional stressors contributing to oppression. In fact, most empowerment theorists tend to be highly suspicious of theories that imply biological determinism. Unfortunately, this suspicion of biological determinism often leads to a total neglect of biological differences and similarities among people. Borrowing from feminist theory, empowerment theories assume that "the personal is (always) political." Thus, psychological difficulties are analyzed in the context of the social structures that generate them. However, empowerment theories do offer a valuable perspective on the dynamic psychological processes that are rooted in the capacity of people to become conscious of their circumstances and to take creative actions to transform them. Empowerment theories see personal and political transformation not only as an ever-present possibility but also as a necessity when conditions of oppression exist.

**TABLE 4.1**    Various Settings and Applications of Empowerment Theories

| Type of Agency | Type of Presenting Problem | Type of Program | Definition of the Helping Situation | Type(s) of Activities |
|---|---|---|---|---|
| Mental health center | Situational depression of LGBTQI clients due to discrimination | LGBQTI individual counseling and support groups | Social issue (consciousness raising and empowerment) | Dialogue; identification of environmental bases of situational depression; group solidarity building |
| Ethnic mutual assistance association | Community-based racism and discrimination | Community outreach | Social issue (antiracist collective action) | Community education; advocacy; racism reduction workshops; ethnic community organizing |
| Community action center | Neighborhood poverty; inadequate housing and employment opportunities | Community organizing and development | Social issue (empowerment and action for justice) | Neighborhood organizing; consciousness-raising dialogue groups; job and housing development; engaging Civil Rights Commission to investigate housing discrimination |
| Catholic social service | Inadequate Spanish-language community services for Hispanic population | Hispanic community service | Social issue (charitable service, liberation) | Advocacy; community action; bilingual interpretation; cross-cultural mediation; bilingual religious services |
| Homeless shelter | Homelessness and poverty | Shelter, transitional care | Social issue (protection and empowerment) | Physical shelter and support; job assistance; advocacy |

In addition, they address important psychological components related to the development of increased personal power or control (Adams, 2008; L. M. Gutierrez, 1990a, 1990b) and the development of a more positive and potent self (J. Lee, 2001). In general, this subjective aspect involves a psychological state that is characterized by a heightened feeling of self-esteem, efficacy, and control (Torre, 1985).

Some have even argued that personal empowerment is a basic human need (Cowen, 1991). Many believe that effective action on the personal or social level depends not only on an awareness of issues of power but also on an increased knowledge about competencies, skills, resources, and opportunities (J. Lee, 2001; Solomon, 1987; Staples, 1990). There is, however, little emphasis on developmental life stages, due to overgeneralized assumptions about culture, gender stereotypes, and the heterosexism inherent in life stage theories.

Although empowerment theories do not directly address personal aspects of spirituality, religious institutions are seen as having a paradoxical role in that they can both facilitate empowerment and perpetuate oppression. This irony is illustrated by the fact that the founders of most world religions were initially perceived as challengers to the predominant social order, but their successors created social institutions that have incorporated patriarchy and other forms of inequality. Canda and Furman's (2010) framework for spiritually sensitive practice offers guidelines for how social workers can work with the personal and community strengths and resources related to religion and spirituality to promote empowerment while avoiding or challenging the oppressive misuses of spirituality and religion.

Further, the development of liberation theology in the past few decades has influenced the development of empowerment theories (Evans, 1992; G. Gutierrez, 1973). Growing out of the social misery of the Catholic poor in Latin America and proclaiming its commitment to the liberation of the poor and oppressed, liberation theology challenges the status quo of the Roman Catholic Church from within a dissident Catholic perspective. It challenges the notion of clerics as a special group of experts and calls those in authority to learn from the poor and oppressed. A similar challenge can be made to social workers who may use the role of "expert" as a barrier that keeps them from hearing the client's "word" or seeing the client's reality (Breton, 1989). Liberation theology rejects the paternalist view of "saving" or "redeeming" the oppressed in favor of a view that encourages people to liberate themselves through a process of consciousness raising and praxis (Freire, 1973).

## Social, Cultural, and Economic Forces

A major strength of empowerment theories is their explicit focus on social, cultural, economic, and political forces that produce inequality and oppression as well as opportunities for liberation. These theories do not merely describe the dynamics of power and oppression; they also prescribe empowering and liberating actions.

Nonetheless, these theories have been criticized for their emphasis on situation-specific understandings of oppression and liberation. Taken to the extreme, empowerment theories implicitly suggest that only those who actually experience oppression can understand it. Under this view, theoretical understanding, empathy, and rapport become difficult for most people (Lengermann & Niebrugge-Brantley, 1992; Wilber, 2000a).

Further, there are numerous factions between and within various types of empowerment theories. Despite their explicit focus on social, cultural, and economic forces, some of these debates have become highly abstruse and hairsplitting, fueled by rival commitments to social justice. J. Lee (2001) has suggested that the development of comprehensive perspectives on empowerment, which attempt to form common cause, solidarity, and cooperative action across disadvantaged or oppressed groups, can help to overcome the danger of factionalism.

## Relevance to Individuals, Groups, Families, Organizations, Institutions, and Communities

As we have seen, empowerment theories attempt to connect micro, meso, and macro levels of social systems. However, when working with individuals, empowerment theories stress that personal problems and successes must be understood within the context of sociopolitical power dynamics. A recognition of the connections between personal problems and structural barriers is central to empowerment theories. Although the primary focus is on oppressed groups, the causes, consequences, and solutions of oppression and inequality are relevant to individuals, families, organizations, institutions, and communities as well. The collective action necessary to effect change can take place at any or all of these levels. Thus, individual empowerment is a necessary component of collective empowerment.

Empowerment theories offer challenges to the organizational and political contexts of human service. The bureaucratic nature of service organizations makes it necessary to standardize services and procedures, which are usually based on guidelines reflecting interests of politically dominant groups and have little application to the diverse needs of oppressed populations. Programs and procedures may reflect negative valuations and biased assessments that further contribute to the victimization of marginalized groups.

Studies that have explored human service organizations have identified barriers to both employee and client empowerment. Gutierrez and colleagues (1995) described empowering organizational contexts as those that encourage the sharing of power between agency administration, staff, and clients. In contrast, Simon (1994a) noted that paternalistic systems lead to powerlessness and dependence. A seven-year ethnographic study of a comprehensive child and family development service agency showed that in practice, an organizational vision of empowerment can change over time in response to increasing staff experience, mandates by federal funders, input from consumers and community stakeholders, and ongoing efforts to resolve competing ideas about economic self-sufficiency (a more individualistic conservative view) and overall family well-being, positive interdependency, and community systems change (a more liberal and social critical view) (Bartle et al., 2002).

According to empowerment theories, macro-level social change requires joining personal and interpersonal levels to the political level. An understanding of communities, organizations, and social institutions is necessary for building coalitions, organizing communities, and impacting social policy. Collective empowerment develops when people join together in action to overcome obstacles and to attain social change (Staples, 1990). Therefore, empowerment is a critical component of contemporary social work practice with communities (Weil, 2005).

## CONSISTENCY WITH SOCIAL WORK VALUES AND ETHICS

Empowerment practice is highly consistent with social work values, because it builds on our traditional commitment to work for justice, especially on behalf of marginalized and oppressed people. It adds political sophistication to the person and environment perspective, recognizing that personal well-being cannot and should not be separate from collective well-being. In addition, these theories specifically reject concepts of victimization and efforts to pathologize the oppressed. Empowerment practice strongly supports a strengths perspective, because it focuses on the creative capacities, strengths, and resources that individuals and communities possess and develop in coping with oppression.

Empowerment practice fosters the wellness of people (Staples, 1990). Perhaps the most important contribution to wellness is "having a sense of control over one's fate, a feeling of purpose and belongingness, and a basic satisfaction with one's self and one's existence" (Cowen, 1991, p. 404). This supports social work's commitment to uphold individual and group self-determination.

Whereas social work's value base is consistent with empowerment, it also involves tensions that can undermine empowerment (Adams, 2008; Mullaly, 2007). The profession's dual role as promoter of social change and protector of society (or privileged groups) involves an inherent ambiguity that is highlighted by empowerment theories. They remind us not to let social work become merely a tool of social control to enforce conformity to norms that may not be relevant or empowering to those who are most in need of liberation and justice.

Empowerment perspectives are especially relevant to issues of diversity, because they have been developed to address issues of oppression experienced by minority and marginalized groups involving ethnicity, race, economic status, gender, sexual orientation, religion, disability, developmental challenge, and other bases for negative stereotyping and inequality (Adams, 2008; Pease, 2002). They challenge the notion that all individuals benefit from the same modality and type of services and assert that attempts to standardize and generalize services may be more harmful and exploitative than equitable. Many social workers are drawing on empowerment perspectives to develop culturally and spiritually appropriate practice (e.g., Al-Krenawi & Graham, 2009; Canda & Furman, 2010; Devore & Schlesinger, 1995; Gray, Coates, & Yellow Bird, 2008; Lee, Ng, Leung, & Chan, 2009; Lum, 2003a, 2003b; Martin & Martin, 2002).

## PHILOSOPHICAL UNDERPINNINGS

Empowerment theories rest on the assumption that all knowledge and worldviews are embedded in particular social and historical contexts and are subject to oppressive power dynamics in their construction. Thus, they tend to be suspicious of theories and claims of fact that are generated by privileged people and institutions that contribute to oppression. In fact, no worldviews are vested with special privilege by empowerment theories. What is important is the collective process of dialogue and interaction between multiple worldviews, value systems, and philosophies as we move toward more comprehensive and just understandings of each other. Despite this seemingly inclusive stance, empowerment theories may give preference to the views of the oppressed, so that they can be given voice and power in overcoming the prevailing philosophies that have created and maintained domination of some groups over others.

Payne (1991, p. 234) has also noted that empowerment theories share with cognitive and humanist approaches the philosophy of "self-control, personal responsibility, and self-actualisation [sic] through empowerment."

## METHODOLOGICAL ISSUES AND EMPIRICAL SUPPORT

Empowerment theories question the fundamental assumptions of conventional positivist science, because it reflects Eurocentric and androcentric biases (Adams, 2008). To the extent that social work research has been dominated by these biases, often associated with positivistic beliefs and quantitative methods, feminists have criticized such research as male focused and patriarchal (L. V. Davis, 1985, 1986). In contrast, empowerment-oriented research focuses on issues that are deemed important by oppressed groups. Empowerment research methods, whether philosophical, historical, qualitative, or quantitative, include research participants in the design, analysis, evaluation, and social action applications of the research process (Adams, 2008). Empowerment-oriented research is aimed at increasing understanding of oppressed people's own experiences, in their own terms, and for their own purposes. Research related to this perspective is generally philosophical, historical, phenomenological, political, qualitative, and naturalistic. Despite the undeniable value of such research techniques, this research is often criticized by traditional positivistic research standards as being "unscientific," because of empowerment researchers' espousal of explicit values and collaboration and solidarity with research participants.

Empowerment theories are most useful in describing and explaining dynamics of power and particular situations of oppression and liberation. From a positivist perspective, these concepts may be difficult to operationalize or test because they are abstract. For example, political power and patriarchy are very real existentially, but they are difficult to operationalize precisely. In addition, many terms related to empowerment have been used inconsistently and without careful definition. This imprecision makes comparisons between studies very difficult. However, the narrower concept of self-efficacy has received much empirical support in the social learning research context. Recently, studies on the process and outcomes of empowerment-oriented programs (e.g., for low-income families and community capacity building) have increased, often demonstrating beneficial outcomes, although these generally do not involve social structural change. Adams (2008) has provided valuable standards for identifying when empowerment is achieved at various system levels.

In their study of organizational and management factors that enhance or hinder the process of empowerment, Conger and Kanungo (1988) found that certain factors may inhibit empowerment. These included organizational factors such as disrupting periods of start-up ventures and chaotic transitions; an impersonal bureaucratic climate with poor communication systems and highly centralized resources; supervisory styles described as authoritarian, negativistic, and lacking in reason for actions and consequences; reward systems that are arbitrary, are low in value, and disregard competence and innovation; and job designs that lack role clarity, training, and technical support, have unrealistic goals and limited participatory opportunities, possess a rigid rule structure, and limit contact with senior management.

A great strength of empowerment theories is their heuristic power. That is, they reveal underlying political processes embedded in all social situations and lead to new ways of understanding and overcoming their limitations through consciousness raising and individual and collective action.

Nonetheless, in an era in which social work is increasingly outcome driven, empowerment theories are frequently subject to criticism for their emphasis on process rather than outcome or on lofty and elusive political goals. Yet, simplistic outcome-driven valuation is fundamentally inimical to the empowerment process. As Solomon (1976), borrowing from Lerner, sardonically pointed out, "if the only measure of the value of a work-therapy program is how many people were put to work, then slavery must have been extremely therapeutic for American Blacks" (p. 359).

## Summary

Empowerment theories have provided an important theoretical base to help us address social work concerns about social justice, human strengths, and resiliency in the face of oppression. Although LGBTQI empowerment theories have received less attention, they are gaining acceptance in education and practice. Action-focused social work empowerment theories, such as those by Adams, Gutierrez, Lee, Mullaly, and Solomon, show much promise for helping us to join theory with practice.

Empowerment theories are especially appealing to those who see social work's primary mission as the promotion of social justice for groups that are oppressed or marginalized. As the profession and professional education increasingly move toward a social justice orientation, it is likely that empowerment theories will become a mainstay of education and practice.

# Feminist Theory

*The feminist struggle continues*
*in countries all over the world*
*You can change the name but the problem's the same*
*Oppression of women and girls*
*Let's get all fired up*
*like feminists will*
*and we'll stay fired up*
*'cause we're feminists still*

© Anne Hills
2008, Raven Heart Music

## FEMINIST THEORY

- helps us understand the connection between the personal and the political
- provides an analytical framework to examine social arrangements that contribute to the oppression and marginalization of people
- describes the interrelationship between material, social, intellectual, and spiritual facets of human existence
- provides a gender lens that can be used to examine and deconstruct systems of power
- can be used as a framework for both micro and macro practice

---

This chapter was coauthored with Bréne Brown, PhD and with contributions by Beverly McPhail, PhD.

Feminist theory is a mode of analysis that involves specific ways of thinking and acting, designed to achieve women's liberation by eliminating the oppression of women in society. Although feminism encompasses different perspectives, it draws on some common empowerment-related themes. In general, feminist theory incorporates a holistic view of the interrelationships between material, social, intellectual, and spiritual facets of human existence. Central to feminist thought is the idea that it is necessary to critique one's social context and deconstruct its discriminatory aspects. Its primary focus is on *patriarchy*, the domination of the major political, economic, cultural, and legal systems by men. Feminist theory stresses the need to identify and name the attitudes, expectations, language, behaviors, and social arrangements that have contributed to the oppression and marginalization of people. It embraces the idea of unity in diversity within community life. Feminist theory recognizes the existence of multiple experienced realities, based in different vantage points, and supports women and other oppressed groups in the formation of their own self-understandings and life aspirations. E. Lewis (1992) held that "the potency of feminist perspectives lies in that they have drawn attention to the subtle, unconscious, and daily exercise of attitudes, beliefs, and behaviors which define and reinforce a despised status" (p. 281).

Feminist theory shares many of the same concerns of conflict and empowerment theories and addresses the way people use power to resist or create change as well as the dynamics of discrimination and oppression. Feminist theory offers robust explanations for human behavior at both the micro and macro levels, embodied in the idea that "the personal is the political." Although born out of political resistance to the historical subjugation of women, feminist theory has applications to all genders. Feminist theory is not limited to "women's issues," but encompasses all human issues. Feminist theory offers critiques of theories developed by and for men (androcentric), but are often applied to women. It also creates new ways to better describe both the female and male experience.

## HISTORICAL CONTEXT

The roots of feminism and feminist theory can be found in the 17th century "revolutionary bourgeois tradition that had equality of mankind as its highest goal" (Phillips, 1987, p. 31). The ideological concept of equality was first introduced in 17th-century revolutionary England and was furthered in the 18th century era of enlightenment. Enlightenment principles eschewed notions of rights rooted in inherited wealth or position and instead focused on individual capacities and merit, which called for governments to be based on the will of its citizens. However, the concept of citizen was slow to include women.

North America's first feminist is often identified as Juana Inés de La Cruz (1648–1695) an intellectual, a poet, philosopher, playwright, and nun who held that all girls and women should be educated, and argued for the right of women to comment on and interpret scripture (Paz, 1988). Another early feminist, Abigail Adams, spoke out for the inclusion of women in the Declaration of Independence. Her husband, John Adams, soon to be the nation's second president, made light of her demand, scoffing at the notion of a "petticoat rebellion" (Cullen-DuPont, 1996).

The first women's rights convention in the United States was held in Seneca Falls, New York in 1848, convened by Elizabeth Cady Stanton, Lucretia Mott, and others. Emerging from this convention, a Declaration of Rights and Sentiments became the founding document of the American women's rights movement (Cullen-DuPont, 1996). Historically, women were barred from education and the professions, could not vote, serve on juries, keep their wages or property, or obtain custody of their children. This document articulated their demands that included the education of women, admission into the trades and professions, the right to speak in public, and the most controversial claim, the right to vote.

Wagner (1996) posits that this convention reflects the little known story of the Iroquois women's influence on early feminists. Although early European American women had few, if any, rights, Iroquois women could divorce their husbands, mothers gained custody in the event of a divorce, property was handed down through the mother's family, and women could nominate and counsel the male chiefs who represented their clan in the Grand Council. Women of color, such as Sojourner Truth and Harriet Tubman, joined the demand for women's rights while also working for the abolition of slavery. Women of all colors and classes gained the right to vote in 1920, after a 72-year struggle that culminated in the passage of the Nineteenth Amendment to the Constitution.

The contemporary wave of feminist thought is frequently attributed to the pioneering work of French existentialist and socialist Simone de Beauvoir. In her book *The Second Sex* (1953) she argued that women have been subjugated to a "second status" that dates back to the stone-age technology of hunter-gatherer societies. She noted that women were "made, not born," that is they were shaped by cultural processes rather than limited by biology. Her analysis of differential evaluations of male and female roles led her to conclude that women are treated and described as objects of men's wishes rather than subjects of their own experiences (Ferree & Hess, 1985).

The Civil Rights and New Left movements of the 1950s and 1960s gave rise to the next wave of the American women's movement. In her book *The Feminine Mystique* (1963), American feminist Betty Friedan critiqued the gender role inequality that was inherent in the socially constructed role imperative of mother and housewife as the only socially acceptable career for women. She also criticized Freudian theory that labeled women's impulses to achieve as neurotic "masculinity striving" and deficient mothering. She argued for gender role equality, stressing the importance of education and career commitment.

The history of the women's movement in the United States is frequently broken into three waves or time periods. The First Wave (1848–1920) focuses on women organizing to obtain the vote and the right to keep their property and wages. The Second Wave (1960s–1980s) is considered the modern women's movement. Despite gains in the early 20th century, women still could not gain credit in their own name or access to birth control, and were limited to lesser paid female-identified professions, jobs they often were forced to give up when they married or became pregnant. Oftentimes they could not wear pants in public, and violence directed against them was often not taken seriously by the criminal justice system. Changes during this period were typically legislative, incremental, and challenged discriminatory practices.

The Third Wave (1990s–present) is viewed as a generational response to failures of the Second Wave, while broadening the feminist agenda to include issues of race, class, and nation, and more fluid notions of gender and sexual identities. Third Wave feminism criticizes the use of a generic category of woman and focuses instead on a number of differences that include inequality in the distribution of goods and services that are based on one's position in the global economy, as well as "class, race, ethnicity, and affectional preference" and their interaction with gender stratification (Lengermann & Niebrugge-Brantley, 1992, p. 480). However, Morgan (2003) and others criticize the notion of three historical waves, arguing that it defines history too narrowly. They contend that its limited focus on political activities that achieved a small number of equal rights by White middle-class women in the United States has served to marginalize international feminist movements (Morgan, 2003).

Not surprisingly, feminism and feminist theory gained prominence in the field of social work, a profession founded and dominated by women. However, despite the major role that women have played, there has been ongoing concern about the lack of women in leadership positions (cited in Giovannoni & Purvine, 1974). Historically, women rarely served on boards of directors, as politicians, or as paid agents, a privilege reserved for men (Rauch, 1975). In fact, in the 1950s, men were actively recruited into the profession in an attempt to professionalize and defeminize social work. During the 1960s and 1970s, the social work literature drew attention to sexism within the profession and decried ongoing sex role stereotyping, sexist assumptions about the nature of the profession, and gendered pay inequities (reviewed in Sakamoto, Anastas, McPhail, & Colarossi, 2008). Ongoing concerns about sexism in the profession are bolstered by current research that shows continued gender inequality, as discussed later in this chapter.

In response to sexism within the profession and to create more women-friendly models and practices, feminist social workers have been prolific authors, theorists, researchers, writers, educators, and activists. Important works within social work include: *Feminist Visions for Social Work Practice* (N. Van Den Bergh & Cooper, 1986), *Feminist Practice in the 21st Century* (Van Den Bergh, 1995), *Building on Women's Strength* (Peterson & Lieberman, 2001), *Understanding Race, Ethnicity, and Power* (Pinderhuges, 1989), *The Role of Gender in Practice Knowledge* (Figueira-McDonough, Netting, Nichols-Casebolt, 1998); *Regulating the Lives of Women* (Abramovitz, 1988), to name only a few. What was first a trickle is now a rich knowledge base that demonstrates how feminist theory can challenge and inform social work practice.

## KEY CONCEPTS

Understanding feminism as a theory is complex and multidimensional because there are multiple feminisms that are both contested and evolving. Marie Shear (1986) defines feminism as "the radical notion that women are people." In 1913, British author Rebecca West noted that she was called a feminist when expressing "sentiments that differentiate me from a doormat or a prostitute" (Marcus, 1982, p. 219). According to bell hooks (2000), feminism is a movement to end sexism, sexist exploitation, and oppression. Second Wave feminist Nancy Hartsock sees feminism as a "mode of analysis, a method of approaching life and politics, rather than a set of political conclusions about the oppression of women" (1981, p. 35). Susan Faludi (1991) contends, "Its agenda is basic: It asks that women not be forced to 'choose' between public justice and private happiness. It asks that women be free to define themselves—instead of having their identity defined for them, time and again, by their culture and their men." (p. xxiii). And Eleanor Smeal, a former president of the National Organization for Women, states: "As its core, feminism is a multi-issue movement committed to extremely long-term goals: the ending of patriarchy; the achievement of economic, political, and social equality for all women; and the creation of a world free from sexism, racism, homophobia, classism, ageism, ableism, violence, and environmental exploitation" (2003, p. 542). In sum, feminism is a theory of power relations that examines male dominance and female subordination, while working to achieve equality and opportunity for women. It is essentially a libratory enterprise, a social justice, empowerment-seeking social movement, that espouses equality of the sexes.

When people are asked about their understanding of the word *feminism*, a very bleak and ugly picture sometimes emerges. Typical negative descriptors include "man-haters, angry, ugly, feminazis, shrill, militant, and radical" (personal communication, Beverly McPhail, May 6, 2010). The number of young women who self-identify as feminist varies, and one research study found that nonfeminist women were more likely to report higher levels of hostility toward men than feminists, contrary to the stereotype that feminists are "man haters" (K. J. Anderson, Kanner, & Elsayegh, 2009). Despite the fact that the feminist movement has literally transformed the lives of both women and men, negative stereotypes and misperceptions abound.

*Feminist* and *gender* are often viewed as synonymous with women, but men have a gender too, and can also be feminists. Feminism is an ideology that seeks to free men from rigid stereotypes of masculinity, as it seeks to free women from rigid stereotypes of femininity.

There are a number of schools of feminist thought that differ in their analysis of what causes gender inequalities and what actions can be taken to end those inequalities. As shown in Table 5.1, *Liberal feminism* holds that men and women are equal, advocates for a rights-based approach, and works to have women join existing institutions in equal numbers to men (Saulnier, 1996). *Radical feminism*, a term borrowed from the Civil Rights and New Left movements, asserts that women are an oppressed class and that patriarchy is at the root of this oppression; patriarchy is enforced through violence against women, and society must be

**TABLE 5.1**    Various Feminist Theoretical Perspectives

| Perspective | Theory | Application |
|---|---|---|
| Liberal feminism | Women are basically the same as men and therefore should have equal rights to men. | On focus of liberal feminists is women's right to control their own bodies through access to sex education and contraception as well as abortion rights. |
| Radical feminism | Women are an oppressed class, patriarchy is at the root of the oppression, and violence against women is a tool of the patriarchy to keep women subordinate. | Radical feminists focus on issues of violence against women, including sexual harassment, rape, battering, and prostitution, redefining such acts as sex discrimination, and how men use power and control to retain their dominant position in the hierarchy. |
| Socialist feminism | Women are oppressed by capitalism and patriarchy, due to their relationships with both the means of production and reproduction. | Socialist feminists focus on women's relationship to the market including unpaid work in the home, childcare, and unequal wages in the paid labor market. |
| Lesbian feminism | Women experience both sexist and heterosexist oppression. | Lesbian feminists seek to make their status as sexual minorities within the women's movement more visible and to address issues of special concern to lesbian women including the understanding of a lesbian identity as a natural variation of human sexuality, and to gain rights for lesbian women including the right to marry, adopt children, be safe from violence, and job protection. |
| Cultural/difference feminism | Women and men are fundamentally different and many unique qualities possessed by women are superior to those qualities inherent in men. | Cultural feminism would elevate women and women's superior feminine qualities to end violence in the world since they believe women are naturally more pacifist than men. |

*(Continued)*

| TABLE 5.1 | Various Feminist Theoretical Perspectives (*Continued*) | |
|---|---|---|
| **Perspective** | **Theory** | **Application** |
| Woman of color feminism | Race, gender, and class interact and intersect to impact the lives of women, and each must be simultaneously addressed. | Addresses the intersection of racism, classism, and sexism. For example, instead of a sole focus on abortion rights and choice, recognizes that poor women of color have fewer choices due to their race, class, and communities as well as gender. Reproductive justice would include a focus on the right to have children as well as the right to not have children, and the right to have support for raising children. |
| Postmodern feminism | Critiques the notion of an essentialist category of *woman* and claims of objectivity, defies the binary categorization of male/female, viewing gender as a continuum rather than binary, but also a performance and a social construction. | Postmodern feminism makes a strong theoretical critique that does not recognize the category of *woman* However, since the category of *woman* is viewed as socially constructed, it can be deconstructed, leading to change in how we theorize gender and sexual identities. |
| Global feminism | Critiques imperialism (including Western feminist imperialism), colonialism, neo-colonialism and globalization, while arguing for the right of women across the globe to define their own oppression and means of liberation. | Women's activism from the ground up rather than imposed from above with a focus on economic solutions such as micro-loans, an emphasis of the education of girls and a focus on ending violence against women including the international trafficking of women. |
| Ecofeminism | Links the domination of women to domination of the environment, including animals, as women are viewed as closer to nature, and both women and nature have traditionally been viewed as under the control of man. | Ecofeminists seek to end the subordination women and the environment, by challenging the hierarchies that traditionally placed men over women and people over nature. The focus is on addressing environmental concerns, including specism. |

*Source:* Saulnier, C. F. (1996). *Feminist theories and Social Work: Approaches and Applications.* New York: The Haworth Press.

completely altered to eliminate male supremacy and other hierarchies (Saulnier, 1996). *Difference or cultural feminism* (discussed in more detail in Chapters 7, 8, and 9) takes a different view and posits that men and women are uniquely different and that the distinctive characteristics of women may be superior to male qualities, such as being more nurturing or pacifist. *Ecofeminist* theory (discussed in more detail in Chapter 2) sees women as being closer to nature than men and argues that the association between women and nature has been used to disempower women. It also creates hierarchies of man over women and people over nature, including the earth and animals. *Women of Color Feminisms*, also known individually as Womanist, Chicana/Latina, Asian American, and Native American feminisms, focus on the intersectionality of oppressions. They examine the ways in which race and class intersect with gender to produce matrices of oppression and theorize that the three cannot be considered separately because they are experienced simultaneously. *Lesbian feminism's* primary concern is the intersection of gender and sexual identity and the way in which homophobia constrains sexual identity and serves as a weapon of sexism. It also decries heterosexism as a key oppressive system (Saulnier, 1996). *Postmodern feminism* questions essentialism in all its forms, describes gender as a social construct, and resists categorizations such as woman or lesbian. *Marxist or socialist feminism* examines how capitalism and patriarchy act to subordinate women. It focuses on women's relationship to the means of production and as a source of reproduction, whose labor is often devalued and whose bodies are often commodified (Saulnier, 1996). *Global and International feminism* believes in the right of women in each country to define feminism for themselves, while also examining economic, colonization, and globalization issues as they relate to gender. This includes resisting Western imperialism and working toward the elimination of women's oppression worldwide (Saulnier, 1996).

Despite the multiple feminisms, there are themes and concerns that are central to all feminist thought. These include the centrality of gender, gender schemas, and developing critical gender awareness; the personal is political, dismantling patriarchy, and confronting oppression; separating gender and sex; and addressing intersectionality.

## The Centrality of Gender, Gender Schemas, and Developing Critical Gender Awareness

Immediately upon the birth or adoption of a baby, the first question posed is: Is it a boy or a girl? This is not without consequence, for the answer will determine the child's name; gifts given and clothing worn; how family, friends, and others will interact with the child; and even the choice of occupations, pay differentials, and risks of poverty. As Kimmel and Messner note that as one of the organizing principles of social life, gender joins class and race ". . . as one of the three central mechanisms by which power and resources are distributed in our society" (2004, p. ix). Acknowledging the importance and *centrality of gender* is a key concept in feminist theory that leads to an examination of all facets of life in order to understand what gender means, how gender works, and the ramifications of both.

The centrality of gender is further perpetuated by *gender schemas*, or mental constructs that we hold, often implicit and unconscious, about an individual, group of people, or events (Valian, 1999). Similar, but not identical to stereotypes, they can be accurate, inaccurate, positive, negative, or neutral. For instance, in Western, middle-class, White society men are often seen as independent, autonomous and action oriented, while women are viewed as expressive, nurturing, and concerned about others. The problem with such schemas is that they oversimplify.

These schemas are often so ingrained in people's thinking that they are rarely challenged or changed. If new or contradictory information is observed or experienced, it is often treated as exceptional or ignored, often by supplying a different interpretation. For example, when we encounter a strong woman leader, we are apt to see her as an exception, rather than changing our schema to acknowledge that both men and women can be strong leaders. According to Valian, gender schemas tend to overrate men and underrate women. So when many women say they have to be twice as good as a man to get ahead, this may be true, for they have to overcome unconscious negative beliefs about their capabilities.

Gender schemas are usually unarticulated; we don't talk about them and may not even be aware that they exist in our repertoire of beliefs. We may even deny that we hold such beliefs, particularly if we see ourselves as being fair and wanting to treat others equally. Despite this, our reactions to an individual are, inevitably, affected by the group the person belongs to and our socially ingrained, unconscious schemas. It is important, then, to discover a schema's content if we are to evaluate people more fairly.

Related, and equally important, is developing critical gender awareness. People are so immersed in the gendered culture that they often do not see the gendered assumptions and ramifications that make up the world. B. Brown (2004) defines critical awareness as the ability to understand how social-community forces shape people's lives and experiences. She notes, "Awareness is knowing something exists. Critical awareness is knowing why it exists, how we're impacted by it, and who benefits from it" (p. 77). As an example, Brown examines how women face many expectations about their physical appearance including their body shape, weight, hair texture, and body odor. Although most women are aware of these expectations on a personal level, they rarely develop critical awareness or consciousness that connects the personal expectations to larger societal demands and influences. Developing critical awareness means asking questions to deepen our understanding of the issues. Similarly, gender consciousness means applying a gender lens to a critical analysis. As seen in Table 5.2, a gender lens is an overlay of questions and concerns that can be used to examine and deconstruct systems of power. Like glasses, they provide a lens through which the world can be viewed more clearly.

## The Personal Is Political

*The personal is political* is an early feminist mantra that provides a more complex analysis of women's concerns. Issues that people might identify as personal inadequacies or individual problems often have their roots in political or societal structures that are beyond an individual's ability to control. Thus, identifying problems, developing solutions, and organizing for change must occur at political and institutional levels as well as the personal level. The way in which a problem is defined is critical, for it leads to how solutions are framed and sought.

For example, women often struggle alone with caring for children, often after being told that if they choose to have children it is their personal responsibility to raise them. However, viewing this as a political, rather than personal issue, reveals gendered sex roles in which women are believed to be naturally suited to raising children. Such gendered roles allow men, governments, businesses, and economic systems to not only minimize their child care responsibilities but also benefit from the unpaid and underappreciated work of women. This also hinders the consideration and implementation of policies that would support women and all parents with family-friendly work policies, including paid maternity/paternity leaves, paid days off, subsidized quality child care, and child allowances.

## Dismantling Patriarchy and Confronting Oppression

Historically and in the present, the dominant gendered system in most societies is patriarchy. *Patriarchy* refers to "rule of the father," but A. G. Johnson (2005) refines this by noting that a society is patriarchal "to the degree that it promotes male privilege by being male dominated, male identified, and male centered" (p. 5, italics in the original), and is also organized around an obsessive control of women that results in the oppression of women. According to Enloe (2004),

**TABLE 5.2**   Gender Lens

**Gender Lens**

1. What gendered assumptions might others or I be making? What stereotypes am I falling prey to?

2. What gender schemas (unconscious gender hypotheses) are operational?

3. How does looking at the intersections of race, class, sexual identity, ability, and gender inform this issue?

4. What is the feminist perspective on this issue? (Which feminism?)

5. Am I treating sex, gender, gender identity, and sexual identity as if they are binaries rather than continuums?

6. Am I reacting to the research on gender or my own gendered assumptions? What does the evidence say?

7. Is this theory/treatment/model applicable to women? Who developed it and for whom? Are there more women-friendly theories/treatment/models that can be applied? What does a feminist perspective bring?

8. What is the history of this issue for women?

9. What is the relational context? The cultural context?

10. How does this impact the "*gendered* person in *patriarchal* environment" perspective?

11. Can I apply the feminist policy analysis to this issue? What does that illuminate?

12. How is the media influencing or informing my perspective? How can I apply the concepts of media literacy to challenge or deconstruct the message?
    a. *Who created this message?*
    b. *What creative techniques are used to attract my attention?*
    c. *How might different people understand this message differently than me?*
    d. *What values, lifestyles, and points of view are represented in, or omitted from, this message? Why is this message being sent? (Center for Media Literacy).*

13. Who has the power in this situation? What are the economic drivers/motives involved?

14. Am I drawing on women's strength, resilience, resistance, creativity, and agency?

15. Am I thinking critically here or just accepting "conventional wisdom"?

16. How am I "performing" and doing" gender when I think gender exists outside of me? What are the consequences for me and others, including my clients or conforming to or resisting gendered expectations?

17. How are my actions reinforcing sexism and heterosexism? (Am I assuming everyone is heterosexual, am I complimenting someone for his or her weight loss or commenting on a little girl's appearance?)

18. How racist am I? More or less? How can I change?

19. What is my position here? One of unearned advantage, privilege, oppression? How does that inform my perspective?

20. Although this issue looks personal/psychological, how it is a political or policy issue for women? What change needs to happen and on what level? What is the "head of the river" solution here?

21. Am I defining another woman or myself by our relationships to men?

22. Am I avoiding male-centered language (mankind, manning the table, man and wife?)

23. What would equality look like?

24. How am I "pledging allegiance to the patriarchy"? (bell hooks).

(*Continued*)

**TABLE 5.2** Gender Lens (*Continued*)

**Gender Lens**

25. Am I treating something like it is reality when it is socially constructed? How can I deconstruct? (Expose a concept as ideological or culturally constructed rather than a natural or simple reflection of reality).

26. What do I have to unlearn before I can learn?

27. Are the barriers external and institutional (discriminatory policies) or internal (my own or others' gender socialization, feelings of inadequacy, lack of confidence, and assertion?)

28. Can I negotiate a more advantageous arrangement for others or myself?

29. How are gender role norms of masculinity or femininity impacting my behavior? What are the risks of under or overconforming?

30. Can I write a letter to the editor, call my elective representative, or run for office myself?

31. How might this be different for different women? Women in other countries?

32. Am I contributing to the rigid gender socialization of children? How and in what way? What, if anything, could I do differently?

33. Are there sex differences here? What does the research say? Are men from Mars and women from Venus, or from North Dakota and South Dakota? Am I exaggerating or minimizing sex differences?

34. Am I assessing for sexual, psychological, economic, and physical violence?

35. Are there double standards operating here? Do I have different expectations for women, men, girls, and boys?

36. How does this issue uniquely impact women, if it does?

37. Are women being sexually objectified? Am I self-objectifying?

38. Am I comfortable with my body and feel as though I have a right to pleasure? If not, how can I change?

39. How can I advocate for others and myself?

40. Can one person make a difference here? How? Or does this require collective action and coalitions?

41. Can I redefine "selfish" to mean "taking care of myself"?

42. Ask Dr. Brown's critical conscious questions:
    a. *Why do these expectations exist?*
    b. *How does it work?*
    c. *How are we impacted by it?*
    d. *Who benefits from it?*

43. Are feminist values and words (choice, empowerment) being co-opted to hide women's lack of real power?

© Beverly McPhail, 2010, reprinted with permission.

patriarchal systems are enduring and adaptable due to the fact that "they make many women overlook their own marginal positions and feel instead secure, protected, and valued" (p. 6).

In patriarchal systems, positions of authority are largely held by men in political, economic, legal, religious, educational, and military institutions. Male dominance is maintained by power differences, with men holding greater power and viewed as superior to women. A male-identified society is one in which the core cultural ideas about what is desirable, preferable, normal, or valued are associated with men and masculinity. Being male-centered means that the focus of attention is primary on men and what they do. Men, for example, typically star in the protagonist role in life as well as in film and theater, while women have limited supporting roles as girlfriends, wives, prostitutes with hearts of gold, or damsels in distress. A final characteristic of a patriarchy is male control, over themselves and women (A. G. Johnson, 2005). Men largely control countries, their own emotions, and women. Women's lives are often constrained by male power and control, and sometimes held in place by violence or threats of violence.

It is important to note that not all men are similarly advantaged in patriarchy because patriarchy intersects with other systems of oppression including race, class, nation, and sexual identity. For example, a poor Black gay man is often not in a privileged position compared to a wealthy White heterosexual woman. Importantly, patriarchy is a system of social arrangements, and this illustrates the necessity of changing systems and institutions, as well as individuals, in order to dismantle patriarchy.

Oppression is the primary tool used to maintain the system of patriarchy, which Frye defines as, "a system of interrelated barriers and forces which reduce, immobilize, and mold people who belong to a certain group, and effect their subordination to another group" (1983, p. 33). Along with her definition she provides a helpful metaphor, a birdcage. She suggests that only looking at one wire in the birdcage makes it impossible to see why the bird is securely trapped. However, when stepping back to see how the wires in the cage relate to one another, it becomes clear that the bird is "surrounded by a network of systematically related barriers, no one of which would be the least hindrance to its flight, but which, by their relation to each other, are as confining as the solid walls of a dungeon" (p. 5). The wires that restrict women are economic, political and social in nature and involve the institutions of marriage, school, and work, to name a few. Thus, it is also important to recognize and confront oppression in order to dismantle patriarchy.

## Separating Gender and Sex

As discussed in more detail in Chapters 4 and 8, it is important to understand the difference between gender and sex when considering issues related to either. *Sex* is the physiological composition of a person and refers to one's biological or natal sex. *Gender or gender role* is an expression of masculinity and femininity that is socially constructed, dictated, and enforced. *Gender identity* is a person's self-concept of their gender, which may or may not be at odds with their biological sex. *Sexual orientation* is one's sexual preference and emotional attraction (Lev, 2004). In its oversimplified and baldest terms, "Gender is what is between your ears and sex is what is between your legs" (Dozier, 2005, p. 298). Significantly, the separation of sex and gender was a major turning point in theorizing about gender.

## Addressing Intersectionality

In the early days of the Second Wave of the women's movement, there was a call for a universal sisterhood based upon the shared oppression of women. The premise was that all women had common experiences due to their membership in a subordinate class. Theory, practice, and activism moved forward on that assumption and women were called to work together to overcome their shared discrimination.

However, the notion of shared sisterhood was challenged, primarily through the work of women of color both in and outside of the United States (Collins, 1991; Lorde, 1984; Moraga & Anzaldúa, 1981; Mohanty, 2003). The primary concern was that White, middle-class women ignored the significant differences in oppression-related race, sexual preference, class, and age. Lorde noted that "There is a pretense to a homogeneity of experience covered by the word *sisterhood* that does not in fact exist." (1984, p. 116, italics in the original). This led women of color to call for a method of analysis that integrates race, class, and gender, as well as nation. Terms used for addressing these interlocking systems of oppression include *multiple oppressions, intersectionality* (Crenshaw, 2003), and *matrix of domination* (P. H. Collins, 2000). The metaphor of an intersection was chosen to illustrate the interactive effects of discrimination that include both structure and process.

## FEMINIST THEORIES

The growth of feminist thought has expanded and now reflects three distinct orientations with different foci: theories of gender differences, theories of gender inequality, and theories of gender oppression (Ritzer, 1988). This "feminist enlightenment" (J. Bernard, 1981) reflects the diverse perspectives of an "interdisciplinary community" comprising sociologists, anthropologists, social workers, psychologists, political scientists, philosophers, historians, biologists, economists, lawyers, literary authors, and theologians. While their particular interests and viewpoints may differ, they write from a woman-centered perspective and reject many of the assumptions inherent in androcentric science and research.

*Theories of gender difference* focus on psychological and relational differences in the way women and men experience both the world and themselves. Basic values, interests, ways of knowing, identity construction, and relational interactions are seen as distinctive from those of men (J. B. Miller, 1986; J. Bernard, 1981; Gilligan, 1982; Ritzer, 1988; Rossi, 1983; Ruddick, 1980). The "different voice" and different vision that women bring to the construction of reality is the main tenet of this set of theories. Although these theories are viewed as conservative by more radical feminists, these theories have made influential contributions to contemporary feminist thought (Ritzer, 1988). They attempt to recast women's development in a positive light rather than accept the deficiencies attributed to women in androcentric theories. We discuss these theories in greater detail in Chapters 7, 8, and 9.

*Theories of gender inequality* largely reject the idea of personality differences between men and women and point instead to commonalities in all humans. Specifically, people are seen as adaptable and characterized by "a deep need for freedom to seek self-actualization" (Ritzer, 1988, p. 296). Differences that exist are seen as structural in nature and are tied to the organization of a society that fosters and perpetuates inequality. In addition, most theories of gender inequality assume that broad-scale systematic change is possible. Chafetz (1989, p. 136), for example, asserted that:

> superior male power, which exists by definition in gender-stratified societies, allows men to coerce women into assuming work roles that reinforce their disadvantaged status, both at the macro and micro levels. . . . Undergirding . . . the process is a gender division of labor that provides unequal power resources to men and women.

It follows, then, that pivotal targets for change are "superior male power" and the "gender division of labor" or the public sphere of social activity. Here lie the true rewards of social life—those of power, status, money, and opportunities for self-actualization. They argue that access to the public sphere is open for men and restricted for women. The private sphere, to which women are relegated, is bound to the role of mother and wife, and the dependency inherent in this limited role denies women the opportunity for self-realization.

Structural change, then, is necessary for the elimination of gender inequality. While theorists with a Marxist orientation may advocate revolutionary action, most take a more conservative liberal stance and advocate working within the system to bring about a more egalitarian social structure.

*Theories of gender oppression* focus more directly on the role of power and domination in creating gender differences and gender inequality. The basic structure of domination and oppression is the patriarchy—a primary power structure that is used deliberately and purposively to control and subjugate women. Ritzer (1988) identified three major strains of feminist theory that focus on oppression: psychoanalytical feminism, radical feminism, and socialist feminism.

Psychoanalytic feminism focuses simultaneously on gender differences and gender oppression. It accepts many of Freud's fundamental assumptions about the nature of the unconscious and the importance of early childhood experiences in personality formation. It rejects, however, his conclusions about the inherent psychological inferiority of women and recasts the differences between men and women as a function of the patriarchy and oppression (Chodorow, 1978). We discuss this more fully in Chapter 7.

In radical feminism, patriarchy is understood to be the root of oppression in all spheres of society. Gender oppression, however, is primary (Al-Hibri, 1981; Deckard, 1979). Violence against women, both physical and psychological, is created and maintained through the lack of control that women are allowed over their lives and choices. Abolishing patriarchy and encouraging sexual freedom are primary goals that require a fundamental change in women's consciousness (Nes & Iadicola, 1989). A new consciousness based on self-worth and strength is necessary if women are to confront and defeat patriarchal domination. Banks (1986) and Valeska (1981) argued for separation and the formation of separate structures that are woman centered (Nes & Iadicola, 1989).

Socialist feminism encompasses a diverse group of theorists who attempt to combine Marxist and radical feminism. Here we see class and gender oppression interlinked. Some have argued that class oppression is "rooted in the production of things" whereas gender oppression is "rooted in the production of people" (Nes & Iadicola, 1989, p. 14). Thus, the "capitalist patriarchy" is of primary concern in the subordination of women (Eisenstein, 1979; H. Hartmann, 1981; Vogel, 1981).

Still other theorists have used class and gender oppression as a base to explore and explain all forms of oppression, including that of race, ethnicity, and sexual orientation. Exploitation and domination are central to this formulation in which "the macro-social structures of economy, polity, and ideology interact with the intimate, private micro-processes of human reproduction, domesticity, sexuality, and subjectivity to sustain a multi-faceted system of domination" (Ritzer, 1988, p. 311).

## CONTEMPORARY THOUGHT IN FEMINIST THEORY

Contemporary feminist theory encompasses a similar diverse set of interests and perspectives. One of the primary advances is a broader definition of the concerns that are included in feminist analysis. Thus, feminist theory has expended to include issues related to all genders, the continuum of sexuality, and the way in which gender is socially constructed. In this sense, feminist theory has, in part, become meshed with gender studies. We discuss these variations and other contemporary feminist theories in the following sections.

## The Social Construction of Gender and the Sex Continuum

Rather than seeing gender as a biological or religious imperative comprised of only two genders that are opposite to each other, feminist theorists (other than postmodern feminists) argue that distinctions must be made between sex and gender; they see one's biological sex as largely immutable, but gender as socially constructed. This means that gender roles are viewed as flexible and dynamic, and change over time and between different cultures.

Understanding gender as a social construction involves the process of deconstruction, which entails exposing concepts as being constructed through ideology or cultural processes rather than seeing them as "natural or a simple reflection of reality" (P. H. Collins, 2000, p. 15). In this view, women's limited and traditional roles as wife and mother are based on discrimination and outmoded cultural stereotypes rather than biological mandates or historical roles (Bem, 1993).

Once the field of gender studies adopted the notion that gender inequalities and roles were socially constructed rather than rooted in biological or divine mandates, attention then turned to exposing *how* gender inequalities were constructed. C. West and Zimmerman (1987) describe gender as routine accomplishment embedded in everyday interaction. Rather than seeing gender as a property of an individual, they view gender as an emergent feature of social situations, which they describe as "doing gender." That is, "a person's gender is not simply an aspect of what one is, but, more fundamentally, it is something that one *does*, and does recurrently, in interaction with others" (C. West & Zimmerman, 1987, p. 140, italics in the original). People are then held accountable for their gender performance based on their sex category. In their formulation, gender becomes a verb rather than a noun, an activity rather than a natural essence.

Not only is gender enacted at the level of personal interactions, but at the institutional level as well. According to Lorber, it "establishes patterns of expectations for individuals, orders the social processes of everyday life, is built into the major social organizations of society, such as the economy, ideology, the family, and politics, and it also an entity in and of itself" (1994, p. 1). Thus, gender difference is used as a means to create a gender hierarchy. Lober notes that not only is gender socially constructed, but gender differences are socially constructed as well. If gender difference can be made to seem natural, then gender inequality must follow and the creation of gender differences is the bedrock on which inequality is built. In this sense, gender differences are a means, rather than an end and set the stage for imposing inequality upon women.

Traditional thought posits that there is a sexual binary with only two sexes, male and female. This model is built on the assumption that "if a person is female she is a woman; if a person is a woman, she is feminine; and if a person is a feminine female woman, she will be attracted to a masculine male man" (Lev, 2004, p. 94). Accordingly, the traditional model also assumes heterosexuality. The fundamental premise of this model is that both sex and gender are universal and fixed and, thus, beyond our control. Based on this, different characteristics are ascribed to each sex. Men are typically viewed as more rational and aggressive than women, and women are viewed as more emotional and nurturing than men. Further, this dichotomy is accepted as being natural and reflecting the given order of things (Alsop, Fitzsimons, & Lennon, 2002). Men and women are often termed the *opposite sex* and their roles can be viewed as complementary.

Lev proposes a more transformational theory/model in which gender identity, gender roles, and sexual orientation are no longer seen as binaries, but rather, as continuums. In this model, each category is not predicated upon another. For instance, a woman could have a female body and a masculine gender identity while adopting a traditionally masculine gender expression and sexually desiring women. To better understand this, Tucker suggests that we, "Think of gender as a rowboat: some people perch carefully in the center, others sit to one side or the other, still others lean out precariously over the edge. And some people cannot keep from tipping the boat over completely" (2005, p. 38).

Another related area in which new theories about women are emerging is that of sexuality and sexual identity. Baumeister (2000) proposes that female sexuality is malleable and mutable, especially when compared to male sexuality, which appears to be relatively rigid. Peplau and Garnets' (2000) work support this premise, stipulating that female "sexual identity, attractions, and behavior can be varied, complex, and inconsistent" (p. 342). In this model, bisexuality is considered as a choice rather than as a transitory state, and relationships, rather than sexual activity, are seen as central to female sexual orientation. For this reason women's sexual orientation is seen as potentially fluid.

Building on the idea of gender and sexual orientation being shaped by forces other than simply biology, *queer theory*, as discussed in Chapter 4, also involves the questioning of sex and gender categories. Although the term *queer* was once used as a derogatory and insulting word for gay people, it has subsequently been reclaimed and used in a more positive and productive way. Queer theory overlaps feminist thought in that it "focuses on mismatches between sex, gender, and desire (Jagose, 1996, p. 3), and suggests that identities are fluid, culture-dependent, and due to social conditioning. In her *performative theory of gender*, J. Butler (1999) describes gender as a performance rather than a noun or a set of attributes. Basing her analysis, in part, on performances of drag queens that play upon the dissonance in anatomical sex, gender identity, and gender performance, she theorizes that if gender can be made, it can be unmade and remade in different, less constricting ways. Butler challenges the notion of the category of *woman*, but suggests that feminists use the category/identity of women as a political tool and strategic practice without attributing ontological integrity to the term.

## Feminist Standpoint Theory

Another significant contribution to critical feminist theory is *feminist standpoint theory*. According to Changfoot (2004), feminist standpoint theory is important in the history of feminist thought because "it at once seeks to become a method and justification for women's epistemological authority" (p. 480). Feminist standpoint theorists propose that research that is centrally concerned with politics and social change and is directed by social values can produce empirically and theoretically preferable results. As an epistemology, the theory asserts that research that begins from the standpoint of particular marginalized groups of human beings yields less partial and distorted understandings of nature and social relations (Swigonski, 1994). Sandra Harding writes, "Standpoint epistemologies and methodologies were constructed in opposition to the all-powerful dictates of rationalist/empiricist epistemologies and methodologies (positivism) in the natural and social sciences and in public institutions such as law, medicine, state economic policy, and so forth" (1997, p. 383).

The term *standpoint* refers to a position in society that involves a level of awareness about an individual's social location, from which certain features of reality come into prominence and from which others are obscured (Swigonski, 1993). To survive, members of marginalized groups must not only understand their life perspective but also develop full knowledge of the life perspective of the dominant group. Swigonski (1994) wrote that this double consciousness or knowledge of, awareness of, and sensitivity to both the dominant worldview of society and their own perspective results in a more complete view of social reality.

Original formulations of the theory were based on the assumptions that all knowledge is located and situated and that the *standpoint*, or position in society, of women provides a vantage point that reveals a more accurate reflection of women's social reality. While the theory originally only addressed the standpoint of women, a reassessment of the theory in the late 1980s and early 1990s resulted in the inclusion of other oppressed and marginalized groups including people of color, gay men and lesbians, children, the poor, and the elderly.

The principal authors who have contributed to the development of feminist standpoint theory come from a variety of academic backgrounds including philosophy, women's studies, political science, and sociology. Many standpoint theorists credit Nancy Hartsock, a professor of political science at the University of Washington, as the first to introduce the theory in her book *Money, Sex, and Power* (1983). Using theory originally proposed by Karl Marx, Hartsock maintained that the concept of a standpoint is built on the proposition that there are some perspectives on society from which, however well intentioned a researcher may be, the real relations of humans with one another and with the natural world remain invisible. Additionally, Hartsock developed the idea of dominant society labeling its perspective as *real* and rejecting the definitions of women. In her examination of the structural differences between men and women, she also drew on object relations theory as espoused by Jane Flax and Nancy Chodorow and their views of the social and psychological processes that lead to different developmental paths (Changfoot, 2004).

Sociologist Dorothy Smith is also identified as one of the original standpoint theorists. Smith advocated an alternative sociology that is based on "insider knowledge" or personal knowledge of one's own lived experience and that exists in the gap between that knowledge and the "objectified knowledge" produced by traditional sociological practices (Longino, 1993).

Patricia Hill Collins, another key theoretical contributor, defined feminist standpoint theory as an "interpretive framework dedicated to explicating how knowledge remains central to maintaining and changing unjust systems of power" (1997, p. 375). Last, Sandra G. Harding, who writes from the perspectives of women's studies, education, and philosophy, has written extensively on standpoint theory from a postmodern perspective.

The following propositions and assumptions of feminist standpoint theory discussed in this section are primarily based on the original works of Patricia H. Collins (1986, 1989, 1990, 1997), Sandra G. Harding (1987, 1991, 1997, 2004), Nancy Hartsock (1983, 1997), and Dorothy Smith (1987, 1997). The synthesis of these ideas and their examination through a social work lens is attributed to and is referenced from Mary Swigonski's work (1993, 1994).

## Propositions and Assumptions of Feminist Standpoint Theory

**LIFE EXPERIENCE STRUCTURES ONE'S UNDERSTANDING OF LIFE**    Feminist standpoint theorists assert that research should be inductive in terms of starting from concrete experiences rather than broad theories. As an example, Swigonski (1993) proposed that developing research from the standpoint of women's lives has made issues such as childbirth, housework, domestic violence, incest, and rape more visible to the public. Collins (1989) went even further and proposed that individuals are more credible as experts if they have had actual experiences in their areas of expertise. Ladner's research (as cited in Swigonski, 1994) with African American adolescent mothers provides a good example of how research based on feminist standpoint theory is guided by life experience. Ladner's personal experiences equipped her to bring the mothers' voices to the center of her research, resulting in her identifying numerous strengths and coping skills of the mothers and their community. The vast majority of past studies on teenage mothers view the participants through the lens of a deviance model, resulting in findings that fail to recognize the strengths of these mothers.

**MEMBERS OF THE MOST AND THE LEAST POWERFUL GROUPS WILL POTENTIALLY HAVE OPPOSED UNDERSTANDINGS OF THE WORLD** P. H. Collins maintained that, "suppressing the knowledge and viewpoint of any oppressed group makes it easier for dominant groups to rule because the seeming absence of an independent consciousness in the oppressed can be taken to mean that subordinated groups willingly collaborate in their own victimization" (1990, p. 5). Often in traditional research, the experiences and worldview of the dominant group is accepted as reality while the views of oppressed groups are dismissed. Feminist standpoint theorists believe that the perspective from subordinate groups often generates less biased analyses of situations because these groups are not as vested in maintaining the idea of their perspective as reality.

**THE LESS-POWERFUL GROUP'S STANDPOINT HAS TO BE DEVELOPED THROUGH EDUCATION** Harding (1991) asserted that in feminist standpoint theory, knowledge is seen as a hands-on procedure. The research process should serve as consciousness-raising for all involved. An understanding of the conflict between the dominant worldview and the marginalized group's worldview is essential for the reinterpretation of reality, which in turn is a prerequisite for effecting social change.

**THE PERSPECTIVE OF THOSE OUTSIDE THE DOMINANT GROUP DEVELOPS FROM THEIR DAILY ACTIVITIES** According to Swigonski (1994), daily activities require marginalized groups to bridge the gap between ideological dualisms such as nature versus culture, professional versus manual work, or intellectual versus emotional work. An example used to illustrate this point is the domestic work of African American women in the homes of White upper-class families. The African Americans' experiences as domestic workers afforded them a standpoint that demystified White power.

**THE APPROPRIATE PERSPECTIVE FOR RESEARCH ACTIVITIES IS EVERYDAY LIFE** Standpoint theory directs researchers to identify research problems within the daily reality of marginalized groups and place their day-to-day reality in the center of research. Working within feminist standpoint theory, researchers find that research problems emerge from the everyday life of marginalized-oppressed groups in relation to the social structure (D. Smith, 1987), which is imposed on less-powerful groups and is the cause of those problems.

**MEMBERS OF MARGINALIZED GROUPS ARE VALUABLE "STRANGERS" TO THE SOCIAL ORDER** P. H. Collins (1986) identified three advantages of outsider status in research: the outsiders' experiences of nearness and remoteness are valuable for objectivity; natives confide in strangers in ways they do not confide in each other; and it is easier for strangers to see patterns of belief or behavior.

The two most fundamental assumptions of feminist standpoint theory are the beliefs that all knowledge is situated and that the standpoint of marginalized and oppressed groups is privileged because it provides a vantage point that reveals an often dismissed perspective of social reality (Hekman, 1997). Feminist standpoint theory also operates out of the assumption that the purpose of all research should be political. Unlike traditional positivist science, which is conducted for purposes of prediction and control, feminist standpoint theory asserts that the purpose of research must be for the subjects of the research to advance their causes (Cook & Fonow, 1990).

Feminist standpoint theory addresses the assumptions of positivist approaches to science and research, specifically the claims that traditional science does not do enough to contribute to the empowerment of the oppressed. Elements of these assumptions were addressed by Fletcher in a comparison of qualities of research design. J. Fletcher (1994) maintained that feminist standpoint theory is grounded in the qualities of vulnerability, reflexivity, receptivity, empathy, collaboration, and appreciation of context. Conversely, the assumptions of the traditional scientific method of knowledge production include subject–object separation, scientific objectivity, and claims of value neutrality.

The scientific approach to knowledge assumes that researchers can and should distance themselves from research participants. Harding (1991) wrote that despite the scientist's attempts to minimize any relationship between herself or himself and the subject of study, both occupy the same causal plane and both are influenced by the same sociocultural factors. Feminist standpoint theory asserts that all research must include reflexivity. Reflexivity is defined as researchers' need to study the role of their own social position as they conduct research. Researchers are encouraged to suspend the role of expert and use the research experience as an opportunity to learn about and understand the experience of others while critically examining the sources of social power in their own lives. Harding (1991) stated that the researcher's class, culture, ethnicity, and gender assumptions, beliefs, and behaviors must be placed in the frame of analysis and in the research reporting.

In addition to the concept of reflexivity, feminist standpoint theory directs researchers to use openness and empathy to connect with and relate to the research participants. According to Shulamit Reinharz (1992), researchers should use the strategy of starting from one's own experience to define the research questions, locate sources of useful data, gain the trust of others in doing the research, and partially test the research findings.

Based on the propositions and assumptions previously discussed, feminist standpoint theorists predict that this theory can transform research into a counterhegemonic process that makes valuable political, social, and cultural contributions while producing empirically and theoretically sound knowledge. According to P. H. Collins (1997, p. 381),

> Standpoint theory argues that ideas matter in systems of power. In this sense, standpoints may be judged not only by their epistemological contributions but also by the terms of their participation in hierarchical power relations. Do they inherently explain and condone injustice or do they challenge it? Do they participate in relations of rule via creating knowledge, or do they reject such rule by generating cultures of resistance? Extracting any claims about knowledge from the power relations in which they are embedded violates the basic premise of standpoint theory because such theory exists primarily to explicate these power relations. Thus, attempts to take the knowledge while leaving the power behind inadvertently operate within the terrain of privileged knowledge.

Many limitations of feminist standpoint theory have been addressed through the creation of multiple versions of the theory. To use this theory to advance social work practice, the profession must embrace the version that recognizes the standpoints of all marginalized groups, not just women. Critics of feminist standpoint theory, especially those within the feminist camp, believe that the theory fails to recognize the issues of difference among group members. Social workers must also acknowledge that differences exist within oppressed groups, and there is not one voice or standpoint that represents an entire group or population.

On an epistemological level, perhaps one of the most valuable contributions of standpoint theory is that it not only validates the knowledge of women but also the idea that women can produce important and useful knowledge. On a practical level, it also provides an important tool for analyzing multiple viewpoints, makes us aware of the need to analyze competing and often incompatible claims of truth and knowledge, and locates power and politics at the center of such claims.

## Relational-Cultural Theory

A relatively new feminist theory, Relational-Cultural Theory, was originally constructed to provide a better understanding of the growth and development of women, but may also include a better understanding of male growth and development. The theory was developed by Jean Baker Miller, a psychoanalyst, and three psychologists, Judith Jordan, Irene Stiver, and Janet Survey (J. V. Jordan & Hartling, 2002), who were dissatisfied with current psychological theory as applied to women. They met informally to reexamine developmental psychology and clinical practice as it related to women, and their meetings expanded into a collaborative theory-building group. They found an institutional home within the Stone Center at Wellesley College and initiated a series of colloquia that attracted additional scholars, clinicians, and researchers who were interested in exploring the complexities of women's psychological development (Jordan & Hartling, 2002).

The core tenets of the theory include: "all growth occurs in connection, that all people yearn for connection, and that growth-fostering relationships are created through mutual empathy and mutual empowerment" (Jordan & Hartling, 2002, p. 49). J. B. Miller (1986) notes that most existing psychological theories focus on the development of a more "separated sense of self" rather than a belief that women's sense of personhood is grounded in "the motivation to make and enhance relatedness to others" (p. 1). Miller even contests the notion of "self-determination" saying there is no such thing, "although we can and do play a central part in our own life—and in others' lives" (p. 2).

Although the theory was initially developed to understand the psychological experience of women, it has expanded to better account for all human experience, both male and female, and on a depth and breadth of topics including depression, trauma, eating disorders, substance abuse, chronic illness, mother–daughter relationships, lesbian relationships, issue of racism, sexism, classism, heterosexism, and a range of other psychological and social problems.

Central to developing relationships is the concept of empathy, or being able to experience the feelings and thoughts of another person while also being able to know and feel one's own. Miller (1986) describes "five good things" that occur in growth-fostering relationships: "1. Each person feels a greater sense of "zest" (vitality, energy); 2. Each person feels more able to act and does act; 3. Each person has a more accurate picture of her/himself and the other person(s); 4. Each person feels a greater sense of worth; and 5. Each person feels more connection to the other person(s) and feels a greater motivation for connections with other people beyond those in the specific relationship" (p. 3).

Disconnection is viewed as an inevitable part of being in relationships, caused by empathic failures, relational violations, and injuries (Jordan & Hartling, 2002). Overcoming these disconnections can lead to an increased sense of *relational competence*. However, when people are unable to effect change in relationships and/or be their authentic selves, they often begin to keep aspects of themselves out of the relationship in order to maintain the relationship, and this is termed a *central relational paradox*. Miller notes that unequal power relationships hinder and even prevent growth-fostering relationships.

Included within this theory is the understanding of how relationships occur within particular cultural contexts such as the devaluation of people due to their gender, race, class, and sexual orientation. Thus, the theory accounts for how discrimination, stereotyping, unearned advantage and privilege impact people's sense of connection and disconnection. Therefore, another central tenet is that people grow (or fail to grow) in relationships that exist within a cultural context. In contrast to other psychological theories that are limited to intrapsychic phenomena, this theory clearly places people not only within the individual or familial level but also within a sociocultural context.

## CONTEMPORARY ISSUES

Contemporary gender issues within the feminist movement are too numerous to count. Inequality and the effects of discrimination and oppression continue to leave most women at a structural disadvantage and some of the more pressing issues include, but are not limited to, intimate partner violence, human trafficking, workplace issues including family responsibilities, the wage gap, occupational segregation, sexual harassment, the feminization of professions, the glass ceiling and escalator, and lack of family friendly benefits. Further, within women's health there is a focus on racial disparities in diagnosis and treatment as well as the medicalization of women's health. Reproductive rights and reproductive justice also continue to be at the forefront of issues that are a focus of feminist concern.

Rather than a more singular focus on abortion services, reproductive justice encompasses a broader vision of rights including (a) the right to have a child, (b) the right not to have a child, and (c) the right for women to parent the children they have, as well as to control their birthing options, such as midwifery (L. Ross, 2007, p. 4). Solinger (2007) notes that engaging in heterosexual sex can become a class privilege when only women with economic means can make the full range of reproductive choices. When "choice" is the major framework for looking at reproductive rights, then women are divided into two classes: women who make "good" choices and women who make "bad" choices. Feminist theory and research will continue to address these and other issues that affect not only women but also men, people of color and gender, and sexual minorities as well. In a real sense, every issue is a woman's issue, and women's issues are human issues as well.

## APPLICATION TO SOCIAL WORK PRACTICE

Feminist theories have direct application to social work practice not only for women, but all persons. Social work and feminism clearly align with their mutual focus on social and economic justice, valuing the worth of all individuals, and goals of social change and empowerment. However, while social work is primarily concerned with a gender-neutral "person in the environment" perspective, feminist social work examines how women and men as gendered beings operate and are often constrained within a patriarchal environment. Such a gender lens brings an additional analysis to social work practice. Feminist theory enriches social work practice by asking and answering additional questions and by recognizing the importance of gender as well as its intersections with race, class, sexual identity, and ability in the distribution of economic and social rewards.

### Definition of the Helping Situation

Practice based on feminist theory defines the helping situation as one that primarily identifies problems in structural, rather than personal, terms. Therefore, using this perspective, women can be viewed as less likely to require treatment for an intrapsychic phenomenon and more likely to require the solutions gained by working at the societal level to change policies and power discrepancies, rather than changing individual women. Thus, there is a primary focus on women's oppression rather than women's depression, although that too demands attention. Removing obstacles to women's growth and opportunities is key, while at the same time building on her strengths. A feminist framework values women's strengths, agency, and resilience, while being knowledgeable about the specific issues that women face, including the unique problems at the intersection of race, gender, class, sexual identity, and physical ability. Women are considered experts in their own lives, needing support, validation, and consciousness raising more than treatment and diagnosis. These theories define situations in terms of social problems and social issues as well as growth. Flowchart 5.1 demonstrates an application of feminist theories derived from these definitions.

## Assessment, Practice Strategies, and Methods

The application of feminist theory to assessment, practice strategies, and methods has the potential to make us question what we believe we know, as gendered assumptions are revealed and challenged. In order to work effectively with clients from a feminist perspective, social workers should be fully conversant with feminist theory and models. Assessment occurs at multiple levels in feminist social work practice. Social workers must first assess their own gender schemas and develop a critical gender consciousness and analysis. They must use critical consciousness to be cognizant of their own positionality and understand how that impacts the helping relationship. Pitner and Sakamoto (2005) define critical consciousness as the "process of continuously reflecting upon and examining how our own biases, assumptions, and cultural worldviews affect the way we perceive difference and power dynamics" (p. 441). For instance, instead of asking themselves if they are or are not racist, Trepangier (2006) suggests that White women ask themselves, instead, how more or less racist they are. This, of course, can apply to people of color as well. Further, in order to address the natural hierarchies that exist in the helping relationship, social workers should act as a guide and facilitator rather than the expert. It is important to recognize that the expert is the woman who is an authority on her own life and experiences. From a feminist perspective, the relationship itself should be valued and viewed as mutually empowering and empathetic.

In assessing women and girls, social workers should use multiple methods of assessment and be knowledgeable about validity, reliability, standardization processes, and norming information to know if such assessments are suitable for women and girls (American Psychological Association [APA], 2007). Because violence is so prevalent in many women's lives, a standard assessment would include questions about her experiences with violence. Assessment within the feminist model also includes a reframing of symptoms and an acknowledgment of oppressive social contexts that may improperly evaluate appropriate responses to oppression as being pathological (Worrell & Remer, 1992).

Practice methods are multiple when undergirded by feminist theory, and can occur at all levels. Methods may include feminist therapy for individuals, groups, and families, although some feminists believe that such therapies are contraindicated because they privatize women's problems instead of politicizing them (Kitzinger, 1996). Feminist therapists often borrow practice methods from other theoretical orientations, but only after subjecting them to a rigorous feminist critique.

Early in the Second Wave of the feminist movement women benefited from consciousness raising groups (Trebilcot, 2002). In these small groups women shared their personal experiences as a tool to analyze the larger structures of male domination with the goal of leading to political action to change the realities of women's lives. Contemporary feminist group work challenges traditional theories on group formation, process, and leadership by noting how gender dynamics can affect group dynamics (L. M. Gutiérrez, Reed, Ortega, & Lewis, 1998). Further, a feminist multicultural perspective on group work involves addressing issues of power, consciousness-raising, self-identification, multicultural socialization, and oppression.

**FLOWCHART 5.1.** A practice application of feminist theory © 2011, Beverly McPhail. Used with permission.

Feminist practice also recognizes the strength and diversity of families and respects diverse arrangements of kinship and social ties, including gay and lesbian families. Finn recommends an assessment tool called the "gendergram" that explicitly assesses the gender and power dynamics in the family (M. B. White & Tyson-Rawson, 1995). Feminist family therapy applies feminist theory and values to work with families and involves examining how gender roles and stereotyping affect individuals in the family as well as their relationships to each other, society, and the therapist (Goodrich, Rampage, Ellman, & Halstead, 1988).

Feminist theory is applicable at the organizational level as well. Rather than seeing institutions and as rational, gender-neutral organizations, gender is recognized as being embedded in organizational processes so that inequalities are reproduced in the mundane work of the gendered organization (Acker, 2006). Intervening at the level of institutions and organizations most often requires policy changes. For example, workplace policies have been adopted that prohibit discrimination based on race and sex, sexual harassment, in addition to the adoption of more family-friendly policies.

Similarly, the goal of feminist organizing "is the elimination of permanent power hierarchies between all peoples which can prevent them from realizing their potential" (L. M. Gutiérrez & Lewis, 1995, p. 98). And, according to Hyde (2003), feminist community practice can offer new ways to conceptualize and implement change strategies as well as uncover and correct the male bias that may be hidden in traditional approaches.

Stall and Stoecker (1998) identify the strength and weakness of the feminist model for practice. One significant strength is the ability to sustain a struggle over the long haul due to the power of the relationships that are built. However, a weakness is it can have difficulty translating its concerns into the public arena. Some possible settings and applications of feminist theory is shown in Table 5.3.

## CRITICAL ANALYSIS

### Biological, Psychological, and Spiritual Factors

Since biological theories of male and female difference have often been used to construct and justify male dominance and female subordination, feminist theory has rightly been suspicious of biological explanations of gender. Historically feminist theory minimized biological explanations and focused, instead, on the structural conditions and the social construction of gender. More recently, Diamond (2006) developed a theory of gender identity development that accounts for both biological and environmental influences.

As noted earlier, a substantial literature on the psychological and moral development of women has emerged from feminist theory and is covered in more detail in Chapters 7, 8, and 9. Although theories of female difference typically eschew biological explanations, they embrace those born in psychology, sometimes uncritically.

Feminist writings have also provided a critique of religion and, in particular, how religious leaders and scholars have used patriarchal interpretations of sacred texts to justify the second-class status of women. However, the feminist critique has also sought to reinterpret religious texts and understandings through a more woman-friendly and gendered lens (Armstrong, 2001, p. vii). According to Warne (2002), a feminist theology challenges male-centered traditional theology and is a creative resource for thinking about God/ultimate reality in relation to women.

Assessing a woman's faith tradition and how it impacts her view of the world and specific difficulties she may be facing, both positively and negatively, is an essential part of a feminist social work practice. Drawing on the wealth of feminist theology, including women of color

**TABLE 5.3**　Various Settings and Applications of Feminist Theory

| Type of Agency | Type of Presenting Problem | Type of Program | Definition of the Helping Situation | Type(s) of Activities |
|---|---|---|---|---|
| Women's shelter | Domestic violence | Shelter; transitional care for women and children | Social issue (protection and empowerment) | Physical shelter and support; legal assistance; advocacy |
| Mental health center | Situational depression of female client | Feminist therapy and women's support group | Social issue (consciousness raising and empowerment) | Dialogue; identification of patriarchal basis of situational depression; solidarity building; setting plans for family/societal change |
| Women's service center | Poverty due to divorce | Multiservice agency for women's issues | Social issue (protection; empowerment; consciousness raising) | Dialogue; identification of patriarchal basis of financial situation; legal assistance; job training |
| Employee assistance program | Sexist work environment | Counseling and assistance for employees | Social issue (consciousness raising and empowerment) | Dialogue, identification of patriarchal basis of work environment; advocacy |
| Women's health services | Unintended pregnancy | Multiservice agency for women's health | Social Issue Medical problem | Female-centered counseling and health services for a range of choices; abortion; adoption; birth control |

theologies, can deepen women's spiritual practices and provide alternative interpretations that transform and reinterpret traditional oppressive religious dogma that typically have kept women subordinate within their faith communities.

## Social, Cultural, and Economic Forces

With its primary focus on power relations, patriarchy and structural inequality, feminist theory has a rich and lengthy history of addressing the ways in which cultural, social, and economic forces impact women and more recently has expanded to include others who are oppressed by a patriarchal social structure. As discussed earlier in this chapter, feminist theory details how the oppression of women is socially constructed at the levels of the personal and the political.

Feminist theories of gender construction and Relational-Cultural Theory, for example, directly address the way in which behavior is gendered through sociocultural norms (Mahalik et al., 2005). Importantly, feminists have long sought to change the culture rather than change the individual women. Similarly, a central concern of feminist theory is the recognition that economic factors have created limited opportunity and roles for women. Traditionally, the economic system represents one more strand of wire in the birdcage that has been used to constrain women.

## Relevance to Individuals, Groups, Families, Organizations, Institutions, and Communities

With its dual foci on the personal and political, feminist theory connects micro, meso, and macro levels of social systems in a similar manner to empowerment theory. Work with individuals is always seen, however, within the context of power dynamics, patriarchy and a gendered society. The primary focus can be on individuals, families, organizations, institutions, and communities as long as a feminist analysis undergirds the analysis of problems. Change efforts can take place at any or all of these levels, although primacy is generally given to changing power relationships that engender inequality and oppression. Importantly, feminist theory is concerned with the nature of justice for all people and systems of all sizes.

## CONSISTENCY WITH SOCIAL WORK VALUES AND ETHICS

Feminist theory and practice are extremely congruent with the social work values and ethics. Social workers are ethically required to become educated about the previously listed range of identities, including issues of sex and gender, as well as refusing to discriminate on that basis. With its focus on the dignity and worth of every individual, social work values align with feminist values that also value each person regardless of gender, gender identity, or gender expression. Feminist values also call for social change and political action rather than accommodation, which is also very congruent with social work values. In fact, with this alignment of values, social workers, female and male, would be hard pressed to explain why they are not feminist in orientation and practice.

## PHILOSOPHICAL UNDERPINNINGS

Feminist theory is undergirded by feminist philosophy. Like most feminist undertakings, feminist philosophy has meant critiquing male theorists and models, reclaiming women in history, and applying the discipline's methods and approaches to feminist concerns. A feminist critique of traditional philosophy finds that false universalizations of male experience often masked male privilege and vested interest in the operation of philosophy (Alcoff & Kittay, 2007). Not content to only critique male bias and misogyny within philosophical traditions, feminist philosophers have sought to reclaim female writers and intellectuals, who often were not recognized as philosophers within the discipline.

However, feminist theory also shares a similar philosophical base with other theories that reject the idea of a totally objective reality and focus, instead, on the social construction of norms, values, and meanings that people assign to both large- and small-scale social phenomena. Similar to empowerment theory, feminist theory sees worldviews as being embedded in particular social and historical contexts and are subject to oppressive power dynamics in their construction.

## METHODOLOGICAL ISSUES AND EMPIRICAL SUPPORT

Methodology in social science research is focused on which processes and procedures for making knowledge are determined to be valid and authoritative. Since feminists are openly politically committed, feminist thought has often been treated as intellectually inferior to existing modes of thought and charged with failing the test of producing generally valid and authoritative knowledge (Ramazanoglu & Holland, 2002). Feminist methodology and critiques of traditional, and often patriarchal, ways of knowing involves questioning "who has the power to know what, and how power is implicated in the process of producing knowledge . . . since the power to produce authoritative knowledge is not equally open to all" (p. 13).

Feminists critique the idea that traditional ways of producing scientific knowledge are objective, about truth, and gender- and politically neutral. They point out that in practice this promoted and reproduced men's appropriation of science and reason, often to the detriment of women (Ramazanoglu & Holland, 2002). As Ramazanoglu and Holland point out, feminist research is not limited to female researchers studying women, using a distinctively feminist research technique, or holding a uniquely feminist ontological or epistemological position. They comment that "what distinguishes feminist researchers (of whatever gender) is some shared political and ethical commitment that makes them accountable to a community of women with moral and political interests in common" (p. 16).

Although feminist researchers retain some elements of the scientific method, they contest the notion of rationality, believe certainty is unattainable, and acknowledge that politics, resources, and the personal enter into the production of scientific knowledge (Ramazanoglu & Holland, 2002).

Similarly, postmodern thought contests the general validity of knowledge production and claims and, ironically, includes a critique of feminist knowledge production and claims. The tensions are multiple, but engaging with the tensions is a hallmark of feminist methodology. Feminists draw on different epistemologies (how researchers can know what they know based on different rules or criteria), while believing politics and epistemology to be inseparable (Ramazanoglu & Holland, 2002). Although feminist researchers are not wedded to particular methods, research endeavors "can be thought of as feminist if they are framed by feminist theory, and aim to produce knowledge that will be useful for effective transformation of gendered injustice and subordination" (p. 147).

Despite contesting traditional, male-centered quantitative research methods, it is those very methods that have shown the disparities in health, mental health, income, education, workplace and other conditions that are the focus of feminist concerns. However, in a systematic review of feminist theory and research Lay and Daley (2007) found over 1,000 published articles that related to feminist theory and only 17 that employed empirical methods in diverse applications of feminist theory. Not surprisingly, these studies were consistent with other research in demonstrating that oppression, control, harassment, and male-privileged environments are still a reality in today's world. However, the authors noted the absence of research that seeks to actually confirm feminist theory in contrast to studying the structural conditions that are at the heart of feminist concerns. They note that "No scholars are refining feminist theory, describing the components of the theory, and showing empirical evidence that demonstrates that the components fit together as hypothesized" (p. 59).

Nonetheless, feminist researchers are now beginning to establish a record of evidence that supports feminist theory and practice. Once undergirding a social movement and political ideology, feminist theory has translated into beginning research results and empirical evidence that adds to the body of knowledge for practice.

## Summary

Feminist theory presents a mode of analysis and practice principles that fulfill the profession's call to social justice and empowerment. Feminist theory acknowledges the power of the social construction of gender and how gender is one of the ways society distributes resources and opportunities. At its core, it is a mode of analysis, a way of looking at the world and asking questions. Importantly, feminist theory adds a gender lens as an overlay to social work policy and practice.

The understanding of gender continues to evolve with notions of sexual and gender binaries giving way to gender and sexuality continuums. Such new theorizing has the potential to radically change the way social work views women and men and affect policy and practice as well. Feminism benefits men as well as women, for as it seeks to liberate women from constraints of a limited female sex role, it also seeks the same for men and people of all genders, races, and sexual identities.

However, achieving these goals means awareness and then action. Men in power did not suddenly give women the right to vote, own property, or gain credit in their own names. Women agitated, demanded, resisted, and organized over decades and that work continues today. For as Coretta Scott King (n.d.) once said, "Struggle is a never-ending process. Freedom is never really won, you earn it and win it in every generation."

# Theories of Assimilation, Acculturation, Bicultural Socialization, and Ethnic Minority Identity

> *The white man tried to tame you*
> *And they put you in a fence*
> *They hunted down the buffalo*
> *And you haven't seen 'em since*
> *No trail of tears prepared you*
> *For reservation life*
> *Your spirit is your mistress*
> *A warm and loving wife.*

> © BILL WARD AND ALLEN DAMRON
> 1992, POST NO BILLS MUSIC (BMI)

## THEORIES OF ASSIMILATION, ACCULTURATION, BICULTURAL SOCIALIZATION, AND ETHNIC MINORITY IDENTITY

- address the interaction, conflict, and cultural change that result from contact between minority and dominant cultures
- explain different modes of adaptation of racial and ethnic minorities to the dominant culture
- describe the stressors involved in socialization to two cultures
- guide assessment and practice with racial and ethnic minorities

This chapter was coauthored by Fernando J. Galan, PhD.

In recent years, the dynamics of acculturation and bicultural socialization in the lives of ethnic and racial minorities has received increasing attention in the literature. As the United States has become more racially and ethnically diverse, changing demographics have led social scientists to question the universal applicability of early theories of culture change that were formulated to describe the adaptation of ethnic Whites to American society (Jenkins, 1988). This chapter presents theories that address the dynamics of intercultural relations and the psychosocial and political effects of differential power and privilege that exist between members of minority groups and the majority European American culture.

## HISTORICAL CONTEXT

The term *culture change* has traditionally referred to the modifications, revisions, and new manners of expression that result from the process of interaction between cultures. We believe that any examination of culture change in the United States must begin with the understanding that intercultural and race relations in America historically involved "conquest, slavery and exploitation of foreign labor" (Steinberg, 1989, p. 5). The colonization of America brought with it the ideal of *Anglo conformity*, based on the assumption that the maintenance of English cultural patterns, institutions, and language was both desirable and necessary for colonists to prosper in the new world. Although specific practices were somewhat modified by the American Revolution, M. M. Gordon (1964) noted that within the ideology of assimilation, the ideal of Anglo conformity has been the most prevalent philosophy. Despite varying definitions, the process of assimilation is essentially one in which "subordinate individuals or groups give up their way of life and take on the characteristics of the dominant group and are accepted as a part of that culture" (Ramakrishnan & Balgopal, 1995, p. 14). This may involve assimilation at the cultural, structural, psychological, and biological levels (Marger, 1994).

Assimilation ideology rests on the doctrine of "manifest destiny." This doctrine has been a major political and religious rationalization in the United States *for territorial expansion by European settlers* from coast to coast, requiring the assimilation, containment, or annihilation of everyone else in between, especially First Nations (Indigenous) peoples and Mexicans. From the earliest English settlements in Virginia during the 1600s, colonists were encouraged to take Indigenous children from their parents and teach them English and Christianity because they were deemed to be "so wrapped up in the fog and misery of their iniquity" (Takaki, 1993, p. 33). A congressman in the 1800s expressed the ideal of colonialist conquest succinctly: "This continent was intended by Providence as a vast theater on which to work out the grand experiment of Republican government, under the auspices of the Anglo-Saxon race" (cited in Takaki, 1993, p. 176). Thus, assimilation ideology has been used not only to justify pressuring immigrants to conform to Anglo standards but also to disenfranchise Indigenous people. According to M. M. Gordon, the process of assimilation has historically encompassed three main philosophies: Anglo conformity, the melting pot, and cultural pluralism.

Melting pot theory, an early model of culture change, was first proposed in the 18th century by J. Hector St. John Crèvecoeur, a French-born writer and agriculturalist living in New York. He suggested that, in the United States, "individuals of all nations are melted into a race of new men" (cited in M. M. Gordon, 1964, p. 116). America was seen as a totally new meshing together of people rather than a modified England. It was a new blend, culturally and biologically, "in which the stock and folkways of Europe were, figuratively speaking, indiscriminately mixed in the political pot of the emerging nation and melted together by the fires of American influence and interaction into a distinctively new type" (M. M. Gordon, 1964, p. 115). This formulation viewed all ethnic groups as eventually "melting" into one common pot or group. Still, this implied a privileging of Anglo cultural and linguistic patterns.

Assimilation ideology became further popularized with the massive immigration of ethnic Whites to America at the turn of the 20th century. Through contact with and participation in American society, it was theorized that culturally diverse groups would become "Americanized" and come to conform to the predominant Anglo-Saxon culture (Park, 1950). Emphasis on Anglo conformity was seen by some as necessary for the socialization of new immigrant groups. The prevalent attitudes toward Americanization were best summarized by Samuel Rea (cited in M. M. Gordon, 1964, p. 101):

> They (the foreign born) must be induced to give up the languages, customs, and methods of life which they have brought with them across the ocean, and adopt instead the language, habits, and customs of this country, and the general standards and ways of American living.

This type of assimilation ideology proposed a linear continuum in which minority culture lay at one end of the continuum and the dominant culture at the other (Figure 6.1). In the process of becoming assimilated, minorities would give up their original culture and heritage to adapt to American values and culture. The end result would be the elimination of all original cultural differences. According to Lesser, "In assimilation the tendency is for the ruling cultural group to enforce the adoption of certain externals. . . . The adopting culture is not in a position to choose" (cited in Herskovits, 1938, p. 6).

Although both melting pot and Anglo conformity formulations called for assimilation of immigrants, one viewed them as melting into a new national character whereas the other saw them as conforming to a predefined national character.

Rejecting the utility of Anglo conformity and melting pot theories, philosopher Horace Kallen first introduced the idea of *cultural pluralism* in 1915. However, as M. M. Gordon (1964, p. 135) has noted, "cultural pluralism was a fact in American society before it became a theory." Kallen viewed the United States "as a cooperation of cultural diversities, as a federation or common wealth of national cultures" (1924, p. 115). He proposed that cultural pluralism was based on a process of acculturation rather than assimilation. *Acculturation* refers to the changing of one culture by incorporation of elements of another culture. The end result is a new culture containing elements of both cultures. Rather than a "one-way street of WASP-conformity, it implies mutual accommodation of variant groups" (Huang, 1995, p. 105). In acculturation, cultural groups are involved in a reciprocal give-and-take relationship. Despite the proposed

**FIGURE 6.1.** Assimilation of minorities.

A = Minority Culture
B = Majority Culture
C = Shared Values and Norms

**FIGURE 6.2.** Acculturation of minorities.

reciprocity, the model is still one of linear change because it is based on the assumption that people must give up a part of their original culture to become acculturated (Figure 6.2). It also does not challenge the privilege of politically dominant groups to sway acculturation in favor of their cultural standards.

M. M. Gordon (1964, p. 158) suggested that the "presumed goal of cultural pluralists was to maintain enough subsocietal separation to guarantee the continuance of the ethnic cultural tradition and existence of the group, without at the same time interfering with the carrying out of standard responsibilities to the general American civic life." In his contribution to pluralist theory, M. M. Gordon (1964) considered psychological, cultural, and societal factors in assessing the type and degree of assimilation of ethnic persons. In contrast to assimilation theories that assumed equal access to opportunity structures, M. M. Gordon's formulation also assessed both the degree of access to these structures and the degree of intergroup and majority–minority conflict. Despite the fact that M. M. Gordon's model was difficult to use because of the complex nature of the variables and their interrelationships, his conceptualization focused attention on the complexity of acculturation for minorities. He also suggested that there is no single prevailing pattern of cultural adaptation and that the degree of assimilation to American society may be low, moderate, or high.

Linear models of culture change based on assimilation ideology were, in fact, shortsighted because they failed to take into consideration the crucial roles that language, religion, and history play in preserving family and group culture. Further, they did not fully examine the impact of culture on personality and human development. Of equal concern, they either directly or indirectly promoted assimilation, cultural and racial separatism, or genocide as being socially functional and unproblematic. Importantly, Van den Berge (1967) has pointed out that the emergence of Western racism required "the presence of racially distinct groups, different enough so that at least some of their members can be readily classifiable." Another important consideration noted by Ramakrishnan and Balgopal (1995, p. 15), is that "Not all seek assimilation, and not all who seek it obtain it."

Broader conceptual models of culture change based on acculturation and cultural pluralism did not fully emerge until the last few decades. But even these more current models have been criticized as being limited because they fail to focus on "the character of the relations between ethnic groups and the larger society, or on those between ethnic clients and social workers" (Green, 1982, p. 11). In contrast, power-conflict models of race and ethnic relations have focused more directly on power inequality, class and economic stratification, and oppression (O. C. Cox, 1948; W. E. B. DuBois, 1948; Marable, 1983). Unlike assimilation and acculturation theories that typically portray such processes as voluntary, power conflict theories stress the role of "coercion, segregation, colonization and institutionalized discrimination and highlight the forced nature of cultural and economic adaptation" (Feagin & Feagin, 1993, p. 45). Due to their conflict and neo-Marxian orientation, however, these theories have likely received less attention in the professional literature.

Recently, social work scholars have called greater attention to the history of colonialism and genocide in North America and elsewhere as well as the continuing structural injustices and harmful impacts of historical trauma (e.g., Gray, Coates, & Yellow Bird, 2008). Some scholars are also challenging the continuing legacy of White privilege and its insidious effects on social work practice and education (Pewewardy, 2007).

## KEY CONCEPTS

Anthropologists and other social scientists have given numerous definitions of culture (Brislin, 1993). For our purposes, *culture* refers to the organized pattern of values, beliefs, and behaviors developed and transmitted over time by a social group. Culture is constructed by groups from their symbolic representations of themselves and their environments and built up into languages, codes of conduct, and social institutions. Culture is a quality of all human social groups at all social system levels. For example, each family develops distinctive patterns of child rearing, norms for communication, and rituals to deal with life events such as birth and death. Similarly, organizations develop distinctive patterns of mission, values, interpersonal relations, administrative structure, and styles of decision making, leadership, and regulations for staff and client behavior (Marques, Dhiman, & King, 2007).

Culture is so pervasive and it is like the air we breathe. We are completely dependent on it for a sense of meaning, order, and regularity in social life, but we are also usually unaware of its influence. And, like cutting off air, if we were suddenly removed from our culture of origin and introduced into another culture, the limitations of our cultural knowledge would immediately become obvious. We might not know how to speak, act, or think in ways that make sense and enable us to accomplish our goals within the new cultural context.

A related concept, *ethnicity*, was first used by social scientists W. Lloyd Warner and Loe Srole (1945) to draw distinctions between groups based on cultural rather than racial differences. The study of ethnic groups has historically focused on minority groups embedded within a larger culture. Thus, ethnic groups not only share values, norms, customs, rules of interaction, and linguistic patterns, but also they are culturally different to varying degrees and generally set apart from the majority group and are devalued by them. The term *ethnicity* has also been given numerous definitions. We use the term here to refer to shared values, behaviors, and customs as well as patterns of thinking and feeling that distinguish one cultural group within a given society from another. When ethnicity and minority status overlap, the group is generally subordinate in power and often becomes a target of prejudice and discrimination. Although ethnicity is based on a social definition rather than a biological one (Feagin & Feagin, 1993; Phinney & Rotheram, 1987; Rex & Mason, 1986), biologists and anthropologists have cautioned that there are no "pure" races in a biological sense. Due to centuries of intermarriage and interbreeding, there is a tremendous amount of variation between people who share similar physical characteristics, such as skin color and facial features. Thus, attempts to group people into racial categories is not only scientifically flawed but often embedded with racist ideology that assumes superiority or inferiority of one group when compared to another (Feagin & Feagin, 1993).

Not coincidentally, terms used to refer to group differences are inherently controversial and emotion-laden because of the societal context of racism and oppression. The terms *majority* and *minority* refer to groups of unequal power in which one group is dominant and the other subordinate (Aguirre & Turner, 1995). In this chapter, the term *minority* is used to refer to ethnic, racial, and cultural groups within the United States who are both relatively powerless and in the numerical minority. All have experienced some degree of racism and discrimination. We use this term to highlight the need for solidarity, empowerment, and group self-determination in responding to inequality. The term *majority* refers to the larger dominant European American social context that has been strongly influenced by Anglo-Saxon values. Majority groups are predominant in terms of both population numbers and political and economic privilege and power. However, as Lum (2003a, 2003b) has cautioned, this terminology should not be used to imply superiority/inferiority or to draw assumptions about disempoweredness or poverty for people of color or other ethnic groups. Further, within the world as a whole, it is important to recognize that people of European descent are in the numerical minority, as will be the case within the United States if current demographic trends continue. In many communities people of color already outnumber Anglo Americans.

To understand the dynamics of culture contact, one must examine the dangers of stereotyping, prejudice, discrimination, ethnocentrism, racism, and genocide directed at members of minority ethnic and racial groups by the predominant Anglo society (Canda, Carrizosa, & Yellow Bird, 1995; Lum, 1996). Although discriminatory and oppressive assumptions are not limited to European Americans, they have been embedded in the historical context of our social work and social welfare systems. As such, social work is often shaped by implicit or explicit forms of cultural limitation and bias.

A *stereotype* is an overgeneralized and rigid definition of group characteristics that is assigned to people based on their membership in a group. Even well-intentioned efforts to understand cultural characteristics of groups run the risk of stereotyping. For example, Hispanic family patterns are sometimes summarized without regard for the tremendous variation between and within different Hispanic groups and individuals. A related concept, *prejudice*, refers to preconceived and poorly informed judgments about people, such as, "She's Asian American, so she'll be an A student" or "He'll be a bad student because he's Appalachian." It is important to recognize that prejudiced and stereotypical ideas can be stated in either positive or negative terms. Although both are problematic because they are based on overgeneralization, it is usually the negative attitudes toward members of a racial or cultural group that lead to their exclusion from mainstream society. Yet, positive stereotypes also contribute to misunderstanding, neglecting within-group variations, and denying members of so-called model minorities access to resources, power, and assistance when needed to overcome adversity or oppression. According to Allport (1958), prejudice is "an antipathy based upon a faulty generalization. It may be felt or expressed. It may be directed at a group as a whole, or toward an individual because he or she is a member of that group" (p. 7). Feagin and Feagin (1993) have noted that prejudice is an old phenomenon and has deep roots in human history. In contrast, stereotyping (as a well-developed racist ideology) is relatively new and most likely developed with European colonization. Prejudice and stereotyping serve to justify the exploitation of others.

*Discrimination* refers to "actions carried out by members of dominant groups, or their representatives, that have a differential and harmful impact on members of subordinate groups" (Feagin & Feagin, 1993, p. 15). Discrimination may be intentional or unintentional as well as overt or covert. Further, it may be based on the practices of individuals and based on personal bigotry and prejudice (*individual discrimination*), or it may be institutional and embedded in the prescribed policies and practices of an organization, community, or governmental structure (*institutional discrimination*). The relationship between prejudice and discrimination is complex, and many theorists agree that they are mutually reinforcing. Thus, prejudice can lead to discrimination, just as discrimination can lead to prejudice, with each reinforcing the other.

*Ethnocentrism* means considering one's own ethnic or national group to be superior to others and using one's own standards to evaluate all other groups. For example, the belief that "The United States is the most advanced country in the world and all other countries should strive to become just like us" is ethnocentric because it uses one country as the standard for measuring all others and promotes conformity to that standard. *Racism* is an ideology that portrays members of another group as being inferior based on unchangeable physical attributes such as skin color.

Racism may manifest itself in individual actions as well as in institutional policies and activities that deny access, opportunity, power, or privileges to members of the so-called inferior group. According to the United Nations' definition, *genocide* involves acts committed with intent to destroy in whole or in part a national, ethnic, racial, or religious group. This can include killing group members, causing them serious harm, inflicting destructive living conditions, coercing birth prevention, and forcibly transferring children from one group to another. Two vivid examples in U.S. history can be seen in the slavery imposed on African people and the forced removal of Indigenous children from their parents for placement in boarding schools and Anglo adoptive homes.

Theories of acculturation, assimilation, bicultural socialization, and ethnic minority identity all address the complex task of having dual membership in a majority and minority culture. Central to these theories are the concepts of Anglo conformity, assimilation, acculturation, cultural pluralism, melting pot, and culture change previously discussed. The dominant majority culture has disproportionate and predominant influence in determining the norms, rules, laws, and ideologies that govern society. Thus, minority cultures are expected to conform to externally mandated norms of social interaction as well as norms of psychological and social growth and development. Participation in the economic mainstream is often dependent on cultural conformity. Hence, to maintain its privileged position, the majority culture tends to perpetuate institutional racism, ethnocentrism, and other forms of discrimination.

The term *Anglo* is commonly used to denote mainstream American culture that is derived historically from the Western European, White, Anglo-Saxon, and Protestant heritage that was most influential in forging the character of American society. Inasmuch as these Anglo norms are assumed to be superior to those of other cultures, people who fail to conform are usually seen as pathological, marginal, or deficient. We discuss this in greater detail throughout this chapter.

More recent formulations of culture change have included a broader variety of concepts in an attempt to describe the complexity of culture change and identity development in an increasingly global economy. Concepts specifically related to deficiency theory, ethnic, racial/cultural, and minority identity, the dual perspective, transculturality, cultural competence, and a multidimensional transactional model of culture change, are discussed next.

## DEFICIENCY THEORY

To date, the vast majority of theory and research on racial and ethnic minorities in the United States has reflected the values, paradigms, and ideology of the majority culture rather than the cultural and social reality of the people being studied. In addition, the most widely accepted theories of social and psychological growth and development have claimed varying degrees of universality, while reflecting primarily Anglo-dominant norms (Cortese, 1990; E. H. Erikson, 1963; Kohlberg, 1969a, 1969b). The problems associated with using theories and research that are both formulated on Anglo assumptions and embedded with Anglo norms can be most clearly seen in the tendency to view minority people and their personality structures as deficient. The deficiency formulations that are a result of such research and theory introduce a systematic bias into the description of minority individuals and families. In a thorough review of the literature, Valentine (1968) termed this bias the *pejorative tradition*.

| TABLE 6.1 | Deficiency Formulations | |
|---|---|---|
| | **Majority Group Members** | **Minority Group Members** |
| Valued behaviors | Present | Absent |
| Devalued behaviors | Absent | Present |

*Deficiency formulations* are based on two interrelated types of biases that permeate the literature (A. Howard & Scott, 1981). Both of these biases are based on the acceptance of Anglo-based norms, values, and behaviors as overriding criteria from which comparisons are drawn. Endemic to such formulations is the underlying acceptance of assimilation as the normative mode of culture conflict resolution.

As shown in Table 6.1, the first type of deficiency formulation looks at behaviors and traits that are valued by the majority culture and are found to be absent or weakly represented in minority people and their cultures. The second type of deficiency formulation focuses on behaviors and traits that are devalued by the dominant culture; these are believed to be representative of minority groups. Terms such as *hedonistic*, *matricentric*, or *present-oriented* are typically used with pejorative connotations. These two types of formulations are often intertwined with each other and, to complicate matters further, are often linked together in a causal chain (A. Howard & Scott, 1981).

A classic example of causally linked deficiency formulations that are built upon one another can be seen in Daniel Moynihan's classic 1965 essay, "Employment, Income, and the Ordeal of the Negro Family." In essence, Moynihan asserted that blocked opportunity for Black workers has led to a weakening of the family structure. He proposed that unemployment, underemployment, and low-paying jobs have resulted in the breakup of the family that, in turn, has led to an increased dependency on welfare and pathology in the children. This type of reasoning is readily accepted because much of it is based on commonsense notions that most people see as indisputable. Certain social conditions (such as broken homes) are assumed to have intrinsic pathogenic or criminogenic effects and, as Hirschi (1969) pointed out, no amount of evidence to the contrary can shake the presumed validity of these ideas.

This reasoning is also seductive because it initially cites the lack of opportunity for the current plight of the Black family. In fact, it is the Black family structure that is seen as deficient and as giving rise to the conditions that further economic dependence. There is an inherent assumption that if given the choice, Black families would choose a family structure different from the one they now have, and further, it would conform to Anglo values (A. Howard & Scott, 1981).

In addition to theoretical essays that posit minority deficiencies, there has been a long-standing history of similarly flawed empirical research. As A. Howard and Scott (1981, p. 128) noted, part of the problem is that ". . . so much of the conceptual apparatus of social science is infused with (Western) value assumptions." A consensus view of society is reflected in the very epistemologic assumptions that undergird the social scientific enterprise; this view does not necessarily reflect the reality of minority persons. They further asserted that:

> This basic orientation towards groups whose values and lifestyles are at variance with those of the dominant culture are strongly buttressed by certain assumptions of physical science that many social scientists have come to accept as axiomatic. Imputed to social phenomena are the same qualities and characteristics other

disciplines impute to the physical universe. Most basic of all is the assumption that the goal of science is to reveal "the truth" about "reality." (p. 129)

"Social reality," then, becomes constructed by consensus and is based on the norms of majority groups. It is not surprising that minority persons whose values, behaviors, and cultural patterns differ from the majority appear deficient when measured on a continuum that accepts mainstream norms as a fixed reality. A very problematic aspect of deficiency formulations is the fact that they judge the behaviors, values, and norms of minority group members on criteria that are not likely to be culturally relevant. By accepting dominant Anglo values and life ways as the norm, all other forms of behavior and social organization that derive from cultural values at variance with those of the majority society are devalued (Norton, 1993; Triandis, 1990).

This leads to the concept of White privilege (Pewewardy, 2007). *White privilege* refers to social structural and interpersonal benefits and advantages given to White Americans of European descent based on their racial identification. Often, White Americans take these advantages for granted because they have been raised to experience and believe this arrangement to be normal within their cultural milieu.

## THE DUAL PERSPECTIVE

To more accurately understand the life context of minority persons, Norton (1978) has suggested that they must be viewed within two separate contexts, the nurturing system and the sustaining system (Figure 6.3). The *nurturing system* is the primary context and includes the individual, the immediate family, the extended family, and the immediate community (Chestang, 1972; Norton,

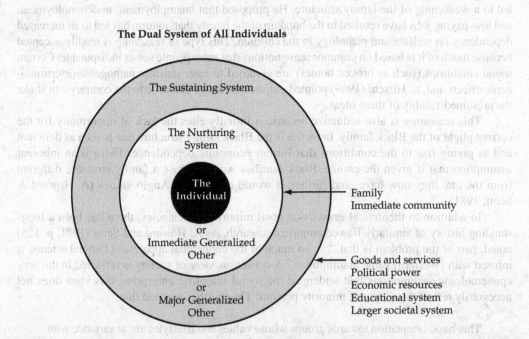

**The Dual System of All Individuals**

**FIGURE 6.3.** The dual perspective. *Source:* D. Norton (1978). Reprinted with permission of the Council on Social Work Education.

1978). The *sustaining system* is the secondary context (or larger society) and comprises political power, the educational system, goods and services, and so on.

Because all persons (minority and majority) have membership in both systems, these systems do not have the same impact on minority and majority groups. The literature in the social sciences has long documented the differences that exist between mainstream Anglo norms, values, and behaviors and those of minority groups (Berman, 1990; A. Howard & Scott, 1981; Phinney & Rotheram, 1987; Red Horse, 1980; Robbins, 1984). Although majority group members likely experience congruence between these two systems, the opposite is true for minorities, who likely find varying degrees of incongruence (T. T. Gibbs, Huang, & Associates, 1989; Norton, 1978).

Children are first raised in their primary context and learn the values, beliefs, attitudes, and behaviors of their family and immediate community. The degree of intimacy within this primary context is usually high, and the bond formed within the family and community ideally conveys love, approval, security, and safety. In minority cultures, tradition, history, language, values, ethnicity, and identity are communicated through family relations. It is this heritage, passed on from one generation to the next, that preserves group distinctiveness. Within the nurturing system, children may have well-defined and valued roles and receive strong reinforcement for adhering to and internalizing cultural values. It is in this context that they first learn appropriate and correct behavior.

As children become exposed to the sustaining system, the values, attitudes, and behaviors that are required by majority society may conflict with those learned in the primary context. The result may be overt or covert messages of racism and inferiority. Behaviors that are valued in one context are often devalued in the other; self-esteem that is high in the nurturing system may become eroded in the sustaining system.

From a *dual perspective*, human development is seen as a combination of cultural influences from both systems. Norton (1978) argued that the "conflict grows out of the degree of incongruence between the two systems, since the frames of reference of the minority group, though embedded in and affected by the major society, can be quite different" (p. 6).

In a more recent work, Norton has added to this model by emphasizing the importance of the temporal framework in which people "act, think, and relate to the world around them" (1993, p. 85). In a prospective study of growth, development, and early socialization of inner-city African American children, she has found that differential socialization to physical time (objective time such as minutes, hours, and days) may have an impact on a child's functioning in majority social contexts. Concepts of time learned in the home may not match those that are needed to function successfully in school.

Norton cautioned, however, that differential socialization must be viewed within its ecological context. Lack of congruence between majority and minority cultures should not be viewed as inherent deficits or pathology.

## BICULTURAL SOCIALIZATION

An outgrowth of Norton's (1978) view of dual cultural influences was the emergence of the bicultural perspective (Chau, 1991; de Anda, 1984; Ho, 1992), which allows family culture to be viewed as one that may operate independently from the larger societal culture. Early theories of bicultural conflict suggested that conflicting cultural norms left minorities with a deficit in socialization. Rather than becoming fully socialized into either culture, they were seen as marginal people who straddled both worlds and were incompletely socialized into either

(Atonovsky, 1956; Stonequist, 1937). More current thought has suggested that a dual or *bicultural socialization* process may occur and that mastery of both cultures can be achieved (de Anda, 1984; Robbins, 1984; Robbins, 1985a). A person who gains bicultural competency "integrates positive qualities of his or her culture of origin and the dominant society's culture. The outcome is a functional way of relating and surviving in both cultures" (Lum, 1995, p. 60).

To more fully understand the developmental tasks of racial and ethnic minorities, one must first understand the relationship between bicultural conflict and bicultural tension (Galan, 1985). *Bicultural conflict* "occurs when an individual's family values and behaviors are different from those of the society at large; there is a high degree of incongruence or contrast between family values and societal values" (Galan, 1992, p. 236). To function in both the majority and minority contexts, ethnic minorities must develop coping skills in both contexts to help them adapt to dual sets of demands. Persons who are unable to do so may experience bicultural tension. *Bicultural tension* "occurs when an individual's available coping skills are based on only one value system: either that of the family or that of society. The individual is not able to use his or her coping skills in both family and societal situations" (Galan, 1992, p. 236). It is the result of a coping repertoire that is inadequate for functioning in both cultures. Bicultural conflict is a fact of life; bicultural tension is not.

Developing a coping repertoire to deal with bicultural conflict is not only a matter of personal choice. It also depends on the degree of support or rejection experienced from the culture of origin and the new cultural context. A bicultural person must have a clear and secure sense of self-identity and multigroup affiliation to deal with messages of rejection or criticism that may come from both cultural contexts. For example, people with racist and ethnocentric attitudes within the majority culture may demean the bicultural person for failure to assimilate completely. People from the culture of origin may label the bicultural person as a traitor or "sell-out" because he or she operates within majority contexts and situationally adopts majority norms and values. It is a significant challenge for people to achieve competence and comfort within two cultural contexts.

However, the minority person who masters two cultures, is able to speak in two languages, and understands two different sets of values may find that a new sense of power emerges from this broader repertoire of adaptive skills. In contrast, the individual who continuously encounters bicultural conflict, straddles two sets of values and norms, and is not able to discern how to manage dual skills likely experiences bicultural tension. How one refines, evaluates, uses, and manages these skills determines whether the struggle of biculturality leads to an adaptive bicultural identity. People who achieve biculturality are in a position to mediate and advocate between cultural contexts.

Because linear models of culture change did not adequately explain the complexity of the American minority experience, historical concepts of assimilation and acculturation eventually came to be seen as insufficient. As an initial response, two-dimensional models (in the form of $2 \times 3 \times 2$ tables) attempted to bring greater clarity and understanding to an expanded view of minority life through description of the minority experience in a categorical manner (Bennett, 1975; English, 1984; Padilla, 1980). These models explained cultural differences "according to the degree to which individuals or groups manifest specific, distinctive traits" (Green, 1982, p. 9). Although cultural differences were named, explained, and enumerated, they were based on discrete categories containing cultural content or traits. According to Green (1982), categorical explanations that rely on a list of group traits easily lend themselves to stereotyping.

Even though many models of culture change have been categorical in nature, few have examined or included the transactional element. Citing anthropologist Frederik Barth's (1969) work, Green argued that transactional explanations provide a fuller description, because they concern themselves with "the ways in which people who are communicating maintain their cultural distinctiveness" (1982, p. 9). The transactional view suggests that one's cultural adherence is dynamic rather than static, and the "degree to which a person is 'acculturated,' therefore, is situational rather than absolute and can be modified to suit the needs of different kinds of cross cultural encounters" (p. 12).

Green further cautioned against using categorical models in which the relations between a family culture and a societal culture were the focus of investigation. Placing importance on the boundaries, lines of separation, and their management, he believed that models of ethnicity were best served if they helped explain the points where individuals confront others who are culturally different. He noted that "the ways in which that distinctiveness is defended, asserted, preserved, or abandoned amount to the stuff of ethnic identity" (p. 12).

## ETHNIC, RACIAL/CULTURAL, AND MINORITY IDENTITY

The concepts of *ethnic identity*, *racial/cultural identity*, and *minority identity* have received increasing attention in the social science literature. Early theorizing in this area emerged in the 1970s and 1980s to describe the development of Black racial identity (Cross, 1991), White racial identity (Hardiman, 1979, Helms, 1984), and racial identity of diverse groups from non-European backgrounds (Sue & Sue, 1981). Much of the impetus of these models was based on a need for understanding clients from non-European backgrounds. Since that time a number of theories and models have emerged to describe identity development for a variety of racial and ethnic groups. Although terminology and foci differ slightly among the various authors, all of these models view development of minority groups within the broader cultural and historical context of oppression, racism, and marginalization of people of color in the United States. Sue and Sue (1999) observed that "the sociopolitical dynamics related to the treatment of marginalized or oppressed groups in our society share many similarities. Prejudice, stereotyping, and discrimination and their negative effects on these groups operate from a common foundation with frightening effects" (p. 304).

*Ethnicity* refers to "one's sense of belonging to an ethnic group and the part of one's thinking, perceptions, feelings, and behavior that is due to ethnic group membership" (Phinney & Rotheram, 1987, p. 13). Similar to the acquisition of other types of identity, ethnic identity involves both social and psychological processes including cognition, perception, patterns of social interaction, and social learning and internalization. As Spencer (1993) has observed, "The critical socialization task of minority-status children is the acquisition and internalization of positive identity elements in a non-minority preferred society" (p. 107). Similarly, theories of *racial identity* describe stages of identity formation related to racial characteristics and examine the degree to which people of color affiliate or disassociate with others from the same racial heritage (Helms, 1993).

Several authors have proposed stage models of ethnic, racial/cultural minority identity development in which the person moves from immersion in the minority culture to eventually recognizing that his or her culture is devalued by majority society. This initially may lead to identity diffusion, typified by rejection of the culture of origin and immersion in the majority culture. As the person grows older, she or he develops an awareness of the importance of primary group ties and becomes immersed in the culture of origin. Finally, the internalization of personal and group identity leads to acquisition of a positive ethnic or racial/cultural identity (Aboud, 1984; Cross, 1985, 1991; Helms & Cook, 1999; Katz, 1976; Phinney, 1990; Phinney & Rotheram, 1987; Porter, 1971; Sue & Sue, 1999, 2003).

Cross (1991), delineated the following five stages of racial identity development that help us understand heterogeneity among African Americans: *pre-encounter, encounter, immersion-emersion, internalization*, and *internalization-commitment*. In this model, people move from denigrating Anglo, Eurocentric definitions of Blackness and gradually evolve to self-prescribed definitions that value African American worldviews, values, and other cultural orientations.

According to Cross, movement to the second stage must be preceded by the experience of a catalytic event such as a racial slight or indignity. People must then internalize the event by challenging preencounter conceptions of Blackness. During the second stage, people experience cognitive dissonance and begin a commitment to an active search for their identity. Positive exposure to African or African American culture can assist people in shedding ingrained stereotypes and help move them to more positive and Afrocentric definitions of their own racial identities. Not all Blacks progress to stage five, but those who do not only adopt African Americans as their primary reference group but also commit themselves to eradicating oppression.

Helms and Cook (1999) proposed somewhat comparable stages in an identity model for people of color (POC). Their POC model broadens the scope to include other American minority racial groups such as Asian, African, Latino/Latina, Native Americans, and African Americans. They propose a series of statuses that POC move through to attain healthy emotional and social functioning. These statuses include *conformity, dissonance, immersion/emersion, internalization*, and *integrative awareness*. Similar to Cross' model, the final and most sophisticated stage is one in which the person develops a positive racial self and is able to integrate aspects that may be characteristic of other groups as well (Comstock, 2005).

Similarly, Sue and Sue (1999, 2007) proposed a racial/cultural identity development (R/CID) model to describe the experience of the oppressed as they "struggle to understand themselves in terms of their *own culture,* the *dominant culture,* and the *oppressive relationship* between the two cultures" (1999, p. 128). They delineated five stages of development: conformity, dissonance, resistance and immersion, introspection, and integrative awareness. In this model, people move from initially having a preference for the dominant culture and experiencing feelings of internalized shame and embarrassment about their own culture to considering positive aspects of their own racial/cultural groups as they confront issues of racism and oppression. They begin challenging previously held beliefs and attitudes to move toward endorsing minority-held views and rejecting dominant values of society. As their feelings intensify, they develop a need for positive self-definition and, in the last stage, they are able to develop an "inner sense of security" that allows them to appreciate unique aspects of their culture, themselves, other minority groups, and select aspects of American culture (p. 136).

Consistent with Norton's (1978) dual perspective, developmental models of this type suggest that the prejudices of the sustaining system (mainstream society) toward minority groups may result in racist messages of inferiority that can become internalized into one's self-concept. Those who move beyond this and attain a positive ethnic identity have been successful at resolving the conflicts and tension stemming from these dual cultural influences. Not all are able to do this, however. Some may continue to reject their culture of origin and never achieve ethnic integration. Cross (1987) has noted that "the price of assimilation . . . is not necessarily 'poor mental health,'" but that an assimilated worldview leaves people unable to identify with and advocate for those who are not assimilated (p. 133). Research has found that despite diversity in minority groups, racial/cultural and ethnic identity in newcomer youth generally takes one of three or four paths: a strong ethnic identity, a hyphenated American identity, an assimilated American identity, or a pan-ethnic minority group identity (Delgado et al., 2005). Further, Rotheram and Phinney (1987) have suggested that those who develop an ethnic identity through biculturality achieve *bicultural competence* rather than a bicultural identity.

In contrast, Taylor and Usborne (2010) see cultural identity clarity as being the primary factor that promotes psychological well-being in individuals and groups that have experienced racism, oppression, and other forms of collective trauma. They propose that self-concept is comprised of four components: personal identity, personal (self) esteem, collective identity, and collective esteem (p. 95). They argue that collective (cultural/religious) identity is necessary for a healthy sense of self and well-being and that it takes precedence over the other three components. Collective identities are primary because individual identity can only arise in relation to specific groups and cultures. Thus, individual identity is shaped by the social, environmental, and cultural forces that include "social norms, gender stereotypes, historical events, and cultural assumptions" (McAdams cited in Taylor & Usborne, p. 97). They propose that a clearly defined collective (cultural) identity is a "necessary prerequisite for engaging in the process of defining a personal identity, and, by extension, personal (self) esteem" (p. 100).

Notably, Rotherman and Phinney (1987) have cautioned, that "ethnic identity is not a static attribute, but evolves with personal identity in response to . . . changes and new environmental challenges" (p. 215). Camino (1994) has also suggested that ethnic identity is fluid and that there is "no single or static form of ethnicity" (Camino, cited in Delgado, et al., 2005). Additional research on ethnic socialization and cultural identity clarity is needed to help us further understand the way in which culture interacts with the changing social structure in contemporary society.

## A MULTIDIMENSIONAL TRANSACTIONAL MODEL OF BICULTURAL IDENTITY

Models of culture change based on acculturation ideology, linear logic, deficiency formulations, or categorical models are, by their very nature, doomed to fall short in their description of ethnic minority development and functioning. We submit that a fuller explanation of minority life must include, at a minimum, an understanding of ethnic identity, the dual perspective, the dynamic nature of bicultural socialization, the existence of bicultural conflict and bicultural tension, and the contextual nature of cultural adherence.

Galan (1978, 1990) proposed a multidimensional transactional model of bicultural identity in which bicultural socialization is viewed as a process that incorporates the elements of person-in-situation-across-time. In addition to the cultural and behavioral value choices that become present in any possible social situation, this model introduces the element of time and, in doing so, provides a framework that considers both the contextual and temporal aspects in the development of a dynamic bicultural identity. Galan argued that this can result in a higher level of personal integration and cultural adaptability.

To consider the contextual aspects of bicultural identity, Galan argued that it is necessary to examine the degree of adherence to both the norms and values of the ethnic family culture *and* those of the larger majority American culture. To avoid the faulty assumptions of assimilation ideology, these must be considered separately. Implicit here is the notion that there are multiple possibilities for adaptation that lie on a continuum of time, referred to here as the Z *axis*. For example, one can have high adherence to both, low adherence to both, or high adherence to one and low to the other. This can be more easily understood categorically if we plot this out on two separate Z and Y axes and transactionally when value and behavioral choices are plotted across time on a Z axis.

An X axis (Figure 6.4) can be used to measure adherence to ethnic family cultural norms and values, with high adherence on the far right of the continuum and low adherence on the far left. A Y axis can be used to measure adherence to majority American culture, with

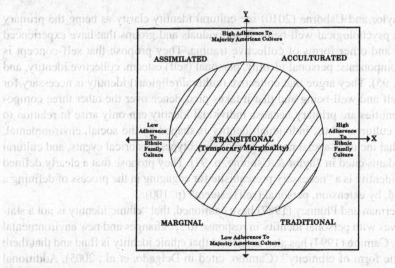

**FIGURE 6.4.** A two-dimensional model of bicultural identity. *Source:* Adapted from F. J. Galan (1978). © F. J. Galan.

high adherence to norms and values at the very top and low adherence at the very bottom. This model now enables us to consider different types of adaptation that are contextually based.

### Traditional Adaptation

First-generation-born ethnic minorities and new immigrants typically have strong family cultures that are steeped in tradition. The language used at home is usually the language of origin, and family ties are closely connected to the country of origin. Religious views are strong, values and beliefs are usually inflexible and unwavering and reinforce clearly delineated status and gender roles. Behavior patterns are prescribed by mores and are likely culturally distinct from those of the larger society. In addition, extended families are strong and children are expected to marry within the group. This results in a clear sense of peoplehood based on the ethnic group, and in this context, individuals gain a strong sense of ethnic identity that is traditionally defined.

High adherence to the values and behaviors of the ethnic family culture is generally evident, as well as a low (or absent) adherence to values and behaviors of the society (see Figure 6.4). As individuals identify with and incorporate minority group norms, while separating themselves from those of the larger society, they develop a strong ethnic identity and traditional orientation in coping and adaptation. In this form of adaptation, skills learned from the family are used in all situations—in both the cultural context (nurturing system) and in the societal context (sustaining system).

### Marginal Adaptation

As ethnic minorities come into contact with the larger societal system, they are introduced to the values and norms of that system, many of which are incongruent with their culture of origin. Thus, they are likely to experience culture conflict. Some are unable to deal with the conflictual demands of the two systems and ultimately end up rejecting the norms and values of both. Individuals who become marginal are those who, having been introduced to both cultural and dominant societal norms, feel uncomfortable with either set of coping responses. Individuals who develop a marginal orientation experience a high degree of cultural tension and do not possess or use adaptive skills in either their nurturing system or sustaining system. Ethnic minority persons with marginal orientations have a low adherence to both ethnic family cultural values and behaviors and societal values and behaviors (Figure 6.4).

## Assimilation Adaptation

As ethnic minorities become schooled through the system of formal public education, they become subject to socialization to the values and norms of the larger society. In other words, to some extent they become acculturated. As minorities become acculturated, they also become exposed to a wider variety of values and behaviors and, if they embrace these new values and behaviors, they increase their repertoire of adaptive responses.

New ways of defining, viewing, and responding provide them with new skills for adapting, particularly in situations away from the family. Ethnic minorities learn quickly to recognize their levels of competence in mainstream society as soon as they are tested in school. To succeed in school, they must learn to communicate in the language of the school. In addition, they must be able to understand how another adult (the teacher) views and responds to the world and to them.

Ethnic minority children from traditional families who attend school are immediately separated from those who do not. Those in school begin to relate outside the boundaries of tradition; those who are not bound by the monolingual and monocultural skills of their nurturing system.

In the process of acculturation, however, some minority persons come to value the norms of the sustaining system and devalue the norms of their nurturing system. In doing so, they either lose or give up the adaptive skills from their nurturing system and adopt skills that are adaptive only in the majority societal context. This assimilation orientation results in a repertoire of adaptive skills that are monolingual and monocultural and solely based on the norms and values of the majority sustaining system.

Ethnic minority persons who choose assimilated orientations may feel pressured to drop their cultural values and behaviors to survive the perceived or actual discrimination of being ethnically different. Wishing not to be outcasts in a society that devalues ethnic differences, some assimilate culturally. Others who assimilate may come to judge their nurturing system values as being deficient and "less than." Still others may decide that assimilation is necessary to succeed in the economic mainstream. Often, minorities who are assimilated endure the ridicule of those who are not, as they are perceived as traitors, labeled as *sell-outs*, and judged harshly by those who are either more bicultural or traditional. As seen in Figure 6.4, ethnic minorities with assimilation orientations have a low (or no) adherence to values and behaviors of their culture of origin and a high adherence to majority societal values and behaviors.

## Bicultural Adaptation

As we have already noted, contact between minority and majority cultures may result in a variety of outcomes and a broad range of adaptive skills. In this model, individuals who acculturate (i.e., become socialized to the norms of the larger society) do not necessarily give up their original cultural values and behaviors in the process of learning new ones. Instead, for some it is possible to retain their original cultural values and identity while learning, adopting, and integrating the values and norms of the majority societal system. Because values and behavior are largely related to context, the individual who embraces both is able to develop bicultural adaptation skills, bicultural competency, and a bicultural identity. This individual is culturally integrated.

In contrast to the individual who straddles both worlds and is not well integrated into either (marginal adaptation), the truly bicultural person is comfortably integrated into both and possesses a full range of adaptive skills for both the nurturing and sustaining systems. Adaptive skills learned in the original cultural setting are used when interacting in the nurturing system, whereas adaptive skills learned in the majority societal setting are called on when interacting in the sustaining system. This dual set of values, behaviors, and coping responses becomes so totally integrated into the individual that the "appropriate" response for each context becomes almost second nature. Robbins (1984) has suggested that this is a much more complex process of socialization than of that to a single culture.

It follows, then, that ethnic minority persons with a strong bicultural orientation have high levels of adherence to both nurturing group values and behaviors and sustaining societal values and behaviors. Within boundaries of acculturated values and behaviors, ethnic minority persons range in levels of biculturality. They also range in levels of assimilation, traditionality, and marginality. Not surprisingly, several researchers interested in biculturality have focused their work on developing measures to determine levels of adherence to values and behaviors of both the culture of origin and those of larger society (Cuellar, Harris, & Jasso, 1980; Inclain, 1979; Szapocznik, Scopetta, & King, 1978).

Further, it is not uncommon to find different modes of acculturation occurring within one family. Grandparents (and sometimes parents) may be traditional in a family in which the children are assimilated or bicultural. Normative conflicts that result from generational differences are often compounded by differences in acculturation. People who are totally assimilated are likely to experience bicultural tension resulting from an inadequate repertoire of coping skills necessary for transactions in the primary context. In contrast, those who are traditional are likely to experience bicultural tension resulting from an inadequate repertoire of coping skills necessary for transactions in the larger societal context.

Thus far we have discussed four different orientations and types of adaptation that may occur as a response to culture conflict. This model, however, depicts a categorical and static view of behavior. Both commonsense and scientific theories remind us that behavior is neither static nor simplistic. To obtain a fuller appreciation of the complexity of bicultural socialization, we now add three important concepts: (a) ethclass, (b) transitional marginality, and (c) the continuum of time.

## Gender, Social Class, and Ethnicity/Race

No discussion of acculturation, assimilation, bicultural socialization, and ethnicity/race would be complete without a concomitant discussion of gender and social class. Of particular importance is the way in which these multiple aspects of identity intersect. Amott and Matthaei (1996) have argued that "the concepts of gender, race-ethnicity, and class are neither trans-historical nor independent . . . it is artificial to discuss them outside of historical time and place, and separately from one another" (p. 12).

According to Amott and Matthaei, the interconnection between gender, class, and ethnicity/race is complex in its relationship to oppression and one's sense of identity. Women do not experience separate identities based on each of these three domains independently, but rather as an integrated whole. Historically, European colonization and Anglo domination defined not only the roles and economic fate of people of color but also of women. This not only marginalized racial and ethnic minorities but also negatively affected gender and family roles, especially within minority communities.

The combination of ethnicity and social class has been termed by M. M. Gordon (1964) as *ethclass*. As Devore and Schlesinger noted, "Members of different ethnic groups with a history of poverty and discrimination move into certain segments of the middle class at varying rates and paces" (1991, p. 34). While numerous variables may impact social mobility, identifiable physical characteristics (such as skin color) remain a primary barrier. Additionally, they pointed out that social class distinctions—even for minority persons who are behaviorally assimilated or acculturated—often result in their being labeled as *inferior* because their work, often as blue-collar laborers, is devalued. In general, women of color experience discrimination and oppression in the workplace to a greater degree than do Anglo women (Ammot & Matthaei, 1969). Figure 6.5 provides a rough approximation of the relationship between ethnic minority adaptation and economic class, as determined by placement on the Y axis. As we can see on this continuum, persons with strong marginal and traditional orientations (very low on the Y axis) usually have disproportionately high representation in the lower economic class; those with less marginal or traditional orientations and those with more assimilated or bicultural orientations (slightly higher on the Y axis) usually are most common in the working class. Middle economic class status is generally reserved for those who are assimilated or biculturated and who are, by definition, moderate to high on the Y axis. And finally, upper-middle economic class status is usually reserved for the most assimilated or most acculturated (biculturated), who are placed highest on this axis.

Although there are always exceptions to the model presented here, we agree with Devore and Schlesinger that "the extent to which groups continue to be oppressed and experience discrimination is in an ongoing process of transformation" (1991, p. 32). Accordingly, the nature and extent of stratification and oppression (which directly affects ethclass) continue to change as society changes.

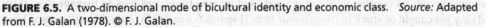

**FIGURE 6.5.** A two-dimensional mode of bicultural identity and economic class. *Source:* Adapted from F. J. Galan (1978). © F. J. Galan.

Not all ethnic minority groups, however, experience the same degree of oppression. The degree of oppression can be quite variable and is based on differential access to property, power, and prestige. Some groups are denied power and prestige but are allowed to accumulate enough wealth (or property) to occupy middle-class status (Turner et al., 1987). The impact of racism in the United States means that, in general, people of color have continued to experience greater institutional barriers to upward social mobility than have European American immigrants, and this is especially true for women of color.

A particularly subtle form of discrimination occurs in the idea of a *model minority*, as Asian Americans have often been called in the popular press (Takaki, 1993; Uba, 1994). The model minority myth praises Asian Americans for their relatively high achievement of educational and income levels and their emphasis on hard work and educational advancement. It is often accompanied by positively framed stereotypes. At the same time, the myth ignores the institutional barriers that continue to exist for Asian American upward mobility into political and economic leadership positions. In terms of personal income, Asian Americans have not reached equality (Takaki, 1993). Further, the extreme generalization that occurs when dozens of distinct language and ethnic groups are placed into catchall categories obscures the significant differences between groups. For example, Southeast Asian refugees from Vietnam, Cambodia, and Laos (especially the post-1976 arrivals), have a relatively greater disadvantage in terms of economic and educational attainment as well as in coping with postrefugee flight trauma (Ishisaka, Nguyen, & Okimoto, 1985; Uba, 1994).

Further, the history of anti-Asian discrimination is blurred over in the model minority myth. This myth is often used to support the exclusion of Asian Americans from affirmative action and minority-student recruitment programs. The final irony is that the myth is an implicit insult to other minority groups, who are defined as "less than model," all from an Anglocentric perspective.

Although Figure 6.5 shows that social class closely parallels high adherence to both family and societal values, it should be pointed out that the upper level is theoretical. Racial and ethnic minorities are rarely, if ever, granted access to the highest echelons of class in the United States. What they do, however, is set up structures that parallel American ideals; their success in achieving middle-class status on their own attracts a high degree of acceptance.

## Transitional States of Adaptation

As already noted, bicultural identity evolves from a dual process of socialization, first to the primary cultural context and second to the dominant societal context. A key variable that impacts the process of acculturation is that of age. As Matsuoka (1990) and Lum (1995) have pointed out, problems related to acculturation that involve age and generation can create disunity among family members. Not surprisingly, the young typically acculturate more quickly, while older adults retain traditional cultural values, roles, and behaviors.

Several problems are apparent in this regard. First, cultural transition and socialization to Anglo norms may be particularly difficult during critical growth periods. This is especially true during adolescence, when the minority child is struggling to integrate both cultures into a newly emerging identity. The Anglo norm of individual identity may be contrary to norms in many cultures, which stress group identity and responsibility to the family rather than to oneself (Cortese, 1990; Kiefer, 1974; Lum, 1995; Triandis, 1990). Adolescents, who may experience continual bicultural conflict at this stage, may not be able to discern how to manage dual skills and may get caught or stuck in *transitional state* (Figures 6.4 and 6.5). *Transitional*, as used here, refers to a temporary state of marginality that results from inconsistency in values and norms. *Temporary marginality* is (a) acculturation stress brought about by competing interests, values, and behavioral choices of a social situation and (b) the accompanying emotional discomfort and cognitive dissonance experienced by the individual.

Given that adolescence in Western society is by its very nature and definition a period of transition, transitional marginality is, to a certain extent, expectable for most adolescents during this stage. Transitional marginality is usually resolved as the adolescent adopts behaviors and forges an identity that is ego-syntonic and meets with social approval.

Ethnic minority children, however, are doubly affected by transitional states as they attempt to master not only the transition to adulthood but also the transition to bicultural adaptation while forming an ethnic identity. The adolescent who may be struggling to cope with physiological and emotional changes, increasing demands for individuation, and bicultural tension, may find a refuge in transitional states as a temporary coping mechanism (Figure 6.5). Those who, for complex reasons, are unable or unwilling to go beyond this to develop alternative coping mechanisms for either the cultural or societal context may adopt a permanently marginal adaptation.

Second, adults who encounter the demands of acculturation as a result of recent immigration may find refuge in transitional marginality as they are faced with both ethnic identity– and social role–related dilemmas. As previously mentioned, ethnic identity and personality development in many ethnic minority cultures are based on a collective, rather than an individual, responsibility. This dramatic shift may serve to weaken existing support structures that have traditionally aided in solidarity and mutual aid.

Another common stressor for adults confronting acculturation is that of loss of status. Traditional family roles prescribed by cultural norms carry with them specific statuses and privileges, some of which may be lost or undermined in the process of acculturation. While women undergoing an acculturation process may, in fact, experience more options for independence and personal growth, this often results in the disruption of the traditional family system. As Matsuoka (1990, p. 342) noted, "Changes in family functioning reduce the supportive value of family involvement." Galan previously observed that "as the children develop coping responses and skills in the majority culture and, as they discover a new power to manage societal situations, they may find themselves in conflict with one or both parents, whose coping repertoire is limited to family situations" (1992, p. 237).

A third factor that may lead to temporary marginality in transitional states is *intergenerational conflict* caused by differential acculturation. As already noted, children may acculturate faster than their parents and grandparents. As adults try to retain their native culture while their children acculturate, differences in education, language, and values become more pronounced.

Two common problems that result from differential *acculturation* are *adultification* and *spousification*. Adultification occurs "when a child assumes adult roles before adulthood." Spousification occurs when a child becomes adultified and subsequently bonds emotionally as a spouse with a parent (Galan, 1992, p. 238). An adultified child is one who assumes and carries out adult roles in the family that are not normative in either the nurturing or sustaining system. A spousified child is one who, as a result of carrying out adult roles in the family, becomes emotionally bonded to the opposite sex parent (Galan, 1992; Rinsley, 1971). Manifestations of tension experienced by Mexican American adolescents who have been spousified have been discussed in the literature (Galan, 1992).

Children who possess bicultural coping skills are often called on to be advocates, cultural translators, or problem solvers in a family. Galan (1992) observed from clinical cases of Mexican

Americans that "bilingual/bicultural children who navigate between two languages and two cultures often develop incredible mediation abilities and sophisticated code-switching responses, as well as a high level of social sensitivity and an appreciation of the difficulties encountered by those who speak only Spanish. That they are referred to as 'being like two people' is a tribute to an adaptive biculturality" (p. 239).

## The Continuum of Time

To appreciate the complexity of developmental tasks involved in bicultural socialization, it is necessary to go beyond the categorical model of adaptation choices presented in two-dimensional models. The continuum of time is represented by the Z axis in a three-dimensional transactional model of bicultural identity developed by Galan (Figure 6.6) and adds the dimension of the context of social situations over the continuum of time. True biculturality is defined as cultural adaptability, a developed ability to individualize and own or use all of one's values and behaviors and to appropriately choose those that maximize coping in a particular social situation. It is most accurately analyzed when there is a consideration of (a) the variety of social situations across time that bicultural persons encounter and (b) the way in which their value and behavioral choices in transactions protect and preserve their cultural distinctiveness. The Z axis represents the transactional field and illustrates how bicultural identity is developed over time, is dynamic, and results from one's coping in the situational struggles involved. It is a continual measure of ethnic identity and group membership.

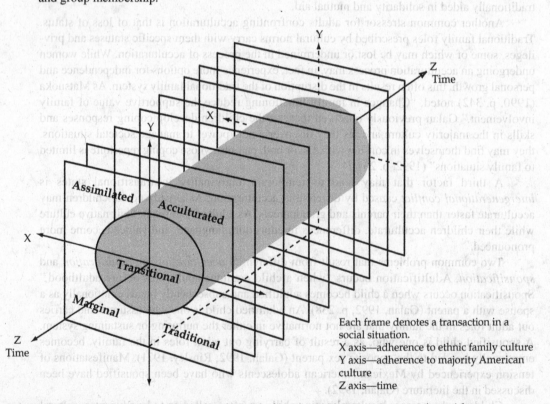

Each frame denotes a transaction in a social situation.
X axis—adherence to ethnic family culture
Y axis—adherence to majority American culture
Z axis—time

**FIGURE 6.6.** A multidimensional transactional model of bicultural identity. *Source:* Adapted from F. J. Galan (1978). © F. J. Galan.

Some situations, such as those at the workplace, may require adapting and acting in more acculturated or assimilated ways, whereas other situations, such as those in family gatherings, may call for more traditional behaviors. As the individual comes to understand that the social context provides various value and behavioral choices, cultural adaptability is learned as a result of learning to choose the behaviors that maximize adaptability.

The Z axis allows us to consider the different coping responses that are used in varying cultural, family, and societal situations across time. As Szapocznik, Kurtines, and Fernandez (1980, p. 356) suggested, "The process of becoming bicultural involves learning communication and negotiation skills in two different cultural contexts, each with a separate set of rules." Accordingly, bicultural adaptation involves a high degree of flexibility in coping with the entire cultural and societal milieu. Cultural adaptability is the ultimate cultural coping skill and is a result of being integrated in the values and behaviors of both ethnic family culture and majority societal culture. It is skill to use them appropriately to maximize coping in a social situation. A higher level of personal integration is often observed among ethnic minority individuals with a bicultural adaptation, especially among those with a developed sense of cultural adaptability.

## Achieving Cultural Integration Through Dual Identification

Most current personality theories stress consistency and integration of self as a measure of healthy functioning. When judged by majority societal norms, bicultural adaptation may be viewed as dysfunctional and deficient. This, of course, is not a surprising bias, as most aspects of ethnic minority life are seen as inferior when judged by majority societal norms.

Although consistency is an important element in a culturally integrated personality, it is *consistency within self* rather than consistency of self that is critical. *Cultural identity integration* is the degree of internal consistency among one's values, behaviors, and identity within a given context.

As ethnic minority persons become acculturated into the larger social system, they begin a process of dual identification. As societal values and behaviors are learned, they must also become fully internalized for true integration to be achieved. In bicultural socialization, two distinct sets of values and behaviors become internalized, and thus, the entire set of values, norms, and behaviors from both cultures becomes a resource from which individuals can draw. Persons who simply use adaptive behaviors without internalizing them, on the other hand, may experience transitional temporary marginality at various times throughout their development.

Rather than "straddling" two cultures, ethnic minorities can, in internalizing and identifying with both, become free to use all of their values in guiding their decision making and behavior in a wide variety of contexts. Through this they can gain competence in the majority societal context as well as ethnic competence in the ethnic family context. The dual identification process may, in fact, prepare the stage for the gradual development of an empowered personality, capable of cultural adaptability.

## TRANSCULTURALITY

Given the reality of cultural conflict and tension, it is important to examine models that allow us to find a common point between us, even in difficult circumstances. Most spiritual traditions emphasize that human experience is characterized not only by difference and divergence but also, on a deeper level, by commonality and unity. Drawing on the concept of the Medicine Wheel in Indigenous spiritual traditions and the meditation design called a mandala in Hindu and

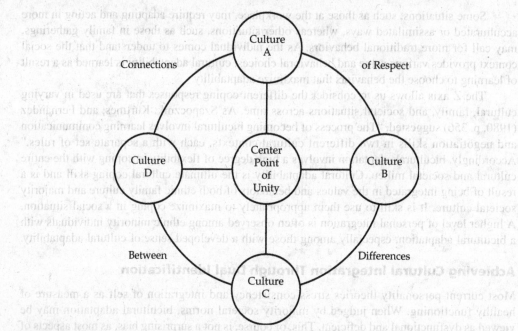

Connections of Respect

Between Differences

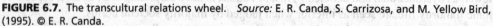

**FIGURE 6.7.** The transcultural relations wheel. *Source:* E. R. Canda, S. Carrizosa, and M. Yellow Bird, (1995). © E. R. Canda.

Buddhist traditions, a model of transculturality has been proposed (Canda et al., 1995; Canda & Furman, 2010; Lee, 1982). *Transculturality* means that a person is able to relate respectfully, comfortably, and competently in many different cultural contexts, while appreciating both differences and commonality. This is more than just a mastery of technical skills or a recognition of pancultural or universal human characteristics (Lum, 2003a, 2003b). It is a deep and abiding sense of connection with others, resting on our common humanity and common needs for love, meaning, supportive community, and justice. Medicine Wheels and mandalas depict this idea through a design that typically involves variations on a circle divided by four directions and unified by a common center point (Figure 6.7). Following this insight, the transcultural relations wheel symbolizes diversity with unity (Canda et al., 1995).

Connections of respect between diverse cultures are represented by the four direction circles connected by the circumference of the circle. This encompasses the ideals of biculturality and multiculturality. A social worker who is genuinely multicultural respects and appreciates all forms of human diversity and is able to connect or mediate across various cultural contexts through a flexible, knowledgeable, and skillful behavioral repertoire (such as familiarity with culturally appropriate ways of relating, multilingualism, and use of interpreters, translators, and cultural brokers). This is not easy to achieve. For example, when a social worker is early in the process of becoming culturally flexible and increasing engagement in cultural contexts beyond the culture of origin or primary affiliation, he or she could begin to feel confused, marginalized, or lost in between. At various times, members of the social worker's primary affiliation group might become critical of her or his changes of lifestyle and social activity. Likewise, members of groups with whom the social worker seeks contact may be suspicious or unwelcoming. This process requires continuous dedication to personal and professional growth, a good social support system, and skill at making mutually enjoyable and beneficial relationships within one's culture of origin and with people across cultural differences.

In addition, the center circle, "The Center Point of Unity," is the position that unites diverse cultures simultaneously. Achieving transculturality means being aware of this common human connecting point within oneself and being able to relate to others from this center. In many Indigenous North American spiritual teachings, this common point is described as the heart or spiritual center of the person. Gene Thin Elk (1991), a Lakota trainer in substance abuse treatment, refers to this as the *Sacred Mystery* or *Higher Power* within each person that unites us all. To use another metaphor, the Chinese character for mind is based on a symbol for the heart. Centered relating is heart-to-heart connectedness. When professional values and culturally appropriate skills and knowledge flow from this centered mind, one's manner naturally conveys respect, comfort, interest, empathy, and rapport (Canda & Furman, 2010).

Another way of reflecting on this transcultural perspective is to visualize an outer circle that encompasses all the various cultural standpoints. This reflects a mode of consciousness that includes and transcends the various diverse vantage points. As we will see in Chapter 13, this is a transpersonal scope of consciousness from which we appreciate and operate within the variety of particular cultural standpoints (including our own) but we are not limited to them. In terms of Fowler's faith development theory (see Chapter 9), this relates to the stages of conjunctive and universalizing faith.

Achieving transculturality is fundamentally an ongoing lifelong spiritual endeavor of growth that is not limited to any particular religious or cultural expression. It is a challenge and promise open to people of all cultural backgrounds. Transculturality can be especially challenging to achieve with regard to spiritual diversity, since many people invest their religious beliefs and worldviews with a sense of ultimate truth and authority that might exclude or denigrate others. Transculturality involves a commitment to honoring one's own cultural and spiritual standpoint and also honoring others.

## CULTURAL COMPETENCE

Given the cultural diversity in contemporary society and the projected growth of ethnic cultural minority populations in the United States, achieving cultural competence has become one of the most pressing issues for professional practice in a variety of fields including social work. For professionals to work effectively with members of culturally distinct groups, they must develop an understanding of and respect for a variety of cultures, values, and worldviews. While *cultural competence* has been defined in a variety of ways, we use Haley's (1999) definition: "the ability to work effectively across cultures in a way that acknowledges and respects the culture of the person or organization being served" (p. 10). This involves possessing and enacting awareness and a congruent set of skills, attitudes, knowledge, behaviors, practices, and policies that fosters successful interactions and outcomes despite cultural differences (Fong & Furuto, 2001; Lum, 2003a, 2003b). Cultural competence is an ingredient in achieving biculturality, multiculturality, and transculturality, as previously discussed.

Cultural competence is mandated by the National Association of Social Workers (NASW) as a prerequisite for ethical and effective social work practice (1999, 2001). In NASW's view, cultural competence is important in work across all kinds of diversity, including, groups distinguished by race, ethnicity, culture, class, gender, sexual orientation, religion, physical or mental disability, age, and national origin. NASW's standards for cultural competence address ethics, values, self-awareness, knowledge, skills, service delivery, empowerment and advocacy, diversity in the workforce, professional education, language diversity, and cross-cultural leadership. They address qualities of social workers and their human service organizations. Cultural competence is set within the context of understanding and responding to oppression.

Although the literature has focused on the need for professionals to possess cultural competence, it would seem that this is also necessary for nonprofessionals. Children are growing up in an increasingly multicultural society, and the ability to traverse cultures with cultural awareness and sensitivity will likely be an important social and life skill. We believe that the ability to function effectively in the context of cultural difference will increasingly become a requisite skill in interpersonal relationships as well as in the workplace.

Most models of cultural competence are based on the conceptual work of Pedersen (1994) and Mason, Benjamin, and Lewis (1996), and utilize developmental stages in which a person or organization progresses from lower to higher levels of functioning. The higher the level, the more proficient one is at integrating culturally appropriate knowledge and values and working skillfully with culturally different people and groups. Some models address the attainment of knowledge and skills at the individual level, while others focus on changes within the institution or organization that are derived from changes in the individual. At a minimum, cultural competence includes valuing diversity, conducting cultural self-assessments, managing the dynamics of difference, institutionalizing cultural knowledge, and adapting services to fit the cultural needs of the community.

Pederson's model (1994) involves the acquisition of cultural competencies in *awareness* (recognizing one's own biases and gaining knowledge about sociopolitical issues affecting those from other cultures), *knowledge* (culturally factual information about other groups), and *skills* (action that results from integrating awareness and knowledge).

Mason et al. (1996) defined a five-stage model in which people move from culturally damaging practices to those that respect and deliver culturally relevant services. The five stages or statuses include: *cultural destructiveness*, *cultural incapacity*, *cultural blindness*, *cultural precompetence*, and *cultural competence*. The first stage is typified by attitudes, policies, and practices that are harmful to individuals and their cultures. In the second stage, the person or organization is not intentionally destructive but may lack the capacity to work with different cultures. In the third stage there may be expressed intent of being unbiased, but differences in culture fail to get acknowledged. Movement toward the fourth stage consists of acknowledgment of cultural differences and clear efforts to improve. The final stage is one in which there is acceptance and respect of cultural differences and an ongoing attempt to find ways to encourage and respond to these differences. Services at this stage become culturally relevant, and there is also a commitment to initiating structural changes to improve people's lives. This involves awareness of sociopolitical factors, constructs, and forces that underlie oppression, racism, power, and privilege.

More recently, Ramsey and Latting (2005) and Latting and Ramsey (2009) suggested that despite the widespread interest in cultural competence, the literature has been lacking in concrete descriptions of specific skills or action strategies that are attainable for most professionals. They noted that the incredible diversity of groups and subgroups within each distinct culture makes it difficult, if not impossible, for professionals to attain such a broad base of knowledge. They also held that "focusing on separate social groups may also obscure complex intersections among different sources of social identity (e.g., a disabled, third-generation Latina lesbian) or how dominant or nondominant group memberships vary from setting to setting" (2005, p. 3). To overcome these and other limitations, they developed a set of *intergroup competence* skills that are generic across all social groups. Rather than focusing on specific cultural competencies, their model addresses skills that assist people in ending ingrained habits that foster cultural animosity (such as stereotyping) and skills that enhance better intergroup relations and valuing of diversity

| TABLE 6.2 | A Typology of Intergroup Competencies | | | |
|---|---|---|---|---|
| | **Focus** | | | |
| **Approach** | **Self: Rescripting Our Individual Story** | **Relationships: Revealing Each Other's Stories** | **Context: Building Critical Consciousness** | **Organization: Repatterning Systems** |
| Reflection | Becoming aware of own cultural values/ assumptions | Empathizing with multiple perspectives | Connecting the personal to the cultural and societal | Identifying systemic patterns |
| | Committing to personal change | Differentiating intent from impact | | Identifying own role in perpetuating patterns |
| Action | Processing emotions | Engaging in inquiry and openness | Addressing dominant/ nondominant group dynamics | Surfacing undiscussables |
| | Reframing mental models | Engaging in responsible feedback | | Advocating and engaging in systemic change |

© Jean Kantambu Latting and V. Jean Ramsey, 2004.

in organizations. As seen in Table 6.2, their model addresses the emotional, cognitive, and behavioral domains and applies to ourselves, our relationships with others, the larger societal context, and the organizational context.

The specific skills and tasks delineated in Table 6.2 provide an excellent base for people to examine their own ethnocentric biases and assumptions and a process by which they can begin to gain cultural sensitivity and competence through reflection and action.

## CONTEMPORARY ISSUES

As most traditional cultures have historically devalued or restricted the role of women and, in many cases, relegated them to second-class citizenship or defined them as property, we are faced with an interesting dilemma. Similar concerns relate to marginalization and oppression of any stigmatized members of many traditional and contemporary cultures, such as LGBTQI (Lesbian, Gay, Bisexual, Transgender, Queer, Questioning, and Intersexed) people and people with disabilities. Cultural sensitivity mandates that we accept diverse cultural norms and practices as valid alternate forms of social organization. In doing so, must we also accept sexist and other oppressive policies and practices that are a part of these cultures? We do not have an easy answer for this. On the one hand, to be "invited in" to the nurturing system requires an understanding of and respect for the traditional culture. On the other, we cannot ignore social conditions (in either the primary or secondary context) that foster oppression. Above all, we must recognize the changing nature of society at large and in ethnic communities, in particular. As Robbins (1985a) has suggested, we have a misguided notion that traditional cultures remain static while only the larger society changes. Thus, we fault the others for not keeping pace. Cultural transformation varies from society to society, and we must learn to balance the competing ideologies of constancy and change. Galan's notion of contextual adaptation is particularly relevant here. The norms and values that must be internalized for interaction in the nurturing system are not necessarily the same ones used in the dominant society. As ethnic minorities become more bicultural, their traditional values become transformed as well.

In addition, when identifying a cultural group's values, one must consider whose perspective within the group is being used. For example, male anthropologists have often used male informants and their perspective to define cultural norms. But women may have a very different view of what is normal or desirable. The 1995 United Nations conference on women held in China demonstrated an impetus to develop universal standards of human rights applied to both women and men. Yet this remains controversial, because contemporary views of universal human rights tend to privilege Western cultural assumptions, skewed by individualism and capitalism (Gray & Fook, 2004; Ife, 2001; Kreitzer, 2006; Yip, 2004). The International Federation of Social Workers (IFSW) and the International Association of Schools of Social Work (IASSW) have created a set of global standards for social work that are part of an ongoing process to sort out this dilemma (2005).

When considering the diversity that exists in contemporary society, even the most dynamic views of bicultural socialization presented here are somewhat oversimplified. As noted, people of color, collectively, are fast becoming the majority group in the United States. In addition, many European Americans are becoming more bicultural through interracial and intercultural marriages. However, the ideal of bicultural socialization should be a two-way street; if ethnic minority persons are expected to become bicultural while European Americans are not, that in itself is discriminatory. One must recognize that intercultural interaction and mutual learning are extremely complex, especially when considering the many regions with highly diverse populations that exist in the United States. In addition, the world has become a global community, with a high level of international economic and military interdependency, international travel and communications, and marriage and adoption across national boundaries.

Increasingly, many people have ancestry from multiple ethnic and racial origins. As a result, multiracial-multicultural people are advocating for their right to define their own identities and ethnic affiliations, rather than being pressured by others to identify with one group. Opposition is being voiced to the simplistic, exclusive racial and ethnic categories used to define ethnic identity in census surveys and affirmative action forms. For example, a person whose mother is Korean and father is Mexican American is forced to choose a self-description that excludes one or the other.

Tremendous cultural diversity raises the challenge of *multiculturalism*, a genuine appreciation for and participation in multiple cultural contexts, for both minority and majority persons (Canda et al., 1995; Lum, 1996, 2003). Achieving multiculturality, that is, comfort and competence to function in multiple cultural contexts, is a challenge compounded by the many different values, life ways, and languages that one needs to connect. Some people have reacted against this by retreating into racism and ethnocentric and exclusionary policies, such as English-only education or anti-immigrant scapegoating for social problems. Living in a multicultural society and world poses a great challenge as well as a great opportunity for mutual enhancement and mutual support between people of all cultural groups.

## APPLICATION TO SOCIAL WORK PRACTICE

With the exception of the Dual Perspective and occasional references to deficiency theory and bicultural socialization, the theories presented here, and cultural content in general, have historically received relatively little attention in the social work literature (Devore & Schlesinger, 1995,

1998; Green, 1999; Lum, 1996, 2003; McMahon & Allen-Meares, 1992). This content is most notably absent or minimally covered in most textbooks on human behavior in the social environment. Instead, it is found most often in discussions of majority–minority relations and in journal articles and textbooks that discuss issues and strategies for culturally sensitive practices. Further, in social work education it is not unusual for theories and practice approaches developed primarily by and for White Americans and Western Europeans to be taught with little questioning of the cultural limitations and inadequacies when these are applied to other cultural groups. Minority and international students in North America are challenged to make continuous special efforts to grapple with relevancy to their own cultural and linguistic groups, while English-speaking White students are given the luxury of thinking about diversity as an occasional topic.

We believe that an understanding of cultural conflict and tension; the interrelatedness of gender, class, religion, and ethnicity/race dual identification; and differential modes of adaptation are central to an understanding of growth, development, and socialization for ethnic minorities. When an individual's frame of reference is based in only one culture, the level of incongruence between the two cultures is heightened. An inability to manage bicultural tension may lead to alienation that is manifested physically, emotionally, or interactionally. To address the issue of culture and ethnicity more clearly, Devore and Schlesinger (1995, 1998) have suggested a series of "ethnic sensitive adaptations" that include a wide range of approaches for social work practice.

As noted earlier, both NASW and the international social work organizations IFSW and IASSW mandate that social workers work in a culturally competent manner, refrain from negative discrimination, and work toward social justice for all peoples. This poses significant challenges for social workers to engage in continual personal and professional growth, to develop cultural flexibility and appropriateness, to appreciate both human differences and commonalities, and to link with international efforts that balance universal human rights with locality-specific priorities.

Some social work scholars are concerned that the term *cultural competence* implies a set of skills that someone (typically focusing on White social workers) can achieve to interact with different people, as though Euro-American social workers should be the center point of social work perspective in the United States and around the world. This itself is ethnocentric. Actually, all social workers who assent to professional standards of ethics are committed to work in a culturally appropriate manner within and across any relevant cultural groups. This can take many different forms in various cultures and countries. There is also a concern that cultural competence might be reduced to a set of objective criteria of behaviors that can be scored, rather than as a continuous process of growth, relationship building, and active challenging of social injustices. So some scholars prefer terms such as *culturally appropriate*, *culturally relevant*, *locality specific*, or *indigenous* (Gray, Coates, & Yellow Bird, 2008).

## Definition of the Helping Situation

The contemporary theories presented here view ethnic identity formation and acculturation as being dynamic, adaptive, and self-affirming. Minority persons are seen as potentially flexible, variable, and self-transforming. The focus becomes supporting the individual, family, or community with their hopes and goals rather than forced assimilation, strict adherence to cultural traits, or congruence with a stereotypical typology. The helping situation is client centered and is defined as one relating to *growth* or the alleviation of *problems* related to adaptation, bicultural tension, and forced assimilation. It may also be defined as a *social issue* if the difficulties lie in structural features of either the sustaining system or the nurturing system. Flowchart 6.1 demonstrates practice applications derived from these definitions.

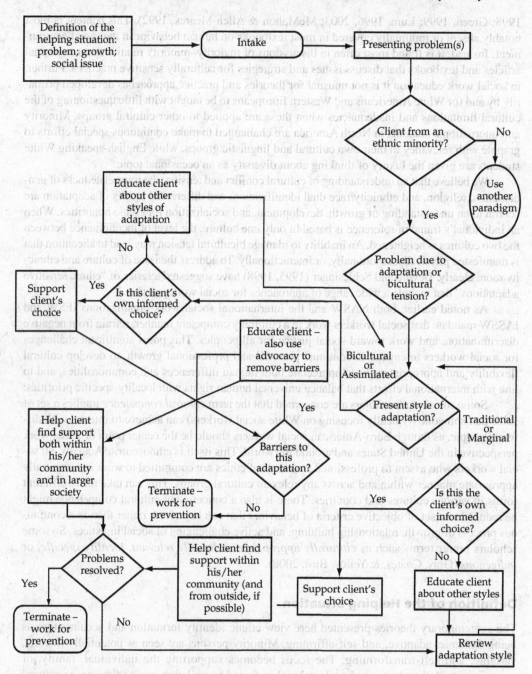

**FLOWCHART 6.1.** Adaptation of racial and ethnic minorities.   © 1998, S. P. Robbins, P. Chatterjee, & E. R. Canda.

## Assessment, Practice Strategies, and Methods

As the Dual Perspective (Norton, 1978) suggests, dual assessments of both the majority and minority cultures are necessary to get complete information about the norms, values, and behaviors that are socially sanctioned in each context. Areas of congruence and incongruence are then assessed. In addition, when working with individuals and families, information about the adaptation orientations of all family members is necessary to assess potential conflict due to differential acculturation. This must also include information about the level and variety of coping skills available to people in their situations. One must remember that Americans of European ancestry may also engage in various modes of adaptation through intercultural and international contact. As previously noted, bicultural conflict is not, in itself, a necessary source of tension. However, lack of cultural proficiency often leads to feelings of guilt, anger, grief, shame, and bitterness. Likewise, sexism, classism, racism, and discrimination compound the challenge of biculturation and call for empowering responses to overcome institutional or interpersonal constraints.

Dual assessments of the nurturing and sustaining systems are also necessary to yield information about change that may be essential in either or both systems. For example, if majority communities are unresponsive to the bicultural needs of their residents, a community needs assessment may be necessary to determine the supports that are lacking. Likewise, one must assess the availability of support systems in the nurturing system. Are natural helping networks available for persons grappling with issues of dual identity? How might these best be promoted, used, and maintained? Social workers often overlook the strengths and resources available in minority cultures because we are either unaware of their existence or we believe them to be deficient. Above all else, the models presented here suggest that we, as practitioners, must have a high level of cultural knowledge, awareness, and sensitivity when working with culturally diverse populations. The dual assessment of the nurturing and sustaining systems must accurately reflect the resources, strengths, and limitations of both systems. This requires the ability to set aside prejudicial attitudes based on deficiency formulations when assessing the primary culture. The Anglo value assumptions that underlie our traditional ideas about what is normal, healthy, and functional may not apply cross-culturally. As Norton cautioned (1993), cultures must be viewed within their own ecological context.

Clearly, an understanding and appreciation of the bicultural perspective helps us define appropriate practice methods in work with ethnic minority clients. Practice methods derived from these theories cover a broad spectrum that includes individual, family, organizational, or community intervention. Legislative advocacy may also be a focus of practice.

On the individual and family levels, a primary task may be helping clients develop skills that will assist them to achieve optimal functioning in either the nurturing or the sustaining system or both. This may include, but is not limited to, educational activities aimed at skill development, bicultural effectiveness training, values clarification, involvement in cultural studies programs, involvement in formal education, and counseling aimed at cultural and identity integration. For those choosing bicultural adaptation, practice methods and interventions should be aimed at helping clients develop the flexibility necessary to manage their entire cultural milieu.

In addition, community organizing and legislative advocacy may be necessary to effect change in larger social systems. Schools that force assimilation while simultaneously devaluing the minority culture, for example, may become a target for change. Similarly, state or national policies that provide barriers to adaptive choices may be a point of focus as well.

Finally, the Dual Perspective suggests that we must be invited in to the nurturing system if we are to be effective. This may be problematic as a specific situation (e.g., child or spouse abuse) or agency policies may mandate immediate action. We must understand the limitations this places on us in the helper role. Clients are too often labeled *resistant* when they do not accept us and the help we offer. However, acceptance rarely occurs on our timetable and may be a very lengthy process; we must learn to be patient if we are committed to gaining the trust necessary to be invited in.

For social work agencies to foster clients' cultural self-determination and goal achievement, the agency itself must reflect multicultural competence (Canda et al., 1995; Canda & Furman, 2010; Green, 1995; Harrison, Wodarski, & Thyer, 1992; Iglehart & Becerra, 1995; Lum, 1996). Agency staff composition should reflect the cultural and linguistic diversity in the client population. The hiring and promotion of biculturally skilled workers should be a priority. Agency services should be designed to be accessible and culturally relevant. To accomplish this, links and cooperative teamwork arrangements with formal and informal support systems, such as kinship groups, religious organizations, ethnic mutual assistance organizations, and traditional healers, need to be maintained. In addition, trained interpreters, translators, and cross-cultural mediators need to be employed as staff and consultants. Table 6.3 illustrates a variety of settings and applications of the theories discussed here.

## CRITICAL ANALYSIS

### Biological, Psychological, and Spiritual Factors

The theories covered here have their primary focus on social and cultural processes and their impact on psychological and social adaptation and functioning. They do not address biological processes.

The classic theories emphasize the social and psychological dysfunction that result from culture conflict. Despite this, little attention is paid to specific psychological processes involved. Linear models of assimilation and acculturation are based on the idea of psychological adaptation but fail to specify the psychological mechanisms through which adaptive change occurs. The more current theories attempt to minimize the negative impact of culture conflict on individual and family functioning. Instead, they emphasize the development of ethnic and bicultural identity, transculturality, and adaptive functioning.

Although issues related to spirituality receive little attention in most theories of culture change, the formulation of transculturality focuses on inclusive spirituality as a key to achieving respectful, skillful, and mutually beneficial multicultural relations (Canda et al., 1995; Canda & Furman, 2010; Lee, 1982).

### Social, Cultural, and Economic Forces

Theories of culture change place their primary focus on social and cultural forces and processes. Both Norton's and Galan's models give an additional emphasis to situational context and the continuum of time. Issues relating to power relations and cultural pluralism that were obscured in classical theories due to their assimilation ideology have been corrected by current theories that explicitly address these issues. The concept of ethclass adds an understanding of economic forces and the ways in which people become economically marginalized for failure to assimilate or acculturate. One of the realities of living in a complex industrial or postindustrial society is that a certain degree of acculturation is necessary to achieve any degree of economic stability or success. Too often, however, we confuse economic acculturation with cultural assimilation. Theories that stress bicultural competency and contextual behavior do not demand a linear progression in which people are forced to abandon their cultural norms and identity to achieve economic stability.

**TABLE 6.3**  Various Settings and Applications of Cross-Cultural Interaction Theories

| Type of Agency | Type of Presenting Problem(s) | Type of Program | Definition(s) of the Helping Situation | Type(s) of Activities |
|---|---|---|---|---|
| Mental health center | Anxiety and identity confusion of transracial adoptee | Individual/family counseling, transracial adoptee support group | Crisis Social issue | Culturally competent counseling and group work; support bicultural socialization process |
| Social work department of hospital | Non–English-speaking patient facing surgery | Medical services, discharge planning | Sick Problem Crisis | Language interpretation, translation; cross-cultural consultation; linkage to culture-specific support systems |
| Statewide human services department | Overrepresentation of minority children in foster care | Child welfare, foster care | Social issue | Cultural-competence training of staff; recruitment of minority adoptive homes; community outreach |
| United Nations High Commission for Refugees | Warfare, genocide, and refugee flight | Refugee services | Crisis Social issue | Provide protection and asylum; resettlement and/or repatriation; intercultural conflict mediation |
| Tribal government, human services department | Increased incidence of youth suicide | Community-based prevention | Crisis Social issue | Family/community outreach, education; collaboration with elders and spiritual leaders; cultural revitalization activities |

## Relevance to Individuals, Groups, Families, Organizations, Institutions, and Communities

This group of theories simultaneously focuses on the individual, primary and secondary groups, the family, the culture of origin, cultural organizations, communities and institutions, as well as institutions in the larger society. Although interaction and membership within these contexts is

| TABLE 6.4 | Levels of Application of Cultural Conflict Theories |
| --- | --- |
| **Level** | **Examples of Application** |
| Individual | Cognitive, psychological, social, or religious conflict due to cultural differences in norms and role expectations. Resolution of conflict through adaptive functioning, biculturality, and transculturality. |
| Family | Conflict between traditional family structures, norms, and roles and expectations by the dominant culture. |
| Small group | Conflict between different cultural groups due to different norms and expectations. |
| Organizational | Conflict between organizational expectations and minority group norms. Conflict between organizations due to different cultural norms and expectations. |
| Community | Conflict between communities due to differences in cultural norms. |
| Larger social structures | Conflict between majority and minority cultures due to differences in norms. Conflict between minority cultures. Resolution of conflict through transcultural unity. |

stressed to varying degrees, the primary contextual focus is on individual and family adaptation and the impact of culture conflict between minority cultures and the dominant society.

The theories discussed here address the inherent conflicts in norms and values between minority and dominant cultures. Their application, however, extends to the community, organizational, small group, and individual levels as well (Table 6.4).

## CONSISTENCY WITH SOCIAL WORK VALUES AND ETHICS

Embedded in the early theories of assimilation and acculturation was the notion that optimal health and well-being could be achieved only if people gave up a part of their cultural identity to become American. Contemporary theories reject this approach and stress the importance of some degree of bicultural adaptation, multiculturality, or transculturality.

Despite the fact that the models presented here directly address racial, ethnic, and cultural minorities, they largely ignore the influence of gender and other aspects of human diversity that are not embedded in the culture of origin. The notion of deficiency formulation, however, can be directly applied to all oppressed groups and is certainly applicable to women. The Anglo biases inherent in negative views of ethnic minorities are also prevalent in our most accepted theories of psychological development, which portray women as deficient. However, the concept of bicultural socialization has been applied to minorities other than racial and ethnic groups. For example, bicultural socialization has been described in relation to homosexuals' experience within the majority heterosexual societal context (Lukes & Land, 1990). The transcultural perspective and the NASW standards for cultural competence are relevant to people of any type of group membership.

There are now many resources to help social workers develop culturally appropriate practice, including books and journals that specialize on social work with diversity and international contexts, such as the *Journal of Ethnic and Cultural Diversity in Social Work, Social Development Issues,* and *International Social Work.* Lee and colleagues (2009) have developed a comprehensive model of integrative body–mind–spirit social work that draws on Eastern and Western theories, philosophies, and evidence-based practices that is consistent with cultural competence and a transcultural perspective. Other recent works explore issues pertaining to theories and practices that address intersecting issues of cultural appropriateness, Indigenous cultures, and macro justice matters of colonialism and genocide (e.g., Al-Krenawi & Graham, 2009; Gray, Coates, & Yellow Bird, 2009).

## PHILOSOPHICAL UNDERPINNINGS

Early theories of assimilation and acculturation assumed deficiencies and pathology in ethnic minority cultures, families, lifestyles, and persons, as judged by the objective reality of Western scientific thought. In contrast, more current formulations reject the notion of an objective reality and point to the social construction of all norms and values. In doing so, they assume neutral, rather than pathological, differences between cultures. Thus, standards of deviance and dysfunction are not viewed as being inherent in behavior but are imposed on relatively disenfranchised minorities by the majority culture and theorists who are part of that culture.

Norton's Dual Perspective, originally developed as a conceptual framework for social work practice with racial and cultural minorities (1978, 1993), contains a unique blend of philosophical assumptions from systems theory, conflict theory, symbolic interaction, and Erikson's developmental theory. Perhaps most importantly, the conservative assumptions of functionalist and ecological theory are well balanced with the conflict formulation that recognizes the ideological control of the dominant society and that rejects the deficiency formulations that are imposed on minority cultures. This position is very consistent with the assumptions of dynamic system theory. Similarly, Galan's model assumes an interactionist adaptive view of the self. Inasmuch as self is seen as related to context, and contexts can be numerous, multiple selves are possible and are not necessarily dysfunctional. Finally, transculturality assumes that it is possible and desirable to attain a deeper commonality and unity of human experience that approaches cultural diversity and conflict through mutual understanding and mutual benefit.

## METHODOLOGICAL ISSUES AND EMPIRICAL SUPPORT

Although the early theories were not derived from empirical research, a positivistic view was inherent in the assumption of an objective reality as defined by Anglo standards. Later empirical studies relied heavily on quantitative data that used mainstream norms for standardized measurement. Not surprisingly, ethnic minorities were shown to display a vast array of deficiencies that were thought to be reflective of their "objectively inferior" social structures and personalities. Empirical research that stresses quantification not only serves to exaggerate differences between minority and majority groups but also tends to minimize intragroup differences and ignores the true diversity that exists in society. In addition to these inherent problems, there has also been sharp criticism of sloppy research methods, defective reasoning, and flawed findings (Howard & Scott, 1981; Robbins, 1985b; Valentine, 1968).

Clearly, when research is conducted from a culturally sensitive stance, it can provide valuable information on the ways in which people from minority cultures can successfully adapt to their environments. Research on biculturalism has shown that people can, indeed, thrive when they can successfully negotiate multiple cultural identities (Berry, 2005; Ryder, Alden & Paulhus, 2000).

However, most theory in this area rejects the totally positivistic approach and promotes postpositivistic research based on the paradigm of social construction. In this regard Howard and Scott believe that qualitative methodology is necessary to construct positive ethnographies of culturally diverse people (1981). This view, however, is not widely popular among the agencies that fund research, and it is doubtful that the ethnographic approach will become more accepted than quantification.

Norton's research on the growth and development of African American children is providing good prospective data on cultural differences in early childhood socialization. The dual perspective that guides her data analysis provides a positive view of cultural differences and a nonpejorative assessment of problems in functional competence that need to be ameliorated. We believe that this approach will continue to yield critical information about functional competence and adaptation in both contexts.

All of the theories discussed here are better at explanation than prediction and better at a probabilistic level of explanation than a deterministic level. They are adequately suited for explaining properties of both individuals and groups. However, although these related theories do address the impact of macro-level systems on one another, they are most often used to explain behavior at the individual, family, and community levels. There are currently extremely few studies in this field, however, from which we can draw generalizations about bicultural identity and adaptation.

## Summary

Early assimilation theories, based on national pride and belief in the superiority of the Anglo American way of life (which was synonymous with progress and upward mobility), held great appeal for a wide variety of people including the middle class, the growing professional middle class, and the poor who aspired to upward mobility. Although these theories still appeal to many, the technological advances in the last 20 years have created an increasingly diverse "global society," typified by cultural diversity. The more contemporary theories discussed in this chapter will probably be more accepted, as cross-cultural contact continues to increase.

Those with a strong feminist or Marxian orientation may have difficulty accepting models that promote adaptation and incremental change, as many of these do. While the contemporary theories proposed here do not ignore structural inequality, they suggest simultaneous focus on mainstream social institutions, minority cultural institutions, and the individual. For some, this may not be radical enough. On the other hand, there is great value in the multiple foci that can encompass all levels of social work practice and address the entire micro–macro continuum.

# Psychodynamic Theory

*She lies awake at night*
*Too afraid to dream*
*The images that haunt her*
*Are real, or so they seem*
*Afraid of memories*
*Of things she can't recall*
*Alone at night she wonders*
*If they're memories at all.*

© SUSAN MARTIN
1997 (BMI)

## PSYCHODYNAMIC THEORIES

- describe the intrapsychic processes involved in personality development
- emphasize the importance of early childhood experiences on psychosocial development
- delineate the role of defense mechanisms in adaptive functioning
- focus on either pathological or adaptive functioning
- assist us in formulating questions used in a psychosocial history
- have been widely used in social work practice with individuals and groups

Psychodynamic theory proposes a model of personality development based on the existence of opposing forces that strive for a dynamic balance. Originating with the psychoanalytic formulations of Sigmund Freud, theories based on this model assume either intrapsychic conflict or psychosocial conflict. Theories of intrapsychic conflict point to dynamic conflict between psychic structures within the person, whereas theories of psychosocial conflict focus on dynamic conflict between internal and external (societal) forces (Corsini & Marsella, 1983; Maddi, 1980).

## HISTORICAL CONTEXT

Although Austrian neuropathologist and psychoanalyst Sigmund Freud is widely regarded as the "grandfather" of psychodynamic theory, many of his ideas and concepts were based on the works of earlier philosophers and theorists. Philosophical thought on the unconscious, dream interpretation, and techniques of free association date back to the writings of Aristophanes and Plato in the fourth century B.C. Abnormal psychology is believed to have originated with Hippocrates (Corsini & Marsella, 1983; Ellenberger, 1970).

A number of 19th-century German philosophers expanded on these early works. Ideas about the "unconscious" were elaborated by Gotthilf Heinrich von Schubert and Carl Gustav Carus and later by Friedrich Nietzsche, who coined the term *id*. The primacy of the sex instinct was noted by Arthur Schopenhauer, as were beginning conceptions of the id, ego, and repression, all of which are central themes in Freud's theory.

Other theorists such as Pierre Janet and Richard von Krafft-Ebing were writing in a similar vein. Janet theorized about the *subconscious* and Krafft-Ebing about the *libido*, a term he used prior to Freud. Likewise, the use of hypnosis to access the unconscious began in the late 1700s with the work of Franz Anton Mesmer and continued with the work of Jean Charcot (Ewen, 1988).

According to Corsini and Marsella (1983), four major ideological trends of the 19th century can also be found in Freud's work: Victorian morality, the primacy of science, Rousseau's vision of society, and Darwin's vision of human evolution. These combined to form a view of human behavior that placed the biological drives of sex and aggression at the center of human nature and motivation. According to Freud, psychopathology occurs because society, with its demands for sociality and civility, artificially imposes restrictions on this "true" nature. As we examine Freud's theory, this historical and ideological context becomes a critical factor in understanding his early scientific theorizing about the determinants of personality and behavior. His theory is considered "scientific" rather than "philosophical" because it "stems from observations made within a consistent frame of reference" (Corsini & Marsella, 1983, p. 27).

## KEY CONCEPTS

Although psychodynamic theorists may vary in their individual descriptions of intrapsychic and psychosocial processes and forces, most adhere to the following concepts from Freudian psychoanalysis (Konopka, 1983):

1. The importance of early childhood experiences in personality development
2. Existence of unconscious and preconscious motivation
3. Existence of the ego, which assists in rational action

**4.** Existence of defense mechanisms

**5.** Feelings of ambivalence, in which people concurrently experience opposite emotions such as love and hate

We explain these in more detail in our discussion of Freudian and neo-Freudian theories.

## SIGMUND FREUD: PSYCHOANALYSIS

Psychoanalytic theory was an outgrowth of Freud's clinical experience as a neuropathologist treating patients whose disorders had no apparent physical causes. In his private practice, Freud encountered patients who exhibited symptoms of paralysis despite the fact that there was no corresponding structural damage. The medical specialists of his day believed that "hysterical paralysis" of this sort occurred only in women (*hysteria* is Greek for "uterus" or "womb") and was caused by either irritation of the sexual organs or "play acting" (Appignanesi & Zarate, 1979; Ewen, 1988).

In his earlier studies with French neurologist and hypnotist Jean Charcot, Freud had witnessed demonstrations in which hypnotic suggestion reduced, removed, or modified symptoms of hysteria. The mechanistic thinking of the time, however, insisted on physical rather than psychological causation. Though trained as a mechanist, Freud eventually abandoned this approach in favor of a more holistic view of behavior that included psychological causation of psychopathology.

In reviewing Freud's theory of psychosexual development, one must understand his views about the relationship between society and the individual. Freud rejected philosophical beliefs that people were born good or bad, moral or immoral. Rather, he believed infants to be amoral, and, thus, inherent "goodness" or "badness" could not explain human nature. He turned, instead, to the physiological nature of humans for his explanation of behavior. Central to his theory is the idea that all human behavior is motivated by two primary biological drives or instincts that are present at birth—sex and aggression. Society, of course, must put restrictions on these, and in doing so, a conflict is created between our biological needs and our social environment (Freud, 1930, p. 62):

> If civilization poses such great sacrifices not only on man's sexuality, but on his aggressivity, we can understand better why it is hard for him to be happy in that civilization. In fact, primitive man was better off in knowing no restrictions of instinct.

Given this inherent conflict between the needs of the individual and the needs of society, it is not surprising that people become neurotic (Martindale, 1988).

## THE CONSCIOUS, PRECONSCIOUS, AND UNCONSCIOUS

Freud originally theorized that the mind was made up of three parts: the unconscious, the preconscious, and the conscious. The *unconscious* is the part of the mind that holds ideas, thoughts, and memories that we cannot access and bring into our conscious awareness. Because we cannot access these ideas, we are unaware of their existence. In contrast, the *preconscious* holds ideas, thoughts, and memories that we are not currently thinking of, but if we concentrate, we can bring these to our *conscious,* or aware, part of the mind.

Jones (1953) has noted that the "important dividing line was not between consciousness and the rest but between the unconscious and the other two" (p. 402). Freud deliberately avoided using the term *subconscious* because he thought it was misleading (Jones, 1953).

Freud believed that the "hysterical" paralysis he observed in his patients was the result of a traumatic experience that they had repressed, or pushed back, into their unconscious. The conscious memory of the event was too painful to deal with, so the mind resolved the problem by pushing it out of consciousness. Because it had not disappeared, but was instead repressed, it manifested itself in a physical symptom such as paralysis (R. M. Thomas, 1985). The cure, then, involved techniques that would unmask the repressed memories and bring them to the conscious level. After abandoning his early techniques involving hypnosis, he used free association and dream interpretation to help his patients uncover these unconscious memories.

### The Structure of the Mind: The Id, Ego, and Superego

To the three levels of consciousness Freud added the constructs of id, ego, and superego (Figure 7.1). The *id* corresponds to the unconscious and is present at birth. The id comprises basic drives and instinctual energies, the most basic of which is sexual; Freud called this *libido* (Latin for "desire"). The *ego* includes both the conscious and preconscious and develops out of the id from experiences that help the child distinguish "self" from "other." The *superego* is the last to develop and is a "special part of the ego that observes and sits in judgment above the rest" (Ewen, 1988, p. 38). Just as the ego develops out of the id, the superego develops out of the ego. Although the ego and superego are largely conscious and preconscious, they are, in part, unconscious as well. The ego and superego may at times "dip into the id and make judgments as to what aspects of the id should be admitted into ego territory" (Corsini & Marsella, 1983, p. 32).

Freud believed that the drives and instincts that originate in the id were primarily sexual and antisocial. The id, which is present at birth, begins to build up libidinal (sexual) energy that demands release. Once this energy is released (or expended), it is experienced as pleasure. The newborn, in Freud's view, was all id, seeking satisfaction of its immediate needs—food, warmth, affection, and so on. The biological needs of the infant are transformed by the id into psychological

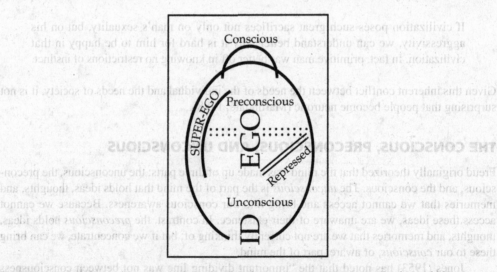

**FIGURE 7.1.** Freud's psychic structure. *Source: New Introductory Lectures on Psychoanalysis* by Sigmund Freud, translated by James Strachey. Translation copyright © 1965, 1964 by James Strachey. Used by permission of W. W. Norton & Company, Inc.

tension or wishes. As the id's needs are satisfied, the infant stores in its memory pictures of the objects that bring it pleasure. This primary process of wish fulfillment is based on the *Pleasure Principle*. It is irrational, chaotic, and amoral, and stems entirely from the id's need to expend libidinal energy.

The Pleasure Principle, however, does not take into account the external reality of the world outside the infant. The ego, fueled by libidinal energy, arises from the id to accomplish this, because the primary process cannot indefinitely satisfy the infant (R. M. Thomas, 1985). According to Freud, "It is to this ego that consciousness is attached; the ego controls the . . . discharge of excitations into the external world" (1922, p. 7). The conscious ego can now consider the demands of reality and can control or defer the demands of the id, at least temporarily. This disciplined thinking represents the secondary process, which is based on the *Reality Principle*. In contrast to the irrational, chaotic thought of the primary process, the secondary process is rational, problem solving, and pleasure delaying (Ewen, 1988).

The final part of the psychic structure, the superego, emerges through the child's identification with parents. As the ego begins to introject (internalize) parental values, the superego develops out of the ego. Thus, concepts of right and wrong, should and should not, become internalized in the emerging superego. Although children are not "born" moral, they "become" moral as they introject parental and societal values. The two aspects of the superego are the *conscience* (the should-nots) and the *ego ideal* (the shoulds). The superego punishes or rewards the child with feelings of guilt or shame when internalized values are not followed and with pride and self-praise when they are (R. M. Thomas, 1985). Thus, the superego is critical to the perpetuation of civilized society and the status quo. This, however, is not unproblematic as the demands of civilized society run counter to the individual's natural instincts (sex and aggression) (Freud, 1930). Accordingly, the id and the superego are in perpetual conflict and the ego serves as a mediator between the two.

## Stages of Psychosexual Development

Superimposed on the levels of consciousness and structure of the mind are developmental phases that are psychosexual in nature. Freud suggested that as people grow and develop, they pass through a series of five sequential phases, each of which is dependent on proper resolution of psychosexual conflicts at the previous stage. Freud believed that libidinal instincts in the infant were bisexual and, as such, were polymorphously perverse. In other words, the infant could gain sexual satisfaction in any part of the body. He believed that development of the psyche (personality) depended on the way in which the child expended libidinal energy in the erotogenic (sexually sensitive) zones of the body at different phases of development. Further, the lasting feelings the child gains about self and others are dependent on the resolution of conflict at each stage. Freud proposed five stages with corresponding *erotogenic zones*: oral, anal, phallic, latency, and genital.

In the *oral stage* (from birth through 12 or 18 months) the infant explores the world through the mouth, which is also the primary source of gratification. As the infant invests libidinal energy in objects that bring pleasure (mommy's breast or a substitute), the child "cathects" that object. Instinctual gratification such as satisfying hunger, the need for tactile support, and the need for comfort is primary in this stage. If the infant receives too much or too little need satisfaction, this is reflected in later personality development. Freud divided this stage into two phases, the oral passive (characterized by sucking) and the oral aggressive (characterized by biting).

As a rudimentary ego begins to grow, the infant starts to distinguish "self" from "not self." Things that give pleasure are experienced as "self"; things that do not are experienced as "not self." The infant begins to develop ambivalent feelings toward mother who is not always available to meet the id's demands. The ambivalence of love and hate is often expressed through biting during the latter part of this stage (R. M. Thomas, 1985).

The *anal stage* (roughly ages 2 to 3) corresponds with toilet training, a time when the child learns that the rectum is an important means of self-expression. Although the child is still investing libidinal energy through the mouth, the rectum and urethra become the dominant zones of gratification. This stage is also divided into two phases: expulsion and retention. In the first phase the child receives pleasure through the expulsion ("letting go") of urine and feces. The parents, however, are urging the child to control these instinctual urges. To do so, the ego (which is still rudimentary) must borrow libidinal force from the id to accomplish countercathexis. In the latter phase, the child now receives pleasure from "holding on" (or retaining) the feces and urine at will. Again, the role of the parents is critical, as they must not be too harsh or too lax in their demands. If they are, the child may become anal retentive (withholding) or anal aggressive (freely letting go). These tendencies may later manifest themselves as withholding or letting go of inner feelings, many of which are hostile. Persons who are miserly or overly possessive may be characterized as anal retentive. Those who show frequent rejection or abandonment may be seen as anal aggressive. The idea that things have value comes from this stage (R. M. Thomas, 1985).

The *phallic* (or Oedipal) *stage* (roughly ages 3 to 5) moves the erotogenic zone to the genitals; the penis for boys and the clitoris and vulva for girls. Children now discover that they can get erotic pleasure from masturbation. As they do, they connect the pleasure with a desired love object, a specific person. At this point however, psychosexual development takes a different path for boys and girls. Boys turn to their first love object, their mother, who gave them their first pleasure in the oral stage. They develop a sexual desire for mother and a corresponding fear of father, who is now a rival for mother's affection. This is called the Oedipus complex (named after the Greek king Oedipus who unknowingly killed his father and married his mother). As children are inherently bisexual, boys also develop attachments to father and jealousy toward mother. As boys learn (through normal experimentation) that they have a penis and girls don't, they incorrectly conclude that girls once had a penis, which was taken away as a form of punishment. Boys become convinced that the same thing will happen to them, and they develop *castration anxiety*. This anxiety forces boys to give up their Oedipal wishes, and instead, they begin to identify with their father. As boys turn away from the opposite-sex parent and identify with the same-sex parent, these "identifications and prohibitions are incorporated into the superego and help to bring about its formation" (Ewen, 1988, p. 41). The Oedipal urge then becomes repressed into the dark recesses of the unconscious.

Girls, Freud believed, follow a slightly different path. Like boys, they also develop ambivalent attachments to both parents, with mother as the primary sex object. As girls discover that they have no penis, they begin to feel inferior and develop penis envy. When they then find that mother shares the same deficiency, they begin to develop resentment toward her and a corresponding wish to have their father's child (Freud, 1925, in Gay, 1989, p. 676):

> Now the girl's libido slips into a new position along the line—there is no other way of putting it—of the equation "penis-child." She gives up her wish for a penis and puts in place of it a wish for a child: and with that purpose in view she takes her father as a love object.

Girls, then, lacking the motivation of castration anxiety, never fully develop a superego. They remain, in Freud's opinion, narcissistic and display inferior character traits. Although they may, at some point, abandon or repress the Oedipal conflict, they never do so in a satisfactory manner as "their superego is never so inexorable, so impersonal, so independent from its emotional origins as we require it to be in men" (Freud, 1925, in Gay, 1989, p. 677).

In the *latency stage* (roughly ages 5 or 6 through puberty) the erotic drives are still located in the genitals but are fully repressed. Here we see a continuation of identification with the same-sex parent, and the superego becomes strengthened as parental values continue to be incorporated.

The *genital stage* begins at puberty and lasts through adulthood. Freud did not make any distinctions between adolescence and adulthood, and this final stage represents adult genital maturity. Libidinal energy is now directed toward appropriate members of the opposite sex. Freud believed that the erotic zone for women shifted from the clitoris to the vagina as "the female genital organ for the first time meets with the recognition which the male one acquired so long before" (Freud, 1933, cited in Ewen, 1988, p. 44).

Satisfactory progression through these psychosexual stages requires parents to play a major role in providing satisfaction for the child's instinctual urges. These must be handled with great care and understanding, as too much or too little need satisfaction can create pathology that is manifested in adulthood. If the child's needs are too satisfied, there is little impetus to move to the next stage and the child becomes fixated. Fixation also occurs if the child's needs are insufficiently satisfied, and the child continues to gain satisfaction symbolically of these unmet needs as an adult.

Freud also stressed the importance of body image. As the ego develops, so does an awareness of one's body. During primary process, the infant normally transfers libidinal instincts onto others. If, however, the libidinal attachment is to the ego, *narcissism* (self-love) may occur. Although narcissism is normal in infancy, the libido becomes transferred to other people (objects) in normal development. Conversely, if normal infantile narcissism does not occur, the child may become ambivalent about his or her own body. Primitive body images from early developmental stages may later result in self-destructive behavior as an adult. Given the heavy emphasis that Freud placed on the unconscious id, it is not surprising that he believed most behavior to be based on unconscious motivation.

Although Freud was most interested in psychopathology and early childhood experiences that led to neuroses in adulthood, he did acknowledge that psychologic normalcy was possible for some people. Here, he distinguished between neuroses that were situational and brought on by external events and those that were caused by internal psychic conflict and characterized by anxiety.

## Anxiety

The concept of anxiety is central to Freudian theory. In his early formulations, Freud held that anxiety originated in the id and was caused by an overabundance of libido or sexual feelings that became discharged as anxiety. In his later writings, he placed its origins in the ego where it serves as a warning of internal danger. Anxiety may be caused by external stimuli, habitual patterns, or feelings of guilt and self-denigration when one violates the codes of the superego. The ego generates anxiety to warn the psyche of unacceptable impulses (Corsini & Marsella, 1983).

## Defense Mechanisms

When the ego experiences internal danger, it defends itself with a variety of defense mechanisms that are ultimately aimed at repression. When an impulse, idea, or event is repressed, the ego

| TABLE 7.1 | Common Defense Mechanisms of the Ego |
|---|---|
| Denial | A refusal to believe or perceive reality. |
| Displacement | Transferring feelings and behaviors to a substitute object. |
| Identification* | A conscious or partly conscious taking on of character traits of another person to reduce self-hatred. |
| Projection | Attributing unacceptable characteristics of the self to another person. |
| Rationalization | Superficial but rational explanations that are used to justify unacceptable behavior and maintain self-esteem. |
| Reaction formation | Repressing an unacceptable impulse and replacing it with its opposite, such as replacing hate with love. |
| Regression | Adopting behaviors from an earlier period of development. |
| Repression | The ego threatening impulses, ideas, and acts into the unconscious. |
| Sublimation | A form of displacement that is a normal adjustment process and does not lead to repression; diverting sexual impulses to acceptable outlets. |

*Identification with the aggressor* is believed to be a very powerful defense mechanism in psychodynamic theory. It occurs not only during childhood while dealing with the sexual feelings toward a parent but also throughout the life span when a person encounters other persons holding substantial power.

pushes it back into the id's unconscious, where it cannot be accessed. As Corsini and Marsella (1983) noted, repression is "both a defense and the aim of defenses" (p. 44). Although the concept of ego defenses appeared in Freud's earlier works, his daughter, Anna, was responsible for the development of a more comprehensive list (Freud, 1966). Table 7.1 presents a partial list and explanation of commonly used defense mechanisms.

## Transference

Another unconscious process particularly relevant to psychoanalytic therapy is that of transference. Freud believed that patients unconsciously project repressed emotions and desires, meant for their parents, onto the analyst. He believed it to be an inevitable and necessary focus of treatment. Other psychodynamic theorists have since revised, altered, and extended the definition of transference and a few believe that it is not necessary at all.

## The Life and Death Instincts

In his early writings, Freud identified only one primary instinct—the *life instinct*, named "Eros," after the Greek god of love. The life instinct, fueled by the libido, motivates the desire for food, water, sex, shelter, and so on. In addition, it guarantees biological survival by governing reproduction. In his later writings, he identified a second instinct, the *death instinct*, or "Thanatos," which is Greek for "death." The death instinct is seen in repetitive acts that result in self-destructive behavior. Thanatos also shows itself in aggression. As a pair of basic motivating forces, Eros and Thanatos remain in constant conflict—self-preservation versus self-destruction. Freud believed that although Eros was prominent during most of the life span, Thanatos eventually wins as people, at the end of life, return to an inorganic state (Freud, 1922). Table 7.2 summarizes Freud's key concepts.

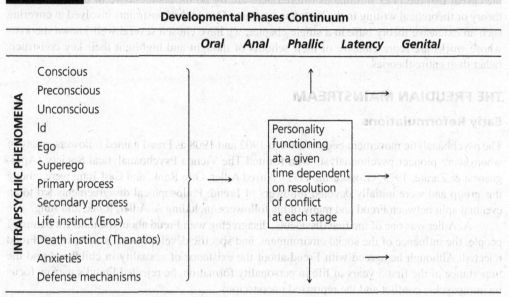

TABLE 7.2   Key Concepts of Sigmund Freud

**Developmental Phases Continuum**

Oral    Anal    Phallic    Latency    Genital

INTRAPSYCHIC PHENOMENA

Conscious
Preconscious
Unconscious
Id
Ego
Superego
Primary process
Secondary process
Life instinct (Eros)
Death instinct (Thanatos)
Anxieties
Defense mechanisms

Personality functioning at a given time dependent on resolution of conflict at each stage

## ROADS FROM FREUD

Similar to Karl Marx, Sigmund Freud's theories have led to several generations of Freudian scholars who can be divided into two groups. Robinson (1969) has suggested that they form a dichotomy of "conservatives" and "radicals."

The conservatives, or the *Freudian Mainstream*, are those theorists who accept many of Freud's basic assumptions about the intrapsychic nature and structure of personality but have modified and reformulated his original works. Among this group are Alfred Adler, Carl Jung, Otto Rank, Helene Deutsch, Karen Horney, Anna Freud, and Harry Stack Sullivan, to name a few.

Within the Freudian Mainstream there is an additional split between the more traditional psychodynamic theorists and the ego psychologists. In breaking with Freud's view of the genesis of the ego, the ego psychologists believe, among other things, that the ego emerges as a separate structure rather than grows out of the id. Perhaps the most well known of the later neo-Freudian ego psychology theorists is Erik Erikson. We discuss his work in Chapter 8 in our presentation of life span theories.

The most popular contemporary wave of neo-Freudian thought can be seen in two offshoots of psychodynamic theory, object relations theory and self-psychology. Theorists Otto Kernberg and Heinz Kohut have built on the works of earlier mainstream theorists such as Rene Spitz, Melanie Klein, Margaret Mahler, and John Bowlby. In addition, Nancy Chodorow has formulated a feminist perspective on object relations.

In contrast, the radicals, or the *Freudian Left*, are theorists who diverged from mainstream thought, especially in their views on sexuality and the role of economic and ideological forces on personality. Some attempted to combine the works of Sigmund Freud and Karl Marx. Several noted theorists in this group are Wilhelm Reich, Erich Fromm, and Herbert Marcuse. We discuss the Freudian Left later in this chapter.

As we review the works of the Freudian Mainstream and the Freudian Left, we do so with the caveat that the brief summaries offered here are by no means inclusive of the full array of theory or theoretical writing in the Freudian tradition. Due to the constraints involved in covering such an extensive theory base in a single chapter, we have chosen several well-known theorists whose works are representative of their schools of thought and highlight their key constructs rather than entire theories.

## THE FREUDIAN MAINSTREAM

### Early Reformulations

The psychoanalytic movement began between 1902 and 1908 as Freud gained followers, many of whom were pioneer psychoanalysts who formed The Vienna Psychoanalytical Society (Appignanesi & Zarate, 1979; Grosskurth, 1991). Alfred Adler, Otto Rank, and Carl Jung were among this group and were initially devoted followers of Freud. Philosophical disagreements led to an eventual split between Freud and many of his followers, including A. Adler, Rank, and Jung.

A. Adler was one of the first dissidents, disagreeing with Freud about the inherent nature of people, the influence of the social environment, and specific developmental stages, which Freud rejected. Although he agreed with Freud about the existence of sexuality in childhood and the importance of the first 5 years of life in personality formation, he rejected Freud's narrow focus on intrapsychic conflict and the repressed unconscious.

In his theory, called *Individual Psychology*, he proposed that intrapsychic processes involved the creative self, which he believed to be innately social, cooperative, and active in seeking goals, the most primary of which is *self-perfection* (A. Adler, 1927, 1929). Central to his theory is the idea that behavior is often shaped by anticipation of future events and the goals we set, rather than past experiences. He also believed that expectations related to birth order and memories of childhood (rather than actual experiences) play a crucial role in shaping the personality (Ewen, 1988). A. Adler also dismissed the Freudian view of women as biologically and psychologically inferior and he was one of the first psychodynamic theorists to suggest that the structure of society, with its attendant power disparities and gender inequality, was responsible for creating inferiority complexes in women. He held that all psychopathology involved an inferiority complex, but that psychopathology was the product of a misguided lifestyle, rather than fixations and regressions. This theoretical break with Freud clearly placed him in the "enemy" camp, as did his resignation from the Vienna society in 1911, "to protest Freud's autocratic control" (Grosskurth, 1991, p. 42).

Freud's onetime heir apparent and chosen successor, Carl Gustav Jung, was both a psychoanalytic psychiatrist and mystic who became interested in the occult and parapsychology. In contrast to A. Adler, who rejected the repressed unconscious, Jung embraced it, but substantially revised the Freudian concept of repression. He held that repressed material could, in fact, be accessed because repression is not an actively maintained process. He also agreed with Freud's position that instincts motivate behavior and libidinal energy fuels mental activity. However, he sharply disagreed with Freud's overemphasis on sexuality and argued that the psyche comprises more than just the libidinal life instinct. He did, however, accept the importance of the intrapsychic processes of the ego and the unconscious and further delineated two types of unconscious (Ewen, 1988). Freud, however, demanded total loyalty, and as Jung began to distance himself theoretically from Freud, he too came to be seen as a traitor. When Jung finally severed his ties to the psychoanalytic movement, Freud authored two papers in which he delineated his theoretical differences with both Jung and A. Adler (Freud, 1914a, 1914b; Grosskurth, 1991). We discuss several of Jung's theoretical concepts in more detail in Chapters 8 and 13.

Later theorists carrying on the psychodynamic tradition diverged from the primarily intrapsychic focus of Freud. Most attributed a greater importance to the role of the social and cultural environment in shaping human behavior. Citing other scholars, Corsini and Marsella (1983) have suggested that theorists such as Karen Horney and Harry Stack Sullivan, among others, were "really neo-Adlerians, since Adler . . . strongly stressed the importance of understanding the individual in a social context or milieu" (p. 332).

Karen Horney, an eminent female psychoanalyst, focused her theory on the causes of neurotic behavior. In addition to her belief that society plays a major role in personality development, she rejected Freud's biological determinism and held that people had the capacity to develop and change (Horney, 1945, p. 9). She proposed that people are guided by two "selves," the real (inner) and the ideal (outer). The ideal self, based on societal values and beliefs that are not attainable, keeps us from knowing our inner or "true" self (Corsini & Marsella, 1983). Central to Horney's theory is the concept of basic anxiety, or the feeling of isolation, helplessness, and concern about one's capacity to get love. Basic anxiety leads to coping strategies or styles that may become relatively permanent and assume the form of needs. Horney proposed ten neurotic needs that people develop over time and later related these needs to three associated personal styles: moving toward people (dependency); moving against people (domination); and moving away from people (detachment). Arising as defenses to basic anxiety caused by problems in childhood, she suggested that children cope with their environment by moving toward, against, or away from their parents, which leads to dependent, dominating, or detached personalities (Horney, 1937, 1939, 1942, 1945, 1950).

Horney was a pioneer in pointing out that the primary conflict in the development of women is between dependency and ambition. Further, she reexamined the concept of penis envy and suggested that while penis envy is an empirically observable phenomenon, it is caused by the status associated with the possession of the penis rather than a biologically inherited envy. In other words, if society values males more than females, the penis becomes a symbolic representation of that status superiority (Horney, 1967; Sayers, 1991).

Harry Stack Sullivan, a psychiatrist and personality theorist, was strongly influenced by theoretical perspectives from psychodynamic psychiatry, anthropology, sociology, and psychobiology. Much of his work revolved around understanding the causes of schizophrenia from a multidisciplinary perspective (1953, 1964). He was the first theorist with a psychodynamic orientation to suggest that individual personality cannot be separated from interpersonal relations (H. S. Sullivan, 1953). He theorized that interpersonal interaction with others leads us to develop images (or personifications) of ourselves and others. Although these images may not be accurate, we act on them and they influence our behavior. Interaction with others also gives rise to "dynamisms," or enduring behavior patterns.

Although H. S. Sullivan largely abandoned the intrapsychic, biologically deterministic approach of Freud in favor of a more social and interpersonal theory, their developmental models share some similarities. For example, H. S. Sullivan proposed sequential developmental stages in which "significant others," such as parents, teachers, or friends, play a large role in creating or preventing pathology. He identified three modes of cognition (thought) through which people experience the world: prototaxic, parataxic, and syntaxic. As children grow, they move from the undifferentiated "stream of consciousness" prototaxic mode as an infant to the logical, rational syntaxic mode that is based on symbolic communication. The syntaxic mode first emerges as children begin to master language at age two or so, and it becomes their dominant mode around age five. H. S. Sullivan believed that schizophrenics regressed to one of the two earlier modes. Like Freud, H. S. Sullivan attributed maladjustment in many cases to early experiences within the family and believed that poor adjustment in early stages could lead to problems in adult life. In contrast, however, H. S. Sullivan attributed the development of personality to interpersonal rather than intrapsychic factors.

## Later Reformulations

As theorists continued to apply, extend, and reformulate Freud's original works, an increased emphasis on the role of the environment led to a more optimistic view of human behavior. Blank and Blank (1974) suggested that contemporary psychodynamic theory begins with Heinz Hartmann's reformulation of the ego as an autonomous structure. Subsequent contributions by Rene Spitz, Melanie Klein, and Margaret Mahler, to name a few, have added to the growing literature on psychodynamic theory, especially in the field of object relations. David Rapaport later synthesized traditional Freudian theory with the new concepts of ego psychology.

E. G. Goldstein (1984) has noted the emergence of two major streams of ego psychology. The first stems from classical Freudian theory and emphasizes the unconscious and instinctual forces of personality. The second stresses the adaptive capacity of the ego and minimizes the unconscious. H. Johnson (1991) has more recently argued that "opinion is diverse as to the boundaries of the theories" (p. 404). We agree with H. Johnson and acknowledge the somewhat arbitrary division that is made in our discussion of ego psychology, object relations theory, and self-psychology.

**EGO PSYCHOLOGY**    A primary focus in ego psychology is the process of adaptation. For the ego psychologists, life itself is an adaptation to the genetic, geographical, cultural, spiritual, and social environment. Secondly, continued adaptation requires a series of choices that are actively made by the ego. Although there are numerous theorists writing in this vein, the two we review here are Heinz Hartmann and Robert White.

Heinz Hartmann is widely regarded as the "father" of ego psychology for his revolutionary view of the ego. In contrast to Freud, who believed that the ego grew out of the id, H. Hartmann proposed that both the ego and id were present at birth in an "undifferentiated matrix" and each, containing its own energy source, develops independently of one another. As the id and ego emerge, there is, he acknowledged, some conflict between the instinctual urges of the id and the reality orientation of the ego. Not all functions of the id, however, are conflict-prone. He believed that ego functions such as language, motor, and intellectual development were conflict-free. He called the part of the ego not in conflict with the id the conflict-free ego sphere (1958).

According to H. Hartmann, the ego performs two sets of functions: autonomous functions and acquired functions. Autonomous functions are conflict-free and arise within the biological "undifferentiated matrix" at birth. Acquired functions, on the other hand, emerge from conflicts with the id that are dominated by drives and primary process thinking.

For H. Hartmann, adaptation was "a reciprocal relationship between the organism and its environment" (1958, p. 24). In discussing the environment, he addressed the reciprocity of the mother–infant relationship and acknowledged the family, the social structure, and the intergenerational evolution of tradition, all of which aid in adaptation. His term for the environment, *average expectable environment*, placed a primary focus, however, on the mother–infant dyad and led to an elaboration of what would later become object relations theory.

He also proposed a process of *neutralization*, whereby energy derived from libidinal and aggressive id drives is transferred to the ego and is used for negotiation with the environment. H. Hartmann redefined psychosis as a failure of neutralization rather than a conflict between the ego and the outside world (Blank & Blank, 1974). Finally, he theorized a developmental progression that went from primary infantile narcissism to object constancy and laid the foundation for later object relations theorists.

Robert White, a contemporary of H. Hartmann, introduced the idea of competence as an important ego construct. According to him, competence is an individual's "fitness or ability to carry out those transactions with the environment which result in its maintaining itself, growing, and flourishing" (1963, p. 60). He suggested that parallel to Freud's developmental phases, a drive toward competence and mastery produces specific competencies that correspond with each stage. According to White, these competencies are coping with the environment during the oral stage; efforts to work independently during the anal stage; language acquisition, communication skills, and role-playing (thereby role-learning) during the phallic stage; social skills during latency; and identity and life skills acquisition during the genital stage.

The works of H. Hartmann and White have contributed greatly to ego psychology due to their emphasis on the conflict-free sphere, the development of competency, and the idea of conscious determination. Table 7.3 summarizes key concepts of H. Hartmann and White.

**OBJECT RELATIONS THEORY**   Theories of object relations are derived from Freudian psychoanalytic theory and ego psychology. In Freudian theory, the infant stores and internalizes images of objects that satisfy libidinal drives; these objects are generally persons. Object relations theory focuses on this process and its impact on personality and interpersonal relations in later life (E. G. Goldstein, 1984; Polansky, 1982). E. G. Goldstein (1984) delineated two different meanings of object relations in current use: (a) interpersonal relationships and (b) intrapsychic structures. We discuss here the work of Rene Spitz, Margaret Mahler, John Bowlby, Otto Kernberg, and Nancy Chodorow.

**TABLE 7.3**   Key Concepts of Heinz Hartmann and Robert White

**Developmental Phases Continuum**

| | | Oral | Anal | Phallic | Latency | Genital |
|---|---|---|---|---|---|---|
| **INTRAPSYCHIC PHENOMENA** | **Heinz Hartmann**<br>Conflict-free ego sphere<br>Autonomous functions<br>Acquired functions<br>Neutralization | Infantile narcissism | Object constancy | Personality as adaptation of the ego in an average expectable environment | | |
| | **Robert White**<br>Ego competence<br>Drive toward competence and mastery | | | Personality as mastery of stage-related competencies | | |

Rene Spitz focused on the "reciprocal relationship" between the mother and child in his work on ego functions. He introduced two theoretical constructs from his studies of foundling, abandoned, and hospitalized children: hospitalism and anaclitic depression. He found that infants display developmental problems when confined in hospitals or other impersonal environments and deprived of close emotional and tactile support from their mothers. They are often undersized and sluggish in their movements, speech, and toilet training (Polansky, 1982; Spitz, 1945, 1946a, 1946b). Spitz referred to this as *hospitalism* (Spitz, 1945, 1946a). Polansky has pointed out that this condition can also emerge in infants raised at home who have been severely neglected (1982, p. 176).

Anaclitic depression develops in infants who initially received early care and support from a mother and were then removed from her care (Polansky, 1982, pp. 177–178; Spitz, 1959). Spitz believed that this type of depression in infants is parallel to that found in adults when they experience loss.

Spitz attributed these infant pathologies to a disruption in the psychic organization of the infant during critical periods of development. In normal development the ambivalence the infant feels toward the libidinal object (mother) results in the "realization that the formerly 'good' (gratifying) object and the 'bad' (frustrating) one are, in fact, one and the same person" (Blank & Blank, 1974). At roughly 6 months, the infant's drives of libido and aggression come together with these two "object representations" in a process Spitz calls fusion. Accordingly, it is failure in fusion that creates pathology.

Margaret Mahler's theory has become increasingly popular as clinical social workers, psychologists, and psychiatrists have adapted it for work with borderline patients. Mahler's original work, however, was with psychotic and autistic children. In Mahler's work the phrase *object relations* is a foundation concept (Mahler, 1952; Mahler, Pine, & Bergman, 1975). It refers to the way an infant's rudimentary ego becomes organized during the first 3.5 years of age. During these early years, the infant struggles to differentiate between what is self and what is other. The various mental representations of this self–other differentiation and their consequences on the personality structure during the first 36 months of life, lie at the heart of her work.

Mahler's developmental theory was influenced by the works of John Bowlby (1969, 1973, 1975), Jean Piaget (1936), and Rene Spitz (1959, 1965). Her developmental stages do not correspond to those of Freud. Instead, she proposed her own model, a four-stage theory that begins with autism (birth to one month), progresses to normal symbiosis (1 to 4 months), and then to separation-individuation (4 to 36 months). Successful completion of these stages leads to the establishment of *identity* at about age three or four. Identity, for Mahler, is "not a sense of who I am but that I am" (Mahler et al., 1975, p. 8).

According to Mahler, the child arrives at birth with normal autism, a fragmented sense of self, and little manifest awareness of any other person. Responsive to primarily internal stimuli, the infant begins to separate pleasurable and painful feelings.

At about one month, normal autism gives way to the formation of symbiosis or attachment to mother. The infant now perceives that an external object (mother) is the source of gratification. At the beginning of this stage attachment-seeking behavior is displayed in which the infant shows anticipation of pleasure or pain in relation to the mother's actions.

At about 3 months, the infant forms a symbiotic bond with mother, the central feature of which is delusional "fusion with the (mental) representation of the mother and . . . the delusion of a common boundary of the two" (Mahler, 1968, pp. 7–8). Critical in the stage is a match between the mother and infant, as later development is dependent upon symbiotic gratification. Severe symbiotic deprivation may result in symbiotic psychosis. Alternately, the child may regress to autism. Insufficient (but not severe) symbiotic deprivation leads, instead, to developmental distortions.

Stage three, separation-individuation, begins at about four to 8 months of age and encompasses four substages. The first is that of differentiation from the mother. Mahler refers to this process as *hatching from the symbiotic partner* and *expansion beyond the symbiotic orbit.* Now the infant begins to perceive herself or himself as separate from the other. Naturally, this differentiation creates separation anxiety, and the infant continues to need close physical contact with mother.

Practicing the second substage is linked to the development of locomotion at 8 to 15 months. The infant now "practices" separation by physically moving away from and returning to mother. At about 15 to 24 months rapprochement occurs. In what Mahler calls "rapprochement crises," the child struggles to assert his or her will against the objects present, including the former symbiotic partner. The child now displays autonomous behavior and begins the acquisition of language and representational thought. At the end of this crisis, the child begins to develop a greater sense of self.

Achievement of individuality, the final substage, is marked by the ability to perceive mother as a separate being, and the child now develops object constancy. During this stage, at about 24 to 36 months, the child internalizes the cohesive image of the mother (both good and bad objects), and this internalization (object constancy) leads to a healthy individuation. Of this phase, Anna Freud observed earlier (1968): "Object *constancy* means . . . to retain attachment even when (the symbiotic partner) is unsatisfying." Completion of this stage leads to a consistent self-image by age three or four.

Althea Horner, who further developed Mahler's theory, has suggested that failure of earlier attachment may lead to primary infantile autism; failure of attachment in very early childhood may lead to secondary autism or to the formation of a psychopathic personality (no commitment to a moral code); failure to resolve the rapprochement crisis may lead to a narcissistic personality; and failure to arrive at identity formation and object constancy may lead to a preneurotic personality (A. J. Horner, 1979). Table 7.4 summarizes the key concepts of Margaret Mahler.

---

**TABLE 7.4**    Key Concepts of Margaret Mahler

**Developmental Phases Continuum**

*Autism    Symbiosis    Separation-Individuation    Identity*

INTRAPSYCHIC PHENOMENA

Primitive ego at birth

Good and bad object representations

Self–other differentiation

Object constancy

Personality as an outcome of self–other differentiation during first three years of life

John Bowlby's contributions, rooted in the psychodynamic mainstream, are based on ethology, cross-cultural, and clinical observations. His seminal works, *Attachment* (1969), *Separation* (1973), and *Loss* (1980), have added to the growing literature on object relations theory.

Bowlby emphasized that "attachment behavior is regarded as a class of social behavior of an importance equivalent to that of mating behavior and parental behavior" (Bowlby, 1969, p. 179). While there are various reasons as to how and why attachment occurs, by the end of the first year almost all children show attachment behavior, and its absence is a symptom of a serious developmental problem. Bowlby rejected the idea of a return-to-the-womb drive and was more sympathetic to ideas about primary object sucking and clinging (i.e., the infant desires mother's breast and tactile support derived from contact with her).

Bowlby theorized that *separation anxiety* is a universal phenomenon and is based on an instinctive feeling of danger. He also acknowledged the role of real-life experiences in the creation of anxiety. During normal development, the infant *splits good and bad object images* and *internalizes* the good ones. This, in his opinion, minimizes anxiety as the internalized image provides the child with a sense of security. In contrast, children who have been separated from their parents develop *anxious attachment*, as they do not have internalized good objects to rely on.

In his observations of infants he noted three phases that follow the separation of the child from the mother. The infant first *protests* in anger at the mother's absence, then *despairs* and *becomes depressed* when crying does not bring her back. Finally, the infant becomes *detached*, by using repression as a defense. Detachment, for most, is a useful coping mechanism. For some, however, it becomes pathological if overused (Polansky, 1982). Bowlby also argued that instinctual drives and attachment are separate processes. Further, he believed that attachment behavior "does not disappear with childhood but persists throughout life" (Bowlby, 1969, p. 350).

Otto Kernberg, a contemporary theorist, has integrated traditional Freudian drive theory with object relations theory. His particular interest was in the diagnosis and treatment of borderline personality disorders.

Kernberg accepted Mahler's developmental stages of autism, symbiosis, and separation-individuation, and added three corresponding levels of pathological fixation and regression that lead to psychosis, character disorders, or neurosis in adulthood. In contrast to other theorists, however, he believed the aggressive drive to be the cause of developmental failures.

According to Kernberg, psychosis is the result of fixation or regression during the autistic or symbiotic stages. This occurs if the infant fails to introject good self-objects or aggressively projects "all bad" self-objects with no self-other differentiation. In some cases, cognition may compensate and a "superficial adaptation to reality" may occur (Blank & Blank, 1974). Although psychosis is avoided, this developmental failure results in a diminished capacity for guilt, love, or empathy.

Personality disorders, especially borderline pathology, are linked to fixation or regression at the third stage. Developmental failure is characterized by the pathological defensive splitting of good and bad self and object images. At the beginning of this stage, the child achieves differentiation so that boundaries between self and others are developed. The final integration of good and bad images is thwarted, however, due to an abundance of aggression. Finally, Kernberg attributed neurotic character disorders to a failure to resolve the Oedipal conflict.

**OBJECT RELATIONS THEORY: A FEMINIST REVISION**  Nancy Chodorow offered a feminist revision of Freudian theory. She held that it is male, rather than female, development that is problematic and conflictual. Her focus, true to object relations theory, is on pre-Oedipal, self-other differentiation. Building on Mahler's developmental stages, Chodorow theorized that infants experience a "primary oneness" with mother. As children begin to differentiate self from other, girls experience a sense of "femaleness" that creates a close emotional bond in the mother–daughter relationship. Mothers, recognizing the similarities between themselves and their daughters, likewise develop close attachments to them. Thus, core gender identity for girls builds upon the primary oneness, and they grow up with "a sense of continuity and similarity to their mother, a relational connection to the world" (Chodorow, 1979, p. 53).

Boys, on the other hand, recognize that mother's femaleness is different from their own maleness and learn their gender identity as "being not-female." To individuate, they must reject feminine identifications and emotions and emphasize their differences. Mothers, of course, recognize and experience their sons as different from themselves and form looser attachments to them as they begin to separate and form patterns of autonomy.

Because men are less emotional (having rejected early female identification), they do not fulfill women's deep emotional needs for attachment. Thus, in heterosexual relationships, women seek to re-create their primary oneness with mother through intense bonding to their children (Chodorow, 1978). This, Chodorow believed, provides women with an emotional connectedness that they cannot get from their emotionally detached mates.

Chodorow also pointed out that in our society men have the power to define women's lives and identities. Thus, they "have come to define maleness as that which is basically human, and to define women as not-men" (1979, p. 55). Gender difference becomes interpreted in this transformed manner during the Oedipal conflict as an unconscious defense. It then becomes institutionalized as a developmental norm of separateness, individualism, and autonomy, and becomes equated with mental health and self-fulfillment.

Chodorow held, however, that a change in power arrangements and parenting practices would also bring about fundamental changes in psychological characteristics of children. Table 7.5 summarizes key concepts of Chodorow.

**SELF-PSYCHOLOGY**   Heinz Kohut, the leading proponent of self-psychology, developed his theory as an outgrowth of his work with narcissistic clients. In contrast to object relations

---

**TABLE 7.5**   Key Concepts of Nancy Chodorow

**Developmental Phases Continuum**

| | *Infancy and Childhood* | *Rest of Life* |
|---|---|---|
| **INTRAPSYCHIC PHENOMENA** | Primary oneness with mother<br>Being female<br>Being not-female<br>Oedipal conflict | Personality as an outcome of gender identification based on biological differences/similarity to primary caretaker and social definition of gender roles |

theorists, he held that models of psychological autonomy based on separation and individuation do not reflect the reality of life. Instead, the human condition is characterized by psychologically healthy interdependence (H. Johnson, 1991).

Perhaps his most profound divergence from most mainstream reformulators lies in his acknowledgment of the interrelationship between the social structure and personality development. Kohut tied the character disorder of narcissism to societal changes of the 20th century and the isolated nature of the nuclear family. He contrasted Freud's "Guilty Man" (the product of sexual repression) with contemporary society's "Tragic Man" (the product of alienation and isolation). In a Marxian sense he viewed pathology of the human condition as tied to specific historic and structural changes in society. However, here is where the Marxian analogy ends as he shifted the specific blame for individual pathology to the unempathic mother and absent father (J. K. Gardiner, 1987; Kohut, 1984).

Kohut proposed a model of personality development in which the infant's drives and instincts are separate from the attainment of a cohesive self, which develops during the first few years of life. He believed that children are born into empathic environments comprised of self-objects. The empathic environment is a warm, nurturing environment with a nurturing parent who assists the child's development through "empathic mirroring." This is a process in which the child is "confirmed in its vitality and assertiveness by the mirroring self-object" (Kohut, 1984, p. 23). The term *self-object* denotes the child's perception of other people (and objects) as part of self, inasmuch as the functions they perform are perceived to be the child's own. According to Kohut it is the self–self-object relationship rather than the self-object relationship that is at the core of psychological functioning throughout life. Although the nature of the relationship with self-objects changes, the need for them does not (H. Johnson, 1991).

During the process of development the child attains a cohesive self through transmuting internalizations. This is a process whereby the child incorporates into self "the functions which the object used to perform for the child" (Kohut, 1971, p. 50). This must be done gradually, and the child must shift attention from the whole person to the specific function to be internalized (Blank & Blank, 1974).

In his work on narcissistic personality formation, Kohut diverged from Freud's Oedipal focus. Instead, he suggested two separate lines of development: "(1) from autoerotism to narcissism to object love, and (2) from autoerotism to narcissism to higher forms and transmutations of narcissism" (Blank & Blank, 1974, p. 80). Clearly, he regarded narcissism as necessary in both normal and abnormal development. Pathological narcissism occurs when the child is deprived of an empathic environment. In the absence of empathic mirroring, the child is unable to integrate into a realistic self-image the early grandiose self-images and the idealized parent images.

J. K. Gardiner has noted that "although self-psychologists adopt non-sexist language, speaking of the 'nurturing parent' or the 'child's caretaker,' they assume that the mother has the primary role in the infant's life" (1987, p. 226). Thus, deficiencies in a child's self-structure are directly attributable to deficient and unempathic mothers. Table 7.6 summarizes Kohut's key concepts.

There are numerous other authors who have made substantial contributions to contemporary psychodynamic thought. Greenspan (1989), for example, proposed a six-stage comprehensive theory of object relations. Fairbairn (1952) and Guntrip (1961, 1969) have elaborated on the schizoid position and the depressive position. Koenigsberg (1977) has suggested that racism, revolution, and nationalism can be explained by constructs used in ego psychology. In addition, E. G. Goldstein (1984) and Polansky (1982) have made substantial contributions in relating ego psychology to social practice. Strean has long been a leading proponent of traditional psychodynamic thought (L. Freeman & Strean, 1987).

**TABLE 7.6**  Key Concepts of Heinz Kohut

**Developmental Phases Continuum**

*Infancy and Childhood*      *Rest of Life*

INTRAPSYCHIC PHENOMENA

Self-object
Transmuting
internalizations
Self-structure
Cohesive self

Self as an
outcome of
empathic
environments

## THE FREUDIAN LEFT

The "radical" reformulators, or Freudian Left, depart from mainstream thought in several ways. Some, like Geza Roheim, believed that sexual permissiveness is an indicator and aim of human happiness. In his reformulation, it is the repression of libidinal urges that leads to unhappiness and misery. In essence, he rejected the antisocial nature of Eros as posited by Freud.

Others sought a form of synthesis between the works of Freud and Karl Marx. Within this group there are two distinctive "camps" or orientations. The Marxist Freudians, such as Wilhelm Reich and Erich Fromm, are primarily psychoanalysts, trained in the Freudian tradition, who attempted to incorporate Marxian concepts into Freudian theory. In contrast, the Freudian Marxists, such as Herbert Marcuse (first discussed in Chapter 3), are primarily Marxian theorists attempting to explain the psychological dynamics of oppression in capitalist societies. To this end, they incorporate Freudian concepts into Marxian theory.

The Freudian Left, however, has not gained great popularity among professional helpers. Reich was discredited by a legal and political system, Roheim was isolated by most of his colleagues, and Marcuse became the chief ideologue of the student rebels in the United States during the 1960s. Only Fromm attained credibility in Europe and America. We discuss the ideas of Reich, Fromm, and Marcuse here.

Wilhelm Reich, a psychoanalyst and former active Marxist, believed that sexual energy (or libido) is at the core of human functioning and determines an individual's character. He theorized three levels of personality structure. At the surface level was the "mask of self-control," "politeness," and "artificial sociality." Immediately under the surface was the Freudian unconscious, with "sadism, greediness, lasciviousness, and envy." At the third (and deepest) level was one's "natural sociality and sexuality, spontaneous enjoyment of work, and capacity for love" (Reich, 1960, pp. 2–4).

Reich criticized Freud's notion of the death instinct, which, according to Reich, "implied that human suffering was inevitable, under socialism as well as capitalism" (Robinson, 1969,

p. 36). However, Reich argued that Freud and Marx shared some things in common: "The underlying dialectical theme in all of Freud's work was the notion of psychic conflict. As Marxism was a conflict sociology, so Freudianism was a conflict psychology" (Robinson, 1969, p. 42). Reich was also keenly aware of the role of ideology on character. For Reich, ideology of the external environment became anchored in the character structure (personality) and internalized by the individual. Further, he held that the family is produced by a certain economic environment and political ideology. It, in turn, helps nurture certain ideologies in the character structure of infants who later are supportive of that economic order and ideology.

Erich Fromm was a psychoanalyst who preferred the term *humanist*. His work, *Marx's Concept of Man* (1961), illustrated his admiration of Marx, and in *Beyond the Chains of Illusions* (1962) he compared Marx with Freud. This theme was also articulated in *Escape from Freedom* (1941), in which he suggested that human beings, when finding themselves incapable of handling their freedom, escape to ideologies like fascism.

Fromm's concern about the individual was, in most of his writings, centered on the concept of identity and need (1955). Identity is the process by which one's personality is forged not by being someone, but by belonging to someone. He also proposed that people have extra-biological needs: the need for creative outlets, for natural roots, to define one's own identity, and for a frame of reference. Fromm was responsible for the formulation of a new idea: It is not the individual who is sick, but a certain kind of society that makes people sick. He argued that mental or emotional sickness in individuals is brought about by a sick society.

According to Fromm, social character is cultivated in an individual during childhood by the cultural prescriptions of child rearing. He argued that social character is formed during the developmental phases and is structured by the interaction between psychological, cultural, macroeconomic, and technical bases of society. When social character makes demands on the individual that are unfulfilling to his or her extra-biological needs, a "sickness" ensues.

Herbert Marcuse became interested in psychoanalytic theory later in life. Trained in Hegelian and Marxist thought, he sought a synthesis between Marxism and Freudian psychoanalysis. For Marcuse, the Freudian concept of the unconscious was important, given that his concern with human consciousness predated his interest in psychoanalysis. The unconscious, he believed, could be used to view the fundamental conflicts in society.

Marcuse (1966) also extended the Freudian intrapsychic process of repression and the reality principle in his creation of two new concepts: surplus repression and performance principle. Surplus repression was an extension of Marx's concept of *surplus value*, which refers to profits made through the exploitation of a person's labor. Surplus repression is an intrapsychic process whereby repression is used to justify the domination of one group (class) over another. In this he discussed the quantification of human relationships that facilitated a certain social order (capitalism). The *performance principle*, Marcuse's term for Freud's reality principle, is a process by which "body and mind are made into instruments of alienated labor" (Marcuse, 1966, p. 46). In his discussion of the performance principle, Robinson (1969, pp. 205–206) observed:

> (The) desexualization of the body resulted in a radical reduction of man's potential for pleasure. . . . Libido became concentrated in one part of the body, namely the genitals, in order to have the rest of the body free for use as an instrument of labor.

In an earlier version of *Eros and Civilization* (1955), Marcuse also argued that the story of Oedipus became popular in the Western world because it sustained the patriarchal family, as did the story of Prometheus because it supported the performance principle. The stories of Narcissus

| TABLE 7.7 | Areas of Difference Between the Marxians and the Freudians | |
| --- | --- | --- |

| Conflicts | Marxian | Freudian |
| --- | --- | --- |
| Sources | Class conflicts<br>Ideological conflicts<br>"Sick society" | Intrapsychic conflicts<br>Sexual conflicts<br>"Sick individual" |
| Focus | Society: Its class structure | Individual: His or her<br>psychic structure |
| **Inequality, due to** | | |
| Social class | Main concern (alienated labor) | Ignored |
| Gender | Secondary concern | Primary concern<br>("anatomy is destiny") |
| Age | Secondary concern | Primary concern<br>(identification and transference) |
| Disability | Another main concern ("from each<br>according to his ability, to each<br>according to his need") | An important concern<br>(disturbances of body<br>image—"sick individual") |
| Race/ethnicity | Translated to problem of class—<br>Is this a have or have-not<br>group? | Translated to disturbances of<br>body image—problems of<br>identification |
| Origin of human<br>problems | Role in production process<br>Ownership of means of production | Psychosexual adjustment |

(used by Freud to describe neurotic self-love called narcissism) and Orpheus "the voice that does not command but sings" were unpopular because they were too far from the "reality principle" that supports the work ethic (Marcuse, 1966, p. 161).

For most theorists in the Freudian mainstream, the pleasure principle is seen as undesirable and must be held in check by the reality principle. For Marcuse, the pleasure principle is held in check by performance principle, which, in turn, is a source of human suffering. The slogan "make love, not war," used by student rebels in the 1960s, was based on Marcuse's writing.

In their efforts to synthesize the works of Marx and Freud, the Freudian Left has drawn analogies between the two theorists. Although both are, in fact, conflict theorists, there are numerous differences that we highlight here. Table 7.7 summarizes the differences between the two theoretical orientations.

## CONTEMPORARY ISSUES

One of the most controversial and divisive debates in contemporary psychodynamic thought relates to the issue of repressed memories of childhood sexual abuse. In Freud's early clinical work with hysterical conversion, he became convinced that repressed memories were based on real experiences of sexual molestation by a parent, other adult, or older sibling. Child sexual abuse, at that time, was not a topic that was openly discussed or acknowledged. Some now contend that Freud's retraction of his initial "seduction theory" was based on peer pressure rather than on his own misgivings that the "memories" of abuse were his own constructions

(S. L. Bloom, 1995; Rockwell, 1995). Others have clearly documented the basis for his doubts and, using Freud's own writings, have demonstrated the coercive nature of the methods he used to elicit such memories (Crews, 1995; Esterson, 1983; MacMillan, 1991; Pendergrast, 1996; Schimek, 1987). His later revision portrayed the act of molestation as an incestuous fantasy rather than a real occurrence. In his subsequent writings, he held that children fantasize about sex with their parents and repress, instead, this fantasy. Articles and books by psychoanalyst Jeffrey Masson and others have charged that Freud turned his back on what he knew to be actual abuse because of censure from the psychoanalytic community (Masson, 1984, 1990).

This debate initially created major rifts within the fields of social work, psychology, and psychiatry, with both clinicians and researchers often finding themselves polarized by their strongly held personal beliefs. Due to our growing awareness of the reality of childhood sexual abuse, many have uncritically accepted the claim that memories of such abuse are routinely repressed or dissociated (Bass & Davis, 1995; Benatar, 1995; Blume, 1990; Bradshaw, 1992). Despite this belief, there is little if any scientific evidence to support this position.

In a thorough review of the literature, Robbins (1995, 2002, 2007); found that theories of repressed trauma are supported only by retrospective case studies, similar to those used by Freud. Case studies, although valuable in their own right, should not be confused with validated scientific findings. The few studies that initially were believed to provide evidence of repression (Briere & Conte, 1993; Herman & Schatzow, 1987; Loftus, Polonsky, & Fullilove, 1994; Williams, 1994) are restricted by serious methodological limitations (Robbins, 1995). A number of studies (Grassian & Holtzen, 1996; Herman & Harvey, 1996; Kluft, 1996; Whitfield, 1996) claimed to provide scientific evidence of repression or dissociation. These claims are questionable, however, due to the methodological limitations inherent in the retrospective nature of the research (Robbins, 1995, 2002).

This does not mean, however, that childhood abuse cannot be forgotten and later remembered; clearly, in some cases, it can. The question that remains to be answered is whether forgotten memories of abuse are due to processes involving repression or dissociation, as proposed by contemporary traumatologists, or if they are due to a variety of more common processes related to delayed recall. Significantly, in a review of 60 years of research, Holmes (1990) was unable to find any controlled studies that supported the concept of repression. Although we cannot yet rule out the possibility of repression, neither can we confirm its existence. To test the repression/dissociation hypothesis, we need well-designed studies that are conducted with methodological rigor.

Unfortunately, those who voiced skepticism about widespread repression were often accused of being in denial (in the true Freudian sense) and of engaging in antifeminist backlash that seeks to deny the reality of childhood abuse. Robbins (1995), however, has pointed out that the issue of child sexual abuse and the debate about recovered memories are, in fact, two distinct issues: one is about the reality of abuse that has now been widely documented, whereas the other is about the existence of repression and the reliability of memories that are "recovered" through abreactive techniques or spontaneous environmental cues.

This debate was fueled by hundreds of retractors who claim that their therapists used suggestive and coercive methods to evoke false memories of abuse. Perhaps even more troubling is the fact that a growing number of women claimed that their therapists ignored their accounts of remembered abuse, while digging for repressed memories. This has been damaging not only to the clients themselves but also to their families. The False Memory Syndrome Foundation, a support and advocacy organization that promotes and sponsors scientific research on memory, has been a source of support to families who claim that they have been falsely accused.

Due to the emotionally charged nature of this controversy, as well as the numerous lawsuits that it spawned, it is critical that social workers learn about memory and avoid the use of techniques that are likely to evoke specious memories. Significantly, a 1996 National Association of Social Workers' (NASW) policy on recovered memories cautioned social work practitioners that the therapist's opinions, suggestions, and techniques can have a significant influence on their clients' impressions and beliefs.

During the last decade, much of the research in this field has taken a different approach, and researchers are now examining the ways in which false memories can be created (Bjorklund, 2000; Gallo & Seamon, 2004; Schacter, 1999; A. K. Thomas & Loftus, 2002). It is essential that social workers be familiar with the most current research in this area as there is now a growing consensus that therapy aimed at recovering memory is not scientifically sound. Issuing a cautionary note, Robbins, paraphrasing D. B. Klein (1977), suggested that "we must avoid confusing what a theorist has merely claimed or believed with what s/he has actually proved or demonstrated" (1995, p. 483).

A contemporary application of object relations theory can be seen in the field of addictions. Efforts to explain alcoholism, other forms of substance abuse, adult children of alcoholics, as well as a variety of bad habits and compulsive behaviors that are now termed *addictive disorders*, have led to a widening popularity of object relations theory (Wood, 1987). The popular (albeit simplistic) notions of the "dysfunctional family" and "codependency" fit well with theories that trace current illnesses and pathologies back to the family of origin and failures in pre-Oedipal development. In the last two decades, contemporary psychodynamic theory has been embraced by addiction specialists and persons in recovery who seek insight into the genesis of their "damaged selves" (Wood, 1987). Consequently, theoretical concepts derived from psychodynamic thought have become enmeshed in self-help ideology and popular psychology. Kaminer (1993) has argued that the willingness to label all life problems as symptoms of a disease and to attribute bad parenting as its cause, seriously impedes efforts to identify and address serious patterns of abuse and human suffering. We point out that such ideology is not only reductionistic and deterministic but also antithetical to the strengths perspective in social work practice.

Finally, there has been a renewed interest in the relational paradigm, and Borden (2000) has suggested that despite its problematic aspects, there is potential to "enlarge the concepts of the person, relationship, social environment and psychosocial intervention in continued development of theory, research and practice methods" (pp. 370–371). Groundbreaking work by Siegel (2001) is likely to generate a continued interest in further development and refinement of attachment theory.

## APPLICATION TO SOCIAL WORK PRACTICE

Psychodynamic theory has provided a substantial core of knowledge about intrapsychic and interpersonal behavior that has been applied to social work practice for more than half a century. Emphasis on the individual and on Freudian psychoanalysis led to the embracing of diagnostic casework and functional casework in the late 1920s and mid-1930s, respectively. Diagnostic casework rested on the metaphor of "diagnosis and treatment," while functional casework rejected the illness metaphor and believed in the human capacity for problem solving and the capacity for growth.

By the 1950s the newer concepts of ego psychology broadened our theoretical base. More recent contributions of object relations theory and self-psychology continue to add to this rich heuristic tradition. Although it is no longer the predominant theory used in practice, psychodynamic theory, alone and in combination with other theories, has produced enduring practice models. One does not have to embrace psychodynamic theory as a basic paradigm to acknowledge its contributions, such as knowledge about defense mechanisms and stages of human development. In addition, much of the information that we gather in contemporary psychosocial histories is a direct outgrowth of these theories.

## Definition of the Helping Situation

The theories presented here offer five potential definitions of helping. The theories of Freud and most mainstream theorists (both traditional and contemporary) rely on the definition of the *patient* as *sick*. In their focus on the pathologies of psychosis, neurosis, narcissism, borderline personality, and other character disorders, they are based on the medical model of illness that mandates treatment by an expert therapist.

In contrast, ego psychology most often leads to a definition of *problem* or *growth*, inasmuch as people are seen as inherently adaptive and able to change their situations through their own will or creative self, if provided the opportunity.

The Freudian Left, on the other hand, is primarily based on a social issues definition. While specific individuals may have problems, they are usually defined within the context of the larger society. Thus, it is the "sick society" or social structure that creates the sick individual. We note here that some ideas from the Freudian Left were embraced by the feminist movement in the 1970s and 1980s and led, in part, to the development of "gender consciousness," resulting, for example, in feminist support groups and shelters for battered women. However, the definition here partially switches from social issues to one of self-help. Flowcharts 7.1 and 7.2 demonstrate applications of contemporary psychodynamic theory and theories of the Freudian Left.

## Assessment, Practice Strategies, and Methods

Clinical assessment derived from these theories would include detailed psychosocial histories emphasizing family history and constellation, developmental history, sibling relationships, emotional development, memories of early childhood, and current functioning, at a minimum. Dreams and projective tests may also be used.

Treatment is generally a form of insight-oriented therapy with individuals, small groups, and families, and the primary focus is on uncovering unconscious feelings and motives for behavior. In recent times, techniques such as hypnosis and guided imagery have been used to evoke abreaction of childhood traumas. Transference is typically used as a therapeutic device to counter resistance. Depending on the therapist's specific orientation, free association and dream analysis may be used. Some approaches may also include an educational focus aimed at the adaptation of social demands and needs. In self-psychology, empathic mirroring is used to help the client attain a cohesive self. Table 7.8 illustrates a variety of settings and applications of psychodynamic theory.

## CRITICAL ANALYSIS
### Biological, Psychological, and Spiritual Factors

Psychodynamic theories are primarily concerned with internal psychological processes. Although these theories largely stem from biological foundations (drives of sex and aggression), they ignore current empirical knowledge about the infant's biological development. As Rossi (1981) has

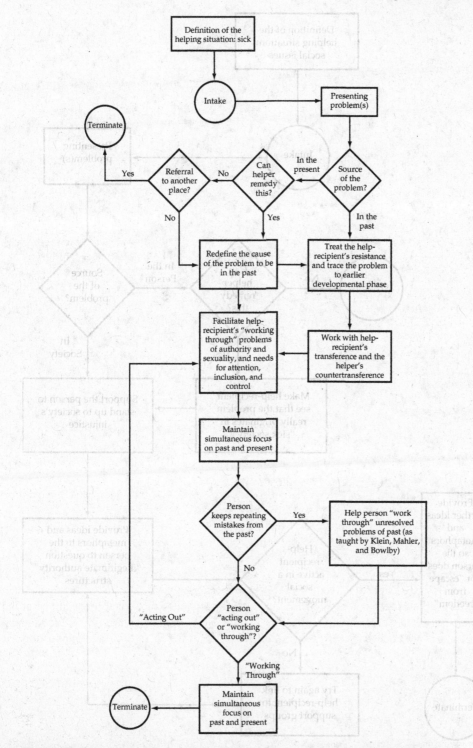

**FLOWCHART 7.1.** An example of pathways in contemporary psychodynamic treatment.
© 2004, S. P. Robbins, P. Chatterjee, & E. R. Canda.

**FLOWCHART 7.2.** An example of pathways from the Freudian Left. © 1998, S. P. Robbins, P. Chatterjee, & E. R. Canda.

| TABLE 7.8 | Various Settings and Applications of Psychodynamic Theories | | | |
| --- | --- | --- | --- | --- |
| **Type of Agency** | **Type of Presenting Problem(s)** | **Type of Program** | **Definition(s) of the Helping Situation** | **Type(s) of Activities** |
| Private practice | Intense sense of shame and guilt | Individual psychotherapy | Problem, Deviance Crisis | Personal history taking; talk therapy; catharsis |
| Mental health center | Anxiety disorder | Individual psychotherapy | Problem, Deviance Crisis | Medication as needed; psychoanalysis of repressed impulses; talk therapy |
| Mental health center | Low self-esteem | Group psychotherapy | Problem Deviance | Mutually reflective dialogue; esteem-building group exercises; dissolving defense mechanisms |
| Family services agency | Parent–child conflict | Family therapy | Problem Growth | Family dialogue; ventilation of feelings; analysis of family psychodynamics |

pointed out, the neurological connections necessary for representational thought are not present in the pre-Oedipal stage. Physiological factors such as myelinization of brain matter must be considered when evaluating the validity of intrapsychic theories. Thus, constructs such as "ego" and emotions of "envy" are inconsistent with empirical evidence about brain development in early infancy. Rossi argued that an ego or sense of self, cannot exist in the absence of cortical functioning.

The emphasis in most psychodynamic theory is on the unconscious, on intrapsychic structures and processes, and on developmental tasks in infancy and early childhood. Most also emphasize pathology rather than normalcy. There is some variation, however, as ego psychologists as well as theorists writing in the Adlerian and Jungian tradition emphasize adaptation and competence.

Despite the internal focus, there is little attempt among the theorists discussed here (with the exception of Jung) to address spiritual concerns. In *Future of an Illusion* (1961), Freud argued against what he considered to be the irrational and unverifiable beliefs of religious systems. He held that religious ideas develop as a psychological defense against anxiety aroused by the awesome and sometimes destructive power of nature as well as by the problems generated by society itself. He astutely observed, however, that such beliefs can promote immaturity of development, irrationality, and justification for social problems and prejudices. He recommended rationality and scientific inquiry as healthy alternatives to religion.

Although these insights are important, there are serious flaws in his arguments that demonstrate an underlying Eurocentric bias and a superficial and insulting portrayal of tribal and totemic belief systems. First, his concept of religion was limited to a narrow interpretation of the Judeo-Christian context. Because of this, he failed to recognize that not all religious claims are held beyond question. Mystical traditions, for example, emphasize that faith be rooted in direct experiential confirmation. We discuss this in more detail in Chapter 13. Second, in his position that rationality is the highest form of cognition, he ignored other cognitive modes such as intuition and holistic thinking. Finally, he reduced all religious behavior and experience to defense mechanisms based on childish feelings of helplessness and anxiety.

Recognizing these limitations, Jung, in fact, had criticized Freudian and Adlerian theories for being one-sided: "It is psychology without the psyche, and thus it suits people who think they have no spiritual needs or aspirations" (Jung, 1984, p. 198). Some contemporary trends in psychoanalytic thought, however, are more congenial to religion and spirituality. Author M. Scott Peck, for example, has written a series of popular books that combine insights from Freudian theory with his own version of nondenominational Christianity. His first book, *The Road Less Traveled* (1978), set a record for number of weeks on the best-seller list.

## Social, Cultural, and Economic Forces

Due to the heavy emphasis on intrapsychic processes, most mainstream reformulators do not adequately address social, cultural, or economic forces. There is slight variation, however, with A. Adler's and Horney's focus on structural aspects of gender inequality and status superiority, Chodorow's focus on power disparities, H. S. Sullivan's interpersonal focus, and Kohut's recognition of societal changes. Despite this, psychodynamic theories retain a largely psychological focus, with primary attention paid to developmental tasks in childhood or infancy.

In contrast, the Freudian Left places its primary emphasis on the impact of the social, economic, and political structure on individual personality. The Marxian influence adds the economic dimension that is usually absent in psychodynamic thought.

## Relevance to Individuals, Groups, Families, Organizations, Institutions, and Communities

The primary focus in most psychodynamic theory is on the individual. Specific contextual focus is placed on the mother-child dyad. Theorists acknowledge the contextual setting of society to varying degrees but focus primarily on the individual within that context. Despite this, psychodynamic thought has been widely applied to small groups, particularly in the context of group therapy. It has also been applied to organizations and societies in an attempt to explain pathology at the macro level.

In contrast, the Freudian Left often focuses simultaneously on the society and the individual within the context of a specific economic and political order (capitalistic democracy) and social structure (patriarchy).

## CONSISTENCY WITH SOCIAL WORK VALUES AND ETHICS

Psychodynamic theory has made some important contributions that are consistent with social work values. Freud, for example, emphasized the importance of psychosexual development at a time when "polite society" wished to keep sexuality from public view and discussion. Countering the prevailing view that human behavior is rational and volitional, Freud pointed out that people do not often fully understand their own motivations. Further, when Christians sought religious hegemony over the world, Freud criticized the hypocrisy, confused thinking, and irrational dogmatism of religion in general and Christianity in particular.

Despite these contributions, mainstream Freudian thought is riddled with problems that run counter to many social work values. The overriding focus of most psychodynamic theory is on pathology rather than well-being and on deficiency rather than strengths. H. Johnson (1991) for example, has noted the tendency in psychodynamic theory to adultomorphize and pathomorphize. She argued that theorists incorrectly use characteristics of adults as their basis for inferred infant experiences and ascribe to normal infants the later states of adult pathology. Further, the prescribed role of the expert therapist, especially the power imbalance that is endemic to maintaining expert authority in the helping relationship, does not fit well with client self-determination. Similarly, it does not fit well with empowerment practice.

In addition, the Freudian view of women is not, to say the least, a very positive one. Freud characterized women as deficient—biologically, morally, and interpersonally. He attributed their failures in life to their biology, and their failure as mothers to their weak personality structure (rooted in their biology). While most contemporary theorists reject his ideas about female deficiency, some have tried to defend him by arguing that he was merely reflecting, in his analysis, the prevailing views of women at that period in time (Freeman & Strean, 1987; Mitchell, 1974).

We note here that while Freud may indeed have been a product of his time, and that his views were shared by many, other theorists writing in the same time period were able to shed the blinders of sexism that so constrained his view of women. Although there have been corrective efforts with the advent of ego psychology and feminist reformulations, there is little evidence that most psychodynamic theorists adhere to a pro-feminist stance. The tendency to pathologize women—particularly mothers—remains a central problem for psychodynamic theory.

Surprisingly, perhaps, Freud's view of homosexuality was not as negative as his view of femininity. Inasmuch as he fully accepted the bisexual nature of the infant, he saw homosexuality as a developmental fixation that resulted in the retention of polymorphous perversity. Freud defined homosexuality in terms of unresolved Oedipal conflict and, in the case of male homosexuality, possible anal fixation (J. Mills, 1990). He did not, however, necessarily equate this with neuroses or psychological disorder. Contemporary psychoanalytic views of homosexuality attempt to integrate the conclusion that homosexuality is (a) a normal, adaptive behavior with (b) the view that homosexuality is, nonetheless, a product of "conflicted libidinal wishes and deficiencies due to early developmental disturbance in object relations" (J. Mills, 1990, p. 916).

Importantly, psychodynamic theories do not adequately address diversity. Due to their inherently intrapsychic and interpersonal focus, issues of diversity in race, ethnicity, culture, and social class (to name a few) are largely ignored. The exceptions here are the theories derived from the Freudian Left. These theories, however, have not received much attention in the social work literature.

Clearly, from a social work perspective, the complexity of human behavior and the internal, interactional, and environmental factors that shape the individual cannot and should not be reduced to intrapsychic processes and early childhood experiences. However, in the dialectical sense, we also argue that they cannot be ignored as they are part of the larger puzzle of both normal and pathological development.

## PHILOSOPHICAL UNDERPINNINGS

Despite the wide variety of theorists writing from a psychodynamic perspective, shared philosophical assumptions are apparent throughout. While authors may give varying weight to the role of the environment, their focus is primarily intrapersonal. That is, they believe that human behavior can be best understood through the study of psychological phenomena such as intrapsychic structures, drives transformed into psychological needs, psychical processes, and so on. Further, most attribute adult pathology to developmental failures in early childhood. In doing so, they promote a deterministic and reductionistic view of people, one that leaves little room for growth and change without professional help.

Some, such as Freud and Kernberg, are even more narrowly deterministic, suggesting that "biology is destiny." Determinism can be found, however, at many levels. The interpersonal focus of self-psychology and most object relations theorists place blame on the mother–child relationship and vilifies mother for her inability to meet the child's needs. In fact, most of the theories in this group simultaneously reify and vilify mother. They bestow on her almost omnipotent powers in shaping the child, then blame her for failing to do a good job. This, perhaps, is not surprising as ambivalence toward mother is an intrinsic feature of, perhaps, both the theories and the theorists. We have suggested previously that theories are often extensions of the histories, attitudes, and beliefs of their authors.

Although some theorists implicitly assume a rather dismal view of the human infant (greedy, aggressive, self-serving), others are more optimistic about the nature of self and the potential for free will. Most, however, implicitly assume that intrapersonal conflict or struggle is a necessary part of development—especially the development of morality (superego).

Finally, there is an underlying assumption that the problems people encounter create a state of illness that requires professional help. In the context of this professional help, incremental changes based on insight are considered to be desirable. Sudden change is not trustworthy and may be seen as a prelude to another form of acting out or regression.

Although it is rarely addressed in the social work literature, there is a coercive nature embedded in traditional psychodynamic thought. Because the analyst or therapist has the expertise (i.e., power) to reinterpret and define our true motivations (which are hidden to us), any attempt at disavowing, disproving, or criticizing their constructs is defined as denial or pathology on our part. Given the power superior position of the therapist, the patient's ability to question the validity of the concepts being applied is nullified.

In traditional psychoanalysis it is further assumed that all psychoanalytic practitioners must go through analysis themselves to become aware of their own unconscious conflicts that may impact their therapeutic relationships. Traditional psychoanalysis is assumed to be a lifelong process, as the unconscious conflict is lifelong as well.

## METHODOLOGICAL ISSUES AND EMPIRICAL SUPPORT

Rooted in positivism and the scientific method, psychodynamic theory presents numerous methodological problems, not the least of which are the ideas of unconscious motivation and repression.

Although empirical evidence of the unconscious has been found in post-hypnotic suggestion and parapraxes (Freudian "slips of the tongue") (Corsini & Marsella, 1983), the influence of the unconscious on behavior has yet to be proved.

In a thorough review of recent empirical studies on psychoanalytic theory, H. Johnson (1991) looked at two types of studies—those on defense mechanisms and those on subliminal psychodynamic activation. Studies on defense mechanisms have yielded mixed results, at best, and they have not demonstrated that unconscious processes work to constrain our impulses. Rather, the methodological constraints of psychodynamic constructs render them difficult, if not impossible, to measure. Inasmuch as they are unobservable processes, they must be inferred and are not available for empirical verification. H. Johnson noted that while adaptive mechanisms may be used in coping, "the study of such psychological mechanisms does not require the theoretical framework of psychoanalysis" (1991, p. 416).

Studies of subliminal techniques are often referred to as *Oneness Studies* based on their stimulus message "Mommy and I are One." Reviewing the results of more than seventy studies of this type, H. Johnson concluded that while "the notion of an unconscious mental life (is supported) . . . it would be stretching this finding to infer that . . . particular unresolved conflicts give rise to specific kinds of clinical pathology" (1991, p. 414). Further, the concept of repression has failed to find support in any controlled studies (Holmes, 1990).

Historically, validation from clinical observations was considered sufficient by the analytic community. Well-constructed empirical studies were rare and, when conducted, would often yield little if any support for the efficacy of analytically oriented therapy. Despite this, most mainstream theorists remain committed to the psychodynamic paradigm and some contend that case studies are sufficient for the purpose of validation. In his later years Freud himself eschewed scientific support and believed that "his theory needed no validation" (cited in Torrey, 1993, p. 216).

H. Johnson's (1991) review of empirical studies in developmental psychology, however, raised serious questions about the validity of psychodynamic constructs. In contrast to the narcissistic omnipotence, fusion, and nondifferentiation of pre-Oedipal infants portrayed in contemporary psychodynamic literature, current research shows them to be perceptually complex, active initiators with distinct preferences who are responsive to their environment at an early age. In addition, H. Johnson noted that "far from being 'fused,' they appear to sense their ability to alter the behavior of others" (p. 418). A related but perhaps more basic issue is the fact that there is little if any empirical evidence to support the existence of the proposed stages. A. Kohn (1991) has also noted that research has demonstrated that personality is not necessarily formed at an early age.

Overriding problems cited in most empirical studies on psychodynamic constructs are serious methodological flaws, including problems in experimental design, inconsistent results, questionable measurement procedures and instruments, a failure to consistently establish interrater reliability, and problems with operational definitions (H. Johnson, 1991).

Masson's resurrection of Freud's seduction theory has created a burgeoning literature on repressed trauma. It has also led to several works that evaluate the scientific basis of Freudian theory (Crews, 1995; S. Fisher & Greenberg, 1996; MacMillan, 1991; Pendergrast, 1996; Torrey, 1993). Not surprisingly, studies have consistently failed to support most of Freud's main ideas about the centrality of childhood experiences in determining adult personality and psychopathology. Although S. Fisher and Greenberg (1977, 1996) have claimed to find support for several Freudian concepts, a close examination of their methodology and data suggests that these claims cannot be taken for granted. Many of the studies cited are based solely on clinical validation of psychoanalytic concepts and involve subjective judgments made by psychoanalytically oriented therapists who are predisposed to provide confirmatory evidence.

More recently, limited empirical support has been found for transference-focused therapy and mentalization-based therapy, both of which utilize psychodynamic principles (Bateman & Fonagy, 2008, 2009; Clarkin, Levy, Lenzenweger, & Kernberg, 2007; Levy et al., 2006). In addition, a few meta-analytic studies have found lasting positive changes that increased with time in patients who underwent psychodynamic therapy (de Maat, de Jonghe, Schoevers, & Dekker, 2009; Shedler, 2010). Given the lengthy history of psychodynamic therapy and the limited empirical support that it has garnered over the last 100 years, additional research is needed to support the efficacy of these methods.

All of the theories discussed here are better at explanation than prediction; better at a probabilistic level of explanation than a deterministic level; and better suited for explaining properties of individuals than properties of groups, with the exception of the Freudian Left, whose theories are well suited for both. In addition, deviant case analysis is often necessary for explanation of cases that run contrary to theoretical propositions.

## Summary

Early psychodynamic theory found broad appeal in diagnostic and functional casework and group work. Although this appeal has waned in recent years, the contemporary offshoots of object relations and self-psychology have again gained acceptance, primarily in the field of addictions and in some psychiatric settings.

Given the diversity among the theorists writing from a psychodynamic stance, we anticipate a strong appeal for specific theorists, if not for the group of theories as a whole. Jungian psychology, for example, has had a small but steady following for years and has been an important influence on transpersonal theory (discussed in more detail in Chapter 13).

Although the Freudian Left has not received much attention in social work practice, the fusion of Marx and Freud may appeal to those with a more sociological orientation. Their combined emphasis on personality and social structure parallels, in some ways, Chodorow's concerns.

With her psychoanalytic feminist synthesis, Chodorow has been a seminal influence in the growth of "gender difference" theories and may appeal to many who are interested in women's psychology or in the genesis of the "gendered personality." J. K. Gardiner (1987) suggested that feminists may also find Kohut's self-psychology appealing as it "points to empathy, creativity, love, and humor as characteristics of the mature self" (p. 245).

Finally, the creative, adaptive self in ego psychology may likely appeal to many. H. Hartmann's definition of adaptation is a foundation concept in Germain and Gitterman's ecosystems theory (Chapter 2), widely used in contemporary social work practice.

# Theories of Life Span Development

> *He's getting a little thicker*
> *'round the middle now, aren't we all?*
> *His long hair's getting grey*
> *and I can see the back roads in his face,*
> *It's weathered by the rain that he's seen fall.*
>
> © BILL MUSE
> 2 MUSES (ASCAP)

## THEORIES OF LIFE SPAN DEVELOPMENT

- describe processes of individual growth and development over the life cycle
- delineate stages of development that correspond to specific age periods
- focus on the individual's mastery of skills and tasks
- are useful in formulating assessment and intervention plans for individuals, families, and small groups

The content on gay and lesbian development was coauthored by Mende Snodgress, JD, LCSW and Barbara Becker, MPH. The section on shame resilience theory was authored by Brené Brown, PhD (© 2004), and is used here with her permission. The section on bisexual identity development was authored by Tom Brown, MS, PsyD.

Theories of life span development examine a wide variety of factors that contribute to developmental processes and outcomes over the life span. Some theories address the entire life cycle from birth to death, whereas others focus on specific stages such as infancy or old age. Most address the mastery of skills and tasks related to biological, psychological, and social development associated with specific age periods.

## HISTORICAL CONTEXT

Early concepts of life stages can be found in Eastern and Western religious thought. The Talmud described 14 stages, detailing a progression of development that encompasses religious, moral, and cognitive learning as well as desired social roles and psychological traits. For example, age 5 is delineated for reading scripture, age 13 for assuming moral responsibility, age 15 for abstract reasoning, age 20 for seeking a livelihood, age 60 for becoming an elder, and age 80 for demonstrating special wisdom (Levinson, 1978, p. 325).

Sanskrit scholars depicted six stages of humanity: *Saisav*, childhood and the time of innocence; *Kaisore*, late childhood and adolescence and the time for learning; *Yauvan*, early adulthood and the time for marriage and occupation; *Gaarhastha*, the time for raising a family; *Vaanaprastha*, the beginning of disengagement from life; and *Sanyas*, the completion of disengagement and preparation for union with cosmic spirit. Literary references to life stages can also be found in Shakespeare's *As You Like It*, in which he portrayed the world as a stage, men as players with many parts, and "acts being seven ages," from infancy to old age and senility.

Scientific theories of life span development emerged in the early 20th century with Sigmund Freud's theory of psychosexual development and G. Stanley Hall's study of adolescence, published in 1904. Hall emphasized the biological basis of adolescent development and characterized it as a time of turbulence, or "storm and stress" (Santrock, 1989).

Traditional theories emphasized developmental tasks during infancy, childhood, and adolescence and characterized adulthood as a period of stability. Early theories portrayed personality and character traits formed in childhood as the determining factors of adult adjustment and functioning. In contrast, contemporary theories, sometimes known as the life cycle perspective, focus on change during adult years and recognize the potential for growth and development throughout life. Although they reject the notion that childhood experiences determine later life, they acknowledge the role of early development as a foundation for adulthood (Datan, Rodehaver, & Hughes, 1987; Hetherington & Baltes, 1988; Santrock, 2005). Interest in adult development and the life cycle (or life span) perspective is relatively new and has emerged in the latter half of the 20th century (Havighurst, 1972; Santrock, 2005). Friedan (1993) has pointed out that recent interest in adult development is linked to the increase in life expectancy; life expectancy increased by 30 years for men and almost 40 years for women since 1900, when life expectancy was 46 years. Thus, interest in development after early adulthood is a result of longer life.

## KEY CONCEPTS

Central to all theories of life span development are the concepts of growth and development. R. M. Thomas (1985) noted that *growth* usually refers to a "change in size," whereas *development* refers to "change in the complexity and functions of the individual" (p. 39). These terms, however, are often used interchangeably to denote changes in both size and function. Santrock

(1989) expanded this definition by pointing out that in addition to growth, development can include decay and deterioration (as in the process of death).

The nature of human development consists of complex interaction between biological, psychological, and social processes. These processes involve changes in physical structure and function and changes in perception, cognition, emotion, reasoning, personality, language, and relationships with others. They are interwoven and interdependent and are impacted by both genetic inheritance and environmental factors.

Life span theories usually divide the life cycle into age-related stages or phases. Approximate age "bands" are used to define the beginning and end of each stage. Although theorists vary in their descriptions of tasks related to each stage, most are in close agreement with Santrock's (1989) delineation of developmental periods: *prenatal* (conception to birth), *infancy* (birth to 18 or 24 months), *early childhood* (18 or 24 months to 5 or 6 years), *middle and late childhood* (6–11 years), *adolescence* (10 or 12 to 18 or 22 years), *early adulthood* (18 to early 20s to 30s), *middle adulthood* (35 or 45 to 45 or 65 years), and *late adulthood* (60 or 70 years to death).

In an analysis of life span research in developmental psychology, Baltes (1973, 1987) delineated additional characteristics of the life span approach. Development is seen as contextual, multidirectional, and malleable. The social, cultural, economic, political, physical, and biological contexts that shape development theoretically allow for numerous paths and directions as well as opportunities for change. As development takes place over the entire life span, no one period or stage is necessarily dominant. Further, many believe that the multidimensional aspects of development (biological, psychological, and social) necessitate a multidisciplinary and interdisciplinary approach. Finally, human development is embedded in a historical context and must be viewed in relation to historical events that shape the context of society.

As Neugarten (1985) has noted, however, the terms *life span* and *life course* (which are sometimes seen as synonymous) differ in their basic intellectual concerns and foci. Life span, as used by psychologists, focuses on the inner life, while life course, as used by sociologists, "emphasizes turning points when the 'social persona' undergoes change," such as "age-sex-related role transitions" (p. 297).

As already noted, life span theories encompass numerous aspects of development. The primary focus of this chapter is on theories of personality and social development from a psychological perspective, many of which build on the works of Sigmund Freud and Erik Erikson. We include here basic information on physical development throughout the life cycle and suggest that more complete content can be found in textbooks that focus exclusively on life cycle development.

Other theories of human development (cognitive, moral, phenomenological, symbolic interactionist, behavioral, and transpersonal) are discussed in the following chapters. We realize that this division is somewhat artificial, given the interrelatedness of developmental processes. It does, however, reflect the nature of theory development in academic disciplines that are increasingly specialized and somewhat fragmented. We strongly agree with Baltes (1973), however, that the study of human behavior mandates a multi- and interdisciplinary approach.

## THEORETICAL KNOWLEDGE ABOUT PHYSICAL DEVELOPMENT

Our knowledge about biological, physical, and motor development is increasingly linked to technological advances in genetics, neurophysiology, neurotransmission, biochemistry, and medicine. Traditional research, based on clinical observations and physiological studies with animals, has been greatly advanced by technology that now allows us to study in utero development, biochemical processes of the brain, and genetic predisposition to a variety of diseases. Consequently, our knowledge about prenatal development, the perceptual and cognitive abilities of infants, brain functioning, disease, and aging processes has advanced greatly in the last 25 years. It is safe to anticipate that there will be similar, if not greater, advances in the coming decades as well.

It is important to note that the physical changes described here are not based on an inevitable universal pattern of growth and decay. Rather, they reflect a pattern of development typical of persons living in modern industrial and postindustrial societies. There is wide variation in "normal" human aging, and cross-cultural research has shown that it is the interaction between our genetic endowment and our social, cultural, and physical environment that determines how we age.

As Eaton (1989–1990, p. 86) noted, "In the U.S. our expectations about aging are based on parochial and inaccurate ideas. Many of the older Americans we see are handicapped by chronic illnesses and the culturally sanctioned disuse of their mental and physical facilities." Changes in diet, fitness, and lifestyle will likely produce older people who are "more fit, less constrained and more involved." Given this caveat, Tables 8.1 and 8.2 summarize current knowledge about biological, physical, and motor development over the life span and the critical periods during infancy and childhood that provide windows of opportunity for the development of vision, feelings, language, and movement.

## THEORETICAL KNOWLEDGE ABOUT SEXUAL DEVELOPMENT

As discussed in Chapter 7, the first theory of childhood sexuality is attributed to Freud (1962/1905) and his essays on the theory of sexuality. Although this theory has been criticized for being unverifiable and for not reflecting the real world of children, he is credited with being the first theorist to acknowledge the existence of childhood sexuality (Santrock, 2008). Kinsey, Pomeroy, and Martin (1948/1998) and Kinsey, Pomeroy, Martin, and Gebhard (1953/1998) published reports that provided initial information on childhood sexuality, although the primary focus of these reports was on adult sexuality. Research conducted by Borneman (1994) and translated from German provided the first systematic look at childhood sexual development, but it was heavily influenced by Freudian thought and has been criticized for its lack of empirical rigor (Okami, Olmstead, & Abramson, 1997).

There was scant research on children's normal sexual development until the 1990s when Friedrich, Grambsch, Broughton, Kulper, and Ubeilke (1991), Friedrich and colleagues (1992), and Friedrich and Trane (2002) conducted longitudinal studies using items from two validated instruments, the Child Behavior Checklist and the Child Sexual Behavior Inventory. This research was an attempt to determine normative sexual behaviors in children aged 2–12 who were not part of a clinical sample and who had no known or confirmed history of sexual abuse. The studies relied on parent's reports of their children's sexual behaviors and provides a valuable information about normal childhood development in preadolescents.

Friedrich et al. (1991, 1992) and Friedrich and Trane (2002) found that, in general, children between 2 and 6 years exhibit a wide range of sexual behaviors and the variability is quite extensive. However, they become more modest as they enter elementary school and the reported frequency of sexual behaviors decreases with age until puberty. Further, they found that children's sexual behaviors are strongly influenced by their family and culture.

| Age | Physical/Biological Changes | Motor Development |
|---|---|---|
| **TABLE 8.1** | Life Span Physical and Motor Development | |
| **Prenatal** | | |
| 1 month | Embryo forms. Beginning of nerve growth. | |
| 2 months | Rudiments of brain and backbone emerge. Ear begins to shape. | Reflexive responses react to stimuli. |
| 3 months | All organs are in place. Nerve cells multiply. Synapses begin to form. | Touch reflex develops on mouth, hands, feet, and eyelids. Fetus's body can jerk, move, and hiccup. |
| 4 months | Synapses develop in brain. Modeling of facial features begins. Eyelids close. | Fetus can frown, squint, grimace, swallow, and suck thumb. |
| 5 months | Nerve cell production slows and cells enlarge and make complex connections. Nerve cells are developing into specialized brain areas. Beginning senses of taste, smell, and hearing. Begins to react to sound. | |
| 6 months | Responds to sound. | Sense of touch develops enough to feel movement. |
| 7 months | Nerve and muscle motivation. More consistent response to sound. Beginning function of optic nerve. Eyelids open. Physical development is almost complete. | |
| 8 months | Neural circuits as advanced as a newborn. Brain scans show periods of dream sleep. Awareness starts at 32 weeks. | Grasping reflex develops. |
| 9 months | Hearing is mature at 35 weeks. Vision improves. | Fetus begins to develop daily activity cycles. |
| **Infancy (birth to 24 months)** | | |
| Newborn | Rapid weight gain. Sensory development (i.e., oral and visual). | Primary reflexes (i.e., moro reflex). Sucking reflex. |
| 1 month | Increase in muscle strength and control. | Reflexive movements of arm, leg, and hand. Rolls partially from side to back. Stares at object—does not reach. |

*(Continued)*

| TABLE 8.1 | Life Span Physical and Motor Development (*Continued*) | |
|---|---|---|
| **Age** | **Physical/Biological Changes** | **Motor Development** |
| 2 months | Increase in hair growth. | Chin up, tries to hold head up. Swipes at objects, holds objects for a few moments. |
| 3 months | | Voluntary control begins to replace reflexes. On tummy, holds chest up briefly. |
| 4 months | Teething. | Turns head in all directions, sits briefly with support. Reaches with arms. |
| 5 months | Increase in hand–eye coordination. | May locomote by rolling, twisting, and rocking. Sits on lap, sits alone momentarily, seated, can grasp object. |
| 7 months | | Sits with light support, balances well. Hands reach for objects, holds two objects—one in each hand. |
| 8 months | Brain growth. | Crawls, pivots. Gets self to sit. Stands and gets down with help. Grasps partially with fingers, clasps hands. |
| 9 months | | Walks while being held by hand. |
| 11 months | | Climbs chairs and tables. Stands alone. Climbs up steps with help. Squats and stoops. Holds crayons and makes marks. |
| 12 months | | Pulls self up to stand. Walks when supported but prefers crawling. Steps off low objects, walks up and down steps with help. Takes covers off containers. Begins to show hand preference. |
| 13 months | | Walks in side-step pattern along furniture (cruises). Moves to rhythms. Pokes, pulls, turns, and twists objects. |
| 14 months | | Stands alone. Climbs stairs on hands and knees. Reaches for objects with smooth motion and no spatial errors. |
| 15 months | | Walks alone, using rapid "running-like" walk. Throws ball. Can open small hinged box. |
| 16 months | | Trots well. Can walk sideways. Squats smoothly. Seats self. |
| 18 months | | Jumps off floor with both feet. Shows hand preference. |
| 19 months | | Climbs onto everything. Fully developed grasp and release. |

| Age | Physical/Biological Changes | Motor Development |
|---|---|---|
| 20 months | | Jumps forward, runs. Hangs from bar grasping with hands. |
| 23 months | | Throws objects overhand. Pedals small bicycle. Strings large beads. |
| 24 months | Development of language. | Walks alone on stairs, can walk backward. Capable of bladder control.<br>Turns book pages, one at a time. Fully developed hand preference. |
| **Early Childhood (2–6 years)** | | |
| 2–3 years | 6 inches average growth.<br>16 pounds average weight gained from 3 to 6 years. | Scribbles, walks rhythmically, jumps, opposes thumb, grasps. |
| 4–4½ years | Muscles undergo more rapid growth than rest of body. | Hops, runs, draws circles.<br>Dresses self. |
| 6–6½ years | First permanent teeth. | Prints name, gallops (if shown how).<br>Walks balance beam.<br>Rises from ground from prone position without use of hands, punches or hits. |
| **Middle and Late Childhood (7–11 years)** | | |
| | Growth of 2–3 inches per year.<br>Weight gain of 3–5 pounds per year.<br>Legs increase in proportionate length.<br>Fat tissue develops more rapidly than muscle.<br>Slimming of trunk. | Throws, swims, climbs, skips rope, skates, rides bicycle.<br>Marked sex differences in gross motor skills.<br>Females develop fine motor skills more rapidly (drawing, penmanship, etc.).<br>Rhythmic skills. |
| **Adolescence/Pubescence (12–15 years)** | | |
| | Maximum growth and abrupt deceleration.<br>Most permanent teeth.<br>Primary sex organs develop rapidly.<br>Hormonal secretion.<br>Pubic hair.<br>Rapid gain in height.<br>Menstruation in females. | Initially may have lack of coordination due to uneven physical development.<br>Motor activity becomes more integrated and coordinated.<br>High physical performance, but with lack of judgment and discretion. |
| **Post-Pubescence (16–18 years)** | | |
| | Height and weight growth slows.<br>Muscular growth increases.<br>Maturation of sex organs.<br>Increase in facial hair in males. | Continued high level of coordination and motor skills. |

(Continued)

| TABLE 8.1 | Life Span Physical and Motor Development (*Continued*) |

| Age | Physical/Biological Changes | Motor Development |
|---|---|---|
| **Early Adulthood (18–30 or 35 years)** | | |
| 18–22 years | Adult proportions reached. High point in vigor and physical fitness. | Continued high level of performance. |
| 22–30 or 35 years | Decrease in height. Increase in body fat. Less physical activity. | |
| **Middle Adulthood (35–60 years)** | | |
| | Vision and hearing begin to decline (high tones, especially in men). Fat accumulation. *Heart and coronary arteries become less efficient. *Loss of elasticity in muscle tone. Settling of joints. Graying. Hair loss. Menopause in females. | Reaction time slows. Fine motor skills continue at a high level, enhanced by experience. Decrease in gross motor skills. |
| **Late Adulthood (60–70 years)** | | |
| | Wrinkled skin. *Hair and teeth loss. *Sensory defects. Continued decrease in height. Bowing of shoulders and back. *Stiffness in joints. *Decreased muscle tone and endurance. *Movement slows. Circulatory system slows. | *Decrease in overall motor control. *Increasing lack of agility (but experience may compensate for decreased physical ability). |
| **Old Age (70 to death)** | | |
| | *Rapid deterioration of the muscles and bones. *Loss of hearing and vision. *Loss of ambulatory functions. Neurological breakdown. Weight loss. | *Loss of coordination and reaction. *Eventual loss of gross and fine motor skills. |

*Source:* Adapted from M. Bloom, 1985; Caplan & Caplan, 1997; Nilsson & Hamberger, 1990; The Princeton Center for Infancy and Early Childhood, 1993.

*Note:* This chart is not a rigid timetable. Some babies develop earlier, some later, and some skip behaviors (i.e., walking without ever crawling).

*Changes may be due to individual genetic predisposition, lifestyle, diet, and/or lack of physical or mental activity.

| TABLE 8.2 | Critical Periods of Development: Windows of Opportunity |
|---|---|

| Area of Development | Approximate Ages of Developmental Windows | |
|---|---|---|
| | **Initial Development** | **Later Development** |
| **Vision** | | |
| Visual acuity | Birth to 4 years | 4 to 8 or 9 years |
| Binocular vision | 4–6 months to 3 years | 3–4 years |
| **Feelings** | | |
| Stress response | Birth to 3½ years | 3½–10 years |
| Empathy and envy | 1½–10 years | 10+ years |
| **Language** | | |
| Syntax and recognition of speech | Birth to 6 years | 6–10 years |
| Second language | Birth to 6 years | After 6 years (with declining ability) |
| Vocabulary | 1½ years onward | Throughout life |
| **Movement** | | |
| Basic motor skills | Birth to 4 years | 4–8 or 9 years |
| Fine motor activity | 2½ or 3 to 10 years | 10–10½ years |

*Source:* Adapted from Nash, 1997.

Tables 8.3 and 8.4 summarize the variety of normal sexual behaviors that American children between ages 2–6 and 7–12 openly display. Table 8.5 shows the most infrequent sexual behaviors in children of all ages. These behaviors are a potential cause for concern because they are relatively infrequent and more closely mimic adult sexual behavior and possible sexual violence.

T. C. Johnson (1999) has urged caution in interpreting children's sexual behaviors because young children do not experience sexuality identically to adults due to significant age-related cognitive and developmental differences. According to him, children's sexual feelings are linked to attachment and sensuality and it is easy to misinterpret the meaning of children's sexual actions when we place adult sexual constructs on child behavior. Although we are now beginning to understand children's sexual development, more research is needed to help us understand the full range of normal and problematic sexual behaviors in children (Rademakers, Laan, & Straver, 2000; Thanasiu, 2004).

## THEORETICAL KNOWLEDGE ABOUT NEUROBIOLOGY AND NEUROTRANSMISSION

As we have seen thus far, most theories of human behavior used in social work examine social and psychological processes and fail to account for the roles of biological processes that are central to human behavior and functioning. Although it is beyond the scope of this book to cover the vast fields of current knowledge about genetics, heritability, brain development, and the complexities of brain functioning, excellent sources for social workers are Saleebey's *Human Behavior and Social Environments: A Biopsychosocial Approach* (2001) and Ginsberg, Nackerud, and Larrison's *Human Biology for Social Workers: Development, Ecology, Genetics &*

**TABLE 8.3**    Normal Child Sexual Behavior Age 2–6

- Touches sex parts at home
- Undresses in front of others
- Sits with crotch exposed
- Kisses nonfamily members
- Touches breasts
- Tries to look at people undressing
- Interest in opposite sex
- Touches sex parts in public
- Shows sex parts to adults
- Looks at nude pictures
- Masturbates with hand
- Shy with strange men
- Walks around in underwear
- Walks around nude
- Shy about undressing
- Pretends to be opposite sex
- Talks flirtatiously
- Overly aggressive, overly passive
- Uses sexual words
- Shows sex parts to children
- Hugs strange adults
- Rubs body against people
- Touches others' sex parts

*Source:* Adapted from Friedrich et al., 1991, 1992; Friedrich & Trane, 2002.

*Health* (2004). In addition, an excellent discussion of brain development and the implications for understanding human behavior can be found in DeMoss's *Brain Waves Through Time: 12 Principles for Understanding the Evolution of the Human Brain and Man's Behavior* (1999). According to him, with the advent of technological advances that allow us to study the brain, scientific research has increasingly shown the central role of the brain in human behavior. As Mohr (2003, p. 113) has noted:

> the brain is the starting point for why and how we process all "mental" information—not just cognitive, but interpersonal communications, self-concept, emotional reactivity, personality, learned responses, etc. Research findings have made it abundantly clear that the brain is the organ of the mind, and one of its products is behavior.

Growing knowledge of the brain and the ways in which brain function affects mood, cognition, and behavior have led to increased interest in the plasticity of the brain and the role of neurotransmitters, the chemicals that carry messages between nerve cells (Beatty, 2001; Cynader &

| TABLE 8.4 | Normal Child Sexual Behavior Age 7–12 |
|---|---|

- Shy with strange men
- Walks around in underwear
- Walks around nude
- Shy about undressing
- Scratches crotch
- Touches sex parts at home
- Undresses in front of others
- Sits with crotch exposed
- Kisses nonfamily adults and children
- Touches breasts
- Tries to look at people undressing
- Interest in opposite sex
- Looks at nude pictures
- Uses sexual words

*Source:* Adapted from Friedrich et al., 1991, 1992; Friedrich & Trane, 2002.

| TABLE 8.5 | Most Infrequent Sexual Behavior for Children |
|---|---|

**Under 4% or less for all ages and for both boys and girls**

- Puts mouth on sex parts
- Asks to engage in sex acts
- Masturbates with an object
- Inserts object into the vagina/anus
- Imitates intercourse
- Makes sexual sounds

*Source:* Adapted from Friedrich, et al. 1991, 1992; Friedrich & Trane, 2002.

Frost, 1999; Elbert, Heim, & Rockstroh, 2001; Le Doux, 2002). Neurotransmission has been linked not only to normal developmental processes but also to psychiatric disorders and substance abuse and dependence. Although research in this field has yielded exciting new discoveries, DeMoss (1999, p. 9) has warned that "the sheer volume of information about the brain is one of the biggest impediments to understanding and applying that information." Although knowledge in this field is still in its infancy, Table 8.6 summarizes current thinking about some of the ways that selected neurotransmitters work in the body and the brain.

It is important to remember that many neurotransmitters interregulate each other, and the ways in which various neurotransmitters work in concert with or against each other, as well as their role in regulating behavior, is just recently beginning to be understood. That said, it is critical to recognize that neuroscience alone cannot provide a full or adequate understanding of

TABLE 8.6  Neurotransmitters

| Neurotransmitter | What It Probably Does | Problems If It Is Out of Balance |
|---|---|---|
| Serotonin (5-HT) | In the body, 5-HT is involved with blood pressure and gut control. | Surplus 5-HT can make you feel sick, less hungry, get headaches or migraines. |
| | In the brain, it controls mood, emotions, sleeping/waking, feeding, temperature regulation, etc. | Deficient amounts can make you feel depressed, drowsy, etc. |
| Dopamine (DA); there are four pathways of DA neurons in the brain | In the brain, one pathway controls muscle tension and another controls emotions, perceptions, and sorts out what is real/important/imaginary, etc. | Deficient amounts of DA in one pathway can cause loss of smooth, controlled muscle movement (as in Parkinson's disease). |
| | | Surplus DA in another pathway can cause alterations in perception (e.g., you may see, hear, or imagine things that are not real). |
| Noradrenaline (NA); sometimes called norepinephrine (NE) | In the body, it controls the heart and blood pressure. | Surplus NA can make you feel anxious, jittery, etc. |
| | In the brain, it controls sleep, wakefulness, arousal, mood, emotion, and drive. | Deficient NA may make you feel depressed, sedated, dizzy, and have low blood pressure. |
| Acetylcholine (ACh) | In the body, ACh passes messages that make muscles contract. | Surplus ACh in your body can make your muscles tighten up. |
| | In the brain, it controls arousal, the ability to use memory, learning tasks, etc. | Deficient ACh can produce dry mouth, blurred vision, and constipation, as well as confusion, drowsiness, slowness at learning, etc. |
| Glutamate | Acts as an "accelerator" in the brain. | Surplus glutamate can make you anxious, excited, and some parts of your brain may become overactive. |
| | | Deficient glutamate may make you drowsy or sedated and may cause alterations in perception. |
| Gamma-aminobutyric acid (GABA) | Acts as a "brake" in the brain. | Surplus GABA may make you drowsy or sedated. |
| | | Deficient GABA may make you anxious, excited, and may contribute to mood instability. |

*Source:* Adapted from Bazire, 2001; J. J. Mann, 2004; McFarlance, 2002.

human behavior because the human mind works with meaning, not just facts, and subjective experience plays a large role in behavior. According to DeMoss, "Just as we are social creatures, our brains are social brains" (1999, p. 227) and external social influences can impact the development of both the mind and the brain. In groundbreaking work, Siegel (1999) synthesized concepts and findings from the fields of neurobiology, child development, cognitive science, communication, and object relations among others to show that "human connections shape the neural connections from which the mind emerges" (p. 2).

The current fascination with neuroscience is, at least in part, an outgrowth of the rapidly growing psychopharmaceutical industry and its ties to psychiatry and the *Diagnostic and Statistical Manual of Mental Disorders* (*DSM-IV-TR*) (Cosgrove, 2010, Wood & Lowes, 2010). We anticipate that this will continue with the *DSM-V* that is scheduled for publication in 2013. Attempts to link mental illness and substance abuse to specific neurochemical processes have led to an increasingly biological model of behavior. Although an understanding of neurobiology certainly adds to our knowledge base, it is inherently reductionistic and fails to recognize the social and relational nature of both human development and brain development. A fuller understanding of human behavior must include an understanding of the way in which the brain, the physical environment, the social environment, and behavior interact with one another (DeMoss, 1999).

## THEORIES OF PSYCHOSOCIAL DEVELOPMENT: THE LIFE SPAN APPROACH

The life span approach to psychological development originated in the 1950s with the work of Erik Erikson. Although his theory falls clearly within the framework of the Freudian mainstream, Erikson was one of the first reformulators to fully extend the idea of developmental stages to the entire life span. Erikson's delineation of adult developmental stages, combined with marked increases in life expectancy, gave rise to a growing interest in old age, adult development, and psychosocial changes between adolescence and old age (Hunter & Sundel, 1989; Santrock, 1989).

### Erik Erikson: Eight Ages of Man

Erik Erikson was born in Germany in 1902 and became a naturalized American citizen in 1939. Although initially hired as a tutor in a progressive school for children of Freud's inner circle, he was quickly "adopted" by them and he began training in child psychoanalysis. His reformulation of Freud's theory has become one of the most accepted and popular theories of human development in contemporary times.

Using Freudian concepts for his theoretical base, Erikson expanded the developmental paradigm to include three additional stages of adult development from young adulthood through old age. He also minimized the importance of id drives and focused on the healthy, adaptive qualities of the ego. For Erikson, the ego played a significant role in the mastery of psychosocial tasks and mastery of the environment. The ego was also critical in establishing and preserving one's *identity*, which Erikson saw as crucial for human existence.

As Roazen (1976) has pointed out, Erikson not only de-emphasized libidinal drives but also desexualized the Oedipal conflict. In his revision of Freudian theory, he saw the Oedipal conflict as a phase of development that was historically anchored in the context of Freud's culture. Although Erikson retained a modified version of this stage, he stressed the ambivalent feelings children experience during this conflict.

In *Childhood and Society* (1950), Erikson proposed an epigenetic model of human development. He coined the term *epigenesis*, derived from epi (upon) and genesis (emergence), to indicate development based on a "ground plan" out of which "parts arise" during specific times of "ascendancy" until "all parts have arisen to form a functioning whole" (p. 53). Thus, Erikson fashioned his model of psychosocial development after the growth of the infant in utero. The psychological unfolding of personality, he believed, takes place in a prescribed sequence as we adapt to and interact with "a widening social radius, beginning with the dim image of a mother and ending with mankind" (p. 54).

According to Erikson, each stage of development is characterized by a crisis in which the ego assists the individual in attaining a balance in a "series of alternative basic attitudes," such as trust and mistrust. The crisis in each life stage is marked by a conflict between two opposing personality traits or basic attitudes, one of which is ego "syntonic" and the other, ego "dystonic." Healthy resolution involves a balance toward the syntonic quality while maintaining some of the dystonic tendency. The resolution of each crisis further leads to the development of ego qualities that he originally described as "virtues," which are related to the specific crisis of each stage. He later changed the term *virtues* to *strengths*.

As we review Erikson's theory, it is important to remember that his first five stages are closely tied to those of Freud, with emphasis shifted from the instincts of the id to the reality orientation of the conflict-free ego.

**STAGE 1: BASIC TRUST VERSUS BASIC MISTRUST**    During infancy (birth to 1 year), the child is dependent on mother for food and care. As the child incorporates or takes in through sucking and swallowing, there is a receptivity to what is being offered. The mother is responsible for coordinating the child's experience of getting and hers of giving. At the later part of this stage, the child's eyes begin to focus, and incorporation becomes more active as the child bites to hold on to things. If the mother provides a predictable environment in which the child's needs are met, a sense of basic trust develops. This sense of trust implies not only sameness and continuity from the caretaker but also self-trust in one's capacity to cope with urges. According to Erikson, it is the quality rather than the quantity of maternal care that is critical at this stage. Successful resolution leads to a lasting ego quality of *hope*, an enduring belief that wishes can be fulfilled. Unsuccessful resolution leads to a sense of mistrust in other people and the environment.

**STAGE 2: AUTONOMY VERSUS SHAME AND DOUBT**    During early childhood (age 2–3), the child learns a sense of autonomy through retention and elimination of urine and feces. As the child's muscles mature to the point that bodily wastes can be retained or expelled at will, the child experiments with two simultaneous social modalities—holding on and letting go. Parents must be firm and tolerant so that the child can gradually learn bowel and bladder control and a "sense of self-control without loss of self esteem" (Erikson, 1950, p. 70). From this emerge a sense of autonomy and pride and the lasting ego quality of *willpower*, the determination to use free choice and self-restraint. Unsuccessful resolution of this stage leads to lifelong feelings of shame and doubt.

**STAGE 3: INITIATIVE VERSUS GUILT**    During the play age (3–5 years), increased locomotor mastery (walking and running) gives the child a wider radius of goals. In addition, language skills add to the ability to imagine "so many things that he cannot avoid frightening himself with what he himself has dreamed and thought up" (Erikson, 1950, p. 78). The Oedipal wishes and the ambivalent feelings that accompany them must be repressed to temporarily mask the *initiative* toward the opposite-sex parent. While this initiative is a prerequisite for masculine and feminine behaviors later in life, it is now repressed out of necessity—to avoid the guilt that would accompany knowledge of incestuous thoughts. Parents assist the child in learning appropriate roles, including gender roles, as the child diverts the sexual drive into acceptable activities. At this point, conscience, or superego, becomes established to govern the initiative. Proper resolution of this stage leads to a lasting ego quality of *purpose*, the courage to pursue goals. Unsuccessful resolution leads to feelings of shame.

**STAGE 4: INDUSTRY VERSUS INFERIORITY**    The child now enters the school age (6–12 years) and is enmeshed in the world of school and opportunities for new types of mastery. As children develop their abilities in new skills and tasks, they desire recognition gained from producing things. Through this, they develop a sense of industry and a lasting ego quality of competence. Unsuccessful resolution of this stage leads to lifelong feelings of inferiority and inadequacy.

**STAGE 5: IDENTITY VERSUS ROLE CONFUSION**    As the child approaches adolescence (12–18 years or so), physical and hormonal changes mark the beginning of puberty. Rapid growth and physical genital maturity disrupt the earlier continuity of childhood. This stage is perhaps the most important for Erikson, as the adolescent must now forge a lasting ego identity through aligning his or her basic drives, endowments, and opportunities. A sense of ego identity is (1950, pp. 94–95):

> the accrued confidence that one's ability to maintain inner sameness and continuity . . . is matched by the sameness and continuity of one's meaning for others. Thus, self-esteem grows to be a conviction that one is learning effective steps toward a tangible future, that one is developing a defined personality within a social reality which one understands.

As the adolescent struggles to integrate past and future views of self and begins to define new appropriate sex roles, an *identity crisis* may emerge from this confusion. New expectations from parents may add to this stress. Tolerance, understanding, and guidance in the home can assist the adolescent in achieving an integrated identity. Unsuccessful resolution can result in either role confusion or identity diffusion, a state in which the individual is left with strong doubts about who he or she is. This may lead to delinquency, psychotic incidents, or overidentification with others. Youths who emerge with a strong sense of identity and individuality gain a lasting ego quality of *fidelity*, or freely pledged loyalties.

**STAGE 6: INTIMACY VERSUS ISOLATION**    Young adulthood (early to late 20s) brings an end to the years of childhood and youth. It is now time for choosing a career, socializing with the opposite sex, and eventually marriage and raising a family. Interpersonal intimacy is the task of this stage, encompassing both psychological and sexual intimacy. Failure to achieve intimacy leads to isolation, an inability to develop intimate and meaningful relationships. The person who cannot be intimate will likely be self-absorbed. Proper resolution of this stage leads to a lasting ego quality of love, or mutuality of devotion.

**STAGE 7: GENERATIVITY VERSUS STAGNATION**    During adulthood (late 20s to 50s), mature genitality (in the Freudian sense) leads to procreation and establishing guidance for the next generation. Those who do not apply this to their own offspring must sublimate and find outlets in altruistic activities. According to Erikson, simply wanting or having children is insufficient for completion of this stage. Rather, an active role and a "belief in the species" leads to efforts to make the world a better place for future generations. Unsuccessful resolution of this stage results in a sense of stagnation or self-indulgence that reflects interpersonal impoverishment. Successful resolution of this stage can be seen in the lasting ego quality of care, or concern for others.

**STAGE 8: INTEGRITY VERSUS DESPAIR** Late adulthood (after 50 years) is a period of retrospective reflection about one's own life and acceptance of the eventual end of life. If, at the end of the life cycle, one can accept responsibility for past choices and find meaning and contentment in the road that was traveled, a sense of integrity is achieved. Unsuccessful resolution of this stage leads to a sense of despair. This may be exhibited as disgust and anger at external sources but is an indication of self-contempt. The lasting ego quality that emerges from proper resolution of this stage is wisdom. Erikson's stages of development are summarized in Figure 8.1.

With focus on the ego rather than the id, Erikson emphasized the ability of the individual to achieve mastery in each stage. Although his early concept of stage development reflected a Freudian model of traditional psychopathology, his later writings focused on the healthy personality. His emphasis on the historical context of ego development tied the concept of ego pathology to specific historical, economic, and cultural phenomena. In this regard, he was historically specific in linking his epigenetic model to personality development in industrial societies. His pervasive interest in social structure and culture is clearly reflected in his cross-cultural research (1963).

Erikson was one of the few psychosocial developmentalists who conducted detailed studies of religious development. He believed that some people concentrate intensely on a spiritual theme as the main focus of their lives and, even in childhood, precociously attend to existential concerns more typically associated with midlife. Referring to this sort of person as *homo religiosus* (Latin for "the religious person"), he used this term to distinguish a deeply spiritual person from one who merely conforms to conventional religious beliefs and expectations. His psychobiographical studies present Martin Luther and Mohandas Gandhi as exemplars of the *homo religiosus* (1962, 1969).

Erikson's ideal of religious development can be seen in the person who is able to integrate understanding of what is factually correct with actuality, that which feels true and effective in action. *Actuality* involves a way of living that results in mutual benefit between one's self and others in the process of seeking growth and edification. Actuality not only leads one to confront the personal quandaries of mortality, temporality, and limitedness but also propels one to work for societal welfare and to act against social injustice. The sense of responsibility to one's own household and society that is achieved by ordinary people is extended to a sense of responsibility for all humanity and a fascination with the significance of the entire cosmos by the *homo religiosus*.

In addition, his later writings expanded on ideas set forth in his early theories, continuously modifying his life cycle theory. He further delineated the psychosocial tasks of ego identity, explored themes of adulthood related to love and work, extended Freud's genitality of early adulthood into sensuality and sexuality in later life, and later added detailed descriptions of parallels between early and later life development.

In a 1983 interview, Erikson revealed that, "30 years ago I lacked that capacity for imagining myself as old, and the general image of old age was different then" (E. Hall, 1983, p. 22). In collaboration with his wife Joan, the additions made to his original stages reflected, at least partially, their experience with old age. In a 1988 interview, they discussed their most recent theoretical additions to his developmental model. The psychosocial crisis of old age now more fully delineated concerns related to physical disintegration, which Erikson termed *the law of life*.

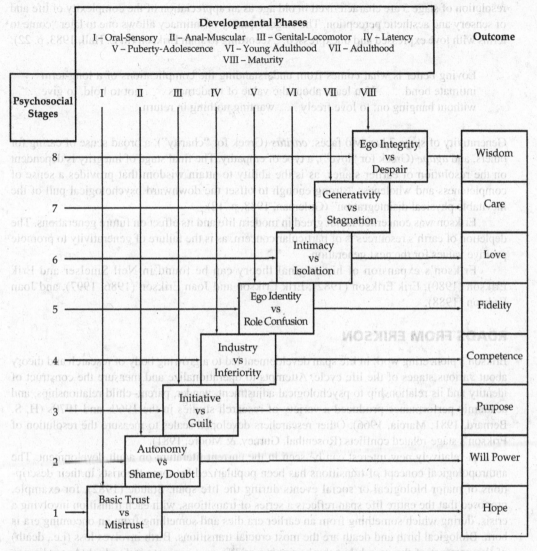

**FIGURE 8.1.** Erikson's epigentic chart.  *Source: Childhood and Society* by Erik H. Erikson. Copyright 1950, 1963 by W.W. Norton & Company, Inc., renewed © 1978, 1991 by Erik H. Erikson. Used by permission of W.W. Norton & Company, Inc.

They specified the way in which ego qualities that emerged through early tasks are paralleled in old age. For example, the basic trust developed in infancy becomes "an appreciation of human interdependence." Learning control over one's body in stage 2 becomes a mirror image as physical deterioration sets in. They believe that acceptance of this fact is critical. The lessons of stage 3, initiative, purpose, and playfulness, lead to empathy and resilience, and the "child's playfulness becomes a sense of humor about life. I can't imagine a wise old person who can't laugh," states Erikson. The industry of stage 4 leads to "a lifelong sense of effectiveness" and "humility . . . a realistic appreciation of one's limits and competencies." The identity crisis and resolution of stage 5 are characterized in old age as an appreciation of the complexity of life and of sensory and aesthetic perception. The stage 6 quality of intimacy allows one to later "come to terms with love expressed and unexpressed." According to Joan Erikson (in E. Hall, 1983, p. 22):

> Loving better is what comes from understanding the complications of a long-term intimate bond. . . . You learn about the value of tenderness . . . not to hold, to give without hanging on; to love freely . . . wanting nothing in return.

Generativity of stage 7 has two faces: *caritas* (Greek for "charity"), a broad sense of caring for others, and *agape* (Greek for "love"), a type of empathy. The final stage of integrity is dependent on the resolution of earlier stages, as is the ability to attain wisdom that provides a sense of completeness and wholeness "strong enough to offset the downward psychological pull of the inevitable physical disintegration" (Goleman, 1988, p. 12).

Erikson was concerned about greed in modern life and its effect on future generations. The depletion of earth's resources is of particular concern, as is the failure of generativity to promote positive values for the next generation.

Erikson's expansion of his original theory can be found in Neil Smelser and Erik Erikson (1980), Erik Erikson (1982), Erik Erikson and Joan Erikson (1986, 1997), and Joan Erikson (1988).

## ROADS FROM ERIKSON

Erikson's pioneering work in life span development led to a growing body of research and theory about various stages of the life cycle. Attempts to operationalize and measure the construct of identity and its relationship to psychological adjustment, gender, parent–child relationships, and academic performance produced a variety of research studies in the 1960s and 1970s (H. S. Bernard, 1981; Marcia, 1966). Other researchers developed scales to measure the resolution of Erikson's stage-related conflicts (Rosenthal, Gurney, & Moore, 1981).

A relatively new interest can be seen in the current literature on adult development. The anthropological concept of transitions has been popularized by some theorists in their descriptions of major biological or social events during the life span. Staude (1982), for example, proposed that the entire life span reflects a series of transitions, with each transition involving a crisis, during which something from an earlier era dies and something from an oncoming era is born. Biological birth and death are the most crucial transitions. Birth involves loss (i.e., death) of the comfort of the womb but the beginning of life as a separate individual. According to Staude, the next major transitions are those in adolescence, midlife, and finally, late life, followed by death. Transitions occur through a cultural process and involve culturally prescribed transition rituals that denote role exit from an earlier phase and role entrance into a new one. Golan's (1981) work reflected this theme as well.

Robert Havighurst (1972), influenced by Erikson, suggested that development is based on mastery of age-related tasks. Of interest here is his description of adult life cycle tasks. In early adulthood (age 18–30), developmental tasks entail selection of one's mate, reference group, and occupation and beginning a family. The tasks between age 30 and 60 are assisting children to become responsible, happy adults; relating to one's spouse as a person; achieving adult civic and social responsibility; establishing an economic standard of living; developing leisure activities; accepting the physical changes of middle age; and adjusting to aging (and dying) parents. The tasks from age 60 on are discussed later in this chapter.

According to Havighurst (1952), developmental tasks are the things a person must learn to be a reasonably happy and successful person. Erikson's influence is clearly seen in the biological, psychological, and cultural dimensions that lie at the source of Havighurst's tasks. Hunter and Sundel (1989) suggested that clear-cut expectable tasks such as these may help individuals adjust to adult life.

Popular interest in adult development is generally attributed to the publication of Gail Sheehy's best-selling book *Passages: Predictable Crises of Adult Life* (1976), in which she popularized the idea of *midlife crisis*. Citing studies by Daniel Levinson, George Vaillant, and Roger Gould, in addition to her own interviews with 115 adults, she proposed an age-stage theory based on transitions and "predictable crises" of adult life. Sheehy's work, however, never gained scientific credibility because she provided no information about her samples, research methods, or instruments and offered no statistical analyses. Although her road map of adult life may be less than scientifically sound, it created great interest in, and identification with, life cycle stages and crisis at midlife. As we will see, many of the prominent midlife theories that emerged in the 1970s and 1980s were empirically based. They were not, however, free of methodological limitations.

## THEORIES OF MIDLIFE DEVELOPMENT

In *The Seasons of a Man's Life*, Daniel Levinson, with colleagues Darrow, Klein, Levinson, and McKee (1978), investigated the development of the *life structure*, an underlying life pattern consisting of goals, lifestyles, roles, interests, values, personal meanings, and intrapsychic dynamics. Blending theoretical concepts of Jung, Havighurst, and Erikson, Levinson proposed a model of adult development based on challenges and crises at various stages in the life cycle. Based on an analysis of interviews conducted with 40 men and self-selected biographies of great men, Levinson described male adult development from 17 to 65 years of age.

He proposed four age-related eras and three transition periods, which he called the "seasons" of a man's life (Figure 8.2). Levinson proposed that life is a series of alternating *stable* (structure-building) and *transitional* (structure-changing) periods. Stability, however, does not necessarily mean tranquility. As in childhood, each transition involves separation and individuation, and as each transitional phase ends, a new era is begun.

Most interested in midlife, Levinson proposed that *early adult transition* involves questioning "the nature of the world and one's place in it" and making and testing initial choices necessary for adult life (1978, p. 56). Early adulthood involves two contrasting tasks: exploring possibilities in personal and occupational settings and creating a stable life structure such as marriage or a career. The substage of "age 30 transition" leads one to question the first adult life structure and may initiate efforts to change it, sometimes with substantial difficulty. At the end of this era, settling down involves the second adult structure.

*Midlife transition* may entail, for some, a serious crisis in the workplace or in personal relationships. For others, it is uneventful. Significantly, 70–80% of the men in Levinson's sample experienced great difficulty during this time. As middle adulthood begins, people experience new challenges involving marriage, career, and family. If, during the previous transition, a person is defeated, there is little emotional energy left with which to confront new challenges. At the close of this era, the developmental task is overcoming "the splitting of youth and age" and balancing the two.

Embracing Erikson's concern about generativity versus stagnation, as well as Carl Jung's concept of development in adulthood, Levinson saw the potential for "continuing self-renewal . . . through the afternoon and evening of life" (1978, pp. 28–33). As Friedan (1993, p. 111) has

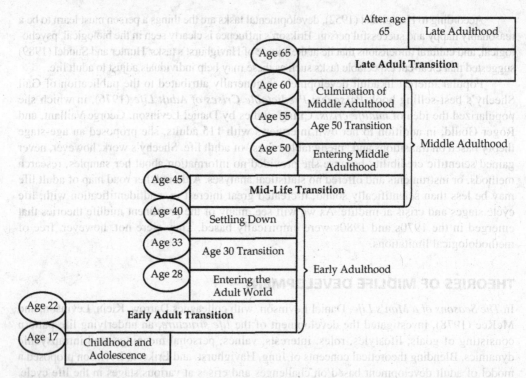

**FIGURE 8.2.** Levinson's stages of adult development. *Source: The Season of a Man's Life* by Daniel Levinson. Copyright 1978 by Daniel Levinson. Used by permission of Alfred A. Knopf, a division of Random House, Inc.

pointed out, however, Levinson believed this renewal ended in one's late 50s with the "reality and experience of bodily decline" around age 60.

George Vaillant's *Adaptation to Life* (1977) built on a combination of psychodynamic theory, Erikson's principle of epigenesis, and an extension of Norma Haan's work on personality to examine adaptation mechanisms in healthy adult development.

In a longitudinal study of 95 Harvard sophomores, an interdisciplinary team interviewed and evaluated this group of men from their college days until age 47. Ego defenses (called creative adaptations) were placed in a hierarchy ranging from least adaptive (Level 1) to most adaptive (Level IV), as displayed in Figure 8.3.

Vaillant found that as the men aged, their coping mechanisms became more adaptive. The best outcomes for the group were found among those who were happiest in their midlife, although unhappy in early adulthood. Conversely, the least well adapted were those who found the "storms" of midlife too painful and "longed for the relative calm of their young adulthood." Further, he found that the quality of long-term friendships was more important in predicting later adaptation than early childhood traumas. Finally, he found support for Erikson's epigenetic stages, as most men successively achieved identity formation, intimacy, generativity, and a search for ego integrity. Importantly, most did not show signs of midlife crisis.

In a more recent work, Vaillant (1995) reaffirmed his belief in the importance of psychodynamic theory and argued that "It is time for the ego and its defenses to be seen as facets of psychobiological reality, not as articles of psychoanalytic faith" (p. 5). Using longitudinal

| Level | Developmental Stages | Common in |
|---|---|---|
| | Infancy   Childhood   Adolescence   Adult Life Cycle   Death | |

| Level | | Common in |
|---|---|---|
| Four | **Mature Mechanisms of Defense**<br>Altruism: Service to others<br>Humor: A form of displacement<br>Suppression: A stiff upper lip<br>Anticipation: Planning for future<br>Sublimation: Indirect or attenuated expression of instincts | "Healthy"<br>individuals<br>between 12 and 90 |
| Three | **"Neurotic" Mechanisms of Defense**<br>Intellectualization: Instinctual wishes in formal, affectively bland terms<br>Repression: Inexplicable memory loss<br>Displacement: Redirection of feelings toward a less cared for object<br>than the person arousing the feelings<br>Reaction Formation: Behavior opposed to an acceptable instinctual impulse<br>Dissociation: Drastic modification of one's personal identity to avoid<br>distress—neurotic denial | "Healthy"<br>individuals<br>between 3 and 90<br>(To the user they<br>alter private feelings.<br>To the beholder<br>they appear as<br>quirks or neurotic<br>hang-ups.) |
| Two | **Immature Mechanisms of Defense**<br>Projection: Attributing one's own feeling to others<br>Schizoid Fantasy: Fantasy and autistic retreat for conflict resolution<br>Hypochondriasis: Transformation of reproach to others into<br>self-reproach and somatic illness<br>Passive-Aggressiveness: Aggression to others indirectly and passively<br>Acting Out: Direct expression of an unconscious impulse | "Healthy"<br>individuals<br>between 3 and 15<br>(To the user they alter<br>distress due to<br>intimacy or loss.<br>To the beholder<br>they appear socially<br>undesirable.) |
| One | **"Psychotic" Mechanisms of Defense**<br>Delusional Projection: Frank delusions about external reality<br>and experiences of persecution<br>Denial: Denial of external reality<br>Distortion: Grossly reshaping external reality to suit inner needs | "Healthy"<br>individuals<br>before age 5<br>(To the user they<br>alter reality. To the<br>beholder they<br>appear crazy.) |

**FIGURE 8.3.** Vaillant's four levels of adaptive mechanisms.   *Source:* Vaillant, 1977.

research that includes a psychobiography of an artist and a prospective study of adult development conducted at Harvard University, he proposed that defense mechanisms reflect an adaptive response rather than evidence of an illness. Building on his earlier work, he suggested that adaptive defenses are not only necessary to our well-being, but that they play a central role in resilience, spiritual growth, and maturation of the ego.

Sigmund Freud, when asked what a human should be able to do well, answered "Lieben und Arbeiten" meaning "love and work" (Erikson, 1950, p. 102; Liebert & Spiegler, 1990). It is these midlife tasks, love and work, which are the central concerns in Roger Gould's *Transformations: Growth and Change in Adult Life* (1978). Using a combination of empirical studies and clinical insights, he prepared a questionnaire on normal growth and change in adulthood by initially gathering life histories from psychiatric residents under his supervision and subsequently engaging in systematic observation of age-homogeneous outpatient therapy groups. Questionnaires were then administered to 524 nonpatient, White, middle-class subjects, age 16–60. In his analysis of the data, Gould found clusters of responses within specific age groups (Figure 8.4). He found that subjects in his study were constantly transforming themselves from legacies of their childhood and past situations to an adult orientation or consciousness. With each step forward into adulthood, interactions with family members, spouses, friends, lovers, colleagues, and superiors at work aided in these transformations. Although different issues emerged at each stage, the pursuits of liberty and external social conditions were central to their responses.

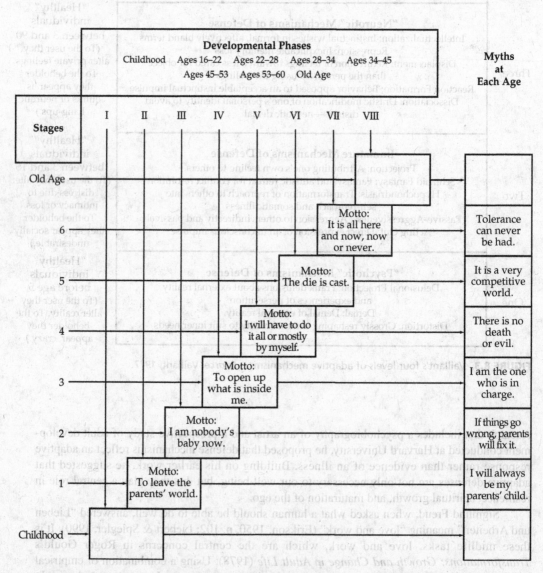

**FIGURE 8.4.** Gould's six stages of adult development.  *Source:* Adapted from R. L. Gould, 1978.

Gould also found midlife at around age 40 to be particularly stressful for many and concluded that unreasonable expectations of adulthood must be changed if we are to avoid frustration and dissatisfaction in adult life. He suggested that certain "myths" exist in each period of development, and mastery of these myths leads to personal liberty and happiness.

Also expanding and building on the themes of work and love, Sharon B. Merriam and M. Carolyn Clark examined the interaction of work, love, and learning in adulthood in their book *Lifelines: Patterns of Work, Love, and Learning in Adulthood* (1991). In an exploratory study of over 400 adults, Merriam and Clark supplemented their data with in-depth interviews and questionnaires, administered over a 20-year span, to 19 men and women. In their analysis of key life events, they found three distinct patterns in the life arena of love and work:

1. *parallel*, where both love and work move in tandem
2. *steady/fluctuating*, where one is steady and the other is not
3. *divergent*, where both are independent and sometimes change in opposite directions

They found no significant gender differences among these patterns and concluded that learning may have a crucial role in adult development. They found that both work and love can be a stimulus for learning as well as a "source of learning in and of themselves."

Examining personality at midlife, Norma Haan (1981, 1989) and Haan, Hartka, and Millsap (1986) utilized a longitudinal study of personality stability and change. They followed two samples, age 5–55 and age 11–62, respectively, of approximately 100 White, middle-class people from Northern California (commonly called the Berkeley study). Observations, interviews, and test scores were gathered at seven points in time, and additional in-depth interviews were used during the adult years.

Their findings ran contrary to predictions of psychodynamic life stage theory. Moderate shifts in personality were found in the transition to midlife and again in the transition to later maturity. In contrast, childhood and adolescent personality traits were more stable and predictable. In addition, they found that some aspects of personality may be more flexible than others, and that critical life events may be partly responsible for these changes in adulthood. The most stable dimensions of personality were those relating to intellectual interest and values. Significant changes found at midlife, for both men and women, were an openness to knowing themselves, becoming less self-defensive and less conventional. As Haan concluded, "Older dogs evidently do learn new tricks" (cited in Hunter & Sundel, 1989, p. 154). Finally, they found little evidence of midlife crisis, as most of their subjects functioned comfortably in middle age. In a similar vein, earlier studies had also shown elements of both stability and change in personality between adolescence and late 30s (Block & Haan, 1972).

In a study of men at midlife, Michael Farrell and Stanley Rosenberg (1981) collected data from 300 men, age 38–48, from different social classes. An in-depth, follow-up interview was used to gather more extensive data from a subsample of 20 men and their families. Analysis of their data showed a relationship between social class and alienation (i.e., crisis). Stress, dissatisfaction, and alienation were found predominantly among the working class. Middle- and upper-class subjects ranked lower on all of these measures.

In addition, they defined four personality types and several developmental paths. Some of the men thrived at midlife, some of them experienced crisis, but many denied their problems and "buried their heads," avoiding the pressures around them. In sum, they found no evidence for a universal midlife crisis.

Most recent research on midlife crisis has found that midlife is not universally stressful and relatively few men or women experience a crisis in midlife (Horton, 2002; Powell, 1998; Rosenberg, Rosenberg, & Farrell, 1999; Wethington, 2000). Despite this, myths about midlife persist. Wethington found that among those who did report a midlife crisis, the way in which they defined the term was much broader than the definitions used by researchers. She also found that crises that occurred both earlier and later than midlife were referred to as midlife crises and that crises were attributed to challenging life events rather than aging.

Current research continues to support both stability and change in personality in midlife. However, as Heatherton and Nichols (1994a) have noted, the way in which personality is defined strongly influences whether it is seen as stable or adaptive. Research that defines personality in terms of basic traits is not likely to find significant change, in comparison to research that utilizes a wider array of personality characteristics such as overall psychological functioning.

In a review of over 150 longitudinal studies, B. W. Roberts and DelVecchio (2000) found that stability in personality traits increased in early and middle adulthood. They also found that stability peaks for people when they are in their 50s. Stability is found in five basic factors that comprise most aspects of personality: neuroticism, extroversion, openness to experience, agreeableness, and conscientiousness. Changes, however, are commonly seen in other aspects of personality that may be independent from these five traits. According to Berk (2004), "An evolving mix of competencies and experiences leads certain personality traits to change in middle adulthood" (p. 519). Some of the traits that have been found to be amenable to change are introspection, self-acceptance, autonomy, and environmental mastery. Many also experience a change toward a more androgynous gender identity as they approach midlife. Further, it is believed that the ability of adults to envision *possible selves* may greatly assist people in making major changes in midlife. Possible selves is the temporal dimension of self-concept and refers to future-oriented representations of what one hopes to become and what one is afraid of becoming and reflects both hopes and fears (p. 518). Thus, some degree of flexibility and change in self-concept and personality may be achieved through the creation of possible selves that can be redefined as needed by the individual. It is important to remember that contextual factors and life events that are often not accounted for in research can also influence personality and personality change. Not surprisingly, there is also some degree of cultural variation regarding personality stability and malleability.

## LIFE SPAN DEVELOPMENT AND LATE ADULTHOOD

In comparison to the wealth of theory on midlife development that has grown rapidly since the 1970s, there are relatively few theories about psychosocial development in late adulthood. Although numerous studies have explored a wide variety of factors involved in the aging process and in adjustment to aging, few theories have been generated from these data. Most research recognizes, however, that social factors play a critical role in psychological functioning and adjustment.

Not surprisingly, studies of life satisfaction among older adults have found factors such as income, health, close personal attachments, and extended social networks to be important predictors of satisfaction in later life. Other studies have suggested that life satisfaction is a function of personality, which is believed by some to be stable throughout life (Atchley, 1997; Santrock, 1989). Although there is some controversy in the literature about whether personality throughout life is characterized by stability or change, most researchers accept the idea that personality becomes relatively stable after middle age (McCrae & Costa, 1982; Neugarten, 1977).

Studies on personality in late adulthood have found broad patterns of personality related to aging. Neugarten (1977), for example, identified four patterns: integrated personalities, who are highly adaptive to aging; armored or defended personalities, who are frightened and defensive; passive-dependent personalities, who rely too much on others or withdraw; and disorganized or unintegrated personalities, the most maladjusted. She found that life satisfaction and morale decrease as one moves from an integrated to unintegrated personality.

Kermis (1986) has noted that the study of late-life personality is difficult. Among other things, "the effects of past experiences and expectancies on present behavior are a challenge to disentangle" (p. 61).

Some theorists have chosen, instead, to focus on developmental tasks of late life. Havighurst (1972) defined six: (a) adjusting to declining health and physical strength, (b) adjusting to retirement and reduced income, (c) adjusting to changes in spouse's health or his or her death, (d) establishing an affiliation with one's age group, (e) adopting and adapting social roles flexibly, and (f) establishing satisfactory living arrangements. Similar to Erikson, he believed that acceptance of one's physical deterioration is necessary for adjustment in late life. The losses that one experiences in the physical realm can be partially compensated for if one buttresses resources in the social arena. He recommended active participation and affiliation with other elderly persons and active political participation in advocating for improved health and social services.

In an adaptation of Havighurst's model, Clark and Anderson (1967) delineated five normative tasks for late life and old age: (a) recognition of aging and definition of one's instrumental limitations, (b) redefinition of social and physical life span, (c) substitution of alternate sources of need satisfaction, (d) reassessment of criteria for evaluating the self, and (e) reintegration of one's values and life goals. Their tasks are more general than Havighurst's and are seen as necessary for adaptive functioning.

Similarly, in an extension of Erikson's eight stages of ego development, M. S. Peck (1978) delineated three challenges of this stage: (a) ego differentiation versus work role preoccupation, (b) body transcendence versus body preoccupation, and (c) ego transcendence versus ego preoccupation.

In coming to terms with late life, Peck echoed Erikson's and Havighurst's concerns about exit from the work force and physical disintegration. To achieve ego transcendence, one must find new outlets for fulfillment in view of the social and physical losses one endures. Establishing valued activities to replace the work role and finding activities that transcend the physical body are primary challenges of old age. The final task of ego transcendence represents a psychological closure similar to Erikson's attainment of wisdom. In this last stage, one recognizes and accepts one's mortality and gains a sense of comfort in recognizing contributions made earlier in life.

The concept of *ego transcendence* in late life was first conceptualized by Carl Jung in his description of the development of the ego and the Self. The word Self is capitalized to distinguish the true or whole Self from the ordinary ego. In contrast to Freud and Erikson who saw individuation as an early developmental task, Jung believed that true individuation usually began after the age of 40 and extended over the second half of life. As one of the first post-Freudian reformulators to conceptualize development from birth to death, he saw life as "the story of the self-realization of the unconscious" (Jung, cited in Whitmont, 1969, p. 265) and interwove a spiritual component (based on Eastern and Western thought) into his developmental model. He divided ego evolution into three phases: in childhood, the ego (conscious) and Self (unconscious) separate from their undifferentiated state to produce a first personality; in middle adult life, the ego and Self separate and the ego becomes primary, leading to ego–Self estrangement; and in late life, the ego reestablishes a relationship to the Self to fulfill the personality potential. If the last stage is successful, the ego establishes an expansion of consciousness and identity to the total Self. This stage "prepares consciousness for its ultimate limitation: physical death" in which the "ego returns to its original identity with the Self" (p. 285). As a critical developmental task of aging, Jung believed that ego transcendence was necessary to establish a "new rooting in the Self" in which an integral wholeness leads to the self-realization that God is within us and allows us to comprehend the mystery of the transpersonal Thou (Baker & Wheelwright, 1983; Hampden-Turner, 1981; Whitmont, 1969). We discuss transpersonal concepts of the Self and development more fully in Chapter 13.

Betty Friedan (1993) developed a comprehensive perspective on aging regarding "vital people over 65" in order to expose the myths of aging. Older adulthood has long been portrayed as a period of decline from youth, a pathological state that led to irreversible deterioration in physical and mental abilities. Thus, age has become equated with illness and the dread of age has become pervasive. With this view in mind, it was seen as normal and functional for older people to disengage from previous life roles and activities to prepare for death (Cumming & Henry, 1961). According to Friedan, this view of catastrophic decline, however, was based on pathological rather than normal aging. Within the last two decades, research has shown that changing one's diet, exercise, lifestyle, or environment can prevent, modify, or reverse much of the decline associated with age. Friedan noted that we must break out of the "youthful definitions" that describe earlier phases of development in order to accurately gauge continued development in later adulthood.

Friedan argued that late-life development should not be viewed simply as a recapitulation of earlier stages, as the Eriksons suggested, but as development that encompasses a more open-ended view of maturity. Citing research by Jane Loevinger (1976) and Bernice Neugarten (1968), and Jung's theory of individuation, Friedan posited that "midlife, rather than childhood or adolescence, represents the pivotal time of individuation, autonomous self-definition, and conscious choice" (1993, p. 113).

In her interviews with vital older people, she found that many had forged creative adaptations that allowed them to experience continued growth through late life. Many of these adaptations were in direct contrast to the developmental imperatives suggested by theorists such as Erikson. For example, intimacy in older age need not be expressed solely through the bonds formed in a long-term marriage. Instead, Friedan suggested that the "ties of intimacy, the bonds of the truly shared self" may consist of deep relationships with people whom we include in our new "families of choice" and may consist of friends and, sometimes, relatives. This is an especially important issue for older women who have outlived their spouses or for those who could not find intimacy in marriage or in other early relationships. She noted that new possibilities of intimacy may "have to evolve beyond the ways of our youth—inside or outside the old forms of marriage, friendship, family, community—if they are to nourish us in age" (Friedan, 1993, p. 257). Similarly, she argued that the rigidly prescribed sex roles that dominated our earlier years are not as pervasive in older age. This may allow us to more freely reclaim and affirm what she sees as the "missing pieces" of ourselves. Late adulthood may give us the opportunity to go beyond and stretch ourselves to do things that we have not previously done. We must forge new roles and definitions for ourselves in the process of seeking the "empowerment of age."

Recent gerontologists' efforts to counter negative stereotypes of aging as merely a process of decline and social disengagement have led to the popularity of a more strengths-oriented view of *successful aging*. The perspective of successful aging recognizes that there are many ways of experiencing physical, mental, and social aspects of aging not always characterized by severe functional impairments (Berkman & D'Ambruoso, 2006; Dillaway & Byrnes, 2009). Indeed, Americans are on average living longer with fewer health problems than in previous generations. Successful aging refers to ways that people can age well by adapting to the processes of growing old through behaviors that reduce risk of disease and disease-related disability, maintain a high level of physical and mental functioning in daily life, and continue active enjoyable social engagement. Continuity theorists emphasize ways that people who successfully age carry forward adaptive lifestyles and relationships from midlife into late life. Some successful aging theorists point out that even if older adults experience decline or disability, they might not view themselves as unsuccessful, but rather they might find ways to continue or refine their lifestyles and sense of identity in ways that acknowledge, cope with, and give meaning to age or illness-related changes.

The Swedish gerontologist, Lars Tornstam, developed a theory of *gerotranscendence*, based on studies of elders (aged 50s through 90s) who use the aging process as a positive opportunity to grow beyond the typical materialistic, pragmatic, rational, and ego-focused perspective of adulthood (Binstock, 2006; Tornstam, 2005; Tornstam & Tornqvist, 2000). This is a developmental shift in dimensions of worldview. In the *cosmic dimension*, the border between past and present is transcended, there is increased sense of attachment to the stream of life across generations, fear of death disappears, the mystery of life is appreciated, and profound joy in nature and in ordinary events grows. In the *self dimension*, there is a more balanced awareness of one's good and bad aspects, decrease of self-centeredness, an ability to care for the body without being obsessed with its changes, a growth in altruism (especially for men), and a sense of personal wholeness. In the dimension of *social and personal relationships*, there is a decrease of interest in superficial relationships, increasing appreciation for solitude, a willingness to be unstuck from roles and social conventions, freedom from desire for excessive wealth and possessions, and a greater nonjudgmental and tolerant broad-mindedness.

Interestingly, Joan Erikson, during her early 90s, expanded Erik Erikson's stages to a ninth relating to old age in the 80s and 90s (Erikson & Erikson, 1997). Drawing on the work of Tornstam and the experience of herself and her husband Erik, Joan described the challenges of increasingly severe physical and mental limitations common in this age group. She said that elders who come to terms with these difficult life experiences and who have supportive social environments might make their way to gerotranscendence. She emphasized the importance of changes in social institutions and values to create supportive physical and social environments for elders that would also encourage younger people to learn from their accrued wisdom.

Spirituality can be an important aspect of successful aging because it can assist coping with hardships and loss, support resilient response to chronic illness, enhance the feeling of a life well lived, and encourage preparation for completing life (Nakashima & Canda, 2005; Nelson-Becker, Nakashima, & Canda, 2006a, 2006b). As elders become more acutely aware of their mortality, they often become more reflective about their life accomplishments in relation to their priorities that are often influenced by religious beliefs and personal spiritual commitments. Elders might reflect on the quality of their past and current life, including a sense of how their experiences relate to the meaning and purpose of life, moral standards, implications for their beliefs about existence after death (if any), and expectations of family, religious community, and culture. They might become less involved in formal religious participation (sometimes due to reduced mobility), but often engage in private or family-based spiritual practices, such as prayer and watching televised religious programming. Relatives, clergy, and lay members of religious support systems might provide home-based companionship and religious activity, such as provision of material and social support, discussion of life review, prayer, ritual, assistance with planning for possibility of medical crises, and preparation for death and funeral. Dedication to spiritual development may contribute to gerotranscendence.

## LIFE SPAN DEVELOPMENT OF WOMEN

It is now widely recognized that the vast majority of theory and research on life span development has been based on all male samples and male models of development. This was not as well known, however, when Carol Gilligan (1977, 1978, 1982) first criticized normative developmental models for not reflecting women's development. In her critique of Erikson's ego identity model, Gilligan (1982) noted that on the one hand, Erikson proposed that ego identity occurs in adolescence as children become autonomous and individuated in preparation for adulthood. On the other hand, females are supposed to wait until they attract a mate to fill their "inner space" and loneliness before they can become whole (Erikson, 1968). As Gilligan (1982, p. 12) pointed out, "for men identity precedes intimacy and generativity . . . for women these tasks seem instead to be fused." She also noted that the only stage of childhood that prepares one for intimacy is the first one—trust versus mistrust; all other stages relate to separation and individuation. In his male model of the life span, "development itself comes to be identified with separation, and attachments appear to be developmental impediments" (pp. 12–13). Women were thus portrayed as developmentally deficient due to the attachments that were developmentally required of them.

Recognition of the androcentric (male-centered) bias within developmental theory (Chasseguet-Smirgel, 1970; J. H. Williams, 1977) led to the beginning of feminist writing that not only critiqued the androcentric basis of mainstream ideas but also celebrated the notion of female difference. Building on the earlier works of Jean Baker Miller (1976) and Nancy Chodorow (1978, 1979), a growing branch of feminist theory has stressed the ways in which women think, reason, and act in accordance with a sense of interdependence, intimacy, nurturance, connectedness, and relatedness to others. This has been referred to as women's "voices" (Gilligan, 1982), "ways of knowing" (Belenky, Clinchy, Goldberger, & Tarule, 1986), "standpoints" (Harding, 1986), and "talk" (Schaef, 1985). Due to this sense of interconnectedness, feminist theorists contend that women have a better understanding of and abiding concern for harmony and mutual empowerment. In direct contrast to the individuated, separate self-identity that androcentric developmental models define as the ideal, woman-centered theorists portray female development as being not only different from, but equal or superior to male development.

As Bem (1993) has pointed out, although most feminist theorists agree that the male emphasis on separation, domination, and hierarchy is problematic, there is less agreement about the sources of male–female difference. Theorists have alternately described these differences as being due to biological factors (Daly, 1978; Rich, 1976), developmental factors (Chodorow, 1978; Gilligan, 1982), or social-psychological and structural factors (Aptheker, 1989; Eagly, 1987; Epstein, 1988; Harding, 1986; Hooks, 1984; H. Rose, 1983).

In her analysis of theoretical perspectives on the construction of gender identity, Bem (1993, p. 133) observed that, for the past 50 years emphasis in the social science literature has been on:

> socialization, situational constraint by the social structure, psychodynamic conflict, or identity construction by the individual. The first and second emphasize something that the culture does to the individual, whereas the third and fourth emphasize something that goes on within the individual's psyche.

However, not all feminist theorists have embraced the idea of male–female differences. Some, like Bem, have argued that although woman-centered discourse has been valuable in illuminating the ways in which men in power androcentrically define science, morality, and all of our social institutions, it has nonetheless reproduced gender polarization. Rather than minimizing conditions of inequality, Bem concluded that gender polarization "aids and abets the social reproduction of male power" (1993, p. 194). Although the idea of male–female developmental differences may be intuitively appealing, there is little evidence to demonstrate that such gender differences exist. In a thorough review of the literature, Tavris (1992) concluded that power, rather than gender, is primary in understanding the differences that exist between men and women.

Additional research on female development has focused on adolescent girls, a population that had previously not received much attention in psychological studies or feminist literature. In a review of the literature on adolescence, Petersen (1988) found that a loss of self-worth, poor body image, eating disorders, depression, and suicidal ideation increased for girls during adolescence. They also lose optimism (Seligman, 1991) and resiliency (Block, 1990). In her research, Gilligan (1986, 1991) called attention to a "relational crisis" that begins for girls in adolescence and often remains at the center of their later development. In this crisis, their voices become buried within them, they lose confidence and courage, and they separate from themselves. More recently, Mary Pipher's best-selling book, *Reviving Ophelia: Saving the Selves of Adolescent Girls* (1994), has brought national attention to the social and cultural pressures that lead teenage girls to "split into true and false selves" and lose confidence and self-esteem. Gilligan (1991) has described this adolescent crisis and subsequent psychological development as "profoundly transformational" (L. M. Brown & Gilligan, 1992; J. B. Miller, 1976, 1988).

In contrast to theories of gender differences and the view of women's development as being transformational, a review of contemporary research and theory by Wrightsman (1988, pp. 120–126) found that women's development in adulthood primarily differs from that of men's in four ways:

1. Male developmental models address four early adulthood tasks for men—finding a dream, an occupation, a mentor, and a mate. Some research suggests that, for women, finding a mate is a primary concern.
2. In contrast to men, women at midlife increase their desire for autonomy.
3. Women may follow one of the three following paths: homemaker-mother, career woman, and a combination of both. Accordingly, their role expectations and tasks are different.
4. Sheehy suggested a fourth possible pathway—that of the nurturer who postpones her own achievement until after raising a family.

In addition to these four issues, M. S. Horner (1968, 1972) had earlier delineated two other points:

1. Men are socialized, from childhood onward, to seek achievement or to compete, whereas women are socialized to be affiliation oriented, to be agreeable, and to seek solidarity.
2. Men experience anxiety when they face a "fear of failure," whereas women experience anxiety when they attain success in competitive situations, and they face a "fear of success."

It is now recognized that gender-based fears of success and failure have not been empirically well established. Further, if this has any validity at all, it may be related to life span decisions women make. That is, women who choose the role of wife-mother or the dual role of wife-mother and career woman may, in fact, experience fear of success. On the other hand, women who choose only the career role in early adulthood may not experience this fear at all. The problem, if it exists at all, may be inherent in *gender role socialization* rather than gender. Gender stratification related to role and socialization has been well documented (Abramovitz, 1988).

A developmental model that illustrated these different role expectations was proposed by Riegel (1975), who suggested that people are required to deal with two types of transitions throughout life—biophysical and psychosocial. He noted that the role of gender is important in defining these transitions, and, accordingly, different developmental paths are experienced by men and women.

An emerging body of literature on women's health has recently addressed the biological transition of menopause. As Dan and Bernhard (1989) noted, the medical community has portrayed menopause as a disease and sign of decay. In contrast, many women who have experienced menopause have come to define it in neutral or positive terms. With her best-selling book *Menopause: The Silent Passage* (1992/1995), author Gail Sheehy shattered many long-standing myths about menopause and defined this normal transition as a stage in a woman's life that she dubbed the "Second Adulthood" (p. xix). In doing so, she helped destigmatize open discussion about the changes that accompany menopause. And perhaps just as importantly, she provided solid data on the pros and cons of hormone replacement therapy, an issue that continues to be divisively debated today.

Two additional studies using exclusively female samples provide us with good data on adult development for women. Grace Baruch, Rosalind Barnett, and Caryl Rivers examined contemporary patterns of love and work in *Lifeprints: New Patterns of Love and Work for Today's Women* (1983). They use the term *lifeprint*, the pattern of a life, to describe pleasures, problems, conflicts, and issues that face women at midage (p. 7). In their survey of 300 White women, age 35–55, the authors found significant social and environmental factors that had an impact on their lives. In contrast to women in young adulthood whose primary concern is finding a mate, the women in this sample were more likely to discuss themes of achievement and work when describing their lifeprints (Barnett & Baruch, 1980; Baruch et al., 1983). Only 20% of the women identified marriage as a marker event or turning point. In addition, the authors found that multiple roles enhance a woman's well-being. Their data did not support the idea of a midlife crisis. In fact, the authors suggest that "If the study of midlife had begun with women, perhaps the midlife crisis would never have become a part of our vocabulary" (Baruch et al., 1983, p. 241).

Ravenna Helson, Valory Mitchell, and Geraldine Moane conducted a longitudinal study of 132 women from Mills College in California. The researchers found a psychological "shift" toward attitudes that have typically been associated with "male" characteristics—"greater dominance, higher achievement motivation, greater interest in events outside the family, and more emotional stability" (cited in Rosenfeld & Stark, 1991, p. 233). The midlife concerns expressed by these women were similar to those expressed by men. The researchers, however, describe this as "midlife consciousness" rather than "crisis." The best psychological outcomes were found in women who committed themselves to tasks involving family or career, or both. Those who committed themselves to neither one experienced less growth.

Although contemporary theory and research reflect an ongoing controversy about similarities and differences between men and women especially in the area of psychological and moral development (see Tavris, 1992), there are clear differences in gender roles, expectations, and biology. Alice Rossi (1978, p. 79) reminded us that:

> we cannot toss out the physiological equipment that centuries of adaptation have created. We can live with the biological heritage or try to supercede it, but we cannot wish it away.

Rather than denying biological differences, she urged a radical societal change in which people are "more respectful of natural bodily processes . . . differences between individuals, more concerned for its children, and committed to both achievement in work and in personal intimacy" (p. 79).

The issue of similarities and differences in female and male development remains a central concern in feminist theory and has given rise to numerous debates. We explore this more fully in our upcoming analysis as well as in Chapter 9.

## SHAME RESILIENCE THEORY

A new theoretical model that contributes to our understanding of emotional factors that affect women's development can be found in the work of Brené Brown and her research on the role of shame in women's lives. *Shame resilience theory* (SRT) (B. Brown, 2004) emerged from a grounded theory study of 215 women on shame and the impact it has on women's lives.

According to Brown, once largely misunderstood and discounted by social scientists, a growing number of researchers and practitioners are examining shame and its role in a wide range of mental and public health issues including self-esteem/concept issues, depression, addiction, eating disorders, bullying, suicide, family violence, and sexual assault (Balcom, Lee, & Tager, 1995; Hartling, Rosen, Walker, & Jordan, 2000; Jordan, 1989; Kalafat & Lester, 2000; D. Lester, 1997; Mason, 1991; Nathanson, 1997; Sabatino, 1999; Talbot, 1995; Tangney & Dearning, 2002). As mounting empirical evidence points to shame's importance, some researchers have described shame as "the master emotion of everyday life" (Scheff, 2003) and "the preeminent cause of emotional distress in our time" (Karen, quoted in Trout, 2000).

SRT proposes that shame is an intensely painful feeling or experience of believing that we are flawed and therefore unworthy of acceptance and belonging. Women were found to most often experience shame as a web of layered, conflicting, and competing expectations. *These expectations tell women who they should be, what they should be, and how they should be.* At their core, these ideal expectations are products of very rigid social and cultural expectations. The expectations are based on socially constructed interpretations of who women are "supposed to be" based on demographics (i.e., their gender, race, class, sexual orientation, age, religious identity) and/or our roles (i.e., a mother, an employee, a partner, a group member). The expectations are often born in our larger society, then filtered through our various cultures and communities of race, ethnicity, social class, group membership, ideology, faith, politics, and so on.

Many, if not most, of the expectations are impossible to meet. They are ideals and myths that no individual could possibly embody. But more than that, what makes them even less attainable is the way the layers of expectations often conflict and compete with one another. Varying sociocultural expectations can be enforced by family members, partners, friends, coworkers, children, helping professionals, membership groups, and faith communities. Many times individuals internalize the expectations and impose them on themselves. These sociocultural expectations and the way they are enforced are, in turn, constantly reinforced by society's very powerful media culture including television, advertising, marketing, film, music, and print.

SRT maintains that shame is a very contextualized experience—why one experiences it and around what issues is very specific to individuals. There is no comprehensive list of "universal shame triggers"; however, categories that represent the areas where women appear to be the most vulnerable did emerge from the data. These categories include identity, appearance, sexuality, family, motherhood, parenting, health (mental and physical), aging, religion, and speaking out on public or private issues. While the triggers are very specific to individuals, feeling or experiencing shame appears to impact women by leaving them feeling trapped, powerless, and isolated. While each of these concepts is, in themselves, a formidable issue, it is the intricate weaving of these concepts that makes shame so powerful, complex, and often difficult to overcome.

The concept of "trapped" is best understood as a ratio of expectations to options. Women are faced with numerous conflicting and competing sociocultural expectations and very few real options for meeting the layers of expectations. The concept of trapped is very similar to Marilyn Frye's concept of the "double bind." Frye (2001) describes double binds as "situations in which options are reduced to a very few and all of them expose one to penalty, censure or deprivation." The concept of being trapped expands the concept of double bind by combining limited and punitive options with layers of competing expectations to form a complex web that traps women.

The concept of powerlessness emerged with three properties: consciousness, choice, and change. As defined in *The Merriam-Webster Dictionary* (1997), *power* is "the ability to act or produce an effect." For women experiencing shame, the ability to produce an effect that could effectively countershame is very difficult because shame often evokes overwhelming and painful feelings of confusion, fear, anger, judgment, and/or the need to hide. It is difficult to identify "shame" as the core issue when trying to manage these intense feelings. Even when women are able to identify shame, the silencing and secret nature of shame makes it very difficult to identify and act on the choices that would facilitate change.

Isolation emerged as the product of feeling trapped and powerlessness. Relational/cultural theorists, Miller and Stiver (1997, p. 72), fully capture the concept of isolation when they write:

> We believe that the most terrifying and destructive feeling that a person can experience is psychological isolation. This is not the same as being alone. It is feeling that one is locked out of the possibility of human connection and of being powerless to change the situation. In the extreme, psychological isolation can lead to a sense of hopelessness and desperation. People will do almost anything to escape this combination of condemned isolation and powerlessness.

There appears to be no evidence in the literature to indicate that individuals can develop resistance or immunity to shame. To the contrary, there is overwhelming evidence that demonstrates that shame is a universal human experience (Balcom et al., 1995; Hartling et al., 2000; Nathanson, 1997; Scheff, 2000, 2003; Tangney & Dearning, 2002). While shame resistance may be unattainable, SRT does propose that individuals can demonstrate shame resilience and that this resilience is an effective and constructive strategy for moving through shame and shaming experiences.

SRT utilizes the relational view of resilience proposed by relational/cultural theorists. Unlike many traditional definitions of resiliency that focus on an individual's ability to rebound or adapt to stress, the relational view of resiliency encourages transformations from isolation and pain to relatedness and growth through empathic mutuality, vulnerability, relational confidence, and relational awareness (Jordan, 1992). The focus on mutuality is central to the concept of resilience that emerged from the original data.

As seen in Figure 8.5, SRT proposes that shame resilience is best understood on a continuum that represents, on one end, the products of shame—feelings of being trapped, powerless, and isolated. Located on the opposite end of the continuum are the components of shame resilience—empathy, connection, power, and freedom.

The research participants clearly identified "experiencing empathy" as the opposite of "experiencing shame." Empathy is described as the ability to perceive a situation from the other person's perspective—"to see, hear, and feel the unique world of the other" (Ivey, Pederson, & Ivey, 2001).

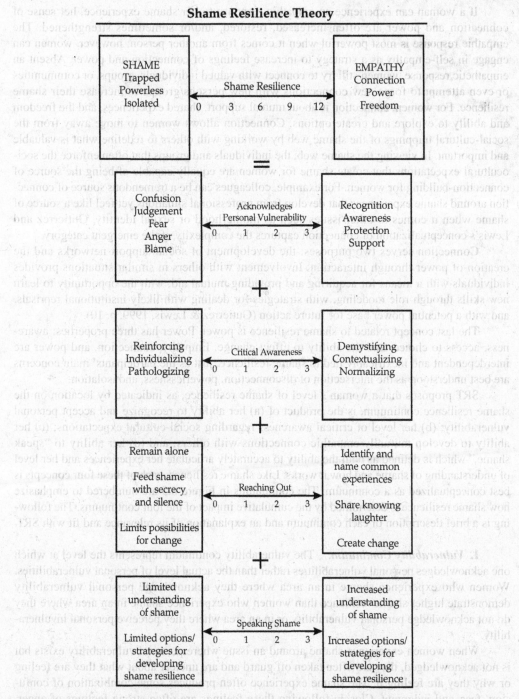

**FIGURE 8.5.** Shame resiliency theory. *Source: Women & Shame: Reaching Out, Speaking Truths, & Building Connection* by Brené Brown. Copyright 2004 by Brené Brown. Reprinted by permission.

If a woman can experience an empathic response to her shame experience, her sense of connection and power are often increased, restored, and/or sometimes strengthened. The empathic response is most powerful when it comes from another person; however, women can engage in self-empathy as a strategy to increase feelings of connection and power. Absent an empathetic response, women still try to connect with valued individuals, groups, or communities or even attempt to forge new connections with new persons/groups to increase their shame resilience. For women, connection is about mutual support, shared experiences, and the freedom and ability to explore and create options. Connection allows women to move away from the social-cultural trappings of the shame web by working with others to redefine what is valuable and important. In viewing the shame web, the individuals and groups that often enforce the sociocultural expectations that create shame for women are equally capable of being the source of connection-building for women. For example, colleagues can be a tremendous source of connection around shame experiences that develop from professional situations yet feel like a source of shame when it comes to other issues such as motherhood or sexual identity. Gutierrez and Lewis's conceptualization of connection captures the complexity of the emergent category.

Connection serves two purposes: the development of social support networks and the creation of power through interaction. Involvement with others in similar situations provides individuals with a means for acquiring and providing mutual aid, with the opportunity to learn new skills through role modeling, with strategies for dealing with likely institutional reprisals, and with a potential power base for future action (Gutierrez & Lewis, 1999, p. 10).

The last concept related to shame resilience is power. Power has three properties: awareness, access to choice, and the ability to effect change. Empathy, connection, and power are interdependent and inextricably tied to shame resilience, just as the participants' main concerns are best understood as the intersection of disconnection, powerlessness, and isolation.

SRT proposes that a woman's level of shame resilience, as indicated by location on the shame resilience continuum, is the product of (a) her ability to recognize and accept personal vulnerability; (b) her level of critical awareness regarding social-cultural expectations; (c) her ability to develop mutually empathic connections with others; and (d) her ability to "speak shame," which is defined as both the ability to accurately articulate her experiences and her level of understanding of shame and how it works. Like shame resilience, each of these four concepts is best conceptualized as a continuum. The continuums in Figure 8.5 are numbered to emphasize how shame resilience is determined by the cumulative impact of the four continuums. The following is a brief description of each continuum and an explanation of its relevance and fit with SRT.

**1. *Vulnerability Continuum.*** The vulnerability continuum represents the level at which one acknowledges personal vulnerabilities rather than the actual level of personal vulnerabilities. Women who experience shame in an area where they acknowledge personal vulnerability demonstrate higher shame resilience than women who experience shame in an area where they do not acknowledge personal vulnerability or in an area where they perceive personal invulnerability.

When women experience shame around an issue where personal vulnerability exists but is not acknowledged, they are often taken off guard and are unclear about what they are feeling or why they are feeling it. The shame experience often produces some combination of confusion, fear, and judgment. Closely following these feelings are often strong feelings of anger, rage, and/or blame. If shame is experienced around an issue where there is perceived invulnerability, the reaction can be even more painful and confusing. In both instances, the feelings of fear, judgment, anger, rage, and blame can be directed both inward and/or outward. When women experience shame in an area of acknowledged vulnerability, they are significantly more likely to be aware of what they are experiencing and why it is happening. They are also more likely to seek support and appropriate protection.

**2.** *Critical Awareness Continuum.*    There appears to be a positive relationship between a woman's level of critical awareness regarding her "shame web" and her level of shame resilience. The concept of critical awareness (also referred to as *critical consciousness and/or critical perspective*) is both the process and the cognitive state of linking personal experiences with social-cultural issues (Bricker-Jenkins, 1991; P. H. Collins, 2000; Freire, 1970; L. M. Gutierrez, 1995; Hooks, 1990; Stout & McPhail, 1998). The critical awareness continuum represents both the level of awareness a woman has about the social-cultural forces that shape her experiences and her ability to critically assess her personal experiences in the context of those forces. Women with little or no critical awareness often lack the skills necessary for deconstructing and contextualizing shame experiences. Rather than linking their experience to larger issues, they individualize the situation, reinforcing the idea that they are bad or flawed persons unworthy of acceptance. Without a larger context, the issue becomes a personal flaw rather than a collective issue. This, in turn, leads women to pathologize the shaming behavior or thought—"something is inherently wrong with just me."

**3.** *Reaching Out.*    SRT proposes that women increase their shame resilience when they are able to develop empathy, connection, and power with others. As stated earlier, mutuality is a critical component in developing shame resilience. When women reach out to offer support to others, they increase their own resilience by building support networks that allow them to identify shared experiences and demystify the isolating properties of shame. These networks also become important sources of ideas and strategies that elevate their critical awareness of the shame web and their understanding of shame. One of the most important benefits of developing empathy, connection, and power with others is recognizing how the experiences that make us feel the most alone, and even isolated, are often the most universal experiences.

**4.** *Speaking Shame.*    Speaking shame is about the importance of developing an emotional vocabulary that allows individuals to engage in thought and dialogue about shame and shame resilience. To develop shame resilience, we must know and have some fluency with the language (words and concepts) that give meaning to shame and the strategies of shame resilience. When we are unable to speak shame, we have limited opportunities to expand our understanding of shame and this, in turn, decreases our options for creating change.

This last element, speaking shame, is a necessary component to building an effective and lasting connection network. Most of us don't naturally acquire the vocabulary we need to identify, describe, and discuss the actual process of experiencing shame or increasing shame resilience. Shame is a complex language—learning it requires practice and skill. Speaking shame requires us to develop names and terms to describe some of the most painful and abstract concepts that we, as humans, have to confront.

Literature on shame can be found in almost every area of the social sciences and humanities. In the social sciences, there are psychoanalytic, self-psychology, bio-psychosocial, sociological, and combined approaches. In the humanities, there are cultural, anthropological, art, literary, philosophical, and theological approaches. As expected, each contribution to our understanding of shame is made through the lens of a particular discipline or field.

SRT is probably best supported by and lends the most support to relational-cultural theory (RCT), which we discussed in Chapter 5. The fact that connection, empathy, and isolation play central roles in RCT and the SRT might be attributed to the highly inductive methods used to generate both theories. Similar to the grounded theory methodology used in the study that produced SRT, RC theorists allowed their theory to emerge from qualitative data collected from women. Miller and Stiver (1997, p. 16) write:

> If we observe women's lives carefully, without attempting to force our observations into preexisting patterns, we discover that an inner sense of connection to others is the central organizing feature of women's development. By listening to the stories women tell about their lives and examining these stories seriously, we have found that, quite contrary to what one would expect based on the governing models of development emphasizing separation, women's sense of self and of worth is most often grounded in the ability to make and maintain relationships.

The two fundamental differences between the SRT and RCT are the SRT's focus on critical awareness and education. The theoretical foundation for critical awareness and education can be found in feminist social work practice (Bricker-Jenkins, 1991; Stout & McPhail, 1998), critical pedagogy (Freire, 1970; Hooks, 1994, 2000a), and empowerment theory (L. M. Gutierrez, 1995; Gutierrez & Lewis, 1999).

SRT proposes a new approach to understanding shame and its impact on women. Future research is necessary to fully develop and test its practice applications. Studies are currently being conducted on the application of the SRT with African American women and lesbian women. Data are also being collected from adolescents and men. SRT must be continually tested and modified if it is to remain a theory grounded in data.

In her most recent work, Brown has expanded on her shame research. In the process of collecting data for SRT, she identified new patterns that required further inquiry. A subset of research participants spoke about the importance of embracing imperfection and vulnerability. They reported trusting themselves and discussed authenticity, love, and belonging in a way that provided a new perspective to her previous research. Her current work (2010) proposes a framework for *wholehearted living* that is based on courage, compassion, and connection. It is from practicing these tenets that one is able to cultivate a sense of worthiness. We anticipate that this theory will be further refined with additional research and will be seen as a ground-breaking theory for social work due to its consistency with social work values and the strengths perspective.

## LESBIAN, GAY, BISEXUAL, TRANSGENDER, QUEER, QUESTIONING, AND INTERSEXED IDENTITY DEVELOPMENT

Definition of the terms *sexual orientation*, *sexual identity*, *gender identity*, *lesbian*, *gay*, *bisexual*, *transgender*, *queer*, *questioning*, and *intersexed* is essential to any discussion of identity development in sexual minorities. According to Lev (2004), *sexual orientation* is "the self-perception of one's own sexual preference and emotional attraction . . . [it] is less of an internal sense of self and more of an external desire for another person, although . . . [it] becomes integrated as an identity construct" (pp. 85–86). In contrast, *gender identity* is how a person sees himself or herself socially—as a man, a woman, or a combination of both. Thus, sexual orientation and sexual preference are parts of one's broader *sexual identity*, which also includes gender identity.

Sexual orientation, gender identity, and sexual identity are independent of one another and may be expressed in a variety of ways and combinations (Nangeroni, 1996).

When sexual orientation is directed at members of the same sex, it is *homosexual*, and when it is directed at members of both sexes, it is *bisexual*. Sexual orientation can also be *heterosexual*, directed toward the opposite sex, or *nonsexual*, directed toward neither sex. Importantly, forms of sexual orientation that are not heterosexual are stigmatized (Lev, 2004).

Early definitions of homosexuality described such behaviors as "inversions" of normal human sexual behavior (H. Ellis, 1922). Other early theories defined lesbians more specifically as a "third sex," embodying characteristics of both males and females (Hirschfields, 1936). Monique Wittig (1992), a contemporary lesbian feminist, identified herself as "not a woman, but a lesbian." Many contemporary views define lesbianism and male homosexuality according to sexual and affectional connections. For example, D'Augelli (1994, p. 120) defined lesbians and gay men as individuals "who express their needs for closeness and intimacy more consistently with people of the same gender." Golden (1994) described lesbians as either "primary" or "elective," distinguishing between individuals who believe they have no choice in their orientation and those who perceive themselves as having consciously chosen a lesbian orientation. However, Golden's primary and elective attributions may not be as generalizable to gay men. According to Golden, feminism plays a significant role in creating the distinction between elective and primary lesbian orientation. Still other theorists have defined lesbians and gay men strictly in terms of self-definition. If individuals self-identify as lesbian or gay, regardless of their sexual practices or asexuality, they are treated by some definitions as lesbian or gay (Ferguson, 1981).

Although bisexuality has received less attention in the literature than homosexuality, historically bisexuals have experienced discrimination from both the heterosexual and the gay/lesbian communities (Comstock, 2005). Bisexuality occurs on a continuum and some who identify as bisexuals are equally attracted to both sexes while others are more attracted to one sex or the other. Some may self-identify as bisexual prior to coming out as gay/lesbian while others later become involved in strictly heterosexual relationships and give up their bisexual identity (2005). Many, however, retain a bisexual identity throughout life. Both homosexuals and bisexuals can also be transgendered.

*Transgender* is a much more complex term and refers to a broad category of people who are gender variant. Transgendered people can be gay, lesbian, bisexual, heterosexual, or nonsexual (Lev, 2004). Transgendered people have self-identified as *transsexual* (a person whose sexual identity is opposite to their biological sex at birth—some undergo sex reassignment surgery, some do not), *transvestite/crossdresser* (a person who wears clothing identified with the opposite sex and is frequently, but not always, heterosexual), *drag queen* (a male who emulates a female, is generally campy, and is often—but not always—gay), *intersexed* (a person born with mixed sexual physiology—also called a hermaphrodite—who is often surgically reassigned at birth), *androgyne* (a person appearing/identifying as neither man nor woman and presenting a gender either mixed or neutral), *masculine-identified females*, and *feminine-identified men*. The term *transgenderist* usually refers to a person who lives as the gender that is opposite his or her anatomical sex while retaining his or her biological birth anatomy. They feel that they are more than crossdressers but are not transsexuals. Transgendered persons can be *MTF* (male to female) or *FTM* (female to male) (Lev, 2004; Nangeroni, 1996).

As a better understanding of the varieties of sexual and gender identities and orientations has emerged in recent years, terminology describing these variations has also evolved. As discussed in Chapter 4, the term *queer*, popularized in the 1990s by Queer Nation, is now commonly used as an umbrella term to describe all sexual and gender minorities. In fact, some prefer it because it is not gender specific. The letter Q in LGBTQI can also denote those who are questioning their sexual or gender identity, or sexual orientation. A more recent term, *gender queer* (GQ) refers to people who do not identify as either male or female or who identify as both. Those who are GQ may or may not see themselves as transgendered and the term *androgyne* is often used synonymously with GQ (Aizura, Walsh, Pike, Ward, & Jak, 2010). There is scant research or theory on GQ and intersexed (the letter I in LGBTQI) identity development, and due to this the remainder of the discussion will focus on people who identify as LGBT.

Due to the significant differences between gay/lesbian, bisexual, and transgender persons, separate models of identity development have been proposed by authors and researchers in the field, and we discuss these groups independently from each other while, at the same time, comparing and contrasting the similarities and differences where appropriate.

## Gay and Lesbian Identity Development

Traditional life stage theories defined homosexuality in terms of the failure to resolve developmental conflicts at certain stages of development. E. Erikson (1954) viewed homosexuality as the formation of a "negative identity" or role confusion in which the adolescent, failing to master the tasks of this stage, identifies completely with the opposite gender, essentially giving up all efforts to successfully complete the tasks traditionally associated with gender (J. Mills, 1990).

In fact, homosexuality was believed to be a form of psychiatric disorder and was treated as such until 1973, when the American Psychiatric Association removed the diagnosis of homosexuality from the *DSM* (Herek, 1995). By 1975, the American Psychological Association adopted a formal policy stating that homosexuality was not a function of mental illness or emotional or psychological deficiency (B. Greene, 1994). Other professional associations, such as the National Association of Social Workers, followed this lead and depathologized homosexuality. This marked the beginning of an era in which psychotherapists began to focus less on curing homosexuality and more on healthy lesbian and gay development over the life cycle (L. Brown, 1995; B. Greene, 1994).

Life stage theories abound in the literature about lesbian and gay development (Cass, 1979; E. Coleman, 1982; D. C. Kimmel, 1978; L. A. Lewis, 1984; Troiden, 1989). These stage theories center on sexual identity and the coming out process. Coming out is most simply defined as the process by which, over time, individuals come to identify, acknowledge, and, ultimately, accept themselves as lesbian or gay. Lev (2004) has noted that although the concept of *coming out* was developed within the gay and lesbian community, it has drifted into mainstream culture and is now used to describe personal disclosures that generally have stigmas attached to them. Most gay and lesbian coming out theories include the following elements: identity conflict or confusion; self-recognition; identity exploration and experimentation; disclosure to others; acceptance of identity and establishing long-term relationships; separatism, pride in identity, and wider disclosure; reconciliation with heterosexual culture; and expanding the focus of development beyond the scope of sexual orientation (Table 8.7). These theories share with other life cycle models the fact that many of the stages are reached as a result of crises. These crises, however, involve clashes with the heterosexist values of the larger society, individual expectations, lack of meaningful role models, and internalized homophobia (Gonsiorek, 1995).

Following neo-Freudian tradition, coming out theories require successful resolution at each stage to produce well-adjusted lesbian and gay individuals. Unsuccessful resolution of identity conflicts or ongoing confusion about sexual identity may prevent an individual from self-acknowledgment of a lesbian or gay sexual orientation. If self-recognition of orientation never occurs, identity exploration and experimentation either does not take place or continues to

| TABLE 8.7 | Stages of Coming Out |
| --- | --- |
| **Stage 1** | *Wonders "Could I be lesbian or gay?"* |
| Identity confusion | Fights against possibility of difference |
| Being different | Feels confused and alienated |
| Recognition | Seeks and absorbs relevant information about own behavior |
| | Seeks and absorbs relevant information about lesbians and gays |
| | Private awareness of thoughts, feelings, and behaviors |
| | Shut down self-awareness |
| | Gains different understanding of past behavior |
| **Stage 2** | *"I may be lesbian/gay"* |
| Identity comparison | Admits attraction to some people of the same sex |
| Coming out to self | Tentatively shares feelings with select others |
| | Confronts conflict between homosexual feelings and heterosexual indoctrination |
| | Changes expectations for future/grieves |
| | Changes expectations for behavioral rules |
| | Rationalizes or stops behavior |
| | Fears or denies possibility of negative reactions |
| **Stage 3** | *"I probably am lesbian/gay"* |
| Identity tolerance | Explores sexual, romantic, and other connections/relationships |
| Exploration | Looks for community/ideology |
| Relationships | Decides who, where, when, and how about coming out |
| Coming out to others | Segregates from heterosexuality |
| **Stage 4** | *"I am lesbian/gay"* |
| Identity acceptance | Learns about same sex partners |
| Significant relationships | Relaxes |
| | Builds families of choice |
| | Participates in lesbian/gay community |
| | Passes or self-discloses with some comfort |
| **Stage 5** | *Generally abandons passing* |
| Identity pride | Overemphasizes gay/lesbian identity and beliefs |
| | Discounts heterosexuality |
| | Develops "us" and "them" worldview |
| | Becomes identified with lesbian/gay community |
| **Stage 6** | *Eliminates dual identity* |
| Integration of identity | Develops sense of self that extends beyond homosexuality |
| | Abandons "us" and "them" worldview |
| | Focus shifts to issues beyond sexual identity |

*Source:* Adapted from Cass, 1996; E. Coleman, 1982; L. A. Lewis, 1984; Sophie, 1988.

feed identity conflicts. If sexual orientation is never disclosed to others, it is unlikely that a gay or lesbian individual can ever achieve acceptance of his or her identity. Failure to establish lesbian or gay relationships or to achieve some sense of pride in identity may perpetuate identity conflicts or confusion and internalized self-hatred.

Although establishing lesbian or gay identity as sequential and linear has distinct organizational and descriptive advantages, lesbian and gay identity formation does not always fit into such a tidy framework. In practical experience, some individuals with unresolved identity confusion do experiment with same-sex sexual activity over the life span but do not move on to make disclosures to others or to self-identify as a lesbian or gay. While it is true that lesbians and gays may, for example, struggle with identity confusion and eventually resolve this struggle, it is also true that this struggle can be resurrected at subsequent points in time. In fact, many lesbians and gay men live with identity conflict throughout their lives. It is also the experience of many gays and lesbians that pride in identity may be intact, but within certain social contexts (such as employment) individuals choose to conceal their sexual orientations because of social proscriptions against homosexuality and the lack of legal protection for this status. Each time a lesbian or gay man meets a new person or appears in a new environment, she or he may be faced with renewed conflicts relating to sexual identity, self-acceptance, and disclosure. Mastery of the conflicts attendant to coming out seems virtually impossible when an individual is faced with coming out each time a new person or situation is encountered.

It is particularly problematic that coming out stage theories do not generally address the unique experiences of lesbians, and most are modeled on the experiences of gay men. Research generally supports the conclusion that men come out more abruptly than women, and the primary focus of their coming out is sexual behavior (Gonsiorek, 1995). For women, the process of coming out seems to be more gradual and less associated with sexual behavior than with emotional and affectional attractions to same-sex partners (L. Brown, 1995). Vivienne Cass (1996), one of the originators of coming out developmental models, has modified her original work that described the identity formation of lesbians and gay men as virtually identical. Cass now describes the identity formation process for lesbians and gay men as being a function of Western European indigenous psychology. Western European psychology informs the identity formation of lesbians differently from that of gay men in two significant areas: (a) women understand emotions more easily than sexual feelings, and identification of sexual feelings is relatively easy for gay men and (b) women have more difficulty than men in the process of individuating and establishing their own sexual identities. In these two respects, Cass has found identity formation to be significantly different between lesbians and gay men. Cass has recognized that for lesbians, sexual identity and sexual behavior are distinct and different. At least with respect to these differences, Cass seems to have partially repudiated her own coming out stage theory.

Further, coming out stage theories do not appear capable of describing developmental tasks completed by gay men directly, and by lesbians indirectly, in the era of the AIDS pandemic. This pandemic has impacted the lesbian and gay community more directly than any other population. Gay men and lesbians have been faced with the experiences that Erikson attributed to the late stages of life in which one witnesses the loss of spouses and friends, loss of employment, loss of economic standing, and loss of control over one's own body. These events often occur during the years when Erikson's other developmental stages should be being resolved. Long before they can achieve "intimacy" or "generativity," many gay men in their early 20s and 30s are facing "integrity versus despair." Although it appears that many such men achieve a sense of wisdom, this achievement would be impossible based upon Erikson's formulation.

None of the early stage theories applicable to lesbians and gays account for gay and lesbian development in later life. Recent theories have attempted to bridge this gap by considering lesbian and gay development over the life span in terms of age cohort groups (D'Augelli, 1994). In view of the fact that cultural attitudes toward lesbians and gays have a significant impact on development over the life span, and cultural attitudes have changed over time, the age cohort model is likely to produce a more accurate description of gay and lesbian development.

## Bisexual Identity Development

Although bisexual men and women share some similarities in issues related to identity and coming out with gay men and lesbians, there are sufficient differences that are not adequately addressed by gay/lesbian coming out theories (Blumstein & Schwartz, 1993; F. Klein, 1993, 1999; Lev, 2004; Markowitz, 1995). Based on a series of research studies conducted in San Francisco between 1983 and 1988, Weinberg, Williams, and Pryor (1994) developed a model of bisexual identity development for both men and women. Most of the people interviewed described their bisexuality as an evolving process that began with first forming and establishing a heterosexual identity. Subsequently, most experienced homosexual attractions and encounters and, after experiencing concomitant heterosexual and homosexual attractions, many began to self-label as "bisexual." Gender differences, however, were apparent. For men, having sex was easier than falling in love, and for women, falling in love was easier than having sex. By the time of the 1988 follow-up interviews, many who participated in prior interviews reported changes in their romantic feelings, sexual feelings, and sexual behaviors. For example, bisexual women and men tended to seek out women as sexual partners following the discovery of HIV, because bisexual men were considered more of an HIV risk than women.

The model developed from this research has four stages: initial confusion, finding and applying the label, settling into the identity, and continued uncertainty. *Initial confusion*, the first stage, can last for years. Some feel confused because their attractions to members of both sexes are strong and anxiety provoking. Also, some assume that their same-sex attractions ends their attractions to the other sex. Another source of confusion may result when one's conceptual options include only "heterosexual" or "homosexual" as self-labels and not "bisexual." A final source of confusion found by Weinberg et al. (1994) was difficulty acknowledging one's same-sex attraction, a phenomenon more common in men than women.

The second stage is *finding and applying the label*. One way in which some participants were able to accomplish this was by having enjoyable sex with members of both sexes only *after* becoming aware of the bisexual label. However, others experienced such strong attractions to both sexes that they felt compelled to more quickly acknowledge they were bisexual. The encouragement of others was another important factor and, although this was more common for women than men, it was most likely to occur when men pressured their women partners to engage in a sexual threesome or group sex. Some women learned about bisexuality in a less pressured way, in contexts such as therapy, involvement in organizations, friendships, social events, or exposure to literature. However, even after the label was discovered and applied, many reported negative attitudes about bisexual behavior, and stereotypes about bisexuals added to their intermittent self-doubt or confusion (Weinberg et al., 1994). In addition, some experienced attractions more toward one sex, causing them to wonder if they might be gay or lesbian.

In the third stage, *settling into the identity*, people became more comfortable with their sexuality, often through social support. However, during this stage, some wondered whether bisexuality was a phase or transition (e.g., from heterosexual to homosexual, or homosexual to heterosexual), and some believed that if they were in monogamous relationships, then transition to a monosexual identity would occur. Because those in the self-described transition process did not mention the gender of their monogamous partners, Weinberg et al. (1994) concluded that the quality of these relationships was likely to be a more important factor than the actual gender of the partner. Others cited relational breakups as a factor precipitating their transition from bisexual identification to homosexual or heterosexual. That said, changes in sexual behaviors were more prominent than changes in self-labels. In other words, some continued to self-label as bisexual even though they were in monogamous relationships. Due to this, this stage appears to be more strongly related to peoples' acceptance of their bisexual feelings rather than sexual or emotional involvement with members of both sexes.

The final stage in this model is *continued uncertainty*. Weinberg et al. (1994) found that, even though participants self-labeled as bisexual, it was common for them to experience periodic confusion about their sexuality. For some, insufficient social validation, including a lack of bisexual role models and communities, was believed to be a contributing factor. For others, confusion may result from the need to change to a lesbian or gay self-label to be accepted in homosexual communities. For women, a lack of social support may carry over into some feminist communities or negatively impact their feminist identity. For example, feminist bisexual women also felt as though they were being "acculturated" into liking men or "selling out the world of women" by their attractions to men (p. 35). Furthermore, some men reported feeling uncertain about how to have multiple partnered (e.g., nonmonogamous) relationships or how to be in relationships at all. For both sexes, being in a monogamous relationship contributed to continued uncertainty about their bisexuality. Similarly, those who were inhibited about acting on their attraction to both sexes or who had weaker feelings for one sex also experienced this uncertainty.

Due to the dearth of bisexual resources and communities outside of San Francisco, Weinberg et al. (1994) wondered whether it is possible for bisexuals in other cities to reach the later stages of bisexual identity development. The authors also recognized the simplicity and broadness of their model, acknowledging that there may be alternate pathways by which bisexual identity develops.

Building on the work of Weinberg et al. (1994), T. Brown (2000) extended their model in an attempt to integrate research from the literature on lesbian and gay identity development to describe better how members of both sexes experience the process of bisexual identity development. One of the major contributions of this model is a clear articulation of possible gender differences for each stage separately and for the developmental process of bisexual identity as a whole. In addition, Brown reconceptualized Weinberg et al.'s fourth and final stage, continued uncertainty, and relabeled it *identity maintenance* to more accurately describe the behavioral features described in this stage. In Weinberg et al.'s follow-up study, the vast majority (75%) were found to have continued self-labeling as bisexual, despite occasional emotional or cognitive uncertainty. They proposed that affiliation with a bisexual community and/or serial or concomitant involvement with members of both sexes would be important for maintaining a bisexual identity.

For the remaining 25%, they found that those who were monogamous were more likely to adopt a self-label congruent with their current relationships and adopt a homosexual identity and that this was also associated with concomitant uncertainty about their bisexuality. Those who remained confused lacked social validation, role models, and social support and reported an absence of sexual activity with members of both sexes.

Other reasons for questioning their self-label as bisexual were associated with vacillations in their attractions to women and men and social pressure to change their self-label. And yet other reasons included a new or deepened involvement in a monogamous relationship, a belief that bisexuality represented a transition to homosexuality, a loss of interest in members of one sex, and a disinterest in self-labels about sexuality.

Clearly, not all who reach *identity maintenance* remain there. For those who experience uncertainty, several factors may contribute to this. For example, some who are monogamously involved may experience a type of cognitive dissonance associated with uncertainty or change in their self-label. Just as Golden (1987) reported that self-labeled lesbians may continue to have sexual contact with men, it would be anticipated that not all bisexuals would necessarily experience this dissonance. Another possibility is that some proceed through bisexual identity in the process of exploring and discovering their own sexuality. Alternately, some may experience bisexuality as a means of foreclosing homosexual identity, as suggested by Cass (1979) and Troiden (1988). Finally, Cass and Troiden both posited that gays/lesbians who progress to the final stage of homosexual identity development may revisit earlier stages, and this may be the case for those who are experiencing uncertainty about their bisexuality as well.

## Transgender Identity Development

Although the coming out process for gays, lesbians, and bisexuals has received a fair amount of attention in the literature, less is known about coming out and identity development for transgendered persons. As previously noted, this population is characterized by incredible diversity, and much of the scant research has been devoted to transsexuals who are seeking sexual reassignment surgery.

Early work by anthropologist Ann Bolin (1988, 1992) described the process of transitioning from one sex to the other and identified a three-stage process that included separation, transition, and incorporation. This transition includes a sense of "rebirth" that occurs prior to sex reassignment surgery. Other researchers have also studied male-to-female transsexuals and delineated stages of transition that begin with distress, confusion, and anxiety and culminate in acceptance and incorporation of a new identity (Lewins, 1995; Rachlin, 1997). Lev (2004) has noted that "unlike gay, lesbian, and bisexual people who have the option to remain closeted if they choose about their desires, their behaviors, and even their lifestyles, transgendered and transsexual people who do modify their bodies must engage in a transaction process with others who will witness and react to these visible body changes" (p. 233). However, she also recognized that there is a psychological, sociological, and possibly spiritual process involved in accepting a gender variant identity, even though many transgender people fail to fully "transition" biologically from one sex to another.

In her work on transgender emergence, Lev formulated a six-stage process that is built on both gay and lesbian coming out theories as well as transsexual transition theories but was developed to include a "wider range of identities and pathways to resolution" (2004, p. 233). Fully acknowledging variation within this population, her model was designed to describe emergence as it is experienced by transsexual and transgendered adults.

**STAGE 1: AWARENESS**    In this initial stage, gender variant people are frequently in great distress as they become conscious of feeling different and realize that they may be different. For many this awareness may go back to early childhood, while others may not recognize their gender variance or feel distress until puberty or adulthood. Most, however, experience *gender dysphoria*, "a profound discomfort with their birth sex and confusion over what this means" (Lev, 2004, p. 236). When people become consciously aware of their gender variance, intense emotions may be experienced. Lev warned that overwhelming feelings and possible terror that are felt should not be underestimated or ignored. In contrast, others experience this stage with joy and a sense of release. Importantly, in this extremely emotional stage, it is premature to make decisions about transitioning.

**STAGE 2: SEEKING INFORMATION/REACHING OUT** As people progress to stage 2, they seek education and support about issues related to transgenderism. Fortunately, this is now relatively easy due to the growing transgender liberation movement and access to the array of information found on the Internet. Many spend hours absorbed in web pages and reading literature on trans-genderism. Some go online and experiment with "virtual gender," which gives them the ability to change their identity at will without the fear of getting caught or exposing themselves. This second stage may actually precede stage 1, as some people first learn about transgenderism on the Internet and subsequently enter the awareness stage.

In reaching out to others, people begin to understand that they are a part of a wider commu-nity, and this facilitates a shifting of identity from one of isolation and distress to feeling that they are a part of an identifiable group. As people gain more knowledge and a sense of belonging, they often begin reexamining their own histories in a way that allows them to restructure the past and come to a positive resolution of their emerging identity as a transgendered person. In some communities, transgender support groups are available and some people reach out by calling or attending these groups. For others, it may be difficult to find a group or person with whom they can identify, and Lev points out that simply finding other transgendered people does assure that there are sufficient similarities to break through feelings of isolation. Some may experience other transgendered people as being sufficiently different from themselves and come to feel further isolated if this occurs. The dominant themes in this stage for most are growth, expansion, and the development of a more solid sense of identity.

**STAGE 3: DISCLOSURE TO SIGNIFICANT OTHERS** Even as transgendered people begin to gain an awareness of this fundamental and normal part of themselves, they are also rightfully cognizant of the distress that this may create for significant others in their lives. Although most have already disclosed to a therapist or other transgendered people, disclosing to loved ones is usually a frightening prospect. For some, disclosure brings a significant release of anxiety and tension, and many are relieved, regardless of the response. However, this may also evoke an array of negative emotional reactions from significant others that can be devastating. Although the emotionality of stage 1 may resurface, it is now bolstered with the knowledge and support gained in the second stage. Quite commonly, families have been aware of at least some of the issues related to gender variance, but many have failed to outwardly acknowledge that awareness and have relied on denial, avoidance, and silence instead. In addition, there are significant potential conflicts involved in coming out to partners, spouses, and significant others, not the least of which involve issues related to custody of minor children and potential dissolution of the mar-riage or partnership. Some, however, cannot afford to self-disclose and, despite this, may be discovered by loved ones or the police. When this occurs, they may experience disclosure before experiencing the awareness of stage 1 or gaining access to the resources of stage 2.

**STAGE 4: EXPLORING IDENTITY AND TRANSITION** As people enter this stage, they begin to explore various transgender identities in the search for an identity or label that "fits" who they are. Rather than talking about what is wrong with them or remaining preoccupied with approval from others, they become "engaged in a self-reflective process of authenticity . . . and come to terms with a great truth about who they are" (Lev, 2004, p. 254). Central to this stage is resolu-tion of their gender dysphoria and coming to accept their gender identity. It is common now to experiment with new roles, clothing, and mannerisms appropriate to their gender identity. They may get more involved in crossdressing, begin to risk exposure as they start to crossdress in pub-lic, and some may display more outwardly visible signs of masculinity or femininity. Outward changes in this stage are generally easier for transgendered females to manage, as unisex clothing is already common, and wearing pants, baseball caps, or other masculine clothing can also be interpreted as a fashion statement unrelated to transgenderism. In addition, many of these changes are not glaringly apparent and, instead, involve subtleties of gendered mannerism such as gestures, sitting and walking postures, and the use of voice.

In this stage, people also begin to look to the future and consider the impact of their transition on family members as well as on their future employment and financial status. Although some may consider the use of hormones and total transsexual transition, the real-life implications of these decisions lead many to reject these options. Others may take hormones in low doses to achieve better body congruence but do not choose to fully transition to the other sex. In this regard, Lev has warned that "it is important to not attribute a hierarchy to the emergence process, and sometimes people do feel pressure from within the transgendered community to 'move ahead,' when they are unsure if this is what they want or what is best for them" (2004, pp. 255–256). Because the consequences for gender transition can be personally and socially damaging, people must be allowed to explore and choose the degree of transition that best fits with their personal needs and desires.

**STAGE 5: EXPLORATION—TRANSITION ISSUES/POSSIBLE BODY MODIFICATION**   This stage involves consolidating gender presentation, exploring options for transition and body modification. Technically, those who do not desire body modification are not considered to be "transsexual," and this has prevented them from being considered as candidates for hormones or surgery. According to Lev, "Transgendered people have often felt stuck between two untenable realities—living in bodies that felt dissonant or having a full sex change. Middle-ground positions were not seen as options" (2004, p. 259). Most, but not all, explore the possibility of body modification (e.g., hormones, electrolysis, surgery), and some compromise by living between genders, take pride in this, and enjoy switching back and forth. Lev noted that this is more common among transgendered youth, and people who have chosen to live alternative and unconventional lifestyles. For some, fluidity of gender presentation allows them to explore both their masculine and their feminine sides. However, many transsexuals are now choosing full transition and are more likely to be out and open due to the growth of the transliberation movement. Importantly, one significant difference between coming out as gay, lesbian, or bisexual and emerging transgendered is that "once body modifications begin, transgendered people are forced out of the closet" (p. 263).

**STAGE 6: INTEGRATION AND PRIDE**   In this final stage, identity as a transgendered or transsexual person becomes integrated and synthesized. Transmen and transwomen become comfortable with their current identities, do not deny their previous selves, and no longer experience gender dysphoria. Importantly, in contrast to most gay/lesbian models, identity integration does not necessarily mandate that they come out to be integrated. As Lev noted, "there are many paths towards integration; some people choose to live 'stealth' and others choose to be more 'out' about their transsexual history, or current transgendered status" (2004, p. 267). Some live fully as the opposite sex while others do not. For transsexuals, gender identity is based on "who they know themselves to be" rather than on their genitals. Different people use different strategies, and the key issue for this stage is resolving gender dysphoria and making necessary adjustments to life in a gender-polarized world. However, they choose to define themselves, "they have become comfortable with who they are, and where they stand in the transgendered continuum. They have synthesized . . . their gender identity . . . into the greater whole of who they are (artist, parent, business owner, chef, accountant, attorney, etc.)" (p. 268). Lev also cautioned that resolution at this stage does not mean that the current life choices are permanent and the way that transgender people choose to live may change at some point in the future.

Lev's work is particularly important because it helps us understand the complexity of sexual and gender identity and illuminates the problems inherent in the traditional conceptions of gender identity, gender role, and sexual orientation. It also points to the fluidity of the process of identity transformation and the reality that as people's lives, needs, self-identifications, and circumstances change, gender identity can change as well.

Although there is a growing body of research and theory on gay, lesbian, bisexual, and transgender identity, less scientific attention has been given to identity development of other sexual minorities. With the advent and growth of the Internet, persons with sexually variant orientations and interests have begun to discover that they are not alone, reach out to each other, and reinforce each other's identities. According to Lev (2004, p. 162), the Internet has become a "gathering place" for information and communication, and sexual variation that was "previously thought to be 'rare and unusual' . . . may be fairly common" (Apostolides, 1999; Martins & Ceccarelli, 2003; Moser, 1999).

In much the same way that social scientists and researchers have begun to question our assumptions about narrowly constructed gender roles, they are also examining the complexities of a variety of sexual practices and orientations that were once considered to be perversions or paraphilias. Erotic power exchange (EPE) or BDSM (bondage/discipline, domination/submission, sadism/masochism) refers to eroticized, consensual, noncriminal sexual play and acts that were historically categorized as "deviant" and "pathological" forms of sexuality. EPE and BDSM may also include a variety of fetishes such as crossdressing and other forms of transgenderism. Scholarly works by a variety of authors (Brame, Brame, & Jacobs, 1996; Bullough & Bullough, 1993; Bullough, Bullough, & Elias, 1997; T. P. Lester, 2003; Weinberg, 1995; Wells, 2003) have begun to examine the dynamics of these traditionally unconventional forms of sexuality, and it is becoming clear that there is a growing community of people who identify at least part of their sexual orientation in relation to BDSM practices. Despite the variety of subcultures *within* the BDSM community (e.g., gay, lesbian, transgender, heterosexual, bisexual, male dominant, female dominant, and fetish, among others), the identity issues that many people in this lifestyle encounter are not dissimilar to those previously discussed. At a minimum, identity emergence involves some degree of questioning and uncertainty, connection to others, some degree of coming out, and self-acceptance. Clearly, more research is needed in this area to better understand the specific issues and diversity within this sexual minority group so that practice with this population does not rely on outdated pathological concepts of sexual difference (Kleinplatz & Moser, 2004).

Numerous authors have pointed to shortcomings inherent in coming out theories. Although some theorists indicate that their theories are not intended to be construed as linear and sequential, this ignores the fact that implicit in each of these theories, issues such as identity confusion are expected to be successfully resolved at a certain point in each individual's life. It is presumed that when the conflicts associated with each coming out stage are resolved, individuals are then able to move to the next successive stage until they reach the stage in which they have achieved such comfort with sexual orientation that the focus of development shifts to different issues, unrelated to sexual orientation. In other words, coming out stage theories are, by definition, more than merely descriptive.

The stage theories that have developed around sexual identity formation or coming out do not appear to be widely applicable outside of Western European culture (Cass, 1996; Chan, 1995; D'Augelli, 1994; Gonsiorek, 1995). Social constructionists generally view coming out theories as mere fabrications that are a product of European American thought but that do not accurately depict identity formation outside of Western European culture (Kitzinger, 1995).

Coming out stage theories do not have a great deal of significance among other racial and ethnic groups in which individuals are often conflicted between their birth cultures and LGBT cultures. As Chan (1995) illustrated, many Asian cultures stress the intense privacy of sexual behavior. To discuss such behavior, even in front of family members, might be perceived as bringing shame to the family. To identify one's self according to one's sexual behavior would be viewed as utterly inappropriate. European American views of the coming out process, which hail disclosure to others as a stage in healthy development, are completely antithetical to appropriate behavior within Asian cultures. Similar issues impact African Americans and Hispanics. Stage theories of coming out impose the expectation on members of other cultural groups that they must, in effect, choose between their birth cultures and their sexual orientations.

Stage theories that have been created to describe life span development of oppressed cultural groups such as African Americans and Hispanics are not generally applicable to LGBT persons, despite their status as members of oppressed populations (Pope, 1995). Three factors set LGBT persons apart from other cultural minorities: (a) they do not usually have familial support to assist in their developmental processes; (b) most lesbians, gay men, bisexuals, and some transgendered persons can "pass" as heterosexual and are thus constantly confronted with the question whether to come out in any given setting; and (c) sexual orientation is not always viewed as an immutable characteristic, and it is often perceived as a matter of choice that can be changed.

Because of the central focus on sexual behavior, coming out theories do not account for other developmental issues affecting LGBT persons, such as widespread expressions by many that throughout childhood and/or adolescence, they have always felt "different" from their peers (Kaufman & Raphael, 1996). This feeling of "differentness" is described as broader in scope than the feelings of differentness attributable to a different sexual identity (D'Augelli, 1994).

Coming out stage theories also do not take into account the distinction between sexual behavior and sexual identity. Many lesbians, bisexuals, and some gay men experience changes in their sexual identity over time (Golden, 1987). The well-known singer Holly Near is an excellent example of an individual who had early sexual experiences with women, and who identifies herself as lesbian, but whose primary romantic and sexual attractions have generally been to men (L. Brown, 1995). Many men engage in same-sex sexual practices but do not identify themselves as gay or bisexual. This issue has only recently received media attention on *The Oprah Winfrey Show*, regarding African American men who identify as heterosexual but have sex with men, and in the film media (*On the Down Low* by Iconoclast Films) about Latino men who do the same. Two recent books by King and Hunter (2004) and King (2005) have also explored this topic. In some cultures, same-sex sexual practices are employed as a form of birth control, where other forms of birth control may be prohibited by religious strictures.

Life span stage theories are generally problematic when applied to LGBT development because they focus most specifically on sexual behavior that is not necessarily reflective of sexual identity. In addition, stage theories applied to this population are overly simplistic. These theories require resolution at each stage, but many aspects of coming out cannot be resolved because the conflicts constantly recur as each new situation is encountered. LGBT development over the life span must be viewed as fluid and as limited and shaped by the context in which it occurs. Stage theories do suggest fluidity but do not take into account the impact of contextuality.

Finally, as noted earlier, coming out stage theories lack cultural sensitivity, and are thus of limited utility with other populations. Nonetheless, stage theories do offer useful descriptive information about the barriers involved in coming out and play an important role in sensitizing us to the heterosexist bias that permeates most developmental theory.

## STAGE THEORIES: POPULARITY VERSUS VALIDITY

Life span developmental stage theories have made an important contribution to the study of human behavior by helping us move away from the idea that "lifescripts are written in childhood." They do us a disservice, however, in telling us that development is primarily a function of chronological age. Dannefer (1984a) has elaborated on the problems inherent in ontogenetic models. The term *ontogenetic* is applied to developmental psychology when human behavior is seen as a function of age. According to Dannefer (p. 104):

> the basic structure of adult development theory involves one primary independent variable, age, and one dependent variable, the developmental sequence. . . . In sum, ontogenetic stage theories conceive of the developmental process as uniform and constant. Since the sequence is invariant, the causal factors must be invariant as well: the enormous range of environmental variability is thus logically required to be causally unimportant.

Numerous studies have shown that environment varies by race (Lieberson, 1980b), class (Elder & Liker, 1982; Farrell & Rosenberg, 1981; M. L. Kohn, 1969), gender (Sokoloff, 1980), the structure of labor markets (Doeringer & Piore, 1971), and career paths (Spillerman, 1977). Stage theories do not allow for this full range of variation and their impact on development. Often, environment is acknowledged as a factor but given little or no weight in developmental outcomes.

Why, then, are stage theories so popular? Sociologist Orville Brim, Jr., suggested that they are "a little like horoscopes. They are vague enough so that everyone can see something of themselves in them" (in Rosenfeld & Stark, 1991, p. 231). Popularity, however, should not be confused with validity. Universal life stages for psychosocial development probably do not exist despite the growing literature in the field.

Alice Rossi (1985) has pointed out, for example, that there are more similarities between those in the same birth cohort (a group that experiences historical events at about the same age as they move through the life cycle) than between groups of people born in different generations. Demographic and economic factors, rather than psychological ones, may have a significant impact on major life events. Our dreams, expectations, values, and opportunities are shaped as much by external factors as internal ones. The size of a birth cohort is influential in determining the degree of competition and, therefore, the amount of opportunity and quality of life.

The concept of similarities among members of birth cohorts was popularized in the 1990s by authors William Strauss and Neil Howe in their book *Generations: The History of America's Future, 1584–2069* (1991), in which they proposed that in the four centuries of American history (dating from early colonial times), there have been recurring patterns of four "peer personality" types that describe attributes of people belonging to specific generational cohorts. Although they acknowledged that the identified attributes may not fit everyone in a given generation, they posited that people sharing the same "age location" in history are influenced by their generation's "collective mind-set." The idea of generationally shared psychological characteristics became further popularized with the term *generation X*, now commonly used to describe the group of then young adults who are currently in their 40s. Although the idea of similarities within birth cohorts sensitizes us to the fact that there are shared experiences among people born in the same generation, this has unfortunately led to overly simplistic stereotyping that fails to look at both individual and subgroup differences. In fact, the peer personality of generation Xers has been commonly portrayed as one of disenfranchisement, uninvolvement, and laziness, denoted by the term *slackers*. The popular media's role in furthering this negative stereotype has been a point of contention with those who do not believe that personality types can be attributed solely to one's birthdate.

Further, in looking at contemporary society, Bernice Neugarten argued that the life cycle has become fluid; age is no longer a good predictor of specific life events. She pointed to the fact that massive changes in society have brought with them a new timing for life events as well as inconsistencies in age-appropriate behavior. The complexity of society has led to a change in the meaning of social age. Distinctions that once may have been valid are now blurring as the lines between developmental stages fade. Children, for example, now have knowledge of sex, drugs, and nuclear war, topics that were once "reserved" for adults. They also engage in more adult-like sexual behavior and adult-like crime. In contrast, the emergence of the "young-old," those who are healthy, physically active, financially stable, and politically active, has caused us to question when old age begins. Although age norms have not totally disappeared, they are becoming less relevant in determining the course of our lives.

In a similar vein, Nancy Schlossberg pointed to the unpredictable nature of our contemporary lifestyles. The traditional timetables used in developmental theories are not in congruence with the reality of our social lives. According to Schlossberg, "No one is doing things on time any more" (in Tavris, 1989). Accordingly, she believes that it is specific events that occur, or fail to occur, that shape our lives and development.

One thing is clear as we review the works of contemporary developmental theorists: There is little consensus among them. The research is often contradictory, suggesting that there are no universal stages or principles.

## CONTEMPORARY ISSUES

The models of development presented here underscore the necessity of recognizing contemporary social conditions that create stressors for people and decrease their ability to cope effectively with transitions. One example in modern society is the increasing number of persons caught in the "sandwich generation"—those who care for both children and elderly parents. Although this may be sequential rather than concurrent, it is nonetheless a stressor, and disproportionately so for women who are usually the primary care providers (Hunter & Sundel, 1989).

Erikson's attempt to be historically specific in describing development in industrial societies is admirable. His recognition that behavioral norms, family structure, interpersonal relationships, and societal expectations are related to the economic structure of society added an important dimension that was notably lacking in Freud's earlier formulation. Erikson's most recent theorizing, however, largely ignores the massive social change that has occurred in the past 50 years. Instead of expanding his theory to reflect the structural changes involved in a service-oriented (rather than industrial) society, he remained entrenched in his original theory, refining the stages that he first wrote about in 1950. The fluidity of the life cycle that is apparent to many contemporary writers received no recognition in his most current work.

The same has been true for most theorists writing about the family life cycle as well (Carter & McGoldrick, 1980, 1989; Duvall, 1971, 1988; Hill, 1986; Rhodes, 1977). This is significant because, historically, theories of family life cycle were intricately tied to notions of individual development based on autonomy and were centered on factors such as the birth of a child, child rearing, and the "empty nest," as children leave home. The significant ways in which family structure has been impacted by social, economic, and technological changes have been largely ignored in most family stage theory, which continues to portray the family as being a White, middle-class, nuclear, child-centered, heterosexual couple, often divorced and remarried, with children and/or stepchildren. Coontz (1992) has pointed out that the "traditional" nuclear family was, in fact, a new phenomenon in the 1950s and " a historical fluke, based on a unique and temporary conjuncture of economic, social and political factors" (p. 28).

Although some theorists have recognized the reality of divorce, remarriage, and blended families, few have addressed the variety of diverse and flexible family forms that now exist (Frazier, 1994; Schriver, 2010; Slater & Mencher, 1991; Weston, 1991; Zinn & Eitzen, 1993). In addition, technological advances such as birth control, in vitro fertilization, and surrogacy have made the family life cycle considerably more fluid; this fluidity has a significant impact on individual development as well. Roger Gould, who once accepted the idea of formal stages, now calls them "hogwash." His clinical observations have led him to revise his thinking, and he now believes that instead of progressing through stages, people "change their ways of looking at and experiencing the world over time" (cited in Rosenfeld & Stark, 1991, p. 232).

Rapidly advancing technology and the pervasiveness of computers, the Internet, video games, smart phones, texting, and social media sites such as Facebook have recently raised concerns about the ability of the current "Net Generation" (also called N-Gens, Generation Y, or the Millennial Generation), born in the late 1970s and early 1980s, to balance real-life demands with the constant distraction of the virtual world. Some fear that memory, school performance, sleep patterns, self-control, the ability to focus, and face-to-face social interactions are being compromised by constant electronic stimulation and multitasking (Beuerlein, 2008; Richtel, 2010). However, researcher and author Don Tapscott, who has surveyed over 10,000 young people, contends that there is little concrete evidence to support this negative view. In his books *Growing Up Digital: The Rise of the Net Generation* (1999) and *Grown Up Digital: How the Net Generation Is Changing Your World* (2008), he discusses the behavioral norms of N-Gens and the potential effects that these may have on the culture, workplace, family structure, and education. Citing his research and that of others, he argues that the use of technology is actually making many young people smarter as well as equipping them with crucial mental and interactional skills necessary for succeeding in a digital age. Although some believe that his view may be unduly optimisitc, it provides a serious counter to the overly negative view of the effects of technology on the motivation and behavior of today's youth.

Finally, an important issue that has received little attention in life span theories is that of resilience. Although most life span theories see growth and change as possible, there has been little attempt to examine individual or group differences that lead to resilience for those who experience multiple stressors during childhood and adolescence. A growing literature in this area (Andrews, 1997; Gelman, 1997) is now documenting the "protective" factors that allow some children to thrive in spite of adversity. Although the research points to a cluster of factors that include genetic predisposition and personality, the single most consistent factor is a trusting relationship with an adult. Resilient children often seek out relationships with adults outside of their family when family members are abusive, mentally ill, or unavailable. Further research in this area will likely help us understand the ways in which we can foster resilience to help produce better developmental outcomes for multiple risk children.

## APPLICATION TO SOCIAL WORK PRACTICE

Life span theory and Erikson's epigenetic model, in particular, have been widely embraced by social work practitioners and educators alike. Erikson's model continues to be one of the most prevalent models of psychosocial development used in practice today. Although Erikson's later work became more focused on health and adaptation, his initial theory and basic developmental schema was heavily rooted in the Freudian tradition. Thus, the initial leap from Freud to Erikson was a small one. Subsequent focus on adaptation of the conflict-free ego led to a more positive view that mastery could be achieved despite a struggle against tremendous odds. The expanded radius of environment proposed by Erikson also fit well with a renewed interest in person-in-environment, much of which had been ignored by classic psychoanalytical thought.

Authors such as Neugarten, Gould, Rossi, Schlossberg, and Friedan (to name a few) are examples of contemporary theorists whose works are underrepresented in social work textbooks and journals. Fortunately, in the past 10 years, there has been a significant increase of research and practice guidelines for gerontological social work (e.g., Berkman & D'Ambruoso, 2006). Although there is increasing attention to competing paradigms relative to women's development and ways of knowing and, more recently, theories of LGBT development, traditional theories based on Eurocentric and heterosexist male developmental models continue to predominate both human behavior textbooks and questions on social work licensing exams.

## Definition of the Helping Situation

The theories presented here are all based on models of adaptation and transformation and lend themselves to two definitions of the helping situation: *problem* and *growth*. People are seen as inherently adaptive and creative and able to transform themselves and their lives, if given access to the necessary social supports. However, despite the fact that most of these theories are not rooted in an illness model of behavior, it is not uncommon for adult psychopathology to be identified with incomplete resolution of intrapsychic conflict during infancy or childhood. This is likely a holdover from Erikson's early epigenetic model that tied such psychopathology to childhood stages. Flowchart 8.1 illustrates a possible road map of the helping situation.

## Assessment, Practice Strategies, and Methods

Stage theory-based practice is generally defined in terms of an "expert" clinician who assesses whether clients are adequately and normally meeting their life tasks. If problems are identified, causes may relate to earlier unresolved life stages, thus requiring a sort of archeological dig into the person's past through psychotherapy.

Many of Erikson's therapeutic goals were similar to those of Freud, although his methods were somewhat different. The model of practice derived from his theory is largely based on insight, aimed at strengthening the rational capabilities of the ego. Many therapeutic techniques are identical to those described previously in our discussion of ego psychology. Assessment is based on detailed psychosocial histories, and treatment often focuses on uncovering unconscious material that impedes healthy ego functioning.

In contrast to traditional psychoanalysis, Erikson did not place a major focus on childhood experiences in the family of origin and preferred to stress personal responsibilities. Because a strong focus is on unconscious material, free association may be used with adults. In his work with children, Erikson placed a great reliance on the use of play to uncover the child's unconscious. The types of configurations that children build with blocks, or the play scenes they create with dolls, are believed to reveal aspects of the ego that are representative of their unconscious conflicts (Ewen, 1988).

Another direct application of his theory can be seen in work with adolescents struggling with identity crisis. Educational models aimed at assisting adolescents in their struggle for identity may employ courses in life adjustment and self-understanding (R. M. Thomas, 1985). Erikson's most current theory expansion on development in late adulthood and old age will likely lead to practice models that assist the elderly in coming to terms with their own mortality and help them to adapt to physical degeneration. Therapeutic methods that facilitate a "life review" may help people gain a sense of closure on life that leads to adaptive functioning and "wisdom."

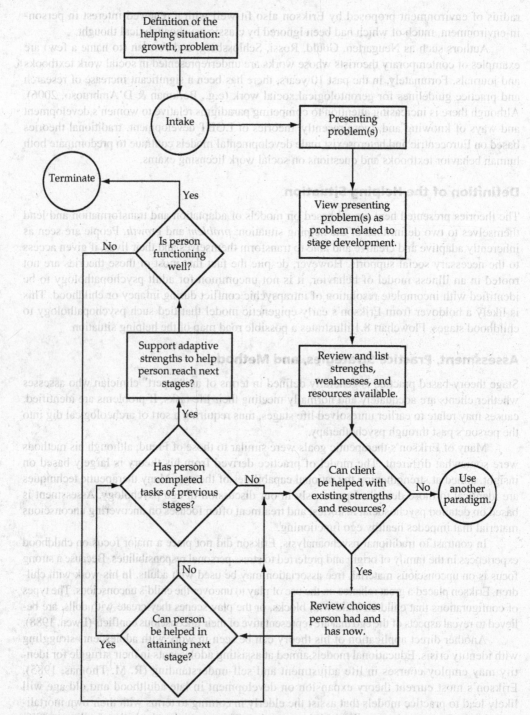

**FLOWCHART 8.1.** One possible road map for applying developmental stage theories. © 1998, S. P. Robbins, P. Chatterjee, & E. R. Canda.

The contemporary body of life span theory and research that focuses on middle and older age presents a fairly optimistic model for practice because it points to the possibility of change after early adulthood. This perspective underscores the importance of life circumstances and external events more than intrapsychic phenomena, although they are interrelated. Accordingly, therapeutic techniques would be targeted at continual growth and development throughout life and would focus on the way in which life conditions impact intrapersonal and interpersonal dynamics.

In contrast, theoretical knowledge about women's development and the development of LGBTQI persons suggest models of practice that focus more on individual and group empowerment as a way to overcome barriers endemic to an androcentric, heterosexist society.

Finally, inasmuch as the idea of universal patterns of development is, at best, questionable, it is important that practice models reflect a strong focus on individual adaptation and coping that is reflective of the specific social conditions, contexts, and transformations in the client's life. Table 8.8 illustrates settings and applications of life span theories.

## CRITICAL ANALYSIS

### Biological, Psychological, and Spiritual Factors

Biological factors are recognized as being important factors in development but are not the primary area of emphasis in most psychosocial developmental theories. Accordingly, there is little elaboration of the specific biological processes that underlie most developmental processes. In addition, more attention is given to physical growth and development occurring between birth and adolescence than in middle age and later life. Biological changes are seen as being interrelated with psychological and social growth in most developmental theories.

Biology has sometimes become the primary focus of recent attempts to uncover the "causes" of homosexuality. This is not surprising, as "deviant" behavior is easier to explain if a biological cause can be attributed to it. In contrast to the earlier psychological theories of Freud and Erikson that attributed homosexuality to incomplete psychosocial resolution of crises in early developmental stages, biological explanations tend to focus on either genetic transmission or structural differences in the brain. It is unlikely, however, that a single cause will be found to uniformly explain as complex a phenomenon as sexual orientation. One must also recognize that biological explanations are commonly used in an attempt to rationalize discriminatory beliefs and practices.

Most of our concepts of physical and biological changes in late life, unfortunately, have been based on models of pathological illness (such as Alzheimer's disease) rather than on normal change. This is now being recognized and corrected in the contemporary literature on successful aging, aging well, and gerotranscendence.

The primary focus of life span theories is on psychological growth and adaptation over the life span. Some theories emphasize the full range of stages, whereas others emphasize a specific stage such as midlife or later adulthood. Further, there is an emphasis on successful crisis resolution and adaptation as a major factor in psychosocial development. One must recognize that the tasks described by Erikson (and those writing in the Eriksonian tradition) refer to what an individual should do, rather than what is scientifically likely. Finally, some theories emphasize development in males, whereas others emphasize developmental processes in females. More recently, a growing body of theory has focused specifically on LGBT development, with specific attention to the psychosocial factors and consequences of coming out. A growing body of theory is now addressing gay and lesbian parenting as well (Weston, 1991).

| TABLE 8.8 | Various Settings and Applications of Life Span Development Theories | | | |
|---|---|---|---|---|
| Type of Agency | Type of Presenting Problem(s) | Type of Program | Definition(s) of the Helping Situation | Type(s) of Activities |
| Private practice | Individual's difficulty with intimacy | Individual psychotherapy | Problem Growth | Psychosocial history; stage development assessment; talk therapy |
| Women's services center | Women's frustration of life goals | Women's Psychosocial support counseling | Problem Growth | Psychosocial history and goal assessment; examination of gender-based roles and restrictions; assertiveness training and action |
| Area council on aging | Elder's sense of isolation and anxiety about mortality | Individual counseling | Problem Growth | Psychosocial history; life review; re-connection with significant others; referral to community center |
| Family services center | Gay adolescent questions identity and life goals | Individual counseling | Problem Growth | Assessment of ego-identity, peer and family relations, and comfort with sexual orientation; clarification of life goals and action plans |

Life span theories that address spirituality generally focus on the emergence of spiritual themes in mid to later adulthood. They typically ignore the spiritual development of children and youth or address it only indirectly as an aspect of ego formation and enculturation. The recent interdisciplinary movement of positive youth development has turned significant attention to the spiritual development of children and youth (Cheon & Canda, 2010; Kvarfordt & Sheridan, 2007; Lerner, Roeser, & Phelps, 2008). The positive youth development field has an affinity with the social work strengths perspective in that it examines the factors that prevent or reduce risk factors and that promote the optimal psychosocial-spiritual development of youth for successful transition into adulthood. Recent studies suggest that while most contemporary American youth are affiliated with religions, many place a higher priority on personal spiritual meaning and exploration of various religious and nonreligious options. Youth who are actively engaged in a search for meaning and those who are involved in a satisfying religious community tend to be at lower risk of health, mental health, and social problems and also tend to have a clearer sense of personal identity and a higher sense of life satisfaction and optimism about transition toward adulthood.

## Social, Cultural, and Economic Forces

The social environment in Erikson's theory covered a broad range of social contexts, beginning with the infant mother dyad and extending to community and then "humankind." Erikson additionally included a historical context in his description of development within industrial societies. However, Erikson's early writings suffer from a restricted and culturally biased view of the environment and, despite his attempt to be sensitive to issues of culture, he portrayed minorities as deficient by European American standards. For example, in his cultural analysis of Sioux and Yurok Indian tribes (1963), he compared Native People to "compensation neurotics" who could not adapt to modern-day life. He painted an image of their romantic past and dismal present, as embodied by a "parasitic life" of government entitlements and psychological dependency, and focused on their intrapsychic ambivalence and failure to embrace the "full benefit of government boarding school education." He, of course, did not acknowledge that this "full benefit" included forced assimilation and cultural disintegration. Nor did he acknowledge the continued governmental exploitation of Indian land and mineral rights in exchange for "entitlements" that perpetuated poverty. Clearly, the realities of modern-day racism and paternalism toward Indian people escaped Erikson's clinical observations. Failure to recognize the political and ideological context of human development is a problem that continues to plague most developmental theories today. Tornstam's research on gerotranscendence has mainly been with Swedish and Danish older adults; he acknowledges this cultural limitation and encourages more cross-cultural research.

Most life span theories include a variety of social contexts that typically include familial, occupational, and gender roles as well as interpersonal ties, group affiliations, and community roles. Primary emphasis, however, is on the way in which the individual functions in these social contexts.

Strikingly absent from most life span theories is any discussion of social class differences or economic forces that shape people's lives. The one exception to this is in the literature about older age, where poverty is seen as having a significant impact on one's health and well-being. Likewise, cultural differences are largely ignored or minimized in mainstream theory due to the tendency of theorists to claim universality of their proposed stages of development.

## Relevance to Individuals, Groups, Families, Organizations, Institutions, and Communities

Life span theories place their primary focus on growth and development of the individual. However, it is through interaction within the family, peer groups, organizations, institutions, and communities that people learn to resolve developmental psychosocial conflicts and come to internalize moral values and normative behaviors and to gain a lasting sense of ego identity.

# CONSISTENCY WITH SOCIAL WORK VALUES AND ETHICS

Due to the focus on adaptive functioning and the psychosocial perspective, life span theory has an inherently good fit with social work values. Life span theories recognize the potential for creativity and growth throughout life and the resiliency of people moving through transitions and crises. This is consistent with the strengths perspective. Nonetheless, these theories have been criticized by proponents of the strengths perspective due to the tendency to focus on developmental problems and rigidly defined life stages.

In addition, the failure of life span theories to adequately address issues of diversity has been noted by theorists who question the validity and universality of stage models because they ignore or minimize differences in gender, class, culture, and sexual orientation. Erikson's theory has been accused of assuming a deficiency model of female development. In fact, Roazen (1976, p. 144) noted that Erikson broadened "Freud's famous claim that anatomy is destiny . . . into the assertion that 'anatomy, history, and personality are our combined destiny.'" Erikson's assumption that the individuated, autonomous self represented the norm for healthy psychosocial development has since been found to contain cultural biases as well.

As discussed in Chapter 6, most cultures define "self" in relation to family and community and the individuated self is the *exception* rather than the norm. Yet individuated (i.e., individualistic) self is the benchmark of healthy, adaptive functioning in most life span theory. Thus, diversity is devalued by the European American biases that permeate most historical and contemporary models of development.

The corrective efforts of feminist and LGBTQI developmental theory have likewise been criticized for ignoring issues of race, ethnicity, and social class. The Anglo middle-class bias is just as prevalent in these theories as it is in traditional models of development. Not surprisingly, most forms of diversity are often portrayed as deficiency when judged by the developmental standards set forth in these models. This is especially true for gay men and lesbian women who, by definition, cannot accept the "mature genitality" of heterosexual intimacy. There is little room for normal individual variation despite the focus on adaptive functioning.

However, Erikson's writing on Gandhi and Luther suggests that psychosocial maturation may lead, for some, to a commitment to action for social justice. The recognition of the importance of the social environment in affecting personal development also suggests that social critique should follow from these theories. However, these political implications have been poorly developed in conventional life span theories. At best, there is recognition of economic and social barriers encountered by the aging. And, despite their psychosocial focus, psychological components of empowerment such as positive self-esteem and a sense of efficacy are largely ignored as well. However, recent theories that address the development of women and lesbian and gay people are pointing out the need to examine the political context of discrimination and oppression.

## PHILOSOPHICAL UNDERPINNINGS

Theories of life span development share common philosophical assumptions about the nature, duration, and direction of human development. In contrast to the pathology orientation of most psychodynamic theories, most life span theories are wellness oriented and assume potential for adaptive functioning.

Brennan and Weick (1981, pp. 16–17) have identified five assumptions that they found common in the theoretical writings of Erikson, Levinson, Vaillant, and Gould. First is the assumption that human development is lifelong. In contrast to psychodynamic theories that suggest that personality is formed by early childhood, and theories of cognitive development that portray adulthood as a period of "irreversible deterioration," life span theories assume that positive growth and change are possible throughout life.

Second is the assumption that development unfolds in stages. As discussed in Chapter 7, this assumes a model of discontinuous change that is generally based on the idea of invariant sequentiality. The qualitative changes in each stage emerge from the resolution of crises, conflicts, or challenges of earlier stages. Thus, in an additive fashion, the building blocks of earlier stages provide the foundation for later stages. These are generally believed to be related to chronological age and emerge in a predictable age-stage sequence.

Third, some theories assume a transition period between stages in which a "crisis" is common. As we have seen, midlife crisis has been described as a normative experience in several of these theories.

Fourth, transition periods, even when marked by crisis, are assumed to provide opportunities for growth. The tasks of adapting to new roles, expectations, demands, and the constantly emerging self, are believed to inherently create new possibilities for growth and change.

Finally, adulthood is seen in terms of health rather than pathology, and people are assumed to have strengths that allow them to adapt and cope. In sum, change throughout life is seen as normative, persistent, and healthy and follows a predictable sequence related to age.

To this list, we add several other assumptions. Most traditional theories assume a universal path with little, if any, regard for differences in gender, social class, lifestyle, culture, sexual orientation, or other factors that may influence development. Although some theories acknowledge biological and environmental influences, it is the ontogenetic unfolding and psychological adaptation that are assumed to be the primary forces in development. Related to this view, poor adaptation and coping are assumed to be related to intrapsychic rather than environmental factors.

Finally, emphasis on personal responsibility, free choice, and the material rather than spiritual world (i.e., the here and now rather than the hereafter) permeate descriptions of the tasks essential to satisfactory development and reflect an ideology that Max Weber (1948) termed the *Protestant work ethic*.

## METHODOLOGICAL ISSUES AND EMPIRICAL SUPPORT

Most life span theories are based on a positivistic tradition. Many of the constructs are derived from empirical research that uses a variety of research techniques and study designs. Some studies have been based on clinical observations, whereas others have used medium to large samples in cross-sectional or longitudinal designs. Content analysis of biographical materials is sometimes used in conjunction with quantitative data.

Recent empirical challenges to Erikson's theory explored the applicability of his life stage model across several class and ethnic groups in the United States, New Zealand, Romania, and India (Chatterjee, Bailey, & Aronoff, 2001; Chatterjee & Curl, 2003, 2004). Using the Human Development Index of 1995, the authors calculated rates for the respective countries as well as rates for several ethnic and social class groups within each country. The results showed that low ethnic or social class position was related to low life expectancy at birth as well as a shorter life span. It was also related to the disappearance of adolescence as a transitional phase between childhood and adulthood. This suggests that adolescence is a socially constructed rather than biologically determined phase in human development. Further, between-country comparisons maintained the same trend and two different trajectories of human development emerged in a world system: one for the privileged, with high social capital (see Chapter 12), and another for the substantially less privileged, with low social capital. The authors concluded that Erikson's stages are more appropriate for understanding development of the privileged. This research complemented earlier and current ethnographic work by MacLeod (1995, 2008), who also found that Erikson's theory is not as applicable to those who have low social capital.

Despite the positivistic orientation of life span theories, the supporting research has been criticized as being seriously limited in both "scope and scale" (Lacy & Hendricks, 1980). In addition, methodological problems have raised questions about the validity and reliability of the studies. For example, central constructs such as "personality" have been given varying and contradictory definitions by different researchers. In addition, retrospective recollections of past experiences and feelings are often compared with subjects' descriptions of their present functioning. Further, comparisons of different age groups are often used to describe distinctive features of one group (Haan, 1989). Most of the studies from which developmental theory is derived have been based entirely on White, middle- to upper-middle-class subjects, many of whom only include men. The development of feminist theory has succeeded in including women's voices but often overgeneralizes from very small samples and elevates gender to the position of a primary causal variable while minimizing or ignoring class, race, and ethnicity. Similar problems have been noted in theories of LGBT development as well.

Most researchers acknowledge that there is little empirical evidence to support the existence of uniform age-related stages that unfold in an epigenetic sequence (Chiriboga, 1989; Lacy & Hendricks, 1980). There is also little evidence supporting the universality of midlife crisis as a developmental stage. Instead, research has shown that gender, social class, and, to a lesser extent, race are significantly related to developmental paths and outcomes (Baruch et al., 1983; Farrell & Rosenberg, 1981; Lacy & Hendricks, 1980; Neugarten & Datan, 1974).

Further, as R. M. Thomas (1985) noted, Erikson's theory has "the same basic problems of scientific validation . . . [as] Freud's theory . . . many of his proposals . . . must be accepted on faith, faith in the theorist's interpretive skills and in his authority rather than on experimental and observational evidence" (pp. 254–255). Unfortunately, it is often perceived as a factual model of development rather than a theoretical one. This is a critical distinction because, as a theory, it has received relatively little empirical validation (Ewen, 1988).

Many other developmental theories share the same dilemma of validation. Despite the relative absence of supportive research, age-stage and coming out developmental models continue to permeate social work textbooks on life span development—often uncritically, and all too often presented as "fact." Popularity is, indeed, mistaken for validity.

Their popularity is, perhaps, partly due to their heuristic value. Life span theories provide a simple yet comprehensive view of development that makes common sense (to those who share the assumptions of the theorists) and leads to many developments for research and practice. Yet this very appeal can be dangerous when social workers accept the theories uncritically and attempt to fit clients into a preconceived developmental mold.

A case in point is the current popularity of the concept of successful aging. Although it is a helpful counterpoint to negative stereotypes of aging, the concept is often used in an uncritical way that can actually increase ageism (Dillaway & Byrnes, 2009). The concept of successful aging emerged from the idea of productive aging that emphasizes avoidance of disease and disease susceptibility, high cognitive capacity, active social engagement, and even continued wage earning in the workforce. This can lead to expectations that older adults should not become ill or disabled, they should continue wage earning, and they should reduce use of social security and the welfare system. Even on a practical level, these expectations become less tenable for elders who are not members of relatively wealthy and privileged groups. The successful aging concept can be co-opted into a political agenda to reduce government responsibility for older adults, delay age of retirement, and place more burden on the private market and individual self-sufficiency. At worst, it can lead to a portrayal of elderly people as undeserving poor who refuse to work or who are unwelcome burdens on the state. Admirably, Tornstam's (2005) qualitative and quantitative studies have endeavored to present an understanding of positive aging from the emic perspectives of elders themselves, freed from the assumptions of White, middle-class male researchers. Social workers need to be cautious to apply the concept of successful aging in a way that recognizes the natural conditions of aging and death, avoids ageism or ableism, and takes into account the particular personal and cultural understandings and ideals of aging for clients.

As is the case with psychodynamic theory, ego psychology and theories of life span development are (a) better at explanation than prediction, (b) better at a probabilistic level of explanation than a deterministic level, and (c) better suited for explaining properties of individuals than properties of groups. However, these theories are substantially better than psychodynamic theories in explaining properties of groups (such as specific cohorts at a given time). In addition, deviant case analysis is often necessary for explanation of cases that run contrary to theoretical propositions.

## Summary

Erikson's theory of epigenetic life span development has found broad appeal in social work, psychology, and educational psychology. As previously mentioned, it has been one of the most accepted models in social work practice and continues to be the "standard" against which psychosocial development of clients is often gauged.

Contemporary life cycle theories that focus on midlife have received greater attention and appeal among the general public, spurred on by the success of Gail Sheehy's best seller, *Passages: Predictable Crises of Adult Life*. The concept of midlife crisis, derived from several of these theorists, has become a widely accepted catchphrase and explanation of difficulties at midlife.

As we noted previously, the popularity of these theories is widespread because they offer explanations to which people can easily relate. Ego strengths such as competence and wisdom are positive traits that most people would probably identify with and hope to achieve. Finally, with an emphasis on mastery, adaptation, transformation, possible selves, and growth throughout life, there is great appeal in the optimistic view that we are not prisoners of our biology or childhood—change is possible!

# Theories of Cognitive and Moral Development

*You should watch the way you eat,*
*I think you're eating too much meat*
*I think that you should change the clothes you wear*
*You should change your TV channels,*
*Those polyester sheets to flannels*
*You should change the way you do your hair.*
*I only want what's best for you, why ever won't you listen*
*I should know by now what you should put your emphasis in*
*We should both know better than to tell each other what to do*
*Don't should on me and I won't should on you.*

© DAVID ROTH 1986,
DAVID ROTH/MAYTHELIGHT MUSIC

## THEORIES OF COGNITIVE AND MORAL DEVELOPMENT

- describe the changes in conscious thought processes and moral reasoning from infancy through adulthood
- examine the way in which socialization leads to the internalization of social rules
- help us understand the relationship between the development of logical thought and moral reasoning
- help us examine possible gender differences in moral reasoning
- help us understand stages in the development of faith
- are useful for formulating assessments and interventions for individuals, groups, and families

This chapter was coauthored with David Hussey, PhD.

Theories of cognitive and moral development describe the ways in which thought and moral reasoning change and develop from infancy through adulthood. We include these theories together because the development of moral reasoning is inseparably tied to the developmental maturation of cognitive capacities during childhood and adolescence. These theories are based on a developmental framework that stresses the interaction between innate biological factors and the social environment. In contrast to psychodynamic theories that stress unconscious thought, theories of cognitive and moral development focus on conscious thought processes and reasoning.

## HISTORICAL CONTEXT

Although philosophers had long been interested in matters related to the mind and morality, the field of cognitive development is generally attributed to Swiss biologist and psychologist, Jean Piaget. According to Siegler (1986), "Before Piaget began his work, no recognizable field of cognitive development existed" (pp. 21–22).

Piaget's work was heavily influenced by his early interests in both biology and philosophy, and he referred to himself as a *genetic epistemologist*. The genesis of his work reflects a particular interest in the development of intellectual structures and knowledge. Through his early work in biology and the observation of mollusks, Piaget concluded that the environment had an important effect on biological development and maturation. He came to see biological development as a process of adaptation to the environment that could not be explained solely by hereditary factors. He later extended this view to the process of mental development in humans as well (Piaget, 1952), positing that cognitive development was both a process of adaptation as well as an extension of ontogenetic biological development (Wadsworth, 1979).

Piaget believed that knowledge was *constructed* through a *process* in which children physically and/or mentally *act* on objects, images, or symbols. While working in Alfred Binet's laboratory school in Paris (1919–1921), he became fascinated with the reasoning process that children used when they gave the wrong answers. Using a clinical method of interview adapted from psychiatric interview techniques, his subsequent research focused on qualitative differences in the methods of logical thinking used by children of different ages. He later modified his research techniques to emphasize "the role of the child's activity in the formation of thought" (Ginsburg & Opper, 1979, p. 7). In addition, he became interested in the way in which the passage of time changes the relationship between the knower and the known (R. M. Thomas, 1999). Piaget's work influenced all subsequent theories in cognitive development.

According to Santrock (1989, p. 275) moral development, in one sense, has a longer history than any other topic traditionally associated with human development. Debates about whether children were born innately good, evil, or tabula rasa (a blank slate) were popular subjects for philosophers and theologians. Early theoretical formulations about moral development in young children can be seen in Sigmund Freud's concept of the *superego* and in George Herbert Mead's concepts of the *me* and the *generalized other* (discussed in Chapter 10). However, Piaget is credited with stimulating the current interest in moral development. His initial work in cognitive development led him to ask questions about the process through which children developed ethical rules in playing games. Although he wrote only one book on this topic (Piaget, 1932), this early work stimulated numerous studies and provided the basis for Lawrence Kohlberg's popular stage theory of moral development.

## COGNITIVE DEVELOPMENT

Cognitive development is concerned with the changes in intellectual abilities, mental activities, and behaviors through which knowledge of the world is attained. This requires an understanding of a variety of interrelated factors including biological, social, environmental, experiential, and motivational factors as well as the emotional life of the individual. According to Piaget, children take an active role in constructing their knowledge of the world. Children construct their knowledge through action on the environment and the objects with which they interact. A closer look at Piaget's work identifies some of these important elements of cognitive activity and growth.

### Key Concepts

Central to all theories of cognitive development is the idea of intelligence. Although the parameters of *intelligence* are being questioned and debated in the contemporary literature, this term is typically used to denote conceptual ability based on abstract thought and effective problem solving and is measured by standardized intelligence quotient (IQ) tests designed to systematically measure such ability. Even though Piaget's theory is based on the development of logic and abstract reasoning, his definitions of intelligence were deliberately broader. For Piaget, human intelligence is a type of evolutionary biological adaptation that enables people to successfully interact with the environment. Intelligence is the instrument that allows people to achieve a harmonious adjustment, or *equilibrium*, between self and environment and is based on mental activity that is constructed by people through actions. In addition, Piaget believed that intelligence involves competence, the best that someone can do at a given developmental stage (Ginsburg & Opper, 1979).

According to Piaget, intellectual development in humans is largely based on biological factors related to specific heredity. For example, biologically transmitted differences in physical structures (such as the nervous system, the eye, or the brain) are inherited by different species. These physical structures determine the type and degree of intellectual functioning. Physical maturation is another example of specific heredity that is biologically controlled by genetic codes. Although physical maturation (including brain growth) is necessary for psychological development, in general, and cognitive development, in particular, Piaget argued that environmental factors also played a large role. Thus, he saw physical maturation alone as a necessary but not sufficient cause of cognitive development (Ginsburg & Opper, 1979).

For people to grow intellectually, Piaget theorized that the mind had a structure similar to other structures in the body such as the stomach or the heart (Wadsworth, 1979). He named the basic structure of the mind the *scheme* (also called *schema* in the singular or *schemata* in the plural). He proposed that schemata are the cognitive or mental structures by which individuals intellectually adapt to and organize their environment. It is important to recognize that the concept of schemata is a theoretical construct of the mind that is inferred, rather than a physical structure of the brain that can be observed. In this sense, Piaget's concept of schemata is similar to Freud's concepts of the id, ego, and superego; they must be inferred because there is no corresponding empirical physical structure. In a simpler sense, schemata can be viewed as constructs or concepts that help to identify and process incoming stimuli; they help organize events into categories according to shared characteristics. The newborn has a few schemata, but as the child matures, these schemata become more generalized, differentiated, and qualitatively refined. For example, early schemata of the infant involve reflexive motor activities such as sucking. As the child develops, the schemata slowly become more organized into sensorimotor activities such as looking, grasping, and hitting. With further development, the schemata are refined and differentiated from the early sensorimotor schemata of the infant to the mature cognitive schemata of the adult (Wadsworth, 1979).

Piaget also proposed two inborn biologically invariant functions for all species based on general heredity: organization and adaptation. *Organization* refers to the tendency to blend and coordinate physical or mental structures into more coherent, complex, and higher order systems or structures. A young infant, for example, either grasps an object or looks at it. These two structures (grasping and looking) eventually become organized into a more complex structure that allows the infant to grasp and look at the same time.

*Adaptation*, the second function, refers to the process by which structures of the mind develop over time to achieve a better fit with the environment and external reality. Adaptation consists of two processes, assimilation and accommodation. *Assimilation* is a cognitive process through which new perceptual events and understandings of the external world are incorporated into existing schemata. As children assimilate, they attempt to explain new information based on their current frame of reference. A young child who is familiar with dogs, for example, may first assimilate a horse into an existing dog schema, thinking that the horse is a big dog due to their shared characteristics (four legs, a tail, bigger than a cat). However, not all new stimuli can be assimilated and the child must alter or change schemata to adapt to new stimuli, perceptions, and experiences through the process of accommodation.

*Accommodation* is the creation of new schemata or the modification of old ones for placing new stimuli that do not fit into already existing cognitive schemata. In doing so, the child revises old ways of thinking to fit new information and situations. Of primary importance is the ability to adapt and organize the environmental stimuli. This occurs constantly in people, as we are bombarded with a multitude of new sensory input. Thus, assimilation and accommodation are ongoing processes.

Whereas assimilation explains the quantitative change involved in placing new input and information into existing ways of knowing, accommodation helps account for the qualitative development of new understandings. Together, they produce cognitive and intellectual adaptation through the development of intellectual structures (Wadsworth, 1979). Due to his focus on the development of intellectual structures, Piaget's theory is known as a structural approach to cognitive development.

Finally, *memory* involves retaining information over time and plays a crucial role in all cognitive and intellectual development (Santrock, 1989). It is also central to learning and having a sense of self; without memory, there is no self. Although there are many different ways of categorizing memory, Piaget distinguished between two types of memory: recognition memory and evocation memory. Recognition occurs in the presence of an object that has previously been encountered and is one of the first types of memory that infants exhibit. This is easily seen in infants' recognition of their parents when they are in within their sight. Evocation (also called recall) depends on the ability to evoke a mental image of something that is not present. Piaget believed that evocation, mental images, and language began more or less at the same time (Piaget & Inhelder, 1969). As the child grows and develops, memory becomes more complex and the quantity of memories increase with maturation (R. M. Thomas, 1985). Due to the fact that maturation and additional experiences alter the mind, Piaget held that the act of remembering is not simply a repetition of the original experience but involves a "reconstitution of the past" (Piaget, cited in R. M. Thomas, 1985, p. 263).

**JEAN PIAGET'S THEORY OF COGNITIVE DEVELOPMENT**    Based initially on the observation of his own three children and eventually of larger groups of children, Piaget proposed that four underlying causal factors determined cognitive development. First is maturation, which leads to physical growth. Second is physical experience, or action with the environment, which is necessary for assimilation and accommodation of the environment. The third factor is social interaction, or the interchange of ideas between people. For example, ideas such as justice and honesty are social in nature; they are forms of knowledge dependent on social interaction for concept construction and meaning. The final factor is equilibration, or the "internal self-regulating system that operates to reconcile the roles of maturation, experience, and social interaction" (Wadsworth, 1979, p. 35). Equilibration is the keystone of developmental change and refers to the "overall interaction between existing ways of knowing and new experience" that leads to a more stable equilibrium between the cognitive system of the child and the external world (Siegler, 1986, p. 27). It is the force that maintains a harmonious balance.

In addition to these broad factors, Piaget identified four major developmental stages of cognitive development. He believed that these stages are universal, or the same for all children in all cultures. He also held that they were based on invariant sequentiality, that is, they occur in a specific sequence, or the same, invariant, fixed order. He believed that stages could not be skipped and must occur in a fixed order because each new stage builds on previous stages. Although he paid little attention to individual differences, he acknowledged that it is possible for children to progress through these stages at different rates due to either experiential or hereditary factors, and he recognized that there is a rather large range of intellectual behaviors within a particular stage. Although the ages given below for each stage are approximate, it is assumed that these are normative expected ages for each stage.

*Stage 1: Sensorimotor Period (Birth to about Age 2):*    During the sensorimotor period there are six substages of gradual, progressively more complex behavior and learning. Despite the fact that infants typically do not speak until the end of this period, they exhibit enormous cognitive growth in the first two years. Perhaps most significant is the fact that they immediately exhibit goal-directed behavior and learning. At birth, infants have no concept of external objects other than on a reflexive level such as sucking, grasping, or looking. However, they quickly progress from reflexive sucking to purposive sucking to get fed. As infants mature and begin to gain control over their reflexes, muscles, and sensory organs, they learn to reproduce pleasurable events, first in relation to their own bodies (such as opening and closing their hands, imitating their own sounds) and then in relation to other people or objects (such as imitating sounds made by others or moving small objects out of their path). They openly experiment with objects, picking them up and dropping them, or pulling them, to watch the effect. Experiments in this stage are done externally, as infants act on the environment.

As they become gradually able to follow objects visually and anticipate their positions, an awareness of the permanence of objects develops; Piaget called this *object permanence*. For example, in his experiments, Piaget showed that infants younger than 9 months do not look for an object when it is completely concealed. According to Piaget, children begin to demonstrate object permanence at about 12 months, but it is not until the very last substage of the sensorimotor period (18–24 months), that children obtain true object permanence. Finally, able to draw conclusions about unseen objects, children look for hidden objects because they have developed *representational ability*, the ability to mentally represent objects and actions in memory (Papalia & Olds, 1992). They can now evoke memories that are not directly linked to immediate perception.

As the beginnings of symbolic thought and representation necessary for language emerge from the more primitive sensorimotor intelligence, children begin to solve problems internally. Children now begin to exhibit an understanding of causality, and the relation between goals and the means to attain those goals.

**Stage 2: Preoperational Period (Ages 2–7):**   As the use of symbolic thought increases, the child is able to produce mental symbols that mediate her or his performance. Conceptual-symbolic behavior replaces sensorimotor behavior. Although perception still dominates over reason, behavior sequences can now be played out mentally rather than just physically. Piaget further divided the preoperational phase into two subperiods: the preconceptual period (2–4 years of age) and the intuitive period (4–7 years of age). The preconceptual period is characterized by the development of language and imaginative play. According to Piaget, "cognitive development promotes language development, not vice versa" (Shaffer, 1993, p. 247). Once language develops, it enhances children's problem-solving abilities and allows children to learn from the verbalizations of others. Imaginative and symbolic play is important in this stage because it allows children to act out their conflicts in a nondistressing manner, and they become aware of themselves as objects.

During the intuitive period we see the beginning emergence of skills in the areas of numbers, classification, and interrelationships. In addition, behavior eventually becomes less egocentric and more social.

Although preoperational thought represents an advancement over the previous sensorimotor period, it is still quite limited. For example, children display egocentric thinking, a cognitive state in which the world is seen only from the view of the self; children are not yet able to view the world from the perspective of others. Children also display animistic thinking in which they attribute life or human characteristics to inanimate objects. Importantly, thinking at this stage is confined to momentary perceptions as children are not able to take into account changes from one moment to the next. In addition, they cannot center or focus on more than one aspect of a problem when several aspects are present.

During the preoperational period, social interaction and communication with others provide a medium to test ideas to verify or contradict their legitimacy. He saw this social behavior as an important form of accommodation. Socialization is progressive in that children's behavior always becomes more social (Piaget & Inhelder, 1969).

**Stage 3: Concrete Operations (Ages 7–11):**   This stage is distinguished by the primacy of reason over perception. Thought becomes less egocentric and children gain two cognitive operations necessary for logical thought: reversibility and compensation. With *reversibility*, children gain the ability to reverse, or undo an action in their mind. When they acquire *compensation*, they are able to decenter their perceptions and focus on more than one aspect at a time. With these operations, logic and objectivity increase and reasoning now can be applied to observable, concrete problems. As deductive thinking begins, children gain cognitive skills for *conservation*, the recognition that properties of an object do not change when its appearance is altered. For example, children can now see that when a ball of clay is rolled into the shape of a narrow sausage, it contains the same amount of clay as when it is rolled into a round ball. As children come to understand the relationship between successive steps, they remember the sets of changes that have taken place. Examples of other cognitive skills that Piaget charted at this stage are *seriation* (the ability to arrange items according to their increasing or decreasing size, such as lining up people according to height); *classification* (the ability to group objects into categories and subcategories according to their characteristics); and *transitivity* (the ability to understand reciprocal concepts such as if A is greater than B, then B is less than A). In addition, cognitive development during this period leads to improved concepts of causality, space, and time.

***Stage 4: Formal Operations (Ages 11–15):*** During this period abstract thought and scientific reasoning emerge. Problems are now approached using logic, reason, and combinational thought. Hypothetical reasoning and a growing appreciation of interactions among multiple factors are now possible. Adolescents are now able to reason correctly from hypothetical data, as they begin to solve problems and then check their answers. There is also greater importance attached to a language-based system of representation. Individuals with formal operations can think about their own thoughts and feelings and think about thinking; they can operate not only on concrete objects and events but also on ideas (Shaffer, 1993).

Piaget believed that no cognitive structural advances in the quality of reasoning occurred after this period (Wadsworth, 1979). Instead, he held that further changes in cognitive abilities are quantitative. As each structural change incorporates and improves upon the previous structures, the development of schemata in adulthood demonstrates major differences from those of childhood in the sheer number of cognitive structures or schemata. Despite the lack of qualitative change after attaining formal operations, Piaget believed that adults continue to develop and refine new schemata and ideas.

Hetherington and Parke (1986) have noted that because formal operations are influenced by IQ level as well as educational and cultural factors, not everyone attains the level of formal operations. For example, if groups do not emphasize symbolic skills or if educational experiences are limited, the stage of formal operations may occur late in development or may even be absent. In addition, several theorists have suggested that Piaget's formal operational stage does not adequately reflect mature thinking in adulthood. They have proposed that the flexibility and adaptiveness that characterizes adult thought represents an advanced stage of postformal thought that transcends formal logic (Labouvie-Vief, 1985; Labouvie-Vief & Hakim-Larson, 1989). As Papalia and Olds (1992) have pointed out, postformal thought is characterized by an integration of concepts that include reliance on subjectivity, intuition, and logic. Experience contributes to our ability as adults to solve practical problems, while personalizing our reasoning and drawing from our experiences. They propose that the integration of logical conclusions with emotion better enables us to deal with ambiguous situations and think differently about moral issues (Papalia & Olds, 1992). Table 9.1 summarizes Piaget's key concepts of cognitive development.

## Roads From Piaget

Today, while few psychologists would call themselves strictly Piagetian, the combination of Piaget's formulations, theories that stress biological or environmental influences on cognition, information-processing models, and contemporary theories of intelligence offer a growing body of knowledge on cognition. As Gardner (1991, p. 30) has noted, these "competing visions of human development" can be seen as commentaries "on Piaget's central conceptualizations." Post-Piagetians fall into several different camps, with neo-Piagetians adhering most closely to his original theory, but expanding on the array of behavior that they examine to now include, for example, emotional development and the importance of social roles.

| TABLE 9.1 | Piaget's Stages of Cognitive Development |

| Stage Description | Examples of Performance | Object Concept |
|---|---|---|
| **Stage 1: Sensorimotor (birth–about 2 years)** | | |
| Reflex activity (0–1 month) | Learns to suck. | Tracks moving object but ignores its disappearance. |
| Primary circular reactions (1–4 months) | Repetitive movements; opens and closes fist; moves thumb to mouth; moves hand and watches it. | Looks at spot where object disappeared. |
| Secondary circular reactions (4–8 months) | Imitates own sounds if made by someone else; repeats movements that have an effect. | Searches for a partly concealed object. |
| Coordination of secondary schemes (8–12 months) | Imitates new sounds; moves objects that are in the way. | Searches for an object in the last place it was found. |
| Tertiary circular reactions (12–18 months) | Drops objects to see effect; reaches a toy by pulling an extension of it. | Searches for and finds objects that are hidden while watching. |
| Invention through mental combinations (18–24 months) | Can evoke memories not linked to perception; experiments are done internally. | Searches for and finds objects that are hidden out of sight. Object constancy is complete. |
| **Stage 2: Preoperational (age 2–7)** | | |
| Preconceptual (age 2–4) | Language; symbolic thought; pretend play; conscious of self as an object. | Can mentally visualize things that are not present. |
| Intuitive (age 4–7) | Centers on one thing at a time; thinking is confined to momentary perceptions. | |
| **Stage 3: Concrete operations (age 7–11)** | | |
| | Reasoning and logical thought begin; is able to perform reverse operations mentally; exhibits conversation, seriation, classification; transitivity; centers on more than one thing at a time; remembers changes that have taken place. | |
| **Stage 4: Formal operations (age 11–15)** | | |
| | Hypothetical deductive reasoning; combinational thought. | |

*Source:* Adapted from *Development Psychology: Childhood and Adolescence*, 4th edition, by D. R. Shaffer. Copyright © 1996. Reprinted with permission of Wadsworth, a division of Thomson Learning.

Post-Piagetian scholars have also taken sides in the nature/nurture debate about the relative importance of biological and environmental factors on cognitive development. Linguist Noam Chomsky, for example, was critical of Piaget's failure to emphasize the role of language in cognitive development. Writing primarily in reaction to the traditional stimulus–response and social learning theories that emphasized reinforcement and imitation, Chomsky took a radical stance in proposing that language acquisition was an innate, genetic phenomenon and not the product of external influences. In Piaget's view, language development reflected the more general processes of cognitive development. According to Chomsky, however, children possess a number of sophisticated, innate, linguistic mechanisms that compose a language acquisition device. These innate mechanisms depend on the development of mature cells in the cerebral cortex during the first 2 years of life. These mechanisms allow the brain to perform mental operations that encode sounds and enable infants to produce grammar and invent sentences. Because certain phases of language development coincide with specific motor skill accomplishments, Chomsky held that children easily acquire their native languages during similar, critical stages of language acquisition. Although there is some neurological support that language acquisition is related to the increasing specialization of neural structures within the brain, Gardner (1991, p. 33) has noted that "the verdict is still out on the study of rules governing human language."

In contrast, anthropologist Clifford Geertz, Soviet psychologist Lev Vygotsky, and American psychologists Jerome Bruner and Michael Cole argued for the importance of cultural factors in development. In rejecting the "mind-centric" theories of Piaget and Chomsky, they pointed to the way in which culture, with its "rich interpretations and meanings" shapes people, language, and cognitions through interpersonal interaction with parents and significant others as well as through exposure to cultural artifacts and inventions (Gardner, 1991, p. 39). In their view, human development is impossible in the absence of culture.

According to R. M. Thomas (1999), most developmental theorists now accept that both biology and culture play significant roles in development, and this stance is captured in Peter Medwar's quip that "human behavior is 100 percent under the control of genes and 100 percent under the control of the environment" (cited in Gardner, 1991, p. 41).

Later refinements and advancements of Piaget's foundational work assisted in the growth and development of information-processing models that provided more systematic examinations of cognitive task performance. Information-processing theory views the mind and processes of human cognition as similar to that of a computer and examines on the perceptions (individual interpretations of sensory input) and symbols (representations based on consensual meanings that we assign to things) that people use to process information. It focuses heavily on the processes involved in memory and in the selection, coding, and storage of information. Information-processing theory has contributed greatly to our understanding of memory in young children and adults.

We previously discussed the differences between recognition and recall memory. Current research on infants, for example, has shown that infants as young as 2 to 3 months can spontaneously recall an overhead mobile that they were previously taught to kick. Also, in contrast to Piaget's theory, some researchers have claimed that by 8 to 9 months, infants show the beginnings of object permanence and deferred imitation (imitating the actions of live models viewed a day earlier) (Kail, 1990; Shaffer, 1993).

However, conclusions about object permanence have been questioned by L. Cohen (1996), whose research failed to support the finding of object permanence in either 4- or 8-month-old infants. In contrast to the view that infants are smarter than we think, Cohen (1996) concluded that infants are dumber than many researchers think.

It has been well established that recall improves steadily in the first 2 to 3 years and, by age 2, toddlers can recall some events that happened a few months earlier. Even more dramatic improvements in memory occur between ages 3 and 12, with the ability to recall becoming stronger as the child matures. Throughout most of childhood, however, recognition memory is stronger than recall, and many theorists now believe that advances in logical reasoning are strongly related to memory development.

A growing body of literature has demonstrated that infants are capable of nonverbal memory. In fact, there is evidence that auditory stimuli (such as a voice) presented to a fetus during the last trimester can be recognized within the first 2 days after birth (De Casper & Spence, 1986; Spence & De Casper, 1987). However, despite the fact that infants are capable of remembering, most adults have very few, if any, independent memories prior to age 2 or 3, and only sketchy memories up until age 5. This normal phenomenon has been termed *infantile amnesia*, and, in contrast to Freud, who believed that all such memories were repressed due to psychosexual emotional conflicts, most cognitive theorists attribute this lack of recall to normal developmental processes. Some have suggested that this involves the reorganization of the central nervous system or differences in the way infants encode information and the way adults retrieve it (Siegler, 1986). However, in a thorough review of the literature on memory in infants and young children, Howe and Courage (1993) proposed that infantile amnesia is linked to the emerging sense of self rather than to problems with storage or retrieval. They argued that because "autobiographical memory, by definition, is memory for information and events pertaining to the self . . . knowledge of the self as an independent entity . . . is perhaps the minimum criterion for the existence of autobiographical memory" (1993, p. 306). Very significantly, the time frame for the development of autobiographical memory is between 2 and 3 years of age. This coincides with both the development of an independent sense of self and linguistic achievement that allows the child to designate experiences in the past tense.

Information processing has also given us important insights into adult memory. Discussions about developmental changes in adult memory generally distinguish between four different storage systems: sensory memory (in which the brain stores what we see, hear, smell, taste, or touch); immediate memory (in which we retain information for up to 10 seconds); short-term memory (in which we retain unrehearsed information for 20 to 30 seconds and rehearsed information for 5 to 10 minutes); and long-term memory (in which we retain information for long periods of time, perhaps days, weeks, and years). Despite the belief that equates failing memory with natural aging, Poon (1985) has shown that long-term memory for past events is generally not affected by aging, while long-term memory for recent events typically is (Papalia & Olds, 1992). However, according to Loftus (personal communication, 1997), old experiences are usually remembered because we have rehearsed them before. When people have trouble remembering recent experiences, it is generally because these experiences have not been stored efficiently into long-term memory. When the experiences are equated, both older and younger people "remember more recent things better than older things" (Loftus, personal communication, 1997).

Related research in this area has also suggested specific strategies to improve memory. Studies have shown, for example, that memory rehearsal techniques are critical to memory and that exceptional memory is dependent on what we already know. Thus, memory may be more dependent on experience than on age. In addition, researchers have shown that young children and poor problem solvers can be taught skills of logic that aid in solving complex problems (Siegler, 1986).

Direct application of this can be seen in Reuven Feuerstein's (1979, 1980) work in mediated learning. Based on the view that the mind is continually modifiable, Feuerstein uses an assessment tool, the Learning Potential Assessment Device, to assess a *person's* potential for learning and then devises a specific mediated learning experience that utilizes hands-on modeling and instruction as an intervention to modify cognition. His program, called *Instrumental Enrichment*, is aimed at modifying cognitive structures so that people can become autonomous and independent thinkers. In contrast to interventions that only seek to change behavior, Feuerstein's method changes the actual cognitive processes that people use. His work is especially significant in that he has successfully demonstrated the ability to teach teenagers and adults more advanced logical thinking and reasoning. This runs contrary to the Piagetian model that proposed a natural biological unfolding of cognitive complexity with maturation and experience.

Despite the many valuable insights gained from information-processing theory and research, one of the basic assumptions of this model has been called into question by contemporary cognitive research. Specifically, the analogy that likens the mind to a computer has been shown to be fundamentally flawed. As neuroscientist Steven Rose (1992, p. 91) has cautioned:

> Brains do not work with information in the computer sense, but with meaning (which) is a historically and developmentally shaped process . . . because each time we remember, we in some senses do work on and transform our memories; they are not simply being called up from the store. . . . Our memories are recreated each time we remember.

In addition, contemporary research on the brain has shown that contrary to the computer analogy, the brain itself becomes transformed with experience and environmental and social interaction (DeMoss, 1999; Nash, 1997; Siegel, 1999). Table 9.2 provides a summary showing some of the interrelated changes that occur in brain, cognitive, emotional, and social development from birth through older adulthood.

In contrast to traditional thought that linked the concept of human intelligence to logical, rational thought, several contemporary theorists have proposed new theories of intelligence that expand our understanding of human mental processes, cognition, and intelligence. Noting that cognitive psychologists study intelligence through the use of experimental tasks rather than standard IQ tests, theorist Robert Sternberg (1988) suggested that Jean Piaget, "One of the greatest intelligence theorists of all time" used obscure tasks to determine children's level of intellectual functioning. Observing that our ideas about intelligence are based on how well people perform in school, Sternberg argued that we have a limited understanding of intelligence because we have asked a limited set of questions about it. To gain a fuller understanding of intelligence, it must be viewed in relation to three factors: "the internal world of the individual, the external world of the individual, and the experience with the world that mediates between the internal and the external worlds" (p. 58). He proposed a *Triarchic Theory of Intelligence*, in which he delineated three subcomponents of intelligence based on these three factors.

*Componential intelligence* is typified by the ability to do well on tests that require analytical thinking. People who possess componential intelligence generally do well on IQ tests and succeed at school. *Experiential intelligence* is typified by people who are creative thinkers. Although they may not do well on tests, they are able to insightfully combine disparate experiences. *Contextual intelligence* is typified by people who possess "street smarts" and are able to succeed in almost any context. Although they don't usually have high test scores, they quickly learn how to "play the game" and manipulate the environment around them (Trotter, 1986). Sternberg held that although there are different aspects to intelligence, they are not independent of one another.

This contrasts with Howard Gardner's (1983, 2006) *Theory of Multiple Intelligences*, in which he proposed eight (originally seven) separate types of intelligence. Similar to Sternberg, Gardner argued that we have a narrow conception of intelligence and held that "reason, intelligence, logic and knowledge are not synonymous" (1983, p. 6). His theory attempts to expand the

| TABLE 9.2 | Some Major Changes in Brain, Cognitive, Emotional, and Social Development over the Life Span | | | |
|---|---|---|---|---|
| **Stage (age in years)** | **Brain** | **Cognitive** | **Emotional** | **Social** |
| Infancy and toddlerhood (0–2) | Rapid significant spurts in brain weight and size<br><br>High plasticity<br><br>Gains in brain weight and size<br><br>Beginning lateralization | Sustained attention improves<br><br>Recall memory emerges<br><br>Categorization emerges<br><br>Autobiographical memory emerges<br><br>Emergence of language | Development of basic emotions<br><br>Basic understanding of feelings of others<br><br>Self-conscious emotions<br><br>Emerging emotional self-regulation | Attachment to others<br><br>Self as object<br><br>Emergence of social categories<br><br>Emergence of empathy<br><br>Movement from nonsocial activity to parallel play |
| Early childhood (2–6) | Continued large gains in brain weight and size<br><br>Increased formation of synapses, myelination, and synaptic pruning<br><br>Continued lateralization | Recall improves<br><br>Autobiographical memory becomes more organized and detailed<br><br>Representational ability and language skills improve | Understanding of causes, consequences, and behavioral signs of basic emotions<br><br>Increased emotional self-regulation | Shift to associative and cooperative play<br><br>First friendships<br><br>Shift to make-believe play<br><br>Emergence of gender identity<br><br>Emergence of conscience |
| Middle childhood (6–11) | Continued formation of synapses and synaptic pruning | Development of concrete operational thought<br><br>Gains in recall and autobiographical memory<br><br>Gains in information processing and attention<br><br>Gains in vocabulary<br><br>Gains in self-understanding | Self conscious emotions such as pride, shame, and guilt become governed by personal responsibility<br><br>Appreciation of mixed emotions<br><br>Gains in emotional self-regulation | Games with rules become common<br><br>Gains in perspective taking<br><br>Experimentation with cooperation, competition, winning, and losing<br><br>Formation of peer groups and importance of peer acceptance<br><br>Continued development of friendships |

*(Continued)*

**TABLE 9.2**   Some Major Changes in Brain, Cognitive, Emotional, and Social Development over the Life Span (*Continued*)

| Stage (age in years) | Brain | Cognitive | Emotional | Social |
|---|---|---|---|---|
| Adolescence (12–18) | Growth spurt in frontal lobe; increased myelination and continued synaptic pruning<br><br>Hormonal changes that are stimulated in the brain | Development of abstract thinking<br><br>Development of scientific reasoning | Fluctuating emotional states linked to hormonal changes and social forces | De-idealization of parents and move toward autonomy<br><br>Peer conformity<br><br>Gender intensification<br><br>Sexual, self, and ethnic identity becomes more solidified |
| Early adulthood | Myelination continues and may develop into middle and later adulthood | Fast and abstract reasoning, and memory is at its prime<br><br>Development of post-formal relativistic thought possible (thought is qualitatively different) | Emotions and emotional well-being may be related to a variety of factors<br><br>Focus on romantic love | Same-sex and other sex friendships<br><br>Siblings as friends<br><br>Romantic partnership<br><br>Transition to parenthood for many<br><br>Diversity of adult lifestyles |
| Middle adulthood | Gradual reduction in weight and volume of brain<br><br>Atrophy of some neurons<br><br>Continued plasticity, myelination, and neuronal growth in parts of brain | Processing speed in working memory may decline and create some memory problems*<br><br>Better practical problem solving<br><br>Possible increase in vocabulary<br><br>Cognitive skills can be improved with training | Emotions and emotional well-being may be related to a variety of biological, psychological, social, and cultural factors<br><br>Emotional adaptations to physical changes of mid Life | Adaptation to entry and exit of family members<br><br>Possible kinship care<br><br>Possible divorce and remarriage<br><br>Sibling contact and support may decline<br><br>Social groups may depend on career development<br><br>Number of friends may decline with age<br><br>Friendship may become more selective |

| Stage (age in years) | Brain | Cognitive | Emotional | Social |
|---|---|---|---|---|
| Later adulthood | Continued gradual reduction in weight and volume of brain<br>Continued atrophy of some neurons<br>Continued plasticity, myelination, and neuronal growth in parts of brain | Possible impaired processing of context*<br>Attention deficits may slow mental performance*<br>Possible decline in explicit memory*<br>Modest forgetting of remote memories<br>Possible increase in vocabulary<br>Can improve a wide range of cognitive skills with training | Emotions and emotional well-being may be related to a variety of biological, psychological, social, and cultural factors<br>Social support and social interaction may be key factors for many<br>Possible enhanced emotional understanding and emotional self-regulation<br>Emotional reactions may be more complex and personalized<br>Mature sense of faith | Friendships may increase in importance<br>New relationships with grown children and grandchildren |

*Sources:* Berk, 2004; DeMoss, 1999; Giedd, Blumenthal, Jeffries, et al. (1999); Neurobiology of Aging Center, 2003; Santrock, 2005; Sowell, Peterson, Thompson, et al., 2003; Thompson, Giedd, Woods, et al., 2000.

*Note: Some declines may be due to poor health and/or illness.

areas of cognitive and developmental psychology by delineating a variety of skills and capacities that display cognitive competence. He defines *intelligence* as a psychologically and neurally based computational capacity to process a certain kind of information (2006). Different types of intelligences include: *linguistic intelligence*, a facility for syntactic and pragmatic language ability, as exemplified in poetry; *musical intelligence*, the ability to perceive and create patterns in pitch (or melody) and rhythm; *logical-mathematical intelligence*, the prototypical Piagetian intelligence that involves ordering and reordering the world of objects and statements in logical ways; *spatial intelligence*, an amalgam of abilities that include the ability to accurately perceive the visual world and cognitively manipulate it (as in mentally rotating objects), as well as the ability to find your way around in an environment; *bodily-kinesthetic intelligence*, facility with fine motor movement of one's body and the skillful handling of objects to solve problems or make things; *intrapersonal intelligence*, the ability to "access one's own feeling life," and to know oneself; and *interpersonal intelligence*, the ability to understand others, to "notice and make distinctions among other individuals and . . . (read) their moods, temperaments, motivations and intentions" (p. 239). Gardner later added to this list *naturalist intelligence*, the ability to engage keen awareness of and distinctions between the diverse plants, animals, mountains, cloud formations, and other features of the physical/natural environment (Gardner, 2006, 2009). Recently, he has been considering adding a ninth type—*existential intelligence.* This refers to the ability to ask and ponder the biggest questions of human nature, life, death, and other deep concerns.

Gardner accepts a candidate for a type of intelligence only if that candidate meets certain criteria. It must be related to a skill universal to the human species and based in biological proclivity and neurology. An intelligence is an ability to solve problems and perform tasks that are relevant to particular cultural and community settings, so various social groups might prioritize and reward specific kinds of intelligence. An intelligence must be encodable in a symbol system (such as language, picturing, or mathematics). There must be support for existence of a proposed intelligence from multiple areas, such as normal cognitive development, breakdown of cognitive abilities due to organic pathology, existence of abilities in special populations such as prodigies and people with autism, valuation in various cultures, and various empirical studies (Gardner & Hatch, 1989). In his view, there is strong evidence for the first seven types of intelligences.

Although individuals and groups might emphasize certain intelligences, everyone has the full range of intelligences. Yet, no two people have the same profile of development of particular intelligences. Further, a high level of an intelligence does not mean that a person will always act intelligently. For example, a person who has strong mathematical skills might use them to gamble wastefully (Gardner, 2006). Gardner also notes that some people have a *laser profile*, meaning that they draw heavily on a single or a pair of intelligences, for example, a scientist who has highly developed logical-mathematical and spatial abilities. Other people have a *searchlight profile*, meaning that they have roughly equivalent strengths in three or more intelligences and do not have a single pronounced strength. For example, a politician might be adept at drawing on linguistic, interpersonal, and intrapersonal intelligences. To some extent, there is choice or social pressure about which intelligences to prioritize and whether to cultivate a laser or searchlight profile. However, he suggested, that some people might not be able to alter their predisposition, such as a person with autism with a laser profile or a person with attention-deficit disorder with a searchlight profile and short-term focus.

Moran (2009) describes three ways that intelligences interact within a person. In *bottlenecking*, one expression interferes with another, as when a school rewards linguistic and mathematical abilities but ignores or suppresses others. In *compensation*, a person uses one intellectual strength to compensate for another weak area, as when a person with dyslexia cultivates interpersonal intelligence to maximize school and social performance. In *catalysis*, growth in one intelligence stimulates growth in another, as when a poet cultivates musical intelligence, thus making the poetry more rhythmic. Further, every person (with various intellectual strengths and profiles) mutually shapes intelligences of everyone who interacts with him or her. Further yet, each culture prioritizes certain intelligences and, through intercultural interaction, shapes the priorities and expressions of other cultures.

Gardner noted that IQ tests measure only two of these intelligences, linguistic and logical-mathematical, which he sees as being time-bound and culture-bound. Because we place such great emphasis on this narrow range of intelligence, we miss the full range of capabilities and intelligences that people have. Gardner proposed that children are born with varying amounts of these different intelligences, and it is therefore important to assess intellectual profiles early in life. Education, then, should be geared toward fostering the abilities and aptitudes that are innate, while, at the same time bolstering the necessary areas in which they show low aptitude.

Daniel Goleman proposed a theory of *emotional intelligence* (1995), based on the idea that people have "two different kinds of intelligence: rational and emotional" (p. 28). Emotional intelligence is a type of "meta ability" that governs our ability to use our rational capacity and is involved in areas such as "self-control, zeal and persistence, and the ability to motivate oneself" (p. xii). Based on his own work and that of others, he proposed five areas of emotional intelligence: *knowing one's emotions,* or self-awareness; *managing emotions*, the capacity to "soothe oneself" and shake off feelings of distress; *motivating oneself*, by "marshaling emotions in the service of a goal"; *recognizing emotions in others*, or empathy, "a fundamental 'people skill' "; and *handling relationships*, the ability to manage the emotions of others with social competence. According to Goleman, we must pay attention to the emotional aspects of cognition and foster what he calls "emotional literacy," if we are to effectively address and prevent problems such as depression and violence that are prevalent in today's society.

In more recent works, Goleman has expanded on the concept of intelligence to include social and ecological intelligence. Goleman proposes that we are wired to connect with others and sees social intelligence as the ability to recognize and read cues from other people in the course of social interaction and, based our reading of these cues, structure our actions accordingly (2007). He provides anecdotal and scientific evidence for this process as being both based in neurological reactions and socially learned abilities that involve individual choice and agency. Social intelligence involves several interrelated processes that include *primal empathy* (being able to sense emotional signals and feelings of others); *attunement* (the ability to listen while being fully receptive); *empathic accuracy* (the ability to accurately understand the thoughts, feelings, and intentions of others); *social cognition* (knowing how the social world works and how we structure our actions based on this); *synchrony* (the ability to interact effortlessly at the level of nonverbal communication); *self-presentation* (the ability to present ourselves effectively); *influence* (the ability to shape the outcome of social interactions); and *concern* (being able to care about the needs of others and acting accordingly). His subsequent work on ecological intelligence (2009) is less about internal or social processes. It addresses the hidden impact of the choices that we make that threaten the long-term sustainability of the planet. He proposes a "radical transparency" that will be brought about by new technologies that will not only help people make better decisions about goods that they purchase but also encourage businesses to engage in practices that are ecologically sound.

As we can see, the contemporary work of post-Piagetian theorists and researchers is bringing us closer to a holistic view of people that, hopefully, allows us to draw on a fuller array of their strengths and abilities. We turn now to an area that historically has received a great deal of attention—moral development and its links to cognitive development.

## MORAL DEVELOPMENT

In all societies there is an expectation that people conform to social and cultural norms and rules regarding acceptable behavior and ethical conduct. Moral behavior is concerned with the shoulds and should-nots of individual conduct, as dictated by such norms. Theories of moral development describe the qualitative changes in moral reasoning that occur as people grow and mature from childhood to adulthood.

### Key Concepts

Moral development is generally viewed as an important aspect of *socialization*, the process by which children learn to conform to societal norms and rules (R. M. Thomas, 1999). Through socialization, these rules become *internalized*, and children come to incorporate these rules into their own personal values. Once rules are internalized, children are no longer dependent on external sources of rewards or punishment to ensure conformity.

Central to most theories of moral development is the idea that changes in moral reasoning are dependent on changes in cognitive development. As children mature, cognitive egocentrism is gradually replaced by social reasoning developed through interaction with others. Children begin to display reciprocity by considering the intentions, viewpoints, and situations of others. Because moral stages are closely linked to cognitive development, there is also a corresponding assumption of *invariant sequentiality* (Eckensberger, 1994).

Theorists and researchers who study moral development are generally concerned with three aspects of morality: how people reason or think; how they actually behave; and how they feel about moral issues. Most theories, however, focus on the development of moral reasoning rather than on the way in which people behave or feel.

**PIAGET'S THEORY OF MORAL DEVELOPMENT**    Building on his earlier work in cognitive development, Piaget believed that children's understanding of right and wrong is molded by their cognitive awareness. He was particularly concerned with the way in which children come to respect and internalize rules as well as gain a sense of social justice. For Piaget, social justice involves the fair and equal treatment of people under socially defined rules.

In studying the stages of children's moral reasoning, Piaget played marbles with children of different ages and asked them questions about the rules of the game. In addition, he presented children with stories of moral dilemmas to understand their ideas about social justice. Based on this research, he proposed a two-stage theory of moral development that coincides with his preoperational and operational stages of cognitive development (Piaget, 1932).

Prior to about age 5, Piaget proposed that children are *premoral* and have a limited awareness of rules and reasons for them. Children play games for the fun of it, often making up their own rules.

In the first stage of moral development, *moral realism* or *heteronomous morality* (ages 5 through 10), rules are laid down by parents and authority figures; children don't really understand the reasons for the rules. However, through socialization they develop respect for rules and perceive the rules as untouchable, absolute, and sacred. They believe that rules must always be followed. At this stage, children believe that a consequence of punishment defines the wrongness of an act.

In the second stage, *moral relativism* or *autonomous morality* (ages 10 through adulthood), children become aware of meanings and reasons for rules, and rules are regarded as a product of mutual consent and respect. The shift to this stage occurs due to cognitive maturation, social experience, and the development of role-taking skills. Social rules are now seen as arbitrary agreements, made by people, which can be challenged, questioned, and changed. Children now consider the feelings and viewpoints of others in judging their conduct and administering punishment for rule breaking. At this stage, children are able to judge acts by intentions, not just by their consequences.

Piaget saw moral reasoning as a form of social knowledge that children construct out of their interactions with other people, particularly other children. Adult models present children with early, dominant authority figures that constrain children's behavior. However, these relationships with adults do not foster the concepts children need to develop a sense of justice, which he believed could only come from reciprocity, cooperation, and mutual respect (Piaget, 1932). It is through childhood and adolescent peer interactions that children are forced to discover that other children may have values different from their own, and through consensus and cooperation these differences can be accommodated. Children experience a healthy conflict in this discovery that can stimulate the advancement of autonomous moral reasoning. Authority in and of itself is insufficient for the development of a mature sense of moral justice.

In Piaget's investigations, younger children often saw the fairest punishment as the harshest and most retaliatory, while older children adopted the punishment that most fit the crime because it served a preventive function that helped the people see the consequences of their actions. However, Piaget believed that it was difficult, at best, to gain a clear understanding of moral development that can be applied universally. He suggested that concepts of justice are possibly influenced by cultural or local conditions that may encourage one form of reasoning over another. Such reasoning may prioritize arbitrary and harsh expiatory punishments and deprioritize "punishment by reciprocity," which, by contrast, assumes that severe punishment is not necessary and attempts, instead, to look at the content of rules and the natural consequences for breaking those rules.

**LAWRENCE KOHLBERG'S THEORY OF MORAL DEVELOPMENT**    Seeking to extend and modify Piaget's theory, Lawrence Kohlberg believed that moral reasoning was not fully developed by ages 10 to 11, as Piaget had proposed. Kohlberg based his theory on his initial research in which he verbally presented a series of moral dilemmas to 50 American boys, age 10 to 28. Rather than focusing on the answers that his subjects gave, he probed further to determine the actual reasoning that they used in deriving their answers. Although Kohlberg saw moral development in a more detailed way than did Piaget, he agreed that mental restructuring of experience was a necessary component.

Kohlberg proposed that moral development was a longer and more complex process. Like Piaget, he believed that each successive stage integrates and builds upon the reasoning of the previous stage, and the qualitatively distinct style of moral reasoning that emerges is applied across a broad range of situations. However, for Kohlberg there is no direct association between age and moral maturity. Advancement through stages is motivated by two main factors. First is a cognitive disequilibrium that develops due to the progressive awareness of one's own inadequacies in moral reasoning. Second is the advances in perspective taking that result from an increased capacity to understand others' viewpoints. His theory consists of six stages divided into three levels, with two stages at each level.

The first level is the *preconventional level*, which lasts roughly from birth to age 9. At this level there is no internalized awareness of right and wrong. Rules are externally imposed by authority figures and children obey rules to avoid punishment or to gain rewards.

During stage 1, the *obedience and punishment orientation*, children follow rules to avoid punishment. Moral behavior is based on fear of punishment or the consequences associated with rule violations. Children are unaware of the motives or intentions of others in judging actions. Similar to Piaget's thinking, the severity of punishment is believed to depend on the extent of wrongdoing.

In stage 2, the *naively egoistic orientation*, children follow rules to earn rewards or favors. However, they do the right thing to satisfy their own egocentric needs, with little regard for the needs of others. There is a beginning sense of reciprocity in social interactions, as children learn that if they behave in a certain way, they can get their needs met.

The second level, the *conventional level*, lasts from approximately ages 9 through 15. Moral behavior at this level is guided by conventional rules and norms and is aimed at winning approval from others or conforming to the existing social order. The motive, however, is one of conformity rather than an autonomous sense of ethics or morality.

During stage 3, the *good boy/nice girl orientation*, older children conform to rules to avoid social disapproval or negative evaluations by others. They now anticipate others' thoughts and feelings in an effort to seek approval and praise. In contrast to the egocentric reasoning at stage 2, children now become concerned about the opinions that others hold about them and they want to be seen as good people. In addition, children begin to understand the concept of intent; rule breaking is seen as less serious if the intention of the actor was good.

In stage 4, the *authority-maintaining morality*, people want to avoid criticism from authority figures. To avoid guilt and shame from criticism, they conform to the social order rather than to individual standards. They can now step outside of a two-person relationship and consider the larger perspective of societal laws and rules in determining their course of action. They believe in uniform, fair application of laws and they identify with and show respect for social institutions. Moral rules are viewed in a more rigid, legalistic way that serves to support and preserve the prevailing social order.

The final level is the *postconventional level*, from age 16 onward. In this level we see an autonomous, self-accepted moral maturity. Kohlberg believed that most adults do not achieve this level.

In stage 5, the *contractual legalistic orientation*, people choose moral precepts to guide their lives based on the morality of contracts. Contracts that are fair and just should be followed; those that are based on externally imposed laws that compromise human rights should be challenged and modified. Distinctions between legality and morality begin to emerge, and there is greater flexibility in moral beliefs. Emphasis is placed on democratically accepted law and consensus as well as an understanding of the greater good and the potential to modify an unjust social contract.

Finally in stage 6, the highest moral stage, the *universal ethical principle orientation*, there is the emergence of truly autonomous morality based on individual conscience. Broad moral guidelines are based on abstract principles such as justice, compassion, equality, and human dignity. The development of true conscience based on such principles transcends any legal formulations that conflict with these larger moral guidelines.

Despite the fact that Kohlberg included this third level in his theory, he believed that very few people ever reach this level. In fact, he proposed that practically no one ever functions consistently at stage six, which was his ideal. Table 9.3 summarizes Kohlberg's key concepts of moral development and illustrates typical reasoning at each stage in relation to questions posed about a moral dilemma involving Heinz, a man whose wife is dying and needs expensive medication that he can't afford to buy. The respondent must provide a rationale for whether Heinz should steal the medicine.

## Roads From Piaget and Kohlberg

Although Kohlberg's theory received greater acceptance than Piaget's and has long been portrayed in most psychology and social work textbooks as the normative standard for moral development, his work has led to both further developments as well as stinging critiques. Robert Coles, a psychoanalytically trained psychiatrist and Harvard University professor, for example, has documented children's spiritual life, moral thought, and moral intelligence through his direct interaction and conversations with a wide range of children (Coles, 1990, 1991, 1997). However, unlike many theorists and researchers, he deliberately has not used traditional survey research or attempted to make "general psychological statements without reference to idiosyncrasies and exceptions" (Coles, 1990, p. 22). He is critical of traditional research methods that attempt to measure children's thinking, moral development, and faith development, noting that "If the child fails to respond to a researcher's predetermined line of questioning, the researcher is likely to comment on a 'developmental' inadequacy" (1990, p. 23). Although Coles' work has made a significant contribution to our understanding of children and has been considered groundbreaking, it has not led to a testable body of theory.

| TABLE 9.3 | Kohlberg's Stages of Moral Development | |
|---|---|---|
| **Stage Description** | **Examples of Moral Reasoning: Why He *Should* Steal the Drug** | **Examples of Moral Reasoning: Why He *Should Not* Steal the Drug** |
| **Preconventional** | | |
| Stage 1: Avoid punishment | If he lets his wife die, he'll get in trouble. | He might get caught and sent to jail. |
| Stage 2: Seek rewards | If he gets caught, he could give the drug back and he wouldn't get a long jail sentence. | The druggist needs to make money. |
| **Conventional** | | |
| Stage 3: Gain approval/ avoid disapproval | He should show his wife how much he loves her. | If his wife dies, he can't be blamed. It's the druggist's fault for being selfish. |
| Stage 4: Conformity to rules | It would be his responsibility if she dies; he can pay the druggist later. | It's always wrong to steal; he'll always feel guilty. |
| **Postconventional** | | |
| Stage 5: Social contract | Because he vowed to take care of his wife, he is justified in taking it, even though stealing is wrong. | Extreme circumstances don't justify stealing. He'll lose respect for himself. He should think about the long-term consequences. |
| Stage 6: Individual principled conscience | His wife's life is more important than the druggist's profits. | Other people may also need the drug. He should consider the lives of everyone involved— not just his wife. |

*Source:* Adapted from *Life Span Development* by John W. Santrock, Copyright © 1989. Used with permission of The McGraw-Hill Companies.

In the following sections we review Matthew Kanjirathinkal's ideological critique of Piaget and Kohlberg, Carol Gilligan's feminist critique and subsequent model of women's moral development, and James W. Fowler's model of faith development that builds on the theories of Piaget and Kohlberg.

**KANJIRATHINKAL'S SOCIOLOGICAL CRITIQUE**  Drawing on the works of Marx, Mannheim, and Lukacs, Matthew Kanjirathinkal (1990) utilized a sociology of knowledge perspective to critique the prevailing theories of cognitive and moral development. In particular, he criticized the use of reason in ethics, positing that ethics and ideology cannot be understood apart from their sociohistorical origin. Knowledge is a social product because it results from a cooperative process of group life. Agreeing with Karl Marx that the conditions of life interpret thought, he held that, "It is not consciousness that determines life, but life that determines consciousness" (Kanjirathinkal, 1990, p. 3). He argued that reason is portrayed as the ultimate legislator of moral laws, while, at the same time, reason is disconnected from the conditions that it is studying.

Kanjirathinkal concluded that this separation supported the bourgeois class' culture, values, and economic interests.

Piaget, like philosopher Immanuel Kant, believed that knowledge is constructed by the subject through logical thinking that cognitively transforms experience. What Piaget further added to the equation is a biological, genetic structuralism that grounded the a priori categories (schemata or reason) as an almost autonomous entity unaffected by sociohistorical conditions. Kanjirathinkal argued that Kant's individualistic epistemology and transcendental method involves "turning to the structure of the subject to seek answers for the problems one experiences in society" (p. 15). In essence, Piaget biologized Kant's transcendentalism by identifying the necessary and universal a priori conditions of knowledge with forms of biological structure. The biologization of transcendentalism, thus, serves as a powerful ideology to group the structures of modern society and its socioeconomic operations (p. 55).

In terms of morality, he argued that Piaget implicitly advances the thesis that morality is an expression and function of formal operations because it stems from a rational being's adaptive effort of assimilating and accommodating to the environment. Autonomous morality is the fully equilibrated form of consciousness that results from biological maturation and reciprocal inter-action (p. 67).

Piaget held that cooperative reason cannot develop under social pressures and can come to pass only under conditions of mutual respect and cooperation among equals. The implication, therefore, is that nondemocratic countries are morally and socially underdeveloped and inferior. For Kanjirathinkal, this was tantamount to a defense of the ideals of Western democracy, with democracy, morality, rationality, and biology being equated with one another. Rather than democracy being a matter of intellectual development, he argued, it is a political system of power distribution tailored to suit corporate capitalism. In Piaget's theory, Western moral values are argued to be universal and superior because they are autonomously produced by transcendent reason, are biologically determined, or because they are presupposed within the context of rational discourse (p. 9). The substantial values that undergird all varieties of ethical cognitivism (found in the works of Kant, Piaget, Kohlberg, and Habermas) are equality, freedom, progress, and democracy. Thus, moral judgment becomes a vehicle of reason to carry out its mission of advancing the causes of the bourgeoisie.

For Kohlberg, progress through the moral levels and stages is characterized by increasing differentiation and increasing integration. Once again, cognitive development is the yardstick by which to measure moral development. Despite the genetic structuralists' claims that cognition is based on interaction, Kanjirathinkal asserted that it is portrayed as essentially individualistic, in that morality in psychological theory is grounded in the internalized dialogue of individual consciousness rather than social processes and factors. Hence, thought and the conditions that produce thought (that is, culture) become separated. The exclusive reliance on biology and concomitant disregard for social factors to explain the formation of cognitive categories assumes that individuals are isolated from a social and cultural context. This separation is further highlighted when democracy is posited by Kohlberg to be the proper milieu and method for moral development, because education in a free society forestalls the dangers of cultural indoctrination (Kanjirathinkal, 1990, p. 94). Thus, cognitive-moral developmental theory essentially amounts to an argument that the capitalistic style of life is superior and that it is universally and logically necessary.

**CAROL GILLIGAN'S FEMINIST CRITIQUE AND THEORY**    In her book *In a Different Voice: Psychological Theory and Women's Development*, Carol Gilligan (1982) criticized Kohlberg for failing to account for gender differences in moral development. Building on the earlier works of

Nancy Chodorow (discussed in Chapter 7), Gilligan proposed that women develop a moral orientation that is grounded in relationships and responsibilities rather than in the more male concern for rules and abstract principles. Consequently, females typically scored lower in Kohlberg's interviews (usually at stage 3) and failed to reach a higher level of moral functioning. Gilligan argued that when women are studied using a more relevant frame of reference, a different and less biased portrayal of moral judgments is revealed.

Gilligan's initial research was based on three studies: a study of college students that examined identity and moral development; research interviews with women who were faced with the difficult decision of whether to have an abortion; and a larger study of men and women, ages 6 to 60, that focused on conceptions of rights and responsibilities. In contrast to Kohlberg's methodology that focused on the way in which people *thought* and *reasoned* about moral dilemmas, Gilligan expanded her research design to learn how people actually *defined* moral problems and to determine the specific situations that they saw as constituting moral conflicts (Gilligan, 1982). Terming the differences that she found as a *different voice*, she proposed that it was theme rather than gender that characterized such differences. Nonetheless, she argued that women, more so than men (although not exclusively), revealed a different voice in moral reasoning.

Using examples from her studies, Gilligan proposed a three-stage developmental process, beginning in early childhood and culminating in adulthood. In contrast to Kohlberg, however, she did not place age bands around the emergence of each stage. Instead, she described the perspectives that characterized each stage and the transitional phases that led to the eventual development of the next stage.

**Stage 1: Self-survival:** Moral reasoning is initially concerned with caring for one's self. At this stage women are involved with the pragmatics of self-survival; lacking power and feeling disconnected and all alone, the self becomes the "sole object of concern." However, this leads to a transitional phase in which caring only for one's self comes to be seen as selfish, and women begin to acknowledge their responsibility toward others.

**Stage 2: Caring for Others (Feminine Goodness):** As women begin to understand the connection between self and others, they come to accept conventional definitions of women's maternal roles and define morality in terms of their responsibility to care for others—especially for those who are dependent and unequal. At this stage they totally exclude themselves from the equation and are concerned only with their acceptance by and responsibility toward others. This imbalance eventually leads to another transition, as the total exclusion of self in moral formulations begins to create a disequilibrium.

**Stage 3: Interdependence of Self and Others:** In this final stage women recognize that the needs of self and the needs of others must be balanced; this leads to a recognition of interconnection, interdependence, and an appreciation of the dynamics of relationships. According to Gilligan (1982), this involves a "critical reinterpretation of the conflict between selfishness and responsibility" (p. 105). As women shift from an ethic of feminine goodness to that of responsibility to self *and* others, the *ethic of care* that emerges from this reflective understanding is universal in condemning exploitation and hurt. Instead of seeing interdependence as a weakness, women come to appreciate relationships as a source of moral strength.

Gilligan's formulation on women's moral stages initially received a great deal of support among writers and theorists seeking to develop a feminist knowledge base about women's development. However, theories that propose psychological developmental differences based on

| TABLE 9.4 | Gilligan's Stages of Moral Development |
|-----------|----------------------------------------|
| **Stage Description** | **Basis of Moral Reasoning** |
| Stage 1: Self survival | Morality is based on what is best for oneself and the pragmatics of survival. |
| *Transition from selfishness to responsibility for others* | |
| Stage 2: Caring for others (feminine goodness) | Morality is based on meeting other people's needs and caring for the dependent and unequal. |
| *Transition from feminine goodness to truth* | |
| Stage 3: Interdependence of self and others | Morality is based on caring for self and others; it involves an ethic of care based on nonviolence. |

gender have received widespread criticism from feminists who argue that it is structural differences (in opportunities)—not psychological differences—that should be the focus of feminist inquiry. Further, given that power continues to reside in patriarchal structures, psychological differences (if they even exist) are not seen as neutral differences, but as deficiencies on the part of women. Perhaps even more problematic is the fact that her theory has received little empirical support, which we discuss later in this chapter.

In an updated preface to *In a Different Voice* (1993), Gilligan has taken a more overtly political stance and, in reflecting on her work, has more clearly addressed the relationship between women's psychology and the prevailing social order. According to Gilligan, "a new psychological theory in which girls and women are seen and heard is an inevitable challenge to a patriarchal order that can remain in place only through the continuing eclipse of women's experience" (1993, p. xxiv). Because the perpetuation of the existing social order is dependent on theories of development and morality that link goodness and progress with disconnection or detachment, Gilligan argued that women's psychology, grounded in the feminine voices of attachment and relationships, is a potential revolutionary threat. In a clever turn of the feminist phrase "the personal is the political," Gilligan asserted that "the political has become the psychological." It is unlikely, however, that this stance will satisfy the critics who continue to point to structural rather than psychological differences.

Although Gilligan is best known for her books and articles on women's moral development, her subsequent research on female adolescent development has yielded important insights about psychological distress and a loss of self-confidence that girls encounter in their teenage years (Gilligan, 1990; Gilligan, Rogers, & Tolman, 1991). As discussed in Chapter 8, these observations have been replicated by a growing body of research that paints a troubling picture of female adolescent development in contemporary society. Table 9.4 illustrates Gilligan's key concepts of women's moral development.

**JAMES W. FOWLER'S THEORY OF FAITH DEVELOPMENT**   Building on the ideas of Piaget and Kohlberg, as well as insights from Erik Erikson, James W. Fowler, a contemporary professor of theology and human development, proposed a theory of faith development. Although he is a committed Christian, he attempted to make his theory applicable to people of all beliefs, whether religious or nonreligious. In this respect, his definition of faith is similar to the idea of spirituality commonly used in social work, as defined in Chapters 1 and 13.

Fowler (1996) defined *faith* as the "pattern of our relatedness to self, others, and our world in light of our relatedness to ultimacy" (p. 21). The concept of *ultimacy* refers to whatever a person understands as the ultimate or most profound basis of reality that gives orientation to her or his life. This may take theistic, agnostic, or atheistic forms. Faith, therefore, is generic and universal to human beings and "may be characterized as an integral centering process, underlying the formation of beliefs, values, and meanings, that (1) gives coherence and direction to persons' lives, (2) links them in shared trusts and loyalties with others, (3) grounds their personal stances and communal loyalties in a sense of relatedness to a larger frame of reference, and (4) enables them to face and deal with the limit conditions of human life, relying upon that which has the quality of ultimacy in their lives" (p. 56).

Faith has strong cognitive and moral aspects; it is developmental, dynamic, and relational. Fowler (1996) distinguished faith from belief and religion. *Belief* is defined as "an intellectual assent to propositions" (p. 55). *Religion* is defined as "a cumulative tradition composed from myriad beliefs and practices that have expressed and formed the faith of persons" (p. 56). Thus, evaluation of a person's faith development does not involve judgment of any particular beliefs or religious affiliations; faith can be expressed either inside or outside of religious institutional contexts. Building on Piaget and Kohlberg, Fowler asserted that faith development relates to an increase in the complexity and comprehensiveness of how we understand ourselves and the world, and the ability to take the perspectives of others. The contents of faith are the things and qualities of greatest value to us, the images of power that give us support in challenging times, the master stories we tell ourselves to interpret events, and our locus of authority for defining what is true and right.

Faith development can include transformations in the contents of faith over time, which he called conversion (Fowler, 1981). *Conversion* is a significant and often dramatic change of our values, images, sources of authority, and master stories. He cited, for example, the case of a 1930s White sharecropper who felt an intense personal experience of call by God to protest against the racist attitudes and behaviors of his social milieu. Sometimes such conversion involves a process of critical self-reflection that leads to a change of stage, rather than just changes in contents of faith.

A *stage of faith* is a pervasive pattern of knowing and valuing that orients us to ourselves, the world, and ultimacy. Transition through stages is affected by challenges to the prevailing faith orientation that require more complex, sophisticated, and comprehensive understandings. These challenges ordinarily come from physiological changes (such as biological maturation or physical injury) or significant changes in the social environment or crises of meaning that may occur at a time of bereavement (Fowler, 1996). From a Christian framework, Fowler (1981, 1996) also suggested that change can be stimulated by unpredictable and disruptive manifestations of God's grace that can call people to fundamentally reevaluate their lives. Fowler's stage theory, however, focuses on the ordinary and expectable developmental experiences rather than on these revelatory possibilities.

Fowler (1981) derived his stage theory from a study conducted from 1972 to 1981 to determine how people viewed their personal history, how they worked through problems to solutions, and how they formed moral and religious commitments. He and his collaborators conducted 359 in-depth interviews with mostly White men and women, primarily Christian and Jewish, ranging in age from early childhood to past age 61. He refined his description of these stages over time, and the following summary integrates ideas from both his original study and his most recent writing (1981, 1984, 1996).

**Stage 1: Primal Faith (Infancy):**   As the infant is dependent upon caretakers for survival, experience of maternal and paternal presence shapes pre-images of ultimacy. Ideally, consistent nurturance by parents yields a basic sense of mutuality and trust about the universe and the divine.

Harmful experiences at this stage can result in later images of a punitive or arbitrary and unde-pendable God. This stage, however, is speculative because Fowler recognized that his research technique could not verify empirically the internal experience and pre-images of the infant.

**Stage 2: Intuitive-Projective Faith (Early Childhood, Beginning about Age 2):** The young child's rapidly developing capacity for language and symbolization gives rise to imagina-tive fantasy about the mysterious and the ultimate, drawing on symbols learned from family and people who are experienced as powerful. As the young child has not yet developed a capacity for critical self-reflection, it is difficult to distinguish fantasy from factuality.

**Stage 3: Mythic-literal Faith (Middle Childhood, Beginning about Age 6, and Beyond):** The child is able to develop and learn more sophisticated stories, morals, and values from the family's community. Contents of faith are shaped primarily by the beliefs of and loyalty to the child's identified community. For believers in a personal God, God is seen as a being who gives just rewards and punishments.

**Stage 4: Synthetic-Conventional Faith (Adolescence and Beyond):** Many adoles-cents expand the capacity for self-reflection to examine the meaning of one's life and significant relationships. A personalized myth of identity and ideas about ultimacy are formed with greater influence from social reference groups beyond the family.

**Stage 5: Individuative-Reflective Faith (Young Adulthood and Beyond):** Some young adults and adults question the beliefs and stories they have received from family, friends, and other social groups. They engage in critical reflection to arrive at a greater sense of personal accountability and responsibility for their faith, especially in response to conflicts of values and beliefs between themselves and others. They demythologize their learned master stories and seek to construct a deeper sense of life vocation and ideology.

**Stage 6: Conjunctive Faith (Early Midlife and Beyond):** For some adults, critical reflection gives rise to a sense of the ambiguity and paradoxes in life that takes into account tensions between apparently contradictory qualities within the self and the world. For exam-ple, the person recognizes both symbolic and rational qualities of experience and attempts to integrate them. Competing faith traditions and claims of truth are appreciated. Truth is seen as multiform and complex, rather than dichotomous or simplistic. Conjunctive faith brings a clearly articulated commitment to particular beliefs and values together with an openness to other faiths and personal choices. Significantly, only one person in Fowler's sample was rated as having achieved this stage.

**Stage 7: Universalizing Faith (midlife and Beyond):** This final stage involves resolv-ing many of the tensions and paradoxes associated with stage 6 by moving beyond the limits of one's own ego perspective and cultural and religious constraints. Although people continue to have difficulties and personal foibles, they seek to rise above them. They are able to take the perspective of other people, nationalities, and faith traditions, as well as their own. They develop a sense of nonjudgmental love and valuing for all people and all beings. Those who believe in a personal God feel able to relate to the world from the standpoint of God's unconditional love for all and are open to fellowship with people of other faith stages or traditions. This love for all beings gives rise to a commitment to social action for justice. The transcendent perspective challenges egoistic, ethnocentric, and religiously fundamentalist norms and may therefore be perceived as subversive by people who uphold conventional social and religious views. As we will see, this stage is similar to the transegoic stages of development in Ken Wilber's theory, which we discuss in Chapter 13.

Similar to Kohlberg's final stage that few ever achieved, Fowler considered attainment of this last stage to be very rare. Examples of people who achieved this stage of faith, cited by Fowler, are Mahatma Gandhi and Reverend Martin Luther King, Jr. Not surprisingly, no one in Fowler's sample was rated at this stage. However, Fowler held that the contemporary postmodern situation of religious pluralism and global interdependence challenges people to become ever more complex, sophisticated, and inclusive in their faith. His theory, therefore, not only describes stages of faith but also advocates for active efforts in religious education and education in general to encourage development to the last two stages.

## CONTEMPORARY ISSUES

Perhaps one of the most contemporary issues in cognitive development involves the relationship between the mind and the brain. In contrast to the philosophical tradition that separated the mind from the physical body, current research is increasingly attempting to delineate the connections between genetic determinants of behavior as well as the neurochemical brain processes that give rise to cognition. Due to advances in technology, coupled with heavy funding of brain research, the 1990s was dubbed the "decade of the brain." Thus, cognitive scientists have begun to get a clearer picture of the way in which neurochemical transmitters (the substances that relay electrical impulses between neurons in different parts of the brain) govern memory, emotion, thought, alertness, and a variety of other human functions. There is increasing evidence, for example, that men and women do process information differently, and that memory is much more complex and less localized than previously thought. In addition, there is speculation that a better understanding of these processes will lead to eventual cures for a variety of psychiatric and behavioral disorders, including schizophrenia, depression, phobias, and drug addiction.

The preeminent influence of biology and genetics also has been a cornerstone of sociobiology and evolutionary psychology, both of which attribute biological causation not only to cognitive functioning but also to many areas of social behavior. In addition, a number of studies on identical twins have frequently been cited as evidence to support a biological view of human behavior, and some researchers continue to argue about the relative weighting of biological and environmental factors in determining behavioral and personality factors such as openness to experience, conscientiousness, extroversion, political and social attitudes, body fat, optimism and pessimism, religiosity, sexual orientation, substance abuse, and attention deficit disorder, among others. Despite amazing similarities that have been found in identical twins, critics cite an equally impressive arsenal of research that demonstrates that environment—both shared and unshared—has more of an influence than genetics (Neimark, 1997).

As we discussed in Chapter 8, although research on genetics and neurotransmission is certainly an invaluable area of inquiry, it can also lead to an extremely reductionistic view of people that portrays all behavior as genetically determined and all mind processes as essentially biochemical; this leaves little room for human agency, free will, or the interpretive process. As Harvard University psychologist Jerome Kagan (1997) has noted, "some psychiatrists and neuroscientists are moving too quickly toward a biological determinism that is as extreme as the earlier loyalty . . . to an environmental explanation." Inherent in the "new romance with biology" is the danger that we award biology and inherited temperament "too strong a voice" and ignore the fact that "we also inherit the human capacity for restraint" (p. A64). A more realistic view (and one that is accepted by most behavioral scientists) is that nature and nurture interact in complex ways. According to Kagan (1997, p. A64), in his rephrasing of philosopher W. V. O. Quine, "every behavior can be likened to a pale gray fabric composed of black threads, for biology, and white threads, for experience, but it is not possible to detect any purely black threads nor any purely white ones."

One significant finding related to cognitive developmental theory is that experience and environmental factors are much more important in shaping the mind than Piaget proposed. Direct links are now being made between the development of specific brain processes and functions that were previously attributed to the mind (Nash, 1997). Although there are "windows of learning" that appear to be biologically based, it is the flood of sensory experiences that actually shape and progressively refine the brain. The physical structure of the brain has been found to produce trillions of neuronal connections (synapses) during the first years of life that die off in the absence of environmental stimulation. Thus, researchers are paying increasing attention to the effects of stimulating environments on infants and toddlers with the recognition that "rich experiences . . . really do produce rich brains" (Nash, 1997, p. 51). As a result, there is increasing attention to early childhood education and day care.

This raises interesting questions about previous assumptions in mainstream developmental theory about the supposedly negative effects of early infant-stimulation programs. Originally developed for use with infants with developmental disabilities (such as those with Down syndrome), "infant-stim" programs provided rigorous and methodical environmental stimulation to infants and toddlers to capitalize on the brain's plasticity in early years. These programs were initially lauded as successful and cost-effective educational efforts that increased children's developmental abilities and cognitive outcomes (Pines, 1982). However, they were quickly applied to "normal" children without disabilities, for the purpose of enhancing and hastening development. Child developmental psychologist David Elkind (1987), in particular, has been highly critical of this application of infant-stim programs. He proposed that programs, such as those developed by Glenn Doman (1963, 1982) and Siegfried Engelmann and Therese Engelmann (1966), among others, that advocated formal instruction in reading and math for preschoolers would put them at risk of lasting psychological and physical harm due to the social pressures imposed by parents. Dubbing the boom in early childhood education as "miseducation," Elkind argued that "healthy education supports and encourages . . . spontaneous learning" (based on children's natural exploration of the world) and that "Early instruction miseducates, not because it attempts to teach, but because it attempts to teach the wrong things at the wrong time" (1987, p. 25).

Although there has been little replicable research to support the efficacy of such infant-stim programs when applied to developmentally normal children, there is also a dearth of replicable research to support Elkind's position that such programs cause irreparable damage to children's self-esteem and ability to learn. We note that this controversy has been mired in ideology on both sides. It will be especially interesting to follow the emerging applications of contemporary brain research that point to the importance of early childhood education.

## APPLICATION TO SOCIAL WORK PRACTICE

The traditional theories of cognitive and moral development, as espoused by Piaget and Kohlberg, have received wide acceptance in social work practice and have been an integral part of human behavior theory. Unfortunately, they too often have been portrayed as fact, rather than theory. Sadly, the work of contemporary theorists such as Sternberg and Gardner is overlooked by most human behavior textbooks. H. Goldstein (2001) commented on the importance of appreciating the multiple intelligences proposed by Gardner in relation to social work education and practice and its applicability to both experiential learning and supporting individual differences. Carol Gilligan's work has received wider acceptance in the field. It has been less common, however, to find contrasting views of other contemporary cognitive and moral theorists and researchers in the mainstream social work literature, although some current textbooks are now beginning to correct this oversight (see, for example, Ashford & Le Croy, 2010).

Two additional related areas, in particular, have also been notably missing from the literature: (a) theory and research on memory and memory development and (b) the development of morality linked to religious or spiritual beliefs. We view knowledge about memory as particularly important and timely, given the contemporary controversy about recovered and false memories (discussed in Chapter 7) and the numerous lawsuits against social workers and other mental health professionals that may have resulted from the use of suggestive therapeutic techniques. Also timely is an expansion of our knowledge of religious and spiritual factors involved in moral judgment. Traditionally, religious institutions have been portrayed as a mechanism of socialization, and the primary focus of moral development has been on its relationship to cognitive development, with both seen from an internal, individualistic view. We believe that these emerging areas of knowledge for social work practice will, hopefully, gain more widespread acceptance in the near future.

## Definition of the Helping Situation

In examining the helping situation, there are several applications for the cognitive and moral developmental models discussed. The dominant definition of the helping situation is one of growth and self-actualization. People are seen as having their own unique, latent capacities that need to be stimulated and developed by others who can act as facilitators for this process. Alternately, the helping situation could be defined from the problem perspective. In this case, the helper, in collaboration with the client, relies on the client's intellect to find a solution. A further definition that has applicability is that of deviance, when it is assumed that a lack of cognitive skills or moral reasoning is the cause of deviant behavior. Here the social worker assists the client in advancing his or her cognitive and moral thinking beyond its current level through a variety of confrontational individual and group techniques. An assumption in the two latter models is that the helper is cognitively and morally advanced (superior) to the person receiving help (T. Howard & Wilk, 1986; Kohlberg, 1981). Flowchart 9.1 demonstrates an application of cognitive and moral developmental theory derived from these definitions.

## Assessment, Practice Strategies, and Methods

Assessment of cognitive skills and moral reasoning is typically based on methods similar to those used by Piaget, Kohlberg, and Gilligan. To date, Gardner's assessment methods for determining multiple intelligence have received less attention in social work but may become more widely used in school settings in the future. In direct practice, the use of the clinical interview is primary, and this may be supplemented with validated instruments used to assess cognitive functioning and moral reasoning. Although psychological testing is typically the domain of psychologists rather than social workers, the results of such tests, once interpreted, can provide a basis for social work assessment and intervention.

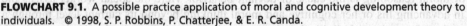

**FLOWCHART 9.1.** A possible practice application of moral and cognitive development theory to individuals. © 1998, S. P. Robbins, P. Chatterjee, & E. R. Canda.

In addition, an understanding of cognitive and moral development can aid social workers in examining a client's growth process and suggest the level of intervention needed. For example, when examining a young victim's reaction to a violent assault, Carol Mowbray (1989, p. 198) indicated:

> Combined with young children's egocentrism, their primitive sense of moral development may have some serious consequences for how they react to traumatic events. First, if serious damage or injury has occurred to others but not themselves, children may blame themselves, whether or not they had any culpability—and the more serious the damage, the greater the self-blame. If adult reactions are to blame the victims, children will undoubtedly accept this. . . . Young children may also experience more self-blame and guilt and consequently more fears of retribution because their egocentrism leads them to attribute real power to their thoughts and fantasies; so if they wished something bad would happen to their sister, parent, etc., and it did, they would

feel responsible. Because of their absolutist morality and orientation to authority figures, young children may also feel that if something bad happens to them (e.g., as a victim), then they must have deserved it.

Thus, an understanding of children's cognitive and moral development can play a critical factor in the development of an intervention plan.

Other practice strategies and methods using a cognitive/moral developmental approach might include exposing clients to conflicting information just above their current reasoning capacity for the purpose of creating cognitive conflict and challenging them to advance their moral thinking. Recently, efforts in this area related to the development of victim empathy have been used in an attempt to promote the acquisition of prosocial skills in perpetrators of sexual offenses, domestic violence, and violent crimes. The compounding of more advanced moral reasoning with confrontive, prosocial peer group discussions, interactions, and role-playing is the basis of many violent offender treatment programs. Most commonly used are a variety of confrontational individual and group techniques.

Currently, it is very common in the mental health field to use treatments that combine elements of behavioral and cognitive theories, such as dialectical behavior therapy (DBT) that is widely applied in work with people who have been diagnosed with borderline personality disorder, suicidal ideation, eating disorders, and difficulties with impulse control and managing disturbing thoughts or feelings (S. C. Haynes, Follette, & Linehan, 2004). Cognitive-behavioral therapies (CBTs) emphasize the way people learn, unlearn, and relearn their ways of experiencing and resolving problems, especially as mediated by cognition. Therapeutic activities may target changes in behavior through classical and operant conditioning (see Chapter 12) and/or habits of thinking, self-talk, and clarity of awareness. In any case, cognitions are seen as key to understanding a person and helping her or him to change and to enhance ability to achieve goals (Keegan Eamon, 2008).

Fowler's theory can be extremely relevant to developmental assessment. Using a similar model, Joseph (1987, 1988) pointed out the importance of images of God and religious stories in social work clients' lives in helping them form worldviews and standards for moral reflection. She found that those with images of God as being punitive, rigid, and authoritarian, experienced feelings of excessive shame and guilt; they also exhibited inflexible and simplistic ways of thinking about life issues. Social work practitioners can use Fowler's model to help people critically reflect on these God images and develop more sophisticated and life-affirming views, while still keeping their faith commitments and traditions. Clinical practice in this area could encourage clients to move toward Fowler's faith stage 4 and beyond if spiritual development is relevant to their life goals (Canda & Furman, 2010).

It is important, however, to realize that use of the theories discussed here may result in a tendency to psychologize the helping situation and blame people for what is seen as their inherent deficiencies. Although often overlooked, a critical consideration from a macro perspective is whether the perceived deficiency is individual or societal. Are problems in cognitive and moral functioning due to individual shortcomings, or can they be attributed to structural barriers that people face due to differences in social class and gender? In assessment, for example, it is important to consider whether the elimination of structural barriers to higher education would reduce such deficiencies.

In addition, authoritarian models and structures in the family, school, and society may run contrary to the development of higher-level cognitive and moral thinking. This is important because a large body of evidence suggests that higher stages of cognitive and moral development

| TABLE 9.5 | Various Settings and Applications of Cognitive and Moral Development Theories |

| Type of Agency | Type of Presenting Problem(s) | Type of Program | Definition(s) of the Helping Situation | Type(s) of Activites |
| --- | --- | --- | --- | --- |
| Junior high school | Adolescent steals from other students | School social work | Growth Problem Deviance | Developmental assessment; peer support group to raise perspective-taking and moral reasoning. |
| Family service center | Death of parent, self-blame of child | Individual and family counseling | Growth Problem | Developmental assessment; child counseling to reduce ego-centric self-blame and fantasies; family grief work. |
| Mental health center | Unrealistic, debilitating guilt of religious client | Individual counseling | Growth Problem | Spiritually sensitive assessment of religious beliefs, images of God, and relation to guilt; dialogue; collaboration with clergy. |
| Community action center | Hostility between opposing interest groups | Community organizing and development | Growth Problem Social issue | Conflict mediation; community "speak outs" and dialogue groups; nonviolent activism. |

are best realized when appropriate environmental supports exist on multiple levels, including family, peers, schooling, and institutions of the wider society (Berk, 1989). Although cognitive/moral developmental models are most often seen in the context of interventions with individuals, small groups, and families, this evidence suggests that macro-level considerations and interventions may be appropriate as well. Table 9.5 illustrates a variety of settings and applications of cognitive and moral developmental theory.

## CRITICAL ANALYSIS

### Biological, Psychological, and Spiritual Factors

Piagetian developmental theory is heavily based on factors that are portrayed as innate and biological in nature. Despite his interactionist stance and belief that cognitive structures themselves are not innate, he proposed invariant stages that epigenetically unfold in an age-stage sequence according to innate biological timing. Although environmental factors and social interaction are necessary for development to proceed, it is the biological mandate that determines the timing and the sequence of development. Although Kohlberg does not as closely subscribe to age-stage correlations as does Piaget, his theory, nonetheless, is based on the sequentiality of stages.

These models have been criticized by psychodynamic theorists for ignoring emotional and affective development. By emphasizing only the cognitive basis of moral judgments, neither Piaget nor Kohlberg adequately addressed the emotional basis of moral behavior. In contrast, because Gilligan's theory is partially based on Nancy Chodorow's object relations theory, she addressed emotional factors to a greater extent than other theorists. Nonetheless, in all theories discussed here, with the exception of Goleman's theory on emotional intelligence and Gardner's theory of multiple intelligences, emotions are given less weight than conscious reasoning.

Fowler's work on faith development is the only cognitive theory to address in detail the spiritual implications of cognitive and moral development. As such, it provides an important starting point for consideration of the spiritual development of individual clients. However, because it builds upon the assumptions of the Piagetian tradition, it retains the other limitations discussed here.

Gardner is not yet sure whether to include existential intelligence in his list of separate intelligences. However, he recognizes the importance of dealing with the big questions of life, whether or not that is distinct to a separate intelligence or represents an amalgam of multiple intelligences. While Goleman is best known for his theory of emotional intelligence, he has more recently addressed social and ecological intelligences. All of these interests relate to his long-term interests in spirituality, Buddhism, meditation, and mindfulness practices (Goleman, 1988, 2009). Indeed, mindfulness-based practices, derived from Buddhist meditation, have become widely used and researched in health and mental health fields and are becoming better known in social work (Baer, 2006; Hick, 2009; McBee, 2008). Mindfulness-based therapeutic practices are usually taught to clients without explicit reference to Buddhism. They help the person learn how to pay attention to the present moment with a clear mind, acknowledging what is without judgment and without being carried away by thoughts and feelings. These practices help free people from anxieties, angers, and obsessions while promoting compassion, acceptance, and forgiveness (Canda & Furman, 2010).

## Social, Cultural, and Economic Forces

Theorists discussed in this chapter all emphasize the importance of social interactions and role-taking behavior. Children are seen as playing a very active role in learning through experience within their social environments. Perspective-taking skills involve complex evaluations of people's intentions, thoughts, emotions, and the situations that elicit them. However, in contrast to psychodynamic theory, there is a definite deemphasis on parents and past. Piaget is quite similar to George Herbert Mead (discussed in Chapter 10) in assigning primacy to the influence of peer group interactions in the development of autonomous moral reasoning.

Although the importance of environmental influences is stressed, the primary focus is on interpersonal interaction. Even Gilligan's dual focus on individual rights and relational embeddedness fails to address structural aspects of the environment. Thus, the scope of environment in these theories is narrowly defined and, with the exception of Gardner's work, is divorced from any sociohistorical context. In addition, cultural variables receive little attention, if any, because these theories are assumed to be universal. Economic factors are largely ignored, as are structural factors related to power that produce inequities in opportunity.

Some of Fowler's theological essays, however, go beyond the descriptive aspects of his stage theory to suggest a postmodern theological response to current issues of social justice. In keeping with the tenets of Christian liberation theology (discussed in Chapter 4), Fowler (1996) described a parallel process in collective human social development to the stages of individual faith development. He suggested that cultural and religious diversity, and situations of social injustice and oppression, challenge both individuals and communities to work out inclusive and respectful modes of faith.

## Relevance to Individuals, Groups, Families, Organizations, Institutions, and Communities

Theories of cognitive and moral development focus primarily on the individual, the family, and peer groups. Although organizations, institutions, and communities are seen as part of the environment, they are portrayed as playing a somewhat less direct role in the development of cognitive and moral reasoning. They are, however, extremely relevant in that the existing social structure of contemporary democratic societies is portrayed as a superior climate for fostering the development of abstract cognition and moral reasoning. Fowler's theory, however, focuses on the spiritual development of individuals and does not give much insight into the dynamics of faith in families and other social groups.

Although the focus of cognitive-behavioral intervention is usually the individual, Keegan Eamon (2008) gives a thorough account of how these therapies can be applied to promote empowerment of vulnerable populations, promoting individuals' well-being, enhancing their social interactions, increasing their capacity for self-determination, enhancing their access to community resources, and encouraging engagement in changing macro social policies. However, they do not directly target changes of social policy or social structure.

## CONSISTENCY WITH SOCIAL WORK VALUES AND ETHICS

Theories of cognitive and moral development reflect a belief in growth and development that, in many ways, has a high degree of consistency with social work values. The achievement of optimal health is linked to a person's inherent ability to achieve increasingly higher stages of development as a part of the normal maturation process. The interactionist stance that focuses on the importance of interpersonal relations in the development of cognitive, moral, and spiritual structures points to the complexity and resiliency of human development in these areas.

Although insights from these theories support a strengths perspective of practice, they are often used, instead, to diagnose deficits in cognitive and moral development. In discussing the strengths perspective, Saleebey (1992, p. 23) has noted, "Theory about human growth and change needs to be unhinged from the lockstep view of what is considered 'normal' development and turn instead to fluid models . . . that recognize the creative and powerful energy underlying all human growth" (also see Weick, 1983). Thus, these theories fail to support a strengths perspective when the creative and adaptive energy of individuals is ignored in favor of internal, interpersonal, and social factors that produce pathology. Cognitive behavioral therapies have been criticized for relying on an expert model of control in which the social worker or therapist impose treatment goals and interventions without due regard for clients' own preferences and for cultural and political issues. However, they can be applied within a collaborative and empowerment framework to avoid this pitfall (Keegan Eamon, 2008).

Gardner's theory of multiple intelligences is more consistent with a strengths perspective because it reframes deficits as differences and points, instead, to the socially constructed nature of our definitions of valued cognitive skills. In a similar vein, Feuerstein's (1979) position that teenagers and adults can, with guidance, learn intelligence, rids us of the biological stage determinism inherent in Piagetian thought.

Further, the unquestioning acceptance of the superiority of the prevailing social order in Kohlberg's theory is problematic from a social justice/empowerment point of view. Cortese (1990) and E. Sullivan (1977) have argued that Kohlberg's lack of attention to injustice in society can be seen as a conservative ideology that supports the status quo. Sullivan held that this can also be viewed as an unconscious "defense of exploitation."

There are also serious problems regarding Kohlberg's lack of attention to cultural differences and his portrayal of stages as universal. As Cortese has noted (1990, p. 95), "the dearth of postconventional scores in underdeveloped and rural cultures" demonstrates not the universality of the theory but, rather, the cultural and ethnocentric bias that permeates it. Thus, cross-cultural application of Kohlberg's theory can easily lead to a deficiency view of clients that inaccurately portrays them and their cultures as inferior.

Fowler's vision of an inclusive universalizing faith, however, is reminiscent of social workers who advocated for an application of Christian values to social work in a way that would foster acceptance of human diversity and a commitment to social justice (Keith-Lucas, 1994; Towle, 1965). Allan Keith-Lucas, who was one of the most prominent writers on Christian social work, described this orientation as a faith of love, which is nonjudgmental and respectful of clients. Keith-Lucas (1985) even suggested that Christians who are theologically rigid, simplistic, and judgmental likely do more harm than good for clients, and, therefore, are not suitable to be social workers.

Fowler emphasized the importance of accommodating faith to an appreciation for human diversity and used examples of people from non–Judeo-Christian traditions to illustrate the higher stages of faith development. He was also careful to include both males and females in his research and to avoid negative gender bias. In appreciation for Carol Gilligan's critique of Kohlberg's work, Fowler (1984, p. 46) wrote, "Gilligan teaches us that moral maturity . . . means balancing responsibility and care with a keen sense of rights and justice." His ideal stage of universalizing faith is characterized by unconditional love for all people and all beings. This unconditional appreciation of diversity is central to our professional values and ethics.

## PHILOSOPHICAL UNDERPINNINGS

Gardner (1987, p. 50) has noted that "philosophers have wrestled for centuries with such currently fashionable issues as the nature of mental representation, the extent to which human thought is merely a mechanical (as opposed to a spiritual) process, and the relationship between reason and feeling." Philosopher Rene Descartes, the "prototypical antecedent of cognitive science" viewed the mind as "central to human existence" but which "stands apart from and operates independently of the human body" (p. 51). This view of the "rational mind" and the separate "mechanical body" became the source of ongoing debate in philosophy and an underlying premise in early cognitive psychology. Cognitive and moral stage development theories are further based on the assumption of human growth and self-actualization. In addition, both Piaget and Kohlberg assigned a high priority to subjective reason.

However, at the base appears to be belief in the existence of certain innate, underlying mental structures, biologically referred to by the term *genetic structuralism*. These structures, for the most part, are assumed to be predetermined and therefore lack strong social and cultural antecedents. Additionally, the stages proposed are assumed to be linear, invariant, sequential, and universal.

Kanjirathinkal (1990) has argued that implicit in Kohlberg's moral dilemmas is the assumption that they constitute either a private problem of an individual or a public problem that an individual has to solve without public process or consultation. In the end, moral problems are basically subjective, individual cognitive conflicts.

The assumptions that underlie Fowler's theory come both from the Piagetian school of structural cognitive development and liberal Christian theology. Most notably, Fowler adopted a postmodern theology of ecumenism, justice, and liberation. His philosophical perspective would likely not be comfortable for social workers who are either positivistic or fundamentalist. However, it is quite consistent with the philosophical assumptions shared by many writers about connections between social work, spirituality, and transpersonal experience (for a wide review, see Canda & Furman, 2010).

## METHODOLOGICAL ISSUES AND EMPIRICAL SUPPORT

Theories of cognitive and moral development are built on a strong positivistic base that allows for replication. The ability of Piaget's theory to be empirically studied made it extremely viable for scientific verification. However, Piaget did not operationally define many of his constructs and failed to employ rigorous methodological criteria. Another shortcoming is that much of his research involved small samples, including extensive observations of his own children. In addition, his failure to use standardized interviewing techniques makes his research difficult to replicate independently.

A number of studies have shown that Piaget seriously underestimated the cognitive abilities of young children. His theory has been especially criticized for an inaccurate portrayal of preoperational children's representational abilities, egocentrism, perceptual perspective taking, causal reasoning, and ability to conserve (Shaffer, 1993).

Further, critics have contended that the global nature of his theory presents cognitive development as being too homogeneous and unified. Flavell (1985) and others believe that the Piagetian model is incomplete and cannot account for the "complexity and variety of human thought phenomenon." In particular, research has found that experience may be an especially important factor because cross-cultural studies indicate that the sequence of intellectual growth may be more diverse than Piaget proposed (Dasen & Heron, 1981; Glick, 1975). Although Piaget assumed children's thinking to be homogeneous, contemporary studies have found children's thought to be more heterogeneous in that they do not apply the same cognitive mechanism across all problems or tasks and do not necessarily operate on a single, uniform level of cognitive complexity (Papalia & Olds, 1992; Shaffer, 1993; Siegler, 1986).

Probably the most intensely debated issue is the progression of cognitive development through distinct and different stages. Piaget proposed invariant and discontinuous stages in which children display particular competencies not previously available to them. Research evidence indicates, however, that most cognitive changes proceed slowly and gradually. Of even greater significance is the fact that these changes often occur in a back and forth fashion as opposed to incremental advancements. Children's competencies can appear, disappear, and reemerge later in their development, suggesting that a less tightly knit concept of stage is needed (Siegler, 1986).

Both Kohlberg and Piaget used the clinical interview as the preferred method of studying children's moral development. Kohlberg advanced Piaget's interview format by asking children to choose between hypothetical courses of action and to justify their choice based on moral reasoning rather than just commenting on one scenario and the goodness or badness of the character. Other investigators (Rest, 1983) developed less time-consuming and more standardized measures such as the Defining Issues Test to identify subjects' stage of moral reasoning. Still others have suggested that a full understanding of children's reasoning cannot be gained from structured clinical interviews or standardized measures (Coles, 1990, 1997).

Colby, Kohlberg, Gibbs, and Liberman (1983) have argued that Piaget's notion of morality being formed by preadolescence is premature, and that moral development is a long and elaborate process that is not culminated until adulthood. Furthermore, researchers have established that children are able to judge wrongdoings on the basis of harm and not just intent (Surber, 1982). In addition, the focus on intentions and consequences is reductionistic and a fuller understanding of moral reasoning would, of necessity, consider many more dimensions of the human experience. Other critics maintain that Piaget overlooked social, cultural, and economic differences among children.

Researchers have found general support for the premise that children proceed from lower to higher stages of moral development (D. Kuhn, 1976; Rest, 1983). There is even some impressive evidence confirming Kohlberg's stages of progression in a longitudinal study of 58 boys (Colby et al., 1983). However, Kohlberg's model of moral development and Piaget's genetic structuralism offer little in the way of explanation for the historical and ideological structures that may influence and impact cognitive and moral development.

Investigators who question the existence of underlying cognitive structures in moral development are more inclined to explore and highlight the importance of experience and sociohistorical conditions. The ability to understand the perspective of others on different issues and tasks, for example, has been found to increase with age and experience. However, perspective and role-taking skills have shown varied correlations with intelligence (Rest, 1979; Rubin, 1978) and do not tell us the ways in which cognitive variables are related to moral thought.

Results of numerous investigations have also indicated that formal schooling is one of the most powerful predictors of moral change, and adults do not show much advancement beyond that accounted for by formal education (Dortzbach, 1975; Rest, 1979; Rest & Thoma, 1985). Nonetheless, the specific aspects of education that enhance moral development are still unclear. In addition, many critics also think that parents play a more crucial role in moral and cognitive development through discipline than Kohlberg realized (Hetherington & Parke, 1986).

Although Kohlberg's theory initially appeared to have some empirically based cross-cultural support, his methodology and findings have come under increasing attack (Cortese, 1990). His cross-cultural applications suggest that individuals in more intellectually advanced and technologically complex societies are morally advanced because they are capable of higher levels of moral reasoning than those in rural and underdeveloped cultures. The fact that reasoning at the highest three stages of moral development is absent in traditional village cultures (Kohlberg, 1969a) raises important questions about the validity of Kohlberg's methodology and theory; his moral dilemmas may simply be inappropriate for assessing moral development in certain, less technologically sophisticated cultures. Cortese (1990, p. 96) has argued that Kohlberg "erroneously equates the more complex and abstract with the more right and moral" and "reflects an ideological bias rooted in Western culture." He proposed that Kohlberg's research methods are problematical and demonstrate a "lack of understanding the background of [his] subjects."

Gilligan's theory, despite its popularity and intuitive appeal to many feminist scholars, has failed to receive empirical verification. According to Tavris (1992, pp. 85–87), a number of studies, including those by Gilligan herself (when carefully scrutinized), have found little support for gender-based differences in men's and women's moral reasoning or the "value placed on autonomy versus attachment" (see also Colby & Damon, 1987). More recently, a meta-analysis of 113 studies of moral reasoning (Jaffee & Hyde, 2000) found only small effects for gender differences in females using care reasoning and a small effect for men using justice reasoning. They found that moderating variables other than gender can affect the type of moral reasoning a person uses, including the content and context of the moral dilemma. Gilligan's contribution may be more the identification of an "ethic of care" and less the gendered use of such thinking, as it can be employed by both men and women. Martha Mednick (1989, pp. 1119–1120) has noted that "the belief that women have a different voice . . . appears to be a symbol of a cluster of widely held social beliefs that argue for women's difference, for reasons that are quite independent of scientific merit."

Due to Fowler's emphasis on the importance of stories and symbolism in the formation of individuals' faith, it is not surprising that his research methodology is more consistent with the constructivist paradigm and qualitative research based on interviewing people, collecting their life stories, and interpreting them. Unfortunately, his accounts of methodology are insufficiently detailed to allow evaluation of his conclusions, and his sample is very limited in terms of ethnicity and religious affiliation. His interpretations of the empirical data reflect his own psychological and theological assumptions about things for which he presents little evidence. This can be vividly seen in his discussion on the experience of infants and the possibility of universalizing faith.

Even though many of the abstract and overgeneralized features of cognitive theories have been criticized, CBTs, including mindfulness practices, are now some of the most widely researched and empirically supported kinds of helping practices in the health, mental health, and social work fields.

All of the theories discussed here are (a) better at explanation than prediction, (b) better at a probabilistic level of explanation than a deterministic level, and (c) better suited for explaining properties of individuals than properties of groups. As discussed earlier, Piaget's model frequently underestimates children's cognitive abilities based on his somewhat rigid stage formulations, and Kohlberg's theory, despite claims to the contrary, has limited cross-cultural application.

## Summary

Theories of cognitive and moral development have provided a positive and rational view of human behavior and have made important contributions to our knowledge base about life span development (Santrock, 1989). Despite the limitations discussed earlier, Piaget's work remains one of the most well-elaborated and coordinated theories of cognitive development. Cognitive theories provide "an optimistic view of human development, ascribing to children and adults the ability and motivation to know their world and cope with it in constructive ways" (Santrock, 1989, p. 51).

These theories will likely appeal to those who place high value on logical, rational thought and moral reasoning derived from conscious processes. Gilligan's reformulation of Kohlberg has had great appeal in feminist theory for those who are interested in different developmental paths of men and women. Although the more contemporary theories of Sternberg, Gardner, and Goleman have not yet received much attention in the social work literature, they will likely appeal to those who are interested in a broader definition of intelligence and the importance of emotions in daily life. Finally, Fowler's faith development theory should hold high appeal for those who are trying to incorporate contemporary ideas about spirituality into our knowledge base about human development.

The theories discussed here provide a good micro-level framework for social work practice with individuals, small groups, and families. However, the notion of invariant, universal stages has been the subject of much criticism and may weaken the appeal of stage-based theories. Equally problematic is the fact that most of these stage-based theories view cognitive and moral growth as essentially internal processes of the individual mind and thereby fail to give adequate consideration to the structural features of society that may be more directly responsible for differences in cognitive and moral outcomes. Nonetheless, the focus on both internal processes and interpersonal influences on growth and development provides a useful, though not comprehensive, framework for social work practice.

# Symbolic Interaction

*Timothy the mirror maker*
*Made a very special one for me*
*Now I can see with no disguise*
*How I look in someone's eyes*
*What it is exactly that they see.*

© ROD MACDONALD
1997, BLUE FLUTE MUSIC (ASCAP)

## SYMBOLIC INTERACTION THEORIES

- help us appreciate the relationship between the individual and society
- enhance our understanding of the "self" as a social process
- assist us in our understanding of socialization through the life cycle
- give us an alternative view of deviance and psychopathology
- are useful in formulating assessment and intervention plans for individuals, families, and small groups

Termed *microsociology* because of its emphasis on the individual, symbolic interaction focuses on the relationship between the individual and society as it is reflected in the self. In contrast to psychodynamic theory, the self is seen as social rather than intrapsychic in nature. It is the dynamic process of interaction between the person and the environment that results in a self that is continually growing and changing. Symbolic interaction is based on the premise that identity involves shared significant symbols (or shared meanings) that emerge in the process of interaction with others.

## HISTORICAL CONTEXT

Symbolic interaction developed as a synthesis of the dominant philosophical, psychological, and sociological schools of thought in the late 1800s. Although numerous theorists contributed to the interactionist perspective, George Herbert Mead is generally credited with shaping the theoretical development of symbolic interactionism in its early stages (Abraham, 1988; Perdue, 1986).

While European sociologists Georg Simmel, Emile Durkheim, and Max Weber were among the first to explore social psychological processes, most sociologists were primarily concerned with large social structures, institutions, and processes. A growing interest in the individual and the interaction between the person and environment began to emerge at the turn of the century at the University of Chicago. As Perdue (1986, p. 235) has noted, the growth of symbolic interaction is inseparable from the growth of Chicago as an urban metropolis during this era. Sociologists found a living laboratory in the tenements, ghettos, and immigrant neighborhoods. Some, like Mead, became involved with settlement houses like Hull House. According to Forte (2004a), "Academics from the university and social workers from the settlement worked in the turf of their counterparts regularly" (p. 392). The social disorganization that accompanied urbanization, immigration, and industrialization at the turn of the century provided a fertile atmosphere for both scientific inquiry and social reform. Although some theorists were interested in child development, others were concerned with the impact of social change on adult personality (Meltzer, Petras, & Reynolds, 1975).

The philosophical and theoretical thought that emerged as the Chicago School of Symbolic Interaction was a synthesis of a diverse group of writers whose works reflected German romantic idealism and American pragmatism. Philosophers James W. Baldwin and John Dewey, sociologists W. I. Thomas and Charles Horton Cooley, and psychologists Wilhelm Wundt and William James were among the early contributors to the social psychological view of the individual. Although Freudian thought played little, if any, role in the development of symbolic interactionism, there are important similarities in the concepts of Mead and Freud, which we discuss later in this chapter.

## KEY CONCEPTS

Although symbolic interactionism encompasses a broad range of theorists and theories, they all share common assumptions about the nature of human development. People are seen first and foremost as social beings who interact with one another based on shared meanings, or symbols. Thus, human interaction is symbolic interaction.

In contrast to animals whose behavior is largely shaped by reflexes and reinforced responses to stimuli, symbolic interactionists point out that humans do not simply respond to symbols—they also interpret them. Because human interaction is a continuous interpretive process, human life is seen as dynamic and creative. It is through our interpretations that we "construct" our social reality. This is discussed in more detail in Chapter 11.

According to symbolic interactionists, the ability to think, as we know it, is impossible without language. Thinking, to Mead, is a "process of talking to one's self" and involves reflection, discrimination, and analysis. Although physiological and psychological processes are involved in thought, perception, and other mental processes, the meanings that people assign to their experiences are social in nature. Thus, human behavior is seen as a function of social rather than physiological or intrapsychic processes alone. As Mead (1964, p. 121) noted:

> the behavior of an individual can be understood only in terms of the whole social group of which he is a member, since his individual acts are involved in larger, social acts which go beyond himself and which implicate the other members of that group.

Accordingly, individual personality is rooted in the social structure and social processes by which one comes to develop a self-conception. Because humans *reflect* on their experiences, they are able to visualize themselves, evaluate their actions and feelings, and consciously make desired changes. The reflection and evaluation that give rise to self-conception enable people to experience themselves simultaneously as both subject and object. As we reflect and think about ourselves, we are the object of our thoughts. Simultaneously we are also the subject who is engaged in thinking!

Self-conceptions, however, do not arise simply from intrapsychic or physiological processes. Rather, they develop through the process of interaction and are shaped, in part, by the views and attitudes that others hold about us. It is this ability to reflect and respond to ourselves as others respond to us that leads to an awareness or consciousness of one's self. Thus, symbolic interactionists stress the social and interactional processes that contribute to human development and self-conception. The process of socialization, whereby individuals learn the norms, values, roles, skills, and expectations of society, is a primary concept in this theory. Socialization, for the symbolic interactionist, is a "dynamic process that allows people to develop the ability to think, to develop in distinctively human ways" (Ritzer, 1992, p. 349). Also emphasized is the nondeterministic nature of human behavior; people are seen as having reasons for the choices that they make.

Ritzer (1992, p. 348) has summarized the basic principles of symbolic interaction enumerated by Blumer, Manis, and Meltzer, and Rose to include the following:

1. Human beings, unlike lower animals, are endowed with the capacity for thought.
2. The capacity for thought is shaped by social interaction.
3. In social interaction, people learn the meanings and the symbols that allow them to exercise their distinctively human capacity for thought.
4. Meanings and symbols allow people to carry on distinctively human action and interaction.
5. People are able to modify or alter the meanings and symbols that they use in action and interaction on the basis of their interpretation of the situation.
6. People are able to make these modifications and alternatives because, in part, of their ability to interact with themselves, which allows them to examine possible courses of action, assess their relative advantages and disadvantages, and then choose one.
7. The intertwined patterns of action and interaction make up groups and societies.

## THE CHICAGO SCHOOL AND EARLY INTERACTIONISM

The term *symbolic interactionism* was first coined in 1937 by Herbert Blumer, who was a student of Mead. Earlier authors, however, developed many of the core concepts that underlie this theoretical perspective. Philosopher and psychologist John Dewey, for example, proposed that the mind should be viewed as a process rather than a structure. This process involves thinking, defining, imagining, interpreting, and analyzing one's environment and, from this, choosing a course of action (Meltzer et al., 1975; Ritzer, 1992; Stryker, 1980). Likewise, psychologist William James conceptualized consciousness as a process of the mind. Consciousness, he theorized, involved an awareness of one's self and, thus, the self is "partly known and partly knower, partly object and partly subject" (James, 1892/1948, p. 176). He used the term *the me*, or *empirical ego*, to denote the self as *known* and the term *the I*, or *pure ego*, to denote the self as *knower*. These concepts were later adopted by Mead in his theory of development. Sociologist W. I. Thomas was instrumental in extending the interactionist theory of "self" development to adulthood. In his writings, he emphasized the plasticity of human nature as it becomes shaped by social and environmental factors. In collaboration with Florian Znaniecki (1927), he developed a theory of personality that stressed the interdependence of the individual and the environment. He also underscored the importance of the meanings that we attribute to our interactions and surroundings in his concept of the *definition of the situation*. In addition to meanings and definitions that are culturally and socially taught through socialization, Thomas emphasized the ways in which people spontaneously modified their individual meanings and definitions. He saw creative capacity as an integral part of self (Ritzer, 1992).

Although there are numerous theorists and philosophers who can be credited with early contributions to symbolic interactionism, two of the most influential are Charles Horton Cooley and George Herbert Mead, whose works we discuss here in fuller detail.

## Charles Horton Cooley

In his theoretical writings, Cooley was greatly influenced by John Dewey, James Baldwin, and William James as well as the organic view of society, which stressed the reciprocal interaction between the individual and society. In Cooley's view, any understanding of society must be based on an understanding of the individuals in that society. According to Cooley, "self and society are twin-born, we know one as immediately as we know the other, and the notion of a separate and independent ego is an illusion" (1909/1962, p. 30). Although Cooley never taught at the University of Chicago, his work is generally linked to the symbolic interactionist thought of the Chicago school. The term *school* refers to a school of thought rather than a geographic location.

In his attempt to explain the self–society relationship, Cooley focused on the mental processes of individuals that result in self-consciousness and social consciousness. According to Cooley, the "individual mind" and "social mind" are as inseparable as self-consciousness and social consciousness and were rooted in the interpretive process of imagination (Larson, 1973). It is through the "imaginative ideas in the mind" that we know ourselves and others. Two of Cooley's important concepts that help us understand the self–society relationship are the *looking-glass self* and the *primary group*.

All self-conception, according to Cooley, is dependent on interaction with others and based on our imagination of how we appear to them. He proposed a process of self-conception called the looking-glass self that involves three phases. First, we imagine how we appear to others. Second, we imagine the judgments that people make about us. Third, we develop self-feelings that incorporate these perceptions. Pride and shame are two of the most important self-feelings that we develop in response to others. The desire to avoid the self-reflection of shame, he believed, was a primary factor that influenced behavior (Abrahamson, 1990; Martindale, 1988). We see ourselves, in part, as others see us, and it is through this process of reflection that "personality" is formed.

Cooley further theorized that self-conception arises in the context of interaction with groups. *Primary groups* are "characterized by intimate face-to-face association and cooperation" and are "fundamental in forming the social nature of the ideals of individuals" (1909/1962, p. 23). It is through interaction with primary groups that individuals develop shared expectations that link them to the broader social structure. People come to identify themselves in relation to primary groups and develop a feeling of "we" that creates a psychological "fusion of individualities into a common whole." *Secondary groups*, in contrast, are those based on relatively impersonal, contractual, and formal relationships. Although our initial socialization takes place within the primary group, later social interactions occur within both types of groups.

As we will see, Cooley's primary group and looking-glass self are integral components of Mead's theory, which extends and elaborates on these ideas.

## George Herbert Mead

Like Cooley, Mead was heavily influenced by the social thinkers of his time. Four books, published after his death, were based on his lecture notes, which his students collected and edited. The most famous of these, *Mind, Self, and Society* (1934), details his theory of the development of the social self. Mead called his social thought *social psychology* but distinguished it from social psychology written from a psychological standpoint. He believed that membership in a social structure or social order was instrumental in determining individual conduct and experience. Thus, human consciousness, the mind, and the self were considered essentially social products that develop out of existing social processes.

This position was in stark contrast to the behavioral psychologists of the day who denied the importance of human consciousness in the study of behavior. Mead rejected the reductionism of behavioral psychology as exemplified by John B. Watson (discussed in Chapter 12) because it attempted to explain "inner experience in terms of external behavior." Instead, he developed a theory based on the behavioral focus of observable action and interaction and extended it to also include the mind and society (Ritzer, 1992). He called his new social psychology *social behaviorism* to distinguish it from radical behaviorism. He argued that this new approach recognizes the importance of inner experience and emphasizes human action in its natural social situation.

Mead proposed a developmental model of personality that consists of three stages. In the first stage, the stage of imitative acts, the infant (birth to age 2) imitates the gestures, actions, and sounds of others. The infant, for example, imitates a smile or a hand wave. The imitation of gestures and acts is preparatory for the next stage in which the child learns to imitate roles.

In the second stage, the play stage (age 2 to 4 or so), the child begins to manipulate symbols through the acquisition of language. Gestures, which were imitative and nonsymbolic in the first stage, now begin to take on symbolic meaning. During this stage, the child begins to act out or imitate the roles of others through play. Here the child plays at being a mother, father, teacher, cowboy, or ballerina. An important distinction to make is that, at this stage, the child is not responding to the expectations of others. Instead, the child is responding to his or her own social acts (Mead, 1964, p. 215):

> The child says something in one character and responds in another character, and then his responding in another character is a stimulus to himself in the first character.

Thus, the child begins to build self by using his or her own responses. Children, for example, often play side by side with little awareness of each other; a contemporary term for this is *parallel play*. It is through this imitation of roles that the child begins to acquire the roles of society and begins to organize self-responses into a whole.

In the third stage, the game stage (age 4 to 6 or 7), we see a dramatic shift as the child begins to learn and incorporate rules and regulations into the playing of games. The child now becomes aware of the attitudes of everyone else involved in the game and learns to respond to those attitudes.

In doing so, the child takes on the role of the other and is able to assume the different roles and attitudes of all participants in the game and to understand their relationship to one another. In a baseball game, for example, the child "must know what everyone else is going to do in order to carry out his own play" (Mead, 1964, p. 215). In contrast to the play stage where the child's own whim guides the playing of roles, the game stage requires an organization of these roles. This organization takes the form of rules and regulated procedures that the child incorporates into game playing. As Mead notes, children at this stage show a great interest in rules and often make them up on the spot to help themselves out of difficulties.

As the child takes on the roles of others, he or she gains an awareness of an organized reaction to his or her game playing. As this awareness occurs, the child takes on the "generalized other" and begins to internalize the rules of society into the self. According to Mead (1964, p. 218):

> The organized community or social group which gives to the individual his unity of self can be called "the generalized other." The attitude of the generalized other is the attitude of the whole community.

The generalized other is an important aspect of personality development in that it is the part of self that accompanies and guides one's behavior and conduct. In Mead's view, self-consciousness can only exist when one can assume the organized social attitudes of others toward oneself. It is through this process of taking on the generalized other that personality arises. Thus, the structure of self expresses or reflects the general behavior pattern of the social group.

Personality, however, is more complex than the internalization of organized attitudes of others. Building on the work of Cooley and James, Mead proposed two components of the self, the "I" and the "me." The "I" is the individual, spontaneous part of self that responds to the attitudes of others. The "me" is the "organized set of attitudes of others" that the person assumes and is formed through the internalization of the generalized other. The social control of the "me" sets limits for the individual reaction of the "I." The "I" and the "me" are in constant interaction and dialogue with each other, and although they are distinct from one another, they are also parts of a whole and respond to each other. During self-reflection, the "I" reflects on the "me." Their relationship is like the relation between subject and object in sentence structure. For example, when reflecting, "I am a student," the subjective self "I" reflects on self in terms of an objective social role (student), the "me." Thus, the self is seen as a social process with two phases. According to Mead, without these two phases, "there could not be conscious responsibility and there would be nothing novel in experience" (1964, p. 233). The self, in Mead's view, is a dynamic, creative process that is a complex interplay and balancing of internalized social rules and incalculable individual spontaneity. Identity in symbolic interaction is the socialized part of the self (P. L. Berger & Berger, 1979).

Further, the self serves numerous functions for both the individual and the larger social group. As Abraham (1988) has noted, communication, analysis of the situation, self-direction, self-control, self-judgment, problem solving, and identity are all functions of the self.

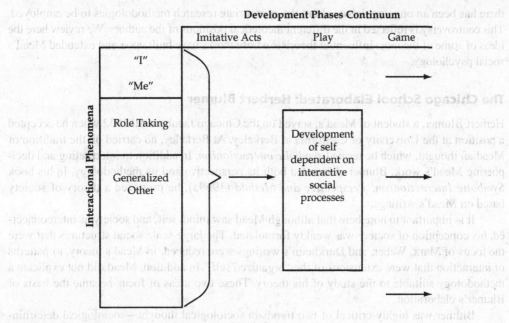

**FIGURE 10.1.** Key concepts of George Herbert Mead.

As previously mentioned, Mead's social psychology did not spring from Freudian thought. In fact, Mead referred to psychoanalytic theory as "the more or less fantastic psychology of the Freudian group . . . dealing with the sexual life and with self-assertion in its violent form" (1964, p. 239). Mead clearly saw self-assertion (as reflected through the "I") as more normal and less violent and antisocial than did Freud. There are, however, interesting points of similarity in their works. Both theorists pointed to the individual nature of the child (Freud's "id" and "ego" and Mead's "I") and to the socialized component of personality (Freud's "superego" and Mead's "me"). In addition, both believed that development during approximately 4 to 6 of age was critical in the internalization of social rules. We have seen in Chapter 9 that theories of cognitive and moral development closely parallel the age/stage correlation of this developmental task.

One important distinction to be made between psychoanalytical and symbolic interactionist theory is that Mead was attempting to explain the genesis of the "normal" self while Freud was seeking answers about the origins of psychopathology. It is not surprising, then, that the springboard for Mead was the behavioral and social psychological theory of his day rather than the psychoanalytical thought of the Freudian group. Figure 10.1 illustrates Mead's key concepts.

# ROADS FROM MEAD

A number of theorists have carried on the theoretical tradition of George Herbert Mead. Inasmuch as Mead's works were published posthumously, an oral tradition developed in which the main ideas were initially handed down by word of mouth. This has declined to a great degree since the publication of Mead's major works. Since that time symbolic interactionism has given rise to a wide variety of subtheories such as self-theory, role theory, and reference group theory (M. H. Kuhn, 1964). In addition to the growth of different variations within symbolic interaction, there has been an ongoing debate about the appropriate research methodologies to be employed. This controversy is reflected in the different theoretical positions of the authors. We review here the ideas of some of the most influential theorists whose works have built upon and extended Mead's social psychology.

## The Chicago School Elaborated: Herbert Blumer

Herbert Blumer, a student of Mead's, stayed on the Chicago faculty until 1952 when he accepted a position at the University of California at Berkeley. At Berkeley, he carried on the tradition of Meadian thought, which he termed *symbolic interactionism*. In addition to interpreting and deciphering Mead's work, Blumer elaborated both its perspective and its methodology. In his book *Symbolic Interactionism: Perspective and Method* (1969a), he proposed a theory of society based on Mead's writings.

It is important to note here that although Mead saw mind, self, and society as interconnected, his conception of society was weakly formulated. The large-scale social structures that were the focus of Marx, Weber, and Durkheim's writings were reduced, in Mead's theory, to patterns of interaction that were extensions of the "organized self." In addition, Mead did not explicate a methodology suitable to the study of his theory. These two areas of focus became the basis of Blumer's elaboration.

Blumer was highly critical of two trends in sociological thought—sociological determinism and an overreliance on quantitative methods—both of which he believed artificially reduced the complexity of social life (Blumer, 1969b; Ritzer, 1992). In keeping with Mead's thesis, Blumer emphasized the interpretive process that results from social action and interaction.

Blumer rejected the macrostructural approach to society because it ignored the interpretive process and fostered an oversocialized view of the individual. Blumer's central thesis is that people "act toward things on the basis of the meanings that things have for them" (1969a, p. 2). The social world comprises objects that are physical (such as buildings), social (such as roles), and abstract (such as customs). Through interaction, people attach meanings to such objects and, in doing so, they actively define and create their world. Thus, the meanings that people attach to physical, social, and abstract objects become the basis for human action. Society, in this view, is symbolic rather than material. People, however, do not act in isolation but, rather, fit "their lines of action to one another." Collective action, therefore, is joint action in which human groups (such as corporations, institutions, nations) construct their actions through interpretation. In Blumer's formulation, society is "created through the joint actions of group life. People make society; society does not make people" (pp. 17–20).

Blumer argued that the existing methodologies employed in the social and psychological sciences were inadequate. He believed that overreliance on quantification and the traditional scientific method led to reductionism, which ignored the interpretative process. Instead, he held that a unique, distinctive methodology was necessary for the study of human behavior.

The methodology that he proposed was based on Cooley's idea of *sympathetic introspection*. This involved the researcher being able to take the points of view of the persons they studied. Qualitative and participative methods are to be employed in the "firsthand" study of social life such as participant observation; nondirective interviewing and examining letters, diaries, and public documents; autobiographies; and case studies. These methods, he believed, would allow the researcher to uncover and understand the interpretive process. Further, he argued that the methodology have a nongeneralizing function. Because people were seen as free actors who create their realities through interpretation, he believed that this uniqueness was inappropriate for universal predictions.

As we can see, Blumer's elaboration of Mead's work focused on "attitudes not ideology, prejudice, not institutional racism, a phenomenological world, not a material one" (Perdue, 1986, p. 254). In this, he remained close to Mead's conception of social action, interaction, and mental processes.

## The Iowa School: Manford Kuhn

In a departure from the traditional symbolic interactionism of Cooley, Mead, and Blumer, sociologist Manford Kuhn developed a school of interactionist thought based on the idea that interactionism could be "operationalized and used successfully in empirical research" (1964, p. 72). In contrast to the qualitative research methods proposed by Blumer, Kuhn believed that traditional quantitative scientific methods were critical and he argued for a uniformity of methods in all scientific fields.

As a faculty member at the State University of Iowa from 1946 until his death, Kuhn developed an empirical approach to the study of self (now called the Iowa School). In this approach, he made a distinction between the nonempirical "I" and the empirically knowable "me." He deliberately abandoned the idea of self as a "process" because it required inclusion of both the "I" and the "me." Instead, he recast the self in structural terms that encompassed only the "me" (Manis & Meltzer, 1967; Martindale, 1988).

Kuhn's methodology is most often associated with his development of the Twenty Statements Test (TST). To test his theory, which he termed *self-theory*, he developed a paper-and-pencil measurement of attributes of the self. In the TST, a person is directed to answer the question "Who am I" with 20 open-ended responses. These responses are then examined by content analysis and can be further analyzed by Guttman-scale techniques. With the TST, Kuhn's theory attempted the task of making the self empirically knowable to outside observers. In doing so, however, he has adopted a conception of self that is predictable and socially determined. Symbolic interactionists of the Mead school criticize it for being reductionistic in that it does not address the subjective processes of the "I" in relation to the objective "me." It also does not emphasize self-reflection as a form of empirical study and knowledge.

The Chicago and Iowa schools diverged on several salient points. Adherents of the Chicago school held that the nature of individuals is subjective and unpredictable, that interaction is based on interpretation, and that social roles are constructed and reconstructed through creating meaning of others' actions. In contrast, the Iowa school held that individuals are generalizable and predictable and that interaction is based on adherence to social roles. The Chicago school believed that the study of people and society should be based on exploratory methods such as participant observation and ethnography to examine the subjective experience of individuals. The Iowa school rejected subjective experience and sought to discover generalizable patterns of behavior using the scientific method. The lack of methodological rigor of the Chicago school was one factor that led to what Stryker (1987) described as a decline in symbolic interaction from the 1960s through the mid-1970s.

## The Dramaturgical Approach: Erving Goffman

In an extension of the ideas of Mead and Blumer, Erving Goffman expanded the processual aspects of self. His symbolic interaction was derived from a variety of influences that include theorists from the Chicago school as well as philosopher-critic Kenneth Burke and phenomenological sociologist Alfred Schutz (discussed in Chapter 11). Burke's "dramatism," which focused on the person as an actor, shaped the dramaturgical metaphor used by Goffman. In *The Presentation of Self in Everyday Life* (1959a), Goffman proposed that the self was constructed through dramatic interaction between the individual actor and the audience. As actors, people manage impressions of themselves in their daily interaction with others. Impression management involves presenting oneself to others in ways that are intentionally guided and controlled by the actor. The "parts" that people play during a "performance" are consciously constructed by the actor in an attempt to present a self that will be accepted by others.

Goffman used a variety of theatrically related terms to discuss various aspects of the performance. Although impression management may fail, Goffman pointed out that most performances are successful. The self that is presented, in most cases, is the one that audience accepts as the "real" self of the actor.

Goffman's dramaturgical model suggests that the self is not static. Rather, it is spontaneous and creative and adapts to the situation. Inasmuch as we have many roles, we may also have many "selves." Goffman also stressed the importance of belief in our role(s). If we are honest, genuine, and sincere, each of the multiple selves that we portray is, in fact, a "true" self. Martindale has pointed out that Goffman's dramaturgy has relocated the internal dialectic between the "I" and the "me" and placed it "between the private and public self in which the real self is a naked, unsocialized, and unsocializable expediency" (1988, pp. 362–363).

Goffman was a prolific writer. In a subsequent book, *Asylums: Essays on the Social Situation of Mental Patients and Other Inmates* (1961), he applied a similar analysis to the residents of total institutions. Total institutions, such as boot camps, prisons, and hospitals, are those in which people are "cut off from the wider society for an appreciable period of time" (p. xii). Goffman examined the transformation of self that people undergo when they are stripped of their normal identities and assigned an institutional or deviant identity. The transition from person to patient, person to prisoner, person to military recruit requires a "stripping process" in which "degradation ceremonies" (such as strip searches) are used to divest people of their sense of self-worth and identity. This divestiture of the self is seen as a necessary first step in the assignment of a new, institutionally prescribed identity.

In *Stigma: Notes on the Management of Spoiled Identity* (1963), Goffman examined the ways in which persons with "spoiled identities" engage in impression management to hide their stigma from others. A stigma is a mark of disgrace (either literal or figurative) attached to characteristics or behaviors that are defined as undesirable in a given society. Goffman identified three different types of stigma: (a) abominations of the body—which include various physical deformities; (b) blemishes of the character—inferred from a person's behavior or past record of institutionalization (i.e., mental disorder, addiction, unemployment, homosexuality); and (c) tribal stigma—of race, nation, and religion.

According to Goffman, "normals" (persons without a stigma) believe that people in these categories are "not quite human." Based on this belief, they create an ideology replete with stereotypes to explain the alleged inferiority and discredit those who fall into these categories. A stigmatized person is thus "reduced in our minds from a whole and usual person to a tainted, discounted one" (1963, p. 3). The "virtual society identity" that is imputed to such individuals is based on stereotypes and may bear little resemblance to a person's "actual society identity"—the attributes and characteristics he or she actually possesses.

Goffman pointed out that during socialization the stigmatized person first "learns and incorporates the standpoint of the normal, acquiring thereby the identity beliefs of the wider society." The person then "learns that he possesses a particular stigma and . . . the consequence of possessing it." The specific timing and interplay of these two phases form the foundation for later development (1963, p. 32).

As stigmatized persons attempt to gain social acceptance, they use a variety of techniques of information management. Some attempt to "pass" and conceal their discreditable characteristics. Those who cannot "pass," because of the visibility of their stigma, use adaptive techniques (such as artificial limbs worn by amputees) to draw attention away from the stigma and to reduce tension in social interactions. Stigma management, however, can create feelings of ambivalence about one's own self, because the stigmatized person does not conform to society's standards of identity. Further, stigma management may lead to one or more of the following outcomes: (a) secrecy, (b) anxiety (about being found out), (c) disloyalty (to others with similar stigma), and (d) dishonesty (to those who are being led to believe that one does not have stigma).

Finally, some may work toward the removal of stigma through consciousness raising and empowerment of the stigmatized. As Goffman suggested, "The stigma and the effort to conceal it or remedy it become 'fixed' as part of personal identity" (1963, p. 65). Consciousness raising is necessary for the stigmatized to reject the stigma from personal identity and to counter the oppressive attempts to enforce stigma by the so-called normals.

In a reformulation of Goffman's work, William Newman (1973) suggested three categories of stigma based on the following: (a) appearance, (b) belief system, and (c) conduct. Table 10.1 summarizes Newman's model.

In later works, Goffman further expanded on the theme of impression management in temporary groups and transitory situations. Although his image of people has been criticized as being cynical, Martindale has noted that in his lifetime Goffman was often heralded as "one of the greatest writers alive" (1988, p. 364).

## Appearance and the Self: Gregory P. Stone

Although Gregory P. Stone may be best known for his research in the sociology of play and sport, his initial work on the role of appearance in the genesis of self is a direct extension of Mead's theory of self-development. Appearance, in Stone's formulation, is as important as discourse in establishing identity, mood, value, and attitude and is critical at every stage of self-development (1962, 1990).

Stone theorized that appearance is central to the "presentation of self" and that our "management" of appearance is interpreted by others. Meaning is established when appearance management coincides with its interpretation. Further, changes in appearance often signal other changes in life (such as a new career).

---

**TABLE 10.1**   Different Types of Stigma

| Stigma Due To | Origins of Stigma | Examples |
|---|---|---|
| Appearance | Physical attributes | Visible minorities, the aged, the disabled |
| Belief system | Cognitive attributes | Jews in anti-Semitic cultures, Hare Krishna sects in Americas, some new sects |
| Conduct | Behavioral attributes | Alcoholics, drug addicts, homosexuals, transgenders, mental patients |

*Source:* Adapted from *American Pluralism* by William Newman. Copyright 1973 by William Newman.

Building on Mead's developmental stages, Stone described the changes in discourse and appearance during the different stages in the emergence of the self. Further, he demonstrated how changes in appearance are linked to the establishment of gender or sexual identity (1990). In stage 1, the infant's appearance is imposed by the parents. The child is invested with masculinity or femininity by virtue of being dressed, for example, in blue or pink, respectively. Stone noted that in America it is the mother who is usually the primary agent of socialization and investiture. In the process of dressing out in stage 2, the child misrepresents the self while wearing the costumes of play. Children typically dress in their parents' clothing, and dressing like the same-sex parent further reinforces gender identity. The costume of play, however, involves collusion on the part of others who allow the child to misrepresent the self in various roles and costumes. As the child becomes socialized in stage 3, the game stage, the process of dressing in entails wearing "uniforms" of the peer circle. This assists in establishing identity linked to the peer group and reinforcing, an "appropriate" and "real" identity (Table 10.2).

Martindale (1988) has noted that Stone's work draws from all of the subbranches of symbolic interactionism and that he is one of the major theoreticians who trained what was then the new generation of symbolic interactionists. In addition, he is credited with being the cofounder and first president of the Society for the Study of Symbolic Interaction.

| TABLE 10.2 | Tentative Model for the Investigation of Processes of Discourse and Appearance in the Early Establishment of the Self | | | |
|---|---|---|---|---|
| **Stages of Early Socialization** | **Discursive Processes** | **Types of Discourse** | **Apparent Processes** | **Types of Appearance** |
| Preplay | 1. Parental representation of infant babbling as verbal symbols (Cooley, Markey)<br><br>2. Progressive curtailment of whole body movement by parental intervention (Latif) | Conversation of gestures (Mead) Prototaxis (Sullivan) Signal communication, or designation, as in "ma-ma" | Investiture | Representation as infant, young child, and gender |
| Play | Identification with discrete differentiated others as in role-playing (Mead)<br>1. Anticipatory socialization<br>2. Fantastic socialization | Egocentric speech (Piaget) Parataxis (Sullivan) | Dressing out | Misrepresentation of the self Costume |
| Game | Generalization and consolidation of other roles Taking the role of the "generalized other" or "team" | Socialized speech (Piaget) Syntaxis (Sullivan) | Dressing in | Representation of peer-group affiliation Uniform |

*Source: Social Psychology Through Symbolic Interaction,* 2nd ed., by Gregory P. Stone. Copyright 1986 by Pearson Education. Reprinted by permission of Allyn & Bacon.

## Labeling Theory

Arising from a symbolic interactionist perspective, labeling theory suggests that deviance is a social, rather than psychological phenomenon. Labeling theorists point to the fact that deviance is not an inherent property of any specific behaviors or persons. Rather, it is a matter of social definition. Behaviors that are defined as normal in one cultural or social context may be defined as deviant in another context. Deviance is thus created through a process of interaction in which moral meanings are assigned to specific behaviors or attributes. Persons who engage in these behaviors or possess these attributes are then selectively chosen and labeled as deviant.

The social audience is a critical variable in labeling theory. The process by which certain individuals are assigned a label of "deviant" is an intricate process of selection that involves the responses of others. It is the social audience, not the individual actor, that determines if a specific behavior is deviant (Erikson, 1962). According to Howard Becker (1973), the process of creating and applying moral meanings (good, bad, normal, deviant) is a moral enterprise conducted by moral entrepreneurs. Moral entrepreneurs are people who create and enforce rules and thereby selectively label certain behaviors and persons as deviant. Rubington and Weinberg (1987) have noted that the highly valued realms of the culture (e.g., psychiatry, law, religion) are responsible for the creation, definition, and control of deviant types and stereotypes.

Labeling theorists are concerned with both the processes and the consequences of labeling. When negative and pathologizing labels are effectively applied, the label impacts all social relations as the labeled person is moved from a normal position in society to a deviant role. This role carries with it a special status and role expectations and the labeled person is expected to fulfill the role requirements of, for example, a "patient" or "prisoner." Often, these role expectations become a self-fulfilling prophecy for both the individual and the social audience. Further, labeling theorists point out that these roles are stigmatized and are usually not reversible. Thus, once labeled, the stigmatized person is rarely, if ever, allowed to resume a normal role or position in society.

## ROLE THEORY, REFERENCE GROUPS, AND SOCIALIZATION THROUGH THE LIFE CYCLE

As we have seen, the development of self depends on interaction, role imitation, and role taking. Although the self is complete once the generalized other is internalized, development continues throughout the life course. To understand the process of later-life socialization, we draw on concepts from role theory, reference group theory, and socialization theory, all of which reflect the interactionist framework.

The concept of role is central to symbolic interactionism. A *role* is a social category or position with a set of expected behavior patterns. Roles, however, do not exist in isolation and are, to a great extent, defined by their relationship to one another. Some roles are ascribed and are based on criteria such as race, ethnicity, sex, or age. In contrast, other roles are achieved through personal effort, accomplishment, or choice (Federico, 1979). The role of woman, for example, is ascribed, whereas the role of wife or mother is achieved. One learns to perceive and enact a variety of roles during the process of socialization. Role socialization ensures that behaviors are somewhat uniform and standardized.

Role theory is related to structural functionalism and symbolic interactionism. Biddle and Thomas (1979) have been instrumental in furthering the concepts and collecting research in this area. Sheldon Stryker (1980) has also used role theory concepts and principles in an attempt to extend symbolic interactionism to the societal level.

The term *role expectation* refers to the rights and obligations of a role as seen by self and others. If the role expectations of an individual are different than the expectations of others, there is a conflict in role expectations. *Role conflict*, on the other hand, refers to contradictory expectations in the roles of an individual. This can refer to two roles that have incompatible expectations or one role with built-in inconsistencies. Role ambiguity may occur when role expectations are unclear or not well defined.

*Role entrance* refers to beginning a role. Marriage, for example, is a transition ritual whereby one enters the marital role of husband or wife. Similarly, divorce is another transition ritual allowing *role exit* from the marital role. Similarly, many other roles have their own procedures for entrance and exit (Z. S. Blau, 1972; Ebaugh, 1984).

The term *role support* refers to the amount of support one has (or does not have) in the enactment of a given role. Take, for example, a young woman who becomes pregnant. Role support for entrance into the parental role may depend on her marital role, her relationship with her husband, and the response of family members. The family's response may well influence *role compliance* (adherence to role expectations) or *role denial* (denial of role expectations). At the least, it may cause *role strain*. Role strain may result from conflicts, ambiguity, or the inability to meet role expectations.

The term *role loss* has been used frequently in relation to the aging and the aged. Retirement or the permanent loss of a job is accompanied by the loss of an occupational role. The death of a spouse brings the loss of a marital role. Such cumulative role losses are a major source of depression (and isolation) in aging persons.

A final pair of concepts in role theory are *task roles* and *socioemotional roles*. Bales (1950) discovered that in group settings certain persons take on roles to complete a task, even though it may create unhappiness among group members. In contrast, others take on roles to soothe and manage the group members' feelings. Both are important because without emphasis on task performance certain chores may get postponed indefinitely. On the other hand, lack of sensitivity to the emotional climate of the group may cause the group to fall apart.

In cultures with narrowly defined rules for sex role socialization, men are often assigned task roles and women socioemotional roles. Women's movements in both industrialized and agrarian societies have engaged in continuous struggle to change this type of sex role stereotyping and socialization.

The term *reference group* was coined by H. Hyman (1942) and refined by Robert Merton (in Merton & Skitt, 1950) and refers to a group that sets the normative and behavioral standards of an individual. Reference groups are important in the socialization process because people modify their attitudes and behavior to fit the expectations of the group. In addition, people evaluate their own behavior and self-concept by taking into account the attitudes of people in their reference group.

A related concept, *reference set*, also helps us understand socialization through the life course. In contrast to a reference group, which is an actual group of people, a reference set is the mental representation of specific individuals whose attitudes are taken into account when a person evaluates his or her behavior. Whereas reference groups are comprised of living people, reference sets may include a wide range of possibilities including friends and parents who are no longer alive, great figures in history, gods, fictional heroes and heroines, and so forth. The reference set helps the individual evaluate the appropriateness of behavior and assists in the maintenance of self-esteem.

*Socialization* is the process by which we learn the roles and rules of society. It is not, however, simply a process of molding or shaping the individual. According to P. I. Rose (1979), it involves not only "learning the tolerance limits of social situations" and "mastering appropriate responses" but also testing limits and, sometimes, breaking away from traditional constraints. In Mead's view, language is the primary vehicle of socialization. This is significant in that language enables us to think abstractly, assign meanings, and reflect on ourselves and our environment. Thus, socialization is not a one-sided process (P. L. Berger & Berger, 1979).

An important dimension in socialization is the distinction between primary and secondary socialization. *Primary socialization* is childhood socialization within the immediate family and community. All later forms (such as professional or adult socialization) are *secondary socialization*. Both primary and secondary socialization vary by society and social class. P. L. Berger and Luckmann (1967, p. 137) have observed that:

> The age at which, in one society, it may be deemed proper for a child to be able to
> drive an automobile may, in another, be the age at which he is expected to have killed
> his first enemy. An upper-class child may learn the facts of life at an age when a
> lower-class child has mastered the rudiments of abortion technique.

Primary socialization ends when the generalized other is internalized in the child's consciousness. At this point, the rules that guide behavior are no longer external and can be experienced internally through one's conscience. Peter Berger (1963) has also suggested that during the process of socialization people come to *like* what they are supposed to do. With the internalization of the generalized other, the child begins the process of secondary socialization (see also Chatterjee, 1990).

As previously discussed, primary socialization first begins with significant others (such as mother, father) and then moves to the generalized other. Secondary socialization now requires movement back to significant others because the general rules and values of society have been internalized. This is accomplished through identification with reference groups and the identification of people in one's reference set. These identifications aid us in evaluating our behavior with regard to specific roles.

Further, as people mature, they move through different stages in the life course. These are not necessarily formal stages, but stages such as childhood or adulthood, as defined by a particular society, that approximately correspond to biological age. From the standpoint of socialization, there is a sequence of statuses that are socially linked to these different stages. In American society, for example, relatively low status is accorded to infants, children, and adolescents. The individual gains status as he or she enters early adulthood and continues to gain status until old age when status once again declines. Inasmuch as people experience their "selves" through reflective interpretation, the statuses attached to stage development may have a profound impact on self-concept. One developmental task in secondary socialization is the adaptation to (or struggle against) changing status and the maintenance of self-esteem. It is important to note that declining status in old age is often accompanied by downward economic mobility and social isolation (Z. S. Blau, 1973). The longer people live past retirement, the greater their chances of becoming impoverished.

As we move through status changes, we are also expected to meet the changed expectations that accompany each stage. One primary expectation is that we make room in our lives for new significant persons. Children in the United States, for example, are expected to slowly disengage from their parents and establish relationships with teachers and friends. Adolescents are expected to strengthen their peer associations and, based on heterosexual assumptions prevalent in society, eventually turn their attentions toward the opposite sex. Similarly, young adults are expected to choose an opposite sex partner and make room for new relationships with coworkers, employers, adult friends, and, eventually, children and in-laws. These increased demands may also be seen as developmental tasks in secondary socialization.

Meeting these increased demands is generally a fluid process for most people because of *anticipatory socialization*. Interaction with others allows us to become familiar with the role and status expectations of future stages. Thus, we are able to change our behavior in anticipation of future expectations.

One of the most significant changes in secondary socialization is that there is a marked shift from concern about basic values to a concern about overt behavior. Because children have already internalized the general rules and values of society, later-life socialization does not usually attempt to influence basic values and motives. Instead, socialization is aimed at role appropriate behavior and, in some cases, values tied to professional roles, such as social work values.

It is important to recognize the social constraints that place limits on later-life socialization. Although some constraints are related to biological capacities and physical decline in old age, others are social in nature. In addition to status changes throughout the life cycle, social policies (such as mandatory retirement) can have a profound impact on one's sense of self. P. I. Rose (1979) has noted that social norms have not kept pace with medical advances that prolong life.

Finally, it is important to remember that role expectations, statuses, and developmental tasks relating to socialization are culturally defined and are not necessarily universal. Figure 10.2 summarizes key concepts of life span socialization.

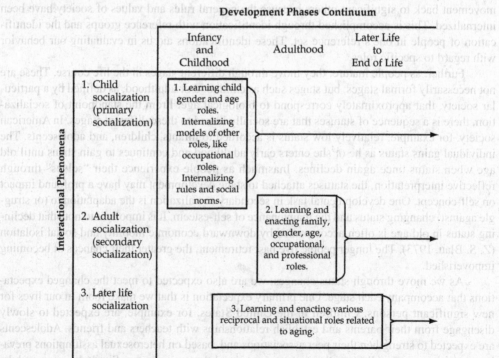

**FIGURE 10.2.** Key concepts in theories of socialization.

## CONTEMPORARY ISSUES

Many theorists have noted that socialization today is much more difficult than it has been in the past. As society undergoes rapid social change, it also becomes increasingly more complex. Technological advances, geographic mobility, cultural diversity, the changing role of women, and increasing mass media are just a few of the many influences that contribute to the complexity of both primary and secondary socialization. Historically, children looked to their parents and other adults for knowledge and skills. Children growing up today, however, are likely to have knowledge and skills (e.g., with computers) that their parents do not have. In addition, our major social institutions (family, education, religion) that have traditionally played a major role in socialization have also undergone a substantial transformation. As we move into the 21st century, we are now experiencing an intense rate of value change and value conflict in society.

The erosion of extended family ties has led to a mode of child rearing that places high demands on the mother and systematically isolates the nuclear family—especially women and children (Flacks, 1979; Keniston, 1974). As Roszak (1979, p. 143) has noted, "The family as we know it is one of the most damaged and pathetic by-products of industrial upheaval." And yet, it is within these damaged, small, isolated family structures that primary socialization continues to take place. According to Keniston and the Carnegie Council on Children (1977), individuals often encounter inherent conflicts in their family roles.

Adding to the complexity of family role expectations are contemporary trends that include high rates of divorce and remarriage. Role strain in single-parent and blended families is further complicated by economic mandates that place women in the dual role of caretaker and breadwinner. In a review of empirical literature on women's multiple roles and mental health, Piechowski (1992) found multiple family and work role demands to be related to poor mental health. Examples cited are disproportionate domestic responsibilities (child care and housework), excessive work loads, and inflexible schedules.

This, of course, has an impact on children as well. For many children, daily life in modern society is also filled with uncertainty and contradictions. Flacks (1979, p. 31) points out the incoherence that exists in our major institutions responsible for socialization:

> In the schools, the media and the churches, such contradictory values as self-denial and self-expression, discipline and indulgence, and striving and being are preached, dramatized, fostered, and practiced all at once. On the one hand, television and magazines advocate hedonism, consumption, and living it up, while schools and churches continue, uneasily, to embody the Protestant Ethic.

Thus, the clarity that is necessary for the transmission of cultural values has been undermined by massive change. As traditional roles and role expectations change, there is an increasing probability of role conflict and role ambiguity. In addition, as the life course becomes more fluid, so do the expectations attached to specific stages in the life course. Clearly, there are positive aspects to these changes, not the least of which are increased choices in roles and role expectations. On the other hand, both primary and secondary socialization become increasingly difficult when role expectations are constantly in flux.

## APPLICATION TO SOCIAL WORK PRACTICE

Like many sociologically based theories, symbolic interaction has not traditionally received widespread attention or acceptance in social work practice. Several recent human behavior texts have, however, acknowledged its contributions toward a fuller understanding of human behavior

(Greene & Ephross, 1991; Greene & Saltman, 1994; Longres, 2000; Zastrow & Kirst-Ashman, 2003). Forte (2004a, 2004b) has suggested that it is an ideal theory base for use in social work assessment, intervention, supervision, and consultation. He also advocated for its use in a variety of settings and to inform policy and research. We agree with Forte and believe it has great utility in that its primary focus is on normal rather than pathological development. It also offers the possibility for creative nonconformity through diverse definitions of normality by individuals and their reference groups.

Role theory has received more attention in the social work literature. Authors such as Perlman (1968), Strean (1971), Munson and Balgopal (1978), and L. V. Davis (1986) have noted the importance of social role in understanding relationships.

## Definition of the Helping Situation

Symbolic interaction and its related theories view the formation of self as dynamic, creative, and adaptive. Because people are believed to use reason in making reflective choices, they are seen as flexible and self-transforming. The focus becomes the client with his or her interpretations, hopes, and goals rather than the intrapsychic structure or environmental barriers. The helping situation is client centered and defined as one involving *growth* or the alleviation of *problems* related to stigmatized or deviant identity, role conflict or ambiguity, perception, interpretation, action, and interaction. Flowchart 10.1 demonstrates an application of symbolic interaction derived from these definitions.

## Assessment, Practice Strategies, and Methods

As a theory for assessment, symbolic interactionism sensitizes us to the social aspects of development. Influences in the individual's environment and the persons and groups with whom he or she interacts become a focal point in a psychosocial history. In addition, the client's view of self and others and the interpretive meanings assigned to people and events are critical pieces of information.

Another area for assessment relates to the roles that people take. Issues related to role conflict, role ambiguity, role strain, and role entrance and exit are also important. Because socialization is viewed as a lifelong process, the various expectations of self and others must be considered over the entire life course. Childhood development is important but does not have primacy over development at later stages.

Further, the interactionist perspective suggests that assessment of persons assigned a deviant label should not focus on the alleged deviant. Because the labelers and agencies of social control selectively apply labels of "deviant" to specific behaviors and persons, an important area for assessment is the interactive process that results in the application of a deviant label or stigmatized identity. Factors such as age, gender, social class, race, ethnicity, and sexual orientation provide important information for assessment. Inasmuch as labeling is seen as the outcome of interaction between the labeled and the labeler(s), information about the labeler is relevant as well. Another important area to be considered in assessment is the systematic bias inherent in control agencies (such as psychiatric hospitals, public welfare agencies, schools) that results in oppressed and powerless groups being labeled as deviant.

One final area for assessment is that of the client–worker relationship. The meanings that clients attribute to their lives, relationships, and situations may be different than those seen by the social worker. It is important for both the worker and the client to clarify their respective definitions and examine areas of congruence and incongruence.

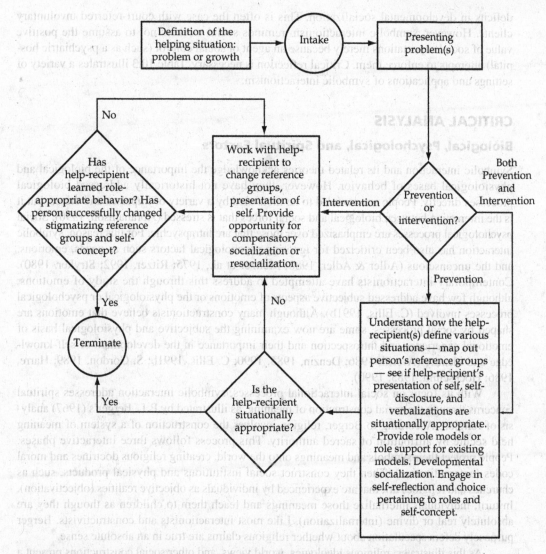

**FLOWCHART 10.1.** One possible practice application of symbolic interactionism in direct practice with individuals, families, and groups.   © 1998, S. P. Robbins, P. Chatterjee, & E. R. Canda.

Symbolic interaction lends itself to direct service methods that include work with individuals, families, and small groups. Specht (1989, 1990) has even suggested that developmental socialization should be the major function of social work practice. By providing "information and knowledge, social support, social skills, and social opportunities," the social worker can assist in developmental tasks of socialization as well as "helping people deal with interference and abuse from others" (1990, p. 354). The worker may also assist the client in alleviating role-related strain and conflicts and problems related to stigmatized or deviant identities.

In some settings, however, the worker may be required to assist in compensatory socialization or to resocialize the deviant actor. Compensatory socialization and resocialization may be necessary when people are unable or unwilling to perform required roles due to impairment or deficits in developmental socialization. This is often the case with court-referred involuntary clients. However, symbolic interactionism reminds social workers not to assume the positive value of social expectations merely because an agent of social control (such as a psychiatric hospital) attempts to enforce them. Critical reflection is necessary. Table 10.3 illustrates a variety of settings and applications of symbolic interactionism.

## CRITICAL ANALYSIS

### Biological, Psychological, and Spiritual Factors

Symbolic interaction and its related theories acknowledge the importance of the biological and physiological bases of behavior. However, they have not historically addressed biological processes directly. People are assumed to be motivated by a variety of impulses and drives, but it is the interaction between biological and social forces that is stressed (Abrahamson, 1990). Social psychological processes are emphasized over those that are intrapsychic. For this reason, symbolic interaction has also been criticized for ignoring psychological factors such as needs, emotions, and the unconscious (Adler & Adler, 1980; Meltzer et al., 1975; Ritzer, 1992; Stryker, 1980). Contemporary interactionists have attempted to address this through the study of emotions, although few have addressed subjective aspects of emotions or the physiological or psychological processes involved (C. Ellis, 1991b). Although many constructionists believe that emotions are shaped by social processes, some are now examining the subjective and physiological basis of emotional experience and introspection and their importance in the development of self-knowledge and identity (Averill, 1986; Denzin, 1985, 1990; C. Ellis, 1991b; S. Gordon, 1989; Harre, 1986; Hochschild, 1983, 1990).

With its focus on social interactional processes, symbolic interaction addresses spiritual concerns through the social construction of meaning, as illustrated by P. L. Berger's (1967) analysis of religion. According to Berger, religion involves the construction of a system of meaning held secure by attribution of sacred authority. This process follows three interactive phases. People project their symbols and meanings onto the world, creating religious doctrines and moral codes (externalization). Then they construct social institutions and physical products, such as churches and religious art, that are experienced by individuals as objective realities (objectivation). In turn, individuals internalize those meanings and teach them to children as though they are absolutely real or divine (internalization). Like most interactionists and constructivists, Berger purposely defers speculation about whether religious claims are true in an absolute sense.

As this illustrates, religious ideologies, world views, and other social constructions present a dilemma, a double-edged sword. One edge of the sword is that this process is a necessary social function to create and maintain a collectively shared sense of meaning, purpose, and order in the world. But the other edge of the sword cuts back, because individual autonomy may be sacrificed to normative social control. A false consciousness may be instilled in people so that they believe social symbolic products are beyond question. This can lead to intolerance or claims that those who do not conform to social prescriptions are immoral or evil, thereby rationalizing stigmatization, persecution, and oppression.

### Social, Cultural, and Economic Forces

Symbolic interaction and its related theories place their primary emphasis on social processes and the meanings that evolve in the course of interaction. The processes of role imitation, role taking, and reflexive learning further emphasize the social and cultural context. Further, because

| TABLE 10.3 | Various Settings and Applications of Symbolic Interaction Theories | | | |
|---|---|---|---|---|
| **Type of Agency** | **Type of Presenting Problems** | **Type of Program(s)** | **Definition(s) of the Helping Situation** | **Type(s) of Socialization** |
| Community center | Lack of recreational facilities for children (age 6–12) | Recreational group work with children | Growth | Primary socialization for good citizenship |
| Community center | Lack of recreational facilities for teenagers (age 12–18) | Recreational group work with teenagers | Growth | Socialization for good citizenship Prevention of delinquency |
| Community center | Delinquent or gang behavior by teenagers | Therapeutic group work with teenagers | Deviance | Resocialize the deviants |
| Community center | Discrimination against area residents | Community group work with adults | Social issues | Socialize area residents to seek empowerment |
| Family service agency | Interpersonal conflict between spouses and generations | Family case work and family group work; family therapy | Problem Growth | Resocialize family members to learn new roles for better family functioning |
| Family service agency or community | Inadequate preparation for parenthood | Family cases work and family group work | Problem Growth | Resocialize unskilled family members to acquire new roles for better functioning |
| Community mental health center | Episodic or chronic mental health problems of individuals | Direct service and supportive service with individuals and groups | Mental disorder Deviance Problem Growth | Resocialize the person for maintenance in the community (without requiring institutionalization) |
| Halfway houses | Integration of discharged mental patients or prisoners in the community | Direct service and supportive service with individuals and groups | Mental disorder Deviance Problem Growth | Resocialize the person for the maintenance in the community (without requiring further institutionalization) |
| Human service departments of public welfare | Child abuse Spouse/mate abuse Elder abuse | Direct service and supportive service with individuals and families | Deviance (for the abusive person) Problem (for the abused person) Growth (for both) | Resocialize the deviants Socialize the victim to deal with the abuse and prevent its repetition |

people create reality, human behavior is portrayed as nondeterministic; people are assumed to have free will in the choices that they make.

In direct contrast to the medical model (and most psychodynamic thought), which assumes that psychopathology is an objective condition, deviance and pathology are believed to be created by the social definitions that people selectively assign to certain behaviors and attributes. Symbolic interactionists point to the fact that definitions of psychopathology vary between cultures and contexts and change over time.

Unlike most personality theories, symbolic interaction suggests that we may have multiple selves. According to Mead (1964, p. 207), "a multiple personality is in a certain sense normal" and is linked to the different relationships we have with different people. In Goffman's formulation, our different selves are linked to the different roles we play. This becomes pathological only when dissociation occurs and parts of the self are left out. Thus, our selves are intricately and normatively part of the social process that gives rise to and reflect a complete self made up of the many.

With its meso-level focus on interaction, symbolic interaction has been criticized for ignoring larger social structures. Structural conditions and economic forces that produce inequality are overlooked (Ritzer, 1992). Perdue (1986, p. 256) asserts that in Blumer's theory:

> society as well as science is spelled with a small s. If Blumer and his heirs have avoided an oversocialized conception of human nature, they have substituted an overpsychologized conception of society. This reductionistic view is especially problematic because nothing appears to exist outside the human mind.

Some have argued, however, that there is nothing inherent in symbolic interactionism to preclude analysis of social structure (Ritzer, 1992; Stryker, 1980). Stryker, for example, has attempted to extend Meadian interactionism through role theory (1980). Perinbanayagam (1985) has also tried to link structure and meaning in his attempt to devise a dialectial interactionism. Forte (2004a) has argued that symbolic interactionism can be used by social workers to "understand culturally different interpretations of similar social experiences, (and) explore meanings such as those of the members of undervalued groups" (p. 393). Future attempts to extend interactionism will need to focus on both smaller- and larger-scale phenomena (Ritzer, 1992).

## Relevance to Individuals, Groups, Families, Organizations, Institutions, and Communities

The theories discussed here simultaneously focus on the individual, the family (as a primary group), peer groups, reference groups, organizations, institutions, and communities (secondary groups) that comprise the larger society. It is through interaction in these primary and secondary groups that people develop shared meanings. The self, as a process, is inseparable from these larger contexts. Additionally, all behavior arises within the context of specific social and cultural environments. These environments, however, are seen as a product of socially constructed meanings that define the roles, rules, and expectations of a society; they are symbolic rather than material.

## CONSISTENCY WITH SOCIAL WORK VALUES AND ETHICS

Although no specific prescriptions for optimal health and well-being can be directly derived from these theories, their focus on the interactional basis of normative development suggests the importance of interpersonal social support from both primary and secondary groups throughout the life cycle. Insights from symbolic interaction support a strengths perspective of social work practice.

Strengths-based practice emphasizes a participatory helping relationship in which the client is given support to define his or her reality and goals. Helpful dialogue is a symbolic interaction that reveals the client's life meaning, especially the talents and resources that have encouraged resiliency. As labeling theory reminds us, this may involve deconstructing negative and confining labels and social expectations that deny or obscure people's strengths (Saleebey, 2002). Symbolic interactionism points out that the helper's every action helps shape the client's understanding of self and world, for better or worse, showing that great care must be taken in the helping relationship. It highlights the importance of supporting a client's development of self-esteem (recognition of one's own strengths and worth) through behavior from the helper that is consistently respectful and affirming.

However, it is important to recognize that symbolic interactionism has been criticized for being ahistorical and apolitical (Kuhn, 1964; Meltzer et al., 1975; Stryker, 1980). Although cultural differences are acknowledged, human diversity is not adequately addressed because differences are seen simply as products of the interpretive process. Similarly, structural conditions such as institutional racism, sexism, and class inequality are reduced to attitudes of prejudice and stigmatization that arise through interaction. Shaskolsky (1970) has noted that the portrayal of people as free and equal actors ignores the fact that some people are more free, or more equal, than others. Symbolic interactionism, especially the forms emphasizing role conformity or normative socialization, can be used to promote an acceptance of the status quo. Gouldner (1970, p. 379) has argued that an avoidance of power differences "entails an accommodation to existent power arrangements." Goffman's dramaturgical model has also been criticized for its avoidance of social stratification and social class, which are taken as "immutable givens" (Meltzer et al., 1975, p. 109). Patricia Clough (1992) has argued for symbolic interaction to include women's voices in both history and everyday life.

When symbolic interactionism is used with a conservative bias, it lends itself to a view of prevailing social arrangements as unproblematic. Socialization to status inferior roles and identities is seen as a process that involves first learning the "normal" and valued roles and then learning how to manage a devalued role. Thus, the stigma attached to gender, race, homosexuality, or physical deformity or disability is portrayed as a characteristic to be managed or concealed, if possible.

In contrast, the interactionist position that pathology and deviance are socially defined and are not necessarily inherent in the person does offer an empowerment perspective for those who are so labeled. It argues against the biological and psychological determinism that often permanently enmesh people in deviant role identities. It encourages people to take an active part in choosing and defining self-definitions, social roles, and reference groups. The interactionist emphasis on the relativity of social standards to particular belief systems and cultural contexts helps to break down ethnocentric assumptions and to open up the possibility of genuine respectful dialogue between people of diverse perspectives (R. Greene, 1994).

## PHILOSOPHICAL UNDERPINNINGS

Several philosophical strains have been identified in the social theory of mind that underlies symbolic interactionist thought: German romantic idealism, American pragmatism, Darwinian evolutionary thinking, and behaviorism (R. Collins, 1994; Perdue, 1986; Ritzer, 1992). From an evolutionary perspective, we see an emphasis on process and change; the mind is portrayed as a process, rather than a structure, and as the self evolves, the mind undergoes a process of change. The theme of process is also a major undercurrent in romantic idealism, which Mead elaborated on in his theory of the self being both subject and object, as well as his notion of self and society being inseparable. Pragmatist thought is evident in the interactionist perspective that reality does not exist independent of meanings that are created, defined, and acted upon by people according to their usefulness. And, finally, the recognition of the importance of observable behaviors is derived from behaviorism.

Symbolic interactionism views human behavior as rational, active, creative, and purposeful. It rejects the idea of an objective reality and points, instead, to the social construction of norms, values, and meanings that people assign to external phenomena.

## METHODOLOGICAL ISSUES AND EMPIRICAL SUPPORT

Symbolic interactionism embraces both positivistic and phenomenological orientations. As previously discussed, theorists from the Chicago school favor qualitative methods, whereas those from the Iowa school stress quantification. It is not surprising that each school finds shortcomings in the other's methods.

"Soft" techniques such as sympathetic introspection have been criticized as being too subjectivist and not sufficiently scientific. The insistence that unique, subjective experiences cannot be generalized is faulted for lessening the utility of the theory. Further, testable propositions cannot be generated from vague concepts that cannot be operationalized (Kuhn, 1964; Meltzer et al., 1975; Ritzer, 1992; Stryker, 1980).

In contrast, traditional methods have been criticized as being inadequate in explaining or describing subjective phenomena. An overreliance on quantification reduces complex social and psychological processes to deterministic cause and effect equations. Quantification is believed to foster a static view of human behavior that is inconsistent with the interactionist view of self as a process rather than a product (Blumer, 1969b; Ritzer, 1992).

Most empirical research in this area has focused on the content of the self. Kuhn's TST has shown that while the self has a great deal of consistency, it is also contextual and situational. In addition, Zurcher (1983) found that changes in society are also related to changes in self-concept. In contrast to the 1950s when people emphasized occupational and familial roles (student, mother), people in the 1970s stressed ways of acting and feeling (happy, worried). Other research has shown that routine transitions in one's life such as getting married, changing jobs, or losing a spouse are related to changes in one's identity (Lund, Carerta, Diamond, & Gray, 1986). Research on the content of self, however, ignores the process through which the self arises (Abrahamson, 1990). Some contend that role theory provides a stronger empirical base for research than symbolic interaction, due to its clearly defined and measureable concepts (West & Turner, 2010).

Although symbolic interactionism accommodates both objectivist and subjectivist orientations, the dominant position is that of Blumer and the Chicago school. Research from this orientation has produced a wealth of information about the nature of everyday reality but has not provided empirical verification of symbolic interaction theory. It is important to note that Blumer does not totally reject traditional methods. Rather, he is critical of their reductionistic tendency (Ritzer, 1992). The ongoing differences between the Chicago and Iowa schools can be found in a heated debate between Blumer (1980) and C. McPhail and Rexroat (1979, 1980). We believe that both orientations are necessary for the future development of this theoretical perspective. Currently, contemporary authors writing in the symbolic interaction tradition have produced works that are methodologically diverse and include studies based on original quantitative and statistical analysis, conversational analysis, and secondary data analysis, among others.

All the theories discussed here are more useful for explanation than prediction and are better at a probabilistic level of explanation than at a deterministic level. Within the limitations noted earlier, they are adequately suited for explaining properties of both individuals and groups. Although these theories posit an interconnection between mental processes, the individual, and the social structure, they are most often used to explain behavior at the individual and small group levels.

## Summary

Despite the fact that symbolic interactionism has not yet been widely embraced as a major theoretical perspective in social work, we believe that it offers an important alternative to the deterministic view of behavior inherent in psychodynamic theory and behavioral psychology. Abraham has noted that "Mead's notion of self is an effective counter to Freudianism and individual psychologies that concentrate on psychic systems and biological drives" as well as a "powerful antidote to structural determinism" (1988, p. 240). With its focus on both internal processes and external action, symbolic interactionism contributes to a fuller understanding of social learning, socialization, and self-concept. We cannot ignore, however, that "What is learned bears some relationship to history and power. Not all interpretations are created equal" (Perdue, 1986, p. 256).

With its roots in philosophy, behavioral psychology, and sociology, symbolic interactionism incorporates several diverse perspectives. Its dual foci on the interpretive process and social context will likely appeal to those interested in both the internal and the external realms of experience.

Symbolic interaction offers a good meso-level framework for social work practice through which we can view individuals, families, small groups, institutions, and organizations. However, its rejection of the material universe in favor of the symbolic introduces a conservative bias that may weaken both the appeal of this theory and its utility for practice based on principles of empowerment. On the other hand, those who seek an alternative to pathology-oriented theories of development will likely be drawn to its phenomenological orientation and concomitant view of the self as dynamic, creative, and adaptive.

# Phenomenology, Social Constructionism, and Hermeneutics

*Well me and John Paul put our heads together*
*But we couldn't think of nothing to say*
*Started thinking early in the evening last night*
*Carried on into the day*
*Then around noon it started making sense*
*And then it wouldn't go away*
*You see, I was always living in the future tense*
*And he was only living today*
*Do you think you can take it, do you think you can make it*
*Do you think it's worth a rusty Goddamn*
*If I'm still thinking when the curtain falls*
*I'll be thinking, therefore I am.*

© MICHAEL ELWOOD 1990

## PHENOMENOLOGICAL THEORIES

- question our everyday assumptions about the nature of reality
- emphasize the primacy of the human mind in the creation of the social world
- provide a critique of positivistic social science and offer an alternative method of scientific inquiry
- are useful in developing assessment and treatment plans for individuals, small groups, and families

---

This chapter was coauthored with Frank Richardson, PhD, and Cynthia Franklin, PhD, LCSW, LMFT.

In Chapter 10, we discussed some of the main assumptions of social constructionist thought that underlie symbolic interactionism. In this chapter, we elaborate the views of social constructionism that are central to phenomenology, existentialism, postmodernism, and hermeneutics. These theories cover broad and distinct perspectives but share in common a belief in the importance of cultural, situational, and socially constructed aspects of human experience. Most specifically, they question our everyday assumptions about the nature of reality and propose that our selves, our identities, our communities, and our social realities are constructions of mind rather than objective entities separate from us (Orleans, 1991). In addition, they also provide a critical analysis of traditional social science. Postmodern or social constructionist thinkers (e.g., Cushman, 1990, 1995; K. J. Gergen, 1985; Heineman, 1981; Saleebey, 1994, 1996; Tyson, 1992; Witkin, 1991) are particularly critical of the positivistic assumptions that underlie the scientific method.

## HISTORICAL CONTEXT

At the end of the 19th century, the "original debate" between positivist and antipositivist views of proper inquiry in the human sciences was still undecided (Polkinghorne, 1983). This debate is often currently framed as a dichotomy between the opposing views of constructionism/constructivism and positivism, as illustrated in Table 11.1. John Stuart Mill, in his very influential *System of Logic Ratiocinative and Inductive* (1884), advocated the use of natural science methods as the only cure for the "backward state" of the human sciences. Wilhelm Dilthey (cited in Rickman, 1976, pp. 170ff.), by contrast, argued that we cannot understand history, human action, or works of art and literature by subsuming them under general laws for the purpose of scientific prediction and control. It was difficult, however, for Dilthey and like-minded thinkers to clarify what kind of knowledge the human science provided. They wished such knowledge to provide an understanding of meaningful, value-laden, ever-changing human action and artifacts and wanted to employ their own unique methods of description and interpretation. They were torn, however, and wished to justify their understandings as being objective and timelessly true, as in the natural sciences. Scientific ideals were prestigious and associated with both the rejection of late-19th-century metaphysical speculation and Enlightenment moral ideals of individualism, democracy, and opposition to dogmatism and arbitrary authority.

However, it was difficult to explain how changing interpretations of changing human phenomena could be regarded as objective, and the debate was won by the followers of Mill. Thus, mainstream social science in the 20th century has been committed to emulating the methods of the natural sciences and seeking theory that would allow us to explain, predict, and control the social realm. This debate, however, has never been conclusively decided and has been kept alive in diverse areas of philosophy and social theory, especially in phenomenology and existentialism.

Phenomenology is a 20th-century philosophical approach developed by German philosopher Edmund Husserl, who is generally credited as the founder of both phenomenology and existentialism. In his last great book, *The Crisis of European Sciences and Transcendental Phenomenology* (1970), first published in 1936, Husserl objected to the positivistic reduction of science and philosophy in the modern world. He claimed that there has gradually taken place a "surreptitious substitution of the mathematically substructed world of idealities for the only real world, the one that is actually given in perception, that is experienced and experiencable—our everyday life-world" (p. 48). Thus, we have mistakenly come to believe that the world of mathematical, objectified nature is the only real world. He argued that natural science itself is rooted in

| TABLE 11.1 | Philosophical Differences Between Positivist and Constructivist and Constructionist Methods | |
|---|---|---|

| Issue or Area | Positivist | Constructivist/Constructionist |
|---|---|---|
| Ontology (the nature of reality) | Realism—reality is singular, stable, and external. | Relativism—realities are individual and collective constructions of and in experience. |
| Epistemology (theories of knowing) | Rationalism—knowledge is authorized as valid by logic or reason; reality is revealed via the senses. | Constructivism—knowing is behavioral and emotional as well as cognitive; the validity of knowledge is less important than its viability; sensation is proactive. |
| Causal processes (theories of causality or change) | Associationism—learning and change are linear chains of discrete causes and effects. | Structural differentiation—learning and development involve refinements and transformation of mental representations. |

| Axioms About | Quantitative/Positivist Paradigm | Qualitative/Constructivist Paradigm |
|---|---|---|
| Nature of reality | Reality is single, tangible, and fragmented. | Realities are multiple, constructed, holistic. |
| Relationship of knower to known | Knower and known are independent, a dualism. | Knower and known are interactive, inseparable. |
| Possibility of generalization | Time and context-free generalizations are possible (nomothetic). | Only time and context-bound working hypotheses are possible (idiographic). |
| Possibility of causal linkages | There are real causes, temporally precedent to or simultaneous with their effects. | All entities are in a state of mutual simultaneous shaping, so it is impossible to distinguish causes from effects. |
| Roles of values | Inquiry is value-free. | Inquiry is value-bound. |

*Source: Clinical Assessment for Social Workers: Quantitative and Qualitative Methods*, by Jordan & Franklin (1995). Chicago: Lyceum/Nelson Hall Books.

and presupposes the everyday life-world, the "intuitive, surrounding world of life, pregiven as existing for all in common" (p. 121).

Husserl's transcendental phenomenology made a radical turn away from naturalism, positivism, and objectivism. Instead of explaining events in our life-world (or *Lebenswelt*) by subsuming them under general laws, he proposed that we should seek to understand the general structures of meaning of that life-world and how they are constituted. To accomplish this, we must "bracket," or suspend, our naive, customary preconceptions about the world so that we can discern the "structure of a phenomenon" or "the commonality running through the many diverse appearances of the phenomenon" (Valle & Halling, 1989, p. 14). Husserl believed that this kind of investigation could eventually lead us to recognize the life-world and humanity itself as a "self-objectification" of a "transcendental subjectivity."

Uncomfortable with the transcendental dimension of Husserl's view, a number of phenomenological thinkers following Husserl held that the starting point is the "*Lebenswelt*, being given directly and immediately in human experience." In this view, "no assumptions are made as to what might be behind or cause the life-world." Rather than being a construction of consciousness, the "world as lived by the person" is "co-constituted or co-created in the dialogue of person and world" (Valle & Halling, 1989, p. 9).

## KEY CONCEPTS

Central to phenomenological thought is the idea that seemingly objective entities, such as society and self, are, in fact, subjectively created by our cognitive processes. Derived from philosopher Rene Descartes' proposal that we should "study reality," phenomenology "studies the creation of what is taken to be real" (Orleans, 1991, p. 173). In contrast to conventional social thought that views norms, roles, attitudes, groups, and social institutions as independent and factual entities, phenomenology proposes that these are essentially human constructs. Although they do not deny the existence of physical or social reality, phenomenologists suggest that all aspects of reality must be studied to determine the ways in which people come to see them as real. This is done through *bracketing*, or "setting aside the idea that the real world is naturally ordered" (Ritzer, 1988, p. 207). Thus, the world of objects and all phenomena must be approached with doubt and question to understand the way in which people construct reality.

There are numerous other concepts that are central to phenomenological thought that are discussed below with their specific authors.

### Alfred Schutz's Phenomenology of Everyday Life

In *The Phenomenology of the Social World* (1967) and in other writings, Vienna-born phenomenologist Alfred Schutz proposed an influential alternative to the positivistic view of social science. One of Husserl's most important followers, Schutz emigrated to the United States and developed his phenomenological stance in the field of sociology at New York's New School for Social Research. Drawing on Husserl's thought, Schutz attempted to develop and improve Max Weber's ideas concerning "interpretive sociology." Weber had argued that the proper subject of sociology was "meaningful behavior." Sociology combines an appreciation of the "subjective meanings" that animate this behavior with a description of the patterns and "ideal types" of human action that it exemplifies. Even though this interpretive activity is different in kind from natural science explanation, Weber still held that its conclusions had to be objective and value-free.

For Schutz, however, an understanding of the structures of meaningful action that are organized around human purposes and goals was quite different from an impersonal cause–effect analysis of the stream of behavior. In addition, Schutz felt it was important to clarify that interpretation (or *verstehen*) has little to do with introspection. Challenging the familiar modern dualism between inner and outer reality, he proposed that we do not "see" only the physical manifestations of inward, meaning-giving acts of interpretation (our own and others'). Rather, our very perception of outward actions involves applying categories of understanding concerning what the actor means from his or her point of view. Schutz identified four realms of the social world: *umwelt*, our physiological and physical surroundings (or directly experienced social reality); *mitwelt*, the social world of other people (or indirectly experienced social reality); *folgewelt*, the future; and *vorwelt*, the past. Although the social construction of reality takes place within the *umwelt*, Schutz believed that the mind could not be studied scientifically because people were unpredictable in their face-to-face interactions with others. He therefore focused on the *mitwelt*, "that aspect of the social world in which people ordinarily deal with types of people or with larger social structures, rather than with actual actors" (Ritzer, 1988, p. 213). He believed that scientific study of "general types of subjective experience" (Schutz, 1967, p. 181) would help us understand the general process that people use in dealing with the world (Ritzer, 1988).

Schutz distinguished between first-order processes by which we interpret our own and others' actions in everyday life and second-order processes by which a social scientist seeks to understand the first-order processes, usually in a more analytical and systematic manner. To permit greater prediction and control of events, most natural science accounts of human action are formulated in any terms whatsoever, even if those terms have nothing to do with our everyday common sense meanings and beliefs. However, Schutz's second-order processes are interpretations that take place to a great extent in terms of the first-order categories by which we make sense out of ordinary life.

The result of second-order processes is a phenomenology of the everyday life-world rather than a transcendental phenomenology. Here, the main feature is its profoundly social or intersubjective character. One's experiences are not identical with those of others in everyday, face-to-face interactions. But in what Schutz terms these concrete "we-relations," we "participate" in each other's conscious life in such a way that there is a "synchronization of two interior streams of consciousness" (1964, p. 26). We-relations are highly intimate face-to-face relations, characteristic of the *umwelt*. Because people rarely reflect on the more routine aspects of day-to-day interaction, they mostly act according to the established recipes and typifications to which they are socialized. *Typifications* are the common sense constructs, or recipes, that we gain through socialization that help us use typical actions for typical situations in daily life (Ritzer, 1988). However, Schutz saw we-relations as being too idiosyncratic for scientific study. In contrast, "they-relations," our interactions with impersonal contemporaries (such as an unseen postal clerk), are anonymous typifications that are dominated by cultural forces (Ritzer, 1988). To study the *life-world*, the taken-for-granted reality of everyday life, this suggests the following general stages in inquiry:

1. Carefully observe certain facts and events within social reality.
2. Construct "typifications" or typical patterns of individuals' purposive behavior or courses of action in various settings.
3. Develop and coordinate to these patterns models of ideal human actors or agents.
4. Ascribe to this "fictitious" consciousness a set of typical motivations, purposes, and/or goals, which are assumed for the purpose of the theory to be invariant. Such a model yields "types" or "puppets" interacting with others in patterns.

Such models and theories should be developed according to the intersubjective norms of the scientific community. Schutz, following Weber, believed that this kind of inquiry would furnish an objective representation and explanation of the structure and dynamics of the life-world. Schutz, however, never specified or clarified what these norms consist of or how they assure an objective knowledge of meaningful action.

Ritzer (1988) has noted that Schutz's theories are extremely complex and have led to a variety of interpretations of his work. R. Bernstein also pointed out that Schutz often "seems to be operating in an orthodox Husserlian context, searching for structures so basic as to be constitutive of any form of social life" (1976, p. 159). However, Schutz generally failed "to distinguish clearly those structures which are presumably . . . permanent . . . and a priori from those which have specific historical roots and causes." In addition, Ritzer (1988, p. 221) has noted that Schutz's deliberate omission of consciousness and mental processes has resulted in a "paradoxical situation of a sociologist who is the field's best-known phenomenologist saying that he is abandoning the subject matter he is best known for."

## ROADS FROM SCHUTZ

Schutz's work came to have a significant impact on the fields of sociology and psychology. Phenomenological thought in psychology helped reveal "how people organize their self interpretations, feel their emotions, create their fantasies, use reason and logic, and generate their actions" (Orleans, 1991, p. 181). By emphasizing that identity, thoughts, feelings, and behaviors are rooted in consciousness, phenomenology unified various aspects of human behavior and provided a base for transactional analysis, existential psychology, Gestalt psychology, Rogerian client-centered therapy, and a variety of other humanistic schools of thought. Orleans has noted that the dissemination of Schutz's ideas led to humans being studied as humans.

Schutz's work was also instrumental in spreading the German antipositivist tradition of sociology in America, especially through the ethnomethodology of Harold Garfinkle on the West Coast and the social constructionism of Peter Berger on the East Coast (Etzkowitz & Glassman, 1991). Phenomenology developed into two branches, microphenomenology, which examines how "everyday life situations are the products of our collective actions," and macrophenomenology, which examines how "the organizations and institutions of society are constructed" through collective actions (Orleans, 1991, p. 173). By the mid-1960s, phenomenology was also embraced as a "Western version of 'mind oriented' philosophies" by scholars interested in non-Western religions. This eventually gave rise to hermeneutic sociology in the 1980s (Etzkowitz & Glassman, 1991, p. 41).

As offshoots of Schutz's work, we examine here some of the central ideas of ethnomethodology, the phenomenological concept of self, the social construction of reality, social constructionism in postmodern thought, and hermeneutic philosophy.

### Harold Garfinkle's Ethnomethodology

Ethnomethodology encompasses both a theoretical and a methodological perspective that places it alternately within symbolic interactionist thought or within phenomenological sociology. Although we agree with Meltzer, Petras, and Reynolds (1975) in support of Wallace's position that "Insofar as ethnomethodology embraces a theoretic . . . viewpoint, it is clearly symbolic interactionist" (1969, p. 35), it is most often associated with a phenomenological line of inquiry. According to Sharrock and Anderson (1986, p. 40), ethnomethodologists believe that "research and theorizing are to be done in conjunction, such that the theorizing is tied to the materials generated by the research."

*Ethnomethodology* is a term that was first coined by Harold Garfinkle to refer to the analysis of commonplace everyday activities in social settings. Like symbolic interactionists, phenomenologists and ethnomethodologists are concerned with the interpretive process and the meanings that arise in social interaction. More specifically, Garfinkle's primary focus was the common sense methods that people use to make sense out of their world.

In his major work, *Studies in Ethnomethodology* (1967), Garfinkle set forth the basic premises of this perspective. Unique to this approach are the techniques of experimentation that are aimed at disrupting the flow of normal events. These experiments, termed *breaching experiments*, are used to illustrate the fragility of social reality and to demonstrate how people construct meanings in their everyday life. For example, in a well-known breaching experiment Garfinkle asked students to act like guests in their own homes. This included acting politely, using formal addresses, and speaking only when spoken to. The reactions of family members demonstrated the importance of shared definitions and common assumptions about "normal" and "proper" behavior.

Another method used by ethnomethodologists is conversation analysis, in which the researcher analyzes audio or videotaped conversations between people to reveal "the procedures by which conversationalists produce their own behavior and understand and deal with the behavior of others" (Heritage & Atkinson, 1984, p. 1). Another goal of conversational analysis is to explicitly examine the ways in which conversation is organized. In general, ethnomethodologists believe that "detailed study of small phenomena may give enormous understanding of the way humans do things" (Sacks, 1984, p. 24). In addition, both phenomenologists and ethnomethodologists believe that macro social structures can be best understood by studying the ways in which meanings are constructed.

## The Self in Phenomenology and Postmodern Thought

Phenomenological thought has led to various conceptions about the nature of self that sharply contrast with perspectives found in mainstream psychological and sociological thought. The self is typically portrayed as a consequence of either social and cultural forces (such as social structure, social organization, roles, norms, and values) or a consequence of internal forces (such as id impulses, ego strivings, attachment needs, or genetically transmitted personality traits). In contrast, phenomenology views the self as a conscious ongoing process, in which the self is the "originator of experience within a biographically determined situation" (M. Lester, 1984, p. 42).

As we saw in Chapter 10, symbolic interaction also portrays the self as a process. However, unlike symbolic interaction, phenomenology focuses on the "intentionality of consciousness" and examines the "self-as-conscious-subject" as well as the practical methods (such as language) that we use to identify or display our "self." Because the self is a process, it is never static, and we consciously create, re-create, and give our self meaning through "accounts, descriptions, assumptions and common-sense-knowledge." Thus, even our biographies can be assembled and reassembled. M. Lester has noted that "seeing and displaying the self as 'consistent' or fixed is itself a situated accomplishment, resulting from using the documentary method of interpretation" (1984, p. 49). The term *situated accomplishment* refers to the fact that we assemble our "selves" for specific situations in everyday life.

Over the last few decades, a number of thinkers, loosely grouped together as "postmodern" theorists, have come to view the ideal of objective, value-free science and theory as a manifestation of the one-sided individualism and technicism of modern times. They complain that 20th-century mainstream social science has uncritically and arrogantly assumed a "self-contained individualism." It pictures a decontextualized, "bounded, masterful self" confronting an objectified world that it seeks to represent and manipulate (Cushman, 1990, p. 599). This, they assert, is at the root of many modern dilemmas in living; it breeds misery at home, imperialism abroad, and is the major source of our confusion about the nature of social science and how it should relate to practical life.

Postmodern theorists reject the idea that there are unchanging foundations for the human sciences that reach beyond the shifting sands of history to identify a metaphysical basis or moral standard for judging our beliefs. They feel that any claim to have found such a basis or standard is simply another historically influenced interpretation, a mere projection of our particular community's viewpoint onto the universe. They contend that it is time to acknowledge the fundamental truth that all our beliefs and values are strictly relative.

Seidman (1994, pp. 5–6) has noted that postmodern thought is characterized by the loss of certainty in what were once assumed to be universal truths about science, society, the mind, and the self. This has been replaced by what Rorty refers to as "multiple vocabularies of self and world." Postmodern theorists such as Derrida (1978), Lyotard (1984), C. West (1995), and Haraway (1991), to name a few, have challenged the "hegemonic Eurocentric, male-dominated, heterosexist culture" that creates inequality and oppression in the name of progress and marginalizes and disempowers individuals and groups. The new cultural "politics of difference" that has emerged in postmodern thought not only questions foundational claims of universality and truth but also "asserts the value of individuality, difference, heterogeneity, locality and pluralism" (Seidman, 1994, p. 7).

Postmodern thinkers generally concur with the philosopher Dreyfus's view that "humanity is a self-interpreting way of being whose practices have enabled it to act as if it had a whole series of different natures in the course of history" (1987, p. 65). In other words, humans do not have a transhistorical or transcultural nature. Rather, culture "completes" humans by explaining and interpreting the world. Culture does not differently clothe the universal human, but, rather, infuses individuals and fundamentally shapes their natures and identities. In Cushman's words, "cultural conceptualizations and configurations of self are formed by the economies and politics of their respective eras. . . . . There is no universal, transhistorical self, only local selves; no universal theory about the self, only local theories" (1990, p. 599).

## Peter Berger and Thomas Luckmann: The Social Construction of Reality

Seeking to extend phenomenology and integrate the individual and societal levels, Peter Berger and Thomas Luckmann (1967, p. 61) proposed that "Society is a human product. Society is an objective reality. Man is a social product" or, as Ritzer (1988, p. 227) has paraphrased, "People are the products of the very society they create." In their influential and now famous book, *The Social Construction of Reality: A Treatise in the Sociology of Knowledge* (1967), Berger and Luckmann attempted to integrate Schutz's work with that of George Herbert Mead, Karl Marx, and Emile Durkheim (Ritzer, 1988). Although, in their view, reality was both subjective and objective, both the self and the social order were produced by subjective processes in interaction with others.

Building on Schutz's phenomenological stance, they held that people perceive their own subjective processes as an objective reality external to them. However, they added to this the idea that reality appears to be objective because it is already objectified through language, which provides people with "the necessary objectifications and posits the order within which these make sense and within which everyday life has meaning" (1967, p. 23). In other words, people are born into a pre-existing society and, through socialization and shared cultural patterns of behavior, they develop habitualized patterns of acting. Thus, behaviors that are constantly repeated become patterns or habits. Although this is helpful because it makes it unnecessary to define each situation anew each time we encounter it, the meanings of our actions become embedded in our routines and come to be taken for granted.

Habitualization leads to institutionalization as our actions become typified in terms of routines that become reciprocal with that of other actors. According to P. L. Berger and Luckmann, "any such typification is an institution" (1967, p. 54). Institutions play an important role in controlling our behavior by "setting up pre-defined patterns of conduct" to which we are expected to adhere (p. 55). Socialization also plays a key role in our internalization of institutional norms for conduct, and it is through this process that socially acquired ways of doing things develop what seems to be an existence of their own. Once our subjective reality is created by internalization, we then reify the external world, and legitimize it, by cognitively ascribing validity to it and come to perceive it as though it were separate from the human processes that created it.

Despite the fact that Berger and Luckmann attempted to portray both objective and subjective aspects of reality, their characterization of the social world and society remained subjective. According to Ritzer (1988, p. 230), "they promised more than simply a subjective sociology . . . and they did not deliver."

## Social Constructionism in Postmodern Thought

One prominent branch of postmodern constructionist thought is represented by American philosopher Richard Rorty (1982, 1985, 1987) and theorist Kenneth Gergen (1982, 1985), who is perhaps the leading social constructionist in contemporary social science. Gergen has argued that the "terms in which the world is understood are social artifacts, products of historically situated interchanges between people" (1985, pp. 267ff.). In both theory and practical life, the "process of understanding is not automatically driven by the forces of nature, but is the result of an active, cooperative enterprise of persons in relationships. In this light, inquiry is invited into the historical and cultural bases of various forms of world constructions." As a result, conceptions of "psychological process differ markedly from one culture to another."

From this perspective, many of the findings and theories of empirical social science are quite distortive. They pretend that the world, the self, and psychological processes are just *one* way, which is not the case, and that they are *our* way, which is ethnocentric and erroneous. The prevalence of a given form of understanding depends not "on the empirical validity of the perspective in question, but on the vicissitudes of social process (e.g., communication, negotiation, conflict, rhetoric)."

According to K. J. Gergen (1985, pp. 270ff.), social constructionism helps us get past the traditional "subject–object dualism." This means that social and psychological inquiry is deprived of any notion of "experience" as a touchstone of objectivity. The so-called reports or descriptions of one's experience are really just "linguistic constructions guided and shaped by historically contingent conventions of discourse." Therefore, there is no "truth through method," and no correct procedure that bestows objectivity on our findings or theories. Moreover, social constructionism "offers no alternative truth criteria." Instead, "the success of [our] accounts depends primarily on the analyst's capacity to invite, compel, stimulate, or delight the audience, and not on criteria of veracity."

Gergen and Rorty have defended their approach against charges of irrationalism or destructive relativism. First, because there is an "inherent dependency of knowledge systems on communities of shared intelligibility," there can be "stability of understanding without the stultification of foundationalism" (K. J. Gergen, 1985, pp. 272ff.). Thus, our practices and values can evolve only gradually through a coordinated effort, rather than chaotically or whimsically. Second, because the "practitioner can no longer justify any socially reprehensible conclusion on the grounds of being a 'victim of the facts,' he or she must confront the pragmatic implications of such conclusions within society more generally." Not being able to hide behind a pretense of objectivity or facade of value-neutrality actually "reasserts the relevance of moral criteria for scientific practice." Because social science theory and professional practice "enter into the life of the culture, sustaining certain patterns of conduct and destroying others, such work must be evaluated in terms of good and evil." Finally, Rorty (1985) has even claimed that this sort of relativism or contextualism does not lead to social fragmentation or personal directionlessness, but to a deepened sense of "solidarity." A sense of the enormous contingency of life actually tends to undermine dogmatism and yields a positive sense of connectedness and shared purpose with fellow practitioners of our particular way of life.

## The Postmodern Thought of Michel Foucault

Many contemporary thinkers in philosophy and the human sciences have been influenced by the penetrating analyses of Michel Foucault (1979, 1980; C. Gordon, 1980). His work on the way in which human science and professional expertise have become mechanisms of social control are especially relevant to social work practice. Foucault presented a more realistic but less optimistic view of our embeddedness in culture than Gergen and Rorty. Initially, Foucault termed his primary unit of analysis *discourse*. In his later writings, he discussed the same realities in terms of "relations of power." Foucault tried to reveal sets of discursive rules that allow us to produce a field of knowledge, including all of its possible statements about what is true or false or good or evil. These rules, however, "operate 'behind the backs' of speakers of a discourse" and the "place, function, and character of the 'knowers', authors and audiences of a discourse are a function" of these rules (Philip, 1985, p. 69). As a result, he held that there can be no overall truth or falsity of a discourse. Rather, truth is simply an effect of the rules of discourse or the power relations that create and constitute a particular form of life. Typically, power relations are neither a matter of explicit consent nor a violent coercion but are the myriad ways people are constrained together to act within a particular, ultimately arbitrary system of power/knowledge. Foucault often characterized them as haphazard, incessant, struggle, and conflict. What we might call "domination" or "justice" is simply truth effects within our cultural order. They are in no way less dominating or morally superior to past or future "regimes of truth" occurring down a directionless historical path; they are only different. Although Foucault's writing focused on the "micropolitics of power" rather than traditional Marxian economic theory, Smart (1983) and Ritzer (1992) have suggested that his analysis was also clearly influenced by Marxian thought.

Foucault suggested that the human sciences (which he termed *dubious sciences*) aim at truth but, in fact, deceptively classify and manage people in line with the current regime. They augment *biopower*, Foucault's term for the kind of detailed surveillance and control that power takes in our era, reflected in our peculiar modern obsession with the creation of a normal and healthy population. In his description of the link between knowledge and power in the fields of medicine and law, Foucault was especially critical about the way in which scientific knowledge is used to exert power and social control over people (1965, 1979, 1980, 1985). According to Foucault, the growth of the human sciences has led to a system of domination in which professionals such as physicians, psychologists, psychiatrists, and educators oppress the mentally ill, the prisoners, and society as a whole. Foucault (1979) was especially critical of the growth of the "scientifico-legal complex" that defines people as the object of knowledge and subjugates them to the professional judgments and actions of "small-scale judges."

Foucault addressed not only how modes of domination form the modern subject, but how certain practices, usually mediated by an external authority figure like a confessor or psychoanalyst, bring individuals' active self-formative processes in line with the current system (1980). In other words, people are induced to scrutinize themselves interminably until they find (or even fabricate) certain problems or tendencies. They are then persuaded to assume individual responsibility for suppressing or managing these desires to conform to current norms of health and productivity. This type of analysis, for example, can be used to shed light on how the emotionally isolated modern individual is trained to adapt to being a cog in the social and economic machinery, to do without lasting social ties, and to criticize only oneself and not the social order for problems in living (Hare-Mustin, 1991, p. 65).

However, instead of social science or ethical discussion, Foucault recommended the practice of *genealogy*. Genealogy limits itself to uncovering the likely origins of "totalizing discourses" and showing how their deceptive claims to unity and truth arose from historical accidents and arbitrary machinations of power. Nevertheless, Foucault often expressed support for those who resist or refuse these operations, in ways that open a space for the rediscovery of particular, fragmented, subjugated, local knowledge or understanding. Toward the end of his life, Foucault felt pressure to articulate some sort of positive ethic beyond merely engaging in the detached genealogy of endless and supposedly equally dominating regimes of truth. He suggested that from the lack of any fixed or universal human nature we could infer a practical program of ceaselessly creating and recreating ourselves "as a work of art" (Foucault, 1982).

## Dilemmas in Postmodern Thought

Phenomenological and constructionist postmodern thought may help to unmask some of our damaging modern pretensions to exaggerated autonomy, certainty, and control. Social constructionism, especially, helps restore a sense of belonging to a historical culture that has formed us. In addition, it provides helpful new tools for recovering diverse and possibly valuable experiences and understandings that have sometimes been "subjugated" by scientistic, rationalistic, or masculinist ways of thinking. Nevertheless, postmodern and social constructionist theory has encountered serious difficulties.

The postmodern outlook seems to set forth a paradoxical and ultimately implausible view of the human self as both radically determined by historical influences and yet radically free to reinterpret itself and social reality as it wishes for its own self-invented purposes. But where would such historically embedded beings get the leverage to reinvent themselves so radically? Where, we might ask, do postmodern theorists stand when they articulate their views? Are these views just another by-product of social forces or entirely optional negotiation of meaning, or are they the truth about human affairs formulated from a distant vantage point? Critics have suggested that postmodern thought reproduces in another guise a characteristically modern view of the distance between self and world as well as modern pretensions to absolute freedom from hampering social and moral ties.

In addition, postmodernists sometime suggest that simply denying all metaphysical and moral universals frees us from tendencies toward dogmatism and domination. But where, then, would we find the conviction or character needed to keep from discarding our ideals of freedom and universal respect in favor of shallow diversions or a comforting new tyranny? How do we find the ethics and commitment necessary to defend the poor and to promote social justice? Postmodern theory leads us to believe that such ideals, when taken seriously, are dangerous illusions. Unfortunately, the social constructionist recommendation that we evaluate our moral beliefs and values in terms of their "pragmatic implications" severely clashes with what we seem to mean by genuine commitment or taking responsibility in everyday life. One wonders if constructionist thinkers have thoughtfully considered what it would mean, for example, to collapse the distinction entirely between feeling guilty merely from the fear of disapproval versus feeling remorse from violating one's authentic personal standards.

Foucault, as we mentioned, clearly sides at times with those who resist or refuse totalizing discourses. But Philip (1985) argued that without a conception of the human good, Foucault cannot explain either *why* people should struggle at all or what they should struggle *for*. Similarly, Taylor (1985) suggested that Foucault's analyses of power/dominion and disguise/illusion make sense only if some critical dimension or genuine goods are implicit in his own analysis. In fact, the denial of any such commitments by postmodern thinkers appears to be belied by their writings. Most oppose arbitrary authority and domination and suggest that it is more enlightened, mature, or wise not to be taken in by false absolutes and ethnocentric moral beliefs. Thus, in the end, it seems they advocate their own brand of wisdom and character ideal just like the rest of us, while denying any such commitments. As a result, critics worry that postmodernism encourages passivity or cynicism and thereby accelerates social atomization and personal malaise.

## Philosophical Hermeneutics

Hermeneutics, the "study of understanding," originated in the study of theological, philosophical, and legal texts. When applied to the social sciences, it attempts to "deal with the problem of meaning" (Wolff, 1991, pp. 187–188). In contrast to phenomenology or constructionism, it is primarily a theory or philosophy rather than a methodology that describes "how to go about the task of interpretation." Philosophical hermeneutics describes "the human phenomenon of interpretation itself." In addition, it encompasses a historical perspective and is able to analyze a broad range of micro and macro structures and processes. For example, hermeneutic analysis can be applied to an individual (as in psychoanalysis) or to a cultural or historical period (Wolff, 1991).

Contemporary philosophical hermeneutics offers a framework for social science, including critical social work, that attempts to go "beyond scientism and constructionism" (Gadamer, 1975, 1981; Guignon, 1991; Heidegger, 1962; Richardson & Fowers, 1994; Ricoeur, 1992; Taylor, 1989; Warnke, 1987). Hermeneutic thinkers agree with critics of postivistic science that we have no direct or immediate access to a "real" world or transcendent norms independent of our interpretation of things. Thus, claims to certain or absolute truths are simply additional interpretations that need to be grounded as well. According to hermeneutics, however, the typical postmodern attempt to get past modern representationalism is overly hasty and incomplete.

Guignon (1991, pp. 96ff.) suggested that when it becomes clear that we can have no direct access to "Nature as it is in itself," distinct from our interpretations, we may experience feelings of loss. This seems to dictate that we are merely "entangled in perspectives" or that "there is nothing outside the text." Paradoxically, though, this "picture of our predicament as cut off from reality makes sense only because of the way it contrasts with the binary opposition of self vs. world it is supposed to replace." Thus, this approach may confusedly perpetuate the very axioms of thought it is trying to replace!

Hermeneutic philosophy views representationalism and a subject–object ontology as more than just a philosophical mistake. It views it as one facet of the whole enterprise of modern emancipatory individualism with its problematic central ethical ideal of "freedom as self-autonomy . . . to be self-responsible, to rely on one's judgment, to find one's purpose in oneself" (Taylor, 1985, p. 7). Hermeneutic thought begins by rethinking ontology. To begin with, humans are "self-interpreting beings" (Taylor, 1985). The meanings they work out in the business of living makes them, to a great extent, what they are, not simply brute influences to be described by natural science. Moreover, individual lives are "always 'thrown' into a familiar life-world from which they draw their possibilities of self-interpretation. Our own life-stories only make sense against the backdrop of possible story-lines opened by our historical culture" (Guignon, 1991, p. 109).

Instead of thinking of the self as an object of any sort, hermeneutic thought follows Heidegger (1962, p. 426) in conceiving of human existence as a "happening" or a "becoming." This is similar to the view portrayed in humanistic psychology. Individual lives have a temporal and narrative structure. They are a kind of unfolding "movement" that is "stretched along between birth and death." In Guignon's (1993, p. 14) words, just as "events in a novel gain their meaning from what they seem to pointing to in the long run . . . so our past lives and our present activities gain their meaning from a (perhaps tacit) sense of where our lives are going as a totality."

In the hermeneutic view, a basic fact about humans is that they care about whether their lives make sense and what their lives are amounting to. Therefore, they have always taken some stand on their lives by seizing on certain roles, traits, and values. Indeed, they "just are the stands they take in living out their lives" (Guignon & Pereboom, 1995, p. 189). This means that humans do not simply desire particular outcomes or satisfactions in living, but rather, they always make "strong evaluations" (Taylor, 1985, p. 3). Even if only tacitly or unconsciously, they evaluate the quality of their desires and motivations and the worth of the ends they seek in terms of how they fit in with their overall sense of a worthwhile or decent life. According to Taylor (1989, pp. 25ff.), frameworks mapped by strong evaluations are inescapably part of human agency or social life.

From the perspective of hermeneutics, this means we are always insiders with respect to some deep, defining set of commitments and identifications, even though their content varies greatly across cultures. In contrast to positivists and postmodernists who believe it is appropriate to try to step outside or distance ourselves as much as possible from historical entanglements, hermeneutic thinkers think this is not only impossible but also somewhat inauthentic. The only sort of human agency we can imagine takes place according to a "logic of question and answer" (Gadamer, 1975, p. 333) within a "space of questions" (Taylor, 1989, p. 26) taken for granted by our culture or elaborated by us in some way.

Outside that dialectic or disengaged from it, we would not gain a better grip on who we are but would simply not know what meanings things have for us on basic matters; this would likely incur a frightening kind of dissociation. Although we can and should profoundly criticize various norms and practices, it is important to recognize that we always critique them on the basis of other taken-for-granted commitments or moral insights from our traditions. Our various cultural and moral traditions are rich resources for such critique. The common view of them as stable, monolithic authorities seems to be a somewhat narrow, prejudiced outgrowth of the perhaps one-sided antiauthoritarianism and antitraditionalism of the Enlightenment. In fact, our actual traditions essentially seem to be multivocal, interminably noisy debates rather than static sets of rules (Fowers & Richardson, 1996).

Interestingly, it seems that positivists, phenomenologists, and postmodernists alike recommend a fairly extensive disengagement from all tradition and authority in a way that, in the hermeneutic view, seems misguided and self-defeating. For example, the position of many postmodernists that detached irony and play are the most appropriate stance toward life seems to perpetuate, rather than overcome, much of the giddy individualism of modern culture. This includes Foucault's view of life as a purely aesthetic self-creation. In trying to think through these issues on freedom and belonging, we have found it helpful to recall Erich Fromm's penetrating analysis of what he termed the profound ambiguity of our modern ideals of freedom.

Fromm, a psychoanalyst who departed from Freudian thought by emphasizing the effect of social and cultural factors on behavior, argued that we suffer from a lag between "freedom from" and "freedom to" (1941/1967, pp. 48–53). He saw this as a "disproportion between the freedom *from* any tie and the lack of possibilities for the positive realization of freedom and individuality." According to Fromm (1947/1975, pp. 75ff.), the "modern market is no longer a meeting place but a mechanism characterized by abstract and impersonal demand." Commodities no longer have "use value" defined by shared community standards and, instead, have only an "exchange value" determined by impersonal market demand and shallow or transient desires. From this, a widespread "personality market" develops in which both professionals and laborers depend on a capricious kind of personal acceptance for their material survival and success, rather than on traditional use value or ethical qualities. Increasingly, people experience themselves as both a commodity to be sold and the seller of it. Thus, "self-esteem depends on conditions beyond [one's] control." The result is "shaky self-esteem," a "constant need of confirmation by others," and feelings of "depersonalization, emptiness, and meaninglessness." With these words, Fromm anticipated today's condition that has been dubbed the "culture of narcissism" (Lasch, 1979).

In addition, Fromm (1947/1975, p. 80) noted that in a society like ours, relationships among people become superficial because it is not really they themselves but themselves viewed as interchangeable commodities that are related. Many seek "depth and intensity of individual love" as a cure for this superficiality and alienation. Unfortunately, however, "love for one person and love for one's neighbor are indivisible; in any given culture, love relationships are only a more intense expression of the relatedness to [others] prevalent in that culture. Hence, it is an illusion to expect that the loneliness . . . rooted in the marketing orientation can be cured by individual love." In the marketing orientation, self-esteem is never secure and one cannot ever get enough acceptance from others. As a result, lasting, satisfying ties of love and friendship become enormously difficult. Hermeneutic thinkers, to use Fromm's terminology, believe that we should ask what freedom is "to" or "for" as well as "from," and that we need to avoid social science and theory that prevents us from addressing this question.

Positivism reflects virtues of healthy skepticism and criticism of merely conventional beliefs. Phenomenology and descriptivist approaches generally restore a sense of life's richness, variety, and deeply emotional character. And postmodern thought, at its best, begins to restore a needed sense of the cultural embeddedness and historical belonging of human life and living. But they all, in the hermeneutic view, preserve a healthy dose of the sharp separateness and detachment of the individual self that modern thought believes to be necessary for human freedom and moral autonomy. This, however, may also be a virtual recipe for emotional isolation and emptiness. Hermeneutic thinkers wonder if these approaches, along with their valuable stress on freedom and healthy skepticism, do not also represent, in part, a flight from life's inevitable risks and responsibilities; it is as if by extreme detachment we could defend or protect ourselves from uncertainty, mistakes, disappointments, and tragedy.

According to hermeneutic thinkers, our moral and political judgments are always tied to specific cultural contexts and issues and, thus, can never be final or certain. There is, however, no reason to think that all moral values are ultimately relative or invalid. In place of the modern "quest for certainty" and a one-sided ethics of "freedom from," hermeneutics advocates the process of hermeneutic dialogue, which parallels what social constructionists refer to as the ongoing negotiation of cultural meanings (Taylor, 1989, 1991; Warnke, 1987, pp. 100ff.).

Hans-Georg Gadamer, a pivotal hermeneutic thinker, referred to this dialogue or interplay of interpretations as a "fusion of horizons." He stressed the essentially dialogic nature of understanding.

From his perspective, the writing of history, the interpretation of a text, much philosophical argument, appreciation of a work of art, political debate, much social science, and psychotherapeutic conversation are best thought of as basically more or less genuine conversations aimed at a shared understanding of some subject matter of practical or existential significance. Although we may only agree to disagree, we often arrive at a reflective and critical integration of views in which the understanding of self and world is transformed. For example, both the meaning of the American Revolution and one's lived understanding of freedom continue to be modified in the dialogue between them. Historical experience changes the meaning events can have for us, not because it alters our view of an essentially independent object, but because history is a dialectical process in which both the object and our knowledge of it are continually transformed. We are immersed in and deeply connected to this process. Thus, moral and political reflection and debate, psychotherapeutic deliberations, and the much less conscious choices and influences of everyday life grow out of a certain kind of dynamic interplay between self and other and between present and past.

In this view, serious moral and political commitments actually encourage us to be as open as possible to challenges and possible insights from others or the past. They motivate us to be open because we want to get things right. And they give us the sense of self needed to withstand uncertainty and doubt. In turn, openness and the constant testing of our beliefs and values against new circumstances and unforeseen challenges deepen our understanding and refine our commitments. However, we can always defensively or dishonestly distort this process, and there is no sure-fire method or social arrangement of checks and balance that can prevent this from happening. But this kind of hermeneutic ontology or general sketch of dialogue and interpretation might help us avoid the extremes of utopian ambition and resigned defeat in modern life. In the hermeneutic view, social science and theory are a "form of practice" (Richardson & Christopher, 1993; Taylor, 1985). They are ethics and politics by other means and an extension of our search for justice, love, and wisdom in practical life.

## CONTEMPORARY ISSUES

Several cultural trends may be responsible for the current proliferation of and return to interpretive, phenomenological, and social constructionist theories. Multiculturalism, feminist thought, and the information industry likely play a part in current cultural practices that lead people to see the inevitability of multiple realities and relativistic moral beliefs (Franklin, 1995). There has also been an increased concern for the cultural basis for psychology, as evidenced in writings such as Cushman's consumer-oriented "empty self" (1995), K. J. Gergen's information overloaded "saturated self" (1994), and Lifton's "protean self" (1993). All express an interest in how history and culture shape the psychology of individuals.

In the past 25–30 years, in particular, there has been an overall social critique of empiricism and science that has left intellectuals more skeptical of progress and science. Embedded in these cultural metaphors is a lack of belief in absolutes and a relativistic view that could be interpreted as portraying groundlessness or even hopelessness. This has led some intellectuals and philosophers to seek answers in social theories such as postmodernism and social constructionism. Yet, due to the limitations of these theories, questions are left unanswered and, ultimately, neither postmodernism nor social constructionism can adequately address many of our contemporary cultural and social concerns. The ongoing debate between those who embrace positivism and those who embrace constructivist thought has intensified with the recent move toward evidence-based practice. We expect that this debate will continue unresolved because of the basic epistemological differences between the two schools of thought.

# APPLICATION TO SOCIAL WORK PRACTICE

As early as the 1970s, phenomenological thought, as expressed in existential psychology, Gestalt psychology, and humanistic therapies such as Rogerian client-centered practice, drew some adherents from social work. Macro applications of phenomenology and constructionism, predictably, received little or no attention. In recent years, however, social work and other helping professions have experienced a resurgence of interest in the theories covered in this chapter. This has led to many critiques of and innovations in social work thinking and practice (Witkin & Saleebey, 2007).

Practice approaches based on the ideas embedded in postmodernism and social constructionism have become especially popular (Brower & Nurius, 1993; Cushman, 1990; Franklin, 1995; Franklin & Nurius, 1996). One of the most widely used practice frameworks to emerge from this is the strengths perspective and related strengths model of case management (Rapp & Goscha, 2006; Saleebey, 2009). The strengths perspective has cross-fertilized with many of the practice approaches mentioned later as well as empowerment practice (see Chapter 4) that emphasize discovery and expansion of clients' and communities' strengths, capacities, and resources; recognition of challenges and oppression without defining people merely as victims, sick, pathological, or problematic; collaborative helping relationship; focus on solutions and creative possibilities; encouraging clients to narrate and reconstruct their life stories; and deconstructing taken-for-granted assumptions about the nature of people and societies.

Finn and Jacobson (2003, 2007) have suggested that social justice work adopt a broader theory base that includes postmodernism among its critical theories. Although hermeneutics has not yet been embraced to the same degree, this may be the next trend, in that it may offer a way to address the hopeless relativism that is found in postmodern and constructionist thought (Franklin, 1995). With its roots in phenomenology and interpretive sociology, constructionist ideas are being applied to clinical social work practice under labels such as the strengths perspective, social constructionism, constructivism, narrative, and postmodernist practice (Franklin, 1995; Franklin & Nurius, 1996).

## Definition of the Helping Situation

The theories discussed here propose that people are interpretive beings who give meaning to their experiences and lives. These meanings, however, are not neutral, and have real effects on the lived experience. In addition, the sociocultural context plays a large role in shaping our common, everyday assumptions and behaviors, despite the fact that we are rarely consciously aware of this. Despite this, people are seen as having the capacity to shape their own lives. Thus, they are seen as creative, adaptive, and with the ability to be self-transforming. The helping situation is client centered and involves "growth" or the alleviation of "problems" that are a result of beliefs and interpretations that restrain a person from achieving his or her full potential. Flowchart 11.1 demonstrates an application of phenomenological, constructionist, postmodern, and hermeneutic thought derived from these definitions.

## Assessment, Practice Strategies, and Methods

As models for assessment, the theories discussed here make us aware of the importance of subjective experience as it is lived in everyday life. Similar to symbolic interaction, the client's view of self, others, and the interpretive meanings assigned to people and events are central to assessment. In addition, subjective, autobiographical accounts of the client's own history take primacy

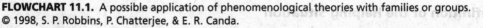

**FLOWCHART 11.1.** A possible application of phenomenological theories with families or groups.
© 1998, S. P. Robbins, P. Chatterjee, & E. R. Canda.

over psychological tests, prior case records, or accounts by significant others. Rather than seeking ultimate, "objective" truths, a person's history is seen in a reconstructive manner. Thus, practitioners use the client's narrative (the stories the client tells us) and a cultural framework as a basis for assessment and treatment.

The theories discussed in this chapter lend themselves to direct service methods with individuals, small groups, and families, as seen in a wide variety of therapeutic methods that have proliferated in the helping professions (Epstein & White, 1991; Franklin & Nurius, 1996; Gergen & McKaye, 1992; Ivey & Gonçalves, 1988; Mahoney, 1991; G. J. Neimeyer & Neimeyer, 1990; Polkinghorne, 1988). In particular, constructionism and postmodernism are used widely in cognitive-behavior therapies and family therapies (Berlin, 1996; Brower, 1996; Brower & Nurius, 1993; Dougher, 1993; Ellis, 1989, cited in Franklin & Nurius, 1996; Franklin, 1995; Granvold, 1996; Mahoney, 1991; Meichenbaum & Fitzpatrick, 1993; R. A. Neimeyer & Stewart, 1996).

Writers contributing to the social constructionist movement in family therapy include Lynn Hoffman (1990), Michael White and David Epson (1990), Harlene Anderson and

Harry Goolishian (1988), Tom Andersen (1991), Insoo Kim Berg (1994, 1996), Steve de Shazer (1991, 1994), and Jill Freedman and Gene Coombs (1996). To describe all the ideas of these authors is beyond the scope of this chapter, but we briefly highlight some of the practice strategies and methods of narrative practice developed by Michael White and collaborators and solution-focused therapy developed by Steve de Shazer and Insoo Kim Berg. Although these are distinct practice approaches, both the narrative and the solution-focused models follow assumptions based on phenomenological and constructionist thought.

Narrative therapy emphasizes storytelling, followed by a series of purposeful questioning techniques, reflections, and probing aimed at introducing new ideas and elucidating parts of the client's story not previously emphasized (M. White, 1993, 1994).

Some commonly used techniques in narrative practice include deconstructive listening (listening for other possible meanings); deconstructive questioning (to help clients see how stories are constructed); questioning assumptions and beliefs (to bring forth problematic beliefs, practices, feelings, and attitudes); building on coping abilities and strengths; understanding internalized conversations (to help clients reframe their experiences into a positive light to find new stories that are more empowering to tell); externalizing the problem (to increase the client's personal agency); constructing unique outcomes (to determine the times when the problems do not occur); and tracking contextual influences (to help clients see how social relationships and other influences facilitate and maintain their problems).

Solution-focused therapy is a strengths-based, behavioral, and goal-directed model that was originally developed at the Brief Family Therapy Center in Milwaukee by Steve de Shazer (1985, 1988, 1991, 1994; de Shazer et al., 1986), Insoo Kim Berg (1994; Berg & DeJong, 1996; Berg & Miller, 1992), and associates (e.g., S. D. Miller, Hubble, & Duncan, 1996; Walter & Peller, 1992). Aligned with social construction theory, it emphasizes how language is used to construct reality. This model is being applied to a wide variety of clinical problems and fields of practice such as in-patient psychiatric disorders (Webster, Vaughn, & Martinez, 1994), alcohol abuse (Berg & Miller, 1992), school-related behavior problems (Metcalf, 1995), crisis-oriented youth services (Franklin, Corcoran, Nowicki, & Streeter, 1997; Franklin, Nowicki, Trapp, Schwab, & Peterson, 1993), sexual abuse (Dolan, 1991), and spouse abuse (Sirles, Lipchik, & Kowalski, 1993, cited in Franklin & Biever, 1996).

Solution-focused therapy is unique and differentiates itself from prescriptive approaches because of its emphasis on process and future behaviors that will help clients accomplish their goals. The primary focus is to help clients construct a set of behavioral tasks that lead to a rapid solution. Consistent with social construction theory, it also addresses how clients talk about their problems and interact with others around the problem. Thus, solution-focused therapists seek to shift conversations, meanings, and relationship patterns into a state of solution, so that all people involved believe and act as if the problem is solved (Franklin & Biever, 1996).

Strategies of solution-focused therapy include tracking solution behaviors, reinforcing the times when the problem is absent and complimenting and attending to small differences in behavioral change, starting from the clients' cognitive frame and working with their meanings to construct solutions to accomplish their goals, focusing on the future instead of the present or the past, and using presuppositional language to help clients restructure meanings about themselves and their problems (Franklin & Biever, 1996). Solution-focused therapists use a wide variety of methods to help clients achieve change. A fuller discussion of these methods and strategies can be found in Franklin and Biever.

Table 11.2 illustrates a variety of settings and applications of phenomenology, social constructionism, postmodernism, and hermeneutics.

| TABLE 11.2 | Various Settings and Applications of Phenomenological Theories | | | |
|---|---|---|---|---|
| Type of Agency | Type of Presenting Problem(s) | Type of Program | Definition(s) of the Helping Situation | Type(s) of Activities |
| Mental health center/private practice | Reevaluating career goals | Vocational counseling | Growth | Narrative therapy; self-reflective journaling; exploring new career options. |
| University-based mental health services | Student anxious over coming out as gay | Student counseling | Crisis Growth | Individual counseling; exploring personal and social beliefs about sexual orientation; referral to gay/lesbian student union. |
| Family services center | Conflict over family roles and rules | Family therapy | Problem Growth | Narrative family dialogue; deconstruction of family patterns; reconstruction of new patterns. |
| City task force on cultural diversity | Racist stereotypes in local business advertising | Community education and outreach | Problem Social issue | Antiracist education and publicity; advocacy with chamber of commerce and businesses; dialogue groups; diversity celebrations. |

## CRITICAL ANALYSIS

### Biological, Psychological, and Spiritual Factors

The theories discussed here pay little attention to the biological basis for behavior. They focus instead on the interpretive process that takes place within the theoretical construct of "mind" and emphasize the way in which culture and society become taken-for-granted realities in our everyday behavior. Although cognitive processes are central, there is little specification of the biological basis of these processes. Hermeneutics sees all human processes as being embodied and a part of human experience, but the focus is not on physiological processes such as neurochemical transmission or the relationship between brain function and behavior. All phenomenologically based theories propose that human behavior can be understood only through the complexity of one's experience.

Phenomenology and social constructionism can also be criticized for ignoring or discounting psychological structures and processes. Schutz totally rejected the study of psychological processes, which he saw as idiosyncratic and unpredictable. Similarly, P. L. Berger and Luckmann (1967) portrayed psychological phenomena as being a social construction of mind but failed to adequately describe the psychological processes involved. They focused, instead, on the social-relational aspects of experience that shape one's cognitions and constructions. In fact, social constructionism has served as a critical voice of modern psychology (K. J. Gergen, 1982). In general, the psychological processes of perception and interpretation are seen in terms of social processes involving socialization.

Phenomenology, social constructionism, and hermeneutics have more to offer regarding spirituality. Each is open to spirituality as a part of human existence and encourages the acceptance and understanding of religious beliefs. In addition, each has a rich spiritual heritage. Phenomenology developed in response to religious and philosophical viewpoints. Peter Berger's primary area was the sociology of religion, which may explain his emphasis on the socialization of prevailing belief systems that are embedded in social institutions. Hermeneutics developed as a method to address the interpretation of religious texts such as the Bible. Practice methods stemming from these theories encourage spiritual exploration and believe in the creative and spiritual capacity of the human being. Insoo Kim Berg (1996), for example, has proposed that the solution-focused therapy is a deeply spiritual approach. Antidogmatism and extreme forms of moral relativism, however, might conflict with some traditional religions as well as the quest for deep spiritual insights, transpersonal modes of consciousness, and standards for universal human rights that include yet transcend particular personal, religious, cultural, and social standpoint–based views (Wilber, 1998, 2000a).

## Social, Cultural, and Economic Forces

Central to a phenomenological understanding of the complexity of human experience is the idea that social, cultural, and economic forces shape us in ways that we are not aware of. It is through the process of socialization that we internalize the prevailing norms of our culture, our society, and our economic system. Although phenomenological and constructionist thought call into question the supposed "objective" reality of such forces, the focus of attention is on the way in which people construct and organize their own world. These theories primarily emphasize the social and relational basis of behavior rather than larger social forces. In contrast, hermeneutics explicitly draws our attention to the way in which social, cultural, and historical forces shape consciousness.

## Relevance to Individuals, Groups, Families, Organizations, Institutions, and Communities

Due to the diverse nature of the theories discussed here, they can be applied at both the micro and macro levels. Although microphenomenology primarily addresses individual consciousness and cognitive processes, Orleans (1991) has pointed out that macrophenomenology can be used to examine large-scale organizations and institutions in a similar but more complex manner. Likewise, social constructionism can be applied to all systems levels, despite its initial macro focus. As previously discussed, hermeneutics, by design, is capable of analyzing both large- and small-scale phenomena.

# CONSISTENCY WITH SOCIAL WORK VALUES AND ETHICS

Numerous aspects of phenomenology, postmodernism, and social constructionism are consistent with social work values and ethics. For example, such theories give preeminence to the client's experience and self-determination and give highest respect to the dignity and worth of individuals and their plight in the world. In addition, because of the emphasis on social constructions, practice theories from these traditions underscore that humans are the architects of their destiny and, therefore, give the highest emphasis possible to the social work ethics of social responsibility. Thus, phenomenological and constructivist thought clearly supports the strengths perspective and client health and well-being.

Most phenomenological theory, however, does not promote social change or social justice (Orleans, 1991), However, practice models such as Michael White's emphasize social justice and the need for changes in broader social institutions and beliefs. According to M. White (1993, 1994), the context of social work practice does not have a privileged location outside of the culture at large and, therefore, is not exempt from the structures and ideology of the dominant culture. The practice context, therefore, is not exempt from the politics of gender, heterosexism, class, race, and culture. Nor is practice free from the politics associated with the hierarchies of knowledge and the politics of marginalization. White borrowed from Foucault in proposing that our clients are in a marginalized position and must be helped to develop new narratives that counter their current stories of oppression.

The relativistic stance of social constructionism, however, poses a problem because it leaves us without a basis for our work. Because, as an underlying premise, social construction-ism rejects objective moral authority and expertise, social workers are left with little basis for the helping relationship. Who decides, and on what basis, that one viewpoint is superior to another? Who determines what is responsible and what is not responsible behavior? Questions such as these remain to be answered and social constructionists have not yet developed a good reply. Such questions imply some type of moral judgment; thus, relativistic theories based on the primacy of subjective consciousness contradict themselves if they try to impose a set of rules for conduct.

Value conflicts also exist between social work practice and direct interpretations of some forms of postmodernism, especially those of a more skeptical rather than affirmative orientation. Historically, social work has emphasized social engineering in one form or another. We are interventionist to the core even if our interventions are couched in language of collaboration with oppressed groups. Some forms of postmodernism, however, suggest that all forms of intervention are wrong. It is not yet clear how these beliefs connect with our tradition, history, and mission to "enhance the social functioning of people." These theories raise challenging questions about the consistency of their tenets with social work values.

## PHILOSOPHICAL UNDERPINNINGS

Perhaps one of the most basic philosophical strains that underlies phenomenology and constructivist thought is philosopher Rene Descartes' proposal that we should "doubt everything except that one was doubting" (Martindale, 1988, p. 544). This is clearly portrayed in his famous statement "I think therefore I am." He held that to explain the world of human beings with certainty, everything should be doubted until self-evident premises could be revealed. Then, reinterpretation would yield truths about the nature of humans and their world (Martindale, 1988).

In addition, Plato's philosophical theory on the importance of ideas, as later embodied in the German epistemology of Kant and Hegel, is seen in the centrality of the processes of the mind and understanding in phenomenological thought. As Etzkowitz and Glassman (1991, p. 25) have noted, "German epistemology came to be called *phenomenology*."

Sharing the same constructionist philosophy as symbolic interaction, phenomenological thought views human behavior as rational, active, creative, and purposeful. All theories discussed here reject the idea of a totally objective reality and point, instead, to the social construction of norms, values, and meanings that people assign to both large- and small-scale social phenomena.

## METHODOLOGICAL ISSUES AND EMPIRICAL SUPPORT

Phenomenology and its related theories eschew positivism and traditional scientific methods. Instead, they propose that a full understanding of the complexity of human behavior can only be gained from alternative methods based on the constructionist paradigm. Their heavily constructionist orientation is based on an epistemological conviction that science can never be objective and value-free.

As previously discussed, ethnomethodology, in the field of sociology, has produced a variety of fascinating studies that support the constructivist paradigm. An additional research basis for constructionism can be found within the psychological sciences (Mahoney, 1995). This includes a broad and diverse array of studies on cognitive and social structures and processes such as memory (Brower & Nurius, 1993); social cognition (Fiske & Taylor, 1991); evolutionary epistemology (Mahoney, 1991); ecological psychology (Greenberg & Pascual-Leone, 1995); narrative psychology (van den Broek & Thurlow, 1991); new social cognitive, applied developmental, and learning theories (Aldridge, 1993; Bandura, 1989; Prawat, 1993); and complexity systems theory (Mahoney, 1995; Warren, Franklin, & Streeter, 1996).

Other studies provide support for many of the tenets discussed in constructivist therapies. Brower and Nurius (1993), for example, reviewed empirical research from cognitive, personality, and social psychology, as well as ecological psychology, and described the importance of the constructionist perspectives (cited in Franklin & Nurius, 1996, p. 2).

Martin further described the socially embedded nature of cognition and the fact that all acts in a social context lend themselves to multiple interpretations and differing outcomes. Studies by Martin, Cummings, and Hallberg (1992) and Martin, Martin, and Slemon (1989) have yielded results consistent with the constructive nature of social situations and cognition (cited in Franklin & Nurius, 1996).

Most of the research that demonstrates the empirical basis of social constructionism is theoretical and comes from ethnomethodology, experimental social and personality psychology, or process research on cognition and psychotherapy. Only recently have practitioners given attention to the evaluation of practice approaches such as the narrative or solution-focused therapy discussed in this chapter. Not surprisingly, there has been a lack of interest in the use of quantitative methods. For reasons discussed earlier, constructionist practitioners prefer qualitative methods such as case studies, ethnography, and discourse analysis (Franklin & Jordan, 1995; Jordan & Franklin, 2003). For this reason, narrative practice has few quantitatively based outcome studies. David Besa (1994), however, performed a series of single case experiments using a multiple baseline design and demonstrated the efficacy of narrative therapy with six families experiencing parent–child conflict. In this research, he showed the effectiveness of techniques such as externalizing the problem.

Franklin and colleagues (1997) have demonstrated several quantitative methods for evaluating the effectiveness of solution-focused therapy and illustrated how to use these methods within an agency serving homeless and runaway youth. At present, however, few outcome studies have been conducted on solution-focused therapy. Existing studies show the model to be a promising approach that deserves further evaluation (De Jong & Hopwood, 1996; Kiser, 1988; Kiser & Nunnally, 1990). See Berg and DeJong (1996) and McKeel (1996, cited in Franklin & Biever, 1996) for reviews.

The theories discussed here are more useful for explanation than prediction and are better at a probabilistic level of explanation than at a deterministic level. In addition, they are adequately suited for explaining properties of both individuals and groups. These theories propose an interconnection between consciousness, cognitive processes, the individual, and larger social and cultural structures. However, with the exception of hermeneutics, they are most often used to explain behavior at the individual and small group levels. They can, however, be used for analysis of larger-scale organizational and institutional structures.

## Summary

Phenomenology, social constructionism, postmodernism, and hermeneutics provide an important perspective on the interpretive process and socially constructed aspects of human experience. Similar to symbolic interaction, the dual foci on the interpretive process and social context will likely appeal to those interested in both the internal and external realms of experience.

Social constructionists have provided the field with a disturbing attack on would-be scientific social science. However, the relativity inherent in constructionist and postmodern thought provides a challenge to practitioners who are called on to make judgments in the face of serious moral and ethical dilemmas. In addition, contemporary hermeneutic philosophy suggests an interpretive approach to understanding human action and social life that may allow us to close the gap between theory and practice.

# Behaviorism, Social Learning, and Exchange Theory

*Hard Changin'*
*To leave the past behind*
*Hard Changin'*
*Gonna take some time*
*Hard changes comin' down*
*Hard changes*
*Takin' higher ground*
*Love always comes around*
*Keep tryin' 'n' tryin'. . . . tryin' 'n' tryin' to change*
*God, it's hard to change.*

© Rex Foster, 1993, Sidestream Music (BMI) and
Rick Beresford, 1993, Mainsqueeze Music (BMI)

## BEHAVIORISM, SOCIAL LEARNING, AND EXCHANGE THEORIES

- focus our attention on observable behavior
- analyze external factors involved in learning
- examine how cognition and emotion mediate behavior
- explain human interaction in terms of the rewards and benefits
- assist us in formulating assessment and treatment plans for individuals and groups

This chapter was coauthored with James McDonell, PhD, Kimberly J. Strom-Gottfried, PhD, and David L. Burton, PhD. Updates and revisions for the second edition were written by Joanne Yaffe Kjosness, PhD.

Behaviorism focuses on learning and the way in which behavior is shaped by its antecedent conditions and consequences. In rejecting mentalistic constructs such as mind, consciousness, and other internal processes, behaviorism stresses the importance of studying observable behavior rather than phenomena that cannot be empirically verified. Social learning theory developed many years later as a reaction to behaviorism's failure to account for internal processes that affect human behavior. Social learning theory posits that learned behaviors are mediated by thoughts, expectations, and emotions and stresses the importance of observational learning or modeling. Exchange theory, which evolved from behavioral psychology, functional anthropology, and utilitarian economics, seeks to explain human interactions through the dynamics of rewards and benefits. Although there are a variety of theorists writing in this tradition, rational, purposive behavior is believed to underlie all exchange.

## BEHAVIORISM

### Historical Context

Behaviorism emerged in the early 1900s primarily through the work of John Watson (1924), Edward Thorndike (1931), and Ivan Pavlov (Gibbons, 1955), among others, and significantly influenced psychological thinking throughout much of the 20th century. Although behavioral theory has experienced a decline in popularity over the past 30 years, behavioral concepts have had a substantial influence on psychology, and the principles of behavioral learning have contributed greatly to the theories and technology of human change. Additionally, radical behaviorism, social learning theory, and an amalgamation of these theories, generally called *cognitive-behavioral* theory, continue to have utility in understanding human behavior (Kendall, 1993; Sheldon, 1995).

Behavioral theories may be classified in two categories: classical behaviorism, as exemplified by the work of John Watson, and neobehaviorism, as seen in the work of B. F. Skinner. Although behaviorism originally represented a shift away from nonobservable events (such as thoughts), social learning placed the internal processes of thought and perception back into behavioral formulations. Since then, a mesh of theories has created what is now termed *cognitive-behavioral* theories, which include aspects of behavioral, neobehavioral, and cognitive conceptualizations of human behavior. The terms *behavior theory* and *learning theory* have been used interchangeably, particularly in the formative years of the development of behaviorism, with certain theorists favoring one term over the other. Social learning theory, however, has moved beyond the purely behavioral perspective and has made substantial contributions to other theoretical areas, such as theories of motivation, attribution, and social cognition.

### Key Concepts

Behavioral theories are primarily interested in learning. Human beings are seen as having multiple processes of acquiring or changing behaviors. Two primary processes through which learning occurs are classical conditioning and operant conditioning. *Classical conditioning* emphasizes learning that occurs on the basis of association, when a naturally eliciting stimulus is paired with a neutral stimulus. *Operant conditioning*, in contrast, stresses the importance of reinforcement rather than association of one stimulus with another. A newly learned behavior may be called a *conditioned response*, *reflex*, or *habit*. Behavior may be motivated by a drive or need and is strengthened or weakened by *reinforcement* in the form of a *reward* or punishment. In social learning theories, behavior is learned through observation or *modeling* and is then shaped by internal cognitive processes prior to performance of learned behaviors. These and other related concepts are discussed in more detail here.

## Classical Behaviorism

John B. Watson is generally credited with the founding of behaviorism as a movement within psychology. Watson defined behaviorism as a natural science aimed at the prediction and control of human behavior and held that behavior could be shaped through the selection and application of appropriate stimuli. In a replication of Pavlov's earlier work on conditioned reflexes, Watson produced a conditioned reflex in an 11-month-old boy who was initially not afraid of a tame white rat (Corsini & Marsella, 1983). Watson showed that the child could be made to fear the rat by simultaneously pairing the sight of the rat with a stimulus that induced a fear response, in this case a loud noise made out of the child's sight. Thus, through *classical conditioning*, sight of the animal alone eventually elicited the same fear response as the noise (J. B. Watson, 1924).

The child came to *associate* fear of the noise with sight of the rat and, over time, the sight of the rat alone became sufficient to produce fear in the child. When responses to stimuli become connected and patterned over time through repetition, this forms a *habit*, which is a stimulus–response (S-R) set that has been conditioned. Watson saw this associational process as being reflexive in nature but did not give much credence to reinforcement as an element in habit formation. Rather, he believed that learning was a function of the immediacy of the relationship between stimulus and response. He further believed that psychopathology was the result of conditioned learning rather than internal conflicts of the id or unresolved Oedipal conflicts.

Watson carried his behavioral position to an extreme by claiming that given an opportunity to control the environment of children, he could raise children to become whatever he wished them to be. He advocated this premise in *Psychological Care of the Infant and Child* (1928), one of the first childcare books ever published. His position reflected an unadulterated behavioral perspective, which explicitly rejected the role of heredity and mentalism in determining human behavior. It also reflected a search for objective laws that govern learning in an attempt to rid psychology of subjectivism. In doing so, distinctions between humans and other species were effectively eliminated.

The S-R basis of Watson's position was first developed by the Russian physiologist Ivan Pavlov, whose theory of the conditioned reflex had a profound effect on psychology (Martindale, 1988). Pavlov showed that an environmental stimulus that was not initially sufficient to produce a response could be made sufficient by pairing it with a stimulus that already elicited the response. Through repetition, the neutral stimulus would come to produce the response on its own.

In his famous experiment with dogs, he placed an *unconditioned stimulus* (meat powder) on a dog's tongue. This produced an *unconditioned response* (salivation), because dogs normally salivate in the presence of food. During *repeated trials*, he paired a ringing bell with the meat powder and found that the bell alone eventually became a *conditioned stimulus* that caused a conditioned response (salivation when the bell was rung). Based on the early work of Watson and Pavlov, classical, or *respondent conditioning* (as it is alternately called), provided the theoretical and empirical basis for behavioral psychology.

In the process of his scientific study, Pavlov developed several other principles that have been applied repeatedly to many theories in this realm. Three commonly used principles are generalization, extinction, and spontaneous recovery. *Generalization* refers to the spilling over of the conditioned response to a stimulus that is similar, but not identical, to the conditioned stimulus. Thus, a bell with a slightly different pitch can elicit the conditioned response of salivation from the dog. *Extinction* of learning refers to a gradual decrease and eventual disappearance of a conditioned response when the conditioned and unconditioned stimuli are no longer paired. After some time, when meat powder is presented to the dog without any bell, the bell loses its ability to elicit salivation. However, if the original conditioning was given sufficient effort trials, *spontaneous recovery* of a response occurs as the conditioned reflex returns. For example, if, after extinction, the food is again paired with the bell, the dog quickly recovers the conditioned response and salivates to the bell alone.

Although Pavlov's work is not an encompassing behavioral theory, and some psychologists do not view him as a behavioral theorist, his work was tremendously influential in shaping the field of S-R psychology. In addition to his direct contribution of the conditioned reflex and its related laws, his legacy includes an emphasis on rigorous experimentation and the systematic collection of data.

A contemporary of Watson, Edward Thorndike independently proposed a theory of learning that similarly was built on the foundation of stimulus and response. He held that although human learning resulted from changes in the internal nature and behavior of people, the changes could only be known by their apparent, observable behavior. For Thorndike, behavior meant anything that humans do, "including thoughts and feelings as truly as movements . . . . (with) . . . no assumptions concerning the deeper nature of any of these" (1931, p. 4). Like Watson, Thorndike eschewed an emphasis on consciousness over observable behavior and rejected introspection in data collection; any activity internal to the person could only be discerned through overt behavior and then could only be known as behavior rather than as consciousness.

Despite this stance, Thorndike was concerned with inner responses and connections as well. He noted that situations could occur wholly in the mind, such as when one emotion or idea evokes another. To explain the more sophisticated skill acquisition and problem solving in humans, he proposed the notion of learning by ideas. He believed that failure to account for these phenomena reflected overzealous behaviorism. In addition, he argued that teaching a dog to salivate at the sound of a tone failed to meet the criteria for a behavioral theory, because the stimulus and response could not truly be said to belong together; rather, one simply followed the other in time. Thorndike also noted that there did not seem to be any reward for the animal that would result in a strong connection between stimulus and response. He believed that Pavlov demonstrated only the prototype of learning and, while valuable in its own right, it fell short of a true learning model. In his reformulation, Thorndike emphasized the role of *consequences* that could serve to strengthen or weaken the S-R connection. He proposed that some consequences could be "satisfyers" (a condition that may be actively sought), while others could be "annoyers" (which are actively avoided). Thus, learning could be "stamped in," or reinforced, by what Thorndike dubbed the "Law of Effect."

Thorndike's work was highly influential; his efforts to move beyond associational learning and conditioned reflexes and to account for behavioral consequences as well as highly complex cognitive processes represented a substantial leap forward for behavioral psychology. In a similar fashion, E. C. Tolman rejected Watson's extreme environmentalism and his concomitant dismissal of mentalism. Rather, he proposed that intervening variables such as expectations, purposes, and cognitions were critical factors in the S-R connection (Tolman, 1951). Many of these later formulations formed the basis for the development of both social learning theories and the neobehaviorist movement. Thorndike's ideas on the consequences of behavior predated the radical behavioral notion of reinforcement and were a central component of the seminal work of Clark Hull in the development of his social learning theory.

## Neobehaviorism

*Radical* or *operant behaviorism* represented an evolutionary extension of the classic behavioral line of thought (Catania, 1988; Skinner, 1974, 1988a, 1988b, 1988c, 1988d; Thyer, 1988). Maddi (1980) has suggested that radical behaviorism, which finds its contemporary expression in the work of B. F. Skinner, is derived more from Watson than from Pavlov. He noted that "what makes radical behaviorism radical is the unwillingness to make assumptions about the existence and importance of drives" and the position that "even the minimally mentalistic concept of habit is unnecessary for understanding" (p. 596).

**B. F. SKINNER**  Concerned with misconceptions about the behaviorist position, Harvard University research psychologist B. F. Skinner attempted to lay a clear foundation for analytic behaviorism. He acknowledged the role of innate endowment in behavioral development in an attempt to counter the claim that behaviorism disregards genetic determinism. Drawing on Darwin and other evolutionists, Skinner held that people are shaped by natural selection, a process through which individual characteristics are favored, or selected, in interaction with the environment. He posited that the drive to survive is a primary motivator and, through evolution, the characteristics that lead to success in the person–environment interaction are favored over those that are less successful. One relationship between behavior and environment concerns reflexes, historically taken to refer to physiological processes such as breathing. For Skinner, however, a reflex was only descriptive of behavior, not a causal explanation, and he believed that person–environment relations were too complex to be understood in reflexive terms.

Skinner believed the conditioned S-R response to be the simplest example of learned behavior, noting that people have evolved the capacity to make connections between environmental stimuli and behavior, drawing on reinforcement as a means of maintaining the behavior over time. In line with the S-R theorists, he held that the process of respondent conditioning was clearly linked to conditioned stimuli, and he concurred with the idea that some behaviors are learned this way.

However, he argued that a different strategy, that of *operant conditioning*, was necessary for people to deal effectively with new environments. In contrast to respondent conditioning, which focuses on the antecedents of behavior, operant conditioning is concerned with the consequences of behavior, what happens *after* the behavior occurs. In line with Thorndike's Law of Effect, he proposed that "Behavior is shaped and maintained by its consequences" (Skinner, 1965, 1972, p. 16). Things such as food, water, sexual contact, and escape from harm are crucial to survival and any behavior that brings these things about has survival value. These environmental factors may be said to be a consequence of the behavior rather than antecedent to it, and behavior with a survival consequence is likely to be repeated. Thus, the behavior is *strengthened by its consequence* and the consequence itself is the *reinforcer* for the behavior. For example, when a hungry person acts in a manner that brings about food, the behavior is reinforced by the food and is thus more likely to be repeated. In sum, when behavior results in a consequence that is reinforcing, it is more likely to occur again. Because *operants* do not depend on an antecedent stimulus, they are said to be emitted rather than elicited. The term *operant behavior* indicates that people operate on their environment to produce desired consequences (Corsini & Marsella, 1983).

The consequences of a response lead to either a strengthening or a weakening of that response. Consequences that increase the likelihood of the response are called *reinforcers*, while consequences that result in a decrease are called *punishers*. It should be noted that punishment is not the same as negative reinforcement because both positive and negative reinforcement leads to a strengthened response. A positive reinforcer is a specific consequence (such as food, money, or praise) that is *added* to the environment. A negative reinforcer is a consequence (such as shutting off a loud alarm clock or getting out of the rain by opening an umbrella) that is *removed from* the environment. In other words, to increase the likelihood that a behavior occurs again, *negative reinforcement* involves the removal of an aversive *stimulus*. In contrast, punishment is the application of an aversive *consequence* (such as a slap in the face) or the removal of a positive reinforcer (such as withholding television privileges) that is added to the environment to weaken the response.

Skinner identified two types of reinforcers for humans: primary reinforcers and secondary (or conditioned) reinforcers. *Primary reinforcers* are unconditioned stimuli like food, water, and warmth that do not require learning to be effective reinforcers. *Secondary reinforcers* are learned and developed through pairing with primary reinforcers. Secondary reinforcers such as money, attention, approval, and affection are extremely important in shaping human behavior. *Aversive stimuli*, like those applied in punishment, are also important, and when people learn to avoid an aversive stimulus, it is called *avoidance learning*.

Skinner also demonstrated the effect of various reinforcement schedules on the strength of a learned response. Responses can be reinforced either continuously or intermittently. In *continuous reinforcement,* reinforcement is delivered after every correct response. *Intermittent schedules* can be based on intervals or ratios and can be fixed or variable. In *fixed interval schedules*, a specific interval of time is identified (e.g., 1 minute), and the first correct response after that interval is reinforced. *Variable interval schedules* vary the amount of time between rewards for correct responses (e.g., from a few seconds to a few minutes) and have been found to produce learning that takes longer to extinguish than that which has been acquired through either continuous or fixed schedules of reinforcement. *Fixed ratio schedules* establish a specific frequency of reinforcement (e.g., every fifth correct response), whereas *variable ratio schedules* vary the frequency of rewards. Skinner also devised other complex reinforcement schedules to study their effect on learning. His rigorous research has shown that each of these different schedules has a different effect on the strength, maintenance, and weakening of the response through extinction.

Skinner's primary contribution to behaviorism was to reduce its dependency on antecedent conditions in explaining human behavior. Additionally, his emphasis on rigorous investigation through experimental analysis lent considerable credibility to his theory. Skinner's work was not, however, without considerable controversy. While acknowledging the importance of higher mental processes in determining behavior, he appeared to disregard the importance of cognition in learning of behavior. For Skinner, reasoning and logic were behaviors like any others that could be understood in terms of the schedules of reinforcement through which they were learned. Although this position may seem to be simplistic, Skinner argued that all behavior could be understood in the same way.

In his rather creative novel entitled *Walden Two* (1948/1976), Skinner described a fictional utopian culture based on behavioral principles, termed *behavioral engineering*, that were applied to behavior change and child rearing. Although Skinner did not believe in formal developmental stages, he did propose specific phases of environmental manipulation that corresponded to learning for different age levels. Essentially, he proposed that in the earliest years, a child's needs

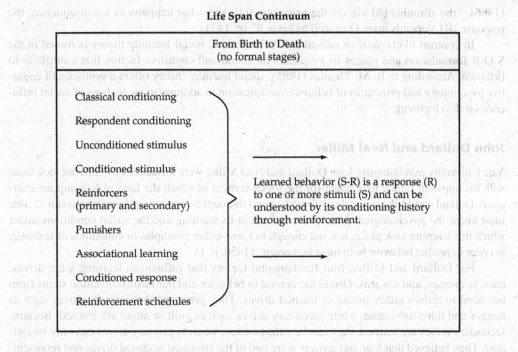

**FIGURE 12.1.** Key concepts in radical behaviorism.

should be quickly and completely fulfilled. Through behavioral engineering, the demands associated with normal life are then gradually introduced at a rate by which the child can master them. This type of controlled operant conditioning, he argued, would strengthen positive emotions such as love and joy, which he believed were critical to producing optimal development that would promote happiness and well-being (Skinner, 1948/1976; R. M. Thomas, 1985). However, due to his assertion that all behavior could be changed through such engineering, Skinner's work has received limited acceptance in mainstream psychology. Figure 12.1 illustrates the key concepts of Skinner's radical behaviorism.

## SOCIAL LEARNING THEORY

*Social learning theory* is the school of behavioral thought that has best combined internal and external processes. Drawing on the work of Pavlov, Watson, Thorndike, and others, Clark Hull (1943) proposed a theory of behavioral learning that influenced the development of the more formal social learning theories of N. E. Miller and Dollard (1941) and Bandura and Walters (1963). Adopting and adapting Thorndike's Law of Effect, Hull was primarily concerned with overt behavioral responses and conditions that serve as reinforcers. In addition, he posited that we can infer the existence of intervening variables such as ideas and emotions (and other internal processes that are not directly observable), as long as they are directly tied to observable input and output. For example, we can directly observe desired changes in a person's performance, but we must infer that learning (an internal cognitive process) has taken place (Hilgard & Bower, 1966).

The postulation of intervening variables based on internal processes led to a new behavioral formulation—one based on S-O-R rather than S-R. According to Hilgard and Bower

(1966), "the stimulus (S) affects the organism (O), and what happens as a consequence, the response (R), depends upon O as well as upon S" (p. 147).

In contrast to classical or radical S-R behaviorism, social learning theory is rooted in the S-O-R formulation and places its emphasis on social and cognitive factors that contribute to behavior. According to R. M. Thomas (1985), social learning theory offers a synthesis of cognitive psychology and principles of behavior modification in addition to an analysis of social influence on development.

## John Dollard and Neal Miller

Yale University psychologists John Dollard and Neal Miller were influenced by Hull but took issue with his apparent failure to account for the social context in which the laws of learning are exercised. Dollard and Miller noted that "To understand thoroughly any item of human behavior . . . one must know the psychological principles involved in its learning and the social conditions under which this learning took place. It is not enough to know either principles or conditions of learning; in order to predict behavior both must be known" (1950, p. 1).

For Dollard and Miller, four fundamental factors that influenced learning were drives, cues, responses, and rewards. *Drives* are central to behavior and our basic motivation stems from our need to reduce either innate or learned drives. They proposed that primary drives such as hunger and thirst are innate, while secondary drives such as guilt or anger are learned. Because secondary drives are learned, they can be extinguished, whereas primary drives can only be satiated. They believed that *fear* and *anxiety* were two of the strongest acquired drives and represented the societal reflection of pain; pain becomes satisfied through its expression as anxiety. Further, they proposed that acquired drives not only represent a conditioned response but also are capable of motivating new forms of behavior (Dollard & Miller, 1950). Drive reduction, according to Dollard and Miller, is the most important form of behavioral reinforcement (Ewen, 1988).

Because drive itself does not suggest the direction of the response, stimulus cues assist in focusing the behavioral response. For example, a person who is hungry (the drive) may go in quest of food by searching for a restaurant (the cue). A *cue* is an environmental stimulus that serves as a signal when a response is rewarded or not rewarded. The connection between *cues* and *responses* are strengthened when the response is *rewarded* either by drive reduction or through socially acquired rewards. When a response is not rewarded, it tends toward extinction, and another response is attempted. The process repeats until a response is rewarded and a connection is established between stimulus and response. On subsequent occasions, there is a tendency to repeat responses that have previously been rewarded.

Central to their social learning theory, and moving toward the S-O-R formulation, Dollard and Miller proposed that the higher mental processes of foresight, language, and reasoning are important factors that determine the individual's ability to engage in adaptive learning. Foresight suggests an ability to formulate a response, not on the basis of the immediacy of a stimulus, but rather on the knowledge of what is likely to happen in the future. Thus, people are able to anticipate environmental events and adjust their responses accordingly. Responses are strengthened when there is a correspondence between actual and anticipated events and when the response results in drive reduction.

They also stressed the role of language, not only as a product of social learning but also as a form of *self-speech* essential to the acquisition of reasoning. *Reasoning* is a type of self-speech that refers to the ability to make necessary connections among discrete stimuli, creating complexes of learning in which drives, cues, responses, and rewards are logically related in a patterned learning sequence. Responses are determined by both the anticipation of future stimuli and the ability to reason to select the most efficacious response.

Dollard and Miller were among the first to address the role of imitation and modeling in learning. Noting that imitation was central to psychological theory and, in particular, to reinforcement theories of social learning, they proposed three mechanisms that they believed to account for most forms of imitation. The first is *same behavior*, which denotes that any two people may respond in the same manner to the same stimulus. This does not necessarily imply any true imitation because the responses of the two people may be entirely independent of each other. Second is *copying*, in which a person learns to model his or her behavior on that of another. The central learning component in copying is the development of knowledge that the copied behavior is the same and that it is within the bounds of social acceptability to engage in copying. However, Dollard and Miller did not believe that either of these imitative forms warranted detailed analysis. Rather, it was the third form of imitation, that of *matched-dependent behavior*, which they found to be central to social life. Matched-dependent imitation occurs when a person attempts to match the behavior of someone else by depending on cues provided by the other person. For example, a physician may suggest lifestyle changes to a patient that will result in better health. The physician's superior knowledge of medicine and health-related issues strengthens the cue value of these suggestions (language stimuli) related to lifestyle changes. The patient, then, tries to follow the suggestions (response demands) by depending on the language cues to determine an appropriate response. Dollard and Miller held that matched-dependent behavior usually involves imitation of a person who holds a status superior position.

In their later writings, they attempted to recast Freudian concepts into behavioral terms, using the term *unconscious conflict* as a core concept. They proposed that unconscious conflict acquired in childhood could become a source of problems in adult life and account for growth patterns in childhood. Grounded in Freudian theory, they proposed four stressful childhood phases that may contribute to unconscious conflict through pathogenic learning: being fed as an infant (on demand or on a schedule, or not being fed properly at all), learning toilet habits and hygienic orientation, learning to manage aggressive impulses and anger, and learning to control sexual expression. However, in contrast to Freud who posited intrapsychic structures and energies as causal, Dollard and Miller viewed neurotic conflict originating in childhood as a form of *learned behavior* that is taught by parents.

Consistent with their behavioral reinterpretation of Freud, Miller and Dollard also postulated that aggressive behavior is a function of experiencing frustration; this is known today as the *frustration–aggression hypothesis*. They suggested that the expression of either aggressive or passive behavior is learned behavior stemming from unresolved anger, fear, or frustration experienced in infancy and early childhood. The need to reduce internal distress caused by these feelings leads the child to stop thinking about the events and issues that elicit such feelings. This is not problematic when it is done consciously. However, when thoughts are unconsciously repressed, they may lead to neurotic symptoms because they are not accessible and, thus, cannot lead to satisfactory resolution of the conflict. Despite this lack of resolution, Dollard and Miller (1950) pointed out that repression in itself is reinforcing, in that it reduces the fear drive.

In their reformulation of psychodynamic theory, Dollard and Miller rejected the metaphysical, abstract Freudian concepts relating to the id–ego–superego structure of the mind. Instead, they proposed that guilt is the result of unlabeled fear responses that became connected to childhood stimuli. When these stimuli recur in later years, the conditioned response (fear) is likewise elicited. Like all conditioned responses, fear can also be generalized to other stimuli that are similar but not identical. They also posited that unconscious repression in infancy and early childhood is due to the child's inability to use language. They proposed that the child's inability to label early conflicts automatically relegates it to the unconscious because, "What was not verbalized at the time cannot well be reported later" (Dollard & Miller, 1950, p. 136; Ewen, 1988). Although their reconceptualization of abstract Freudian concepts into behavioral concepts was widely praised, they never published further in this area. Further extension of their ideas, however, has led to methodological breakthroughs and application by others (Wachtel, 1977; Wolpe & Lazarus, 1966).

In sum, Dollard and Miller drew upon a range of previous theoretical work in developing a behavioral social learning model. Although most of their work represents a classic S-R paradigm, their unique contribution rests in their attempt to synthesize behaviorism and psychoanalysis in behavioral terms and their earlier propositions about social learning (Ewen, 1988). Consistent with earlier behaviorists, their emphasis on empirical rigor in the development of the tenets of social learning reinforced the strong scientific tradition within behavioral psychology.

## Albert Bandura and Social Cognitive Learning

In an early work with Richard Walters, Stanford University psychologist Albert Bandura (1963) took issue with previous learning theories because they relied on a limited number of explanatory principles and were generally derived from animal studies or studies involving one person. The neglect of complex social factors left theorists unable to fully account for the way in which novel social responses are learned. In contrast to Miller and Dollard, Bandura and Walters took exception to any reliance on psychodynamic principles, none of which had been subjected to rigorous scientific analysis. In addition, they were concerned with the emphasis within psychology that attempted to distinguish between normal and deviant development. Such distinctions, they argued, were based on value judgments and were of little theoretical significance. In behavioral theory, undesirable, nonnormative behavior represents a learned behavioral coping mechanism rather than a symptom of psychopathology and, thus, is best addressed through a systematic program of *behavior modification*. Based on principles of operant conditioning, consequences are manipulated so that desirable behavior is reinforced and, if necessary, undesirable behavior is punished. R. M. Thomas (1985) has noted that social learning theory "discourages the application of . . . psychiatric labels" due to its assertion that both prosocial and deviant behavior can be explained by the same set of learning principles (p. 410).

At the core of Bandura's social learning theory is a view of human behavior that shares in common many of the core assumptions underlying George Herbert Mead's symbolic interactionism and Jean Piaget's work on cognitive development: the belief that behavior is based on the interaction between internal and external influences and an appreciation of the role of symbolization in cognition. Bandura (1977, pp. 11–12) proposed that, "people are neither entirely determined by internal causes nor environmental stimuli, but psychological functioning is accounted for by a reciprocal interaction of personal and environmental determinants." This *reciprocal determinism* allows us to control our thoughts and our environments, which, in turn, affects what we do. In contrast to most behaviorally based theorists, he assigned a central role to internal factors such as expectations and thoughts.

In an extension of behaviorism, Bandura and Walters proposed that the central process in social learning was that of *imitation*. They held that "new responses may be learned or the characteristics of existing response hierarchies may be changed as a function of observing the behavior of others and its response consequences without the observer's performing any overt responses himself or receiving any direct reinforcement during the acquisition period" (1963, p. 47). This differs from Miller and Dollard's position in that the actual performance of behavior is not necessary for learning to occur, nor is it necessary for the response to be immediately rewarded. Instead, a person may learn a particular response through *observation* of a *model*. They proposed that after a response has been acquired, social forces begin to influence the learning process by shaping performance.

Bandura and Walters drew on research evidence to suggest three distinct effects of exposure to a model, each of which increases the observer's matching behaviors. First, a modeling effect may result in the transmission of a precisely *imitative response* pattern from model to observer. Here the matched response is novel to the observer, one not previously in the person's behavioral repertoire. They concluded that novel responses to a model are learned almost instantly and in their entirety rather than gradually.

Evidence for this has been found in studies on the acquisition of aggressive responses by children (Bandura, 1986b). In a series of experiments to compare the effects of aggressive and nonaggressive adult models on the aggressive behavior of preschool children, children were exposed to films of either a model who behaved aggressively toward an inflated doll or a model who sat quietly and ignored the doll and other objects in the room. Children who viewed aggressive models displayed more imitative aggressive responses when compared to either the nonaggressive model or the control group. Additionally, the experiments showed that filmed human aggression was as effective as a live model.

Second, the processes of *inhibitory* or *disinhibitory* effects may strengthen or weaken a previously learned response. That is, the model's behavior may suggest whether a previously learned response needs to be tempered. Here the response may not be precisely matched to that of a model but is rather an approximation of the model's behavior. Bandura and Walters cited studies showing that exposure to a cartoon character behaving aggressively resulted in an increase in children's aggression when compared to exposure to a neutral character.

Third, they found that observing a model might prompt a *previously acquired response*. Bandura and Walters noted that "An obvious eliciting effect may be observed in cases in which an adult, who has lost the idioms and pronunciation of the local dialect of the district in which he was raised, returns for a visit to his home. The original speech and pronunciation patterns, which would take a stranger years to acquire, may be quickly reinstated" (1963, p. 79). This is similar to Pavlov's earlier principle of spontaneous recovery, but the initial learning occurs through an observational process of modeling rather than through stimulus pairing.

In later work, Bandura (1977) further stressed the notion that social learning does not depend solely on trial-and-error testing under conditions of reward. Instead, learning occurs as a cognitive process, the symbolic representation of complex human behaviors developed from verbal information and observation of a model. Bandura noted that "from observing others, one forms an idea of how new behaviors are performed, and on later occasions this coded information serves as a guide for action. Because people can learn from example what to do, at least in approximate form, before performing any behavior, they are spared needless errors" (1977, p. 22). Thus, a *cognitive mediational process* allows for *vicarious learning* and corrections in behavioral learning before a behavior is actually performed.

In his most recent book, *Social Foundations of Thought and Action: A Social Cognitive Theory*, Bandura (1986a) offered greater detail and fuller explanation for his theory and specified additional cognitive mediational processes. He prefaced the text with an explanation that he would prefer the theory to be called *social cognitive theory* to emphasize that learning is not a model of conditioning, but of "knowledge acquisition through cognitive processing of information" (p. xii).

In delineating the cognitive and social factors that may affect the process of learning by observation, Bandura categorized the elements of this process into four process domains (1986a, p. 51): attention, retention, production, and motivation. For modeling to take place, the child must first *pay attention* to the relevant stimuli and screen out those that are not important to learning the observed behavior. Second, the process of *retention* is necessary so that the child can remember—either semantically or through visual imagination—the observed behavior. Bandura noted that young children imitate gestures and sounds immediately, whereas older children are better able to store symbols for later recall and reproduction. Consistent with Piaget and Mead, Bandura recognized the importance of language development in the child's ability to store and recall symbolic referents (1977). In this regard, he saw memory permanence as being a critical factor, because memories can fade, become vague, or disappear with time (1969). Memory techniques such as rehearsal, which involves review or practice, may aid the child in retention of observed behaviors. Third, the child must be able to produce the observed behavior. This involves getting the feel of behavioral enactment through repetition and correction, organizing each subskill into a response pattern that can be replicated. Muscular development is especially important in that the child's motor development must be advanced enough to imitate the observed behavior. Finally, *motivation* is necessary to sustain the efforts of these processes. In contrast to Skinner, Bandura believed that reward alone was not sufficient to produce motivation for continued imitation. Instead, he proposed that the child must value the anticipated consequences, rather than simply experience them. Thus, consequences help to regulate the child's behavior by making it possible to predict behavioral consequences and thus select the behaviors to be performed. Importantly, Bandura stressed that the child can learn which behaviors yield the greatest rewards either by observing others or by actually engaging in the behavior.

In early experimental studies, Bandura and Walters found that children are most likely to imitate models whom they regard as prestigious, who receive social recognition and monetary rewards, or who are perceived as similar to themselves and are those of their same gender (1963). Conversely, they tend not to imitate models who are punished for their actions (R. M. Thomas, 1985).

Bandura also proposed that *perceived self-efficacy*, an individual's subjective "conceptions of personal efficacy" is an important factor in regulating behavior. Particularly important are issues of confidence and self-doubt and the way in which they affect our actions. In essence, his research found that people who judge themselves as capable are likely to undertake tasks and challenges that they believe they can perform; they also avoid challenges that they perceive to be beyond their abilities. Self-efficacious people are also more likely to persist in the face of adversity. Bandura, however, did not see self-efficacy as a unitary concept and he believed that self-efficacy varies in different areas. Thus, a person can have high self-efficacy in, say, sports, but low self-efficacy in social situations. The concept of self-efficacy has been incorporated into empowerment theories, as we discussed in Chapter 4.

Bandura also noted that people regulate their behavior based on both external standards set by others and standards that they set for themselves. As people develop standards for themselves, they strive to meet these standards. In doing so, they are rewarded with *self-reinforcement* when these standards are met and are punished by self-imposed feelings such as guilt when self-standards are not met. Thus, to a large extent, behavior becomes self-governed and self-regulated. Although Bandura did not separate development into specific stages, he believed that as people progress toward maturity in cognitive and social growth, they gain increasing self-control over their behavior through self-reinforcement. They also become more able to shape their external environment in ways that they find self-rewarding (Maddi, 1980). In his later work, he also offered more theoretical structure for other cognitive processes such as the automatization of thoughts. These later efforts added more elaborate cognitive aspects to an already socially based conceptualization of human behavior and function.

Bandura (1982a) also recognized that random, chance events could significantly alter a person's life course. For example, chance encounters with previously unknown people can provide new opportunities to be drawn into highly profitable businesses and associations or, conversely, into illicit activities that can lead to detrimental consequences. Although self-efficacy may be an important factor in helping people avoid getting deeply ensconced in bad situations, Bandura noted that "the most important determinants of life paths often arise through the most trivial of circumstances" (p. 749). Figure 12.2 illustrates key concepts in social learning theory.

Bandura and his colleagues moved social learning theory beyond the paradigmatic S-R model, while at the same time they retained its most critical and salient features. The incorporation of cognitive processes as important factors that mediate learning was an affirmation of self-reflective thought and reasoning as key aspects of human development. Additionally, the fundamental rejection of psychodynamic theory, with its emphasis on abnormal behavior, represented a significant break in the development of personality theory. As a result of these efforts, social learning theory became established as a productive theoretical area in its own right, making significant contributions to further development and refinement of social psychological thinking as well as to the development of helping strategies.

For example, the theory of *learned helplessness* developed by Seligman and his colleagues (Abramson, Seligman, & Teasdale, 1978; Hiroto & Seligman, 1975; Seligman, 1975) represented

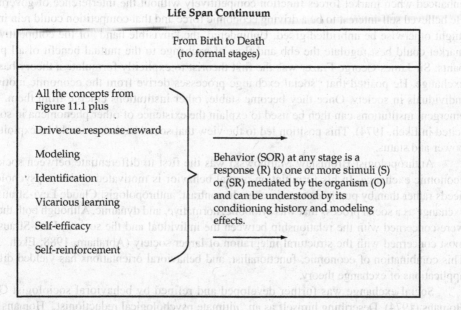

**Life Span Continuum**

From Birth to Death
(no formal stages)

All the concepts from
Figure 11.1 plus

Drive-cue-response-reward

Modeling

Identification

Vicarious learning

Self-efficacy

Self-reinforcement

Behavior (SOR) at any stage is a response (R) to one or more stimuli (S) or (SR) mediated by the organism (O) and can be understood by its conditioning history and modeling effects.

**FIGURE 12.2.** Key concepts in social learning.

an application of social learning theory to a specific area of human functioning. Seligman was intrigued by the experience of helplessness and its relationship to clinical problems. Drawing on a large body of experimental data, Seligman proposed a theory that integrated the motivational, cognitive, and emotional deficits that resulted from helplessness.

The core of the theory holds that when people are faced with outcomes over which they have no control, despite their efforts, they develop a sense of helplessness. For Seligman, this represented an extension of social learning theory, because people learn to become helpless when their efforts to control the outcome of given events meet with continued lack of success.

Seligman's theory of learned helplessness extended the behavioral tradition of drawing on research data derived from experimental studies. This theory also gained increased acceptance as an explanatory model for some forms of clinical depression. This raises interesting questions regarding the extent to which socially oppressive conditions such as racism or sexism may lead to learned helplessness, which may then lead to clinical depression.

Additionally, a conglomeration of theoretical approaches, now subsumed under the label "cognitive-behavioral," has been derived from the work of Bandura and the theorists preceding and following him. This term is now used to describe a variety of current counseling methods and educational practices as well as some innovative corporate personnel policies.

## EXCHANGE THEORY
### Historical Context

Exchange theory evolved from behavioral psychology, functional anthropology, and utilitarian economics as an attempt to explain human interactions through the dynamics of rewards and benefits. The origin of exchange as an economic process is generally attributed to Adam Smith whose 18th-century work, *The Wealth of Nations*, suggested that a nation's resources are enhanced when market forces function competitively without the interference of government. He believed self-interest to be a driving economic force and that competition could rein in what might otherwise be unbridled greed. Unhindered, the "invisible hand" of the competitive free market could best regulate the ebb and flow of exchange to the mutual benefit of all participants. Sir James George Frazer was the first theorist to explicitly formulate a theory based on exchange. He posited that "social exchange processes derive from the economic motives of individuals in society. Once they become stable, other institutions emerge from them. These emergent institutions can then be used to explain the existence of other phenomena in society" (cited in Ekeh, 1974). This position led to the view that social exchange could be exploited for power and status.

Anthropologist Bronislaw Malinowski was the first to differentiate between social and economic exchange. In his formulation, social behavior is motivated by basic psychological needs rather than by purely economic ones. In contrast, anthropologist Claude Levi-Strauss saw exchange as a social process that was symbolic, normative, and dynamic. Although both theorists were concerned with the relationship between the individual and the society, Levi-Strauss was most concerned with the structural integration of larger society (Abraham, 1988; Ekeh, 1974). This combination of economic, functionalist, and behavioral orientations has yielded different applications of exchange theory.

Social exchange was further developed and refined by behavioral sociologist George Homans (1974). Describing himself as an "ultimate psychological reductionist," Homans based his theory on animal models of operant conditioning rather than on symbolic human behavior. His propositions can be summarized as follows: (a) actions increase with rewards and decrease with punishment or absence of rewards, (b) actions are based on the perception of greater rewards, and (c) anger or pleasure result from the unexpected withholding or granting of rewards. Human behavior also involves "distributive justice," the idea that rewards and costs should be distributed fairly; the perception of being at an unfair disadvantage leads to anger. Homans based most of his propositions on the dyad (a group of two), although he believed that these principles were applicable to larger groups as well.

Using basic principles similar to Homans's, sociologist Peter Blau rejected Homans's reductionism and expanded exchange theory to include interactions with larger social systems. He also added consideration of power and social integration, and attempted to find a niche for it in systems theory, conflict theory, and symbolic interactionism.

Sociologist Richard Emerson and his frequent collaborator, Karen Cook, further expanded upon Homans's and Blau's works by developing an exchange analysis of networks and social structures based on a more structured, mathematical approach (1978). Emerson argued, however, that exchange theory is "not a theory at all. It is a frame of reference within which many theories—some micro and some macro—can speak to one another" (1976, p. 336). This is similar to the position that has been advanced about systems theory.

## Key Concepts

According to Abraham (1988), exchange theory applies not only to the process of social exchange "but also all other social relationships namely cooperation, competition, conflict and coercion" (p. 169). Its emphasis on purposive, goal-oriented human behavior covers many theoretical bases. At the heart of exchange is the notion of *profits*. Profits can consist of *benefits* (or *rewards*) less *costs* (or *punishments*). Rewards may be material (economic) or symbolic (such as attention, advice, or status). They are generally defined as things that either have value or bring satisfaction and gratification to the individual (Thibaut & Kelley, 1959, p. 12). Not surprisingly, it is sometimes difficult to predict what, specifically, will serve as a reward, because value may be different from one person to the next.

*Costs* can be considered in two ways—as *punishments* or as *rewards foregone* because a competing alternative was chosen (Nye, 1982, p. 15). Punishments may be physical or emotional and can be administered through the withholding of rewards. In both economic and social exchange, profits accrue when the rewards outweigh cost. *Satiation* or *diminished marginal utility* occurs when a reward has been received repeatedly and its ability to motivate becomes diminished. Conversely, *scarcity* (the less available something is) increases the value of the reward. *Power* is obtained by possessing a skill that is scarce or highly coveted. For example, within a dyad a person has power over another to the extent that one is dependent on the other for a specific outcome. Similarly, the *principle of least interest* suggests that the person who is less eager to preserve the relationship is the one to dominate it. This concept can be used to analyze dominance in the dating relationship, but it also has widespread application to other dyads and larger groups.

The *norm of reciprocity* refers to the expectation that if one receives a reward, the favor will be returned in some way, such as in the exchange of gifts. In contrast to Homans's concept of reciprocity, which assumed that people give something solely for the expectation of receiving something in return, sociologist Alvin Gouldner (1960) expanded his formulation of reciprocity to include the idea that people should not only help those who help them but also avoid hurting them as well. Gouldner believed that reciprocity serves to maintain and stabilize the interaction, keeps the threat of power differentials in check, and has applications to larger groups. Sociologist Marcel Mauss recognized that:

> social exchange processes yield for the larger society a moral code of behavior which acquires an independent existence outside the social exchange situation and which informs all social, economic, and political interpersonal relationships in society. *(cited in Ekeh, 1974, p. 58)*

The morality of social exchange helps to define and regulate exchange processes. This, combined with the norm of reciprocity, is seen as mediating people's natural tendency to act in their own self-interest. The rule of *distributive justice* is based on the idea that rewards should be proportional to their costs, and profits proportional to their investments (Simpson, 1972, p. 5). Investments can be either *achieved* or *ascribed*. Those that are achieved are earned on the basis of past activities or contributions, while ascribed investments are bestowed upon individuals or groups on the basis of some characteristics, such as race or gender. This concept has been used in exchange theory to explain why males, on the average, are paid more than females for the same type of work, or why Whites typically receive higher wages than Blacks or Hispanics. Although the investments of each may be the same, one group's investment is valued more highly because of its ascribed qualities. Clearly, not every person enters the exchange on equal footing.

The term *status* refers to the relative rank of individuals, and *status congruence* refers to the preference for participants to be of the same status. Because one's worth might be diminished by interacting with lower-status people, exchange between people of ranks is discouraged and status congruence is maintained when people of the same level interact; this pairing is believed to be the most comfortable exchange for all parties. Theorists disagree about the extent to which exchanges are consciously evaluated. Most conclude that humans operate with a mix of conscious and unconscious calculations in responding to events or situations.

Thibaut and Kelley (1959) detailed the role of norms in ensuring the smooth functioning of daily exchanges. Cultural norms exist to guide people in their various roles, just as society's rules or laws function to regulate behavior. For example, in romantic and working relationships, people quickly learn or develop norms for carrying out specific household responsibilities or complying with workplace policies. Such normative structure allows people to know what is expected of them and, in turn, they come to trust that the exchange system will yield what they expect. Norms or laws are effective at regulating behavior as long as the people see them as being beneficial to the self-interests of most members of the group or society. In contrast, people may violate norms and laws if they come to believe that there is no benefit in following them. These actions, and their fit within exchange premises, are discussed later in the chapter.

Summarizing concepts based on the theories of Homans, Blau, Gouldner, Emerson, and others, Nye (1982, pp. 20–21) listed 12 theoretical propositions that are useful in understanding the essence of exchange:

1. Individuals choose those alternatives from which they expect the most profit.
2. Costs being equal, they choose alternatives from which they anticipate the greatest rewards.
3. Rewards being equal, they choose alternatives from which they anticipate the fewest costs.
4. Immediate outcomes being equal, they choose those alternatives that promise better long-term outcomes.

5. Long-term outcomes being perceived as equal, they choose alternatives providing better immediate outcomes.
6. Costs and other rewards being equal, individuals choose the alternatives that supply or can be expected to supply the most social approval (or those that promise the least social disapproval).
7. Costs and other rewards being equal, individuals choose statuses and relationships that provide the most autonomy.
8. Other rewards and costs equal, individuals choose alternatives characterized by the least ambiguity in terms of expected future events and outcomes.
9. Other costs and rewards equal, they choose alternatives that offer the most security for them.
10. Other rewards and costs equal, they choose to associate with, marry, and form other relationships with those whose values and opinions generally are in agreement with their own and reject or avoid those with whom they chronically disagree.
11. Other rewards and costs equal, they are more likely to associate with, marry, and form other relationships with their equals, than those above or below them. (Equality here is viewed as the sum of abilities, performances, characteristics, and statuses that determine one's desirability in the social marketplace.)
12. In industrial societies, other costs and rewards equal, individuals choose alternatives that promise the greatest financial gains for the least financial expenditures.

These basic principles apply not only to individuals but also to groups and larger organizations. Although Homans and other theorists focused primarily on dyadic exchange, others believe that interaction cannot be studied or analyzed apart from the larger social structure. Accordingly, some have focused on exchange in small groups (including the family), while others have been concerned with exchange between complex social structures and focused on the link between micro and macro structures (Abraham, 1988; Ritzer, 1992).

## The Dynamics of Exchange, Conformity, and Deviance

In an attempt to understand "how social life becomes organized into increasingly complex structures of associations," Peter Blau extended exchange theory beyond the individual and dyadic level and focused on the process of exchange in groups (1964, p. 2). He theorized a sequence that leads from personal exchange to social structure and eventually to social change. His formulation encompassed four stages in which "(1) exchange transactions between people lead to . . . (2) differentiation of status and power, which leads to . . . (3) legitimation and organization, which lead to . . . (4) opposition and change" (Ritzer, 1992, p. 271).

This reformulation and extension of exchange theory points to the fact that "social interaction exists first in groups" (Ritzer, 1992, p. 271). Groups, then, must offer sufficient rewards to attract people and make them feel accepted. In turn, the relationship between the individual and the group is solidified when the expected rewards are received. This process of exchange generates social and psychological bonds between the people who keep count of benefits that are given, due, and received. For those who cannot engage in equal exchange, a form of debt is incurred in which they are relegated to lower status. Conversely, those who possess resources that others need are accorded higher status. The greater and more consistent a person or group's ability to meet others' needs, the greater the power accrued.

Power, status, norms, and the drive for social approval are important factors in the development of mutually profitable exchanges; they are also central to conformity and group survival. Members must rely on relatively predictable patterns of interaction within their ranks to continue as a unit. Group norms and the individual desire for social approval help ensure conformity among group members and this, in turn, reinforces group cohesion and survival.

Families are a variant of the small group but warrant special consideration within to exchange theory. Transactions may occur among all members within the family as well as between the family and others in the community and society at large. As a segment of larger societal systems, the family interfaces with other individuals such as neighbors, friends, and employers, and formal institutions of society such as the church, schools, and government. Survival of the family depends on its ability to successfully bargain with the structures around it. Table 12.1 summarizes the application of exchange theory to different levels of social system analysis.

## Exchange and the Economic Market

The economic *market* is important when examining exchange in macro-level structures. In contrast to Adam Smith's "invisible hand," Atherton (1990) identified appropriate roles that government may take without improperly confining the free market system. He noted that in

---

**TABLE 12.1**  Exchange Theory—Levels of System Analysis

| Level of Analysis | Exchange Between |
| --- | --- |
| Interpersonal | Persons: by norm of reciprocity, by cost–benefit criteria, by material exchange, by rules of distributive justice. |
|  | (Outcome: either uneven exchange, leading to power of one over another, or even exchange, leading to balance) |
| Within small groups Within families | Group members: by norm of reciprocity, by cost–benefit criteria, by material exchange, by symbolic exchange, by rules of distributive justice. |
|  | (Outcome: either uneven exchange, leading to power of one over another, or even exchange, leading to balance) |
| Between small groups | Groups: by norm or reciprocity, by cost–benefit criteria, by material exchange, by symbolic exchange, by rules of distributive justice. |
|  | (Outcome: either uneven exchange, leading to power of one another, or even exchange, leading to balance) |
| Between various | Symbolic groups: by norm of reciprocity, by cost–benefit ethnic and other criteria, by material exchange, by symbolic exchange, by groups within a nation rules of distributive justice, by ability to maneuver in the marketplace. |
|  | (Outcome: either uneven exchange, leading to power of one group over another, or even exchange, leading to balance) |
| Between nations and | Nations: by norm of reciprocity, by cost–benefit criteria, by other macro-level material exchange, by symbolic exchange, by rules of structures, by distributive justice, by ability to maneuver in the marketplace. |
|  | (Outcome: either uneven exchange, leading to power of one group over another, or even exchange, leading to balance) |

contemporary society some do not have the means to successfully enter and compete in the market system. The commodities or abilities they possess are not valuable (or valued) enough to be exchanged for goods, services, or other advantages. Atherton suggested that when such disadvantages threaten a group's health or safety, the intervention of the government is needed to offer equality of opportunity. Although many exchange theorists would view this as unreasonable intervention on the part of the government, Atherton found it to be consistent with the state's responsibility to protect people; he argued that this does not stifle the free market system but ultimately allows it to function.

Principles of exchange have retained a macro-economic focus in the field of cultural anthropology as well. Economic anthropologists have studied bands, tribes, states, and societies to understand and compare various exchange systems. Kottack (1994) has noted that in contrast to tribal societies that have multicentric exchange systems, contemporary nations have reduced or eliminated different spheres of exchange due to participation in an international economy. When more than one sphere is involved in exchange (e.g., food necessary for subsistence in exchange for items of status), there is increased opportunity for unequal exchange. Studies of this type also sensitize us to the fact that in some cultures people (especially female marriage partners) are used as "items" of exchange (Bohannan, 1955; Plattner, 1989).

An extension of macro-level exchange theory can be seen in the growing popularity of both network theory and rational choice theory. Derived from behaviorism, exchange theory and rational choice theory, *network theory* attempts to describe the interactive pattern of ties that link individuals to larger collective structures in society. Similar to exchange theory, networks can be micro (dyads) or macro (collective groups of individuals) in their focus. As previously noted, Emerson and Cook's exchange theory is based on their empirically based study of exchange network structures.

*Rational choice theory*, derived primarily from the field of economics, shares many of the same assumptions about human behavior that underlie behavioral and exchange theories. People are seen as rational, self-interested actors who seek to maximize their profit through rational thought and action. Although this theory has not been utilized as a major perspective for social work, it has received some recent attention in sociology, primarily as an attempt to build models describing what people do when they act rationally in a specific situation. Further discussion of network theory and rational choice theory can be found in Ritzer (1992) and Craib (1992).

As a more recent outgrowth of exchange theory and rational choice theory, *social capital theory* conceptualizes social relationships as resources that can be used in beneficial exchange to accomplish goals and facilitate collective action. Although many of the concepts used in social capital theory can be attributed to other writers, Coleman (1988, 1990) defined social capital as being a necessary resource for rational choice. Social capital refers to resources available to people by virtue of their membership in a social network and includes nonmaterial (i.e., social) forms of capital such as trust, norms, and networks that are built through obligations, expectations, and trustworthiness (Belanger, 2003). This theory is gaining popularity in social work, and a fuller discussion of the theory can be found in Putnam (2000).

Finally, one must recognize that excessive use of power and privilege in economic exchange may result in rebellion by those who are oppressed. Exchange theory points out that some basic standard of security and satiation is necessary to avoid this and maintain existing power relations. Figure 12.3 illustrates the key concepts in exchange theory.

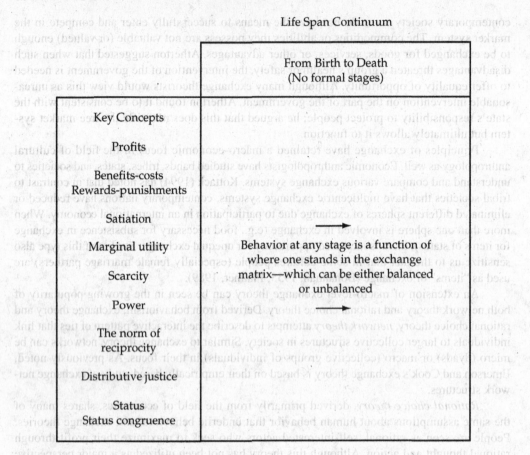

FIGURE 12.3. Key concepts in exchange theory.

## CONTEMPORARY ISSUES

Although behavioral and social learning theories have never received wide acceptance as comprehensive models of human development, practice methods derived from these theory bases have become increasingly popular. With current trends in managed care, there is less time in treatment available, even for those who are insured. Consequently, there has been increased use of behavioral and cognitive-behavioral methods, which are typically brief in application and directed toward the amelioration of specific problems. The tenets of careful empirical evaluation coupled with the clarity of behavioral theories are becoming more popular as the need for cost accountability and service efficiency increases. Currently, behavioral, social learning, and cognitive-behavioral methods are used for a variety of conditions including addiction, aggression, depression, anxiety, as well as classroom behavior management. Additionally, methods of reward and incentive based on behavioral principles are being used in the industrial sector. Companies nationwide have begun to experiment with profit sharing and other innovative reward systems and, thus, behavioral, social learning, and cognitive-behavioral techniques have found application in diverse settings.

One clear trend in the 21st century is that clinical practitioners are more frequently utilizing evidence-based knowledge for the assessment and treatment planning of the people they serve.

Behavioral and cognitive-behavioral interventions, as well as those based on other empirically evaluated social learning theories, are well represented among those treatments that are proved to be evidence based. The move toward evidence-based practice can also be seen in the emerging literature in the field (Bilson, 2004; Briggs & Rzepnicki, 2004; Corcoran, 2000; Gambrill, 1999; Howard, McMillan, & Pollio, 2003; Roberts, & Yeager, 2004; Thyer, 2002). According to Cournoyer (2004) several of the trends responsible for moving social work in the direction of evidence-based practice include legislative mandates for accountability, malpractice lawsuits, and court decisions that have held professionals legally responsible for service outcomes.

## APPLICATION TO SOCIAL WORK PRACTICE

Behavioral and social learning theories have received less attention than psychological stage theories in social work formulations of human behavior. Instead, they have been well received in the practice literature. Thyer and Hudson (1987) reported that behavioral social work has "rapidly become an important and influential perspective" of intervention (p. 1). In addition, effectiveness research has examined more behavioral and cognitive-behavioral approaches than any other (MacDonald, Sheldon, & Gillespie, 1992), and these forms of treatment are reported to be empirically effective (Fischer & Gochros, 1975; Sheldon, 1995). Currently, behavioral approaches are not often clearly labeled as such in social work settings, despite the fact that they are widely used. The use of rewards or incentives in an explicit attempt to change behavior is derived from behavioral theory. Brian Sheldon's (1995) recent text on cognitive-behavioral therapy is currently used in schools of social work around the United States and Great Britain.

In contrast, exchange theory has received little attention in social work. One important and frequently overlooked contribution is in the realm of situational assessments. A useful framework for viewing the motivations of individuals and groups, exchange theory can aid social workers in their understanding of individual and collective behavior and assist them in anticipating resistance to change. Further, the exchange perspective on status and power differences can also offer a meso-level framework for understanding and assessing dysfunctional behavior and nonconformity. In addition, exchange offers an alternative perspective on deviance and the way in which environmental forces might lead to or react to such behavior.

### Definition of the Helping Situation

Behavioral and social learning theories, when used in most social work settings, lead to a "problem" definition of the situation. This theoretical orientation, even in its basic definition of the client, starts with the notion that the social worker is facing a person with a *behavior problem*, which needs to be solved. Behavioral approaches may also lead to a definition of *deviance* if the social worker is in a criminal justice setting. In such cases, it is the client's *deviant behavior* that is the focus of change efforts. Although an illness definition does not stem from behavioral theory, cognitive and behavioral methods are frequently used in the treatment of certain psychiatric disorders. This is especially true when the focus of change is faulty cognition (as in depression) or the elimination of problematic behaviors.

Exchange theories lead to similar definitions of the helping situation. Of primary importance is the exchange orientation. When the exchange matrix breaks down, it may be defined as a *problem, deviance*, or *crisis*. In each of these cases, the helper is expected to offer services and, in turn, receive some form of payment. Flowcharts 12.1–12.3 demonstrate applications of behavioral, social learning, and exchange theories derived from these definitions.

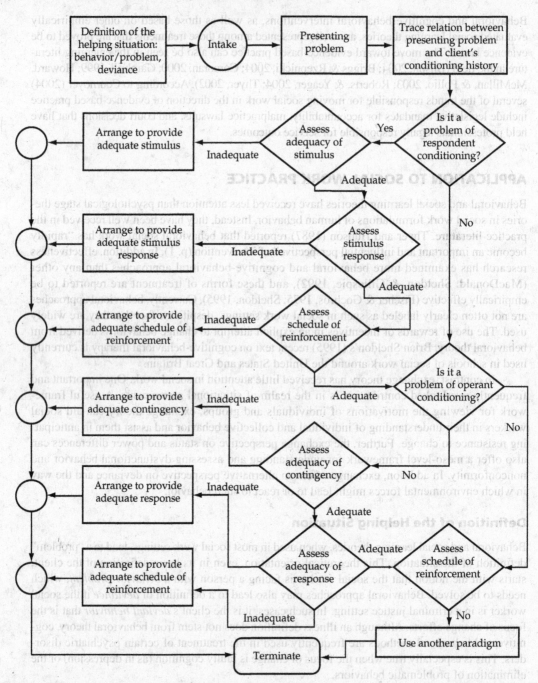

**FLOWCHART 12.1.** Application of radical behaviorism. © 1998, S. P. Robbins, P. Chatterjee, & E. R. Canda.

**FLOWCHART 12.2.** Application of social learning theory. © 1998, S. P. Robbins, P. Chatterjee, & E. R. Canda.

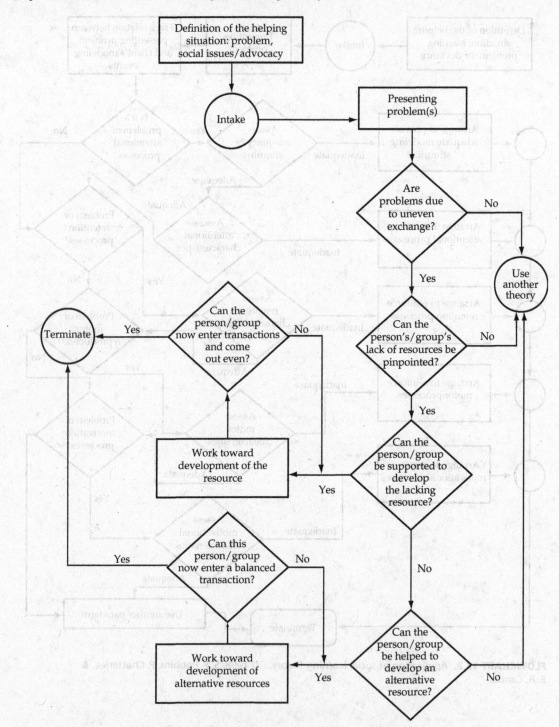

**FLOWCHART 12.3.** One possible road map of empowerment by applying exchange theory.
© 2004, S. P. Robbins, P. Chatterjee, & E. R. Canda.

## Assessment, Practice Strategies, and Methods

Assessment is one of the hallmarks of application of behavioral theory. Currently, and increasingly, assessment measures that are psychometrically sound and valid are in demand for many types of problems. One evidence of this is the success of Fischer and Corcoran's (2007) two-volume text, *Measures for Clinical Practice: A Sourcebook*, which contains over 450 instruments used to measure a variety of behaviors, thoughts, feelings, and symptoms. Most assessment tools in use today are based on the measurement of behaviors and cognitive factors that include thoughts and feelings.

Behavioral, social learning, and cognitive-behavioral methods cover a vast array of strategies used in practice. These include contingency contracting, positive reinforcement, negative reinforcement, punishment, modeling for clients, social skills training, assertiveness training, cognitive restructuring for depression and other problems, and exposure therapy for anxiety. Some specific techniques include relapse prevention (used for substance abuse, sexual aggression, violent aggression, and other behaviors) and biofeedback techniques (used for stress and anxiety). In addition, many institutional settings use some form of token economy through which residents earn privileges based on behavioral principles.

Although rarely used, exchange theories lend themselves to practice application at all systems levels. They are especially appropriate for assessment of power imbalances between persons and groups involved in exchange. All practice strategies and methods derived from exchange theory are based on meso-level assessment, despite the size of the systems involved.

Game theory is based on a special kind of exchange that was proposed for use in the behavioral sciences by psychoanalyst Eric Berne in the "Games People Play in Supervision" (Kadushin, 1968, p. 23). It originally received attention in the social work literature for its application in various situations. Shulman (1968) offered a number of examples in his work with mildly retarded youth. Kadushin looked at the use of gamesmanship in supervisory situations. Exchange theory adds an important dimension of analysis with its focus on interaction between and among people and groups. Table 12.2 illustrates a variety of settings and applications of behaviorism, social learning, and exchange theories.

## CRITICAL ANALYSIS

### Biological, Psychological, and Spiritual Factors

In the behavioral theories, biology has been a point of contention and has received less attention than environmental factors. Although Pavlov studied biological reflexes and responses, Watson, in contrast, utterly rejected the causal role of heredity. Skinner argued that genetic endowment was an important consideration but studied observable behavior instead. Bandura (1986a) focused primarily on experiential learning as the shaping force behind human behavior but respected biology's impact on one's ability to learn and to be affected by cognitive and social processes. At best, internal factors such as neurophysiological processes, cognition, and emotions are seen as "molar behavior" by behaviorists and social learning theorists. Molar behaviors are internal processes that are acknowledged as being intervening variables but are not the focus of study. Although the issue of inclusion of biological factors has not received much attention among behaviorists on a theoretical level, contemporary research on brain functioning and neurophysiology is becoming an important area of inquiry for a holistic understanding of the mind–body connection. Techniques such as biofeedback (which explicitly involve biological aspects of human behavior) have been included in the cognitive-behavioral realm (Sheldon, 1995).

| TABLE 12.2 | Applications of Behavioral and Exchange Theories in Various Settings | | | |
|---|---|---|---|---|
| **Type of Agency** | **Type of Presenting Problems** | **Type of Program** | **Definition of the Helping Situation** | **Type of Behavior Modification** |
| Child guidance centers | Antisocial behavior of children | Direct service to children and their families | Behavior problem Learning problem Deviance | Change from problem behavior to socially acceptable behavior |
| Family service centers | Antisocial behavior of children or family members | Direct service to families | Behavior problem Learning problem | Change from problem behavior to socially acceptable behavior |
| Shelters for abused women and children | Antisocial behavior of abusers | Direct service to the abused women and children | Behavior problem Deviance Social issues | Define abusers as deviant, the abused as problem, and their interaction as a social issue |
| Halfway houses and correctional settings | Asocial and antisocial behavior of inmates | Direct service to inmates | Behavior problem Deviance | Change from deviant to acceptable behavior— develop social control |
| Mental health centers and settings | Asocial and antisocial behavior of patients | Direct service to patients | Sick Behavior problem Learning problem | Change from illness behavior to wellness behavior |
| Human services departments of public welfare agencies | Abusive or victimizing behavior by family members | Direct service to families | Sick Behavior problem Deviance Social issues | Define abusers as deviant, the abused as problem, and their interaction as a social issue |
| Community centers | Asocial and antisocial behavior of community groups | Direct service to communities and community organizations | Behavior problem Deviance | Change from problem behavior to socially acceptable behavior |
| Community centers | Powerlessness of given community groups | Community organization with community groups | Social issues | Develop reward, expert, and legitimate power and their market in community groups |
| Advocacy groups | Powerlessness of given community groups | Community organization with community groups | Social issues | Develop reward, expert, and legitimate power and their market in community groups |
| Social planning agencies | Powerlessness of given community groups | Community planning with diverse groups for equal opportunity | Problem Social issues | Develop reward, expert, and legitimate power and their market in community groups |

Psychological variables are narrowly defined in classical and radical behaviorism and are confined to analysis of observable behavior. Social learning theory expands the psychological realm with its focus on cognition and emotions as mediators of behavior. Exchange theories are more narrowly focused on the dynamics of interpersonal exchange.

Spiritual factors are rarely considered to be relevant to behavioral and exchange theories. Because subjective spiritual feelings and thoughts cannot be observed directly, behaviorism, social learning, and social exchange theories would consider them as relevant only to the extent that they provide a reward or exchange that reinforces behavior. Religious institutions and belief systems can also provide important context for reinforcement and punishment. In radical behaviorism, mind, consciousness, and soul are considered to be unmeasurable and therefore impossible to study. Even existential values, such as freedom and dignity, are considered to be less relevant, since behavior is determined by observable environmental conditions (Skinner, 1972). Not surprisingly, many theorists consider extreme forms of behaviorism to be dehumanizing.

## Social, Cultural, and Economic Forces

Although behavioral theories focus on factors external to the individual, they have been essentially devoid of considerations of culture, social status, economic status, or other macro-level factors. In its infancy, behavioral theory was derived from animal studies and later expanded to describe human behavior. In practice, it has been applied universally to nearly everyone, regardless of cultural, social, and economic differences. Likewise, social learning theories largely ignore many of the macro forces that shape peoples' lives. Instead, they place their emphasis on the interpersonal process of modeling, which retains a distinctly meso-level focus and restricted notion of the social environment.

It is somewhat ironic that a theoretical base so focused on environmental causes of behavior has failed to address salient environmental factors that lie outside of their definitions of a reward structure. Thus, environment, in behavioral and social learning theories, refers only to external factors that provide reinforcement or punishment or opportunities for modeling behavior.

Exchange theory deals more directly with social, cultural, and economic forces within the framework of exchange. One must recognize, however, that the framework of exchange is largely based on interpersonal interaction, even when it is applied to structural features of society and social change. Thus, social, cultural, and economic forces are only important to the extent that they motivate or regulate the behavior of individuals or groups in the exchange matrix. Further, exchange theory maintains capitalistic and ego-centered assumptions about profit-based motivation for individual behavior and social control. These assumptions have been criticized by conflict, empowerment, and deep ecology theorists.

## Relevance to Individuals, Groups, Families, Organizations, Institutions, and Communities

Behavioral, social learning, and cognitive-behavioral approaches have been applied primarily to individuals. In social work, these methods, as reported in the effectiveness literature, are also frequently applied to families and groups (Sheldon, 1995). Organizations and institutions using reward programs and incentives are also using behavioral techniques, even if they are not labeled as such. However, even when used at an institutional level, the focus remains on changing individual behavior.

In contrast, exchange theories focus on the full array of social systems, from individuals, groups, families, and organizations to larger social systems. Interactions, which are the focus of exchange theory, do not take place within a vacuum and therefore, the larger context is also considered. The environmental context attaches value to items of exchange and regulates transactions through norms.

Although all exchange theorists emphasize interaction, emphasis varies from theorist to theorist. Some emphasize the dyad and the behavioral principles that underlie exchange. Others emphasize larger social structures such as networks and societies and the social processes that govern exchange. Most exchange theorists focus on the norms and patterns that govern these interactions. Despite this breadth in scope, exchange theory involves meso-level analysis.

## CONSISTENCY WITH SOCIAL WORK VALUES AND ETHICS

The idea that environment plays a role in the creation of individual problems is consistent with social work's history of working with oppressed populations. Additionally, the focus on behavior rather than the person may assist us in gaining an empathic understanding of clients who exhibit undesirable behaviors. One must recognize that the use of punishment sometimes stems from behavioral theory, although very few behaviorists consider use of aversive stimulation. The use of punishment and negative reinforcement is unethical for social workers if procedures using positive reinforcers can accomplish the same objectives. Additionally, many social workers see behavioral and cognitive approaches as mechanistic, leaving little room for client choice or empowerment. However, because they are so powerful, behavioral methods are often used as an explicit form of social control. Sheldon (1995), however, illustrated that this sort of control is not necessarily the aim, nor the conceptual framework, behind the applications of these theories.

Optimal health and well-being can be seen as the goal of behavioral and social learning approaches when taken from a social work perspective. However, applications of these theories are frequently linked to identification of problem behaviors. Alcoholism and aggression, for example, are typically viewed from a problem orientation rather than from an optimal health orientation. Although behavioral theories are not typically associated with empowerment, they can easily fit within an individual empowerment framework if there is no coercion involved in their application and clients are the primary definers of treatment goals and strategies. Social learning theory's emphasis on self-reinforcement and self-efficacy is consistent with empowerment theory.

However, another potential problem lies in the fact that issues related to diversity have been largely ignored within behavioral and social learning theories. The lack of attention to factors such as race, ethnicity, gender, sexual orientation, and social class, for example, is apparent not only on a theoretical level but also in its practice application. The reductionism and determinism that this engenders is problematic for all behavioral, cognitive-behavioral, and social learning approaches.

Although the principles of exchange theories do not directly address human diversity, several implications can be drawn from the underlying assumptions of the theory. As a meso-level theory that rests heavily on the order paradigm, exchange theories ignore the mechanisms that preserve inequality. Accordingly, women, older people, people with disabilities, people of color, gay men, lesbians, and transgenders, and other disenfranchised populations may be seen as relatively valueless in the economic sphere. As noted earlier in this chapter, the rule of distributive justice fosters a view that ascribed qualities (i.e., race, gender) are a fair (or just) basis upon which to devalue "investments." Because "worth" in the market is based on ascribed characteristics, some people are automatically devalued and given lower status in the exchange process. Downward mobility for those without power is seen simply as a result of uneven exchange.

In addition, the "invisible hand" of Adam Smith easily lends itself to blaming the victim. The assumption that participants in a competitive free market system mutually benefit puts the burden of responsibility on those who do not. This is analogous, on the macro level, to third-world countries whose "underdevelopment" is blamed on its citizens, rather than on neocolonialist policies that exploit their resources for the capitalist gain of wealthy and powerful nations. Although these theories may be used for empowerment at the interpersonal level due to their focus on power imbalances, it is unlikely that they have broad application to macro-level practice and social change due to their inherently conservative nature.

## PHILOSOPHICAL UNDERPINNINGS

The early classical theories of behaviorism assume that behavior is a response to environmental stimuli and that the relationship between stimulus and response is governed by a defined set of constant rules. This suggests that people are subject to the vicissitudes of their circumstances and appears to negate the importance of will or freedom of choice in human behavior. The later classical theories of behaviorism continue the assumption of S-R but make efforts to account for the role of higher mental processes and changing organismic conditions. Thus, there is a strong suggestion that people both act upon and are acted upon by their environment. Social learning theories assume people to be active interpreters of the environment and assume that, while subject to environmental demands, people are capable of acting in accordance with their wants and desires. Radical behaviorism transcends earlier behaviorist assumptions of S-R, adding operant conditioning as a codeterminant process, and assumes that people are subject more to the reward and punishment power of behavioral consequences than to the demands of antecedent stimuli.

Behavioral theories try to be nonjudgmental in nature, neither proposing nor denying a place for morality. Thus, they avoid making explicit assumptions on the basic nature of people. However, this nonjudgmentalism belies the fact that behavioral theories use mechanistic and animal analogies for understanding human behavior and believe human nature to be largely environmentally determined. These theories accept deviant behavior as knowable in behavioral terms but do not judge the behavior itself. This lack of analysis and critique of power and oppression ignores the reality of power relations involved in the definition of acceptable behaviors. Social learning theories, on the other hand, assume that behavior develops from complex cognitive processes applied to real events in the social and physical world. There is ample room for errors in judgment, which may lead to the development of behaviors that lie outside social custom and norm. Although there are no assumptions concerning the basic nature of people, a role is accorded for morality and social judgment.

As exchange theories stem from diverse fields of inquiry, the philosophical assumptions that underlie each reflect this diversity. A fundamental assumption of these exchange theories is that through the consideration of costs and benefits, people seek to profit in their exchanges with others (Abraham, 1988). In addition, exchange theories are based on the viewpoint that humans are actors, not reactors. This presumes rationality on the part of the individual and the ability to calculate behavior and respond accordingly. Most exchange theories are utilitarian in focus and may be termed *Hobbesian* in their view of human behavior. A central assumption is that self-interest is a primary motivating force and that reason is basic to human nature.

The philosophical assumptions that underlie Homans's work are based on the order paradigm that assumes equilibrium and harmony. This equilibrium was found, however, in the principles of exchange rather than in larger society (Perdue, 1986). Blau, on the other hand, tried to integrate functionalism with dialectic conflict theory and symbolic interaction. Accordingly, the philosophical assumptions underlying his notion of exchange include the contradictory forces assumed in the Marxian dialectic and the symbolic nature of behavior (Abraham, 1988).

Theorists who emphasize the symbolic nature of behavior focus on normative behavior shared by those in a value system. Rather than being merely repetitive, symbolic behavior can create new ways of behaving based on the meaning that we give to events and actions. Homans, to the contrary, believed that conditioned behavior was sufficient to explain exchange and *all* of human interaction. Finally, exchange theories make no presumptions about the individual's moral character but view actions based on exchange as reasonable and expectable responses to the need to survive and accommodate the surrounding environment.

## METHODOLOGICAL ISSUES AND EMPIRICAL SUPPORT

Behaviorism and social learning theory are based on the positivist paradigm and include a foundation of rigorous experimentation, typically under highly controlled laboratory conditions. Data are quantitative in nature and often collected through novel means, such as the Skinner box, developed for the purposes of behavioral experiments. Much behavioral research is based on single subject design in which baseline rates of an individual's behavior are established, an independent variable is introduced, and subsequent behavioral changes are measured. In essence, the subject is used as his or her own control, thus eliminating many uncontrolled variables potentially present in designs using experimental and control groups (Corsini & Marsella, 1983). The use of single subjects, however, limits generalizability of the findings. Numerous experimental studies have supported behavioral theory and its diverse applications (Fischer & Gochros, 1975; B. L. Hudson & MacDonald, 1986). Maddi (1980) has suggested that "within its own set of assumptions, radical behaviorism has assumed considerable empirical support" (p. 601). In particular, he notes that there is a large body of research that supports the differential effects of varied reinforcement schedules on learned behavior.

However, research supporting radical behaviorism as well as its theoretical bases has been criticized on several fronts. First, its environmental determinism denies the importance of cognition, emotions, and other causes. Experimental studies that deliberately restrict environmental variables are not likely to be widely generalizable to real-world situations for humans. Thus, the theory has been criticized for being overly simplistic and unrealistically parsimonious (Chomsky, 1967; Ewen, 1988; R. M. Thomas, 1985).

In addition, some central behavioral concepts are either not clearly defined or based on circular reasoning. For example, a reinforcer is defined as anything that strengthens a response and the resulting increased rate of response is what proves that it is a reinforcer (Ewen, 1988). Further, anxiety has been defined as both a primary and a secondary drive. Maddi (1980) has noted that the scales used to measure anxiety often go beyond behavioral predictions that stem from the concept of anxiety as a primary drive. Many anxiety studies have attempted to relate anxiety scores to other performance scores, resulting in R-R correlations, with no attempt to tie responses to antecedent stimuli as proposed by S-R laws.

R. M. Thomas (1985) has also raised important questions about distinctions between punishment and reinforcement, asking "Is withholding a reward a kind of punishment?" (p. 394). Further, radical behaviorism has been criticized for its inability to address species-specific behaviors, due to its reliance on animal studies and its failure to recognize the importance of human symbolization and complex forms of human behavior. These issues have yet to be adequately addressed.

Bandura's social learning theory has received less methodological criticism, particularly due to its explicit acknowledgment of internal processes that impact behavior and its use of human subjects (rather than animals) in research. In addition, it has received a great deal of empirical support, especially in studies that examine modeling, observational learning, and self-reinforcement and self-control (Corsini & Marsella, 1983). However, Maddi (1980) pointed out that some behaviorists would view the emphasis on subjective cognitive processes as being less than fully scientific due to the inability to measure thoughts and ideas directly. Methods used by social learning theorists, such as oral and written verbal reports, do not directly measure the processes themselves but, rather, the behaviors that result from such processes. Further, as self-report data, they introduce a factor of subjectivity into the scientific method. Although this issue should not be dismissed, some believe that the combination of subjective and objective data actually constitutes a methodological strength rather a weakness. One additional problem cited with both social learning and behavioral theory is that they fail to account for individual differences.

The propositions set forth by exchange theorists also reflect a positivistic approach and readily lend themselves to mathematical models and rigorous deductive systems. Emerson (1972) developed a formalized model in which covariance among concepts is precisely defined and represented by symbolic notation. On the other hand, exchange can also reflect a phenomenological outlook, with people viewed as acting in idiosyncratic ways in response to rewards and punishments on which they place value and meaning. Thus, exchange theories embrace both positivism and constructivism.

Early theorists, such as Blau and Homans, were stronger on semantics than methodology. Homans's concepts were not well defined, and this led to subsequent charges of tautological thinking. Blau "does not state a formal set of propositions and is not interested in developing the higher-order axioms of a deductive theoretic system; he only aims to offer a theoretical 'prolegomenon,' or a conceptual sketch" (Abraham, 1988, p. 155).

Homans's theory has been widely criticized for his rigid behavioral reductionism that ignores cognitive factors, or internal mental process. In addition, Talcott Parsons argued that despite his claims, Homans failed to show how behavioral psychology explains large-scale systems (Perdue, 1986). Ekeh (1974) has criticized him for ignoring norms and values and for focusing on dyadic rather than large-scale exchange. Blau's attempt to integrate different sociological perspectives has fallen short as well. Ekeh maintained that Blau's formulation is individualistic with a reductionistic emphasis on economic needs to explain social structures. In contrast, Ritzer (1992) contended that Blau's societal level exchange theory is "no longer identifiable as a behavioristic orientation" (p. 446). In fact, behavioral sociologists have argued that exchange has become a metaphor for interaction (Perdue, 1986).

In Emerson's formalization of exchange, he strengthened the positivistic approach with precise definitions of propositions that are stated in terms of covariance. In focusing his theory away from the motivation of individual actors, he avoided Homans's problems of tautology (Abraham, 1988). Due to its clearly positivistic approach, exchange theory has received a good deal of empirical validation, particularly in its application to social networks. Further, empirically based network analysis has been credited with introducing units larger than dyads into the exchange formulation (Abrahamson, 1990).

With these issues duly noted, exchange has become an important orientation in microsociology. And, as Abraham pointed out, "It has enriched the methodology of various theories of the middle range" (1988, p. 169).

In general, behavioral theories are extremely good at prediction when it is possible to control the relevant environmental determinants of behavior. Predictive power is weakened in the presence of complex environmental factors that contain a large number of random elements. Skinner's radical behaviorism is likewise predictive under highly controlled conditions, as when schedules of operant reinforcement are under experimental control. Bandura's social learning theory is also good at prediction when research is confined to the specific elements of social learning covered by the theory. Similarly, when confined to rigorous experimental design of social networks, exchange theory is good at prediction.

However, as general theories of human behavior, both behavioral and exchange theories are generally better at explanation than prediction and are better at a probabilistic than deterministic level. Behavioral theories best explain behavior at an individual level while exchange theories are better suited for explaining properties of dyads and larger groups. However, the ability to predict future responses, even in a probabilistic sense, is somewhat limited, due to the wide variability of motivators. Even deviant cases may be explained by attributing behaviors to previously unrecognized rewards or costs. One salient criticism of exchange theories is that they are not useful for predicting individual behavior. Likewise, behavioral theories have limited utility for predicting group or organizational behavior.

## Summary

Classical behaviorism has long given way to its radical form and is not widely used in contemporary social work practice. However, some of its fundamental tenets have been incorporated into other mainstream intervention strategies. Behaviorism has generally been subsumed under the rubric of cognitive-behavioral practice and theory, and much of the work that is labeled as behavioral is actually cognitive-behavioral in character. The appeal of behaviorism, however, rests on its explicit simplicity, the ease with which its basic principles may be applied, and its clear effectiveness for impacting certain behaviors. Thus, behavioral practice may be found in settings that provide the means to control the environment in very concrete ways and in which fundamental behavioral change is the stated practice goal.

Social learning theories have gained widespread acceptance within social work and allied mental health disciplines. The appeal of social learning is threefold. First, many of the principles of social learning lend themselves readily to application in a helping context. Second, social learning theory has been shown to have a high degree of validity in understanding human learning. Thus, the principles of social learning theory are found in most comparative approaches to human development. Third, the fundamental tenets of social learning theory may be usefully applied to theoretical development in other areas. Thus, social learning has become, for example, a partial basis for the development of other sociobehavioral theories such as attribution theory and theories

of motivation. In addition, social learning theory frees people from the environmental determinism imposed by radical behaviorism.

Exchange theory analyzes dynamic processes in terms drawn from behavioral psychology and utilitarian economics as well as functional anthropology and, to a lesser extent, dialectical sociology. Thus, it incorporates a variety of theoretical perspectives, allowing for widespread applications, and "offers something for everyone" (Abraham, 1988, p. 169).

Exchange theories offer a useful meso-level framework through which we can view dyads and small groups as well as large-scale social systems. In doing so, they address much of the micro–macro continuum necessary for social work practice. Unfortunately, similar to other meso-level theories, they ignore the reality of rigidly stratified societies, and this conservative bias weakens its utility for practice. Although the behavioral reductionism of Homans fosters a mechanistic view of individuals, the symbolic interactionist stance of Blau should appeal to those with a more phenomenological orientation. With these limitations duly noted, the strength of exchange theories is in their scope, which makes them applicable to a wide range of populations in a variety of settings.

Finally, both social learning and exchange theories are based on the viewpoint that humans are actors, not reactors. This presumption of rationality and foresight on the part of the individual, and the ability to calculate behavior and respond accordingly, will likely hold a particular appeal for social work practice.

# CHAPTER 13

# Transpersonal Theory

*There is a reason, there is a rhyme*
*There is a season, there is a time*
*There is a purpose, there is a plan*
*One day together*
*We'll heal in the wisdom*
*And we'll understand*

© BOBBY BRIDGER
STAREYES MUSIC (ASCAP)

## TRANSPERSONAL THEORIES

- provide a nonsectarian conceptual framework for dealing with spirituality in social work practice
- provide frameworks for holistic and integrative thinking and practice
- address the highest human potential for achieving love, creativity, meaning, and communion
- describe the developmental process of self-actualization and self-transcendence
- describe the variety of states and levels of consciousness
- explain the difference between psychopathological phenomena and spiritual growth experiences

Transpersonal theories address aspects of human behavior that are distinctive to our nature as human beings. They concern our highest aspirations and potentials and our needs for love, meaning, creativity, and communion with other people and the universe. These theories propose that by going deep into ourselves to understand the fullness of who we are, we can transcend the ego by expanding awareness of our true nature, which is connected profoundly with other people and the universe. Going deep into ourselves allows us to experience the common nature that we all share. According to transpersonal theories, the goal of human development is achieving the point at which actualization of self and actualization of others converge. They help us develop a holistic and integrative perspective on human behavior and social work practice.

## HISTORICAL CONTEXT

In 1969, Abraham Maslow heralded the beginning of a new movement in psychology dedicated to understanding "the farther reaches of human nature." This new movement was developed to focus on the distinctive and highest aspects of human potential for development. He called this movement the *fourth force* of transpersonal theory, which goes beyond the earlier three theoretical forces of Freudianism, behaviorism, and humanism.

This fourth force is an outgrowth of humanistic theory (the "third force") that developed in the 1950s and 1960s to focus on the distinctively human strengths and positive qualities of lovingness, spontaneity, meaningfulness, creativity, freedom, and dignity. The humanistic theorists were attempting to counterbalance the dehumanizing and reductionist tendencies of the previously influential "first force" of classical Freudianism and "second force" of behaviorism. In the humanists' view, Freudianism overgeneralized from clinical study of neurosis and created a view of human behavior as being largely determined by unconscious, instinctual, and selfish impulses to seek pleasure and to avoid tension and conflict. On the other hand, behaviorism was seen as a technocratic and mechanistic view that portrayed people as being controlled by environmental forces and denied the capacity for free choice and spontaneity.

Humanistic psychologists studied people who reported a high sense of self-esteem, creativity, and life satisfaction to establish a standard of optimal well-being for human potential. They discovered that many of these highly self-actualized people reported experiences of self-transcendence that were crucial to their sense of self-fulfillment. These experiences are termed *transpersonal* because they transcend the limits of the "persona," or body and ego-bounded self-identity. Transpersonal theories focus on these types of experiences and the developmental process that opens the mind to them. In short, transpersonal theory focuses on the distinctively spiritual aspects of human experience and development.

In addition to humanistic psychology, five other streams of intellectual history have strongly influenced transpersonal theory: existential philosophy born from the despair of industrializing and war-torn Europe, transpersonal psychodynamic theories developed in reaction to Freudianism (such as Jung and Assagioli), study of altered states of consciousness and parapsychology that emerged during the 1960s and 1970s, cross-cultural exploration of diverse worldviews and religious practices, and efforts to join insights from many disciplines into a holistic, integrative perspective (Canda & Furman, 2010; Grof, 2006; Grof & Halifax, 1977; Masters & Houston, 1966; Pelletier & Garfield, 1976; Tart, 2000, 2009; Wilber, 2000a).

Borenzweig (1984) and McGee (1984) introduced transpersonal theory to social work about 25 years ago. It was more widely advocated in the 1990s to early 2000s as a way to develop a more holistic biopsychosocial-spiritual and deep ecological perspective for theory (Besthorn & Canda, 2002; Canda, 1991; Canda & Smith, 2001; Cowley, 1993, 1996; Cowley & Derezotes, 1994). Ken Wilber's transpersonally oriented Integral Theory (discussed later) is being applied to various social work and mental health issues (Larkin, 2005, 2006; Larkin & Records, 2007; Starnino, 2009; P. E. Thomas, 2004). Several holistic frameworks for spiritually sensitive practice inspired in part by transpersonal theory are now available (e.g., Bullis, 1996; Canda & Furman, 2010; Derezotes, 2006; Lee, Ng, Leung, & Chan, 2009). Spiritually sensitive practice addresses the whole person—body, mind, and spirit—in the context of relations with other people, all other beings, and ultimate reality, however a person understands it. Spiritually sensitive practice respects the diverse religious and nonreligious forms of spirituality by working within clients' systems of meaning, supporting them to achieve their highest potentials for development while promoting peace and justice for all people and all beings.

## KEY CONCEPTS

All transpersonal theories focus on experiences and developmental processes that carry a person beyond the sense of an identity bound to the individual body and ego (Washburn, 1994, 1995). Conventional developmental theorists considered a clear sense of distinct self, with mature rational, emotional, moral, and social relational skills, to be the epitome of human development (see Chapters 7, 8, and 9). During the *egoic stage*, the child becomes aware of itself as a separate entity and recognizes caregivers in the environment as distinct objects. Through adolescence, the sense of autonomy is refined. In adulthood, the task of establishing a mature sense of rapprochement and intimacy with others becomes primary. Gilligan's (1982) variation on female moral and cognitive development suggested that gender role socialization of women alters the male-oriented emphasis on autonomy toward connectedness and caring. Yet all these conventional developmentalists focus on the theme of a body and ego-bounded self.

In contrast, transpersonal theorists emphasize that people have the potential to achieve a developmental level beyond the ego-focused level, the *transegoic stage*. In this stage, the self is no longer experienced merely as a separate entity, either autonomous or interconnected. Rather, the self is experienced as fundamentally united with all others. The highest of these experiences are sometimes described as unitive consciousness, cosmic consciousness, or union with the divine.

Wilber (1983) pointed out that this is a crucial distinction for understanding human development and assessing mental health. If mental health professionals do not acknowledge that transegoic experience is possible, they likely interpret descriptions of self-transcendent mystical experiences as evidence of regression to preegoic infantile symbiosis or psychotic ego boundary confusion. Wilber called this the *pre/trans fallacy,* that is, mixing up the preegoic with the transegoic. This fallacy also operates in the reverse when people superficially assume that any statements about mergence or unity with others, even in the context of mental disorganization, delusion, and hallucination, reflect mystical insight (Wilber, 2000a, 2000b).

Transpersonal theorists also highlight states of consciousness. Tart (2000) defined *discrete state of consciousness* as a unique overall pattern of mental functioning such as the way we have self-awareness, sense our body and environment, experience emotions, access memory, and sense the passing of time. An *altered state of consciousness* is a pattern of mental functioning that is significantly different from the ordinary waking state of consciousness, characterized by a high level of rationality and relatively low level of mental imaging. There is a very wide range of states of consciousness that are possible, other than the ordinary waking state, such as those associated with dreaming, deep relaxation, meditation, psychoactive drug use, and hyperstimulation. Each state of consciousness conveys a particular experience of reality, with distinctive perceptual modes. Further, many of these states of consciousness open up transpersonal awareness.

Methods of research into and theorizing about states of consciousness must match the nature of the particular state of consciousness under study. Tart (2000) referred to this as *consciousness state-specific science*. Our understanding of human behavior must take into account the *relativity of consciousness states*. For example, the only way to understand whether a client's report of a vision of a divine being is associated with psychopathology would be to examine the internal experience (i.e., state and content of consciousness), the meaning of the experience for the client within his or her own developmental course and cultural and religious context, and the impact on his or her functioning (Canda & Furman, 2010). Visionary experiences and intensified states of consciousness are entirely expectable, and even desirable, within many ritual contexts that involve prayer, meditation, hyperstimulation, or sensory deprivation. Such transpersonal experiences are not the same as delusions and hallucinations that reflect extreme mental disorganization or rigidity and imperviousness to reality testing, as in some forms of severe mental illness.

One of the main interests of transpersonal theory is *spirituality*. Wilber (2000b) identifies four common meanings of the word spiritual: (a) the highest levels of development going beyond egoic consciousness; (b) a developmental line (such as Fowler's discussion of faith development); (c) a profound or peak experience, for example, through prayer or meditation; and (d) an attitude of love, compassion, and wisdom. Canda and Furman (2010, p. 75) have integrated these and many other ideas about spirituality to form a definition for use in social work. "Spirituality is a process of human life and development focusing on the search for a sense of meaning, purpose, morality, and well-being; in relationship with oneself, other people, other beings, the universe, and ultimate reality however understood (e.g. in animistic, atheistic, nontheistic, polytheistic, theistic, or other ways); orienting around centrally significant priorities; and engaging a sense of transcendence (experienced as deeply profound, sacred, or transpersonal)." Spirituality can express in religious and nonreligious forms. Their more detailed operational model of spirituality encompasses spiritual drives, experiences, functions, developmental processes, and contents of spiritual perspectives. Transpersonal theorists examine all the features of spirituality identified in these definitions.

These key concepts lay the groundwork for the various transpersonal theories to be discussed next.

## TRANSPERSONAL THEORIES

### Maslow's Theory of Self-Actualization and Self-Transcendence

Humanistic theories provide two foundational concepts for transpersonal theory: self-actualization and self-transcendence. *Self-actualization* means that there is a natural inherent tendency of people to express their innate potentials for love, creativity, and spirituality (Maslow, 1968, 1969, 1970a, 1970b). What is needed for self-actualization to proceed successfully is a nurturing environment that provides adequate sustenance and social support, as well as a personal commitment to growth. Self-actualization is like the process of an oak growing from a seed into a full tree. The acorn seed already has within it the potential for the full oak, but adequate sunlight, water, nutrient, and other environmental supports are necessary for the growth to occur. On the one hand, development is like the natural emergence and expansive growth upward of the inborn potentials (self-actualization). On the other hand, development is like the tree striving up toward the light, as when people seek fulfillment by stretching toward their own ideals and aspirations and toward loving and responsible connections with others. As self-actualization continues to its fullest potential, it carries one beyond self-preoccupation, narcissism, and finally ego-focused self-identity; self-actualization then becomes *self-transcendence*. Self-transcendence is not a denial or abandonment of the self. Rather, it is a completion and fulfillment of the self in communion with other beings and the Ground of Being, that is, the ultimate and sacred being or reality, that some call God.

This developmental unfolding, beginning from a necessary focus on survival needs and proceeding to a focus on self-actualization and self-transcendence needs, is termed the *hierarchy of needs* in Maslow's (1968, 1969, 1970a, 1970b) theory. The term *hierarchy* does not imply that subsistence needs are less important than transcendence needs; rather, they must take first priority because without the establishment of survival, security, and sense of being loved, it is difficult to turn attention to matters of creativity and spirituality. Indeed, Maslow (1968) emphasized that needs for belonging and love are as crucial as needs for food and shelter. Also, acquisition of great material wealth, social status, or power do not necessarily make a person self-actualized. On the contrary, Maslow described people who have a constant desire to acquire power and possessions as being oriented toward *deficiency-cognition and motivation* as though they have a bottomless hole inside that can never be filled. Acquisitive and dominating people damage others and restrict resources for others' self-actualization. In contrast, Maslow's ideal was that people should become oriented toward *being-cognition and motivation*. This means living with a sense of inherent personal dignity, worth, and self-love and lovingly accepting others for their own inherent dignity and worth. Being-cognition does not require much wealth to support it; but, it is itself a great spiritual treasure. Figure 13.1 adapts Maslow's hierarchy of needs, taking into account his later work on self-transcendence. From this standpoint, full self-actualization is complementary with other-actualization and leads to self-transcendence.

Maslow stated that self-transcendence needs increasingly come to the forefront in development as basic biological and survival needs are satisfied. These "higher needs" include "need for love, for friendship, for dignity, for individuality, for self-fulfillment" (1969, p. 3); actualization

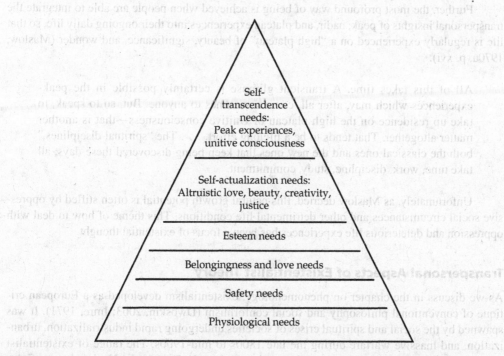

**FIGURE 13.1.** Pyramidal depiction of Maslow's hierarchy of needs, including self-transcendence. *Source:* Adapted from *Toward a Psychology of Being,* 2nd ed., by D. Van Nostrand. Copyright 1968 by Abraham Maslow.

of these needs carries one into a new self-transcending orientation, which is "transpersonal, transhuman, centered in the cosmos rather than in human needs and interests, going beyond humanness, identity, self-actualization, and the like" (1968, pp. iii–iv).

Maslow's research on self-actualizing people found that they often gave accounts of *peak experiences* in which the individual ego boundary loosens or dissolves altogether, opening up a sense of union with other people, nature, and the divine (Maslow, 1968, 1970a, 1970b). People often feel that these are pivotal life-changing events. Peak experiences may occur through a profound sense of empathy and joining with loved ones, awe at the beauty and immenseness of the universe, overwhelming sense of cosmic consciousness, and communion with divinity. Peak experiences are transegoic, that is, they expand awareness beyond the boundaries of the personal ego-based identity. They often are catalysts for growth into an ongoing way of life that is based in self-transcendent awareness and compassionate concern for others.

Maslow (1970a, 1970b, 1971) identified three kinds of transpersonal experiences. The *peak experience* is relatively brief, intense, and shocking. It carries with it a challenge to integrate the insights into ordinary life. Without this integration, peak experiences can be mere transitory "highs" or thrills, without lasting benefits, or they may be crisis-provoking life disruptions that do not lead to growth. Another type is the *nadir experience.* This is an experience of intense encounters with death, medical emergencies, and psychological traumas that can facilitate an opening to transpersonal awareness by breaking the usual sense of identity and worldview. Given the dangerous nature of these crises, however, careful work toward integration of insights and crisis resolution is necessary. A third type is the *plateau experience,* which involves a relatively serene, calm, and poignant sense of enjoyment and happiness.

Further, the most profound way of being is achieved when people are able to integrate the transpersonal insights of peak, nadir, and plateau experiences into their ongoing daily life, so that life is regularly experienced on a "high plateau" of beauty, significance, and wonder (Maslow, 1970a, p. xvi).

> All of this takes time. A transient glimpse is certainly possible in the peak-experiences which may, after all, come sometimes to anyone. But, so to speak, to take up residence on the high plateau of Unitive consciousness—that is another matter altogether. That tends to be a lifelong effort. . . . The "spiritual disciplines," both the classical ones and the new ones that keep being discovered these days, all take time, work, discipline, study, commitment.

Unfortunately, as Maslow decried, this natural growth potential is often stifled by oppressive social circumstances and other detrimental life conditions. This theme of how to deal with oppression and deleterious life experiences has been a focus of existential thought.

## Transpersonal Aspects of Existentialist Theory

As we discuss in the chapter on phenomenology, existentialism developed as a European critique of conventional philosophy and social conformism (Dwoskin, 2003; Imre, 1971). It was spawned by the social and spiritual crises of societies undergoing rapid industrialization, urbanization, and massive warfare during the late 1800s to mid-1900s. The range of existentialist views is wide and divergent, for example, atheists such as the French anti-Nazi resistance fighters Camus and Sartre, Christians such as the Russian novelist Dostoyevsky and the church-critic Danish philosopher Soren Kierkegaard, and Jews who confronted horrors of the holocaust

(Frankl, 1969; Kaufmann, 1956). What these people held in common was a criticism of their contemporary *crisis of meaning*. The concentration of people in large impersonal cities, the subjugation of human labor in mass production of commodities, and the rise of mass destructive and oppressive social movements, such as Fascism, were fracturing the traditional consensus of meaning.

Social malaise and the horrors of war exposed the vulnerability of social conventions and religious beliefs, like castles built of sand, with the ocean tide coming in. The conventional meaning systems were shown to be vulnerable human creations, without essential or ultimate meaning, subject to grossly dehumanizing and callous violent distortions. In short, humanly constructed meaning was shown to be *absurd*, that is, without absolute, essential, or ultimate meaning or divine sanction. Camus (1955, p. 11) described the experience of the absurd as "the revolt of the flesh" at realizing its mortality; a sense of "that denseness and strangeness of the world"; and "discomfort in the face of man's own inhumanity." It does not require cataclysmic events to trigger a crisis of meaning, however. Every person experiences crises of meaning at various points in life when facing the death of oneself and loved ones and other great losses or challenges to the established sense of who one is and what life is supposed to be.

Existentialists assert the need for people to courageously and persistently confront the absurdity of existence. Unflinching awareness of mortality, injustice, and personal confusion can lead to a sense of meaning and purpose and a motivation to form support and solidarity with others. And so we build on our inherent human dignity and caring to assist each other in the search for meaning and to remove oppressive conditions that alienate and dehumanize (Edwards, 1982; Krill, 1978; Lantz, 1993; Lantz & Walsh, 2007; May, 1983). Thus, existentially oriented forms of therapy have contributed to transpersonal theory an interest in the *search for meaning*. Not all existentialist theorists accept the possibility or even desirability of transegoic experience. However, Christian, Jewish, and Zen-influenced existentialists can be considered transpersonally or spiritually oriented theorists, because they emphasize that authentic meaning, which is sought beyond the limits of human understanding, comes from direct experience of a transpersonal or sacred realm. Transpersonally oriented theorists include the Christian philosopher Paul Tillich, the Jewish theologian Martin Buber, the Jewish founder of logotherapy Victor Frankl, and the Christian and Zen-influenced social work theorist Donald Krill.

Krill (1978) described religious responses to the feeling of existential dread (the absurd). Krill explained that Tillich advocated the "courage to be" as a lucid acceptance of meaninglessness as a part of the whole life process. Such faithful perseverance, even with the loss of ego supports, brings one into an experience of the "power of Being." Krill said that mystics go even further by actively courting nothingness to pierce beyond fabricated meaning. For example, Zen meditation involves practicing intentional refrain from mental constructions and distractions, so that one can be completely in touch with the present moment. Krill also gave this traditional Christian example: "Christ reveals the contrasting experiences of life [Nothingness and Being] in two sayings: 'My God, my God, why hast thou forsaken me?' and 'Nevertheless, not my will but thine be done' " (p. 5).

For the transpersonally oriented existentialist, there is a paradox inherent in the mystery of suffering: when we accept the incapacity of human beings to understand our predicament of mortality and meaninglessness, we can grow in spiritual empowerment and wisdom. Kierkegaard described this as *authentic faith*, attained through unflinching confrontation with the absurd, in contrast to hand-me-down, escapist, or conformist belief, called *bad faith*. By consciously willing to be oneself, in exactly the circumstances one finds oneself, no matter how dreadful, one discovers that "the self is grounded transparently in the Power, which constituted it" (quoted in Bretall, 1946, p. 341). The transpersonal and therapeutic quality of this was explained by the social work clinician David Edwards (1982, pp. 49–50):

> Self is the experience of spontaneous consciousness. . . . In states of self-awareness, ego-reflective thinking is suspended and mind is alert to sensory stimuli. . . . The act of faith is the key that unlocks self-transcendence. Faith is not ego belief in illusory fantasy. It is projection of self-expression to make empathic contact; and faith refuses to withdraw even when rejected. It is the unique manifestation of a commitment to spiritual communion meeting and encompassing the being of two individuals. To share my recognition that I have been loved and am able to accept that love is the transforming experience of therapy for both client and therapist.

## Transpersonal Psychodynamic Theories of Jung and Assagioli

Transpersonal psychodynamic theories were formed by people influenced by Freud, but who reacted against his emphasis on pathology and his antipathy toward spirituality. For example, Carl Jung, who at one time seemed an "heir apparent" to lead the psychoanalytic school, broke with Freud largely over disagreements about the role of religion and spirituality in human development (1965). Freud viewed religion primarily as a fantasy system that served to defend against painful awareness of human suffering and provided social and moral controls on potentially destructive id impulses (Gay, 1989). In contrast, Jung saw religion, with or without a formal creed, as involving the human quest for a sense of meaning and the developmental process of achieving personal integration and wholeness (1938). He viewed this quest for meaning and wholeness to be the central theme of psychological development. As he noted, the original meaning of the term *psyche* is soul; so *psychotherapy* means healing for the soul.

Likewise, the Italian psychotherapist, Roberto Assagioli (1965, 1973), emphasized the important role of religion and spirituality in helping people to realize an inner unity between all aspects of themselves and a unity with all in the cosmos. Assagioli named the therapeutic process for assisting in this personal realization of unity "psychosynthesis," in contrast to psychoanalysis, which literally means "splitting apart the psyche."

The integration or unification of the self was described by Jung as a transformational, developmental process, called *individuation,* or the formation of a complete self (de Laszlo, 1990; Ewen, 1988). Individuation involves *a transcendent function* that brings into complementarity, balance, and integration contrasting aspects of the psyche, different styles of relating to the world (introversion and extroversion), and different capacities for perceiving the world (sensation, intuition, feeling, and rational thinking). This transcendent function requires that the conscious ego become more and more open to its unconscious capacities, attributes, and sources of wisdom. As conscious awareness expands, the boundaries of the self grow to encompass the personal unconscious and the collective (transpersonal) unconscious. In this case, full individuation does not mean forming a separate ego-bounded self. It refers to conscious awareness and integration of all aspects of the self in relationship with others and in unity with the true Self, which is one with all.

Jung and Assagioli's theories contained *topographical models* for the structure of the psyche. Jung's view expanded Freud's scheme beyond the personal conscious and personal unconscious to the collective unconscious (Figure 13.2). This model can be pictured as a water well. The opening of the well at the top is the conscious mind, which is open to the environment outside in addition to the depths of the psyche within. Through conscious activity, we can put a bucket down into the water to draw up unconscious contents.

The "well"
of personal psyche

Preconscious

Personal
Unconscious

Underground "water table" connecting all psyches

Collective Unconscious

**FIGURE 13.2.** Jung's topographical model of the psyche depicted as a water well.

The *personal unconscious* includes the *preconscious,* which stores easily retrievable memories, like the surface of the well water. The personal unconscious also includes the deeply submerged contents of repressed and long forgotten memories. With more effort and therapeutic assistance, we can "dip the bucket" of awareness deeper into this well. Beneath these personal levels of the unconscious mind, the individual psyche connects with all others, just as different wells tap into the same ground water at their deepest levels. This is the *collective unconscious* that is a repository of inherited universal potentials for meaning, called *archetypes* (de Laszlo, 1990). The most profound archetype is the *Self,* which means the potential for complete integration and enlightenment, often symbolized in religious terms by sacred exemplars such as Christ or Buddha, and represented in religious designs, such as Buddhist or Hindu meditation diagrams, called mandalas, and First Nations (Native American) Medicine Wheels (Coggins, 1990; Jung, 1959b). When the individual's awareness reaches down deeply into this level, or contents float up unanticipated as in dreams and visions, insights of a profoundly self-transforming nature can occur. This is because the individual self is exposed to energy and messages for growth that feel as though they come from a transcendent, authoritative, and divine source.

Assagioli added to this metaphor a dimension of height as well as depth (1965; Rowan, 1993), creating the shape of an egg (Figure 13.3). At the center of the egg is the conscious "I" of awareness that exerts will and effort to expand the field of consciousness to the full extent of the Self. The complete egg figure represents the complete or true Self. The true Self is commonly spelled with a capital "S" in transpersonal theories to distinguish it from the ego-limited self. The *middle unconscious* is equivalent to the personal preconscious for Freud and Jung. The *lower unconscious* is equivalent to the deep personal unconscious of Freud. It contains basic unconscious process that direct automatic body functioning, as well as fundamental drives and urges, intense

1. The lower unconscious
2. The middle unconscious
3. The higher unconscious or superconscious
4. The field of consciousness
5. The conscious self or "I"
6. The higher self
7. The collective unconscious

**FIGURE 13.3.** Assagioli's model of the psyche.  *Source: Psychosynthesis: A Collection of Basic Writings.* Copyright 1965 by Robert Assagioli. Reprinted by permission of SSL/Sterling Lord Literistic, Inc.

emotional complexes, and disorganized or pathological mental manifestations that may occur through dreams and delusions. The *higher unconscious* (or superconscious) is the source of elevated artistic, creative, and spiritual intuitions, feelings, and revelations.

When we learn to center our awareness in this higher region of mind, we actualize the *Higher Self.* According to Assagioli, once a person does this, he or she realizes that the Higher Self is the true Self, which encompasses but transcends the ego-limited self. When awareness is limited to the egoic level, a person experiences only the realm of the separate personal self as real. Centering awareness in the Higher Self allows contact with the wisdom potential of the collective unconscious. Expansion of awareness to the complete Self results in feelings of personal integrity and balance as well as unity with others because the true Self of everyone is linked in the collective unconscious. Assagioli's distinction between the higher and lower unconscious is intended to avoid confusion between *preegoic,* immature, or psychotic experiences of confusion between self and environment and *transegoic,* mature, mystical experiences of unity with others (Rowan, 1993).

## Holotropic Theory

Holotropic theory was developed by the psychiatrist Stanislav Grof, initially through studies of LSD-assisted therapy in Czechoslovakia and the United States and later through use of nondrug-based techniques to stimulate transpersonal experiences (Grof, 2006; Rowan, 1993). His research revealed that participants reported many transpersonal and life-enhancing aspects, such as helping cancer patients work through psychological and social difficulties associated with the cancer diagnosis and confrontation with mortality (Grof & Halifax, 1977). Stanislav Grof and his wife Christina Grof developed a nondrug-based technique, called *holotropic breathwork,* that often produces transpersonal experiences (Grof, 2006; Grof & Grof, 1989). Holotropic breathwork involves guiding participants through an experience of relaxation paired with mild hyperventilation exercises and bodywork while listening to highly energetic evocative music. By cataloging and analyzing extensive clinical observations and participant reports, a wide variety of transpersonal experiences have been identified, along with a scheme for understanding their place in human development.

Grof (1988, 2006) contrasted two modes of consciousness. In the *hylotropic mode of consciousness,* our experience of reality is limited by our physical sensory faculties, space and time dimensions, and the physical constraints of the environment. Hylotropic literally means "moving toward matter," which is typical of the ordinary waking consciousness that perceives the world as a merely physical realm. In contrast, the *holotropic mode of consciousness* opens awareness to transpersonal and mystical experience. Holotropic literally means "moving toward wholeness." In the holotropic mode, the rules associated with physical limitations are experienced to be transcended. Thus, space and time are no longer barriers.

Grof has developed a detailed categorical classification of transpersonal experiences that are opened through the holotropic mode of consciousness. The first category is "Experiential Extension Within Consensus Reality and Space-Time." This includes experiences that transcend spatial and temporal barriers, so that boundaries between the individual and the universe are not binding. For example, in transcendence of spatial limits, the person may experience merging with other people, animals, plants, the planet, or even the entire universe. This opens the possibility of so-called extrasensory perception such as telepathy. In transcendence of temporal limits, the person may feel identified with his or her own past, including embryonic development or previous incarnations. This opens the possibility of precognition.

The second category is "Experiential Extension Beyond Consensus Reality and Space-Time." It includes experiences that defy conventional Euro-American notions about the inhabitants of the material world entirely. For example, the person may experience communication with the souls of the dead, spirits of plants or animals, or even cosmic consciousness, that is, union with the consciousness of the entire universe. This is the category of experiencing what Jung termed archetypes of the collective unconscious.

The third and final category is "Transpersonal Experiences of Psychoid Nature." In these experiences, the distinction between consciousness and matter is blurred. This category includes synchronistic events, that is, occasions in which there is a meaningful but apparently noncausal link between dreams, intuitions, and visions and material events in one's own life; for example, when a person has a strong dream experience of a particular animal that brings significant meaning and then during wakefulness the animal unexpectedly appears. This category includes spontaneous consciousness-over-matter events, such as hauntings or poltergeists, and intentional consciousness-over-matter events, such as faith healing.

These transpersonal experiences can appear bizarre from the standpoint of the ordinary hylotropic mode of consciousness. Because conventional science and mental health therapy take place within hylotropic assumptions, mental health professionals easily assume that client reports of transpersonal experiences are simply delusional or hallucinatory. However, within the holotropic context, these events can be experienced as real and meaningful and can yield insights applicable to ordinary life. Grof's work emphasizes the importance of taking these experiences seriously within the context of clients' own worldviews and spiritual beliefs.

Grof observed that the holotropic mode of consciousness sometimes opens up awareness to dramatic and rapid experiences of catharsis and self-transformation. Often, this involves a vivid subjective experience of symbolic death and rebirth, which may mirror the stages of literal clinical birthing (Grof, 1985, 1992, 2006). The cathartic aspects may include emotionally powerful memories of related life events. When these events are recalled and the energy is released with therapeutic support, important breakthroughs in personal growth can occur. Whether these "memories" are objectively accurate, or metaphorical imaginations, therapists who use holotropic breathwork help clients to work through these powerful experiences to achieve insight and transformation.

Another important insight stemming from Grof's research is that psychopathological experiences should be distinguished from growth promoting transpersonal experiences, even when these are disruptive. Grof and his colleagues have distinguished between transpersonal growth experiences of spiritual emergence and spiritual emergency (Bragdon, 1990; Grof & Grof, 1990; K. W. Watson, 1994). *Spiritual emergence* is an experience of relatively gradual but progressive expansion of a sense of wellness, freedom, responsibility, and connection with the cosmos. The related experiences and insights are rather easy to integrate into ordinary life. In general, spiritual emergence is felt to be exciting and pleasurable. In contrast, *spiritual emergency* is a critical and difficult phase of intense and profound transformations of the entire being. It usually involves dramatic bursts of energy, altered states of consciousness, explicit spiritual themes, feelings of being plunged into death and rebirth, and serious disruption of daily life. Spiritual emergence is a gradual unfoldment of transpersonal awareness, whereas spiritual emergency is a sudden opening of transpersonal awareness resulting in crisis. Both spiritual emergence and spiritual emergency are important phases of growth, which may alternate with each other. Holotropic theory promotes training for mental health professionals in spiritually appropriate assessment and practice as well as therapeutic techniques that rapidly open transpersonal awareness.

## Wilber's Spectrum Model of Human Development and Integral Theory

Ken Wilber's spectrum model is the most widely cited and comprehensive contemporary transpersonal theory of human development. Wilber (2000a, 2000b, 2001) has integrated a vast array of Eastern and Western philosophical, religious, psychological, historical, and sociological concepts of individual and social development. Wilber brought insights from his own practice of Buddhist meditation, multidisciplinary studies in philosophy, and his personal struggles with life's challenges, including the death of his wife from cancer (Wilber, 1993, 1999).

Wilber's theory offers a spiritually astute alternative to conventional developmental theories. Wilber has been refining his theory through prolific writing since 1977. Given the changes of terminology and refinements of his thinking during this time, the following discussion draws on a wide range of his writing but emphasizes the most recent versions of his model (Wilber, 1996, 1998, 2000a, 2000b, 2001, 2006, 2007; Wilber, Patten, Leonard, & Morelli, 2008).

We have categorized Wilber's model as "transpersonal" because we focus on how it addresses transpersonal aspects of human experience and development. Wilber (2000a, 2000b), however, names his complete perspective as Integral Theory because it includes and transcends the insights and scope of analysis from the "four forces" of psychology (i.e., behavioral, psychoanalytic, humanistic, and transpersonal) as well as from many other disciplines and cross-cultural studies in order to understand subjective and objective aspects individual and collective human experience at all levels of development.

**PRINCIPLES OF DEVELOPMENT**  Wilber's model describes the spectrum of levels of consciousness that emerge in both individual and societal development. It assumes that human beings are the product of an evolutionary process that involves not only biology but also the unfoldment of cognitive capacities, increasingly comprehensive worldviews, more profound forms of spirituality, and corresponding types of social organization (Wilber, 2000a, 2000b). He postulated that individuals and their sociocultural environments exhibit the same basic structures and levels of consciousness, so one can identify parallels of developmental course between micro and macro human systems. This is similar to the biological notion that "ontogeny recapitulates phylogeny." However, the recapitulation is not due to a rigid biological program that controls mental development. Rather, the parallel development occurs because all human holons (system levels) face similar challenges to move toward increasingly sophisticated forms of mental functioning and all human systems influence each other's development. As larger numbers of individuals attain higher levels of consciousness, they influence the formation of collective sociocultural patterns of worldview and institutions to reflect this level of consciousness. A typical mode of functioning in a society operates like a magnet, not only attracting and encouraging its members to come up to this developmental level, but also pulling down and discouraging members from exceeding it (Wilber, 1996). There are always some courageous and gifted people who go beyond the typical mode of functioning, but this is often at the risk of ostracism. Likewise, as technological and sociostructural conditions become more complex, cognitively demanding, and cross-culturally interactive, individuals are challenged to accommodate their modes of consciousness to become broader, more encompassing, sophisticated, and transpersonal. Wilber meant these levels to describe the most typical and common mode of functioning at any developmental period for an individual or society.

Wilber referred to this spectrum model as a *holarchy,* that is, an ordering of increasingly complex, sophisticated, and comprehensive structures of consciousness and social organization. Each level includes the capacities and insights of the previous levels. Each higher level transcends the limitations of the lower levels. *Include and transcend* is an important developmental principle. At each level of consciousness, the person is able to reflect upon the rules, assumptions, and beliefs associated with the lower levels. While functioning from a higher level, a person can modify and transcend the rules, assumptions, and beliefs of the lower levels. Each level reveals greater profundity, self-reflexivity, and comprehensiveness; as Wilber put it, "Greater depth, greater interiority, greater consciousness" (2000a, p. 119). Wilber pointed out that it is not necessary for a person or group to fully master the potential of any given level to progress to higher levels. It is only necessary to achieve sufficient comfort and competence at a given level to be able to explore and move into the higher level of consciousness. For example, one does not have to be a poetic genius to be able to use language very adequately and to have spiritual experiences that go beyond what words can express.

More advanced holons of consciousness have greater *depth,* but less *span,* than the predecessors (Wilber, 1996). Greater depth means that consciousness is able to include more profound and complex aspects of reality. However, fewer and fewer types and numbers of organisms actualize the potential of each higher level of development. Therefore, at each higher level, the population and physical scope (span) of the holon is smaller. For example, according to Wilber, within the vast earth's ecosystem, only humans appear capable of rational and transrational levels of consciousness. Human consciousness can include awareness of the entire earth ecosystem (greater depth), but human organisms compose only a small fraction of the earth's bioecology (smaller span).

Levels of consciousness are holons that include the predecessor levels as component systems. *Level* refers to the epigenetic quality of development, that is, each more advanced level involves a qualitatively different and more comprehensive mode of consciousness and functioning that includes yet transcends the previous levels. These levels of consciousness have universal deep similarities in different places and cultures. For example, people may interpret and express experience of unitary consciousness differently, but the capacity for unitary consciousness seems universal. People may have peak experiences as glimpses into higher levels of consciousness. But a person has achieved a certain level only if his or her consciousness and functioning have been relatively well established with consistent traits and competency at that level.

Each level can be depicted simply as a sequential step, but more precisely, it can be understood as one of many concentric spheres, each of which embraces and includes all the previous ones, or as a widening loop in an ascending spiral. Wilber sometimes uses the sequence of colors of the rainbow to name the levels in order to show that they grade into each other (2006). Indeed, he refers to a level as a *wave* in order to highlight the fluid, flowing, and overlapping qualities of levels. People experience and function in ways that waiver, flow, regress, and progress through the levels. Each level is characterized by a *structure,* that is, the holistic organization of patterns of a person's experience, awareness, and functioning within the level.

Each person, however, has many different capacities and functions, such as cognitive, emotional, motivational, moral, interpersonal, aesthetic, psychosexual, and spiritual (Wilber, 2000b, 2006, 2007). This is similar to the concept of multiple intelligences in Chapter 9. These *lines* or *streams* of development are interrelated but distinct. Each is influenced by a person's genetic and physical makeup, situational and environmental conditions, and choices. They can unfold with some degree of independence, thus making overall personal development a complex pattern of interaction between all these particular aspects of development—not a simple linear progression level to level. Thus, people may show a high level of competence in certain aspects (e.g., spiritual awareness) simultaneous with a low level of competence or even pathology in another aspect (e.g., social relational skills). This situation is exemplified by a spiritual teacher who may have authentic transpersonal insights while being immature emotionally and inappropriate in relations with students, thus posing a risk as a teacher. *Integral development* involves an effort to bring together congruously one's various aspects of development. Yet overall, the general mode of functioning in healthy development is progressive and growth oriented.

As development of an individual proceeds, the sense of self expands while the scope of consciousness becomes deeper and more encompassing. As mind accommodates to each new level, there is a three-phase process. First, the self "steps up to" the next higher level, achieves comfortable functioning at that level and identifies with it. Second, as new experiences are encountered that challenge the existing way of functioning, the self recognizes the limitations of this level and begins to disidentify from it. Third, the self develops upward to the next higher level, bringing with it the accomplishments and abilities of the previous levels. This process leads to the emergence of new *fulcrums of identity,* or sense of self in relation to others, and new *worldviews,* or cognitive maps of the world (Wilber, 1996, 2000a).

In broad terms, according to Wilber, there is a general trend of development through three major stages: preegoic, egoic, and transegoic (also described as prerational, rational, and transrational). Each of these major stages has component levels (to be explained next). The *preegoic stage* involves infancy and early childhood experience focused on the body, physiological needs, and lack of clear distinction between self and environment. The *egoic stage* involves youth to adulthood experience focused on personal identity, social relational needs, and conventional norms of society. Importantly, humans also have the potential for a transegoic stage of development that can culminate in a decentering from the individual self as bounded by bodily, egoic, and ethnocentric perspective to experience the true Self in union with all other beings and ultimate reality. In the transegoic stage, the ordinary limited separate ego-identity is transcended, but the egoic mode of rational functioning is preserved for its utility within conventional reality and the practical limitations of space and time.

Wilber (2000a) identified two major ways that consciousness reflects on the world and engages in developmental change—*translation* (similar to Piaget's concept of assimilation) and *transformation* (similar to Piaget's concept of accommodation). Every conscious holon (e.g., a human individual or social system) reflects on the world, interprets it, and acts upon it from the framework of its worldview, assumptions, cognitive strategies, categories for classifying the world, and rules for action. To maintain self-preservation and to render the world understandable within its present cognitive capacity, a person or social group tends to recognize and respond to only the aspects of the world that conform to expectations and can be operated on successfully within its current capacity and rules. Thus, the world is translated in a self-consistent, relatively egocentric and ethnocentric manner. The translation function allows refinement of sophistication and skill within a level of development (e.g., an egoic understanding of the world), but it cannot succeed easily with more complex and profound aspects of the world (e.g., transpersonal experiences). When a person or social group encounters some issue of complexity that goes beyond its current level of functioning, it is challenged to accommodate itself, that is, expand the sophistication, complexity, and profundity of its rules and worldview. If successful, this results in transformation to a higher level of development (i.e., a more complex, comprehensive, and profound holon of consciousness). When transformation of consciousness is accomplished, the person or social group can access a wider range of experiences and actualize more profound levels of creativity, self-reflection, and inclusive ways of relating with others.

For example, an ethnocentric person uses his or her own culture-bounded rules and norms to judge people of different cultures by inappropriately translating their experience on his or her own terms. The ethnocentrist might also try to reduce his or her discomfort in encountering this differentness by controlling other people, enforcing their conformity to the ethnocentric framework, or destroying them. However, as we have seen with the transcultural perspective (Chapter 6), creative and respectful encounter with the culturally different can lead one to transform oneself toward a more encompassing, inclusive, appreciative perspective that recognizes both cultural relativity and common humanity. Likewise, a social group can define the entire universe in ethnocentric terms, evaluating itself as most central, important, and correct. The danger of inappropriate translation at the collective level is institutional racism, cultural imperialism, and genocide. The promise of cultural transformation is multiculturalism, global perspective, and advocacy for worldwide social and ecological justice (Wilber, 2000a, 2000b, 2003b, 2006).

**LEVELS OF DEVELOPMENT**  The parallel levels of micro (individual) and macro (sociocultural) development can be divided into three main stages described earlier (preegoic, egoic, and transegoic) with component levels (Figure 13.4). Actually, Wilber uses the terms stage and level interchangeably. Here, we use "stage" consistently to signify the three major tiers (Wilber, 2000b) of development, with "levels" referring to their more detailed components. The age ranges given for each level are approximations of typical ages during which people might move to this level. This does not imply that all people develop to any given level or that the age schedule is fixed. In regard to epochs of macro development, these are periods of history at which a certain typical mode of consciousness prevailed for a given society. However, there have always been individuals who exceeded the norm and operated at the "leading edge" of sociocultural and spiritual development for the society. The following summary converges various versions of Wilber's terminology and models, emphasizing his most recent work (2000a, 2000b, 2001, 2003a, 2006, 2007; Wilber et al., 2008). These levels represent "simple orienting generalizations" (2000b, p. 19) about overall development of consciousness.

**PREEGOIC STAGE**

*Level 1: Sensoriphysical/Archaic (ages 0–2).*  Wilber portrays the infant and young child initially as having a physiocentric (body-oriented) self-identity. The physical self and physical environment are relatively indistinct. Bodily needs and urges drive behavior. Thoughts are dreamlike. To develop the capacity for autonomous functioning, the young child is challenged to distinguish between body and mind, self and environment.

In the macro context, Wilber speculated that protohuman hominids (including *Australopithecus, Homo habilis,* and *Homo erectus*) experienced an extreme physical dependence

| Stage | | Individual Level | Societal Level | |
|---|---|---|---|---|
| | 10 | Nondual (as ultimate goal of development) | | |
| Transegoic | 9 | Causal | None yet | Nondual (as process of development) |
| | 8 | Subtle | None yet | |
| | 7 | Psychic | None yet | |
| Egoic | 6 | Vision-logic | Planetary | |
| | 5 | Formal operational | Rational | |
| | 4 | Concrete operational | Mythic | |
| | 3 | Late preoperational | Magic-mythic | |
| Preegoic | 2 | Preoperational | Magical | |
| | 1 | Sensoriphysical | Archaic | |
| | 0 | Nondual (as source and potential of development) | | |

**FIGURE 13.4.** Wilber's holarchy of micro and macro development.

on the natural environment. Therefore, he said that most likely their social structures were small kinship-based bands, limited to about 40 members each by capacity to obtain and store resources. The major form of subsistence was foraging, hunting, and gathering, so there were relatively few possessions and disruption of the natural environment was minimal. Worldview did not clearly distinguish between body, nature, and culture.

***Level 2: Preoperational/Magical-Animistic (ages 2–4).*** The preoperational child develops mental functioning that differentiates self from others. However, there is still a tendency to confuse one's own thoughts and wishes with things in the environment and to believe that one's thoughts can control the environment. Wilber calls this structure of consciousness phantasmic-emotional (1996). With the rapid expansion of language capacity, the young child can use simple symbols and concepts.

In the macro context, societies continued to be organized primarily by kinship-based bands and tribes. Wilber related this to the period of Neanderthal and Cro-Magnon peoples (circa 200,000–10,000 B.C.E.). Worldview distinguished self from environment, but there was still a great deal of indistinction. For example, Wilber believed that magic and ritual were used in a literalistic manner to defend against danger and death and to organize humans' place in the cosmos. Shamans who help maintain this human/nature connection and communicate with the spirit world are the exemplars of spiritual attainment at this level. Cultures tend to define the universe in terms of projections of human characteristics and needs (egocentrism, anthropomorphism). Cultures maintain a closeness to nature, and even venerate it, but primarily through anthropomorphic projections of human fantasies and wishes. The challenge to worldview that characterizes this level is to demarcate society from nature.

**Level 3: Late Preoperational/Magical-Mythological (ages 4–7).**   In middle childhood, the individual gradually diminishes the egocentric belief that one's own thoughts control the world. However, the child tends to transfer this belief in magical control of the environment onto literalistic concepts of supernatural superpowerful spirits or deities who are believed to control the world. Capacity for rational self-reflection begins to develop. The child is able to form more sophisticated mental representations of things, so the structure of consciousness is called representational mind. This sharpens the sense of self as a separate ego and thus marks a transition from the preegoic to egoic stages of development.

In the macro context, around 10,000 B.C.E., during the Neolithic period, the development of horticulture based on the hoe or digging stick allowed larger numbers of people to congregate. The means of food production were easily usable by both men and women, so there was a relatively egalitarian relationship between the genders. Great Mother Goddess religions were common.

By the end of this period, horticulturalism gave way to settled agriculture by means of the animal-drawn plow. The concentration of large numbers of people and the coordination of agriculture on a large scale led to the development of transtribal societies with formalized laws, political organization, and territorialism. Early forms of states arose. Personal identity was strongly determined by social roles and conformance to rules and laws. Complex cosmologies and religious mythologies were codified. Formalized religious institutions with priests and priestesses emerged. Given the increased sense of cultural differentiation from and technological control of nature through agriculture, the cultural challenge became harmonizing society with nature.

## EGOIC STAGE

**Level 4: Concrete Operational/Mythic-Rational (age 7 to adolescence).**   The older child develops a clear sense of autonomous self, but still defined largely by roles in society and pressures to conform to conventional norms of peers and authorities. The structure of consciousness is called rule/role mind. The sense of social membership is keen. The ability to take the perspective of others increases, enhancing empathy. However, people who operate on different norms or belong to different cultures and religions are judged in an egocentric and ethnocentric manner. Although capacity for rational thought grows, concepts and beliefs remain closely tied with concrete things and familiar contexts.

In the macro context, between 4000 and 2000 years B.C.E. and for some time after, agricultural control of the natural environment intensified, creating surplus food stocks. The major sociocultural challenge was to develop institutions for self-regulation of elaborate social systems. The rapid expansion of the size and complexity of states led to stratified social classes, more rigid bureaucratic forms of government, and religion ruled by kings, queens, and elite priesthoods. Because use of the plow for food production was most commonly associated with males, gender polarization and patriarchy emerged. Increased territorialism and competition for land and other resources led to more widespread warfare. Imperialistic empires emerged.

Increasingly, there was a move to recognize the rights of citizens, but the notion of citizenship was defined narrowly to give privilege to males, to exclude classes of exploited members, and to oppose people viewed as outsiders or aliens. However, the intensified interaction across cultures and wide areas of territory led to the emergence of a more global perspective.

### Level 5: Formal Operational/Rational (early to later adulthood).

This is the highest level of cognitive and social development that most people attain in the contemporary world. Many adults develop a sophisticated level of rational cognitive functioning that allows for highly abstract and complex mental representations of the world. The structure of consciousness is called formal-reflexive, because it is no longer necessary for the mind to tie concepts to concrete things when reflecting on self and world. Reason can be applied to operate on the rules and categories of thinking themselves. The sense of separate self is fully formed. This expands the capacity for creative imagination, understanding the relativity of different personal and cultural perspectives, and appreciating the inherent rights and responsibilities of individuals. Paradoxically, while the sense of separate self is sharpened, the capacity for worldcentric identity emerges.

In the macro context, there was a gradual development from agricultural states to industrial and postindustrial nation-states. From around 2500 to 500 B.C.E., with increasing alienation from and domination of nature, patriarchal religious beliefs focusing on a masculine God predominated. However, around the sixth century B.C.E., sages such as Gautama Buddha, Confucius, Lao Tzu, Socrates, and Plato began advocating for a more universalistic and transcendental spirituality.

As social organization and technology became more complex, there was an increasing sense of alienation between elites and exploited members of societies with dominator hierarchies. By the feudal period, the sense of divorce from and even devaluation of nature became more common. Elaborate religious beliefs and institutions continued to be refined. In the so-called Age of Reason, rational analysis, scientific experiment, and political challenges to religious doctrines eventually led to a formal separation between church and state in the modern period. However, these intellectual movements have tended to become reductionistic, relativistic, and materialistic, often involving the rejection of transrational, transpersonal, and mystical experiences.

With the formation of global systems of exchange of resources and information in the modern period, the potential for many people to develop an appreciation for multiculturalism and globalism has expanded. Wilber (2000a, 2000b, 2003b) stated that there is now a tension between cultural forces for postcolonial imperialism and those seeking international justice. Narcissism, ethnocentrism, and nationalism can be reduced as people learn to question their own beliefs and cultural forms and move toward a worldcentric perspective. People can begin to consider themselves as world citizens, with universal transnational rights and responsibilities. Societies become acutely aware of the damaging results of their manipulations of nature, and environmental ethical debates become more widespread. Interreligious sharing stimulates the potential for inclusive approaches to morality and spirituality.

### Level 6: Vision-Logic/Planetary (mid to later adulthood).

According to Wilber, vision-logic is the leading edge of human development at present. Although most people do not attain it, some older adults move to this level in response to reflection on their mortality, the meaning of life, and how to achieve a sense of common humanity that transcends moral and cultural relativism. Vision-logic is a fuller realization of worldcentric identity, engaging in pluralistic appreciation for cultural diversity. For the individual, vision-logic develops from self-reflection upon rationality itself. It shifts beyond linear, analytical, reductionistic ways of understanding toward systemic and holistic understandings. Mind and body become integrated in a quest for total personal wellness. A moral standard of mutuality emerges in which the well-being of oneself is seen to be inextricably related with the well-being of all others, human and nonhuman. So, along with body/mind integration comes a move toward integration of local and global communities and culture and nature. Vision-logic represents a transition from the egoic stage to the transegoic stage.

In the macro context, Wilber projected that postmodernist awareness of the relativity of cultures and value systems are yielding to a transrational, transcultural, global vision. The major sociocultural challenge is to develop mutually beneficial forms of self-regulating exchanges between society, individual members, and the natural environment. Critical reflection on self and society can lead to an understanding that no person should be specially privileged to dominate others. The ideal of political equality is extended to all people and all cultures. Noncoercive ways of conducting international relations are sought.

In the sphere of spirituality, exclusivistic, imperialistic, patriarchal, and ethnocentric forms of religion are in the process of being transcended, according to Wilber. Spiritual claims are tested by reason and experience, but spirituality is not ostracized as superstition or fantasy. Spiritual seekers from many traditions engage in dialogue to share experience and to work toward a communal, transreligious confirmation or rejection of religious claims.

According to Wilber, vision-logic with planetary worldview is a recently emerging potential. Some individuals and organizations are moving toward a planetary worldview and beyond (into transegoic perspectives), forming ethical views based on compassion for all people and all beings. Few people function consistently at this level, and there is no society fully centered in the planetary worldview. Wilber also acknowledged that there is no guarantee of a successful transition to this level or beyond in world development.

In his view, the potential for vision-logic, and the higher transpersonal levels, has always existed for human beings and has been evident in the spiritual adepts throughout the past. It became more practicably attainable with the emergence of the mental-egoic stage, because many people established a cognitive foundation of formal operational thought while complex cross-cultural exchanges challenged ethnocentrism. Wilber stated that vision-logic and the transpersonal levels are available to any person of ordinary intelligence who wishes to continue to progress, because the capacity for transrationality is inherent in the human being.

## TRANSEGOIC STAGE

Levels of the transegoic stage involve the transcendence of egocentrism, ethnocentrism, and rationalism. All the insights and functional capacities of self, culture, and rationality are retained; however, they are encompassed and transcended by well-established worldcentric experience and awareness of interdependency between self and all things in the universe. According to Wilber, there are no societies that function according to a transegoic consensus. Thus, these levels are described in reference to individual development. However, those people who operate at transpersonal levels of consciousness serve as cultural and spiritual innovators, showing the potential for future, as yet difficult to imagine, forms of society and ways of relating society to the planet and the universe.

*Level 7: Psychic.*   In the psychic level, the individual develops a clear sense of an inner Witness, which is a consciousness that can reflect on self and world without being bound to it. The Witness is sometimes called the Soul, or the spiritual essence of a person. The Soul transcends the limitations of personal ego and personal cultural conditioning. It does not belong to any particular individual or culture. It is transpersonal. The transpersonal Self as Soul embraces both culture and nature. The diverse expressions of culture and nature are experienced as manifestations of the divine Spirit, which itself cannot be reduced to anthropomorphic images.

Given this direct experience of communion with other people and all of nature, a moral imperative of compassion arises, not as a forced obligation or externally imposed religious doctrine but rather as an easy and natural result of experiencing connection and identification with others. "Nature mysticism," in which one feels oneself intimately connected with nature, is a common form of spiritual experience at this level.

*Level 8: Subtle.*   At the subtle level, the individual Soul and a personal God are experienced in communion; thus, "deity mysticism" characterizes spirituality. The person has increasing experiences of archetypal themes, such as described by Jung, Assagioli, and Grof. One might experience feelings of divine bliss, love, and compassion. Nature is transcended, yet embraced as an immanental expression of the Divine. This type of spirituality is well expressed in the mystical writing of St. Teresa of Avila, who described the spiritual marriage of the soul with God, in which the bounds of the senses are transcended.

*Level 9: Causal.*   At the causal level, both the Soul and God as separate personalized entities are transcended. This is the realm of "formless mysticism," because all limitations of space, time, and individuality are dissolved in direct experience of pure Consciousness itself. When the divine is described in this context, it may be referred to as the supreme nondual reality, the inseparateness of the true nature of Self and the true nature of the Kosmos. (Wilber spells this word with a capital K to highlight its meaning as the entire universe including its physical, meaningful, and spiritual qualities.) In Hindu Vedantic terms, Self (Atman) and Divinity (Brahman) are One only. The German Christian mystic, Meister Eckhart, described this ultimate Reality as the Godhead beyond God. At this level of spiritual experience, it doesn't make sense to say that someone experiences communion with God, because there is no separation between Self and God in Ultimate Consciousness. At this point, the Witness is experienced as the Ground of consciousness. The true Self is aware of the personal self but is not limited to any particular states or changes in the self. Because this experience transcends any kind of subject/object separation, language cannot express it and no category of thought can contain it. The causal mode of consciousness is a resting in pure Witness without attachment to any content of consciousness. At the causal level, the Witness is aware of space and time without being trapped in them.

*Level 10: Nondual.*   In the causal level, awareness of the oneness of Self and Kosmos conveys a sense of the world of manifested particular forms as being limited and illusory. However, in complete nondual mystical awareness, even the distinction between transcendence and immanence, or unmanifest and manifest, is dissolved. The experience of pure Consciousness is so complete that all forms, all manifestations of the divine, are experienced as pure Consciousness itself. This level is paradoxically the transcendence of all levels, because the Source, Goal, and Process of development are all experienced as One in the same. So this level is really a nonlevel; sometimes Wilber does not list it separately. In Figure 13.4, the Nondual is represented as level 0 (the source and potential of consciousness development), as level 10 (the ultimate realization of pure Consciousness), and as a nonlevel that pervades the entire process of development (the realization of every moment as ultimate). The Witness, or transpersonal Self, *is* everything that is witnessed. The Ultimate Reality is the immediacy of experience, just this, here and now, at all times. So, coming full circle, the culmination of human development opens awareness to the ordinariness of the extraordinary, the blessedness of the mundane, and the unity of the personal and the transpersonal.

**AQAL (ALL QUADRANTS, ALL LEVELS) MODEL**   The preceding discussion of the spectrum of consciousness and human development should be understood within the context of Wilber's overall Integral Theory that attempts to address the development and experience of everything (human and nonhuman). The AQAL model is an important feature of Integral Theory. AQAL is short for all quadrants, all levels, all lines, all states, and all types. So far we discussed levels and lines of development, states of consciousness, and some types of personalities and cultures. We now summarize the four quadrants, or dimensions of (and perspectives on) reality, in which all these occur. We focus on their implications for understanding human behavior and social work.

*AQAL* (pronounced *ah-qwul*) is a framework to organize understanding of the universe in its four major dimensions, the interior (subjective aspect) of the individual and the collective plus the exterior (objective aspect) of the individual and the collective. This is diagrammed as four quadrants (see Figure 13.5). The *Upper Left (UL) quadrant* is the interior of the individual, referring to a person's subjective thoughts, feelings, sensations, and consciousness. This can only be directly experienced from the inside of oneself, for example, in self-reflection and meditation. This is described in "**I**" voice as in "**I** feel peaceful." The *Upper Right (UR) quadrant* is the exterior of the individual, referring to a person's objective features as observed from the outside, for example, in scientific study of the brain. This is described in "It" voice as in "The brain has a certain activity associated with the feeling of peace. **It** (i.e., brain activity) can be measured by an electroencephalogram." The *Lower Left (LL) quadrant* is the interior of the collective, referring to a group's intersubjective awareness, that is, culture. This can be understood from within the shared values, feelings, and worldview of a group. This is described in "We" voice as in "When **we** meditate together **we** feel peaceful; this prepares us to promote peace in our world." The *Lower Right (LR) quadrant* is the exterior of the collective, referring to a group's externally observable organization of forms and behaviors, that is, society. This can be understood by observation of a group's interobjective behavioral interactions. This is described in "Its" voice as in "The Zen Center provides a place for people to meditate together. **It** is located downtown." Wilber refers to this quadrant in terms of "Its" to illustrate that it refers to features of groups.

Any event can be studied or addressed from the perspectives of all four quadrants in order to provide an integral understanding. In the aforementioned example, meditation could be studied in terms of a meditator's self-awareness of subjective experiences (UL), electroencephalograph recording of the activity of her brain while she is meditating (UR), her Zen group's interpretations of the meaning and purpose of meditation (LL), and the systematic rules and procedures for engaging in meditation (LR). The left-side quadrants are studied by fields emphasizing subjectivity such as phenomenology and social constructionism, whereas the right-side

| Upper Left (UL): | Upper Right (UR): |
|---|---|
| Interior-Individual | Exterior-Individual |
| 'I' | 'It' |
| *Consciousness* | *Organism* |
| Lower Left (LL): | Lower Right (LR): |
| Interior-Collective | Exterior-Collective |
| 'We' | 'Its' |
| *Culture* | *Society and environment* |

**FIGURE 13.5.** Wilber's AQAL diagram (simplified and adapted from Wilber, 2006, p. 20 and p. 22).

quadrants are studied by fields emphasizing objectivity such as neurology and positivistic types of social science. The previous discussion of human development focused on the UL quadrant (i.e., development of individual consciousness) and the LL quadrant (i.e., development of cultural worldviews) with some reference to the other quadrants.

From an integral view, all these fields of study can contribute to a fuller understanding of human behavior when they are brought together. For example, Starnino (2009) used the AQAL model to bring together insights from different and sometimes conflicting views within the mental health recovery movement. The mental health consumer movement emphasizes qualities of hope, meaning, and spiritual insight (UL quadrant); the survivor/ex-patient movement emphasizes empowerment to oppose the social construction of mental illness and stigma (LL quadrant); the conventional psychiatric medical model emphasizes use of medications (UR quadrant); and the professional community integration perspective emphasizes development of community-based supports and psychosocial rehabilitation (LR quadrant). He contends that mental health recovery can be strengthened by bringing together the insights of each approach while avoiding their partiality and limitations. Wilber and colleagues are applying the AQAL model to seek integral innovative approaches in many fields of inquiry such as psychology, spirituality, politics, organizational management, social work, and environmentalism as well as to promote personal growth in all lines of development through all stages of consciousness (Larkin, 2005, 2006; Wilber, 2000b, 2006, 2007; Wilber et al., 2008).

## CONTEMPORARY ISSUES

Contemporary conditions in industrial and postindustrial societies have generated social trends focusing on spiritual renewal and religious revitalization. This is illustrated by the rapid growth of membership in evangelistic and charismatic Christian groups, the frequent use of religious polemics in political debate, the rise of the New Age movement, and the growth of spiritually oriented alternative approaches to healing. The emergence of multicultural nations woven together in planetwide cultural and economic networks has challenged people to form worldviews and life ways that embrace multiple views of reality (Wilber, 2000a). This has led to the most extensive efforts toward interreligious dialogue, cross-cultural understanding, and transdisciplinary ways of thinking in human history. Yet, as existentialists have pointed out, the complications and complexities of contemporary life have led many into a crisis of meaning. When the fundamental beliefs and life ways of individuals and social groups are challenged, anxiety and confusion often result. Further, these complex relationships often occur in the context of exploitive, oppressive, and dehumanizing political, economic, military, and religious systems. Unfortunately, the so-called postmodern period seems as much marked by extremes of value relativism, retrenched ethnocentrism, sexism, homophobia, genocidal wars, and religious absolutism as by mutual understanding and accommodation. Transpersonal theory can be seen as an attempt to link ancient spiritual wisdom traditions with contemporary science and philosophy to overcome the many destructive aspects of contemporary life and to take advantage of the potential for personal and social transformation (Wilber, 1998).

Wilber claims that some contemporary societies and innovative groups are beginning to move into the vision-logic level of development, in which the understanding of self expands to include other people and other beings throughout the planet in a vision of interconnectedness and an ideal of international social justice and ecological balance. Transpersonal theory is one manifestation of this trend. However, the danger of this time is that global interrelations will be controlled by "dominator hierarchies," that is, imperialistic, patriarchal, nature-destroying social systems. Transpersonal theory focuses on the study of human psychological, social, and spiritual development to warn of the danger and to support the transformational potential of this time.

## APPLICATION TO SOCIAL WORK PRACTICE

In recent years, transpersonal theories and Integral Theory have been applied to develop detailed frameworks for spiritually sensitive social work practice and to address many particular practice issues, such as adverse childhood experiences, positive youth development, divorce, mental health recovery, coming to terms with death, spiritual developmental crises, counseling with couples, chronic illness, hospice, aging, human service organizational management, and social work education (Bhagwan, 2009; Canda, 1998; Canda & Cheon, 2010; Canda & Furman, 2010; Canda & Smith, 2001; Cowley, 1993, 1996; Derezotes, 2006; Derezotes & Evans, 1995; Larkin, 2005; Larkin & Records, 2007; Nelson-Becker, Nakashima, & Canda, 2006; Starnino, 2009). Integral Theory is also being applied to develop a perspective that can integrate insights from many different fields and research methods and to link micro and macro approaches to practice (Kerrigan, 2006; Larkin, 2006; P. E. Thomas, 2004).

It should be emphasized that the basic transpersonal insight that full human potential includes empathy, creativity, and spirituality has been discussed by social workers since the inception of the profession (Towle, 1965). In the past 20 years of social work, mental health, health and related fields, there has been a rapidly increasing interest in spirituality, including theory-building, empirical research, and practice skills development (Canda & Furman, 2010).

### Definition of the Helping Situation

When clients are struggling with transpersonal experiences, the social worker is challenged as well. For the worker to be able to recognize transpersonal growth crises, or to assist clients to deal with experiences arising from spiritual disciplines such as meditation, the worker must have both theoretical and experiential understanding of the relevant phenomena (Canda & Furman, 2010; Keefe, 1996; Krill, 1990). The worker, therefore, must be engaged in a continuous parallel process between one's own growth and the client's growth. Maintaining a spiritually sensitive helping relationship requires that workers engage in their own constant process of self-reflection, search for meaning, and practice of disciplines that expand awareness to transpersonal levels. From a transpersonal perspective then, the helping situation is an opportunity for both client and worker to deepen their spiritual insight and to grow toward their highest potential, including transpersonal awareness if that is relevant to the client's needs and aspirations. Flowchart 13.1 illustrates possible applications of transpersonal theory for social work practice.

### Assessment, Practice Strategies, and Methods

In addition to having training in the conventional base of knowledge and skill, Hutton (1994) suggested that transpersonal therapists should have the following qualities: openness to transpersonal realms of experience that are healing and transformative; sensitivity to the sacred; knowledge and respect of diverse spiritual paths; and active engagement in spiritual growth. Ideally, the worker regards the client as an irreducible whole with inherent worth and dignity. Although conventions such as diagnostic or assessment categories, standards, and tools may be used to assist practice, the client should never be reduced to mere labels or pathological descriptions. When the worker has a transpersonal vantage on the client, there is a sense of spiritual connection that transcends the personal level of separations based on ego and professional role. Experience of

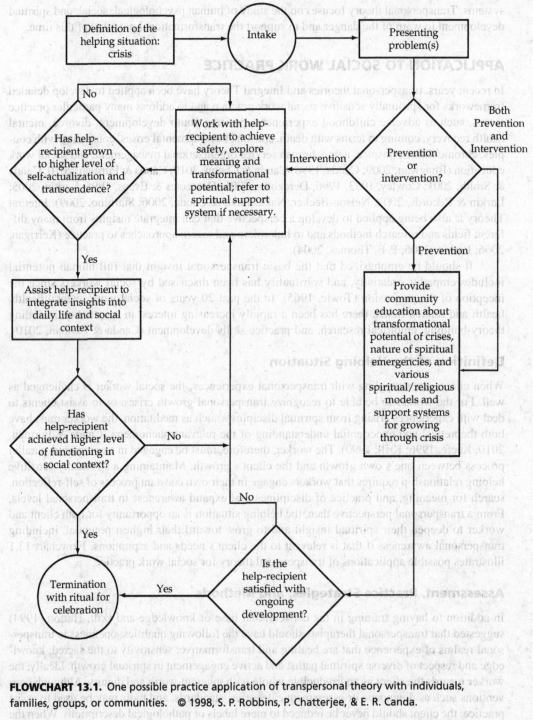

**FLOWCHART 13.1.** One possible practice application of transpersonal theory with individuals, families, groups, or communities.   © 1998, S. P. Robbins, P. Chatterjee, & E. R. Canda.

transpersonal connection with clients heightens the worker's sense of empathy and yields a natural compassionate response (Dass & Gorman, 1985; Wilber, 2000a). Helping should arise from this sense of connection rather than mere technical or bureaucratic requirements.

From a transpersonal view, clients' full potential includes transpersonal possibilities, such as peak experiences, altered states of consciousness, and self-transcendence (Canda & Smith, 2001). Hutton (1994) said that transpersonal therapies encourage the human spiritual quest for sense of personal wholeness and unity with others, ultimate truth, and direct perception of the divine. As Joseph (1987, 1988) has pointed out, social workers may need to assess the ways that clients' benign or punitive conceptions of divinity and their connections with religious support systems affect their sense of well-being throughout the life cycle. Cowley (1993) referred to the transpersonal goal of helping as "spiritual health" in which body, mind, and spirit are integrated and where one achieves a sense of overall satisfaction with life, peace with the world, and communion with the environment. The macro practice implication of this is that the ultimate goal of social work practice would be to create global conditions of justice and bioecological balance that sustain and support everyone's spiritual development (Canda & Furman, 2010).

Transpersonal theory challenges social workers to move beyond the egocentric and ethnocentric assessment standards embodied in conventional development theories (Canda & Furman, 2010; Canda & Smith, 2001). Conventional development theories set up a standard of linear, rational, abstract thinking as the epitome of cognitive development. They posit attainment of separate ego as the pinnacle of identity development. They assume that ordinary waking consciousness, functioning in a dualistic mode (split between subject/object and self/other), is the standard for mental health. This leads to the version of the pre/trans fallacy in which client reports of visionary experiences, altered states of consciousness, and identification with others is reductionistically seen as psychopathological. Certainly mental disorders can involve delusions, hallucinations, and identity confusion. Transpersonal growth can also involve debilitating periods of psychosocial crisis. But transpersonal theory requires that we be able to differentially assess between strengths and pathologies that may occur at preegoic, egoic, and transegoic stages of personal and social development (Nelson, 1994; Wilber, 2000a; Wilber, Engler, & Brown, 1986).

For example, early in the vision-logic level, it is expectable for a person to severely question the meaning and purpose of life and to begin breaking out of conventional egoic self-identity and social conventional roles (Wilber, 1986). This is necessary for transformation to transpersonal awareness to occur. This does not constitute a mere anxiety disorder; if the process were reduced to pathology, the person might be counseled to conform to conventional social norms, accept the ego as the only reality, and be given medications that reduce self-awareness. At the macro level, emergence of a vision-logic worldview involves widespread value confusion in reaction to multicultural and global interactions (Wilber, 2000a). If this is seen as pathological, social policy may move in a reactionary direction of ethnocentrism, isolationism, and imperialism. This would preempt the potential for transcultural and transreligious understanding and cooperation.

In part due to advocacy by transpersonal theorists, the *DSM-IV-TR* has various cautions that clinicians must take into account religious and cultural context and meanings of mental experiences with religious content to determine whether they are "normative" and supportive for the individual or whether they are indicative of psychopathology (Task Force on *DSM-IV*, 2000). This is rather complicated because mystical experiences may or may not overlap with psychotic disorders (Lukoff, 1985; Lukoff, Lu, & Turner, 1995). In addition, V-Code 62.89 has been included since *DSM-IV* for "Religious or Spiritual Problem" that merits treatment but is not related to mental disorder. "Examples include distressing experiences that involve loss or questioning of faith, problems associated with conversion to a new faith, or questioning of spiritual values that may not necessarily be related to an organized church or religious institution" (Task Force on *DSM-IV*, 2000, p. 741). Lukoff, Lu, and Turner (1992) explained that a "psychoreligious problem" involves distressing experiences related to participation in an organized religious institution, such as loss of faith, change of denominational affiliation, and extreme or rigid adherence to beliefs and practices. A "psychospiritual problem" involves distressing experiences associated with reports of relationship difficulties at a transpersonal level or with a transcendent being, such as near death experiences. These may or may not relate to an institutional religion. Further, most of the culture-bound syndromes listed (Task Force on *DSM-IV*, 2000, pp. 898–903) involve religious and consciousness-altering features.

As transpersonal researchers have documented, there are many states of consciousness that involve a wide variety of brain functions and modes of perception. Clinicians need to learn to recognize this variety and to accept the experiential reality of perceptions involved without jumping to conclusions of pathology when these perceptions are at variance with the clinician's own particular view of reality (Tart, 2000, 2009).

Transpersonal theory highlights the growth potential inherent in the crises that social workers must often deal with in practice. From a transpersonal perspective, every life crisis is an opportunity for breakthrough to a higher level of identity and consciousness, precisely because the prevailing psychosocial status quo has been disrupted (Canda and Furman, 2010). Applications of transpersonal theories are shown in Table 13.1.

Peak experiences, nadir experiences, and spiritual emergencies call for a supportive treatment and environment that help the person to move through the crisis of transformation toward a higher level of consciousness and to integrate the insights into ongoing life and satisfying social relations. Also, clinicians need to have skill in a variety of spiritually or religiously derived helping practices that are relevant to particular clients. These could include guided relaxation, meditation, visualization, dreamwork, reading spiritually oriented books, and self-reflective journaling (Canda & Furman, 2010; Derezotes, 2006; Hutton, 1994; Rowan, 1993). At the macro level of practice, the implications for practice described in Chapter 2 on dynamic systems theory, ecofeminism, and deep ecology are relevant here since these reflect vision-logic and transpersonal perspectives. Pyles (2009) summarizes a variety of spiritually based community organizing approaches.

Several social work textbooks present extensive information about how to address spirituality and religious diversity in micro and macro practice in the United States and other countries (e.g., Bullis, 1996; Canda & Furman, 2010; Crisp, 2010; Ellor, Netting, & Thibault, 1999; Lee et al., 2009; Nash & Stewart, 2002; Patel, Naik, & Humphries, 1997; Van Hook, Hugen, & Aguilar, 2001).

## CRITICAL ANALYSIS

### Biological, Psychological, and Spiritual Factors

Most transpersonal development theories do not focus on the details of biology. However, they recognize that biological maturation and neurology affect perceptual, motor, and cognitive abilities throughout the life span. Wilber's Integral Theory addresses biological, physiological, and physical behavioral aspects of the person in the UR quadrant of the AQAL model. Wilber also views biological evolution of the human species as part of a planetary and cosmic evolutionary process in which organisms as species and individuals develop toward greater degrees of complexity and consciousness. This view is rejected, of course, by conventional evolutionary biologists who have a materialistic philosophical base and who see evolution as a process dictated by the intersection of genetics and environment, without any purpose.

**TABLE 13.1**    Various Settings and Applications of Transpersonal Theories

| Type of Agency | Type of Presenting Problems | Type of Program(s) | Definition(s) of the Helping Situation | Type(s) of Activities |
|---|---|---|---|---|
| Mental health center/private practice | Spiritual emergency, crisis | Transpersonal psychotherapy and spiritual support groups | Individual transformational process | Dialogue, spiritual reflection, meditation, ritual |
| Mental health center/private practice | Meditation-related panic attack | Transpersonal psychotherapy and spiritual support groups | Spiritual development | Dialogue, supervised meditation techniques, referral, collaboration |
| Substance abuse treatment facility | Distress due to drug-related visionary experiences | Individual therapy, 12-step programs, other support groups | Spiritual emergency, discernment of hallucinations and visions | Detoxification, dialogue, spiritual reflection, referral, collaboration |
| Family service center | Religious conflict within family | Family counseling | Family transformational process | Family dialogue reframing conflict as opportunity for creativity, referral, collaboration |
| Hospice | Confronting mortality | Grief-work and death preparation | Existential crisis | Dialogue, spiritual reflection, referral, collaboration |
| Religious organization | Questioning faith or religious affiliation | Spiritual direction, individual and family counseling | Spiritual discernment, pastoral counseling | Dialogue, religious reading, referral, collaboration |
| Community action group | High rate of violent crime | Peaceful community organizing and political action | Community transformation process | Networking with neighborhood and religious organizations, win/win conflict mediation, rituals to address collective trauma |

Transpersonal researchers who study states of consciousness are very interested in the neurological and biophysical correlates of subjective experiences. Biofeedback studies and neurochemical studies, for example, have not only identified many of these connections but have also led to the development of techniques for the conscious voluntary control of autonomic body functions (such as in reducing physiological anxiety reactions) through meditation and for inducing rapid altered states of consciousness, such as holotropic breathwork. In the field of medicine, researchers are documenting physical and psychosocial effects of prayer, meditation, healing visualizations, and religious participation on the immune system, disease prevention, and recovery from illness (Koenig, McCullough, & Larson, 2001).

Transpersonal theories make major contributions to the understanding of spiritual development, human potential for creativity and expanded consciousness, and the integration of body, mind, and spirit. Wilber's attempt to link personal and social development offers a conceptual bridge between micro and macro views of the life cycle. His AQAL model has the potential to help social workers integrate many theoretical perspectives and types of empirical evidence for holistic practice.

Some critics reject the possibility and usefulness of any type of theory that seeks universals in human nature and development because of the tremendous variety among human individuals and cultures and the dangers of projecting ethnocentric, sexist, and other biases (Pals, 1996). Some have claimed that Wilber and other transpersonalists overrely on conventional developmental theories to account for preegoic and egoic development, thus carrying in their limitations (Canda, 1991; Walsh & Vaughan, 1994). Yet, Wilber (2000a, 2000b) has refined his theory to take into account insights and empirical evidence from numerous fields of study, cultures, and religions.

There are basic theoretical and philosophical differences and disagreements among transpersonal theorists themselves about the nature of consciousness and reality. Some existentialists view transpersonal theory as a flight into fantasy to escape the tension of mortality and human finitude. On the contrary, as Wilber's account of his wife's death from cancer illustrates, transpersonal theory and Integral Theory can provide a framework for facing mortality with courage and discovering love and meaning in the midst of suffering (1993). Each social worker needs to engage in deep personal reflection to ascertain how he or she would stand on these issues.

## Social, Cultural, and Economic Forces

Transpersonal theorists have leveled many criticisms against social, cultural, and economic forces that restrict individual and societal development. According to Maslow, full human potential can only be attained when supportive environmental conditions are present. Wilber (1996, 2000a, 2000b, 2001, 2006) has warned of the dangers of social pathologies (such as value confusion, religious exclusivism, and militant ethnocentrism) that are risks in the current shift toward a vision-logic, postmodern society. However, in general, as this school of theory is an outgrowth of psychology, most transpersonal theorists emphasize the individual rather than the macro political dynamics and issues of oppression and injustice.

Wilber's work (2000a, 2000b, 2001, 2007; Wilber et al., 2008) has begun to make explicit the implications of an integral approach for social and political action. In broad terms, Wilber proposes that integral politics needs to recognize both the intrapersonal dimension (e.g., moral responsibility, which conservatives have emphasized) and the external sociopolitical dimension (e.g., social justice, which liberals have emphasized). Governance should reflect the vision-logic and transpersonal ideals of worldcentrism (appreciating unity in diversity and going beyond egocentrism or ethnocentrism) and Kosmocentrism (compassion for all beings in all worlds).

As Canda (1991) pointed out, there is the risk of being self-serving by setting up developmental models and standards that reflect the experience of one's own historical and cultural context. For example, when taken literally and simplistically, Wilber's sociocultural development scheme implies that tribal societies and shamanistic forms of spirituality should be (or will be) superseded by supposedly "higher" forms of society and mysticism. In fact, Wilber promotes an approach to global social justice that honors and protects all individuals' and cultures' dignity (2000a, 2000b). The idea of sociocultural evolution should not be misused in ethnocentric and imperialistic approaches to social work practice with Indigenous peoples and international social development. Wilber also posits human beings at the summit of evolution, to which some ecophilosophers object because they advocate for an egalitarian view of all forms of life.

## Relevance to Individuals, Groups, Families, Organizations, Institutions, and Communities

Although transpersonal theories primarily focus on individual consciousness and behavior, they do address macro-social structures in two significant ways. First, the holistic view of Wilber and others is in keeping with the insights of dynamic systems theory that all system types and levels are intricately related. The transpersonalists' advocacy for humane and just social and ecological conditions that support everyone's spiritual development offers a point of connection with deep ecology, ecofeminism, and spiritually oriented macro-change movements. Second, transpersonal theory shows that individuals in many cultures and spiritual traditions report expansion of their awareness and sense of identity to include other people, other beings, and even the entire universe. This yields a moral imperative for compassionate action toward others in the local environment as well as a larger concern for justice and ecological balance for all on the planet and beyond.

   If one were to apply such awareness to social action at any system level, one would seek optimal win/win solutions that maximize the mutual benefit of all involved, human and nonhuman, local and global (Canda & Furman, 2010). Implications for clinical practice have already been described in the previous section. In regard to agency administration and community action, the principles of humanocracy and Gandhian social action presented in Chapter 2 (systems theories) are equally supported by transpersonal theory. For example, the basis of Gandhi's nonviolent action was *satyagraha* (Truth-force), which is an understanding of the inherent worth and dignity of all beings arising from a transpersonal awareness of the transcendent Truth inherent in all (Sharma, 1987). In accord with this, Canda and Chambers (1993) have proposed that social policy debate needs to be conducted from a clear and explicit value position based on an inclusive spirituality. Pyles (2009) describes some types of faith-based and spiritually inclusive community organizing approaches. Bhagwan (2010) describes spiritually sensitive approaches to social development with an international view. Wilber's AQAL model offers potential for innovative social movements and social policies that attend to both micro and macro aspects of practice. Canda and Furman (2010) have developed a model for spiritually sensitive human service organizational culture consistent with transpersonal and holistic management insights.

## CONSISTENCY WITH SOCIAL WORK VALUES AND ETHICS

Because transpersonal theory advocates for the adaptation of helping practices that often derive from religious contexts and have explicit spiritual purposes, this must be done in accord with social work values and ethics. Canda and Furman (2010) have developed a set of guidelines for ethical reflection about the use of prayer, meditation, ritual, collaboration with religious helpers, and other religious and nonreligious spiritually based practices. These take into account principles of nonjudgmental openness to diverse forms of spirituality and religion, establishment of deep rapport and trust, assessing client interest and readiness, and development of worker's competence and comfort. Indeed, social work ethics require that workers practice in a manner that respects religious, cultural, and other forms of diversity. Transpersonal theories can help us to build our knowledge and skills to demonstrate this respect.

Overall, transpersonal theories support an optimistic view of optimal health and well-being. The "farthest reaches of human nature" include high self-esteem, loving and responsible relations with others, sense of meaning and peace with the world, and communion with the ultimate reality. Transpersonalists see this potential as inherent in our nature. Transpersonal practitioners appreciate the internal personal spiritual strengths of clients and cooperate with religious and spiritual resources and support systems in the environment. Transpersonal theories also challenge social work to expand its appreciation for diversity to include the wide variety of religious and spiritual traditions and the full range of states of consciousness. There are many ways of helping and concepts of human behavior that derive from diverse religious and cultural traditions that can expand the helping repertoire (Canda & Furman, 2010; Gray, Coates, & Yellow Bird, 2008; Lee et al., 2009; Mace, 2008; McBee, 2008; Van Hook et al., 2001), for example, collaboration with Christian faith-based organizations, Buddhist mindfulness meditation practices adapted to mental health treatment, Indigenous Medicine Wheel teachings for cultural support and substance abuse recovery, and integration of traditional Chinese philosophy and medicine theory with Western therapies for holistic practice.

Transpersonal theory suggests a concept of empowerment that can expand traditional social work conceptions. Two of the most influential community organizers for human rights and liberation, Mohandas Gandhi and Rev. Martin Luther King, Jr., claimed that the greatest source of power to sustain social justice action comes from beyond the personal, from the universal or divine. In theoretical terms, this is the energy and motivation that arises from transpersonal levels of awareness. Paradoxically, although this type of power requires a well-established ego, it also requires a symbolic death of the ego and transformation to the transpersonal Self. The ego is divested of its autonomous power in order to yield a transpersonal power. Some believe this is consistent with the concept of "surrendering to a Higher Power" in 12-step programs. It does not mean "self-abnegation and subjugation"; it means self-awareness, self-transcendence, and self-fulfillment in meaningful relations with others.

However, as discussed earlier, some transpersonal theories have been criticized for ethnocentric and gender-biased assumptions and language. Although diverse cultures, religions, and worldviews are addressed, they are sometimes viewed through a Eurocentric patriarchal lens. Wilber has made significant efforts to rework his theory to take this into account. He has encouraged the expansion of dialogue between theorists, mystics, and activists of many cultures and spiritual ways to seek consensus of understanding on these complex issues.

## PHILOSOPHICAL UNDERPINNINGS

Transpersonal theories draw on a wide range of philosophical and religious traditions, especially from mystical perspectives within Buddhism, Christianity, Judaism, Hinduism (especially Vedanta), Sufism, Taoism, and various forms of shamanism. In this case, the term *mysticism* refers to a spiritual approach in which people seek direct experience of ultimate reality or of the sacred, rather than relying on borrowed religious or philosophical teachings. Mysticism shares with conventional science a dedication to investigate the nature of reality through direct experience as well as discussion and debate with other investigators. However, it contrasts with conventional science in emphasizing the importance of subjectivity and consciousness and in claiming that egoically based perceptions and linear rationality can be transcended through meditation and other spiritual disciplines.

Therefore, transpersonal theory accepts the conventional scientific view of an objective material reality, limited by causality and temporality, only as a limited egoic mode of understanding. It claims that reality can be understood more comprehensively in terms of holistic philosophies, which recognize the complementarity of opposites and cyclic and systemic processes, as well as monistic philosophies, which posit that, ultimately, all dualistic distinctions between this and that, or self and other, are illusions (Canda, 1991; Canda & Furman, 2010).

## METHODOLOGICAL ISSUES AND EMPIRICAL SUPPORT

Transpersonal theories make important contributions to the expansion of our approaches to research. In particular, they encourage expanding our epistemologies and research methodologies to include quantitative, experimental, phenomenological, qualitative, and mystical disciplines of inquiry into the nature of consciousness and transpersonal experience (Braud & Anderson, 1998; Canda, 1991; Wilber, 1998). As Wilber (1998) pointed out, contemporary conventional science and classical mysticism both share an emphasis on testing claims about reality through direct experience. Transpersonal theories and Integral Theory also bring social work to a more sophisticated level of transdisciplinary and transcultural theoretical inquiry, drawing on concepts from many different fields, cultures, and spiritual traditions.

In terms of conventional scientific empirical support for transpersonal theories, there has been much controversy (Ewen, 1988; Maddi, 1996). Those behavioral scientists who reject the possibility of consciousness independent of body or any transpersonal levels of experience, automatically reject all phenomenological or clinical reports of such phenomena as being illusory. Many transpersonal concepts, such as the collective unconscious, are impossible to operationalize in directly observable terms. However, there is extensive experimental evidence to show that a wide variety of brain functions exist to correspond to subjective reports of states and levels of consciousness (Lukoff & Lu, 1988; Lukoff, Zanger, & Lu, 1990; Tart, 2000). There are numerous qualitative and quantitative studies of the efficacy of participation in religiously based social support systems as well as spiritual practices with transpersonal qualities, such as prayer, meditation, mindfulness, and guided visualization (Canda, 2009; Canda & Furman, 2010; Koenig et al., 2001). Nonetheless, the claims of the superior value of transpersonal experiences and levels of consciousness rest on philosophical assumptions, such as "the more comprehensive, inclusive, and compassionate, the better." This is a matter of philosophy and morality rather than one of empirical support per se.

In general, transpersonal developmental theory is metatheory, in that it integrates many different theories into a more comprehensive theory. The advantage of this is increasing the comprehensiveness and descriptive power of theory. But there is a danger of overrelying on preexisting theories that are embedded with logical and empirical flaws, as described earlier. There is a tendency for some theorists to oversimplify diverse theories and spiritual perspectives in an effort to find common ground. A serious flaw in theoretical reasoning occurs when opponents' views are portrayed in a misleading manner to discredit them. Wilber sometimes has set up "straw figures" through caricatured portrayals of rival views and then ridiculed them (Buhner, 2010). For example, he portrayed deep ecology as an "ecomasculinist" and romanticized view of nature that denigrates human beings (Wilber, 1996). He has since tried to be more precise and less pejorative in his writing (2000a).

Much more careful empirical research of both qualitative and quantitative types is needed to check and refine these theories. In addition, more careful and extensive cross-cultural and comparative religious research is needed to avoid oversimplified interpretations of highly complex and divergent religious traditions and cultures.

# Summary

Transpersonal theories contribute much to our understanding of the spiritual and transegoic aspects of human behavior. Transpersonal theory should hold great appeal for those who have an interest in spirituality and in diverse religious and philosophical conceptions of the self and consciousness. Although the profession began from religious roots that shared these concerns, religion and spirituality have been seriously neglected in social work. If we are to develop an understanding of the whole person and the whole environment, it is crucial that we take the insights of transpersonal theories into account. The social work profession also has a great deal to contribute to the transpersonal theory movement. We can bring our knowledge about the social environment and social action to the task of making transpersonal theory more connected with social justice and ecological concerns. This would provide a broad view of well-being and justice that encompasses the bio-psycho-spiritual-social-planetary and cosmic aspects of the environment.

# Application of Theories

## APPLICATION OF THEORIES TO PRACTICE

- should be based on critical reflection
- helps address all aspects of the person and the environment
- allows making a good fit to various system levels, social work values, and empirical evidence
- provides a wide repertoire for helping in various fields
- draws on great intellectual contributions to understanding human behavior
- opens possibilities for innovation in social work

The wide range of human behavior theories presents a formidable but necessary challenge to the practitioner: how to decide which theory or theories to apply in any given situation. Chapters 1 through 13 have provided both a foundation of theoretical knowledge and critical evaluation of theories, so that students and practitioners have a variety of options. This final chapter builds on this foundation by providing guidelines to help social workers decide which theories to use in practice.

Realistically, in actual social work practice, it is up to the practitioner and agency, in collaboration with the clients as individuals and groups, to decide what theories are appropriate. The preferences of educators, and the authors of this book in particular, are not very significant in that decision. The worker's collaboration with the client is most critical. As we stressed in Chapter 1, "the map is not the territory." In practice, the most crucial reality is not any theoretical precon-ception, but rather the person-to-person encounter with clients in a real situation. In keeping with the strengths perspective, it is from the reality of any particular helping situation, especially the goals, aspirations, strengths, and perspectives of clients, that the helping approach should emerge. For example, hundreds of empirical studies have shown that the particular theory or practice model chosen is not the only key to client satisfaction and positive outcomes in clinical practice and sometimes it is not the main key (Messer & Wampold, 2006). In general, the quality of the helping relationship appears to account for variance in outcomes from 7% to 30% (Cooper, 2004). Three of the strongest factors are a *collaborative relationship* between client and therapist, *consensus and cooperation* on treatment goals, and practitioner *empathy*. This is demonstrated behaviorally when a social worker seeks clear ongoing feedback from clients about the helping relationship and progress toward outcomes, responds authentically to the feedback, and continually strives to improve performance throughout her or his career (S. D. Miller, Hubble, & Duncan, 2008). The helping relationship should demonstrate humanity, empathy, rapport, and genuine caring (Canda & Furman, 2010). Education about theory should help prepare the practitioner to engage in a skillfully caring helping relationship. Theory should not constrain or coerce the relationship.

Education in social work theory and practice skills is analogous to the education of a musician in that both musical theory and technical performing skills need to be mastered. However, if that is all a musician knows, then the performance will be technically excellent but aesthetically dull and lifeless. But when the musician has also a rapport with the musical score and the instrument and is inspired by a love for music, then the performer transcends the limitations of theory and skill to express the musical score with passion, spontaneity, and creativity. Indeed, in that moment of inspired performance, the theory and skill are, in a sense, forgotten at the same time that they give form to the beauty and spontaneity of the music. To achieve such a harmonious expression of theory, skill, and spontaneity, the performer must engage in a continuous process of training, self-reflection, and performance. In social work, this quality of rapport, harmony, and spontaneous insight during helping is often called practice wisdom (Krill, 1990).

In our view, there is no dichotomy between theory and practice application. Rather, there should be a harmonious interplay between thinking and activity, analysis and intuition, planning and spontaneity (Canda & Furman, 2010).

## ALTERNATIVE APPROACHES TO THEORY SELECTION

To help the reader make this link between theory and practice, we offer some suggestions about selecting and applying theories. First of all, we caution against three approaches to theory sometimes promoted in social work. One approach is simply to *reject* theory as useless or irrelevant. As we mentioned in the opening chapter, we believe this position is untenable because all social work practice is informed by values, ideology, assumptions about human nature and behavior, and the organizational structure of service delivery. To ignore this does not enhance practice; instead, it increases the risk of imposing unwitting or hidden agendas on clients.

The second approach to avoid is *theoretical dogmatism*. Some practitioners hold on to a particular theory as though it were an absolute truth that can explain and be applied to everything. Thus, there are social workers who are exclusively loyal Freudians, behaviorists, Jungians, radical feminists, ego psychologists, ecosystems followers, and so on. Such an approach obscures the fact that all theories are social constructions and, as such, have limitations and constraints. Theories are simplifications of reality. Theoretical dogmatism reduces all clients and situations into whatever terms are comfortable to the self-styled expert practitioner. For example, a dogmatic Bowenian family therapist insists on doing genograms with everyone who comes through the door. A dogmatic ego psychology–based social worker is keen to identify the stage of development each client presents and to explore unresolved issues from childhood, whether or not this approach fits the client's present needs. With theoretical dogmatism, the reality of the client becomes submerged in the theoretical assumptions of the practitioner.

The third approach we caution against is *undisciplined eclecticism*. Some social workers recognize the importance of theory but have not achieved a sufficient grasp of any particular theory. They may mix and match whatever bits from different theories and practice approaches they may have encountered. If this process of combining theories is not systematic, self-reflective, well grounded in evidence, and centered in clients' goals and perspectives, it is controlling like the dogmatic approach and it is also less disciplined and well informed.

We propose an approach that is substantially different from ignoring theory, dogmatically adhering to a theory, or choosing a theory in a willy-nilly fashion. In this book, we have promoted the *critically reflective approach* to theory. The critically reflective approach involves cultivating clear awareness about one's own values, goals, practice commitments, strengths, and limitations. It also involves developing a thorough knowledge of a wide range of theories that deal with the whole person and the environment. It requires making informed evaluations about the strengths and shortcomings of each theory, and it requires careful professional discernment about the relevancy of theories to a particular situation in collaboration with the client.

In the following sections, we summarize the particular contributions of the schools of theory covered in this book. The reader should return to each chapter for a more detailed discussion of the theories within these schools and the critical analysis at the end of each chapter. It is also important to remember that most theories have implications for all aspects of human behavior, either directly or indirectly. However, theories have distinctive emphases and relevancy, and it is the distinctive emphasis of each theory that is used for this comparison. This discussion helps summarize and organize the previous presentations of theories to assist the reader in making decisions about how to select a particular theory or to integrate aspects of different theories in a systematic manner.

The discussion also considers how the theories measure up to the critical themes for theory evaluation presented in Chapter 1, the varying emphases on aspects of the person and environment in each theory, and the fundamental great ideas of each school of thought that have made a significant impact on social work and the understanding of human behavior. Then a practice situation is used to illustrate the process and implications of selecting various theories to apply in a particular instance. Finally, emerging trends of innovative thinking about human behavior are discussed to reflect on possible "roads from here" toward future innovation in theory development.

## MEASURING UP TO THE THEMES FOR CRITICAL REFLECTION ON THEORIES
### Person and Environment

A defining characteristic of the social work profession is its commitment to address holistically both people and their environmental contexts. Therefore, the first major theme we consider is the relevance of theories to the biological, psychological, social relational, and spiritual aspects of the individual as well as the surrounding cultural, political, economic, ideological, and physical environment. The review of theories in this book has expanded beyond the common bio-psycho-social definition of person-in-environment to include spirituality, ideology, political economy, and the total planetary ecology. We also do not give primacy to the person over the environment or to the individual over the group, as is common in many discussions of human behavior in social work. We do not give priority to either the person or the environment, but rather we see person *and* environment as inextricably related.

This, of course, does not mean that in every social work activity, practitioners need to address every aspect of the person and the environment. However, it does mean that we need to be cognizant of the entire person and environment constellation to identify the most relevant aspects of the person; the social, cultural, economic, and political systems; and the natural environment. Therefore, in planning practice, it is helpful to consider which theories have the most to say about particular aspects of the person and the environment for a given situation. Indeed, it is important to consider which theories help one think and act in such a holistic way. Once we are familiar with this repertoire of theories, we can begin to make decisions about which theories or aspects of theories might be applied in a particular practice situation.

To assist this, Figures 14.1 and 14.2 show which theories emphasize various aspects of the person and environment. Some theories address many aspects and some are more specialized. For example, Wilber's Integral Theory attempts to address all aspects through the AQAL (All Quadrants, All Levels) model. Among psychodynamic theories, Jung addressed more aspects of the individual than did Freud. Dynamic systems theory, deep ecology, and ecofeminism attempt to integrate a wide range of human and nonhuman systems, whereas cognitive theories focus on the rational, intellectual aspects of human mental functioning. The designations in these diagrams were derived from the authors' assessments and discussions with students who were asked to provide appraisals of the theories that have been most helpful to them with various aspects of human experience. The shapes of the diagrams are based on the mandala and similar symbols such as the Medicine Wheel (see Chapters 6 and 13) in order to show that all these aspects of the person and environment are interconnected. The mandala is a symbol used to depict the harmonious, organic, and cyclic integration of contrasting qualities. Ideally, contrasting aspects can be recognized as complementary and all aspects can be mutually supportive. Therefore, insights from various theories that emphasize different aspects of the person could be integrated to provide a more complete understanding of the person and environment, as long as their principles and practice approaches are consistent with each other.

Traditional mandala and Medicine Wheel symbols show many culture-specific variations and arrangements of aspects of human experience. Although our diagrams are not directly related to any of these traditional symbols, we are indebted to the insights on holistic perspective in Asian and Indigenous cultures (Canda & Furman, 2010; Dumbrill & Green, 2008; Jung, 1959b; Lee, Ng, Leung, & Chan, 2009; Nabigon & Mawhiney, 1996; Verniest, 2006). We are using the mandala as a heuristic device to help the reader visualize the possibility of integrating various theories to achieve a comprehensive understanding of people and their environments.

To highlight the importance of both person and environment, and the possibility of engaging micro and macro systems in practice, we have developed two mandalas of human behavior theories. The first (Figure 14.1) addresses person-focused theories as well as macro theories with particular relevance to individuals. The second (Figure 14.2) addresses environment-focused theories as well as micro theories with particular relevance to macro systems. Figure 14.1 also shows theories that focus on the interface between person and environment, including its social and planetary ecological dimensions. In these diagrams, a theory may be listed either as a general school (e.g., conflict) or as one version within a school (e.g., Marxian).

## PERSON-FOCUSED THEORIES

Figure 14.1 depicts the mandala of person-focused human behavior theories. In the eastern position, metaphorically the place of sunrise and the beginnings of life, we place the biological aspect. From conception and birth through early childhood, the physical and biological frame of the person develops. Due to the relationships of the child to its mother and significant others at the time of emergence and the vigorous expansion of relationships through adolescence,

**Social Environmental Context**

Conflict
Cultural
Deep ecology
Ecofeminism
Empowerment
Exchange
Feminist
Integral
Life span
Moral and cognitive
  development
Social constructionism
Symbolic interaction
Systems

**Planetary Ecological Context**

Deep ecology
Dynamic systems
Ecofeminism
Integral
Transpersonal

**N  Spiritual**

Deep ecology
Dynamic systems
Ecofeminism
Ego psychology
Faith development
Integral
Jungian
Liberation theology
Transculturality
Transpersonal

**W Psychological**

Empowerment
Feminist
Freudian
Integral
Intercultural relations
Life span
Moral and cognitive
  development
Neo-Freudian
Social learning
Symbolic interaction
Transpersonal

**Integration**

Deep ecology
Ecofeminism
Humanistic
Integral
Life span
Systems
Transculturality
Transpersonal

**E BIOLOGICAL**

Behaviorism
Freudian
Integral
Life span
Neo-Freudian
Neurobiological
Social learning
States of consciousness
Transpersonal

**S Social Relational**

Behaviorism
Conflict
Cultural
Empowerment
Exchange
Feminist
Humanistic
Integral
Life span
Moral and cognitive
  development
Neo-Freudian

**FIGURE 14.1.** The mandala of person-focused human behavior theories.

we place the social relational aspect of the person (i.e., the need for connection and belonging) in the next clockwise position, in the south. Social interactions shape continuing biological development as well as the formation of psychological processes. In the west, we place the psychological aspect, in complementary contrast with the biological. The psychological aspect includes

**N Ontological**

Deep ecology
Dynamic systems
Ecofeminism
Integral
Social constructionism
Transculturality
Transpersonal

**W Ideological**

Conflict, especially Marxian
Cultural integration
Deep ecology
Ecofeminism
Empowerment
Exchange
Feminist
Integral
Interactionism
Phenomenology
Social constructionism

**Integration**

Deep ecology/ecofeminism
Dynamic systems
Integral
Marxian
Parsonian functionalism
Transpersonal
Transculturality

**E Physical**

Behaviorism
Conflict
Deep ecology
Ecofeminism
Empowerment
Exchange
Feminist
Integral
Systems

**S Cosmological**

Cultural interaction
Deep ecology
Ecofeminism
Ecosystems
Empowerment
Exchange
Feminist
Integral
Interactionism
Parsonian functionalism
Phenomenology
Social constructionism
Transpersonal

**FIGURE 14.2.** The mandala of environment-focused human behavior theories.

such mental activities as thinking, feeling, and intuiting. In the north, we place the spiritual aspect, in complementary relation with social relations. Preoccupation with spirituality often emerges in later life, as issues of mortality and death become more prominent. North represents the season of winter, during which people tend to become more inward and self-reflective. In contrast, the focus on the social relational aspect of the person (in the south) involves an outward movement of the person's attention to social interaction, similar to the expansion of growth in summer. The center position is the meeting point, or integration, of all other aspects of the person in transaction with the environment. Theories that focus on the holistic or integrated quality of the person are included here. These theories also emphasize the spiritual aspect, because a major theme of spirituality is how we work out a sense of meaning, purpose, and integrity as a whole person. Surrounding this wheel is the field of the total environment, including the political, economic, and sociocultural context, the planetary ecosystem, and the universe. The encompassing environment transacts with all aspects of the person.

## ENVIRONMENT-FOCUSED THEORIES

Figure 14.2 depicts the mandala of environment-focused human behavior theories. Each direction in this mandala relates to themes analogous at a macro level to the themes described in Figure 14.1. These themes are relevant to all human groups, organizations, communities, and societies, as well as the international web of societies, keeping in mind that all these are interwoven with local and planetary ecosystems.

In the east, we place the physical aspect of macro systems, including humanly constructed technological systems and living environments as well as the natural planetary ecosystem of which we are a part. In the south, we place the cosmological aspect of human communities. *Cosmology* relates to the ways in which groups of people understand, feel, think, and act about their interconnections with each other, the world, and the universe. In the first mandala, the south position related to how individuals express their relational needs with others. In the environment-focused mandala, the south position deals with how communities and larger social systems express their relational needs with individual members and with each other. In the west, we place the ideological aspect of communities and societies. All communities and societies form systems of norms and fundamental values that serve to rationalize and organize themselves, especially in political and economic terms. In the north, we place the ontological aspect, which is analogous to the spiritual aspect of individuals. *Ontology* refers to the way in which groups, communities, and societies form worldviews, philosophies, and religious systems that address notions about reality, the ultimate reality, the possibility of divine or nonphysical aspects of the universe as well as philosophical ideas about the purpose and place of human beings in the cosmos. In the center, we place integrative theories that attempt to link these macro aspects with an understanding of the connection between people and the environment.

It is important to note that these mandalas should only be used as metaphors. We do not wish to imply that there is a linear progression of development through these aspects or that they are separate from each other. In his adaptation of the Medicine Wheel for use in substance abuse recovery, Coggins (1990) pointed out that, at any given point in time, a person or social group may focus on any or all of these aspects. In fact, there may be movement in all directions around and within the wheel. Ideally, people work out a sense of completeness and integration in relation with the world through this process.

### Relevance to System Levels, Values, Philosophy, and Empirical Support

In Tables 14.1 and 14.2, we list each school of theory along with our rating of how it emphasizes the major themes for theory evaluation used throughout the text. As preparation for reading these tables, it would be helpful for the reader to review the discussion of these themes in Chapter 1. The explanations that follow assist reading the tables.

Tables 14.1 and 14.2 present a rating of schools of theories. The reader should use this only for a summary of the general orientation of the theories in this book. You will recall that there are many important distinctions and disagreements between theories within each school. It is therefore important to consider the unique qualities of each particular theory when addressing its use in practice. The themes for theory evaluation, presented first in Chapter 1 and, subsequently, person. Surrounding this wheel is the field of the total environment, including the political, economic, and sociocultural context, the planetary ecosystem, and the universe. The encompassing environment transacts with all aspects of the person.

## ENVIRONMENT-FOCUSED THEORIES

Figure 14.2 depicts the mandala of environment-focused and/or behavior theories. Each direction in this mandala relates to themes that are conceptually related to the themes described in Figure 14.1. These theories are relevant to all human groups, organizations, communities, and societies as well as the interrelational web of societies, keeping in mind that all these are interwoven with local and planetary ecosystems.

In the east, we place the physical features that may include humanly constructed technological "forms" and living environments as well as features of the planetary ecosystem of which we are a part. In the south, we place the cosmology of human groups and human communities. Cosmology relates to the ways in which groups of people understand, feel, think, and act about their interconnections with each other and with the natural world. In this mandala, the south position relates to how individuals express their relational needs and values. In the environment-focused mandala, the south position deals with how communities and larger social systems express their relational needs with individuals, groups, and organizations. In the west, we place the development of communities and societies. All communities and societies form systems of norms and fundamental values that serve to rationalize and orient themselves, especially in political and economic terms. In the north, we place the cosmology, which is analogous to the spiritual aspect of individuals. Cosmology refers to the ways in which groups, communities, and societies form worldviews, philosophies, and religious systems that address notions about reality, the ultimate reality, the possibility of divine or nonphysical forces in the universe as well as philosophical ideas about the purpose and place of humanity in the cosmos. In the center, we place integrative theories that attempt to link these macro aspects with an understanding of the connection between people and the environment.

It is important to note that these schools should not be used as metaphors. We do not wish to imply that there is a linear progression of development through these aspects or that they are separate from each other in his application of the Medicine Wheel to the use in substance abuse recovery. Coyhis (1990) pointed out that, at any given point in time, the person or social group may focus on any or all of these aspects. There is a need for movement in all directions around and within the wheel. Ideally, people work out a sense of completeness and balance and interaction in relation with the world through this process.

## Relevance to System Levels, Values, Philosophy, and Empirical Support

In Tables 14.1 and 14.2, we list each school of theory along with our rating of how it emphasizes the major themes for theory evaluation described about in Chapters 1. In preparation for reading these tables, it would be helpful for the reader to review the discussion of these themes in Chapter 1. The explanations that follow assist reading the tables.

Tables 14.1 and 14.2 present a listing of schools of theories. The reader should use this only for a summary of the general orientation of the theories in this book. As we will recall that there are many important distinctions and disagreements between theories within each school. It is therefore important to consider the unique features of each specific theory when addressing its use in practice. The theories for theory evaluation described in Chapter 1 and subsequently

## TABLE 14.1 Emphasis of Theoretical Schools: Systems Levels and Social Work Values

| | Theory | Systems | Conflict | Empowerment | Feminist | Bicultural | Psychodynamic | Life Span | Cognitive/Moral | Symbolic Interaction | Phenomenology | Behavioral/Exchange | Transpersonal |
|---|---|---|---|---|---|---|---|---|---|---|---|---|---|
| Relevance to Systems | Micro | M | L | H | M | H | L | | M | H | M | H | H |
| | Macro | H | H | H | H | H | L | L | M | M | M | M | M |
| Values | Diversity | M | H | H | H | H | L | H | M | M | M | L | H |
| | Empowerment | H | H | H | H | H | L | | L | | M | L | M |
| | Strengths | M | M | H | H | H | | | M | | | M | H |

H = high emphasis, M = medium emphasis, L = low emphasis

**TABLE 14.2  Emphasis of Theoretical Schools: Philosophy and Empirical Support**

| | | Philosophy | | Empirical Support | | |
|---|---|---|---|---|---|---|
| **Theory** | | **Positivist** | **Constructivist** | **Quantitative** | **Qualitative** | **Conceptual rigor** |
| Systems | | L | M | M | | |
| Conflict | | L | M | M | M | H |
| Empowerment | | L | H | M | M | H |
| Feminist | | M | | H | H | |
| Bicultural | | | | | | |
| Psychodynamic | | M | M | L | M | M |
| Life Span | | M | L | M | M | M |
| Cognitive/Moral | | H | | M | M | M |
| Symbolic Interaction | | M | M | H | H | M |
| Phenomenology | | L | H | H | H | |
| Behavioral/Exchange | | H | H | H | H | |
| Transpersonal | | L | H | M | H | H |

H = high emphasis, M = medium emphasis, L = low emphasis.

throughout the text, cover much more detail than can be presented in this table. The themes have been reduced and simplified and an overall judgment about the theory's focus or emphasis (high, medium, low) is indicated for various contrasting characteristics within each theme. These contrasts, however, do not represent dichotomies, and a given theory may address various characteristics with equal or different emphases. For example, although most systems theories attempt to address all levels of social systems with a broadly encompassing perspective, their utility in explaining individual and small-group behavior is somewhat limited. Thus, they are rated as high on macro systems emphasis and medium on micro/meso emphasis.

The various issues for critical reflection on theories are summarized in the two tables in terms of four major themes: systems relevance, social work values, philosophy, and empirical support. In Table 14.1, *systems relevance* refers to the extent to which a theory emphasizes issues pertaining to individuals, families, groups, or organizations (micro and meso systems, designated here as "micro") or communities, institutions, cultures, societies, or the global community and planetary ecology (designated as "macro"). Theories emphasizing micro and meso systems tend to deal more with concepts of individual, small-group, or family well-being, whereas those emphasizing macro systems tend to deal more with issues of social justice. *Social work values* refer to the degree of congruence with key professional commitments and values. This encompasses the degree to which the theory emphasizes the importance of human diversity (designated as "diversity"); personal and collective empowerment (designated as "empowerment"); and consistency with the strengths perspective (designated as "strengths"). Theories rated high in emphasis on diversity, empowerment, and strengths tend to direct social workers toward collaboration, creative innovation, social reform, and significant change rather than merely maintaining the psychosocial status quo.

In Table 14.2, *philosophy* refers to the primary philosophical orientation of the theory. Theories that emphasize positivistic and materialistic assumptions about reality are designated as "positivistic." Theories that emphasize a critique of positivism and propose a more postmodern constructivist world view are considered new paradigms (designated as "constructivist"). In this case, we are not suggesting that all the latter theories are part of the social constructionist or constructivist theories, per se (see chapter 11), but rather, that they attend to the relativity and culturally shaped nature of human understanding. *Empirical support* considers the degree to which theories rely on and are supported by qualitative or quantitative research (designated respectively as "qualitative" and "quantitative"), as well as the degree of conceptual rigor and sophistication (designated as "conceptual rigor"). No theory included in this book completely lacks relevance to any of these themes, so there is no "0" or "none" rating.

There is, of course, disagreement among scholars of human behavior about the rating of these theories. In forming our ratings, we have tried to balance the perspectives of advocates and critics for each theory, as discussed in each chapter. It would be most useful for readers to use these ratings as a starting point for working out their own ratings of a particular theory by thinking about the areas of agreement or disagreement with our ratings, as well as how their evaluation can be supported by current evidence.

## Relevance to Fields of Practice

Because various theories emphasize different aspects of human experience, it follows that they have varying relevance to specific fields and settings of practice. This is indicated in each chapter with tables and flowcharts that give examples of settings and applications to practice. To provide an overall summary, the major schools of theory are listed in Table 14.3 in relation to the fields of social work practice in which they are most likely to be applied. However, this should not imply

| TABLE 14.3 | Relevance of Theories to Fields of Practice |
|---|---|
| **Fields of Practice** | **Schools of Theories** |
| Aging | Ecological, empowerment, feminist, bicultural socialization, life span, cognitive and moral development, symbolic interaction, behavioral, transpersonal |
| Health | Systems, empowerment, feminist, bicultural socialization, life span, cognitive and moral development, behavioral, exchange |
| Mental health | Systems, empowerment, feminist, bicultural socialization, psychodynamic, cognitive and moral development, symbolic interaction, phenomenology, behavioral, transpersonal |
| Hospice | Systems, bicultural socialization, psychodynamic, life span, cognitive and moral development, phenomenology, transpersonal |
| Children and family services | Systems, empowerment, bicultural socialization, life span, cognitive and moral development, symbolic interaction, behavioral, exchange, transpersonal |
| School social work | Systems, empowerment, bicultural socialization, life span, cognitive and moral development, symbolic interaction, behavioral |
| Criminal justice/corrections | Systems, life span, cognitive and moral development, symbolic interaction, behavioral, exchange |
| Administration | Systems, conflict, feminist, empowerment, bicultural socialization, symbolic interaction, exchange |
| Community organizing and development | Systems, conflict, empowerment, feminist, bicultural socialization, symbolic interaction, exchange |
| Political social work | Systems, conflict, empowerment, feminist, bicultural socialization, symbolic interaction, exchange |
| Policy analysis | Systems, conflict, empowerment, feminist, bicultural socialization, exchange |
| International social work | Systems, conflict, empowerment, feminist, bicultural socialization, symbolic interaction, phenomenology, exchange, transpersonal |

that a theory is relevant only to these particular fields of practice, but rather that this is a major emphasis or common use. Indeed, proponents of Integral Theory view it as being relevant to all fields of practice (Esbjorn-Hargens, 2009)

## TWELVE GREAT IDEAS

Another way to sort through the myriad theories is to think about the most compelling ideas they have contributed to social work. Rather than an analytical look at the particular details of each theory, this is a broad-brush painting of the major picture of the world presented by a theory. We suggest that these major insights are important to consider as each of us shapes his or her own understandings of the world and social work practice. In this section we summarize 12 great ideas culled from the schools of theory presented in this book.

### Systems Theories: Everything Is Connected

Although various systems theories disagree about the nature of social systems and social change, they all agree on one powerful insight: that everything is connected. This insight has influenced profoundly the person and environment perspective of social work. In practice, we choose a focal system as client and we focus change activities on particular target systems. We often use genograms and ecomaps to examine significant relationships between people and institutions. And, more recently, we have begun to consider the macro environment of geopolitics and planetary ecology. No matter where we and clients choose to focus our work, we cannot forget to consider the effect of other systems on ourselves and the effect of our work on other systems. For example, if, in collaboration with a psychiatrist, we recommend an antianxiety medication for a highly anxious client, we know that we must also consider whether there are internal psychological conflicts or external environmental conditions that may be exacerbating the anxiety. Therefore, rather than seeking panaceas, we are seeking systemic solutions.

Social work practice in its fullest sense is never just psychotherapy with the individual, group, or family, although it may include psychodynamic or family systems interactions. Likewise, social work practice in its fullest sense is never just institutional change; it must consider the impact of such change on individuals, groups, families, larger communities, and the natural environment. Even though an individual social worker may not be able to address all relevant aspects of the person and environment, systems theories support collaborative work with social workers and other professional helpers who specialize in a variety of areas as well as with other formal and informal support systems to create a comprehensive systems approach.

## Conflict Theories: Social Justice Requires Social Change

Conflict theories highlight two claims: All societies perpetuate some forms of oppression and injustice, and, therefore, our commitment to social justice requires constant attention to oppression and diligent efforts to resist and overcome this oppression. Necessarily, confronting entrenched institutions, policies, programs, and individual behaviors generates conflict. Although this can be highly uncomfortable, and sometimes even dangerous, conflict theories remind us that conflict is a driving force of social change. Conflict theories call social workers to pay attention to oppression, especially in its systemic and institutional forms, and to form strategies for overcoming it. They also challenge us to deal with the dilemmas that confront us as members of an institutionalized helping profession. Although we are committed to social change, we owe our existence and resources to the very social institutions and governmental and private social agencies that we may need to challenge.

## Empowerment Theories: Consciousness-Raising and Collective Action

Empowerment theories in social work have arisen from our profession's commitment to social justice. They extend the broad insights of conflict theory and add particular focus to specific forms of oppression such as those based on gender, social class, age, disability, sexual orientation, race, and ethnicity. They highlight the ways in which stratification creates structural blocks to opportunity and well-being. Empowerment theories in social work add the important insight that significant social change requires the joining together of all people committed to justice in a process of both consciousness raising and practical individual and collective action. To avoid the pitfalls of "blaming the victim" and assuming a "victim mentality," empowerment directs us to build on people's strengths, capacities, and resources to help them accomplish their personal and collective goals and aspirations.

## Feminist Theory: Connections Between the Personal and the Political

Feminist theory provides a mode of analysis for social work that emphasizes gender and the ways in which patriarchy creates and maintains gender-based stratification and oppression. It offers a holistic view of the interrelationships between material, social, intellectual, and spiritual facets of human existence. Feminist theory connects the personal and political and supports women and other oppressed groups in identifying the attitudes, expectations, language, behaviors, and social arrangements that have contributed to the oppression and marginalization of people. At its core, it is a theory of power relations that assists social workers in critical analysis, generating and producing knowledge, and promoting political engagement for the purpose of achieving economic, political, and social equality.

## Culture, Multiculturalism, Cultural Adaptation, and Competence

Theories about culture illuminate the fact that all social work practice is mediated by culture and involves interaction across cultural differences. Culture mediates all person and environment transactions because it is the socially woven fabric of meaning, life ways, and social institutions that defines what it is to be a person and a member of a social group and how people relate to the environment. Theories about culture and cultural adaptation also illustrate the ways in which the dominant society often defines cultural difference as deficiency; they illuminate the tremendous variation in cultural beliefs and norms and emphasize the potential hazards and promises of cross-cultural interaction. In the social work practice context, these theories remind us that cultural diversity and varying modes of cultural adaptation are a fact of life. They guide practitioners in developing culturally competent ways of understanding their clients and engaging in practice.

## Psychodynamics and the Inner World

Psychodynamic theories contribute two enduring major insights: First, that there is an interconnection between the mind and the body; and second, that human behavior may partially be shaped by an inner world of mental processes of which we are often unaware. Psychodynamic theories alert social workers to pay attention to both the mind–body connection and to internal mental processes. They also encourage us to be self-reflective, to aid clients in being self-reflective, and to consider how internal processes interact with the social environment. All psychodynamic theories emphasize that introspection and self-reflective dialogue can engender insight and personal growth. They also suggest that accomplishing major personal change can entail hard, prolonged work. Despite the many limitations of classical psychodynamic theories, some of their basic ideas are still compelling and imply caution against reducing all clinical social work practice to only short-term, task-oriented activity.

## Growth and Development Throughout the Life Span

Life span theories have made an important contribution to social work by describing and analyzing interactions between biological, psychological, and social aspects of development from conception to death. They suggest that experience accumulated by meeting life's challenges can generate personal talents, strengths, and virtues, as well as distress and sense of burden. They suggest that all people are on a life journey and that social workers can provide care and assistance to people on this journey, provide them with help when they are down, and encourage them along the way. Life span theories emphasize that all phases of life can present important opportunities and challenges for growth and that learning and growth are always possible.

## Cognitive and Moral Development

Cognitive and moral development theories emphasize rational, moral, intellectual, and faith development throughout life. They describe intellectual growth as a process in which people strive to make sense of new intellectual challenges and moral dilemmas. Meeting each new challenge requires formation of a more comprehensive and sophisticated way of thinking that can include the previous ways but is not limited to them. As one matures intellectually and morally, one moves beyond egocentrism to an intellectual, moral, and spiritual perspective that appreciates other people's points of view and that can accommodate them within one's own point of view. Cognitive and moral development theories remind social workers to consider how we form our own decisions, how we think about clients, and how we inform our practice with a moral framework of professional values and ethics. They also call attention to clients' ways of understanding the world and how these help or hinder their adaptive behavior and achievement of satisfying relationships with others. Theories that identify multiple intelligences remind us that each person has various capacities (such as in logical thinking, emotional sensitivity, and social relating) and that we can benefit clients by appreciating and tapping their more strongly developed capacities and by helping them to develop other capacities for meeting their goals and for becoming well-rounded.

## Symbolic Interaction and Role Theory

Symbolic interaction and role theory make us aware of the environmental factors, normative expectations, and social processes that give rise to the self. They emphasize the importance of the human capacity to symbolize, to be consciously self-reflective, and to shape one another and society through our social interactions. In addressing the process of socialization throughout life, symbolic interaction and role theory lead us to examine the way in which expectations of significant others and prevailing social institutions guide our behavior, development, and enactment of roles. Labeling theory adds important insights into the deleterious effects of treating clients as objects by assigning them to a stigmatizing diagnostic label or category, which often becomes self-fulfilling. This perspective cautions social workers that when we treat people according to the labels that we assign them, we might ignore their unique characteristics, abilities, and strengths and reduce them from their full stature as human beings.

## Phenomenology, Social Construction, and the Centrality of Consciousness

Phenomenological thought focuses us on that which is rarely the source of our attention—consciousness itself and the nature of reality. The phenomenological stance reveals something that may seem rather shocking at first: that our understandings of self, society, and world are based on social constructions rather than objective, fixed, or absolute things. This insight presents a promising possibility—because self and society are socially constructed, self and society can be deconstructed and reconstructed. Thus, social workers can help clients to identify how their understandings of self, society, and world have come about. Clients can discover that they have a choice to reenvision who they are and what roles they play to achieve their aspirations. These theories also remind us that any such reconstruction process affects other people in *their* socially constructed worlds. Phenomenology also suggests that positivistic research methods are incapable of capturing the complexity and uniqueness of human behavior.

## Behaviorism, Social Learning, and Exchange Theories: Control by the Environment

Behaviorism and exchange theories have been extremely useful in emphasizing the ways in which the social environment shapes behavior. While other theories call attention to the way behavior is shaped by the biological and psychological forces, behaviorism, social learning theory, and exchange theory point out that behavior is often shaped by external conditions, reinforcers, and models that we may not be aware of. On the one hand, this has opened the way for the use of powerful and effective techniques of behavior modification that use empirical measures of the intervention process and its outcomes. On the other hand, these theories also serve as warning to social workers not to mold client behaviors in a manipulative or coercive manner.

## Transpersonal Theories: Self-Transcendence and Fulfillment

Transpersonal theories help us to return to the spiritual and religious aspects of human experience that were important in the foundation of the profession. They provide nonsectarian concepts and models for doing this, by drawing from a wide variety of religious and philosophical traditions around the world. They remind us that to deal with the whole person and environment constellation, we cannot forget about the spiritual aspects of the individual in relationship with the world. They call attention to the positive inner spiritual insights and strengths of people as well as the importance of spiritual and religious support systems for developing a sense of life meaning and direction. They provide guidelines for discussing with clients experiences of a self-transcending nature that may help them to achieve personal and social fulfillment. They expand our professional vision to a worldwide ideal of justice. Wilber's Integral Theory further reminds us to consider all dimensions of the person and environment (subjective and objective aspects of the individual and collective) at all levels (preegoic, egoic, and transegoic) of development as relevant to the practice situation.

These great ideas of the various theories raise many controversial and thought-provoking issues for social workers. We believe that the process of thinking them through and discussing them with others promotes sophistication and refinement of personal and professional development.

## AN EXAMPLE OF INTEGRATING THEORIES FOR A PRACTICE ISSUE

To illustrate how one might think through the relevance of various theories to a specific practice issue, we use an example from the field of social work in health care pertaining to people with disabilities. This helps link the rather abstract discussion so far to a concrete, practical situation. We invite you, the reader, to consider how the method of reflection in this example can shed light on your own practice situations.

Using the mandalas of human behavior theories, we consider how various theories might be useful in practice with people who have cystic fibrosis (CF) and, more broadly, with people with other disabilities. Our descriptions draw on the social work and medical literature about CF; biographical and autobiographical accounts of people with CF; as well as the third author's experience and research with this population (Canda, 2001, 2006, 2009). First, we take a person-focused approach (Figure 14.1) and then we take an environment-focused approach (Figure 14.2). As we move around the directions of the two mandalas and consider their integration, it becomes clear that the various aspects of person and environment overlap and are interrelated inextricably. This approach integrates and transcends insights from two contrasting and sometimes competing perspectives within the field of disability studies: the individual model and the social model. The *individual model* of services for people with disabilities focuses on impairment as personal loss or tragedy, personal problems, individual treatment, expert control of helping, and adjusting clients to social norms (Kim & Canda, 2006). The *social model* focuses on disability as socially constructed oppression, social problems, social action and empowerment, self-help and collaboration, and achieving full potential and rights of consumers. Following the suggestions of Kim and Canda's *holistic model* of services for people with disabilities, our holistic approach relates to the whole person in full life context, views impairments and abilities as only particular facets of people, considers both personal challenges and social oppression, engages collaboration and empowerment in strengths-based practice for individual well-being and social justice, and recognizes both consumers' rights and responsibilities.

## A Person-Focused Approach

**BIOLOGICAL ASPECT** Life span theories lead us to examine developmental issues from conception through death. In this case, given the health challenges that people with CF face, we must pay attention to the biological origin of the disease as well as the possible involvement of medical disability. CF usually has the most severe impacts on lung function and digestion. Symptoms are treatable but not presently curable. CF is one of the most common autosomal recessive genetic diseases in the United States, with the large majority of people with CF being of European descent. Autosomal recessive means that a CF gene must be inherited from both parents for the disease to express in a child. The median life expectancy for people with CF is about 37 years. These medical facts mean that biological aspects of medical care, physical development, disease process, and dying are strongly influenced by CF. This requires consultation and collaboration with health care professionals in a holistic way, in order to avoid the pitfalls of a narrowly construed medical model of disability. Indeed, contemporary holistic medicine includes possibilities for many types of alternative and complementary practices, such as allopathic (conventional) medicine, religious and culturally based traditional healers and support systems, chiropractic, Eastern medicine (e.g., acupuncture), herbalism, and meditation, as may be preferred by the client. (See http://www.socwel.ku.edu/candagrant/Links/links.htm for related Web sites.)

Social workers most often encounter people with CF in hospital and hospice settings. Social workers may also do genetic counseling for prospective parents. Thus, the social worker would need to go beyond the theories presented in this book to understand the more specialized medical theories and treatment procedures specifically related to CF. Importantly, the biological aspects of the illness require major revision of conventional life span theories, because of the shorter median life expectancy and CF-specific developmental tasks at various life stages. Further, as Integral Theory would suggest, the physical well-being of the person can be optimized by attending to all aspects of the person and environment to be discussed next.

**SOCIAL RELATIONAL ASPECT** Systems theories would be beneficial in the development of a holistic assessment and helping strategy for people with disabilities. For example, genograms would be useful for charting the incidence of CF in a multigeneration extended family during genetic counseling. They could also assist family members to discuss the dynamics of relationships within a family that has members with CF. Sometimes, a great amount of time, energy, and money are invested by parents or siblings in the medical care and social support of their family member with a disability. This may result in periods of decreased attention to other siblings or to spouses. Discussion of these issues in the light of symbolic interaction and role theory can help family members to renegotiate roles in a more satisfactory manner and to understand the need for temporary sacrifices of attention by some members. In addition, the social worker could construct an ecomap that identifies important social environmental sources of support and strain that need to be addressed in the helping plan. Focusing on this aspect of the person makes a link to environmental concerns that are dealt with further in the next mandala.

Humanistic theories, derived from phenomenological thought, remind social workers of the importance of empathy and unconditional positive regard for fostering positive self-concept and a therapeutic relationship. Both phenomenology and symbolic interaction caution against seeing the person with CF as merely a patient, confined to a medical label. Empowerment practice can bring together people with disabilities and their allies in order to challenge social stigma and power blocks. Further, in keeping with transpersonal theory, adults with CF sometimes remark that their sense of life meaning and purpose is enhanced when they can use the lessons from dealing with CF for personal insight and to help others. In addition, some people with CF have reported that their religious congregations provide social support.

**PSYCHOLOGICAL ASPECT**    Life span, cognitive, and transpersonal theories address the ways in which challenges in life present opportunities for insight and growth. Most people with CF begin to manifest symptoms in childhood and must deal with them throughout life. This, of course, has important psychological consequences. For example, during acute exacerbations of symptoms, clients might experience anxiety. Behavioral, social learning, and cognitive theories could be used to help clients deal with anxiety as a response to stress that can be managed clinically. For example, training in systematic desensitization and relaxed breathing are methods that can help breathing to return to its optimal level and would support other medical care. Likewise, noting other persons who are coping well with CF as models might aid in learning anxiety management techniques and attitudes and behaviors that promote resilience. Cognitive behavioral therapies that utilize mindfulness meditation could encourage practices that maximize consistent health care and minimize anxiety. Psychodynamic and developmental theories could be useful to help the person work through long-term feelings about dealing with chronic illness to enhance resilience.

**SPIRITUAL ASPECT**    As transpersonal theories suggest, early confrontation with issues of mortality and death might bring about a precocious interest in spiritual issues, such as the meaning and purpose of life, what happens after death, and why one has the disease. Biographical and auto-biographical accounts of people with CF sometimes describe them as having a "wisdom beyond their years," because reflection on mortality can stimulate philosophical and spiritual questions at an early age. Social workers should therefore be prepared to address these concerns. Faith development theory, existentialism, phenomenology, and transpersonal theories can assist the social worker in discussing issues such as these with clients. Unfortunately, some people with CF have reported that social workers (and medical personnel, in general) rarely bring up this topic and may, in fact, discourage it. Significantly, in a survey of 402 patients with CF at a major medical center, about 66% of patients reported that they were using unconventional healing practices, two-thirds of which were religious in nature (R. C. Stern, Canda, & Doershuk, 1992). These included participation in religious support groups, faith healing, group prayer, pilgrimages to holy places, meditation, and use of comforting religious objects, such as wearing scapulars or amulets. Patients generally reported a high level of satisfaction with social and emotional support derived from these practices, which aided and supplemented conventional medical treatments. These internal and external sources of spiritual support could be included in social workers' hospital discharge planning and in general discussions of patients' well-being. Follow-up interviews of 16 adult patients for whom spirituality was highly important revealed that they all reported transpersonal experiences, ranging from awareness of God's presence and communion with nature to revelatory dreams and sustenance from prayer (Canda, 2001, 2006). Participants indicated that their spiritual practices, support systems, and experiences of connection with a sacred source of power and meaning gave them strength to grow in overall sense of well-being, even as their physical symptoms of illness increased. They advocated that social workers be open minded about spirituality as a possible source of meaning, comfort, and physical benefit for people with CF.

## An Environment-Focused Approach

In an environment-focused approach, we consider not only how an individual or family relates to resources and environmental systems but also how collectivities of people, in larger meso and macro systems, might address such practice issues. In fact, the separation between person-focus and environment-focus is a somewhat misleading simplification. We believe that it is critical for social work practice to take into account both the person and environment when faced with any practice issue since they are inextricably interrelated.

**PHYSICAL ASPECT**   Systems theories alert us that physical aspects of the environment are especially important for persons with CF and other disabilities. For example, regarding medical disability issues, access to material resources such as affordable and adequate health care, including insurance and proximity of specialized treatment, is critical. The social worker would need to address the economic implications for the entire family in paying for expensive medical treatments, especially when adults with CF are not able to work due to disability. Further, social and economic justice issues pertaining to people with CF are germane. Empowerment theories can alert the social worker to examine possible structural barriers to people with disabilities, such as employment discrimination, difficulty of transferring medical insurance between jobs, and need for reasonable accommodations in schools and workplace, under the terms of the Americans with Disabilities Act. Also in keeping with empowerment theories, many people with CF and their loved ones use, or would like to use, support groups for both emotional and social support, sharing of information, and collective action. Many such local, national, and international support groups exist that could be used in the helping process. Conflict theories highlight the importance of addressing institutionalized patterns of discrimination and oppression directed toward people with disabilities. They provide guidelines for mobilizing collective action, not only individual efforts, to overcome institutionalized barriers and inequitable social policies.

A social worker who practices from a deep ecological or ecofeminist perspective could identify innovations in professional assistance for people with CF. For example, as a member of a multidisciplinary health care team, the social worker could raise questions about environmentally sound disposal of medical waste. The physical environment of the client in the hospital could be examined to encourage good hygiene and to help the client and hospital staff think about how to make the hospital room aesthetically pleasing and comfortable. From a conflict perspective, the social worker could raise questions to determine who benefits financially from unsound waste disposal practices.

**COSMOLOGICAL ASPECT**   Cosmology addresses more than the physical aspects of the environment. It considers the meanings that social groups attribute to them and the patterns or relationship that individuals and groups establish with them. For example, people with medical disabilities sometimes need to stay in the hospital for prolonged periods. The hospital can come to be perceived as a stressful confinement or even a prison; therefore, at some CF treatment centers, when the client is feeling well enough, periods of leave from the hospital are permitted. The social worker could use ecosystems, deep ecology, or ecofeminist perspectives to help the client to consider what places would feel most replenishing, such as art museums, beautiful public parks, or visits with loved ones in their homes or enjoyable locations. To the extent that medical care permits, visits with pet animals could be arranged in the hospital or at another site. Home-based medical care is actually the most common approach, so social workers can encourage ways for clients to connect with the nurturing, affirming, and beautiful qualities of home and natural places.

Symbolic interaction sheds light on the sometimes negative effects of medical systems' diagnostic labels on social stigma, self-esteem, or sense of hope. This theory could guide social workers to help clients work together in mutual support and advocacy groups to affirm positive self-concept and to proactively be involved in health care decisions and policy formation, with neither unrealistically positive nor negative expectations. In this connection, many advocates prefer not to use deficit-oriented terms, such as *handicapped* or *the disabled*. Many prefer to use terms that are more precise, proactive, and strengths-oriented, such as *people with disabilities* or *differently abled*. The fact that these terms are controversial for various reasons and that individuals and groups with a variety of disabilities prefer various terms itself highlights the importance of social constructionism, phenomenology, and symbolic interactionism.

Structural functionalism might be used to account for the reasons that social systems perpetuate negative portrayals of people with disabilities as well as the reasons for resisting change. In addition, empowerment and conflict theories can provide strategies for collective action for change.

**IDEOLOGICAL ASPECT** The preceding issues are closely tied with group ideologies. For example, the stigmatization of people with medical disabilities plays a role in larger ideological assumptions of society. Society at large, and the medical establishment in particular, form stereotypes and assumptions about people with disabilities that may serve their own self-maintaining functions, while promoting power blocks for clients. For example, it has often been pointed out that American society tends to glorify images of youth, thinness, physical stamina, and so-called able-bodiedness in popular culture and advertising (Robbins, 1997a). As people become preoccupied with conforming to social norms of attractiveness and productivity, many actively seek to avoid or disguise signs of aging or physical vulnerability and thus create vast markets for cosmetics, cosmetic surgery, and medical care. As conflict theory points out, this creates a social ideology (false consciousness) that provides a general context and justification for stigmatization, job discrimination, and other forms of bias against those who fail to meet these norms, in general, and against people with disabilities, in particular. This underscores the importance for social workers to engage in community activism, policy formulation, and the political process as part of an advocacy approach to assist people with disabilities.

**ONTOLOGICAL ASPECT** Just as in the general population, many people with disabilities belong to religious denominations or to other social groups that provide spiritual beliefs. Each religious group, and every culture, form ontological understandings about the causes and purposes of illness. Religious groups might also provide methods of physical, emotional, social, and spiritual support for people with CF. People do not form their spiritual understandings in isolation, but rather in interaction with families, groups, and larger communities. As transpersonal theory would suggest, when community-based understandings of illness provide a sense of hope, meaning, and life purpose, they can enhance the resilience of people with CF. They also highlight that many people believe that death may not be a final end and that it is possible to prepare oneself for death with dignity.

On the contrary, some groups might claim that having CF or other illnesses or disabilities is a punishment from God or a result of personal moral failure, thus adding inappropriate shame, guilt, and ostracism. Therefore, the social worker would encourage a respectful examination of socially and religiously constructed ontological ideas associated with disabilities. People with CF and other disabilities sometimes engage in public speaking to dispel misconceptions that may be prevalent in the community.

**INTEGRATION OF THE PERSON AND ENVIRONMENT** As demonstrated in the mandalas' sections on integration and environmental aspects, many theories contribute to a comprehensive person and environment perspective. For example, Wilber's Integral Theory provides the AQAL model to help connect and organize insights from many theories. When a social worker engages in a collaborative discussion with clients and client groups about such possibilities, they are encouraged to identify their strengths, resources, and aspirations and to draw on the widest possible range of insights and helping strategies to achieve them. Such collaborative discussion also engages clients in a process of self-reflection and dialogue in groups and communities. This promotes both a sense of personal harmony, balance, and integration for individuals and also conditions of justice for communities of people. It promotes recognition of strengths and resources of persons and social groups, encourages resilient responses to adverse conditions, and guides actions to create environmental conditions, resources, and institutions that actualize collective welfare and justice for people with disabilities.

This illustration has certainly not exhausted the possibilities for application of theories to social work practice with people who have CF or other disabilities. However, it has shown the conceptual and practical benefits yielded by integrative and comprehensive thinking about theory. The reader is encouraged to use this example to develop applications of theory relevant to her or his own practice situations.

## ROADS FROM HERE: FUTURE POSSIBILITIES AND CHALLENGES FOR INNOVATION IN HUMAN BEHAVIOR THEORY

*The children of the holocaust still hear the cries of loved ones lost,*
*While the children of Hiroshima must fear the years to come,*
*A heritage of atom bombs burns in their bones, a weight unweighed,*
*But the children of Byzantium, thank God, still got it made!*
*They clean their teeth electrically of miracles they get to eat,*
*And with perfumed hair and jeweled feet . . . they dance to rock and roll,*
*And the wail of guitars, sax, and drums . . . will hide their future as it comes,*
*To children of Byzantium, who never will grow old.*

© TIM HENDERSON,
1985, SNAKE HOLLOW PUBLISHING (BMI)

As we have stressed throughout this book, our knowledge of human behavior historically has been derived from a variety of behavioral and social science disciplines, each with its own ideologies, preferred research methods, and foci. Disciplinary loyalties, as well as increased specialization, have long fragmented our view of both people and their environments. This has been further exacerbated in social work by our professional split into separate areas of clinical and community practice. As Robbins (1994) has noted, the structure of both our organizations and professional education has perpetuated this dichotomy. However, contemporary developments in society and in theory construction are forcing us to see connections that were readily apparent to social work pioneers such as Jane Addams, Lillian Wald, Bertha Capan Reynolds, and the many others involved in the early development of social work. Now, in the 21st century, social work is in a unique position to renew its historical commitment to a holistic view of both people and their environments. This will entail looking outward at the social, economic, political, and natural environmental forces that shape behavior as well as inward toward human consciousness and the spiritual realm of human existence.

We face numerous challenges, however, in our attempt to achieve such a holistic view. First, we must recognize the impact and importance of rapid technological and social change on our social institutions, organizational structures, family forms, and individual values, beliefs, and behaviors. Because all human behavior theory is developed within a specific historical context, we must examine the relevancy of any theory that does not adequately account for life in contemporary society.

One such factor that has been largely ignored in most human behavior theory for social work is the effect of economic globalization, or the global economy, as it is often called. Morell (1997) and Mander and Goldsmith (1996) have aptly noted that global economic and political trends are intricately tied to contemporary social problems such as "unemployment and economic exploitation . . . landlessness, homelessness, violence, alienation, the disintegration of community life and distinct cultures and the near breakdown of the natural world that sustains us all" (Morell, 1997, p. 1). We encourage recent efforts to heighten social workers' awareness of global interdependence and the intersections of national and international social challenges and developments (e.g., Gray, Coates, & Yellow Bird, 2008; Hokenstad & Midgley, 2004; Link & Healy, 2005; Tripodi & Potocky-Tripodi, 2007). We hope that this trend can become more focused on refinement of human behavior theorizing. Macro socio-cultural structures have profound effects on people's values, beliefs, and opportunities for development as well as the ways in which they structure their lives and families. They also affect the type and availability of jobs and the structure of our work environments, educational environments, communities, and social institutions (Chomsky, 1993; Morell, 1997; Wallis, 1995). As R. Fisher and Karger (1997) have argued, such macro contextualization should be put at the base of social work practice. Thus, the role of political economy on human behavior must become central to our understanding of growth, development, and behavior, if social work is to fulfill its mission of achieving social justice.

Another area that has received little attention in most human behavior theory is the spiritual realm of human behavior and belief. This is a particularly challenging area for theory development due to the many controversies inherent in the topic (Canda & Furman, 2010). Social work educational standards set in 1953 and 1962 recognized spiritual aspects to be essential in understanding human behavior and the social environment. However, controversies relating to religious proselytization, interreligious competition, moralistic judgmentalism, and church and state separation in social services led us to avoid the topic in social work education especially during the last 30 years of the 20th century. However, contemporary developments in the popular culture, the social sciences, and human services have been reversing this trend. In fact, the Council on Social Work Education's curriculum policy guidelines revised in 2001 and 2008 (retrieved from http://www.cswe.org, August 9, 2008) require that education promotes nondiscrimination on the basis of religion and knowledge of spiritual development and of religion as an aspect of diversity. The challenge now is how social work can promote theory and practice that are sensitive and competent with regard to spirituality, while honoring professional value commitments to client self-determination and while respecting human rights to freedom of and freedom from religion.

As we have seen in this book, transpersonal theory focuses on the importance of spiritual experiences and religious support systems for individuals. Complementarily, the relatively new fields of ecofeminism and deep ecology are pointing out the links between political, economic, and spiritual issues in macro systems, including the interconnection between human beings and the planetary ecosystem. Given social work's commitment to understanding people and their environments, our profession can make an important contribution by showing the conceptual links between these micro and macro spiritual issues. Importantly, this can lead to practice strategies that simultaneously promote individual fulfillment and international well-being and global ecojustice.

Finally, innovative theory development must take into account both the demographic trends and rapid technological changes that are shaping the lives and circumstances of people in the 21st century. We must be able to question some of our deeply held assumptions about the nature of self, family, institutions, community, society, and world. And we must be open to adopting new theories that more accurately reflect the changing economic, cultural, and psychological landscape of contemporary life.

# REFERENCES

Aboud, F. E. (1984). Social and cognitive basis of ethnic identity constancy. *Journal of Genetic Psychology, 145,* 227–229.

Abraham, M. F. (1988). *Modern sociological theory.* New York: Oxford University Press.

Abrahamson, M. (1990). *Sociological theory: An introduction to concepts, issues, and research.* Englewood Cliffs, NJ: Prentice-Hall.

Abramovitz, M. (1988). *Regulating the lives of women.* Boston: South End Press.

Abramovitz, M. (1993). Should all social work students be educated for social change? *Journal of Social Work Education, 29,* 6–11, 17–18.

Abramson, L. Y., Seligman, M. E. P., & Teasdale, J. D. (1978). Learned helplessness in humans: Critique and reformulation. *Journal of Abnormal Psychology, 87,* 49–74.

Acker, J. (2006). Gender and organizations. In J. S. Chafetz (Ed.), *Handbook of the sociology of gender* (pp. 177–194). New York: Springer.

Adams, R. (2008). *Empowerment, participation, and social work* (4th ed.). New York: Palgrave Macmillan.

Addams, J. (1893). *The subjective necessity for social settlements: Philanthropy and social progress* (pp. 1–26). New York: Thomas Y. Crowell.

Adler, A. (1927). *The practice and theory of individual psychology.* New York: Harcourt, Brace & World.

Adler, A. (1929). *Problems of neurosis.* London: Kegan Paul.

Adler, P., & Adler, P. (1980). Symbolic interactionism. In J. Douglas et al. (Eds.), *Introduction to the sociologies of everyday life* (pp. 20–61). Boston: Allyn & Bacon.

Agger, R. E., Goldrich, D., & Swanson, B. E. (1964). *The rulers and the ruled* (pp. 40–51). New York: John Wiley and Sons. (Reprinted in *The search for community power,* pp. 217–226, by W. D. Hawley & F. M. Wirt, Eds., 1968, Englewood Cliffs, NJ: Prentice-Hall.)

Aguirre, A., Jr., & Turner, J. (1995). *American ethnicity.* New York: McGraw-Hill.

Aizura, A. Z., Walsh, J., Pike, A., Ward, R., & Jak. (2010, March). *Gender questioning.* Trans Melbourne Gender Project, Gay and Lesbian Health Victoria & Rainbow Network Victoria. Retrieved from http://www.glhv.org.au/files/GQv3.pdf

Alcoff, L. M., & Kittay, E. F. (2007). Introduction: Defining feminist philosophy. In L. M. Alcoff & E. F. Kittay (Eds.), *The Blackwell guide to feminist philosophy* (pp. 1–13). Malden, MA: Blackwell Publishing.

Aldridge, J. (1993). Constructivism, contextualism, and applied developmental psychology. *Perceptual and Motor Skills, 76,* 1242.

Aldridge, M. J., Macy, H., & Walz, T. (n.d.). *Beyond management: Humanizing the administrative process.* Iowa City: School of Social Work, University of Iowa.

Alexander, J. C. (Ed.). (1985). *Neofunctionalism.* Newbury Park, CA: Sage.

Alexander, J. C. (Ed.). (1998). *Neofunctionalism and after.* Malden, MA: Blackwell.

Al-Hibri, A. (1981). Capitalism in an advanced stage of patriarchy: But Marxism is not feminism. In L. Sargent (Ed.), *Women and revolution: A discussion of the unhappy marriage of Marxism and feminism* (pp. 165–193). Boston: South End.

Al-Krenawi, A., & Graham, J. R. (2009). *Helping professional practice with Indigenous peoples: The Bedouin-Arab case.* Lanham, MD: University Press of America.

Alinsky, S. (1967, January). Of means and ends. *Union Seminary Quarterly Review, 22(2).* (Reprinted in *Strategies of community organization,* pp. 199–208, by F. M. Cox et al., Eds., 1970, Itasca, IL: F. E. Peacock.)

Allen-Meares, P., & Lane, B. A. (1987). Grounding social work practice in theory: Ecosystems. *Social Casework, 68(9),* 515–521.

Allport, G. (1958). *The nature of prejudice* (abr. ed.). New York: Doubleday, Anchor Books.

Alsop, R., Fitzsimons, A., & Lennon, K. (2002). *Theorizing gender.* Cambridge, UK: Polity Press.

Althusser, L. (1969). *For Marx.* London: Penguin Books.

American Psychological Association. (2007). *Guidelines for psychological practice with girls and women.* A Joint task force of APA Divisions 17 and 35. Washington, DC: Author.

American Psychiatric Association. (2000). *Diagnostic and statistical manual of mental disorders DSM-IV-TR* (text revision) (4th ed.). Arlington, VA: Author.

Amott, T., & Julie Matthaei, J. (1996). *Race, gender, and work: A multi-cultural economic history of women in the United States* (Rev. ed.). Boston: South End Press.

Andersen, T. (1991). Guidelines for practice. In T. Andersen (Ed.), *The reflecting team: Dialogues and dialogues about dialogues.* New York: Norton.

Anderson, H., & Goolishian, H. (1988). Human systems as linguistic systems: Preliminary and evolving ideas about the implications for clinical theory. *Family Process, 27,* 371–393.

Anderson, K. J., Kanner, M., & Elsayegh, N. (2009). Are feminists man haters?: Feminists' and nonfeminists' attitudes toward men. *Psychology of Women Quarterly, 33(2),* 216–224.

Anderson, R. E., & Carter, I. (1990). *Human behavior in the social environment: A social systems approach* (4th ed.). New York: Aldine de Gruyter.

Andrews, V. (1997, August). The art of resilience: Learning to turn crisis into opportunity. *Intuition, 17,* 30–35, 52–54.

Apostolides, M. (1999, September/October). The pleasure of the pain: Why some people need S & M—sadomasochistic sex. *Psychology Today,* 60–65.

Appignanesi, R., & Zarate, O. (1979). *Freud for beginners.* New York: Pantheon.

Appleby, G. A., Colon, E. A., & Hamilton, J. (2007). *Diversity, oppression and social functioning: Person-in-environment assessment and intervention.* Boston: Allyn & Bacon.

Aptheker, B. (1989). *Tapestries of life: Women's work, women's consciousness, and the meaning of daily experience.* Amherst: University of Massachusetts Press.

Armstrong, K. (2001). Foreward. In Y. Y. Haddad & J. L. Esposito (Eds.), *Daughters of Abraham: Feminist thought in Judaism, Christianity, and Islam* (pp. vii–xiii). Gainesville: University of Florida Press.

Arrighi, G., & Drangel, J. (1986). Stratification of the world economy: An explanation of the semiperipheral zone. *Review, 10,* 9–74.

Ashford, J. B., LeCroy, C. W., & Lortie, K. L. (2000). *Human behavior in the social environment: A multidimensional perspective* (2nd ed.). Pacific Grove, CA: Brooks/Cole.

Assagioli, R. (1965). *Psychosynthesis: A collection of basic writings.* New York: Penguin.

Assagioli, R. (1973). *The act of will.* New York: Penguin.

Atchley, R. C. (1997). *Social forces and aging: An introduction to social gerontology* (8th ed.). Belmont, CA: Wadsworth.

Atherton, C. R. (1990). Adam Smith and the welfare state. *Arete, 15(1),* 24–31.

Atonovsky, A. (1956). Toward a refinement of the "marginal man" concept. *Social Forces, 35,* 57–62.

Austin, C. D. (1981). Client assessment in context. *Social Work Research and Abstracts, 17,* 4–11.

Averill, J. (1986). The acquisition of emotions during adulthood. In R. Harre (Ed.), *The social construction of emotions* (pp. 98–118). New York: Basil Blackwell.

Badiner, A. H. (Ed.). (1990). *Dharma Gaia: A harvest of essays in Buddhism and ecology.* Berkeley, CA: Paralax Press.

Baer, R. A. (2006). *Mindfulness-based treatment approaches: Clinician's guide to evidence base and applications.* Boston, MA: Elsevier.

Baines, D. (2008). *Doing anti-oppressive practice building transformative, politicized social work.* Black Point, Nova Scotia, Canada: Fernwood Publishing.

Baker, B., & Wheelwright, J. (1982). *Analysis with the aged.* In M. Stein (Ed.), *Jungian analysis* (pp. 257–258). La Salle, IL: Open Court.

Balcom, D., Lee, R., & Tager, J. (1995, January). The systematic treatment of shame in couples. *Journal of Marital and Family Therapy, 21,* 55–65.

Bales, R. F. (1950). *Interaction process analysis.* Reading, MA: Addison-Wesley Press.

Baltes, P. B. (1973). Prototypical paradigms and questions in life-span research on development and aging. *The Gerontologist, 13,* 458–467.

Baltes, P. B. (1987). Theoretical propositions of life-span developmental psychology: On the dynamics between growth and decline. *Developmental Psychology, 23,* 611–626.

Bandura, A. (1969). *Principles of behavior modification.* New York: Holt, Rinehart & Winston.

Bandura, A. (1977). *A social learning theory.* Englewood Cliffs, NJ: Prentice-Hall.

Bandura, A. (1982a). The psychology of chance encounters and life paths. *American Psychologist, 37,* 747–755.

Bandura, A. (1982b). Self-efficacy mechanism in human agency. *American Psychologist, 37,* 122–147.

Bandura, A. (1986a). *Social foundations of thought and action: A social cognitive theory.* Englewood Cliffs, NJ: Prentice-Hall.

Bandura, A. (1986b). *Aggression: A social learning analysis.* Englewood Cliffs, NJ: Prentice-Hall.

Bandura, A. (1989). Human agency in social cognitive theory. *American Psychologist, 44,* 1175–1184.

Bandura, A., & Walters, R. H. (1963). *Social learning and personality development.* New York: Holt, Rinehart and Winston.

Banks, O. (1986). *Faces of feminism.* Oxford: Basil Blackwell.

Baran, P., & Sweezy, P. (1966). *Monopoly capital: An essay on the American economic and social order.* New York: Monthly Review Press.

**Barker, R.** (1968). *Ecological psychology.* Stanford, CA: Stanford University Press.

**Barnett, R. C., & Baruch, G. H.** (1980). Toward economic independence: Women's involvement in multiple roles. In D. G. McGuin (Ed.), *Women's lives: New theory, research, and policy.* Ann Arbor: University of Michigan Center for Continuing Education of Women.

**Barth, F.** (1969). *Ethnic groups and boundaries.* Boston: Little, Brown.

**Bartle, E. E., Couchonnal, G., Canda, E. R., & Staker, M. D.** (2002). Empowerment as a dynamically developing concept for practice: Lessons learned from organizational ethnography. *Social Work, 47(1),* 32–43.

**Baruch, G., Barnett, R., & Rivers, C.** (1983). *Lifeprints: New patterns of love and work for today's women.* New York: Plume.

**Bass, E., & Davis, L.** (1995). *The courage to heal: A guide for women survivors of sexual abuse.* New York: Harper & Row.

**Bateson, G.** (1972). *Steps towards an ecology of mind.* New York: Ballantine.

**Bateman, A., & Fonagy, P.** (2008). 8-year follow up of patients treated for borderline personality disorder: mentalization-based treatment versus treatment as usual. *American Journal of Psychiatry, 165,* 631–638.

**Bateman, A., & Fonagy, P.** (2009). Randomized controlled trial of outpatient mentalization-based treatment versus structured clinical management for borderline personality disorder. *American Journal of Psychiatry, 166,* 1355–1364.

**Bauerlein, M.** (2008). *The dumbest generation: How the digital age stupefies young Americans and jeopardizes our future (or, don't trust anyone under 30).* New York: Tarcher/Penguin.

**Baumeister, R.** (2000). Gender differences in erotic plasticity: The female sex drive as socially flexible and responsive. *Psychological Bulletin, 126,* 347–374.

**Baudrillard, J.** (1983). *Simulations.* London: Semiotext.

**Baudrillard, J.** (1988). *America.* London: Verso.

**Bazire, R.** (2001). *How antipsychotics probably work.* Retrieved April 23, 2001 from http://bipolar.about. com/health/bipolar/gi/dynamic/offsite.htm?site=http% 3A%2F%2Fwww.nmhc.co.uk%2Fmoa-neur.htm

**Beatty, J.** (2001). *The human brain: Essentials of behavioral neuroscience.* Thousand Oaks, CA: Sage.

**Becker, H.** (1973). *Outsiders: Studies in the sociology of deviance* (Rev. ed.). New York: Free Press.

**Beeghley, L.** (1989). *The structure of social stratification in the United States.* Boston: Allyn & Bacon.

**Beer, S. H. (Ed.).** (1955). *Marx and Engels: The communist manifesto.* New York: Appleton-Century-Crofts.

**Beisser, A. R.** (1973). Models of helping and training for incapacity. *American Journal of Orthopsychiatry, 43,* 586–594.

**Belanger, K.** (2003). In search of a theory to guide rural practice: The case for social capital. In L. Ginsberg (Ed.), *Social Work in Rural Communities* (4th ed.). Alexandria, VA: CSWE Press.

**Belenky, M. F., Clinchy, B. M., Goldberger, N. R., & Tarule, J. M.** (1986). *Women's ways of knowing: The development of self, voice, and mind.* New York: Basic Books.

**Bell, D.** (1960). *The end of ideology.* New York: Free Press.

**Bem, S. L.** (1993). *Lenses of gender: Transforming the debate on sexual equality.* New Haven: Yale University Press.

**Benatar, M.** (1995). Running away from sexual abuse: Denial revisited. *Families in Society, 76(5),* 315–320.

**Benefiel, M.** (2005). *Soul at work: Spiritual leadership in organizations.* New York: Church Publishing Inc.

**Bennett, J. W. (Ed.).** (1975). *The new ethnicity: Perspectives from ethnology.* St. Paul: West Publishing.

**Berg, I. K.** (1994). *Family based services: A solution-focused approach.* New York: Norton.

**Berg, I. K.** (1996). *Solution-focused training.* Milwaukee, WI: The Brief Family Therapy Center.

**Berg, I., & DeJong, P.** (1996). Solution-building conversations: Co-constructing a sense of competence with clients. *Families in Society, 77(6),* 376–390.

**Berg, I., & Miller, S. D.** (1992). *Working with the problem drinker: A solution-focused approach.* New York: Norton.

**Berger, P. L.** (1963). *Invitation to sociology.* New York: Anchor Books.

**Berger, P. L.** (1967). *The sacred canopy.* Garden City, NY: Anchor.

**Berger, P. L., & Berger, B.** (1979). Becoming a member of society. In P. I. Rose (Ed.), *Socialization and the life cycle.* New York: St. Martin's Press.

**Berger, P. L., & Luckmann, T.** (1966). *The social construction of reality.* Garden City, NY: Doubleday.

**Berger, P. L., & Luckmann, T.** (1967). *The social construction of reality: A treatise in the sociology of knowledge.* Garden City, NY: Anchor Books.

**Berger, R. M.** (1986). Social work practice models: A better recipe. *Social Casework, 67(1),* 45–54.

**Berger, R. M., & Kelly, J. J.** (1993). Social work in the ecological crisis. *Social Work, 38(5),* 521–526.

**Berk, L. E.** (1989). *Child development.* Boston: Allyn & Bacon.

Berk, L. E. (2004). *Development through the lifespan* (3rd ed.). Boston: Allyn & Bacon.

Berkman, B. & D'Ambruoso, S. (Eds.). (2006). *Handbook of social work in health and aging.* New York: Oxford University Press.

Berlin, S. B. (1996). Constructivism and the environment: A cognitive-integrative perspective for social work practice. *Families in Society, 77(6)*, 326–335.

Berman, J. J. (Ed.). (1990). *Cross-cultural perspectives.* Lincoln: University of Nebraska.

Bernard, H. S. (1981). Identity formation during late adolescence: A review of some empirical findings. *Adolescence, 62*, 349–358.

Bernard, J. (1981). *The female world.* New York: Free Press.

Bernstein, R. (1976). *The restructuring of social and political theory.* Philadelphia: University of Pennsylvania Press.

Berry, J. W. (2005). Acculturation: Living successfully in two cultures. *International Journal of Intercultural Relations, 29*, 697–712.

Bertalanffy, L. von. (1967). *Robots, men and minds.* New York: George Braziller.

Bertalanffy, L. von. (1968). *General system theory* (Rev. ed.). New York: George Braziller.

Bertalanffy, L. von. (1981). *A systems view of man.* Boulder, CO: Westview Press.

Besa, D. (1994). Evaluating narrative family therapy using single-system research design. *Research on Social Work Practice 4(3)*, 309–325.

Besthorn, F. H. (2001). Transpersonal psychology and deep ecological philosophy: Exploring linkages and applications for social work. In E. R. Canda, & E. D. Smith (Eds.), *Transpersonal perspectives on spirituality in social work* (pp. 23–44). Binghamton, NY: Haworth Press.

Besthorn, F. H. (2002). Radical environmentalism and the ecological self: Rethinking the concept of self-identity for social work practice. *Journal of Progressive Human Services, 13(1)*, 53–72.

Besthorn, F. H. & Canda, E. R. (2002). Revisioning environment: Deep ecology for social work education. *Journal of Teaching in Social Work, 22(1/2)*, 79–101.

Besthorn, F. H. & Pearson McMillen, D. (2002). The oppression of women and nature: Ecofeminism as a framework for an expanded ecological social work. *Families in Society: The Journal of Contemporary Human Services, 83(3)*, 221–232.

Bhagwan, R. (2009). Creating sacred experiences for children as pathways to healing, growth and transformation. *International Journal of Children & Spirituality, 14(3)*, 225–234.

Bhagwan, R. (2010). The interconnectedness of spirituality and social development: Themes for education. *Social Work/Maatskaplike Werk, 46(2)*, 164–174.

Biddle, B. J., & Thomas, E. J. (Eds.). (1979). *Role theory: Concepts and research.* New York: Robert S. Krieger Publishers.

Bilson, A. (Ed.) (2004). Evidence-based practice and social work: International research and policy perspectives. London: Whiting & Birch Ltd.

Binstock, R. H. (2006). Later life and the farther reaches of human nature. *The Gerontologist, 46(5)*, 695–698.

Bjorklund, D. F. (2000). *False-memory creation in children and adults: Theory, research, and implications.* Hillsdale, NJ: Erlbaum.

Blalock, H. M., Jr. (1989). *Power and conflict.* Newbury Park, CA: Sage.

Blank, G., & Blank, P. (1974). *Ego psychology: Theory and practice.* New York: Columbia University Press.

Blau, P. (1964). *Exchange and power in social life.* New York: Wiley.

Blau, P., & Duncan, O. D. (1967). *The American occupational structure.* New York: John Wiley & Sons.

Blau, Z. S. (1972). *Role exit and identity.* Paper presented at the American Sociological Association Meetings, New Orleans, Louisiana.

Blau, Z. S. (1973). *Old age in a changing society.* New York: Franklin Watts.

Blauberg, I. V., Sadovsky, V. N., & Yudin. (1977). *Systems theory: Philosophical and methodological problems.* Moscow: Progress Publishers.

Block, J. (1990, October). Ego resilience through time: Antecedents and ramifications. In *Resilience and Psychological Health.* Symposium of the Boston Psychoanalytic Society, Boston.

Block, J., & Haan, N. (1972). *Lives through time.* Berkeley, CA: Bancroft Press.

Bloom, M. (1985). *Life span development: Bases for preventive and interventive helping* (2nd ed.). New York: Macmillan.

Bloom, S. L. (1995). When good people do bad things: Meditations on the backlash. *Journal of Psychohistory, 22(3)*, 273–304.

Blume, E. S. (1990). *Secret survivors: Uncovering incest and its aftereffects in women.* New York: Ballantine.

Blumer, H. (1969a). *Symbolic interactionism: Perspective and method.* Englewood Cliffs, NJ: Prentice-Hall.

Blumer, H. (1969b). The methodological position of symbolic interactionism. In H. Blumer, *Symbolic interactionism: Perspective and method* (pp. 1–60). Englewood Cliffs, NJ: Prentice-Hall.

**Blumer, H.** (1980). Comment: Mead and Blumer: The convergent methodological perspectives of social behaviorism and symbolic interactionism. *American Sociological Review, 45,* 409–419.

**Blumstein, P. W., & Schwartz, P.** (1993). Bisexuality: Some social psychological issues. In L. D. Garnets & D. C. Kimmel (Eds.), *Psychological perspectives on lesbian and gay male experiences* (pp. 168–183), New York: Columbia University Press.

**Bogue, D.** (1974). *The basic writings of Ernest W. Burgess.* Chicago: Community and Family Study Center, The University of Chicago.

**Bohannan, P.** (1955). Some principles of exchange and investment among the TIV. *American Anthropologist, 57,* 60–70.

**Bolin, A.** (1988). *In search of Eve: Transsexual rites of passage.* New York: Bergin & Garvey.

**Bolin, A.** (1992). Coming of age among transsexuals. In T. L. Whitehead & B. V. Reid (Eds.), *Gender constructs and social issues* (pp. 13–39). Chicago: University of Illinois.

**Borden, W.** (2000). The relational paradigm in contemporary psychoanalysis: Toward a psychodynamically informed social work practice. *Social Service Review, 74(3),* 352–373.

**Borenzweig, H.** (1984). *Jung and social work.* Lanham, MD: University Press of America.

**Borneman, E.** (1994). *Childhood phases of maturity: Sexual developmental psychology.* Amherst, NY: Prometheus Books.

**Bourdieu, P.** (1977a). Cultural reproduction and social reproduction. In J. Karabel & A. H. Halsey (Eds.), *Power and ideology in education.* New York: Oxford University Press.

**Bourdieu, P.** (1977b). *Outline of a theory of practice.* Cambridge, England: Cambridge University Press.

**Bourdieu, P.** (1990). *The logic of practice.* Cambridge, England: Polity Press.

**Bowlby, J.** (1969). *Attachment.* New York: Basic Books.

**Bowlby, J.** (1973). *Separation.* New York: Basic Books.

**Bowlby, J.** (1975). Attachment theory: Separation anxiety and mourning. *American Handbook of Psychiatry.* (Vol. 6, chap. 14, pp. 292–309). New York: Basic Books.

**Bowlby, J.** (1980). *Loss.* New York: Basic Books.

**Bradshaw, J.** (1992, August). Incest: When you wonder if it happened to you. *Lear's Magazine, 5,* 43–44.

**Bragdon, E.** (1990). *The call of spiritual emergency: From personal crisis to personal transformation.* San Francisco: Harper and Row.

**Brame, W., Brame, G., & Jacobs, J.** (1996). *Different loving: A complete exploration of the world of sexual dominance and submission.* New York: Villard Books.

**Braud, W., & Anderson, R.** (1998). *Transpersonal research methods for the social sciences: Honoring human experience.* Thousand Oaks, CA: Sage.

**Braverman, H.** (1974). *Labor and monopoly capital: The degradation of work in the twentieth century.* New York: Monthly Review Press.

**Brennan, E., & Weick, A.** (1981). Theories of adult development: Creating a context for practice. *Social Casework, 62(1),* 13–19.

**Bretall, R. (Ed.).** (1946). *A Kierkegaard anthology.* New York: Random House.

**Breton, M.** (1989). Liberation theology, group work, and the right of the poor and oppressed to participate in the life of the community. *Social Work with Groups, 12(3),* 5–18.

**Bricker-Jenkins, M.** (1991). The propositions and assumptions of feminist social work practice. In M. Bricker-Jenkins, N. Hooyman, & N. Gottlieb (Eds.), *Feminist social work practice in clinical settings* (pp. 271–303). Newbury Park, CA: Sage.

**Briere, J., & Conte, J.** (1993). Self-reported amnesia for abuse in adults molested as children. *Journal of Traumatic Stress, 6,* 21–31.

**Briggs, H. E. & Rzepnicki, T. L.** (2004). *Using evidence in social work practice: Behavioral perspectives.* Chicago: Lyceum Books.

**Brislin, R.** (1993). *Understanding culture's influence on behavior.* Orlando, FL: Harcourt Brace Jovanovich.

**Broderick, C.** (1971, February). Beyond the conceptual frameworks. *Journal of Marriage and the Family, 33,* 139–159.

**Brookey, R.** (1996). A community like Philadelphia. *Western Journal of Communications 60,* 40–54.

**Brooks, W. K.** (1986, Winter). Human behavior/social environment: Past and present, future or folly? *Journal of Social Work Education, 1,* 18–23.

**Brower, A. M.,** (1996). Group development as constructed social reality revisited: The constructivism of small groups. *Families in Society, 77(6),* 336–344.

**Brower, A. M., & Nurius, P. S.** (1993). *Social cognition and individual change: Current theory and counseling guidelines.* Newbury Park, CA: Sage.

**Brown, B.** (2004). *Women & shame: Reaching out, speaking truths, & building connection.* Austin, TX: 3C Press.

**Brown, B.** (2010). *The gifts of imperfection: Let go of who you think you're supposed to be and embrace who you are.* Center City, MN: Hazelden Publishing and Educational Services.

**Brown, L.** (1995). Lesbian identities: Concepts and issues. In A. D'Augelli & C. Patterson (Eds.), *Lesbian, gay and bisexual identities over the lifespan.* New York: Oxford University Press.

Brown, L., Lenssen, N., & Kane, H. (1995). *Vital signs 1995: The trends that are shaping our future.* New York: W. W. Norton.

Brown, L. M., & Gilligan, C. (1992). *Meeting at the crossroads.* New York: Ballantine.

Brown, M. E., & Martin, R. (1991). Rethinking the crisis of socialism. *Socialism and Democracy, 7(3),* 9–56.

Brown, T. (2000, April). *A proposed model of identity development for bisexual persons.* Masters thesis. School of professional psychology, Pacific University, Forest Grove, OR.

Buhner, S. H. (2010). *Ensouling language: On the art of nonfiction and the writer's life.* Rochester, VT: Inner Traditions.

Bullis, Ronald K. (1996). *Spirituality in social work practice.* Washington, DC: Taylor and Francis.

Bullough, V. L. & Bullough, B. (1993). *Cross dressing, sex, and gender.* Philadelphia: University of Pennsylvania Press.

Bullough, B., Bullough, V. L., & Elias, J. (1997). *Gender Blending.* Amherst, NY: Prometheus Books.

Burgess, E. W. (1925). The growth of the city. In Park, R. E., Burgess, E. E., & McKenzie, R. D. (Eds.), *The city.* Chicago: The University of Chicago Press.

Burgess, E. W. (1926). Natural area as the unit for social work in the large city. *Proceedings of the National Conference in Social Work, 53.* Cleveland, OH: 504–510.

Burgess, E. W. (1927, October). The contribution of sociology to family social work. *The Family, 8,* 191–193.

Burgess, E. W., & Wallin, P. (1953). *Engagement and marriage.* Philadelphia: Lippincott.

Burstow, B. (1991, Spring/Summer). Freirian codifications and social work education. *Journal of Social Work Education, 27(2),* 196–207.

Butler, J. (1990). *Gender trouble: Feminism and the subversion of identity.* New York: Routledge.

Butler, J. (1999). *Gender trouble: Feminism and the subversion of identity* (2nd ed.). New York: Routledge.

Butler, R. N. (1975). *Why survive? Being old in America.* New York: Harper and Row.

Camino, L. A. (1994). Refugee adolescents and their changing identities. In L. A. Camino & R. M. Krulfeld (Eds.), *Reconstructing lives, recapturing meaning: Refugee identity, gender, and culture change* (pp. 29–56). Washington, DC: Gordon & Breach.

Campbell, T. (1981). *Seven theories of human society.* New York: Oxford University Press.

Camus, A. (1955). *The myth of Sisyphus and other essays.* New York: Vintage.

Canda, E. R. (1988). Therapeutic transformation in ritual therapy, and human development. *Journal of Religion and Health, 27(3),* 205–220.

Canda, E. R. (1989). Religious content in social work education: A comparative approach. *Journal of Social Work Education, 25(1),* 36–45.

Canda, E. R. (1990). An holistic approach to prayer for social work practice. *Social Thought, 16(3),* 3–13.

Canda, E. R. (1991). East/West philosophical synthesis in transpersonal theory. *Journal of Sociology and Social Welfare, 18(4),* 137–152.

Canda, E. R. (Ed.). (1995). Spirituality [Special edition]. *Reflections: Narratives of Professional Helping, 1(4),* 1–81.

Canda, E. R. (1996). Does religion and spirituality have a significant place in the core HBSE curriculum? Yes. In M. Bloom & W. Klein (Eds.), *Controversial issues in human behavior in the social environment* (pp. 172–177; 183–184). Boston: Allyn & Bacon.

Canda, E. R. (Ed.). (1998). *Spirituality in social work: New directions.* Binghamton, NY: Haworth Press.

Canda, E. R. (2001). Transcending through disability and death: Transpersonal themes in living with cystic fibrosis. In E. R. Canda & E. D. Smith (Eds.), *Transpersonal perspectives on spirituality in social work* (pp. 109–134). Binghamton, NY: Haworth Press.

Canda, E. R. (2006). The significance of spirituality for resilient response to chronic illness: A qualitative study of adults with cystic fibrosis. In D. Saleebey (Ed.), *The strengths perspective in social work practice* (4th ed., pp. 61–76). Boston: Pearson/Allyn and Bacon.

Canda, E. R. (2009). Chronic illness and transilience along my spiritual path. In D. Saleebey (Ed.), *The strengths perspective in social work practice* (5th ed., pp. 72–92). Boston: Pearson A and B.

Canda, E. R., Carrizosa, S., & Yellow Bird, M. (1995). *Cultural diversity in child welfare practice: A training curriculum for cultural competence.* Lawrence, Kansas: The University of Kansas School of Social Welfare.

Canda, E. R., & Chambers, D. (1993). Should spiritual principles guide social policy? Yes. In H. J. Karger & J. Midgely (Eds.), *Controversial issues in social policy* (pp. 63–78). Boston: Allyn & Bacon.

Canda, E. R., & Cheon, J. W. (Eds.). (2010). Spirituality in positive youth development and social work—Special Issue. *Currents: New Scholarship for the Human Services, 9*(1), open access international electronic journal: http://currents.synergiesprairies.ca/currents/index.php/currents

Canda, E. R. & Furman, L. D. (2010). *Spiritual diversity in social work practice: The heart of helping* (2nd ed.). New York: Oxford University Press.

Canda, E. R., Ketchell, A., Dybicz, P., Pyles, L., & Nelson-Becker, H. (2006). *Health through faith and community: A study resource for Christian faith communities to promote personal and social well-being.* Binghamton, NY: Haworth Pastoral Press.

Canda, E. R., Nakashima, M., Burgess, V., Russel, R., & Barfield, S. T. (2003). *Spiritual diversity and social work: A comprehensive bibliography with annotations* (2nd ed.). Alexandria, VA: Council on Social Work Education.

Canda, E. R., & Phaobtong, T. (1992). Buddhism as a support system for Southeast Asian refugees. *Social Work, 37(1),* 61–67.

Canda, E. R., Shin, S., & Canda, H. J. (1993). Traditional philosophies of human service in Korea and contemporary social work implications. *Social Development Issues, 15(3),* 84–104.

Canda, E. R. & Smith, E. D. (Eds.). (2001). *Transpersonal perspectives on spirituality in social work.* Binghamton, NY: Haworth Press.

Caplan, F., & Caplan, T. (1997). *The second twelve months of life: A kaleidoscope of growth.* New York: Pedigree Books.

Capra, F. (1982). *The turning point: Science, society, and the rising culture.* New York: Simon and Schuster.

Capra, F., & Spretnak, C. (1984). *Green politics.* New York: E. P. Dutton.

Carter, E. & McGoldrick, M. (1980). *The family life cycle: A framework for family therapy.* New York: Gardner Press.

Carter, E. & McGoldrick, M. (1989). *The changing family life cycle: A framework for family therapy* (2nd ed.). Boston: Allyn & Bacon.

Cass, V. C. (1979). Homosexual identity formation: A theoretical model. *Journal of Homosexuality, 4,* 219–236.

Cass, V. C. (1996, July). *The coming out process and theoretical consideration.* Symposium presented at the National Lesbian and Gay Health Conference, Seattle, WA.

Catania, A. C. (1988). The operant behaviorism of B. F. Skinner. In A. C. Catania & S. Harnard (Eds.) *The selection of behavior* (pp. 3–8). Cambridge: Cambridge University Press.

Chafetz, J. S. (1987). The role of theory in sociology. In R. L. Curtis, Jr. (Ed.), *Sociology: Persons and process in social context* (pp. 24–38). Dubuque, IA: Kendall/Hunt.

Chafetz, J. (1989). Gender equality: Toward a theory of change. In R. A. Wallace (Ed.), *Feminism and sociological theory.* Newbury Park, CA: Sage.

Chambon, A. S., Irving, A., & Epstein, L. (Eds.) (1999). *Reading Foucault for social work.* New York: Columbia University Press.

Chan, C. S. (1995). Issues of sexual identity in an ethnic minority: The case of Chinese American lesbians, gay men, and bisexual people. In A. D'Augelli & C. Patterson (Eds.), *Lesbian, gay, and bisexual identities over the lifespan.* New York: Oxford University Press.

Changfoot, N. (2004). Feminist standpoint theory, Hegel and the dialectical self: Shifting the foundations. *Philosophy & Social Criticism, 30(4),* 477–502.

Chase-Dunn, C. (1989). *Global formation: Structures of the world economy.* Cambridge, MA: Blackwell.

Chase-Dunn, C., & and Hall, T. D. (1993). Comparing world systems: Concepts and working hypotheses. *Social Forces, 71(4),* 851–886.

Chasseguet-Smirgel, J. (Ed.). (1970). *Female sexuality.* Ann Arbor: University of Michigan Press.

Chatfield, W. F. (1977). Economic and sociological factors influencing life satisfaction of the aged. *Journal of Gerontology, 32(5),* 593–599.

Chatterjee, P. (1985, Winter). Origins of social welfare policy and models of help. *Social Development Issues 9(3),* 27–46.

Chatterjee, P. (1990). *The transferability of social technology.* Lewiston, NY: Mellen Press.

Chatterjee, P., & Bailey, D. (1993). Ideology and social structure in social service settings. In P. Chatterjee & A. J. Abramovitz (Eds.), *Structure of nonprofit management.* Lanham, MD: University Press of America.

Chatterjee, P. Bailey, D., & Aronoff, N. (2001). Adolescence and old age in twelve communities. *Journal of Sociology and Social Welfare 28(4),* 121–159.

Chatterjee, P. & Curl, A. (2003, April). Trajectories of human development. Cleveland, OH: Case Western Reserve Research ShowCASE.

Chatterjee, P. & Curl, A. (2004, January). *Human development and social development.* International University Consortium for International Social Development, Mumbai.

Chatterjee, P., & Hilbert, H. (1986, Fall–Winter). Conceptual models of helping and their functions. *The Journal of Applied Social Sciences, 11(1),* 111–135.

Chau, K. L. (Ed.). (1991). *Ethnicity and biculturalism.* New York: Haworth.

**Checkland, P.** (1981). *Systems thinking, systems practice.* Chichester, England: John Wiley & Sons.

**Cheon, J. W. & Canda, E. R.** (2010). The meaning and engagement of spirituality for positive youth development in social work. *Families in Society, 91(2),* 121–126.

**Chesler, P.** (1976). *Women, money and power.* New York: Morrow.

**Chestang, L.** (1972). *Character development in a hostile environment.* Chicago: University of Chicago Press.

**Chiriboga, D. A.** (1989). Mental health at midpoint. In S. Hunter & M. Sundel (Eds.), *Midlife myths: Issues, findings, and practice implications* (pp. 116–144). Newbury Park, CA: Sage.

**Chodorow, N.** (1978). *The reproduction of mothering: Psychoanalysis and the sociology of gender.* Berkeley: University of California Press.

**Chodorow, N.** (1979). Feminism and difference: Gender, relation, and difference in psychoanalytic perspective. *Socialist Review, 46,* 42–64.

**Choi, J. S., Martin, E., Chatterjee, P., & Holland, T.** (1978). Ideology and social welfare. Indian *Journal of Social Work, 39(2),* 139–160.

**Chomsky, N.** (1967). Review of Skinner's verbal behavior. In L. A. Jakobvits & M. S. Morn (Eds.), *Readings in the philosophy of language.* Englewood Cliffs, NJ: Prentice-Hall.

**Chomsky, N.** (1993). *The prosperous few and the restless many.* Berkeley, CA: Odonian Press.

**Churchman, C. W.** (1971). *The design of inquiring systems: Basic concepts of systems and organization.* New York: Basic Books.

**Clark, M. & Anderson, B.** (1967). *Culture and aging.* Springfield, IL: Charles C Thomas.

**Clarkin, J. F., Levy, K. N., Lenzenweger, M. F., & Kernberg, O. F.** (2007). Evaluating three treatments for borderline personality disorder: A multiwave study. *American Journal of Psychiatry, 164(6),* 922–928.

**Clelland, D. A., & Form, W. H.** (1964). Economic dominants and community power: A comparative analysis. *American Journal of Sociology, 69,* 511–521. (Reprinted in *The search for community power,* pp. 78–114, by W. D. Hawley & F. M. Wirt, Eds., 1968, Englewood Cliffs, NJ: Prentice-Hall.)

**Clifford, D. & Burke, B.** (2009). *Anti-oppressive ethics and values in social work.* Hampshire, England: Palgrave Macmillan.

**Clough, P. T.** (1992). *The end(s) of ethnography: From realism to social criticism.* Newbury Park, CA: Sage.

**Cloward, R., & Ohlin, L.** (1960). *Delinquency and opportunity: A study of the delinquent gang.* Glencoe, IL: The Free Press.

**Coates, J.** (2003a). Exploring the roots of the environmental crisis: Opportunity for social transformation. *Critical Social Work, 3(1),* 44–66.

**Coates, J.** (2003b). *Ecology and social work: Toward a new paradigm.* Halifax, NS: Fernwood Publishing.

**Coates, J.** (2007). From ecology to spirituality and social justice. In J. Coates, J. R. Graham, & B. Swartzentruber, & B. Ouelette (Eds.), *Spirituality and social work: Selected Canadian readings* (pp. 213–228). Toronto: Canadian Scholars Press.

**Coates, J., Gray, M., & Hetherington, T.** (2006). An "ecospiritual" perspective: Finally, a place for Indigenous approaches. *British Journal of Social Work, 36,* 381–399.

**Coggins, K.** (1990). *Alternative pathways to healing: The recovery medicine wheel.* Deerfield Beach, FL: Health Communications.

**Cohen, B. P.** (1989). *Developing sociological knowledge: Theory and method.* Chicago: Nelson Hall.

**Cohen, L.** (1996, April). Infants are dumber than we think. Invited address given at the Forty-Second Annual Meeting of the Southwestern Psychological Association, Houston, TX.

**Cohen, Y.** (1971). *Man in adaptation: The instructional framework.* Chicago: Aldine.

**Colby, A., & Damon, W.** (1987). Listening to a different voice: A review of Gilligan's *In a different voice.* In M. R. Walsh (Ed.), *The psychology of women: Ongoing debates.* New Haven: Yale University Press.

**Colby, A., Kohlberg, L., Gibbs, J., & Liberman, M.** (1983). A longitudinal study of moral judgment. *Monographs of Society for Research in Child Development, 48*(Serial No. 200).

**Coleman, E.** (1982). Developmental stages of the coming out process. In J. C. Gonsiorek (Ed.), *Homosexuality and psychotherapy.* New York: Haworth.

**Coleman, J.** (1988). Social capital in the creation of human capital. *American Journal of Sociology, 94,* 95–120.

**Coleman, J.** (1990). *Foundations of social theory.* Cambridge, MA: Harvard University Press.

**Coles, R.** (1990). *The spiritual life of children.* Boston: Houghton Mifflin.

**Coles, R.** (1991). *Moral life of children.* Boston: Houghton Mifflin.

**Coles, R.** (1997). *The moral intelligence of children.* New York: Random House.

**Collins, J. E.** (1991). *Mysticism and new paradigm psychology.* Savage, MD: Rowman & Littlefield Publishers.

**Collins, P. H.** (1986). Learning from the outsider within: The sociological significance of black feminist thought. *Social Problems, 33(6)*, 14–23.

**Collins, P. H.** (1989). The social construction of black feminist thought. *Signs: Journal of Women in Culture and Society, 4(1)*, 745–773.

**Collins, P. H.** (1990). *Black feminist thought: Knowledge, consciousness, and the politics of empowerment.* London: HarperCollins.

**Collins, P. H.** (1997). Comment on Hekman's "Truth and method: Feminist standpoint theory revisited": Where's the power? *Signs: Journal of Women in Culture and Society, 22(2)*, 375–381.

**Collins, P. H.** (2000). *Black feminist thought: Knowledge, consciousness, and the politics of empowerment* (2nd ed.). New York: Routledge.

**Collins, R.** (1975). *Conflict sociology: Toward an explanatory science.* New York: Academic Press.

**Collins, R.** (1981). On the microfoundations of macrosociology. *American Journal of Sociology, 86*, 984–1014.

**Collins, R.** (1994). *Four sociological traditions.* New York: Oxford University Press.

**Comstock, D. (Ed.).** (2005). *Diversity and development: Critical contexts that shape our lives and relationships.* Belmont, CA: Brooks/Cole.

**Conger, J., & Kanungo, R.** (1988). The empowerment process: Integrating theory and practice. *Academy of Management Review, 13(3)*, 471–482.

**Cook, J. A., & Fonow, M. M.** (1990). Knowledge and women's interests: Issues of epistemology and methodology in feminist sociology and research. In J. M. Nielson (Ed.), *Feminist research methods: Exemplary readings in the social sciences* (pp. 69–93). Boulder, CO: Westview.

**Cook, K. S., & Emerson, R. M.** (1978). Power, equity, commitment in exchange networks. *American Sociological Review, 43*, 721–739.

**Cooley, C. H.** (1909/1962). *Social organization.* New York: Schocken Books. (Originally published by Charles Scribner's Sons.)

**Coontz, S.** (1992). *The way we never were: American families and the nostalgia trap.* New York: Basic Books.

**Cooper, M.** (2004). Towards a relationally-oriented approach to therapy: Empirical support and analysis. *British Journal of Guidance & Counselling, 32(4)*, 451–460.

**Corcoran, J.** (2000). *Evidence-Based Social Work Practice with Families: A Lifespan Approach.* New York: Springer.

**Corsini, R. J., & Marsella, A. J.** (1983). *Personality theories, research, and assessment.* Itasca, IL: F. E. Peacock.

**Cortese, A.** (1990). *Ethnic ethics: The restructuring of moral theory.* Albany: State University of New York Press.

**Coser, L.** (1956). *The functions of social conflict.* New York: Free Press.

**Cosgrove, L.** (November-December, 2010). Diagnosing conflict-of-interest disorder. *Academe*, AAUP, retrieved from http://www.aaup.org/AAUP/pubsres/academe/2010/ND/feat/cosg.htm

**Council on Social Work Education.** (1992). *Curriculum policy statement for degree programs in social work education.* Alexandria, VA: Author.

**Council on Social Work Education.** (2002). *Handbook of accreditation standards and procedures* (2nd ed.) Alexandria, VA: Author.

**Council on Social Work Education.** (2008). *Educational policy and accreditation standards.* Alexandria, VA: Author.

**Cowen, E. L.** (1991). In pursuit of wellness. *American Psychologist, 46(4)*, 404–408.

**Cowley, A. S.** (1993). Transpersonal social work: A theory for the 1990s. *Social Work, 38(5)*, 527–534.

**Cowley, A. S.** (1996). Transpersonal social work. In F. J. Turner (Ed.), *Social work treatment: Interlocking theoretical approaches* (4th ed., pp. 663–698). New York: Free Press.

**Cowley, A. S., & Derezotes, D.** (1994). Transpersonal psychology and social work education. *Journal of Social Work Education, 30(1)*, 32–41.

**Cox, O. C.** (1948). *Caste, class, and race.* Garden City, NY: Doubleday.

**Cox, O. C.** (1970). *Caste, class, and race.* New York: Monthly Review Press.

**Coyle, G.** (1988). *Groupwork with American youth.* New York: Harper.

**Craib, I.** (1992). *Modern social theory: From Parsons to Habermas.* New York: St. Martin's Press.

**Crenshaw, K.** (2003). Traffic at the crossroads: Multiple oppressions. In R. Morgan (Ed.), *Sisterhood is forever* (pp. 43–57). New York: Washington Square Press.

**Crews, F.** (1995). *The memory wars: Freud's legacy in dispute.* New York: New York Review of Books.

**Crisp, B. R.** (2010). *Spirituality and social work.* Burlington, VT: Ashgate Publishing Company.

**Cross, W.** (1985). Black identity: Rediscovering the distinction between personal identity and reference group orientation. In M. Spencer, G. K. Brookins, & W. R. Allen (Eds.), *Beginnings: Social and affective development of Black children.* Hillsdale, NJ: Erlbaum.

*Cross, W. E., Jr.* (1987). A two-factor theory of black identity: Implications for the study of identity development in minority children. In J. S. Phinney & M. J. Rotheram (Eds.), *Children's ethnic socialization* (pp. 117–133). Beverly Hills, CA: Sage.

*Cross, W. E., Jr.* (1991). *Shades of Black: Diversity in African American identity.* Philadelphia: Temple University Press.

*Cuellar, I., Harris, L. C., & Jasso, R.* (1980). An acculturation scale for Mexican American normal and clinical populations. *Hispanic Journal of Behavioral Sciences, 2,* 199–217.

*Cullen-DuPont, K.* (1996). *The encyclopedia of women's history in America.* New York: Facts on File, Inc.

*Cumming, E., & Henry, W.* (1961). *Growing old: The process of disengagement.* New York: Basic Books.

*Cushman, P.* (1990). Why the self is empty. *American Psychologist, 45,* 599–611.

*Cushman, P.* (1995). *Constructing the self, constructing America: A cultural history of psychotherapy.* New York: Addison-Wesley.

*Cynader, M. S., & Frost, B. J.* (1999). Mechanisms of brain development: Neuronal sculpting by the physical and social environment. In D. P. Keating & C. Hertzman (Eds.), *Developmental health and the wealth of nations: Social, biological, and educational dynamics* (pp. 153–184). New York: Guilford Press.

*Dahl, R.* (1961). *Who governs?* New Haven: Yale University Press. (Reprinted in *The search for community power,* pp. 93–114, by W. D. Hawley & F. M. Wirt, (Eds.), 1968, Englewood Cliffs, NJ: Prentice-Hall.)

*Dahrendorf, R.* (1973). Toward a theory of social conflict. In A. Etzioni & E. Etzioni-Halevy (Eds.), *Social change.* New York: Basic Books.

*Dahrendorf, R., & Moore, W.* (1958, September). Out of utopia: Toward a reorientation of sociological analysis. *American Journal of Sociology, 64,* 115–127.

*Daly, M.* (1978). *Gyn/Ecology: The metaethics of radical feminism.* Boston: Beacon.

*Damianakis, T.* (2006). Seeking the spiritual in anti-oppressive organizational change. *Critical Social Work, 7(1).* Retrieved from http://cronus.uwindsor.ca/units/socialwork/critical.nsf/main/E69344834B819BFB852571

*Dan, A. J., & Bernhard, L. A.* (1989). Menopause and other health issues for midlife women. In S. Hunter & M. Sundel (Eds.), *Midlife myths: Issues, findings, and practice implications* (pp. 51–66). Newbury Park, CA: Sage.

*Dannefer, D.* (1984a, February). Adult development and social theory: A paradigmatic reappraisal. *American Sociological Review, 49,* 100–116.

*Dasen, P. E., & Heron, A.* (1981). Cross-cultural tests of Piaget's theory. In H. C. Triandis & A. Heron (Eds.), *Handbook of cross-cultural psychology: Developmental psychology* (Vol. 4). Boston: Allyn & Bacon.

*Dass, R., & Gorman, P.* (1985). *How can I help?* New York: Alfred A. Knopf.

*Datan, N., Rodehaver, D., & Hughes, F.* (1987). Adult development and aging. *Annual Review of Psychology, 38,* 153–180.

*D'Augelli, A. R.* (1994). Lesbian and gay male development. In B. Greene & G. Herek (Eds.), *Lesbian and gay psychology: Theory, research and clinical applications.* Thousand Oaks, CA: Sage.

*D'Augelli, A. R., & Garnets, L. D.* (1995). Lesbian, gay, and bisexual communities. In A.R. D'Augelli & C. J. Patterson (Eds.), *Lesbian, gay, and bisexual identities over the lifespan* (pp. 293–320). New York: Oxford Press.

*Davis, K.* (1959). The myth of functional analysis as a special method in sociology and anthropology. *American Sociological Review, 24,* 757–772.

*Davis, L. E., & Proctor, E. K.* (1989). *Race, gender, and class.* Englewood Cliffs, NJ: Prentice-Hall.

*Davis, L. V.* (1985). Female and male voices in social work. *Social Work, 30(2),* 106–113.

*Davis, L. V.* (1986). Role theory. In F. J. Turner (Ed.), *Social work treatment: Interlocking theoretical approaches.* New York: Free Press.

*de Anda, D.* (1984). Bicultural socialization: Factors affecting the minority experience. *Social Work, 29(2).*

*de Beauvoir, S.* (1953). *The second sex.* New York: Vintage.

*De Casper, A. J., & Spence, M. J.* (1986). Prenatal maternal speech influences newborn's perceptions of speech sounds. *Infant Development and Behavior, 9,* 133–150.

*Deckard, B. S.* (1979). *The women's movement: Political, socioeconomic and psychological issues.* New York: Harper and Row.

*DeHoyos, G., DeHoyos, A., & Anderson, C. B.* (1986). Sociocultural dislocation: Beyond the dual perspective. *Social Work, 31(1),* 61–67.

*DeHoyos, G., & Jensen, C.* (1985). The systems approach in American social work. *Social Casework, 66(8),* 490–497.

De Jong, P., & Hopwood, L. E. (1996). Outcome research on treatment conducted at the Brief Family Therapy Center. In S. D. Miller, M. A. Hubble, & B. L. Duncan (Eds.), *Handbook of solution-focused Brief therapy* (pp. 272–298). San Francisco: Jossey-Bass.

de Laszlo, V. (1990). (Ed.). *The basic writings of C. G. Jung.* Princeton, NJ: Bollingen Series, Princeton University Press.

de Maat, S., de Jonghe, F., Schoevers, R., & Dekker J. (2009, January–February). The effectiveness of long-term psychoanalytic therapy: A systematic review of empirical studies. *Harvard Review of Psychiatry, 17(1),* 1–23.

Delgado, M., Jones, K., & Rohani, M. (2005). *Social work practice with refugee and immigrant youth in the United States.* Boston: Allyn & Bacon.

DeMoss, R. T. (1999). *Brain waves through time: 12 principles for understanding the evolution of the human brain and man's behavior.* New York: Basic Books.

Dembo, R., & Schmeidler, J. (2002). *Family empowerment intervention: An innovative service for high-risk youths and their families.* New York: The Haworth Press.

Denisoff, R. S., & Wahrman, R. (1979). *An introduction to sociology.* New York: Macmillan.

Derezotes, D. S. (2006). *Spiritually oriented social work practice.* Boston: Pearson A and B.

Derezotes, D. S., & Evans, K. E. (1995). Spirituality and religiosity in practice: In-depth interviews of social work practitioners. *Social Thought, 18(1),* 39–56.

Derrida, J. (1978). *Writing and difference.* Chicago: University of Chicago Press.

Derrida, J. (1981). *Positions.* New York: Athlone Press.

Derrida, J. (1994). *Specters of Marx: The state of the debt, the work of mourning, and the New International.* London: Routledge.

de Shazer, S. (1985). *Keys to solution in Brief therapy.* New York: Norton.

de Shazer, S. (1988). *Clues: Investigating solutions in Brief therapy.* New York: Norton.

de Shazer, S. (1991). *Putting difference to work.* New York: W. W. Norton.

de Shazer, S. (1994). *Words were originally magic.* New York: W. W. Norton.

de Shazer, S., Berg, I., Lipchik, E., Nunnally, E., Molnar, A., Gingerich, W., et al. (1986). Brief therapy: Focused solution development. *Family Process, 25,* 207–222.

Devore, W., & Schlesinger, E. G. (1991). *Ethnic sensitive social work practice* (3rd ed.). Columbus, OH: Merrill.

Devore, W. & Schlesinger, E. G. (1995). Ethnic sensitive social work practice: The state of the art. *Journal of Sociology and Social Welfare, 22(1),* 29–58.

Devore, W., & Schlesinger, E. G. (1998). *Ethnic sensitive social work practice* (5th ed.). Boston: Allyn & Bacon.

Diamond, M. (2006). Biased-interaction theory of psychosexual development: How does one know if one if male or female? *Sex Roles, 55,* 589–600.

Dillaway, H. E, & Byrnes, M. (2009). Reconsidering successful aging: A call for renewed and expanded academic critiques and conceptualization. *Journal of Applied Gerontology, 28(6),* 702–722.

Dodd, P., & Gutiérrez, L. (1990). Preparing students for the future: A power perspective on community practice. *Administration in Social Work, 14(2),* 63–75.

Doe, S. J. (2004). Spiritually-based social work values for empowering human service organizations. *Journal of Religion & Spirituality in Social Work, 23(3),* 45–65.

Doeringer, P. B., & Piore, M. J. (1971). *Internal labor markets and manpower anaylsis.* Lexington, MA: Heath.

Dolan, Y. M. (1991). *Resolving sexual abuse: Solution-focused therapy and Eriksonian hypnosis for adult survivors.* New York: Norton.

Dollard, J. (1937). *Caste and class in a southern town.* New Haven: Yale University Press.

Dollard, J., & Miller, N. E. (1950). *Personality and psychotherapy: An analysis in terms of learning, thinking and culture.* New York: McGraw-Hill.

Doman, G. (1963). *Teach your baby to read.* London: Jonathan Cape.

Doman, G. (1982). *Teach your baby math.* New York: Pocket Books.

Domhoff, G. W. (1990). *The power elite and the state: How policy is made in America.* New York: Aldine DeGruyter.

Dominelli, L. (2002). *Anti-oppressive social work theory and practice.* Hampshire, England: Palgrave Macmillan.

Dortzbach, J. R. (1975). Moral judgment and perceived locus of control: A cross-sectional developmental study of adults, aged 25–74. *Dissertation Abstracts International, 36,* 4662B (University Microfilms No. 76-05, 160).

Dougher, M. (1993). Interpretive and hermeneutic research methods in the contextualistic analysis of verbal behavior. In S. Hayes, L. Hayes, H. Reese, & T. Sarbin (Eds.), *Varieties of scientific contextualism* (pp. 211–221). Reno, NV: Context Press.

Dozier, R. (2005). Beards, breasts, and bodies: Doing sex in a gendered world. *Gender & Society, 19(3),* 297–316.

Dreyfus, H. (1987). Foucault's therapy. *Psych Critique, 2(1),* 65–83.

Dubin, R. (1969). *Theory building.* New York: Free Press.

**DuBois, B., & Miley, K.** (1992). *Social work: An empowering profession.* Boston: Allyn & Bacon.

**DuBois, W. E. B.** (1948, May). Is man free? *Scientific Monthly, 66,* 432–434.

**Dubos, R.** (1963). *The cultural roots and the social fruits of science.* Eugene, OR: Oregon State System of Higher Education.

**Dubos, R.** (1968a). *Man, medicine, and environment.* New York: Praeger.

**Dubos, R.** (1968b). *So human an animal.* New York: Scribners.

**Dubos, R.** (1978). *The resilience of ecosystems: An ecological view of environmental restoration.* Boulder, CO: Colorado Associated University Press.

**Duhl, B. S.** (1983). *From the inside out and other metaphors: Creative and integrative approaches to training in systems thinking.* New York: Bruner/Mazel.

**Dumbrill, G. C., & Green, J.** (2008). Indigenous knowledge in the social work academy. *Social Work Education, 27(5),* 489–503.

**Dunbar, M. J.** (1972). The ecosystem as a unit of natural selection. *Transactions of the Connecticut Academy of Arts and Sciences, 44,* 113–130.

**Duncan, O. D.** (1972). From social systems to ecosystems. In J. J. Palen & K. H. Flaming (Eds.), *Urban American conflict and change.* New York: Holt, Rinehart and Winston.

**Durant, W.** (1961). *The story of philosophy.* New York: Washington Square Press.

**Duvall, E. M.** (1971). *Family development* (4th ed.). Philadelphia: J. B. Lippincott.

**Duvall, E. M.** (1988). Family development's first forty years. *Family Relations, 37,* 127–134.

**Dwoskin, J.** (2003). Hannah Arendt on thinking and action: A bridge to the spiritual side of social work. *Journal of Religion and Spirituality in the Social Services, 22(1),* 105–123.

**Dye, T. R.** (1975). *Understanding public policy* (2nd ed.). Englewood Cliffs, NJ: Prentice-Hall.

**Eagly, A. H.** (1987). *Sex differences in social behavior: A social role interpretation.* Hillsdale, NJ: Earlbaum.

**Eaton, S. B.** (1989; 1990, December–January). Aging as we know it: Places it doesn't happen. *Longevity,* 84–86.

**Ebaugh, H. R. F.** (1984). Leaving the convent: The experience of role exit and self-transformation. In J. A. Kotarba & A. Fontana (Eds.), *The existential self in society* (pp. 156–176). Chicago: University of Chicago Press.

**Eckensberger, L. H.** (1994). Moral development and its measurement across cultures. In W. J. Lonner & R. Malpass, *Psychology and culture* (pp. 71–78). Boston: Allyn & Bacon.

**Eco, U.** (1989). *Foucault's pendulum.* San Diego, CA: Harcourt.

**Edwards, D. G.** (1982). *Existential psychotherapy: The process of caring.* New York: Gardner Press.

**Egan, G., & Cowan, M. A.** (1979). *People in systems: A model for development in the human service professions and education.* Monterey, CA: Brooks/Cole.

**Eisenstein, Z. (Ed.).** (1979). *Capitalist patriarchy and the case of socialist feminism.* New York: Monthly Review.

**Ekeh, P. P.** (1974). *Social exchange theory: The two traditions.* Cambridge, MA: Harvard University Press.

**Elbert, T., Heim, S., & Rockstroh, B.** (2001). Neural plasticity and development. In C. A. Nelson & M. Luciana (Eds.), *Handbook of developmental cognitive neuroscience* (pp. 191–202). Cambridge, MA: MIT Press.

**Elder, G., & Liker, J. K.** (1982). Hard times in women's lives: Historical influences across forty years. *American Journal of Sociology, 88,* 241–269.

**Elgin, D. D.** (1985). *The comedy of the fantastic: Ecological perspectives on the fantasy novel.* Westport, CT: Greenwood Press.

**Elkind, D.** (1987). *Miseducation: Preschoolers at risk.* New York: Alfred A. Knopf.

**Ellenberger, H. F.** (1970). *The discovery of the unconscious.* New York: Basic Books.

**Ellis, C.** (1991a). Sociological introspection and emotional experience. *Symbolic Interaction, 14(1),* 23–50.

**Ellis, C.** (1991b). Emotional sociology. In D. Denzin (Ed.), *Studies in symbolic interaction* (Vol. 12, pp. 123–145). Greenwich, CT: JAI Press.

**Ellis, H.** (1922). *Studies in the psychology of sex* (Vol. 2, 3rd ed.). Philadelphia: F. A. Davis.

**Ellor, J. W., Netting, F. E., Thibault, J. M.** (1999). *Religious and spiritual aspects of human service practice.* Columbia, SC: University of South Carolina.

**Emerson, R. M.** (1972). Exchange theory, part 1: A psychological basis for social exchange. In J. Berger, M. Zeiditch, & B. Anderson (Eds.), *Sociological theories in progress* (Vol. 2, pp. 38–57). Boston: Houghton-Mifflin.

**Emerson, R. T.** (1976). Social exchange theory. *Annual Review of Sociology, 2,* 335–362.

**Engelmann, S., & Engelmann, T.** (1966). *Give your child a superior mind.* New York: Cornerstone.

**English, R.** (1984). *The challenge for mental health minorities and their world view.* Austin: Hogg Foundation for Mental Health.

**Enloe, C.** (2004). *The curious feminist: Searching for women in a new age of empire.* Berkeley, CA: University of California Press.

Epstein, C. F. (1988). *Deceptive distinctions: Sex, gender, and the social order.* New Haven, CT: Yale University Press.

Epstein, D., & White, M. (1991). *Narrative means to therapeutic ends.* New York: Norton.

Erikson, E. H. (1950). *Childhood and society.* New York: Norton.

Erikson, E. H. (1954). The problem of ego identity. In A. H. Esman (Ed.), *The psychology of adolescence: Essential readings.* New York: International Universities Press.

Erikson, E. H. (1962). *Young man Luther: A study in psychoanalysis and history.* New York: Norton.

Erikson, E. H. (1963). *Childhood and society* (2nd Rev. ed., enlarged). New York: Norton.

Erikson, E. H. (1968). *Identity: Youth and crisis.* New York: Norton.

Erikson, E. H. (1969). *Gandhi's truth: On the origins of militant nonviolence.* New York: Norton.

Erikson, E. H. (1982). *The life cycle completed.* New York: Norton.

Erikson, E. H., & Erikson, J. M. (1986). *Vital involvement in old age.* New York: Norton.

Erikson, E. H. & Erikson, J. M. (1997). *The life cycle completed: Extended version with new chapters on the ninth stage of development.* New York: W. W. Norton & Company.

Erikson, J. (1988). *Wisdom and the senses: The way of creativity.* New York: Norton.

Esbjorn-Hargens, S. (2009). An overview of integral theory: An all-inclusive framework for the 21st century. *Integral Institute, Resource Paper No. 1,* March, 1–24. Retrieved from http://www. dialogue4health.org/pdfs/3_18_09/E_H_Overview-IT.pdf, August 10, 2010

Esterson, A. (1983). *Seductive mirage: An exploration of the work of Sigmund Freud.* Chicago: Open Court.

Etzkowitz, H., & Glassman, R. M. (1991). *The renascence of sociological theory: Classical and contemporary.* Itasca, IL: F. E. Peacock.

Evans, N. (1992). Liberation theology, empowerment theory and social work practice with the oppressed. *International Social Work, 35,* 135–147.

Ewen, R. B. (1988). *An introduction to theories of personality* (3rd ed.). Hillsdale, NJ: Lawrence Erlbaum Associates.

Eysenck, H. J., & Wilson, G. D. (1974). *The experimental study of Freudian theories.* New York: Barnes and Noble.

Faderman, L. (1991). *Odd girls and twilight lovers: A history of lesbian life in twentieth-century America.* New York: Columbia University Press.

Fairbairn, W. R. D. (1952). *Psycho-analytic studies of the personality.* New York: Basic Books.

Faludi, S. (1991). *Backlash: The undeclared war against American women.* New York: Doubleday.

Farrell, M., & Rosenberg, S. (1981). *Men at midlife.* Boston: Auburn.

Feagin, J. R., & Feagin, C. B. (1993). *Racial and ethnic relations* (4th ed.). Englewood Cliffs, NJ: Prentice-Hall.

Federico, R. C. (1979). *Sociology* (2nd ed.). Reading, MA: Addison-Wesley.

Felten, E. (1993). *The ruling class: Inside the imperial Congress.* Washington, DC: Heritage Foundation.

Fengler, A. P., Little, V. C., & Danigelis, N. L. (1983). Correlates of dimensions of happiness in urban and non-urban settings. *International Journal of Aging and Human Development, 16(1),* 53–65.

Ferguson, A. (1981). Compulsory heterosexuality and lesbian existence: Defining the issues. *Signs: Journal of Women in Culture and Society, 7,* 158–172.

Ferree, M. M., & Hess, B. B. (1985). *Controversy and coalition: The new feminist movement.* Boston: Twayne Publishers.

Feuer, L. (1975). *Ideology and the ideologists.* Oxford: Blackwell.

Feuerstein, R. (1979). *The dynamic assessment of retarded performers: The learning potential assessment device, theory, instruments, and techniques.* Baltimore: University Park Press.

Feuerstein, R. (1980). (In collaboration with Y. Rand, M. B. Hoffman, & R. Miller) *Instrumental enrichment: An intervention program for cognitive modifiability.* Baltimore: University Park Press.

Fiene, J. I. (1987). *Evolution of human behavior and social environment curriculum: 1950 to present.* Paper presented at the Annual Meeting of the Council on Social Work Education, St. Louis, MO.

Figueira-McDonough, J., Netting, F. E., & Nichols-Casebolt, A. (1998). *The role of gender in practice knowledge: Claiming half the human experience.* New York: Garland Publishing Inc.

Findley, P. C. (1978). Critical theory and social work practice, *Catalyst, 3,* 55–67.

Finn, J. (1998). Gender and families. In J. Figueria-McDonough, F. E. Netting, & A. Nichols-Casebolt (Eds.), *The role of gender in practice knowledge: Claiming half the human experience* (pp. 205–239). New York: Garland Publishing Inc.

Finn, J. L. & Jacobson, M. J. (2003). *Just practice: A social justice approach to social work.* Peosta, IA: Eddie Bowers Publishing, Inc.

**Finn, J. L., & Jacobson, M. J.** (2007). *Just practice: A social justice approach to social work* (2nd ed.). Peosta, IA: Eddie Bowers Publishing, Inc.

**Fischer, J., & Corcoran, K.** (2007). *Measures for clinical practice: A sourcebook* (4th ed.). New York: Oxford University Press.

**Fischer, J., & Gochros, H. L.** (1975). *Planned behavior change: Behavior modification in social work.* New York: Free Press.

**Fisher, R.** (1984). *Let the people decide: Neighborhood organizing in America.* Boston: Twayne Publishers.

**Fisher, R.** (1995). Political social work. *Journal of Social Work Education, 31(2),* 194–203.

**Fisher, R., & Karger, H. J.** (1997). *Social work and community in a private world: Getting out in public.* New York: Longman.

**Fisher, S., & Greenberg, R. P.** (1977). *The scientific credibility of Freud's theories and therapy.* New York: Basic Books.

**Fisher, S., & Greenberg, R. P.** (1996). *Freud scientifically reappraised: Testing the theories and the therapy.* New York: John Wiley & Sons.

**Fiske, S. T., & Taylor, S. T.** (1991). *Social cognition* (2nd ed.). New York: McGraw-Hill.

**Flacks, R.** (1979). Growing up confused. In P. I. Rose (Ed.). *Socialization and the life cycle* (pp. 21–32). New York: St. Martin's Press.

**Flavell, J. H.** (1985). *Cognitive development* (2nd ed.). Englewood Cliffs, NJ: Prentice-Hall.

**Fletcher, J.** (1994). Feminist standpoint research and management science. *Journal of Management Inquiry, 3(1),* 74–82.

**Flexner, A.** (1915). Is social work a profession? In *Proceedings of the National Conference of Charities and Correction* (pp. 576–590). Chicago: Hildmann.

**Fong, R., & Furuto, S. (Eds.).** (2001). *Culturally competence practice: Skills interventions and evaluations.* Boston: Allyn & Bacon.

**Fook, J.** (2002). *Social work: Critical theory and practice.* London: Sage Publications.

**Forte, J. A.** (2004a). Symbolic interactionism and social work: A forgotten legacy, Part 1. *Families in Society, 85(3),* 391–400.

**Forte, J. A.** (2004 b). Symbolic interactionism and social work: A forgotten legacy, Part 2. *Families in Society, 85(4),* 521–530.

**Forte, J. A.** (2006). *Human behavior and the social environment: Models, metaphors, and maps for applying theoretical perspectives to practice.* Pacific Grove, CA: Brooks/Cole.

**Foucault, M.** (1965). *Madness and civilization: A history of insanity in the age of racism.* New York: Vintage.

**Foucault, M.** (1974). *The archeology of knowledge.* London: Tavistock.

**Foucault, M.** (1975). *The birth of the clinic: An archeology of medical perception.* New York: Vintage.

**Foucault, M.** (1978). *The history of sexuality: An introduction.* New York: Random House.

**Foucault, M.** (1979). *Discipline and punish: The birth of the prison* (Alan Sheridan, Trans.). New York: Vintage.

**Foucault, M.** (1980). *The history of sexuality: Vol. 1. An introduction* (Robert Hurley, Trans.). New York: Vintage/Random House.

**Foucault, M.** (1982). On the genealogy of ethics: An overview of work in progress. Afterword in H. Dreyfus & P. Rabinow (Eds.), *Michel Foucault: Beyond structuralism and hermeneutics.* Chicago: University of Chicago.

**Foucault, M.** (1985). *The use of pleasure: The history of sexuality* (Vol. 2). New York: Pantheon.

**Fowers, B., & Richardson, F.** (1996). Why is multiculturalism good? *American Psychologist, 51(6),* 609–621.

**Fowler, J. W.** (1981). *Stages of faith: The psychology of human development and the quest for meaning.* San Francisco: Harper & Row.

**Fowler, J. W.** (1984). *Becoming adult, becoming Christian: Adult development and Christian faith.* San Francisco: Harper & Row.

**Fowler, J. W.** (1996). *Faithful change: The personal and public challenges of post-modern life.* Nashville: Abingdon Press.

**Fox, M.** (1979). *A spirituality named compassion and the healing of the global village, Humpty Dumpty and us.* Minneapolis: Winston Press.

**Fox, W.** (1995). The deep ecology–ecofeminism debate and its parallels. In G. Sessions (Ed.), *Deep ecology for the 21st century* (pp. 269–289). Boston: Shambhala.

**Frank, A. G.** (1974). Functionalism and dialectics. In R. S. Denisoff, O. Callahan, & M. H. Levine (Eds.), *Theories and paradigms in contemporary sociology* (pp. 342–352). Itasca, IL: Peacock.

**Frankl, V. E.** (1969). *The will to meaning: Foundations and applications of logotherapy.* New York: World Publishing Co.

**Franklin, C.** (1995). Expanding the vision of the social constructionist debates: Creating relevance for practitioners. *Families in Society, 76(7),* 395–407.

**Franklin, C., & Biever, J.** (1996). *Evaluating the effectiveness of solution-focused therapy with learning challenged students using single case designs.* Unpublished manuscript, The University of Texas at Austin, School of Social Work.

**Franklin, C., Corcoran, J., Nowicki, J., & Streeter, C. L.** (1997). Using client self-anchored scales to measure outcomes in solution-focused therapy. *Journal of Systemic Therapies, 16(3),* 246–265.

**Franklin, C., & Jordan, C.** (1995). Qualitative assessment: A methodological review. *Families in Society, 76(5),* 281–295.

**Franklin, C., Nowicki, J., Trapp, J., Schwab, A. J., & Peterson, J.** (1993). A computerized assessment system for brief, crisis oriented youth services. *Families in Society, 74(10),* 602–616.

**Franklin, C., & Nurius, P.** (1996). Constructivist therapy: New directions in social work practice. *Families in Society 77(6),* 323–325.

**Frazier, S. H.** (1994). *Psychotrends.* New York: Simon & Schuster.

**Freedman, J., & Coombs, G.** (1996). *Narrative therapy: The social construction of preferred realities.* New York: Norton.

**Freeman, L., & Strean, H. S.** (1987). *Freud and women.* New York: Continuum Press.

**Freeman, M.** (1990). Beyond women's issues: Feminism and social work. *Affilia, 5,* 72–89.

**Friedrich, W., Grambsch, P., Broughton, D., Kulper, J., & Ubeilke, R.** (1991). Normative Sexual Behavior in Children. *Pediatrics, 20,* 456–464.

**Friedrich, W. N., Grambsch, P., Damon, L., Hewitt, S., Koverola, C., Lang, R., et al.** (1992). Child sexual behavior inventory: Normative and clinical comparisons. *Psychological Assessment, 4(3),* 303–311.

**Friedrich, W. N. & Trane, S.** (2002). Sexual behaviors across multiple settings. *Child Abuse and Neglect, 26(3),* 243–246.

**Freire, P.** (1970). *Pedagogy of the oppressed.* New York: Seabury Press.

**Freire, P.** (1973). *Education for critical consciousness.* New York: Continuum Publishing Co.

**French, J. R. P., Jr., & Raven, B.** (1959). The bases of social power. In D. Cartwright (Ed.), *Studies in social power* (pp. 150–167). Ann Arbor, MI: Institute for Social Research.

**Freud, A.** (1966). *The ego and the mechanisms of defense* (Rev. ed.). New York: International Universities Press.

**Freud, A.** (1968). *Difficulties in the path of psychoanalysis; a confrontation of past with present viewpoints.* New York: International Universities Press.

**Freud, S.** (1914a). On narcissism. Cited in P. Grosskurth (1991). *The secret ring: Freud's inner circle and the politics of psychoanalysis.* Menlo Park, CA: Addison-Wesley.

**Freud, S.** (1914b). On the history of the psycho-analytic movement. Cited in P. Grosskurth 1991. *The secret ring: Freud's inner circle and the politics of psychoanalysis.* Menlo Park, CA: Addison-Wesley.

**Freud, S.** (1921). *Group psychology and the analysis of the ego.* London: Hogarth Press.

**Freud, S.** (1922). *Beyond the pleasure principle.* London: International Psychoanalytic Press.

**Freud, S.** (1925). Some psychical consequences of the anatomical distinction between the sexes. In P. Gay (Ed.). (1989). *The Freud reader.* New York: W. W. Norton & Co.

**Freud, S.** (1930). *Civilization and its discontents.* New York: DeVinne and Hallenbeck.

**Freud, S.** (1933/1965). *New introductory lectures on psychoanalysis.* Original publication: London: Hogarth Press. Paperback reprint: New York: W. W. Norton.

**Freud, S.** (1953). *The interpretation of dreams.* London: Hogarth Press.

**Freud, S.** (1955a). *Totem and taboo.* London: Hogarth Press.

**Freud, S.** (1955b). *Beyond the pleasure principle.* London: Hogarth Press.

**Freud, S.** (1957). *Leonardo da Vinci: A study in psychosexuality.* London: Hogarth Press.

**Freud, S.** (1960). *Psychopathology of everyday life.* London: Hogarth Press.

**Freud, S.** (1961). *Future of an illusion.* London: Hogarth Press.

**Freud, S.** (1962/1905). *Three Essays on the Theory of Sexuality* (James Strachey, Trans.). New York: Basic Books.

**Freud, S.** (1964a). *An outline of psychoanalysis.* London: Hogarth Press.

**Freud, S.** (1964b). *Moses and monotheism.* London: Hogarth Press.

**Friedan, B.** (1963). *The feminine mystique.* New York: Dell.

**Friedan, B.** (1993). *The fountain of age.* New York: Simon & Schuster.

**Fromm, E.** (1941/1967). *Escape from freedom.* New York: Avon (original work published in 1941 by Rinehart).

**Fromm, E.** (1947/1975). *Man for himself.* New York: Fawcett Premier (original work published in 1947 by Rinehart).

**Fromm, E.** (1955). *The sane society.* New York: Rinehart.

**Fromm, E.** (1961). *Marx's concept of man.* New York: Ungar.

**Fromm, E.** (1962). *Beyond the chains of illusion.* New York: Simon and Schuster.

**Fromm, E.** (1968). *The revolution of hope.* New York: Harper & Row.

**Frye, M.** (1983). *The politics of reality: Essays in feminist theory.* Berkeley, CA: Crossing Press.

**Frye, M.** (2001). Oppression. In M. Andersen & P. H. Collins (Eds.), *Race, class and gender: An anthology.* Belmont, CA: Wadsworth.

**Gadamer, H-G.** (1975). *Truth and method.* New York: Continuum Press.

**Gadamer, H-G.** (1981). *Reason in the age of science.* Cambridge: MIT Press.

**Galan, F. J.** (1978). *Alcohol use among Chicanos and Anglos: A cross cultural study.* Ann Arbor, MI: University Microfilms International.

**Galan, F. J.** (1985). Traditional values about family behavior: The case of the Chicano client. *Social Thought, 11(3),* 14–22.

**Galan, F. J.** (1990). *A multidimensional transactional model of bicultural identity.* Video. McAllen, TX: Whitestar Productions.

**Galan, F. J.** (1992). Experiential focusing with Mexican American males with bicultural identity problems. In K. C. Corcoran (Ed.). *Structuring practice: Effective practice for common client problems* (pp. 234–254). Chicago: Lyceum Books.

**Galaskiewicz, J.** (1979). The structure of community organization networks. *Social Forces, 57,* 1346–1364.

**Gallo, D. A. & Seamon, J. G.** (2004). Are nonconscious processes sufficient to produce false memories? *Consciousness and Cognition 13,* 158–168.

**Galper, J. H.** (1980). *Social work practice: A radical perspective.* Englewood Cliffs, NJ: Prentice-Hall.

**Gambrill, E.** (2004). Contributions of critical thinking and evidence based practice to the fulfillment of the ethical obligations of professionals. In H. E. Briggs & T. L. Rzepnicki (Eds.) *Using evidence in social work practice: Behavioral perspectives* (pp. 3–19). Chicago: Lyceum Books.

**Gambrill, E.** (1999). Evidence-based practice: An alternative to authority-based practice. *Families in Society: Journal of Contemporary Human Services, 80(4),* 341–350.

**Gans, H.** (1972). The positive functions of poverty. *American Journal of Sociology, 78,* 275–289.

**Gardiner, J. K.** (1987). Kohut's self-psychology as feminist theory. In P. Young-Gay (Ed.) (1989), *The Freud Reader.* New York: Norton.

**Gardner, H.** (1983). *Frames of mind: The theory of multiple intelligences.* New York: Basic Books.

**Gardner, H.** (1987). *The mind's new science.* New York: Basic Books.

**Gardner, H.** (1991). The unschooled mind: How children think and how schools should teach. New York: Basic Books.

**Gardner, H.** (2006). Multiple intelligences: new horizons. New York: Basic Books.

**Gardner, H.** (2009). Birth and the spreading of a "meme." In J. Chen, S. Moran, & H. Gardner (Eds.), *Multiple intelligences around the world* (pp. 3–16). San Francisco: Jossey-Bass.

**Gardner, H., & Hatch, T.** (1989). Multiple intelligences go to school: Educational implications of multiple intelligence. *Educational Researcher, 18(8),* 4–10.

**Garfinkle, H.** (1967). *Studies in ethnomethodology.* Englewood Cliffs, NJ: Prentice-Hall.

**Gay, P. (Ed.).** (1989). *The Freud reader.* New York: W. W. Norton.

**Gelman, D.** (1997). The miracle of resiliency. In K. L. Freiberg (Ed.), *Human development 97/98* (25th ed., pp. 180–182). (Originally printed in *Newsweek* [Special edition]. Summer, 1991, pp. 44–47.)

**Gergen, K. J.** (1982). *Toward transformation in social knowledge.* New York: Springer-Verlag.

**Gergen, K. J.** (1985). The social constructionist movement in modern psychology. *American Psychologist, 40,* 266–275.

**Gergen, K. J.** (1994). Exploring the post-modern: Perils or potentials? *American Psychology, 49(5),* 412–416.

**Gergen, K. J., & McKaye, S.** (1992). *Therapy as social construction.* Newbury Park, CA: Sage.

**Germain, C. B.** (1973, June). An ecological perspective in casework practice. *Social Casework, 54,* 323–330.

**Germain, C. B.** (1978, December). General systems theory and ego psychology. *Social Service Review,* 535–550.

**Germain, C. B. (Ed.).** (1979). *Social work practice: People and environments: An ecological perspective.* New York: Columbia University Press.

**Germain, C. B.** (1991). *Human behavior in the social environment: An ecological view.* New York: Columbia University Press.

**Germain, C. B., & Gitterman, A.** (1980). *The life model of social work practice.* New York: Columbia University Press.

**Germain, C. B., & Gitterman, A.** (1995). In *Ecological perspective. Encyclopedia of social work* (19th ed., pp. 816–824). Washington, DC: National Association of Social Workers Press.

*Germain, C. B., & Gitterman, A.* (2008). *The life model of social work practice* (3rd ed.). New York: Columbia University Press.

*Gibbons, J. (Ed.).* (1955). *I. P. Pavlov: Selected works.* Moscow: Foreign Languages Publishing House.

*Gibbs, L. E., & Gambrill, E.* (1996). *Critical thinking for social workers: A workbook.* Thousand Oaks, CA: Pine Forge Press.

*Gibbs, L. E., & Tallent, S.* (1997). Can critical thinking and HBSE course content be taught concurrently? In M. Bloom & W. C. Klein (Eds.), *Controversial issues in human behavior and the social environment* (pp. 81–95). Boston: Allyn & Bacon.

*Gibbs, P.* (1986, Summer/Spring). Human behavior/social environment in the undergraduate curriculum: A survey. *Journal of Social Work Education, 2,* 46–52.

*Gibbs, T. T., Huang, I. N., & Associates.* (1989). *Children of color: Psychological interventions with minority youth.* San Francisco: Jossey-Bass.

*Giedd, J. N., Blumenthal J., Jeffries, N. O., et al.* (1999). Brain development during childhood and adolescence: A longitudinal MRI study. *Nature Neuroscience, 2(10),* 861–863.

*Gilbert, D., & Kahl, J. A.* (1987). *The American class structure.* Chicago: Dorsey Press.

*Gilgun, J. F.* (2002). Completing the circle: American Indian medicine wheels and the promotion of resilience of children and youth in care. *Journal of Human Behavior in the Social Environment, 6(2),* 65–84.

*Gilligan, C.* (1977). In a different voice: Women's conceptions of self and morality. *Harvard Educational Review, 47,* 481–517.

*Gilligan, C.* (1978). Woman's place in man's life cycle. *Harvard Educational Review, 49,* 431–446.

*Gilligan, C.* (1982). *In a different voice: Psychological theory and women's development.* Cambridge, MA: Harvard University Press.

*Gilligan, C.* (1986). Exit voice dilemmas in adolescent development. In A. Foxley, M. McPherson & G. O'Donnell (Eds.), *Development, democracy and the art of trespassing: Essays in honor of Albert O. Hirschman.* Notre Dame, IN: University of Notre Dame Press.

*Gilligan, C.* (1990). *Making connections: The relational worlds of adolescent girls of Emma Willard School.* Cambridge: Harvard University Press.

*Gilligan, C.* (1991). Reframing resistance. In C. Gilligan, A. G. Rogers, & D. L. Tolman (Eds.), *Women, girls and psychotherapy: Reframing resistance* (pp. 1–31). New York: Haworth Press.

*Gilligan, C.* (1993). *In a different voice: Psychological theory and women's development* (with a new preface by the author). Cambridge, MA: Harvard University Press.

*Gilligan, C., Rogers, A. G., & Tolman, D. L. (Eds.).* (1991). *Women, girls and psychotherapy: Reframing resistance.* New York: Haworth Press.

*Ginsberg, L., Nackerud, L., & Larrison, C. R.* (2004). *Human Biology for Social Workers: Development, Ecology, Genetics & Health.* Boston: Allyn & Bacon.

*Ginsburg, H., & Opper, S.* (1979). *Piaget's theory of intellectual development.* Englewood Cliffs, NJ: Prentice-Hall.

*Giovannoni, J. M., & Purvine, M. E.* (1974). The myth of the social work matriarchy. In *Official Proceedings 100th Annual Forum of the National Conference on Social Welfare* (pp. 166–195). New York: Columbia University Press.

*Glendinning, C.* (1994). *My name is Chellis and I'm in recovery from Western civilization.* Boston: Shambala.

*Glick, J.* (1975). Cognitive development in cross-cultural perspective. In F. D. Horowitz (Ed.), *Review of child development research* (Vol. 4, pp. 595–654). Chicago: University of Chicago Press.

*Goffman, E.* (1959a). *The presentation of self in everyday life.* Garden City, NY: Doubleday.

*Goffman, E.* (1961). On the characteristics of total institutions. In *Asylums: Essays on the social situation of mental patients and other inmates.* Garden City, NY: Doubleday.

*Goffman, E.* (1963). *Stigma: Notes on the management of spoiled identity.* Englewood Cliffs, NJ: Prentice-Hall.

*Golan, N.* (1981). *Passing through transitions.* New York: Free Press.

*Golden, C.* (1987). Diversity and variability in women's sexual identities. In Boston Lesbian Psychologies Collective (Eds.), *Lesbian psychologies: Explorations and challenges.* Urbana, IL: University of Illinois Press.

*Golden, C.* (1994). Our politics and choices: The feminist movement and sexual orientation. In B. Greene & G. Herek (Eds.), *Lesbian and gay psychology: Theory, research and clinical applications.* Thousand Oaks, CA: Sage.

*Goldstein, E. G.* (1984). *Ego psychology and social work practice.* New York: Free Press.

*Goldstein, H.* (1990). The knowledge base of social work practice: Theory, wisdom, analogue, or art? *Families in Society: The Journal of Contemporary Human Services, 71(1),* 32–43.

*Goldstein, H.* (2001). *Experiential learning: A foundation for social work education and practice.* Alexandria, VA: Council on Social Work Educaiton.

Goleman, D. (1988). *The meditative mind: The varieties of meditative experience.* New York: Jeremy P. Tarcher/Putnam.

Goleman, D. (1995). *Emotional intelligence: Why it can matter more than I.Q.* New York: Bantam.

Goleman, D. (2007). *Social intelligence: The new science of human relationships.* New York, Bantam.

Goleman, D. (2009). *Ecological intelligence.* New York: Broadway Books.

Gomes, M. E., & Kanner, A. D. (1995). The rape of the well-maidens: Feminist psychology and the environmental crisis. In T. Roszak, M. G. Gomes, & L. R. Brown (Eds.), *Ecopsychology: Restoring the Earth/healing the mind* (pp. 111–121). San Francisco: Sierra Club Books.

Gomory, T. T. (2001). A fallibilistic response to Thyer's theory of theory-free empirical research in social work practice. *Journal of Social Work Education, 37(1),* 26–50.

Gonsiorek, J. C. (1995). Gay male identities: Concepts and issues. In A. D'Augelli & C. Patterson (Eds.); *Lesbian, gay, and bisexual identities over the lifespan.* New York: Oxford University Press.

Goodrich, Rampage, Ellman, Halstead. (1988). *Feminist family therapy: A casebook.* New York: W. W. Norton & Company.

Gordon, C. (Ed.). (1980). *Power/knowledge: Selected interviews and other writings.* New York: Pantheon.

Gordon, M. M. (1964). *Assimilation in American life: The role of race, religion, and national origins.* New York: Oxford University Press.

Gordon, S. (1989). Institutional and impulsive orientations in selectively appropriating emotions to the self. In D. Franks & E. D. McCarthy (Eds.), *The sociology of emotions: Original essays and research papers.* Greenwich, CT: JAI Press.

Gould, K. H. (1987, July–August). Life model versus conflict model: A feminist perspective. *Social Work, 32(4),* 346–351.

Gould, R. L. (1978). *Transformations: Growth and change in adult life.* New York: Simon & Schuster.

Gouldner, A. (1960). The norm of reciprocity. *American Sociological Review, 25,* 161–178.

Gouldner, A. (1970). *The coming crisis in Western sociology.* New York: Basic Books.

Granvold, D. K. (1996). Constructivist psychotherapy. *Families in Society, 77(6),* 345–359.

Grassian, S., & Holtzen, D. (1996, July). *Memory of sexual abuse by a parish priest.* Paper presented at Trauma and Memory: An International Research Conference, Durham, New Hampshire.

Gray, M., Coates, J., & Yellow Bird, M. (Eds.). (2008). *Indigenous social work around the world: Towards culturally relevant education and practice.* Burlington, VT: Ashgate.

Gray, M., & Fook, J. (2004). The quest for a universal social work: Some issues and implications. *Social Work Education, 23(5),* 625–644.

Green, J. W. (1982). *Cultural awareness in the human services.* Englewood Cliffs, NJ: Prentice-Hall.

Green, J. W. (1995). *Cultural awareness in the human services: A multi-ethnic approach* (2nd ed.). Boston: Allyn & Bacon.

Green, J. W. (1999). *Cultural awareness in the human services: A multi-ethnic approach* (3rd ed.). Boston: Allyn & Bacon.

Greenberg, L., & Pascual-Leone, J. (1995). A dialectical constructivist approach to experiential change. In R. A. Neimeyer & M. J. Mahoney (Eds.), *Constructivism in psychotherapy* (pp. 169–191). Washington, DC: American Psychological Association.

Greene, B. (1994). Lesbian and gay sexual orientations: Implications for clinical training, practice and research. In B. Greene & G. Herek (Eds.), *Lesbian and gay psychology: Theory, research, and clinical applications.* Thousand Oaks, CA: Sage.

Greene, G. J., Lee, M. Y., & Hoffpauir, S. (2005). The languages of empowerment and strengths in clinical social work: A constructivist perspective. *Families in Society, 86(2),* 267–277.

Greene, R. R. (Ed.). (1994). *Human behavior therapy: A diversity framework.* New York: Aldine de Gruyter.

Greene, R. R. (1999). *Human behavior theory and social work practice.* New York: Aldine De Gruyter.

Greene, R. R., & Ephross, P. H. (1991). *Human behavior theory and social work practice.* New York: Walter de Gruyter.

Greene, R. R., & Frankel, K. (1994). A systems approach: Addressing diverse family forms. In R. R. Greene (Ed.). *Human behavior theory: A diversity framework* (pp. 147–172). New York: Aldine de Gruyter.

Greene, R. R., & Saltman, E. J. (1994). Symbolic interactionism: Social work assessment, meanings, and language. In R. R. Greene (Ed.), *Human behavior theory: A diversity framework* (pp. 55–74). New York: Aldine de Gruyter.

Greenspan, S. J. (1989). *The course of life.* Madison, CT: International University Press.

Greif, G. L. (1986, May–June). The ecosystems perspective "meets the press." *Social Work, 31(3),* 225–226.

Grof, S. (1985). *Beyond the brain.* Albany: State University of New York Press.

Grof, S. (1988). *The adventure of self discovery.* Albany: State University of New York Press.

Grof, S. *(with Bennet, H.)* (1992). *The holotropic mind.* San Francisco: Harper.

Grof, S. (2006). *When the impossible happens: Adventures in non-ordinary realities.* Boulder, Co: Sounds True, Inc.

Grof, S., & Grof, C. (Eds.). (1989). *Spiritual emergency: When personal transformation becomes a crisis.* Los Angeles: Tarcher.

Grof, S., & Halifax, J. (1977). *The human encounter with death.* New York: Dutton.

Grosskurth, P. (1991). *The secret ring: Freud's inner circle and the politics of psychoanalysis.* Menlo Park, CA: Addison-Wesley.

Guignon, C. (1991). Pragmatism or hermeneutics? Epistemology after foundationalism. In J. Bohman, D. Hiley, & R. Schusterman (Eds.), *The interpretive turn.* Ithaca, NY: Cornell University Press.

Guignon, C. (1993). *The Cambridge companion to Heidegger.* New York: Cambridge University Press.

Guignon, C., & Pereboom, D. (Eds.). (1995). *Existentialism: Basic writings.* Indianapolis, IN: Hackett.

Guntrip, H. (1961). *Personality structure and human interaction: The developing synthesis of psychodynamic theory.* New York: International Universities Press.

Guntrip, H. (1969). *Schizoid phenomena, object relations, and the self.* New York: International Universities Press.

Gutiérrez, G. (1973). *A theology of liberation.* Maryknoll, NY: Orbis.

Gutiérrez, L. M. (1990a). *Empowerment and the Latino community: Does consciousness make a difference?* Paper presented at the annual CSWE meeting. Reno, NV.

Gutiérrez, L. M. (1990b). Working with women of color: An empowerment perspective. *Social Work, 35(2),* 149–153.

Gutiérrez, L. M. (1994). Beyond coping: An empowerment perspective on stressful life events. *Journal of Sociology and Social Welfare, 21(3),* 201–219.

Gutiérrez, L. M. (1995). Understanding the empowerment process: Does consciousness make a difference? *Social Work Research, 19(4),* 229–238.

Gutiérrez, L. M., & Lewis, E. A. (1995). A feminist perspective on organizing with women of color. In F. G. Rivera & J. L. Erlich (Eds.), *Community organizing in a diverse society* (2nd ed., pp. 95–112). Boston: Allyn & Bacon.

Gutiérrez, L. M., & Lewis, E. A. (1999). *Empowering women of color.* New York: Columbia University Press.

Gutiérrez, L. M., & Ortega, R. (1991). Developing methods to empower Latinos: The importance of groups. *Social Work with Groups, 14(2),* 23–43.

Gutiérrez, L., Glenmaye, L., & DeLois, K. (1995). The organizational context of empowerment practice: Implications for social work administration. *Social Work, 40(2),* 249–258.

Gutiérrez, L. M., Parsons, R. J., & Cox, E. O. (Eds.). (1998). *Empowerment in social work practice: A sourcebook.* Pacific Grove, CA: Brooks/Cole.

Gutiérrez, L. M., Reed, B. G., Ortega, R., Lewis, E. (1998). Teaching about groups in a gendered world. In J. Figeuria-McDonough, F. E. Netting, & A. Nichols-Casebolt (Eds.), *The role of gender in practice knowledge: Claiming half the human experience* (pp. 170–204). New York: Garland Publishing Inc.

Haan, N. (1981). Common dimensions of personality development: Early adolescence to middle life. In D. H. Eichhorn et al. (Eds.), *Present and past in middle life* (pp. 117–151), New York: Academic Press.

Haan, N. (1989). Personality at midlife. In S. Hunter & M. Sundel (Eds.), *Midlife myths: Issues, findings, and practice implications* (pp. 145–156). Newbury Park, CA: Sage.

Haan, N., Hartka, E., & Millsap, R. (1986). As time goes by: Change and stability in personality over fifty years. *Psychology and Aging, 1(3),* 220–232.

Haley, J. (1971). *Changing families.* New York: Grune and Stratton.

Haley, J. (1999). Beyond the tip of the iceberg: Five stages toward cultural competence. *Reaching Today's Youth Journal, 3(2),* 9–12.

Halifax, J. (1993). *The fruitful darkness: Reconnecting with the body of the earth.* San Francisco: Harper.

Hall, A. D., & Fagan, R. E., (1956). Definition of system. *General systems, 1,* 18–28. (Reprinted in *Modern systems research for the behavioral scientist,* pp. 81–96, by W. Buckley, Ed., 1968,. Chicago: Aldine.)

Hall, E. (1983). A conversation with Erik Erikson. *Psychology Today, 17(6),* 22–30.

Hall, G. S. (1904). *Adolescence: Its psychology and its relations to physiology, anthropology, sociology, sex crime, religion and education.* New York: Appleton.

Halperin, D. (2003). The normalizing of queer theory. *Journal of Homosexuality, 45,* 339–343.

Hampden-Turner, C. (1981). *Maps of the mind.* New York: Collier.

**Hanlon, W. H., & Weiner-Davis, M.** (1989). *In search of solutions: A new direction in psychotherapy.* New York: Norton.;1

**Haraway, D.** (1991). *Simians, cyborgs, and women.* New York: Routledge.

**Hardiman, R.** (1979). *White identity development theory.* Amherst, MA: New Perspectives.

**Harding, S. G.** (1986). *The science question in feminism.* Ithaca, NY: Cornell University.

**Harding, S. G.** (1987). *Feminism and methodology.* Bloomington: Indiana University Press.

**Harding, S. G.** (1991). *Whose science? Whose knowledge? Thinking from women's lives.* Ithaca, NY: Cornell University Press.

**Harding, S. G.** (1997). Comment on Hekman's "truth and method: Feminist standpoint theory revisited": Whose standpoint needs the regimes of truth and reality? *Signs: Journal of Women in Culture and Society, 22(2),* 375–381.

**Harding, S. G. (Ed.).** (2004). *The feminist standpoint theory reader.* New York: Routledge.

**Hare-Mustin, R.** (1991). Sex, lies, and headaches: The problem is power. In T. Goodrich (Ed.), *Women and power: Perspectives for therapy* (pp. 63–85). New York: Norton.

**Harre, R., (Ed.).** (1986). *The social construction of emotions.* Cambridge: Blackwell Publishers.

**Harrington, M.** (1987). *Who are the poor?: A profile of the changing faces of poverty in the United States in 1987.* Washington, DC: Justice for All.

**Harrison, J., Wodarski, J., & Thyer, B. (Eds.).** (1992). *Cultural diversity and social work practice.* Springfield, IL: Charles Thomas.

**Hartling, L., Rosen, W., Walker, M., & Jordan, J.** (2000). *Shame and humiliation: From isolation to relational transformation.* Work in Progress No. 88. Wellesley, MA: The Stone Center, Wellesley College.

**Hartman, A.** (1993). The professional is political. *Social Work, 38(4),* 365–366, 504.

**Hartmann, H.** (1958). *Ego psychology and the problem of adaptation.* New York: International Universities Press.

**Hartmann, H.** (1981). The unhappy marriage of Marxism and feminism: Towards a more progressive union. In L. Sargent (Ed.),*Women and revolution: A discussion of the unhappy marriage of Marxism and feminism.* Boston: South End Press.

**Hartsock, N.** (1981). Fundamental feminism: Prospect and perspective. In C. Bunch (Ed.), *Building feminist theory* (pp. 32–43). New York: Longman.

**Hartsock, N.** (1983). *Money, sex, and power: Toward a feminist historical materialism.* Boston: Northeastern University Press.

**Hartsock, N.** (1997). Feminist standpoint theory revisited: Truth or justice? *Signs: Journal of Women in Culture and Society, 22(2),* 367–374.

**Hasenfeld, Y.** (1987). Power in social work practice. *Social Service Review, 61(3),* 469–483.

**Hauser, R. M., & Featherman, D. L.** (1977). *The process of stratification: Trends and analyses.* New York: Academic Press.

**Havighurst, R. J.** (1952). *Developmental tasks and education.* New York: David McKay.

**Havighurst, R. J.** (1972). *Developmental tasks and education.* New York: David McKay.

**Hawley, W. D., & Wirt, F. M.** (1968). *The search for community power.* Englewood Cliffs, NJ: Prentice-Hall.

**Haworth, G. O.** (1984). Social work research, practice, and paradigms. *Social Service Review, 58(3),* 343–357.

**Haynes, K. S., & Mickelson, J. S.** (2003). *Affecting change: Social workers in the political arena* (5th ed.). Boston: Allyn & Bacon.

**Haynes, K. S., & Mickelson, J. S.** (2009). *Affecting change: Social workers in the political arena* (7th ed.). Englewood Cliffs, NJ: Prentice-Hall.

**Haynes, S. C., Follette, V. M., & Linehan, M. M. (Eds.).** (2004). *Mindfulness and acceptance: Expanding the cognitive-behavioral tradition.* New York: The Guilford Press.

**Hearn, G.** (1958). *Theory-building in social work.* Toronto: University of Toronto Press.

**Hearn, G.** (1979). General systems theory and social work. In F. J. Turner (Ed.), *Social work treatment: Interlocking theoretical approaches* (pp. 333–360). New York: The Free Press.

**Heatherton, T. F., & Nichols, P. A.** (1994a). Conceptual issues in assessing whether personality can change. In T. F. Heatherton & J. L. Weinberger (Eds.), *Can Personality Change?* Washington, DC: American Psychological Association.

**Heatherton, T. F., & Nichols, P. A.** (1994b). Personal accounts of successful versus failed attempts at life change. *Personality and Social Psychology Bulletin, 20,* 664–675.

**Heidegger, M.** (1962). *Being and time.* New York: Harper.

**Heineman, M. B.** (1981). The obsolete scientific imperative in social work research. *Social Service Review, 55(3),* 371–397.

**Hekman, S.** (1997). Truth and method: Feminist standpoint theory revisited. *Signs: Journal of Women in Culture and Society, 22(2),* 375–381.

**Helms, J. E.** (1984). Towards a theoretical explanation of the effects of race on counseling: A Black and White model. *Counseling Psychologist, 12(4),* 153–165.

**Helms, J. E.** (1993). More psychologists discover the wheel: A reaction to views by Penn et al., on ethnic preference. *Journal of Black Psychology, 19(3),* 322–326.

**Helms, J. E. & Cook, D.** (1999). *Using race and culture in counseling and psychotherapy: Theory and process.* Boston: Allyn & Bacon.

**Herek, G.** (1995). Psychological heterosexism in the United States. In A. D'Augelli & C. Patterson (Eds.), *Lesbian, gay, and bisexual identities over the lifespan.* New York: Oxford University Press.

**Heritage, J., & Atkinson, J. M.** (1984). Introduction. In J. M. Atkinson & J. Heritage (Eds.), *Structures of social action* (pp. 1–15). Cambridge: Cambridge University Press.

**Herman, J. L., & Harvey, M.** (1996, July). *Adult memories of childhood trauma.* Paper presented at Trauma and Memory: An International Research Conference, Durham, NH.

**Herman, J. L., & Schatzow, E.** (1987). Recovery and verification of memories of childhood sexual trauma. *Psychoanalytic Psychology, 4,* 1–14.

**Herskovits, M. J.** (1938). *Acculturation: The Study of Cultural Contact.* New York: Augustin Publisher.

**Hetherington, E. M., & Baltes, P. B.** (1988). Child psychology and life span development. In E. M. Hetherington, R. M. Lerner & M. Perlmutter (Eds.), *Child development in life-span perspective.* Hillsdale, NJ: Erlbaum.

**Hetherington, E. M., & Parke, R.** (1986). *Child psychology, a contemporary viewpoint.* New York: McGraw-Hill.

**Hewitt, N. M., Crane, B., & Mooney, B.** (2010). The family development credential program: A synthesis of outcome research on an empowerment-based human service training program. *Families in Society, 91(1),* 76–84.

**Hick, S. F. (Ed.).** (2009). *Mindfulness and social work.* Chicago: Lyceum Books, Inc.

**Hilgard, E. R., & Bower, B. H.** (1966). *Theories of learning:* New York: Appleton-Century-Crofts.

**Hill, R.** (1986). Life cycle stages for types of single parent families: Of family development theory. *Family Relations, 35,* 19–29.

**Hiroto, D. S., & Seligman, M. E. P.** (1975). Generality of learned helplessness in man. *Journal of Personality and Social Psychology, 31,* 311–327.

**Hirschfield, M.** (1936). The homosexual as an intersex. In V. Robinson (Ed.), *Encyclopaedia sexualis.* New York: Dingwall-Rock.

**Hirschi, T.** (1969). *Causes of delinquency.* Berkeley: University of California Press.

**Ho, M. K.** (1992). *Minority children and adolescents in therapy.* Newbury Park, CA: Sage.

**Hochschild, A.** (1983). *The managed heart.* Berkeley: University of California Press.

**Hochschild, A.** (1990). Ideology and emotion management. In T. D. Kemper (Ed.), *Research agendas in the sociology of emotions.* New York: State University of New York Press.

**Hoff, M. D., & McNutt, J. G. (Eds.).** (1994). *The global environmental crisis: Implications for social welfare and social work.* Brookefield, VT: Avebury.

**Hoffman, E. (Ed.).** (1996). *Future visions: The unpublished papers of Abraham Maslow.* Thousand Oaks, CA: Sage Publications.

**Hoffman, L.** (1990). Constructing realities: The art of lenses. *Family Process, 29,* 1–12.

**Hokenstad, M. C. & Midgley, J. (Eds.).** (2004). *Lessons from abroad: Adapting international social welfare innovations.* Washington, DC: NASW Press.

**Hollingshead, A. B.** (1958). *Social class and mental illness: A community study.* New York: John Wiley & Sons.

**Hollingshead, A. B., & Redlich, F. C.** (1953). Social stratification and psychiatric disorders. *American Sociological Review, 18,* 163–169.

**Holmes, D. S.** (1990). The evidence for repression: An examination of sixty years of research. In J. L. Singer (Ed.), *Repression and dissociation* (pp. 85–102). Chicago: University of Chicago Press.

**Homans, G. C.** (1974). *Social behavior: Its elementary forms* (Rev. ed.). New York: Harcourt Brace Jovanovich.

**hooks, b.** (1984). *Feminist theory: From margin to center.* Boston: South End Press.

**hooks, b.** (1990). *Yearning: Race, gender, and cultural politics.* Boston: South End Press.

**hooks, b.** (1994). *Teaching to transgress: Education as the price of freedom.* New York: Routledge.

**hooks, b.** (2000a, November 17). Learning in the shadow of race and class. *Chronicle of Higher Education,* pp. B14–B16.

**hooks, b.** (2000b). *Feminism is for everybody.* Cambridge, MA: South End Press

**Horner, A. J.** (1979). *Object relations and the developing ego in therapy.* New York: Jason Aronson.

Horner, M. S. (1968). *Sex differences in achievement motivation and performance in competitive and non-competitive situations.* Unpublished doctoral dissertation, University of Michigan.

Horner, M. S. (1972). Toward an understanding of achievement-rated conflicts in women. *Journal of Social Issues, 28(2),* 157–176.

Horney, K. (1937). *Neurotic personality of our times.* New York: Norton.

Horney, K. (1939). *New ways in psychoanalysis.* New York: Norton.

Horney, K. (1942). *Self-analysis.* New York: Norton.

Horney, K. (1945). *Our inner conflicts.* New York: Norton.

Horney, K. (1950). *Neurosis and human growth.* New York: Norton.

Horney, K. (1967). *Feminine psychology.* New York: Norton.

Horton, S. L. (2002). Conceptualizing transition: The role of metaphor in describing the experience of change at midlife. *Journal of Adult Development, 9(4),* 277–290.

Howard, A., & Scott, R. A. (1981). The study of minority groups in complex societies. In R. H. Munroe, R. L. Munroe, & B. B. Whiting (Eds.), *Handbook of cross-cultural development* (pp. 113–149). New York: Garland Press.

Howard, M. O., McMillan, C. J., & Pollio, D. E. (2003). Teaching evidence-based practice: Toward a new paradigm for social work education. *Research on Social Work Practice, 13(2),* 234–259.

Howard, T., & Wilk, R. (1986). Changing the attitudes of social work students: An application of cognitive moral development theory. *Journal of Applied Social Sciences, 10(2).*

Howe, M. I., & Courage, M. L. (1993). On resolving the enigma of infantile amnesia. *Psychological Bulletin, 113(1),* 305–326.

Huang, K. (1995). Tripartite cultural personality and ethclass assessment. *Journal of Sociology and Social Welfare, 22(1),* 99–119.

Hudson, C. G. (2010). *Complex systems and human behavior.* Chicago: Lyceum Books, Inc.

Hudson, B. L., & MacDonald, G. (1986). *Behavioural social work: An introduction.* London: Macmillan.

Hull, C. (1943). *Principles of behavior.* New York: D. Appleton-Century Co.

Hunter, F. (1957). *Community power structure.* Chapel Hill: The University of North Carolina Press.

Hunter, S., & Sundel, M. (1989). *Midlife myths: Issues, findings, and practice implications.* Newbury Park, CA: Sage.

Husserl, E. (1970). *The crisis of European sciences and transcendental phenomenology.* Evanston, IL: Northwestern University Press.

Hutton, M. S. (1994). How transpersonal psychotherapists differ from other practitioners: An empirical study. *Journal of Transpersonal Psychology, 26(2),* 139–174.

Hyde, C. (2003). Gendered perceptions of community needs and concerns: An exploratory analysis. *Journal of Human Behavior in the Social Environment, 8(4),* 45–65.

Hyde, C. (2005). Feminist community practice. In M. Weil (Ed.). *The handbook of community practice* (pp. 360–371), Thousand Oaks, CA: Sage Publications.

Hyde, J. S (2005). The gender similarities hypothesis. *American Psychologist, 60(6),* 581–592.

Hyman, H. (1942). The psychology of status. *Archives of Psychology, 269,* 1–94.

Ife, J. (2001). *Human rights and social work: Toward rights based practice.* Cambridge, United Kingdom: Cambridge University Press.

Iglehart, A. P., & Becerra, R. M. (1995). *Social services and the ethnic community.* Boston: Allyn & Bacon.

Imre, R. W. (1971). A theological view of social casework. *Social Casework, 52(9),* 578–585.

Inclain, J. (1979). Family organization, acculturation and psychological symptomology in second generation Puerto Rican women of three socioeconomic classes. Unpublished doctoral dissertation, New York University.

**International Federation of Social Workers and International Association of Schools of Social Work.** (2005). Ethics in Social Work, Statement of Principles. Retrieved August 2, 2010 from http://www.ifsw.org/f38000032.html

Ishisaka, H. A., Nguyen, Q. T., & Okimoto, J. T. (1985). The role of culture in the mental health treatment of Indochinese refugees. In Tom Choken Owan (Ed.), *Southeast Asian mental health: Treatment, prevention, training, and research.* Washington, DC: U.S. Department of Health and Human Services, National Institute of Mental Health.

Israel, J. (1971). *Alienation: From Marx to modern sociology.* Boston: Allyn & Bacon.

Ivey, A. E., & Gonçalves, O. F. (1988). Developmental therapy: Integrating developmental processes into clinical practice. *Journal of Counseling and Development, 66,* 406–412.

Ivey, A., Pederson, P., & Ivey, M. (2001). *Intentional group counseling: A microskills approach.* Belmont, CA: Brooks/Cole.

*Jaffee, S., & Hyde, J. S.* (2000). Gender differences in moral orientation: A meta-analysis. *Psychological Bulletin, 126(5),* 703–726.

*Jagose, A.* (1996). *Queer theory: An introduction.* Washington Square, NY: New York University Press.

*James, W.* (1892/1948). *Psychology.* Cleveland: World Publishing.

*Jantsch, E., & Waddington, C. H. (Eds.).* (1976). *Evolution and consciousness: Human systems in transition.* Reading, MA: Addison-Wesley.

*Jenkins, D.* (1988). Ethnicity: Theory base and practice link. In Jacobs and Bowles (Eds.), *Ethnicity and race: Critical concepts in social work* (pp. 140–151). Washington, DC: National Association of Social Workers.

*Johnson, A. G.* (2005). *The gender knot: Unraveling our patriarchal legacy* (2nd ed.). Philadelphia:Temple University Press.

*Johnson, H.* (1991). Theories of Kernberg and Kohut: Issues of scientific validation. *Social Service Review, 65(3),* 403–433.

*Johnson, T. C.* (1999). *Understanding your child's sexual behavior: What's natural and healthy.* New York: New Harbinger.

*Jones, E.* (1953). *The life and work of Sigmund Freud* (Vol. 1). New York: Basic Books.

*Jordan, C., & Franklin, C.* (1995). *Clinical assessment for social workers: Quantitative and qualitative methods.* Chicago: Lyceum/Nelson Hall Books.

*Jordan, C., & Franklin, C. (Eds.).* (2003). *Clinical assessment for social workers: Quantitative and qualitative methods* (2nd ed.). Chicago: Lyceum Books.

*Jordan, J.* (1989). *Relational development: Therapeutic implications of empathy and shame.* Work in Progress No. 39. Wellesley, MA: The Stone Center, Wellesley College.

*Jordan, J.* (1992). *Relational resilience.* Work in Progress. Wellesley, MA: The Stone Center, Wellesley College.

*Jordan, J. V., & Hartling, L. M.* (2002). New developments in relational-cultural theory. In M. Ballou & L. S. Brown (Eds).,*Rethinking Mental Health and Disorders: Feminist Perspectives* (pp. 48–70). New York: Guilford Publications.

*Joseph, M. V.* (1987). The religious and spiritual aspects of clinical practice: A neglected dimension of social work. *Social Thought, 13,* 2–23.

*Joseph, M. V.* (1988). Religion and social work practice. *Social Casework, 69(7),* 443–452.

*Jung, C. G.* (1938). *Psychology and religion.* New Haven: Yale University Press.

*Jung, C. G.* (1959). Concerning mandala symbolism. In H. Read, M. Fordham, & G. Adler (Eds.), *The collected works of C. G. Jung* (Vol. 9, Pt. 1, pp. 355–390). New York: Free Press.

*Jung, C. G.* (1965). *Memories, dreams, reflections.* New York: Vintage Books.

*Jung, C. G.* (1984). *Psychology and western religion.* Essays from Volumes 11 and 18 of Jung's Collected Works. Princeton, NJ: Princeton University Press.

*Kadushin, A.* (1968). Games people play in supervision. *Social Work, 13(3),* 23–32.

*Kagan, J.* (1997). The realistic view of biology and behavior. In K. L. Freiberg (Ed.), *Human development 97/98* (25th ed., pp. 54–56). (Originally published in *The Chronicle of Higher Education,* October 5, 1994, p. A64.)

*Kahn, S.* (1991). *Organizing: A guide for grassroots leaders* (Rev. ed.). Washington, DC: National Association of Social Workers Press.

*Kahn, S.* (1994). *How people get power* (Rev. ed.). Washington, DC: National Association of Social Workers Press.

*Kail, R.* (1990). *The development of memory in children* (3rd ed.). New York: W. H. Freeman & Co.

*Kalafat, J., & Lester, D.* (2000). Shame and suicide: A case study. *Death Studies, 24(2),* 157–162.

*Kallen, H. M.* (1924). *Culture and democracy in the United States.* New York: Boni & Liveright.

*Kaminer, W.* (1993). *I'm dysfunctional, you're dysfunctional: The recovery movement and other self-help fashions.* New York: Vintage.

*Kanjirathinkal, M.* (1990). *A sociological critique of theories of cognitive development: The limitations of Piaget and Kohlberg.* New York: Edward Mellen Press.

*Kanuha, V.* (1990). Compounding the triple jeopardy: Battering in lesbian of color relationships. In L. S. Brown & M. P. P. Root (Eds.), *Diversity and complexity in feminist therapy* (pp. 169–184). New York: Harrington Park Press.

*Katz, P. A.* (1976). The acquisition of racial attitudes in children. In P. A. Katz (Ed.), *Towards the elimination of racism.* New York: Pergamon.

*Kaufman, G., & Raphael, L.* (1996). *Coming out of shame.* New York: Doubleday.

*Kaufmann, W.* (1956). *Existentialism from Dostoevsky to Sartre.* Cleveland: World Publishing.

*Keegan Eamon, M.* (2008). *Cognitive-behavioral interventions: Empowering vulnerable populations.* Chicago: Lyceum Books, Inc.

**Keefe, T.** (1996). Meditation and social work treatment. In F. J. Turner (Ed.), *Social work treatment: Interlocking theoretical approaches* (4th ed., pp. 434–460). New York: Free Press.

**Keith-Lucas, A.** (1985). *So you want to be a social worker: A primer for the Christian student.* St. Davids, PA: North American Association of Christians in Social Work.

**Keith-Lucas, A.** (1994). *Giving and taking help* (Rev. ed.). St. Davids, PA: North American Association of Christians in Social Work.

**Kelborn, P. T.** (1995, March 16). Women and the minorities still face "glass ceiling." *The New York Times,* p. C22.

**Kendall, P. C.** (1993). Cognitive-behavioral therapies with youth: Guiding theory, current status, and emerging developments. *Journal of Consulting and Clinical Psychology, 61(2),* 235–247.

**Keniston, K.** (1974). *The uncommitted: Alienated youth in American society.* New York: Dell.

**Keniston, K., & The Carnegie Council on Children.** (1977). *All our children: The American family under pressure.* New York: Harcourt Brace Jovanovich.

**Kermis, M. D.** (1986). *Mental health in late life.* San Francisco: Jossey-Bass.

**Kerrigan, D.** (2006). A brief overview of integral social services. *AQAL: Journal of Integral Theory and Practice, 1(2),* 351–365.

**Kiefer, C. W.** (1974). *Changing cultures, changing lives: An ethnographic study of three generations of Japanese Americans.* San Francisco: Jossey-Bass.

**Kim, K. M., & Canda, E. R.** (2006). Toward a holistic view of health and health promotion in social work with people with disabilities. *Journal of Social Work in Disability and Rehabilitation, 5(2),* 49–67.

**Kimmel, D. C.** (1978). Adult development and aging: A gay perspective. *Journal of Social Issues, 34(3),* 113–130.

**Kimmel, M. S.** (1991). *Review of transforming the revolution: Social movements and the world system* (by S. Armin, G. Arrighi, A. G. Frank, and I. Wallerstein, 1990, Monthly Review Press) in *Social Forces, 70(1),* 253–254.

**Kimmel, M., & Messner, M. (Eds.).** (2004). *Introduction. Men's Lives* (6th ed., pp. ix–xvii). Boston: Pearson/ Allyn & Bacon.

**King, C.S.** (n.d.). Retrieved from http://www.brainyquote. com/quotes/authors/c/coretta_scott_king.html.

**King, J. L.** (2005). *Coming up from the down low: Stop the lies, heal the pain, and get the love and sex you deserve.* New York: Crown Publishing.

**King, J. L. & Hunter, K.** (2004). *On the down low: A journey into the lives of "straight" black men who sleep with men.* New York: Broadway Books.

**Kinsey, A., Pomeroy, W., & Martin, C.** (1948/1998). *Sexual behavior in the human male.* Philadelphia: W. B. Saunders; Bloomington: Indiana U. Press.

**Kinsey, A., Pomeroy, W., Martin, C., & Gebhard, P.** (1953/1998). *Sexual behavior in the human female.* Philadelphia: W. B. Saunders; Bloomington: Indiana U. Press.

**Kiser, D.** (1988). *A follow-up conducted at the Brief Family Therapy Center.* Unpublished manuscript.

**Kiser, D., & Nunnally, E.** (1990). *The relationship between treatment length and goal achievement in solution-focused therapy.* Unpublished manuscript.

**Kitzinger, C.** (1995). Social constructionism: Implications for lesbian and gay psychology. In A. D'Augelli & C. Patterson (Eds.), *Lesbian, gay and bisexual identities over the lifespan.* New York: Oxford University Press.

**Kitzinger, C.** (1996). Therapy and how it undermines the practice of radical feminism. In R. Klein & D. Bell (Eds.). *Radically Speaking: Feminism reclaimed,* Australia: Spinifex Press.

**Klein, D. B.** (1977). *The unconscious: Invention or discovery?: A historical critical inquiry.* Santa Monica, CA: Goodyear.

**Klein, F.** (1993). *The bisexual option.* Binghamton, NY: Haworth Press.

**Klein, F.** (1999). Psychology of sexual orientation. In J. S. Bohan & G. M. Russell (Eds.), *Conversations about psychology and sexual identities* (pp. 129–138). New York: University Press.

**Klein, M.** (1959). *Our adult world and its roots in infancy.* New York: Norton.

**Kleinplatz, P. J. & Moser, C.** (2004). Towards clinical guidelines for working with BDSM clients. *Contemporary Sexuality, 38(6),* 1, 4.

**Kluft, R. P.** (1996, July). *True lies, false truth, and naturalistic false data: Applying clinical research findings to the false memory debate.* Paper presented at Trauma and Memory: An International Research Conference, Durham, NH.

**Koenig, H. G., McCullough, M. E., & Larson, D. B.** (2001). *Handbook of religion and health.* New York: Oxford University Press.

**Koenigsberg, R. A.** (1977). *The psychoanalysis of racism, revolution and nationalism.* New York: The Library of Social Science.

**Koestler, A.** (1967). *The ghost in the machine.* New York: Macmillan.

*Koestler, A.* (1976). Whereof one cannot speak. In A. Toynbee et al. (Eds.), *Life after death* (pp. 238–259). London: Weidenfeld and Nicholson.

*Kohlberg, L.* (1969a). Stage and sequence: The cognitive-developmental approach to socialization. In D. A. Goslin (Ed.), *Handbook of socialization theory and research* (pp. 347–480). Chicago: Rand McNally.

*Kohlberg, L.* (1969b). *Stages in the development of moral thought and action.* New York: Holt.

*Kohlberg, L.* (1981). *Essays on moral development: Vol. 1. The philosophy of moral development.* San Francisco: Harper & Row.

*Kohn, A.* (1991). New studies say birth order means little. *Houston Woman,* March, p. 9.

*Kohn, M. L.* (1969). *Class and conformity: A study in values.* Homewood, IL: Dorsey.

*Kohut, H.* (1971). *Analysis of the self.* New York: International Universities Press.

*Kohut, H.* (1984). *How does analysis cure?* Chicago: University of Chicago Press.

*Konopka, G.* (1983). *Social group work: A helping process.* Englewood Cliffs, NJ: Prentice-Hall.

*Kottack, C. P.* (1994). *Cultural anthropology.* New York: McGraw-Hill.

*Kreitzer, L.* (2006). Social work values and ethics issues of universality. *Currents: New Scholarship in the Human Services,* Retrieved August 2, 2008 from: http://www.ucalgary.ca/SW/currents/articles/kreitzer_v5_n1.htm.

*Krill, D. F.* (1978). *Existential social work.* New York: Free Press.

*Krill, D. F.* (1990). *Practice wisdom: A guide for helping professionals.* Newbury Park, CA: Sage.

*Kuhn, D.* (1976). Short-term longitudinal evidence for the sequentiality of Kohlberg's early stages of moral development. *Developmental Psychology, 12,* 162–166.

*Kuhn, M. H.* (1964, Winter). Major trends in symbolic interaction theory in the past twenty-five years. *Sociological Quarterly, 5,* 61–84.

*Kvarfordt, C. L., & Sheridan, M. J.* (2007). The role of religion and spirituality in working with children and adolescents: Results of a national survey. *Journal of Religion & Spirituality in Social Work, 26(3),* 1–23.

*Labouvie-Vief, G.* (1985). Intellegence and cognition. In J. E. Birren & K. W. Schaie (Eds.), *Handbook of the psychology of aging* (2nd ed.). New York: Van Nostrand Reinhold.

*Labouvie-Vief, G., & Hakim-Larson, J.* (1989). Developmental shifts in adult thought. In S. Hunter & M. Sundel (Eds.), *Midlife myths.* Newbury Park, CA: Sage.

*LaChapelle, D.* (1988). *Sacred land, sacred sex, rapture of the deep: Concerning deep ecology and celebrating life.* Durango, CO: Kivaki Press.

*Lacy, W. B., & Hendricks, J.* (1980). Developmental models of adult life: Myth or reality. *International Journal of Aging and Human Development, 11(2),* 89–109.

*Laird, J.* (1993). *Revisioning social work education: A social constructionist approach.* New York: Haworth Press.

*Lantz, J.* (1993). *Existential family therapy: Using the concepts of Viktor Frankl.* Northvale, NJ: Jason Aronson.

*Lantz, J., & Walsh, J.* (2007). *Short-term existential intervention in clinical practice.* Chicago: Lyceum Books.

*Larkin, H.* (2005). Integral management and the effective human service organization. *AQAL: Journal of Integral Theory and Practice, 1(3),* 2–21.

*Larkin, H.* (2006). Social work as an integral profession, *AQAL: Journal of Integral Theory and Practice, 1(2),* 2–30.

*Larkin, H., & Records, J.* (2007). Adverse childhood experiences: overview, response strategies, and integral theory. *AQAL: Journal of Integral Theory and Practice, 2(3),* 1–25.

*Larson, C. J.* (1973). *Major themes in sociological theory.* New York: David McKay Company.

*Lasch, C.* (1979). *The culture of narcissism: American life in an age of diminishing expectations.* New York: Warner Books.

*Laszlo, E.* (1972). *The systems view of the world.* New York: George Braziller.

*Latting, J. K., & Ramsey, V. J.* (2004, August). *Developing intergroup competency: A model.* Paper presented at the Academy of Management Annual Meeting, New Orleans, Louisiana.

*Latting, J. K., & Ramsey, V. J.* (2009). *Reframing change: How to deal with workplace dynamics, influence others, and bring people together to initiate positive change.* Santa Barbara, CA: Greenwood Publishing.

*Lay, K., & Daley, J. G.* (2007). A critique of feminist theory. *Advances in social work, 8(1),* 49–61.

*Le Doux, J.* (2002). *The synaptic self: How our brains become who we are.* New York: Viking Press.

*Lee, D. B.* (1982). Asian-born spouses: Stresses and coping patterns. *Military Family, 2(2),* 3–5.

*Lee, J. (Ed.).* (1989). *Group work with the poor and oppressed.* New York: Haworth Press.

*Lee, J.* (2001). *The empowerment approach to social work practice* (2nd ed.). New York: Columbia University Press.

Lee, M. Y., Ng, S., Leung, P. P. Y., Chan, C. L. W., & Leung, P. (2009). *Integrative body-mind-spirit social work: An empirically based approach to assessment and treatment.* New York: Oxford University Press.

Leighninger, R. (1977). Systems theory and social work. *Journal of Education for Social Work, 13(3),* 44–49.

Lengermann, P. M., & Niebrugge-Brantley, J. (1992). Contemporary feminist theory. In G. Ritzer (Ed.), *Sociological theory* (3rd ed., pp. 447–496). New York: McGraw-Hill.

Lenski, G., & Nolan, P. D. (1984). Trajectories of development: A test of ecological evolutionary theory. *Social Forces, 63,* 1–23.

Lerner, R. M., Roeser, R. W., & Phelps, E. (2008). *Positive youth development & spirituality: From theory to research.* West Conshohocken, PA: Templeton Foundation Press.

Lester, D. (1997). The role of shame in suicide. *Suicide and Life-Threatening Behavior, 27(4),* 352–361.

Lester, M. (1984). Self: Sociological portraits. In J. A. Kotarba & A. Fontana (Eds.), *The existential self in society* (pp. 18–68). Chicago: University of Chicago Press.

Lester, T. P. (Ed.). (2003). *Gender nonconformity, race, and sexuality: Charting the connections.* Madison, WI: University of Wisconsin Press.

Lev, A. I. (2004). *Transgender emergence.* New York: Haworth Press.

Levinson, D. J. (with Darrow, C. N., Klein, E. B., Levinson, M. H., & McKee, B.). (1978). *The seasons of a man's life.* New York: Knopf.

Levy, K. N., Meehan, K. B., Kelly, K. M., Reynoso, J. S., Weber, M., Clarkin, J. F., et al. (2006). Change in attachment patterns and reflective function in a randomized control trial of transference-focused psychotherapy for borderline personality disorder. *Journal of Consulting and Clinical Psychology, 74(6),* 1027–1040.

Lewin, K. (1951). *Field theory in social science.* New York: Harper & Row.

Lewins, F. (1995). *Transsexualism in society: A sociology of male-to-female transsexuals.* South Melbourne, Australia: MacMillan.

Lewis, E. (1992). Regaining promise: Feminist perspectives for social group work practice. *Social Work With Groups, 17(3),* 271–283.

Lewis, L. A. (1984). The coming out process for lesbians: Integrating a stable identity. *Social Work, 29(5),* 464–469.

Lieberson, S. (1980a). *A piece of the pie: Blacks and whites in America from 1870 to the present.* Berkeley: University of California Press.

Lieberson, S. (1980b). *A piece of the pie: Blacks and white immigrants since 1880.* Berkeley: University of California Press.

Liebert, R. M., & Spiegler, M. D. (1990). *Personality: Strategies and issues.* Pacific Grove, CA: Brooks/Cole.

Lifton, R. J. (1993). *The protean self: Human resilience in an age of fragmentation.* New York: Basic Books.

Lincoln, Y. S., & Guba, E. G. (1985). *Naturalistic inquiry.* Beverly Hills, CA: Sage.

Lindblom, C. (1968). *The policymaking process.* Englewood Cliffs, NJ: Prentice-Hall.

Link, R. J., & Healy, L. M. (2005). *Teaching international content: Curriculum resources for social work education.* Alexandria, VA: Council on Social Work Education.

Lipset, S. M., & Bendix, R. (1961). *Social mobility in industrial society.* Berkeley: University of California Press.

Lloyd, G. A. (1983). *Setpoints and boundaries: Systems and cybernetic perspectives for direct practice.* Paper delivered to the National Association of Social Workers Professional Symposium, Washington, DC.

Loevinger, J. (1976). *Ego development.* San Francisco: Jossey-Bass.

Loftus, E. F., Polonsky, S., & Fullilove, M. T. (1994). Memories of childhood sexual abuse: Remembering and repressing. *Psychology of Women Quarterly, 18,* 67–84.

Longres, J. F. (1995). *Human behavior in the social environment.* Itasca, IL: F. E. Peacock.

Longres, J. (2000). *Human behavior in the social environment* (3rd ed.) Belmont, CA: Wadsworth Publishing.

Longino, H. (1993). Feminist standpoint theory and the problems of knowledge. *Signs: Journal of Women in Culture and Society, 19(1),* 201–212.

Lorber, J. (1994). *Paradoxes of gender.* New Haven: Yale University Press.

Lorde, A. (1984). *Sister outsider.* Freedom, CA: Crossing Press.

Luhmann, N. (1986). *Love as passion: The codification of intimacy.* Cambridge, MA: Harvard University Press.

Luhmann, N. (2000). *Art as a social system.* Stanford, CA: Stanford University Press.

Lukacs, G. (1971). *History and class consciousness.* English translation by R. Livingston. London, England: Cambridge University Press.

Lukes, C., & Land, H. (1990). Biculturality and homosexuality. *Social Work, 35(2),* 155–161.

Lukoff, D. (1985). The diagnosis of mystical experiences with psychotic features. *Journal of Transpersonal Psychology, 17(2),* 155–181.

*Lukoff, D., & Lu, F. G.* (1988). Transpersonal psychological research review: Mystical experience. *Journal of Transpersonal Psychology, 20(2),* 161–184.

*Lukoff, D., Lu, F. G., & Turner, R.* (1992). Toward a more culturally sensitive DSM-IV: Psychoreligious and psychospiritual problems. *Journal of Nervous and Mental Disease, 180(11),* 673–682.

*Lukoff, D., Lu, F. G., & Turner, R.* (1995). Cultural considerations in the assessment and treatment of religious and spiritual problems. *Cultural Psychiatry, 18(3),* 467–485.

*Lukoff, D., Zanger, R., & Lu, F. G.* (1990). Transpersonal psychology research review: Psychoactive substances and transpersonal states. *Journal of Transpersonal Psychology 22(2),* 107–148.

*Lum, D.* (1995). Cultural values and minority people of color. *Journal of Sociology and Social Welfare, 22(1),* 59–74.

*Lum, D.* (1996). *Social work practice and people of color: A process stage approach* (3rd. ed.). Belmont, CA: Brooks/Cole.

*Lum, D.* (2003a), *Social work practice and people of color: A process stage approach* (5th ed.). Belmont, CA: Wadsworth Publishing.

*Lum, D.* (2003b). *Culturally competent practice: A framework for understanding diverse groups and justice issues* (2nd ed.). Belmont, CA: Brooks/Cole.

*Lund, D. A., Carerta, M. S., Diamond, M. F., & Gray, R. M.* (1986). The impact of bereavement on the self-conceptions of older surviving spouses. *Symbolic Interaction, 9,* 235–243.

*Lyotard, J-F.* (1984). *The post-modern condition.* Minneapolis: University of Minnesota Press.

*MacDonald, G., Sheldon, B., & Gillespie, J.* (1992). Contemporary studies of the effectiveness of social work. *British Journal of Social Work, 22(6),* 615–643.

*Mace, C.* (2008). *Mindfulness and mental health: Therapy, theory and science.* New York: Routledge.

*MacLeod, J.* (1995). *Ain't no makin' it: Aspirations and attainment in a low-income neighborhood* (2nd ed.). Boulder, CO: Westview Press.

*MacLeod, J.* (2008). *Ain't no makin' it: Aspirations and attainment in a low-income neighborhood* (3rd ed.). Boulder, CO: Westview Press.

*MacMillan, M.* (1991). *Freud evaluated: The completed arc.* New York: Elsevier Science.

*Macy, J.* (1985). *Dharma and development: Religion as resource in the Sarvodaya self-help movement.* West Hartford, CT: Kumarian Press.

*Macy, J.* (1991). *World as lover, world as self.* Berkeley, CA: Parallax Press.

*Maddi, S. R.* (1980). *Personality theories: A comparative analysis* (4th ed.). Homewood, IL: Dorsey Press.

*Maddi, S. R.* (1996). *Personality theories: A comparative analysis* (6th ed.). Pacific Grove, CA: Brooks/Cole Publishing Company.

*Mahalik, J. R., Morray, E. B., Coonerty-Femiano, A., Ludlow, L. H., Slattery, S. M., & Smiler, A.* (2005). Development of the conformity to feminine norms inventory. *Sex Roles, 52(7/8),* 417–435.

*Mahler, M. S.* (1952). On child psychosis and schizophrenia. *Psychoanalytic Study of the Child, 7,* 286–305.

*Mahler, M. S.* (1968). *On human symbiosis and the vicissitudes of individuation.* New York: International Universities Press.

*Mahler, M. S., Pine, F., & Bergman, A.* (1975). *The psychological birth of the human infant.* New York: International Universities Press.

*Mahoney, M. J.* (1991). *Human change processes.* New York: Basic Books.

*Mahoney, M. J.* (1995). Continuing evolution of the cognitive sciences and psychotherapies. In R. A. Neimeyer & M. J. Mahoney (Eds.), *Constructivism in psychotherapy* (pp. 39–68). Washington, DC: American Psychological Association.

*Mancini, J. A.* (1981). Effects of health and income on control orientation and life satisfaction among the aged public housing residents. *International Journal of Aging and Human Development, 12(3),* 215–220.

*Mander, J., & Goldsmith, E.* (1996). *The case against the global economy and for a turn toward the local.* San Francisco: Sierra Club Books.

*Manis, J. G., & Meltzer, B. N. (Eds.).* (1967). *Symbolic interaction.* Boston: Allyn & Bacon.

*Mann, J. J.* (2004). *The neurobiology of mood disorders.* Retrieved August 26, 2004 from Columbia University psychmed course web space directories. http://www.columbia.edu/itc/hs/medical/psychmed/1_2004/neurobioMoodDisorders.html. 10/24/2004.

*Mann, M.* (1970). The social cohesion of liberal democracy. *American Sociological Review 35,* 423–439.

*Mannheim, K.* (1936). *Ideology and utopia.* New York: Harcourt, Brace & World.

*Marable, M.* (1983). *How capitalism underdeveloped Black America.* Boston: South End Press.

*Marcia, J. E.* (1966). Development and validation of ego identity status. *Journal of Personality and Social Psychology, 3,* 551–558.

*Marcus, J.* (1982). *The young Rebecca: Writings of Rebecca West 1911–1917.* Bloomington: Indiana University Press.

Marcuse, H. (1955). *Eros and civilization: A philosophical inquiry into Freud.* Boston: Beacon Press.

Marcuse, H. (1964). *One-dimensional man.* Boston: Beacon Press.

Marcuse, H. (1966). *Eros and civilization: A philosophical inquiry into Freud.* Boston: Beacon Press.

Marcuse, H. (1974). Re-examination of the concept of revolution. In S. Denisoff et al. (Eds.), *Theories and paradigms in contemporary sociology.* Itasca, IL: F. E. Peacock.

Marger, M. N. (1994). *Race and ethnic relations: American and global perspectives* (3rd ed.). Belmont, CA: Wadsworth.

Markowitz, L. (1995). Bisexuality: Challenging our either/or thinking. *In the Family 1(1).*

Marques, J., Dhiman, S., & King, R. (2007). *Spirituality in the workplace.* Fawnskin, CA: Personhood Press.

Marsiglia, F. F., & Kulis, S. (2009). *Diversity, oppression, and change.* Chicago: Lyceum.

Marson, S. M., & Della Fave, R. (1994). A Marxian review of gerontological literature. *Journal of Sociology and Social Welfare, 21(2),* 109–126.

Martin, E. P., & Martin, J. M. (2002). *Spirituality and the Black helping tradition in social work.* Washington, DC: NASW Press.

Martin, J., Cummings, A. L., & Hallberg, E. T. (1992). Therapists' intentional use of metaphor: Memorability, clinical impact, and possible epistemic/motivational functions. *Journal of Consulting and Clinical Psychology, 60,* 143–145.

Martin, J., Martin, W., & Slemon, A. G. (1989). Cognitive-mediational models of action-act sequences in counseling. *Journal of Counseling Psychology, 36,* 8–16.

Martindale, D. (1988). *The nature and types of sociological theory* (2nd ed.). Prospect Heights, IL: Waveland Press.

Martins, M. C., & Ceccarelli, P. R. (2003, March). *The so-called "deviant" sexualities: Perversion or right to difference?* Paper presented at the 16th World Congress of Sexology, Cuba. Retrieved on September 16, 2004 from http://www.revisef65.org/cuba1.html

Marx, K. (1932/1964). *The economic and philosophic manuscripts of 1844* (D. J. Struik, Ed.). New York: International Publishers.

Marx, K., & Engels, F. (1845–1846/1970). *The German ideology,* Part I (C. J. Arthur, Ed.). New York: International Publishers.

Marx, K., & Engels, F. (1848/1955). *The Communist manifesto* (S. H. Beer, Ed.). New York: Appleton-Century-Crofts.

Maslow, A. H. (1968). *Toward a psychology of being* (2nd ed.). New York: D. Van Nostrand.

Maslow, A. H. (1969). The farther reaches of human nature. *Journal of Transpersonal Psychology, 1(1),* 1–9.

Maslow, A. H. (1970a). *Religions, values, and peak experiences.* New York: Viking.

Maslow, A. H. (1970b). *Motivation and personality* (2nd ed.). New York: Harper & Row Publishers.

Maslow, A. H. (1971). *The farther reaches of human nature.* New York: The Viking Press.

Mason, J. L., Benjamin, M. P., & Lewis, S. A. (1996). The cultural competence model: Implications for child and family mental health services. In C. A. Heflinger & C. T. Nixon (Eds.), *Families and the mental health system for children and adolescents: Policy, services, and research. Children's mental health services* (pp. 165–190). Thousand Oaks, CA: Sage.

Mason, M. (1991). Women and shame: Kin and culture. In C. Bepko (Ed.), *Feminism and Addiction* (pp. 175–194). Binghamton, NY: Haworth Press.

Masson, J. M. (1984). *The assault on truth.* London: Faber and Faber.

Masson, J. M. (1990). *Final analysis: The making and unmaking of a psychoanalyst.* New York: Addison Wesley.

Masters, R. E. L., & Houston, J. (1966). *The varieties of psychedelic experience.* New York: Delta.

Matsuoka, J. K. (1990). Differential acculturation among Vietnamese refugees. *Social Work, 35(4),* 341–345.

May, R. (1983). *The discovery of being.* New York: Norton.

McBee, L. (2008). *Mindfulness-based elder care.* New York: Springer Publishing Company.

McCrae, R. R., & Costa, P. T., Jr. (1982). Aging, the life course, and models of personality. In T. M. Field et al. (Eds.), *Review of human development* (pp. 602–613). New York: Wiley.

McFarlane, W. R. (2002). *Multifamily groups in the treatment of severe psychiatric disorders.* New York: Guilford Press.

McDowell, B. (1994). An examination of the ecosystems perspective in consideration of new theories in biology and thermodynamics. *Journal of Sociology and Social Welfare, 21(2),* 49–68.

McGee, E. (1984). The transpersonal perspective: Implications for the future of personal and social transformation. *Social Development Issues, 8(3),* 151–181.

McMahon, A., & Allen-Meares, P. (1992). Is social work racist?: A content analysis of recent literature. *Social Work, 37(6),* 533–539.

McNamee, S., & Gergen, K. J. (1992). *Therapy as social construction.* London: Sage.

McPhail, B. A. (2002). Gender-bias hate crimes: A review. *Trauma, Violence, and Abuse, 3(2),* 125–143.

**McPhail, B. A.** (2004a). Setting the record straight: Social work is not a female-dominated profession. *Social Work, 49(2)*, 323–326.

**McPhail, B. A.** (2004b). Questioning gender and sexuality binaries: What queer theorists, transgendered individuals, and sex researchers can teach social work. *Journal of Gay and Lesbian Social Services, 17(1)*, 3–21.

**McPhail, B. A.** (2008). Re-gendering the social work curriculum: New realities and complexities. *Journal of Social Work Education, 44(2)*, 33–52.

**McPhail, B.** (2003). Feminist policy analysis: A framework. *The Social Policy Journal, 2(2/3)*, 39–61.

**McPhail, C., & Rexroat, C.** (1979). Mead vs. Blumer, *American Sociological Review, 44*, 449–467.

**McPhail, C., & Rexroat, C.** (1980). Rejoinder: Ex Cathedra Blumer or Ex Libris Mead? *American Sociological Review, 45*, 420–430.

**Mead, G. H.** (1934). *Mind, self, and society* (Charles W. Morris, Ed.). Chicago: University of Chicago Press.

**Mead, G. H.** (1964). *George Herbert Mead on social psychology: Selected papers* (Anselm Strauss, Ed.). Chicago: University of Chicago Press.

**Mednick, M. T.** (1989). On the politics of psychological constructs: Stop the bandwagon, I want to get off. *American Psychologist, 44*, 1118–1123.

**Meichenbaum, D., & Fitzpatrick, D.** (1993). A constructionist narrative perspective on stress and coping: Stress inoculation applications. In L. Goldberger & S. Breznitz (Eds.), *Handbook of stress: Theoretical and clinical aspects* (2nd ed., pp. 233–252). New York: Free Press.

**Meltzer, B. N., Petras, J. W., & Reynolds, L. T.** (1975). *Symbolic interactionism: Genesis, varieties, and criticism*. Boston: Routledge and Kegan Paul.

**Merriam, S. B., & Clark, M. C.** (1991). *Lifelines: Patterns of work, love, and learning in adulthood*. San Francisco: Jossey-Bass.

**The Merriam-Webster Dictionary.** (1997). Springfield, MA: Merriam-Webster.

**Merton, R. K.** (1938). Social structure and anomie. *American Sociological Review, 3*, 672–682.

**Merton, R. K.** (1968). *Social theory and social structure*. New York: Free Press.

**Merton, R. K., & Skitt, A. S.** (1950). Contributors to the theory of reference group behavior. In R. K. Merton & P. F. Lazersfeld (Eds.), *Studies in the scope and method of "the American soldier"* (pp. 70–105). New York: Free Press.

**Messer, S. B., & Wampold, B. E.** (2006). Let's face facts: Common factors are more potent than specific therapy ingredients. *Clinical Psychology: Science and Practice, 9(1)*, 21–25.

**Metcalf, L.** (1995). *Counseling toward solutions: A practical solution-focused program for working with students, teachers, and parents*. Englewood Cliffs, NJ: Simon & Schuster.

**Mill, J. S.** (1884). *A system of logic ratiocinative and inductive: Being a connected view of the principles of evidence and the methods of scientific investigation* (8th ed.). New York: Harper.

**Miller, J. B.** (1976). *Toward a new psychology of women*. Boston: Beacon Press.

**Miller, J. B.** (1986a). *What do we mean by relationships?* Working Paper, Stone Center Colloquium.

**Miller, J. B.** (1986b). *Toward a new psychology of women*. Boston: Beacon Press.

**Miller, J. B.** (1988). Connections, disconnections and violations. Work in Progress No. 33. Wellesley, MA: Stone Center Working Paper Series.

**Miller, J. B., & Stiver, I. P.** (1997). *The healing connection: How women form relationships in therapy and life*. Boston: Beacon Press.

**Miller, J. G.** (1978). *Living systems*. New York: McGraw-Hill.

**Miller, N. E., & Dollard, J.** (1941). *Social learning and imitation*. New Haven: Yale University Press.

**Miller, S. D., Hubble, M., & Duncan, B.** (1996). *Handbook of solution-focused brief therapy*. San Francisco: Jossey-Bass.

**Miller, S. D., Hubble, M., & Duncan, B.** (2008). *Psychotherapy in Australia, 14(4)*, 14–22.

**Mills, C. W.** (1951). *White collar: The American middle classes*. New York: Oxford University Press.

**Mills, C. W.** (1956). *The power elite*. New York: Oxford University Press.

**Mills, C. W.** (1959). *The sociological imagination*. New York: Oxford Press.

**Mills, C. W.** (1963). *The Marxists*. New York: Dell.

**Mills, J.** (1990). The psychoanalytic perspective of adolescent homosexuality. *Adolescence, 25*, 913–920.

**Mirowsky, J., & Ross, C.** (2003a). *Education, social status, and health*. New York: Aldine.

**Mirowsky, J., & Ross, C** (2003b). *Social causes of psychological distress*. New York: Aldine.

**Mitchell, J.** (1974). *Psychoanalysis and feminism: Freud, Reich, Laing, and women*. New York: Vantage Books.

**Mitroff, I. I., & Denton, E. A.** (1999). A spiritual audit of corporate America: A hard look at spirituality, religion, and values in the workplace. San Francisco: Jossey-Bass Publishers.

**Mohanty, C. T.** (2003). *Feminism without borders: Decolonizing theory, practicing solidarity*. Durham & London: Duke University Press.

**Mohr, W. K.** (2003). Discarding ideology: The nature/nurture endgame. *Perspectives in Psychiatric Care, 39(3)*, 113–121.

**Moraga, C., & Anzaldúa, G. (Eds.).** (1981). *This bridge called my back: Writings by radical women of color.* New York: Kitchen Table/Women of Color Press.

**Moran, S.** (2009). Why multiple intelligences? In J. Chen, S. Moran, & H. Gardner (Eds.), *Multiple intelligences around the world* (pp. 365–373). San Francisco, CA: Jossey-Bass.

**Morell, C.** (1997). *Human behavior and capitalist culture: Experiments in politicizing HBSE.* Paper presented at the Council on Social Work Educational Annual Program Meeting, March 8, 1997, Chicago.

**Morgan, R. (Ed.).** (2003). Introduction: New world women. In R. Morgan (Ed.). *Sisterhood is forever* (pp. xv–xvi). New York: Washington Square Press.

**Mosca, G.** (1896/1939). *Elementi di scienze politica* (H. D. Kahn, Trans. & A. Livingston, Ed. & Rev.), *The ruling class.* New York: McGraw-Hill.

**Moser, C.** (1999). The psychology of sadomasochism (S/M). In S. Wright (Ed.), *SM Classics* (pp. 47–61). New York: Masquerade Books.

**Moss, B.** (2005). *Religion and spirituality.* Dorset, England: Russell House Publishing.

**Mowbray, C.** (1989). Post-traumatic therapy for children who are victims of violence. In F. Ochberg (Ed.), *Post-traumatic therapy and victims of violence* (pp. 197–211). Brunner/Mazel: New York.

**Moynihan, D. P.** (1965). Employment, income, and the ordeal of the Negro family. *Daedalus, 94,* 745–770.

**Muldoon, A.** (2006). Environmental efforts: The next challenge for social work. *Critical Social Work, 7(2),* Retrieved from http://www.uwindsor.ca/units/socialwork/critical.nsf/982f0e5f06b5c9a285256d6e006cff78/

**Mullaly, B.** (2002). Challenging oppression: A critical approach to social work. New York: Oxford University Press.

**Mullaly, B.** (2007). *The new structural social work* (3rd ed.). New York: Oxford University Press.

**Munson, C. E., & Balgopal, P.** (1978). The worker/client relationship: Relevant role theory. *Journal of Sociology and Social Welfare, 5(3),* 404–417.

**Nabigon, H., & Mawhiney, A.** (1996). Aboriginal theory: A Cree medicine wheel guide for First Nations healing. In F. J. Turner (Ed.), *Social work treatment: Interlocking theoretical approaches* (4th ed., pp. 18–38). New York: Free Press.

**Naess, A.** (1988). Self-realization: An ecological approach to being in the world. In J. Seed, J. Macy, P. Flemming, & A. Naess (Eds.), *Thinking like a mountain: Towards a council of all beings* (pp. 19–31). Santa Cruz, CA: New Society Publishers.

**Nagel, J. J.** (1988, July–August). Can there be a unified theory for social work practice? *Social Work, 33(4),* 369–370.

**Nakashima, M., & Canda, E. R.** (2005). Positive dying and resiliency in later life: A qualitative study. *Journal of Aging Studies, 19(1),* 109–125.

**Nangeroni, N. R.** (1996). Transgenderism. (Reprinted from the *University of Pennsylvania LGBA B-GLAD Magazine.* Retrieved October 7, 2004 from http://www.altsex.org/transgender/Nangeroni. html)

**Nash, J. M.** (1997, February 3). Fertile minds. *Time,* 48–56.

**Nash, M., & Stewart, B. (Eds.).** (2002). *Spirituality and social care: Contributing to personal and community well-being.* London: Jessica Kingsley.

**Nathanson, D.** (1997). Affect theory and the compass of shame. In M. Lansky & A. Morrison (Eds.), *The Widening Scope of Shame.* Hillsdale, NJ: The Analytic Press.

**National Association of Social Workers.** (1996). *Evaluation and treatment of adults with the possibility of recovered memories of childhood sexual abuse.* Policy statement prepared by the NASW Council on the Practice of Clinical Social Work. Washington, DC: NASW Office of Policy and Practice.

**National Association of Social Workers.** (1999). *NASW code of ethics.* Washington, DC: Author.

**National Association of Social Workers.** (2001). *NASW Standards for Cultural Competence in Social Work Practice.* Retrieved from www.naswdc.org/pubs/standards/cultural.htm

**National Association of Social Workers.** (2006). *Social Work Speaks: NASW Policy Statements, 2003–2004* (6th ed.). Washington, DC: NASW Press.

**Neimark, J.** (1997, August). Twins: Nature's clones. *Psychology Today, 30(4),* 36–44, 64–69.

**Neimeyer, G. J., & Neimeyer, R. A.** (1990). *Advances in personal construct psychology.* Greenwich, CT: JAI Press.

**Neimeyer, R. A., & Stewart, A. E.** (1996). Trauma, healing, and the narrative emplotment of loss. *Families in Society, 77(6),* 360–375.

**Nelson, J. E.** (1994). *Healing the split: Integrating spirit into our understanding of the mentally ill* (Rev. ed.). Albany: State University of New York Press.

*Nelson-Becker, H., Nakashima, M., & Canda, E. R.* (2006a). Spiritual assessment in aging: A framework for clinicians. *Journal of Gerontological Social Work, 48(3/4),* 331–347.

*Nelson-Becker, H., Nakashima, M., & Canda, E. R.* (2006b). Spirituality in professional helping interventions. In B. Berkman & S. D'Ambruoso (Eds.), Handbook of Social Work in Health and Aging. pp. 797–807. New York: Oxford University Press.

*Nes, J. A., & Iadicola, P.* (1989, January). Toward a definition of feminist social work: A comparison of liberal, radical, and socialist models. *Social Work, 34(1),* 12–21.

*Netting, F. E., Kettner, P. M., & McMurtry, S. L.* (2004). *Social work macro practice* (3rd ed.). Boston: Allyn & Bacon.

*Neugarten, B. L.* (1968). *Middle age and aging.* Chicago: University of Chicago Press.

*Neugarten, B. L.* (1977). Personality and aging. In J. E. Birerren & K. W. Schaie (Eds.), *Handbook on psychology of aging* (pp. 626–649). New York: Van Nostrand.

*Neugarten, B. L.* (1985). Interpretive social science and research on aging. In A. S. Rossi (Ed.), *Gender and the life course* (pp. 291–300). New York: Aldine.

*Neugarten, B. L., & Datan, N.* (1974). The middle years. In S. Arieti (Ed.), *American handbook of psychiatry* (pp. 592–608). New York: Basic Books.

*Newman, W.* (1973). *American pluralism.* New York: Harper & Row.

*Nicolis, G., & Prigogine, I.* (1989). *Self-organizing systems in non-equilibrium thermodynamics.* New York: John Wiley & Sons.

*Nilsson, L., & Hamberger, L.* (1990). *A child is born* (completely new edition). New York: Dell.

*Norton, D.* (1978). *The dual perspective: Inclusion of ethnic minority content in the social work curriculum.* Washington, DC: Council on Social Work Education.

*Norton, D.* (1993). Diversity, early socialization, and temporal development: The dual perspective revisited. *Social Work, 38(1),* 82–90.

*Nye, F. I. (Ed.).* (1982). *The relationships: Rewards and costs.* Beverly Hills: Sage.

*Okami, P., Olmstead, R., & Abramson, P. R.* (1997). Sexual experiences in early childhood: 18-year longitudinal data from the UCLA Family Lifestyles Project. *The Journal of Sex Research, 34(4).*

*O'Melia, Michael, & Krogsrud Miley, K. (Eds.).* (2002). *Pathways to power: Readings in contextual social work practice.* Boston: Allyn & Bacon.

*Orleans, M.* (1991). Phenomenological sociology. In H. Etzkowitz & R. M. Glassman (Eds.), *The renascence of sociological theory: Classical and contemporary* (pp. 167–186). Ithaca, IL: F. E. Peacock.

*Padilla, A. (Ed.).* (1980). *Acculturation theory, models, and some new findings.* Boulder, CO: Westview Press.

*Palmer-House, K. E.* (2008). The perceived impact of strengths-based family worker training: Workers' learning that helped empower families. *Families in Society, 89(3),* 428–437.

*Pals, D. L.* (1996). *Seven theories of religion.* New York: Oxford University Press.

*Pandey, R. S.* (1996). Gandhian perspectives on personal empowerment and social development. *Social Development Issues, 18(2),* 66–84.

*Papalia, D. E., & Olds, S. W.* (1992). *Human development* (5th ed.). New York: McGraw Hill.

*Parenti, M.* (1993). *Inventing reality: The politics of news media.* New York: St. Martin's Press.

*Pareto, V.* (1968). *Rise and fall of elites.* Bedminster, NJ: Bedminster Press.

*Park, R. E.* (1950). *Race and Culture.* Glencoe, IL: Free Press.

*Parsons, A.* (1967). Is the Oedipus complex universal? In R. Hunt (Ed.), *Personalities and cultures.* Garden City, NY: Natural History Press.

*Parsons, R. J.* (1991). Empowerment: Purpose and practice principle in social work. *Social Work with Groups, 14(2),* 7–21.

*Parsons, T.* (1951). *The social system.* Glencoe, IL: Free Press.

*Parsons, T., & Bales, F.* (1954). *Family, socialization, and interaction process.* Glencoe, IL: The Free Press.

*Parsons, T., & Smelser, N.* (1956). *Economy and society.* Glencoe, IL: Free Press.

*Patel, I.* (1987). *Vivekananda's approach to social work.* Mylapore, Madras, India: Sri Ramakrishna Math Printing Press.

*Patel, N., Naik, D., & Humphries, B. (Eds.).* (1997). *Visions of reality: Religion and ethnicity in social work.* London: Central Council for Education and Training in Social Work.

*Patrik, L. E.* (1994). Phenomenological method and meditation. *Journal of Transpersonal Psychology, 26(1),* 37–54.

*Payne, M.* (1991). *Modern social work theory: A critical introduction.* Chicago: Lyceum.

*Payne, M.* (2005). *Modern social work theory* (3rd ed.). Chicago: Lyceum.

*Paz, O.* (1988). *Sor Juana or, the traps of faith.* (Margaret Sayers Peden, Trans.). Cambridge, MA. Harvard University Press.

**Pease, B.** (2002). Rethinking empowerment: A postmodern reappraisal for emancipatory practice. *British Journal of Social Work, 32,* 135–147.

**Peck, M. S.** (1978). *The road less traveled.* New York: Simon and Schuster.

**Pedersen, P.** (1994). *A handbook for developing multicultural awareness* (2nd ed.). Alexandria, VA: American Counseling Association.

**Pelletier K., & Garfield, C.** (1976). *Consciousness east and west.* New York: Harper & Row.

**Pendergrast, M.** (1996). *Victims of memory: Sex abuse allegations and shattered lives* (2nd ed.). Hinesburg, VT: Upper Access Books.

**Peplau, L., & Garnets, L.** (2000). A new paradigm for understanding women's sexuality and sexual orientation. *Journal of Social Issues, 56,* 329–350.

**Perdue, W. D.** (1986). *Sociological theory.* Palo Alto, CA: Mayfield.

**Perinbanayagam, R. S.** (1985). *Signifying acts: Structure and meaning in everyday life.* Carbondale: Southern Illinois University Press.

**Perlman, H. H.** (1968). *Persona: Social life role and personality.* Chicago: University of Chicago Press.

**Pernell, R.** (1985). Empowerment and social group work. In Parenes (Ed.), *Innovations in social group work: Feedback from practice to theory.* New York: Haworth Press.

**Petersen, A.** (1988). Adolescent development. *Annual Review of Psychology, 39,* 583–607.

**Peterson, K. J., & Lieberman, A. A. (Eds.).** (2001). *Building on women's strengths: A social work agenda for the twenty-first century* (2nd ed.). New York: The Haworth Press.

**Petr, C. G. (Ed.).** (2009). *Multidimensional evidence-based practice: Synthesizing knowledge, research, and values.* New York: Routledge.

**Petr, C. G., & Walter, U. M.** (2005). Best practices inquiry: A multidimensional, value-critical framework. *Journal of Social Work Education, 41(2),* 251–267.

**Pewewardy, N.** (2007). *Challenging white privilege: Critical discourse for social work education.* Alexandria, VA: Council on Social Work Education.

**Pfuhl, E. H., Jr.** (1980). *The deviance process.* New York: D. Van Nostrand Company.

**Pharr, S.** (1988). *Homophobia: A weapon of sexism.* Little Rock: Chardon Press.

**Philip, M.** (1985). Michel Foucault. In Q. Skinner (Ed.), *The return of grand theory in the human sciences* (pp. 65–82). Cambridge: Cambridge University Press.

**Phillips, A.** (1987). *Feminism and equality.* New York: New York University Press.

**Phinney, J. S.** (1990). Ethnic identity in adolescents and adults: A review of the research. *Psychological Bulletin, 108(3),* 502–503.

**Phinney, J. S., & Rotheram, M. J.** (1987). *Children's ethnic socialization: Pluralism and development.* Beverly Hills, CA: Sage.

**Piaget, J.** (1932). *The moral judgment of the child.* (M. Gabain, Trans.). New York: Harcourt.

**Piaget, J.** (1936). *The origins of intelligence in children.* New York: International Universities Press.

**Piaget, J.** (1952). Autobiography. In E. G. Boring et al. (Eds.), *History of psychology in autobiography,* 4 vols (pp. 237–256). Worcester, MA: Clark University Press.

**Piaget, J., & Inhelder, B.** (1969). *The psychology of the child* (H. Weaver, Trans.). New York: Basic Books.

**Piechowski, L. D.** (1992). Mental health and women's multiple roles. *Families in Society, 73(3),* 131–141.

**Pinderhughes, E. B.** (1983). Empowerment for our clients and for our ourselves. *Social Casework, 64(6),* 331–338.

**Pines, M.** (1982, June). Infant-stim: It's changing the lives of handicapped kids. *Psychology Today* pp. 48–52.

**Pipher, M.** (1994). *Reviving Ophelia: Saving the selves of adolescent girls.* New York: Ballantine.

**Pitner, R. O., & Sakamoto, I.** (2005). The role of critical consciousness in multicultural practice: Examining how its strength becomes it limitation. *American Journal of Orthopsychiatry, 75,* 684–694.

**Piven, F. F., & Cloward, R.** (1973). *Regulating the poor.* New York: Basic Books.

**Piven, F. F., & Cloward, R.** (1977). *Poor people's movements.* New York: Basic Books.

**Plattner, S. (Ed.).** (1989). *Economic anthropology.* Stanford, CA: Stanford University Press.

**Poguntke, T.** (1993). *Alternative politics: The German green party.* Edinburgh, Scotland: Edinburgh University Press.

**Pohlman, M. D.** (1990). *Black politics in conservative America* (Chapter 5). New York: Longman.

**Polansky, N. A.** (1982). *Integrated ego psychology.* New York: Aldine.

**Polkinghorne, D.** (1983). *Methodology for the human sciences: Systems of inquiry.* Albany: State University of New York Press.

**Polkinghorne, D.** (1988). *Narrative psychology.* Albany, NY: State University of New York Press.

**Poon, L. W.** (1985). Differences in human memory with aging: Nature, causes and clinical implications. In J. E. Birren & K. W. Schaie (Eds.), *Handbook of the psychology of aging* (2nd ed.). New York: Van Nostrand Reinhold.

**Pope, M.** (1995). The "salad bowl" is big enough for us all: An argument for the inclusion of lesbians and gay men. *Journal of Counseling and Development, 1(1)*, 301–307.

**Porter, J. D. R.** (1971). *Black child, white child: The development of racial attitudes.* Cambridge: Harvard University Press.

**Poulantzas, N.** (1975). *Classes in contemporary capitalism.* London: NLE.

**Poulantzas, N.** (1978). *Class in contemporary capitalism.* London: Verso.

**Powell, D.E.** (1998). *The nine myths of aging.* NY: W.H. Freeman.

**Prawat, R. S.** (1993). The value of ideas: Problems versus possibilities in learning. *Educational Researcher, 22(6)*, 5–16.

**Presthus, R. V.** (1964). *Men at the top: A study in community power.* New York: Oxford University Press. (Abridged version reprinted in *The search for community power*, pp. 200–216, by W. D. Hawley & F. M. Wirt, Eds., 1968, Englewood Cliffs, NJ: Prentice-Hall.)

**Prigogine, I.** (1989). *Order out of chaos: Man's new dialogue with nature.* Toronto: Bantam.

**The Princeton Center for Infancy and Early Childhood.** (1993). *The first twelve months of life: Your baby's growth month by month.* New York: Bantam.

**Putnam, R.** (2000). *Bowling alone.* New York: Simon & Schuster.

**Pyles, L.** (2005). Understanding the engaged Buddhist movement: Implications for social development practice. *Critical Social Work, 6(1)*. Retrieved from http:www.windsor.ca/units/socialwork/critical.nsf/8c 20das9f1c4be3a8256d6e006d1089

**Pyles, L.** (2009). *Progressive community organizing: A critical approach for a globalizing world.* New York: Routledge.

**Queralt, M.** (1996). *The social environment and human behavior: A diversity perspective.* Boston: Allyn & Bacon.

**Rachlin, K.** (1997, June). *Partners in the journey: Psychotherapy and six stages of gender revelation.* Paper presented at the Second Congress on Sex and Gender, King of Prussia, PA.

**Radcliffe-Brown, A. R.** (1952). *Structure and function in primitive society.* Glencoe, IL: Free Press.

**Rademakers, J., Laan, M., & Straver, C.** (2000). Studying children's sexuality from the child's perspective. In T. Sandfort & J. Rademakers (Eds.), *Childhood sexuality* (pp. 49–61). New York: Haworth.

**Ramakrishnan, K. R., & Balgopal, P. R.** (1995). Role of social institutions in a multicultural society. *Journal of Sociology and Social Welfare, 22(1)*, 11–28.

**Ramanathan, C. S., & Link, R. J. (Eds.).** (1999). *All our futures: Social work practice in a global era.* Boston: Brooks/Cole.

**Ramazanoğlu, C. & Holland, J.** (2002). *Feminist methodology: Challenges and choices.* London: Sage.

**Ramsey, V. J., & Latting, J. K.** (2005). Developing intergroup competencies. *Journal of Applied Behavioral Sciences 41(3)*, 265–284.

**Rapp, C. A., & Goscha, R.** (2006). *The strengths model: Case management with people with psychiatric disabilities* (2nd ed). New York: Oxford.

**Rapp, C. & Wintersteen, R.** (1989). The strengths model of case management: Results for twelve demonstrations. *Journal of Psychosocial Rehabilitation, 13(1)*, 23–32.

**Rauch, J. B.** (1975). Women in social work: Friendly visitors in Philadelphia 1880. *Social Service Review, 49*, 241–259.

**Red Horse, J. G.** (1980). American Indian elders: Unifiers of Indian families. *Social Casework, 61(8)*, 462–467.

**Rees, S.** (1991). *Achieving power: Practice and policy in social welfare.* North Sydney, Australia: Allen and Unwin.

**Reeser, L. C., & Leighninger, L.** (1990). Back to our roots: Toward a specialization in social justice. *Journal of Sociology and Social Welfare, 17*, 69–87.

**Reich, W.** (1960). *Selected writings.* New York: Farrar, Straus and Cudahy.

**Reinharz, S.** (1992). *Feminist methods in social research.* New York: Oxford University Press.

**Rest, J. R.** (1979). *Development in judging moral issues.* Minneapolis: University of Minnesota Press.

**Rest, J. R.** (1983). Morality. In J. H. Flavell & E. M. Markman (Eds.), *Handbook of child psychology: Vol. 3. Cognitive development* (4th ed., pp. 556–629). New York: John Wiley & Sons.

**Rest, J. R., & Thoma, S. J.** (1985). Relation of moral judgment to formal education. *Developmental Psychology, 21*, 709–714.

**Rex, J., & Mason, D.** (1986). *Theories of race and ethnic relations.* London: Cambridge University Press.

**Reynolds, B.** (1951). *Social work and social living.* New York: Citadel. Reprinted, Silver Spring, MD: National Association of Social Workers.

**Rhodes, S.** (1977). A developmental approach to the life cycle of the family. *Social Casework, 58(5)*, 301–311.

**Rich, A.** (1976). *Of woman born: Motherhood as experience and institution.* New York: Norton.

Richardson, F., & Christopher, J. (1993). Social theory as practice. *Journal of Theoretical and Philosophical Psychology, 13(2)*, 137–153.

Richardson, F., & Fowers, B. (1994, August). *Beyond scientism and constructionism.* Paper presented at the annual meeting of the American Psychological Association, Los Angeles, CA.

Richtel, M. (2010, November 21). Growing up digital, wired for distraction. *New York Times.* Retrieved from http://www.nytimes.com

Rickman, H. P. (Ed.). (1976). *Dilthey: Selected writings.* Cambridge: Cambridge Iniversity Press.

Ricoeur, P. (1992). *Oneself as another.* Chicago: University of Chicago Press.

Riegel, K. (1975). Adult life crisis: A dialectic interpretation of development. In N. Datan & L. H. Ginsberg (Eds.), *Life span developmental psychology.* New York: Academic Press.

Riesman, D. (1950/1961). *The lonely crowd: A study in the changing American character* (with N. Glazer & R. Denney, Abr. ed.), New Haven, CT: Yale University Press.

Rinsley, D. (1971). The adolescent in-patient: Patterns of depersonification. *Psychoanalytic Quarterly, 45*, 3–22.

Ritzer, G. (1988). *Contemporary sociological theory* (2nd ed.). New York: McGraw-Hill.

Ritzer, G. (1992). *Contemporary sociological theory* (3rd ed.). New York: McGraw-Hill.

Rius. (1976). *Marx for beginners* (R. Appignanesi, Trans.). New York: Pantheon Books.

Roazen, P. (1976). *Erikson: The power and limits of his vision.* New York: Free Press.

Robbins, S. P. (1984). Anglo concepts and Indian reality: A study of juvenile delinquency. *Social Casework, 65(4)*, 235–241.

Robbins, S. P. (1985a). Commitment, belief, and Native American delinquency. *Human Organization, 44(1)*, 57–62.

Robbins, S. P. (1985b). Indian delinquency on urban and rural reservations. *Free Inquiry in Creative Sociology, 13(2)*, 179–182.

Robbins, S. P. (Ed.). (1994). *Melding the personal and the political: Advocacy and empowerment in clinical and community practice.* Proceedings of the Eighth Annual Social Work Futures Conference. Houston, TX: University of Houston.

Robbins, S. P. (1995). Wading through the muddy waters of recovered memories. *Families in Society, 76(8)*, 478–489.

Robbins, S. P. (1997). Women's self-conception of nutrition: Societal influences on eating behavior. In I. Wolinsky & D. Klimis-Tavantzis (Eds.), *Nutritional concerns of women* (pp. 25–34). Boca Raton, FL: CRC Press.

Robbins, S. P. (2002). Working with clients who have recovered memories. In *Social workers' desk reference.* New York: Oxford University Press

Robbins, S. P. (2007). The social and cultural context of satanic ritual abuse allegations. Reprinted in J. R. Lewis & J. A. Petersen (Eds.), *The encyclopedic sourcebook of satanism.* Amherst, NY: Prometheus Books.

Roberts, A. R., & Yeager, K. R. (2004). *Evidence-based practice manual: Research and outcome measures in health and human services.* New York: Oxford University Press.

Roberts, B. W., & DelVecchio, W. F. (2000). The rank-order consistency of personality from childhood to old age: A quantitative review of longitudinal studies. *Psychological Bulletin, 126*, 3–25.

Robinson, P. A. (1969). *The Freudian left.* New York: Harper & Row.

Rockwell, R. B. (1995). Insidious deception. *Journal of Psychohistory, 22(3)*, 312–329.

Rodway, M. R. (1986). Systems theory. In F. J. Turner (Ed.), *Social work treatment: Interlocking theoretical approaches* (pp. 514–539). New York: Free Press.

Rodwell, M. K. (1998). *Social work constructivist research.* New York: Garland Publishing.

Romer, Governor of Colorado, et al. v. Evans, et al. (1996). (94–1039), 517 U.S. 620. Retrieved November 14, 2003 from http://supct.law.cornell.edu/supct/html/ 94-1039.ZO.html

Rorty, R. (1982). *Consequences of pragmatism.* Minneapolis: University of Minnesota Press.

Rorty, R. (1985). Solidarity or objectivity? In J. Rajchman & C. West (Eds.), *Post-analytic philosophy.* New York: Columbia University Press.

Rorty, R. (1987). Method, social science and social hope. In M. Gibbons (Ed.), *Interpreting politics* (pp. 241–260). New York: New York University Press.

Rose, H. (1983). Hand, brain and heart: A feminist epistemology for the natural sciences. *Signs: Journal of Women in Culture and Society, 9*, 73–90.

Rose, P. I. (Ed.). (1979). *Socialization and the life cycle.* New York: St. Martin's Press.

Rose, S. (1992). *The making of memory: From molecules to mind.* New York: Anchor.

Rose, S. M. (1981). Assessments in groups. *Social Work Research and Abstracts, 17*, 29–37.

**Rose, S. M.** (1990). Advocacy/empowerment: An approach to clinical practice for social work. *Journal of Sociology and Social Welfare, 17,* 41–51.

**Rose, S. M.** (1992). *Case management and social work practice.* White Plains, NY: Longman.

**Rose, S. M.** (1994). Defining empowerment: A value based approach. In S. P. Robbins (Ed.), *Melding the personal and the political: Advocacy and empowerment in clinical and community practice* (pp. 17–24). Proceedings of the Eighth Annual Social Work Futures Conference, May 13–14, 1993. Houston, TX: University of Houston Graduate School of Social Work.

**Rosenberg, S. D., Rosenberg, H. J., & Farrell, M. P.** (1999). The midlife crisis revisited. In S. L. Willis & J. D. Reid (eds.)*Life in the middle: Psychological and social development in middle age* (pp. 47–73). San Diego: Academic Press.

**Rosenfeld, A., & Stark, E.** (1991). The prime of our lives. In L. Fenson, & J. Fenson (Eds.), *Human development: Annual editions 1991/92* (pp. 229–236). Guilford, CT: Dushkin.

**Rosenthal, D. A., Gurney, R. M., & Moore, S. M.** (1981). From trust to intimacy: A new inventory for examining Erikson's stages of psychosocial development. *Journal of Youth and Adolescence, 10(6),* 525–537.

**Ross, L.** (2007, May). What is reproductive justice? In *Reproductive justice briefing book: A primer of reproductive justice and social change* (pp. 4–5). Atlanta, GA: SisterSong.

**Rossi, A. S.** (1978). The biosocial side of parenthood. *Human Nature, 2,* 72–79.

**Rossi, A. S.** (1981). On the reproduction of mothering: A methodological debate. *Signs: Journal of Women in Culture and Society, 6(3),* 492–500.

**Rossi, A. S.** (1983). Gender and parenthood. *American Sociological Review, 49,* 1–19.

**Rossi, A. S.** (1985). *Gender and the life course.* New York: Aldine.

**Roszak, T.** (1979). *Person/planet.* Garden City, NY: Anchor.

**Roszak, T., Gomes, M. E., & Kanner, A. D.** (1995). *Ecopsychology: Restoring the earth/healing the mind.* San Francisco: Sierra Club.

**Rowan, J.** (1993). *The transpersonal: Psychotherapy and counseling.* London: Routledge.

**Rubin, K. H.** (1978). Role-taking in childhood: Some methodological considerations. *Child Development, 49,* 428–433.

**Rubington, E., & Weinberg, M. S.** (1987). *Deviance: The interactionist perspective.* New York: Macmillan.

**Ruddick, S.** (1980). Maternal thinking. *Feminist Studies, 6(2),* 342–367.

**Ryder, A. G., Alden, L. E., & Paulhus, D. L.** (2000). Is acculturation unidimensional or bidimensional?: A head-to-head comparison in the prediction of personality, self-identity and adjustment. *Journal of Personality and Social Psychology, 79,* 49–65

**Sabatino, C.** (1999, Fall). Men facing their vulnerabilities: Group processes for men who have sexually offended. *Journal of Men's Studies, 8,* 83–90.

**Sacks, H.** (1984). On doing "being ordinary." In J. M. Atkinson & J. Heritage (Eds.), *Structures of social action* (pp. 413–429). Cambridge: Cambridge University Press.

**Sakamoto, I., & Pitner, R. O.** (2005). Use of critical consciousness in anti-oppressive social work practice: Disentangling power dynamics at personal and structural levels. *British Journal of Social Work, 35,* 435–452.

**Sakamoto, I., Anastas, J. W., McPhail, B. A., & Colarossi, L. G.** (2008). Status of women in social work education. *Journal of Social Work Education, 44(1).*

**Saleebey, D.** (1994). Culture, theory and narrative: The intersection of meanings in practice. *Social Work, 39,* 351–359.

**Saleebey, D.** (1996). The strengths perspective in social work practice: Extensions and cautions. *Social Work, 41,* 296–305.

**Saleebey, D.** (2001). *Human behavior and social environments: A biopsychosocial approach.* New York: Columbia University Press.

**Saleebey, D. (Ed.).** (2002). *The strengths perspective in social work practice.* Boston: Allyn & Bacon.

**Saleebey, D. (Ed.).** (2009). *The strengths perspective in social work practice* (5th ed.). Boston: Allyn & Bacon.

**Santrock, J. W.** (1989). *Life span development* (3rd ed.). Dubuque, IA: W. C. Brown.

**Santrock, J. W.** (2005). *Life-span development* (10th ed.). New York: McGraw-Hill.

**Santrock, J. W.** (2008). *A topical approach to life-span development* (4th ed.). New York: McGraw-Hill.

**Saulnier, C. F.** (1996). *Feminist theories and social work: Approaches and applications.* New York: The Haworth Press.

**Sayers, J.** (1991). *Mothers of psychoanalysis.* New York: Norton.

**Sayre, W. S., & Kaufman, H.** (1960). *Governing New York City* (pp. 709–716). New York: Russell Sage Foundation. (Reprinted in *The search for community power,* pp. 125–133, by W. D. Hawley & F. M. Wirt, Eds., 1968, Englewood Cliffs, NJ: Prentice-Hall.)

*Schacter, D. L. (Ed).* (May 1, 1999). The cognitive psychology of false memories: A special issue of the *Journal of Cognitive Neuropsychology 16,* 3–5.

*Schaef, A. W.* (1985). *Women's reality.* New York: Harper & Row.

*Shear, M.* (1986, May/June). Media watch: Celebrating women with words. *New Directions for Women.*

*Scheff, T. J.* (1966). *Being mentally ill: A sociological theory.* Chicago: Aldine.

*Scheff, T. J.* (2000). Shame and the social bond: A sociological theory. *Sociological Theory, 18(1),* 84–99.

*Scheff, T. J.* (2003). Shame in self and society. *Symbolic Interaction, 26(2),* 239–262.

*Schimek, J. G.* (1987). Fact and fantasy in the seduction theory: A historic review. *Journal of the American Psychoanalytic Association, 35,* 937–965.

*Schon, D. A.* (1971). *Beyond the stable state.* New York: Norton.

*Schriver, J. M.* (2010). *Human behavior and the social environment: Shifting paradigms in essential knowledge for social work practice* (5th ed.). Boston: Allyn & Bacon.

*Schumpeter, J.* (1950). *Capitalism, socialism, and democracy.* New York: Harper.

*Schutz, A.* (1964). *Collected papers* (Vol. 2). (Avrid Brodersen, Ed.). The Hague: Martinus Nijhoff.

*Schutz, A.* (1967). *The phenomenology of the social world.* (G. Walsh & F. Lennert, Trans.). Evanston, IL: Northwestern University Press.

*Searle, J. R.* (1995). *The construction of social reality.* New York: Free Press.

*Sedgwick, E. K.* (1990). *Epistemology of the closet.* Los Angeles: University of California Press.

*Seed, J., Macy, J., Fleming, F., & Naess, A. (Eds.).* (1988). *Thinking like a mountain: Towards a council of all beings.* Santa Cruz, CA: New Society Publishers.

*Seidman, S.* (1994). *The postmodern turn: New perspectives on social theory.* Cambridge: Cambridge University Press.

*Seligman, M. E. P.* (1975). *Helplessness: On depression, development, and death.* San Francisco: W. H. Freeman and Co.

*Seligman, M. E. P.* (1991). *Learned optimism.* New York: Random House.

*Sessions, G. (Ed.).* (1995). *Deep ecology for the 21st century.* Boston: Shambhala.

*Shaffer, D. R.* (1993). *Developmental psychology: Childhood and adolescence* (3rd ed.) Belmont, CA: Brooks/Cole.

*Sharma, S.* (1987). Development, peace, and nonviolent social change: The Gandhian perspective. *Social Development Issues, 10(3),* 31–45.

*Sharrock, W., & Anderson, B.* (1986). *The ethnomethodologists.* Chichester, England: Ellis Horwood.

*Shaskolsky, L.* (1970). The development of sociological theory in America: A sociology of knowledge interpretation. In L. T. Reynolds & J. M. Reynolds (Eds.), *The sociology of sociology* (pp. 6–30). New York: McKay.

*Sheehy, G.* (1976). *Passages: Predictable crises of adult life.* New York: Dutton.

*Sheehy, G.* (1992/1995). *Menopause: The silent passage.* New York: Pocket Books. First published in America in 1992.

*Sheldon, B.* (1995). *Cognitive-behavioural therapy: Research, practice and philosophy.* New York: Routledge.

*Sheppard, M.* (2006). *Social work and social exclusion: The idea of practice.* Burlington, VT: Ashgate.

*Sheridan, M. J. & Bullis, R. K.* (1991). Practitioners' views on religion and spirituality: A qualitative study. *Spirituality and Social Work Journal, 2(2),* 2–10.

*Sheridan, J. J., Bullis, R. K., Adcock, C. R., Berlin, S. D., & Miller, P. C.* (1992). Practitioners' personal and professional attitudes toward religion and spirituality: Issues for education and practice. *Journal of Social Work Education, 28(2),* 190–203.

*Shulman, L.* (1968). A game-model theory of interpersonal strategies. *Social Work, 13(3),* 16–22.

*Siegel, D. J.* (1999). *The developing mind: Toward a neurobiology of interpersonal experience.* New York: Guilford Press.

*Siegel, D. J.* (2001). *The developing mind: How relationships and the brain interact to shape who we are.* New York: Guilford Press.

*Siegler, R. S.* (1986). *Children's thinking.* Englewood Cliffs, NJ: Prentice-Hall.

*Simon, B. L.* (1994a). *The empowerment tradition in American social work: A history.* New York: Columbia University Press.

*Simon, B. L.* (1994b). Are theories for practice necessary? Yes! *Journal of Social Work Education, 30,* 144–147.

*Simpson, R. L.* (1972). *Theories of social exchange.* Morristown, NY: General Learning Press.

*Sinclair, R., & Albert, J.* (2008). Social work and the anti-oppressive stance: Does the emperor really have new clothes? *Critical Social Work, 9(1).*

*Siporin, M.* (1980). Ecological systems theory in social work. *Journal of Sociology and Social Welfare, 7(4),* 5–7, 32.

*Skinner, B. F.* (1948/1976). *Walden Two.* New York: Macmillan.

*Skinner, B. F.* (1965). *Science and human behavior.* New York: Free Press.

*Skinner, B. F.* (1972). *Beyond freedom and dignity.* New York: Bantam.

*Skinner, B. F.* (1974). *About behaviorism.* New York: Vintage.

*Skinner, B. F.* (1988a). Selection by consequences. In A. C. Catania & S. Harnard (Eds.), *The selection of behavior* (pp. 11–20). Cambridge: Cambridge University Press.

*Skinner, B. F.* (1988b). The operational analysis of psychological terms. In A. C. Catania & S. Harnard (Eds.). *The selection of behavior* (pp. 150–164). Cambridge: Cambridge University Press.

*Skinner, B. F.* (1988c). An operant analysis of problem solving. In A. C. Catania & S. Harnard (Eds.). *The selection of behavior* (pp. 218–236). Cambridge: Cambridge University Press.

*Skinner, B. F.* (1988d). Behaviorism at fifty. In A. C. Catania & S. Harnard (Eds.). *The selection of behavior* (pp. 278–292). Cambridge: Cambridge University Press.

*Skocpol, T.* (1979). *States and social revolutions.* New York: Cambridge University Press.

*Slater, S., & Mencher, J.* (1991). The lesbian family life cycle: A contextual approach. *American Journal of Orthopsychiatry, 61(3),* 372–382.

*Smart, B.* (1983). *Foucault, Marxism and critique:* London: Routledge and Kegan Paul.

*Smeal, E.* (2003). The art of building feminist institutions to last. In R. Morgan (Ed.), *Sisterhood is forever* (pp. 541–550). New York: Washington Square Press.

*Smelser, N., & Erikson, E. (Eds.).* (1980). *Themes of work and love in adulthood.* Boston: Harvard University Press.

*Smith, A.* (1902). *The wealth of nations.* New York: Collier.

*Smith, D.* (1987). *The everyday world as problematic.* Boston: Northeastern University Press.

*Smith, D.* (1997). Comment on Hekman's truth and method: Feminist standpoint theory revisited. *Signs, 22(2),* 392–398.

*Snyder, G.* (1995). The rediscovery of Turtle Island. In G. Sessions (Ed.), *Deep ecology for the 21st century* (pp. 454–462). Boston: Shambhala.

*Sokoloff, N.* (1980). *Between money and love: The dialectics of women's home and market work.* New York: Praeger.

*Solinger, R.* (2007, May). Conditions of reproductive justice. In *Reproductive Justice Briefing Book: A Primer of Reproductive Justice and Social Change* (pp. 77–78). SisterSong, Atlanta, GA.

*Solomon, B.* (1976). *Black empowerment: Social work in oppressed communities.* New York: Columbia University Press.

*Solomon, B.* (1987). Empowerment: Social work in oppressed communities. *Journal of Social Work Practice, 2(4),* 79–91.

*Sophie, J.* (1988). *Gay, straight, and in-between: The sexology of erotic orientation.* New York: Oxford University Press.

*Specht, H.* (1989). *New directions for social work practice.* Englewood Cliffs, NJ: Prentice-Hall.

*Specht, H.* (1990). Social work and popular psychotherapies. *Social Service Review, 64(3),* 345–357.

*Specht, H., & Courtney, M.* (1994). *Unfaithful angels: How social work abandoned its mission.* New York: Free Press.

*Spence, M. J., & De Casper, A. J.* (1987). Prenatal experience with low frequency maternal-voice sounds influences neonatal perception of maternal-voice samples. *Infant Development and Behavior, 9,* 133–150.

*Spencer, M. B.* (1993). Black children's ethnic identity formation: Risk and resilience of castelike minorities. In J. S. Phinney & M. J. Rotheram (Eds.), *Children's ethnic socialization* (pp. 103–116). Newbury Park, CA: Sage.

*Spillerman, S.* (1977). Careers, labor marker structure and socioeconomic achievement. *American Journal of Sociology 83,* 551–593.

*Spitz, R.* (1945). Hospitalization: An inquiry into the genesis of psychiatric conditions in early childhood. *The Psychoanalytic Study of the Child, 1,* 53–74.

*Spitz, R.* (1946a). Hospitalism: A follow-up report. *The Psychoanalytic Study of the Child, 2,* 113–117.

*Spitz, R.* (1946b). Anaclitic depression: An inquiry into the genesis of psychiatric conditions in early childhood. *The Psychoanalytic Study of the Child, 2,* 313–342.

*Spitz, R.* (1959). *A genetic field theory of ego formation.* New York: International Universities Press.

*Spitz, R.* (1965). *The first year of life.* New York: International Universities Press.

*Spitzer, S. P., & Denzin, N. K.* (1968). *The mental patient.* New York: McGraw-Hill.

*Spretnak, C.* (1990). Ecofeminism: Our roots and flowering. In I. Diamond & G. Orenstein (Eds.), *Reweaving the world: The emergence of ecofeminism* (pp. 3–14). San Francisco: Sierra Club Books.

*Stall, S., & Stoecker, R.* (1998). Community organizing or organizing community?: Gender and the crafts of empowerment. *Gender & Society, 12(6),* 729–756.

**Staples, L. H.** (1990). Powerful ideas about empowerment. *Administration in Social Work, 14(2),* 29–42.

**Starnino, V.** (2009). An integral approach to mental health recovery: Implications for social work. *Journal of Human Behavior in the Social Environment, 19,* 820–842.

**Staude, J. R.** (1982). *The adult development of C. G. Jung.* Boston: Routledge and Kegan Paul.

**Steinberg, S.** (1989). *The ethnic myth: Race, ethnicity and class in America.* Boston: Beacon Press.

**Stern, R. C., Canda, E. R., & Doershuk, C. F.** (1992). Use of nonmedical treatment by cystic fibrosis patients. *Journal of Adolescent Health, 13,* 612–615.

**Sternberg, R. J.** (1988). *The triarchic mind: A new theory of human intelligence.* New York: Penguin.

**Stone, G. P.** (1962). Appearance and the self. In A. M. Rose (Ed.), *Human behavior and social processes* (pp. 88–110). Boston: Houghton Mifflin.

**Stone, G. P.** (1990). Appearance and the self: A slightly revised version. In D. Brissett & C. Edgley, *Life as theater: A dramaturgical source book* (pp. 141–162). New York: Aldine deGruyter.

**Stonequist, E. V.** (1937). *The marginal man.* New York: Charles Scribner's Sons.

**Stout, K., & McPhail, B.** (1998). *Confronting sexism and violence against women: A challenge for social work.* New York: Longman.

**Strauss, W., & Howe, N.** (1991). *Generations: The history of America's future, 1584–2069.* New York: William Morrow.

**Strean, H. S.** (1971). The application of role theory to social casework. In H. J. Strean (Ed.), *Social casework: Theories in action.* NJ: Scarecrow Press.

**Stryker, S.** (1980). *Symbolic interactionism: A social structural version.* Menlo Park, CA: Benjamin/ Cummings.

**Stryker, S.** (1987). The vitalization of symbolic interactionism. *Social Psychology Quarterly, 50,* 83–94.

**Sue, D. W., & Sue, D.** (1999). *Counseling the culturally different: Theory and Practice* (3rd ed.). New York: John Wiley and Sons.

**Sue, D. W., & Sue, D.** (2007). *Counseling the culturally diverse* (5th ed.). New York. John Wiley and Sons.

**Sullivan, E.** (1977). A study of Kohlberg's structural theory of moral development. A critique of liberal social science ideology. *Human Development, 20,* 352–376.

**Sullivan, H. S.** (1953). *The interpersonal theory of psychiatry.* New York: Norton.

**Sullivan, H. S.** (1964). *The fusion of psychiatry and social science.* New York: Norton.

**Surber, C. F.** (1982). Separable effects of motives, consequences, and presentation order on children's moral judgments. *Developmental Psychology, 18,* 257–266.

**Svare, G. M., Hylton, M., & Albers, E.** (2007). On our own: Social workers talk about spiritually-sensitive practice within an organizational context. *Journal of Religion & Spirituality in Social Work, 26(4),* 95–113.

**Swift, K.** (1995). *Manufacturing bad mothers.* Toronto, Ontario: University of Toronto Press.

**Swigonski, M. E.** (1993). Feminist standpoint theory and the questions of social work research. *Affilia 8(2),* 171–183.

**Swigonski, M. E.** (1994). The logic of feminist standpoint theory for social work research. *Social Work, 39(4),* 387–393.

**Szapocznik, J., Scopetta, M., & King, O.** (1978). Theory and practice in matching treatment to the special characteristics and problems of Cuban immigrants. *Journal of Consulting Psychology, 6,* 112–122.

**Szapocznik, J., Kurtines, W., & Fernandez, T.** (1980). Biculturalism, involvement and adjustment in Hispanic-American youths. *International Journal of Intercultural Relations, 4,* 353–365.

**Takaki, R.** (1993). *A different mirror: A history of multicultural America.* Boston: Little, Brown.

**Talbot, N.** (1995, Summer). Unearthing shame is the supervisory experience. *American Journal of Psychotherapy, 49,* 338–349.

**Tangney, J. P., & Dearning, R.** (2002). *Shame and Guilt.* New York: The Guilford Press.

**Tapscott, D.** (1999). *Growing up digital. The rise of the net generation.* New York: McGraw-Hill.

**Tapscott, D.** (2008). *Grown up digital: How the net generation is changing your world.* New York: McGraw-Hill.

**Tapscott, D.** (2010, November 23). New York Times cover story on "Growing Up Digital" misses the mark. *Huffington Post.* Retrieved from http://www. huffingtonpost.com/don-tapscott/whats-wrong-with-the-new-_b_787819.html?page=1

**Tart, C. T.** (2000). *States of consciousness.* Lincoln, NE: iUniverse.com, Inc.

**Tart, C. T.** (2009). *The end of materialism: How evidence of the paranormal is bringing science and spirit together.* Oakland, CA: New Harbinger Publications, Inc.

**Task Force on DSM-IV.** (2000). *Diagnostic and Statistical Manual of Mental Disorders* (4th ed., text revision). Washington, DC: American Psychiatric Association.

**Tavris, C.** (1989, Sunday, August 6). Marching in time to a different clock. *Houston Post,* p. 1F.

**Tavris, C.** (1992). *The mismeasure of woman: Why women are not the better sex, the inferior sex, or the opposite sex.* New York: Touchstone.

**Taylor, C.** (1985). *Philosophy and the human sciences: Philosophical papers* (Vol. 2). Cambridge: Cambridge University Press.

**Taylor, C.** (1989). *Sources of the self.* Cambridge: Harvard University Press.

**Taylor, C.** (1991). The dialogical self. In Bohman, J., Hiley, D., & Schusterman, R. (Eds.), *The interpretive* (pp. 304–314). Ithaca, NY: Cornell University Press.

**Taylor, D. M., & Usborne, E.** (2010). When I know who "we" are, I can be "me: The primary role of cultural identity clarity for psychological well-being. *Transcultural Psychiatry, 47(1),* 93–111.

**Thanasiu, P. L.** (2004, October). Childhood sexuality: discerning healthy from abnormal sexual behaviors. *Journal of Mental Health Counseling, 26(4).* Retrieved from http://findarticles.com/p/articles/mi_hb1416/is_4_26/ai_n29132026/

**Theobald, R.** (1987). *The rapids of changes: Social entrepreneurship in turbulent times.* Indianapolis, IN: Knowledge Systems.

**Theodorson, G. A.** (1961). *Studies in human ecology.* New York: Harper.

**Thibaut, J. W., & Kelley, H. H.** (1959). *The social psychology of groups.* New York: John Wiley and Sons.

**Thin Elk, G.** (1991, February). *Red road therapy.* A workshop presented at Haskell Indian Nations University, Lawrence, KS.

**Thomas, A. K., & Loftus, E. F.** (2002). Creating bizarre false memories through imagination. *Memory and Cognition 30(3),* 423–431.

**Thomas, D.** (1979). *Naturalism and social science: A post empiricist philosophy of social science.* New York: Cambridge University Press.

**Thomas, P. E.** (2004). Toward the development of an integral approach to social work: Implications for human behavior theory and research. *Journal of Human Behavior in the Social Environment, 9(3),* 1–19.

**Thomas, R. M.** (1985). *Comparing theories of child development* (2nd ed.). Belmont, CA: Wadsworth.

**Thomas, R. M.** (1999). *Comparing theories of child development* (5th ed.). Belmont, CA: Wadsworth.

**Thomas, W. I.** (1923). *The unadjusted girl.* Boston: Little, Brown.

**Thomas, W. I., & Thomas, D. S.** (1928). *The child in America: Behavior problems and programs.* New York: Knopf.

**Thomas, W. I., & Znaniecki, F.** (1927). *The Polish peasant in Europe and America.* Boston: R. G. Badger.

**Thorndike, E. L.** (1931). *Human learning.* New York: The Century Co.

**Thyer, B. A.** (1988). Radical behaviorism and clinical social work. In R. A. Dorfman (Ed.), *Paradigms of clinical social work* (pp. 123–148). New York: Brunner/Mazel.

**Thyer, B. A.** (1994). Are theories for practice necessary? No! *Journal of Social Work Education, 30,* 147–151.

**Thyer, B. A.** (2001). What is the role of theory in research on social work practice? *Journal of Social Work Education, 37(1),* 9–25.

**Thyer, B. A.** (2002). Evidence-based practice and clinical social work. *Evidence-Based Mental Health, 5,* 6–7.

**Thyer, B. A., & Hudson, W. W.** (1987). Progress in behavioral social work: An introduction. *Journal of Social Service Research, 10(2/3/4),* 1–6.

**Tolman, E. C.** (1951). *Collected papers on psychology.* Berkeley: University of California Press.

**Tornstam, L.** (2005). *Gerotranscendence: A developmental theory of positive aging.* New York: Springer Publishing Company.

**Tornstam, L., & Tornqvist, M.** (2000). Nursing staff's interpretations of "gerotranscendence behavior" in the elderly. *Journal of Aging and Identity, 5(1),* 15–29.

**Torre, D.** (1985). *Empowerment: Structured conceptualization and instrument development.* Unpublished doctoral dissertation, Cornell University, New York.

**Torrey, E. F.** (1993). *Freudian fraud: The malignant effect of Freud's theory on American thought and culture.* New York: Harper Perennial.

**Towle, C.** (1965). *Common human needs* (Rev. ed.). Washington, DC: National Association of Social Workers.

**Trattner, W. I.** (1984). *From poor law to welfare state: A history of social welfare in America* (3rd ed.). New York: Free Press.

**Trebilcot, J.** (2002). Consciousness-raising. In L. Code, (Ed.) *Encyclopedia of feminist theories* (pp. 103–104). New York: Routledge.

**Trepangier, B.** (2006). *Silent racism: How well-meaning white people perpetuate the racial divide.* Boulder, CO: Paradigm Publishers.

**Triandis, Harry C.** (1990). Cross-cultural studies of individualism and collectivism. In J. J. Berman (Ed.), *Cross-cultural perspectives* (pp. 41–133). Lincoln: University of Nebraska Press.

**Tripodi, T., & Potocky-Tripodi, M.** (2007). *International social work research: Issues and Prospects.* New York: Oxford University Press.

**Troiden, R. R.** (1988). *Gay and lesbian identity: A sociological analysis.* New York: General Hall.

**Troiden, R. R.** (1989). The formation of homosexual identities. *Journal of Homosexuality, 17,* 43–73.

**Trotter, R. J.** (1986, August). Robert J. Sternberg: Three heads are better than one. *Psychology Today,* 56–62.

**Trout, P.** (2000). Shame. *National Forum, 80(4),* 3–7.

**Tucker, D.** (2005, Fall). TransAmerica. *FLM Magazine,* 38–39.

**Turner, J. H.** (1986). *The structure of sociological theory* (4th ed.). Chicago, IL: Dorsey.

**Turner, J. H., Singleton, R. S., Jr., & Musick, D.** (1987). *Oppression: A socio-history of black–white relations in America.* Chicago: Nelson-Hall.

**Tyson, K. B.** (1992). A new approach to relevant scientific research for practitioners: The heuristic paradigm. *Social Work, 37(6),* 541–555.

**Tyson, K.** (1995). *New foundations for scientific social and behavioral research: The heuristic paradigm.* Boston: Allyn & Bacon.

**Uba, L.** (1994). *Asian-Americans: Personality patterns, identity, and mental health.* New York: Guilford Press.

**Ungar, M.** (2002). A deeper, more social ecological social work practice. *Social Service Review, 76(3),* 480–497.

**U.S. Department of Commerce.** (1989). *Statistical abstract of the United States, 1989.* Washington, DC: U.S. Department of Commerce.

**Vaid, U.** (1995). *Virtual equality: The mainstreaming of gay and lesbian liberation.* New York: Anchor.

**Vaillant, G. E.** (1977). *Adaptation to life.* Boston: Little, Brown.

**Vaillant, G. E.** (1995). *The wisdom of the ego.* Cambridge, MA: Harvard University Press.

**Valentine, C. A.** (1968). *Culture and poverty: Critique and counter proposals.* Chicago: University of Chicago Press.

**Valeska, L.** (1981). The future of female separation. In C. Bunch & Quest Book Committee (Eds.), *Building feminist theory: Essays from Quest* (pp. 20–31). New York: Longman. Valian, V. (1999). *Why so slow?: The advancement of women.* Cambridge, MA: The MIT Press.

**Valle, R., & Halling, S. (Eds.).** (1989). *Existential-phenomenological perspectives in psychology: Exploring the breadth of human experience.* New York: Plenum Press.

**Van den Berge, P.** (1967). *Race and racism.* New York: Columbia Press.

**Van den Bergh, N. (Ed.).** (1995). *Feminist practice in the 21st Century.* Washington, DC: NASW Press.

**Van den Bergh, N., & Cooper, L. B. (Eds.).** (1986). *Feminist visions for social work.* Silver Spring, MD: National Association of Social Workers Press.

**van den Broek, P., & Thurlow, R.** (1991). The role and structures of personal narratives. *Journal of Cognitive Psychotherapy, 5,* 257–274.

**Vanfossen, B. E.** (1979). *The structure of social inequality.* Boston: Little, Brown.

**Van Hook, M., Hugen, B., & Aguilar, M. (Eds.).** (2001). *Spirituality within religious traditions in social work practice.* Pacific Grove, CA: Brooks/Cole.

**van Wormer, K.** (2004). *Confronting oppression, restoring justice: From policy analysis to social action.* Alexandria, VA: Council on Social Work Education.

**Verba, S.** (1978). *Caste, race and politics: A comparative study of India and the U.S. White Plains.* New York: Books Demand UMI.

**Verniest, L.** (2006). Allying with the Medicine Wheel: Social work practice with indigenous peoples. *Critical Social Work, 7(1).* Retrieved from http://cronus. uwindsor.ca/units/socialwork/critical.nsf/main/9979F6 E595E176DB8525717

**Vidich, A. J., & Bensman, J.** (1958). *Small town in mass society* (pp. 258–267, 272–284). Princeton, NJ: Princeton University Press. (Reprinted in *The search for community power* pp. 65–77, by W. D. Hawley & F. M. Wirt, Eds., 1968, Englewood Cliffs, NJ: Prentice-Hall, Inc.

**Vogel, L.** (1981). Marxism and feminism: Unhappy marriage, trial separation or something else? In L. Sargent (Ed.), *Women and revolution: A discussion of the unhappy marriage of Marxism and feminism* (pp. 195–217). Boston: South End.

**Vosler, N.** (1990). Assessing family access to basic resources: An essential component of social work practice. *Social Work, 35,* 434–441.

**Wachtel, P. L.** (1977). *Psychoanalysis and behavior therapy: Toward an integration.* New York: Basic Books.

**Wadsworth, B. J.** (1979). *Piaget's theory of cognitive development.* New York: Longman.

**Wagner, S. R.** (1996). *The untold story of the Iroquois influence on early feminists.* Aberdeen, SD: Sky Carrier Press.

**Wakefield, J. C.** (1996a). Does social work need the eco-systems perspective?: Part I. Is the perspective clinically useful? *Social Service Review, 70(1),* 1–32.

**Wakefield, J. C.** (1996b). Does social work need the eco-systems perspective?: Part 2. Does the perspective save social work from incoherence? *Social Service Review, 70(2),* 183–213.

**Wallace, W. L.** (1969). *Sociological theory.* Chicago: Aldine.

**Wallerstein, I.** (1974). *The modern world system: Capitalist agriculture and the origins of the European world economy in the 16th century.* New York: Academic Press.

**Wallerstein, I.** (1979). *The capitalist world economy.* London: Cambridge University Press.

**Wallis, J.** (1995). *The soul of politics: Beyond "religious right" and "secular left."* New York: Harcourt.

**Walsh, R., & Vaughan, F.** (1994). The worldview of Ken Wilber. *Journal of Humanistic Psychology, 34(2),* 6–21.

**Walter, J. L., & Peller, J. E.** (1992). *Becoming solution-focused in Brief therapy.* New York: Brunner-Mazel.

**Walz, T., & Canda, E. R.** (1988). Gross national consumption in the United States: Implications for third world development. *International Journal of Contemporary Sociology, 25(3/4),* 165–175.

**Walz, T., & Ritchie, H.** (2000).Gandhian principles in social work practice: Ethics revisited. *Social Work, 45(3),* 213–222.

**Warner, W. L., & Srole, L.** (1945). *The social systems of American ethnic groups.* New Haven: Yale University Press.

**Warner, M.** (1993). *Fear of a queer planet: Queer politics and social theory.* Minneapolis: University of Minnesota Press,

**Warne, R. R.** (2002). Theology, feminist. In L. Code (Ed.)., *Encyclopedia of Feminist Theories,* (pp. 471–473). New York: Routledge.

**Warnke, G.** (1987). *Gadamer: Hermeneutics, tradition, and reason.* Cambridge: Polity Press.

**Warren, K., Franklin, C., & Streeter, C. L.** (1996). New directions in systems theory: Chaos & complexity. *Social Work 43(4),* 357–372.

**Washburn, M.** (1994). *Transpersonal psychology in psychoanalytic perspective.* Albany: State University of New York Press.

**Washburn, M.** (1995). *The ego and the dynamic ground: A transpersonal theory of human development* (2nd ed.). Albany: State University of New York Press.

**Watson, J. B.** (1924). *Behaviorism.* New York: The People's Institute Publishing Co.

**Watson, J. B.** (1928). *Psychological care of infant and child.* New York: Norton.

**Watson, K. W.** (1994). Spiritual emergency: Concepts and implications for psychotherapy. *Journal of Humanistic Psychology, 34(2),* 22–45.

**Watzlawick, P., & Weakland, J. H.** (1977). *The interactional view.* New York: Norton.

**Weber, M.** (1948). *The Protestant ethic and the spirit of capitalism.* (T. Parsons, Trans.). New York: Charles Scribner's Sons.

**Webster, D. C., Vaughn, K., & Martinez, R.** (1994). Introducing solution-focused approaches to staff in inpatient psychiatric settings. *Archives of Psychiatric Nursing, 8,* 251–261.

**Weick, A.** (1983). A growth-task model of human development. *Social Casework 4,* 3.

**Weick, A., Rapp, C., Sullivan, P., & Kisthardt, W.** (1989). A strengths perspective for social work practice. *Social Work, 34(4),* 350–354.

**Weick, A., & Saleebey, D.** (1995). Supporting family strengths: Orienting policy and practice toward the 21st century. *Families in Society, 76(3),* 141–149.

**Weil, M. (Ed.).** (2005). *The handbook of community practice.* Thousand Oaks, CA: Sage Publications.

**Weinberg, M. S., Williams, C. J., & Pryor, D. W.** (1994). *Dual attraction: Understanding bisexuality.* New York: Oxford University Press.

**Weinberg, T. S. (Ed.).** (1995). *Studies in dominance and submission.* Amherst, NY: Prometheus Books.

**Wells, R. H.** (2003, May). Transcending gender: Relations of sexual power roles to gender roles. Masters thesis. Departments of Behavioral Science and Women's Studies, University of Houston, Clear Lake: Houston, TX.

**West, C., & Zimmerman, D. H.** (1987). Doing gender. *Gender & Society, 1(2),* 125–151.

**West, C.** (1995). Doing difference. *Gender and Society, 9(1),* 8–37.

**West, R., & Turner, L.** (2010). Symbolic interaction theory. In M. Ryan & K. Stevens (Eds.), *Introducing communication theory analysis and application* (pp. 76–91). New York: McGraw-Hill.

**Weston, K.** (1991). *Families we choose: Lesbians, gays, kinship.* New York: Columbia University Press.

**Wethington, E.** (2000). Expecting stress: Americans and the midlife crisis. *Motivation and Emotion, 24(2),* 85–103.

**White, M.** (1993). Commentary: The histories of the present. In S. Gilligan & R. Price (Eds.), *Therapeutic conversations* (pp. 121–135). New York: Norton.

**White, M.** (1994). *Narrative theory workshop.* Austin, TX.

**White, M., & Epston, D.** (1990). *Narrative means to therapeutic ends.* New York: Norton.

**White, M. B., & Tyson-Rawson, K. J.** (1995). Assessing the dynamics of gender in couples and families: The gendergram. *Family Relations, 44,* 253–260.

**White, R. W.** (1959). Motivation reconsidered: The concept of competence. *Psychological Review, 66,* 297–333.

**White, R. W.** (1963). *Ego and reality in psychoanalytic theory.* New York: International Universities Press.

**Whitfield, C. L.** (1996, July). *Traumatic memories of 50 adult survivors of child sexual abuse.* Paper presented at Trauma and Memory: An International Research Conference, Durham, NH.

**Whitmont, E. C.** (1969). *The symbolic quest: Basic concepts of analytical psychology.* Princeton, NJ: Princeton University Press.

**Wiener, N.** (1948). *Cybernetics or control and communication in the animal and the machine.* New York: John Wiley & Sons.

Wilber, K. (1983). *Eye to eye: The quest for a new paradigm.* Garden City, NY: Anchor Books.

Wilber, K. (1986). *A sociable God.* Boston: Shambhala.

Wilber, K. (1993). *Grace and grit: Spirituality and healing in the life and death of Treya Killiam Wilber.* Boston: Shambhala.

Wilber, K. (1996). *A brief history of everything.* Boston: Shambhala.

Wilber, K. (1998). *The marriage of sense and soul: Integrating science and religion.* New York: Random House.

Wilber, K. (1999). *One taste: The journals of Ken Wilber.* Boston: Shambhala.

Wilber, K. (2000a). *Sex, ecology, spirituality: The spirit of evolution* (Rev. ed.). Boston: Shambhala.

Wilber, K. (2000b). *Integral psychology: Consciousness, spirit, psychology, therapy.* Boston: Shambhala.

Wilber, K. (2001). *A theory of everything: An integral vision for business, politics, science and spirituality.* Boston: Shambhala.

Wilber, K. (2003a). *Waves, streams, states, and self—A summary of my psychological model.* Boston: Shambhala. Ken Wilber Online: http://wilber.shambhala.com/html/books/psych_model/psych_model1.cfm/

Wilber, K. (2003b). *The war in Iraq.* Boston: Shambhala. Ken Wilber Online: http://wilber.shambhala.com/html/misc/iraq.cfm/. Accessed March 15, 2005.

Wilber, K. (2006). *Integral spirituality: A startling new role for religion in the modern and postmodern world.* Boston: Integral Books.

Wilber, K. (2007). *The integral vision.* Boston: Shambhala.

Wilber, K., Engler, J., & Brown, D. P. (1986). *Transformations of consciousness: Conventional and contemplative perspectives on development.* Boston: Shambhala.

Wilber, K., Patten, T., Leonard, A., & Morelli, M. (2008). *Integral life practice.* Boston: Integral Books.

Wildavsky, A. B. (1964). *Leadership in a small town* (pp. 253–254, 267–275, 276–281). Totowa, NJ: Bedminster Press. (Reprinted in *The search for community power,* pp. 115–124, by W. D. Hawley & F. M. Wirt, Eds., 1968, Englewood Cliffs, NJ: Prentice-Hall.

Williams, J. H. (1977). *Psychology of women: Behavior in a biosocial context.* New York: Norton.

Williams, L. M. (1994). Recall of childhood trauma: A prospective study of women's memories of childhood sexual abuse. *Journal of Clinical and Consulting Psychology, 62,* 1167–1176.

Willie, C. V. (1979). *Caste and class controversy.* Dix Hills, NY: General Hall.

Wilson, W. J. (1980). *The declining significance of race: Blacks and changing American institutions.* Chicago: University of Chicago Press.

Wilson, W. J. (1987). *The truly disadvantaged; the inner city, the underclass, and public policy.* Chicago: University of Chicago Press.

Witkin, S. L. (1991). Empirical clinical practice: A critical analysis. *Social Work, 36(2),* 158–163.

Witkin, S. L., & Gottschalk, S. (1988). Alternative criteria for theory evaluation. *Social Service Review, 62(2),* 211–224.

Witkin, S. L., & Saleebey, D. (Eds.). (2007). *Social work dialogues: Transforming the canon in inquiry, practice, and education.* Alexandria, VA: Council on Social Work Education, Inc.

Wittig, M. (1992). One is not born a woman. *In The straight mind and other essays.* Boston: Beacon Press.

Wolff, J. (1991). Hermeneutics and sociology. In H. Etzkowitz & R. M. Glassman (Eds.), *The renascence of sociological theory: Classical and contemporary* (pp. 187–198). Itasca, IL: F. E. Peacock.

Wolpe, J., & Lazarus, A. A. (1966). *Behavior therapy techniques: A guide to the treatment of neurosis.* New York: Pergamon.

Wood, B. L. (1987). *Children of alcoholism: The struggle for self and intimacy in adult life.* New York: New York University Press.

Wood, S., & Lowes, R. (October 22, 2010). Psychiatrists dominate "doctor-dollars" database listing big pharma payments. *Medscape Medical News.* Retrived from http://www.medscape.com/viewarticle/731028

Worrell, J., & Remer, P. (1992). *Feminist perspectives in therapy: An empowerment model for women.* New York: John Wiley & Sons.

Wrightsman, L. S. (1988). *Personality development in adulthood.* Beverly Hills, CA: Sage.

Yip, K. (2004). A Chinese cultural critique of the global qualifying standards for social work education. *Social Work Education, 23(5),* 597–612.

Zastrow, C., & Kirst-Ashman, K. (2003). *Human behavior in the social environment* (6th ed.). Belmont, CA: Wadsworth.

Zinn, M. B., & Eitzen, D. S. (1993). *Diversity in families* (3rd ed.). New York: HarperCollins.

Zippay, A. (1995). The politics of empowerment. *Social Work, 40(2),* 263–267.

Zorbaugh, H. W. (1926). The natural areas of the city. *Publications of the American Sociological Society, 20,* 188–197.

Zurcher, L. A., Jr. (1983). *Social roles.* Beverly Hills, CA: Sage Publications.

# DISCOGRAPHY

Bobby Bridger. (1981). Heal in the wisdom. On *Heal in the Wisdom*. Independent Release. © Bobby Bridger, Stareyes Music (ASCAP).

Chris Chandler & Phil Rockstroh. (1992). Fast food confederacy. On *Introducing Chris Chandler: As Seen on No Television*. Flying Fish Records. © The Only People That Would (BMI).

Tom Dundee. (1991). A delicate balance. On *Rough Around the Edge*. Flight Records. © Thomas Dundee, Jack of Hearts Music (BMI).

Michael Elwood & Beth Galiger. (1992). Me & John Paul. On *Hemlock Smile: Live at La Casa*. Independent Release. © 1990, Michael Elwood.

Anne Feeney. (1994). Whatever Happened to the Eight-Hour Day? On *Heartland: Anne Feeney Live*. Super 88 Records. © Anne Feeney, 1992 (BMI).

Rex Foster and Rick Beresford. (1993). Hard Changing'. On *Believin': Rex Foster, Artist*. Agarita Records. 1993, Rex Foster/Sidestream Music (BMI), Rick Beresford/Mainsqueeze Music (BMI).

Tim Henderson. (1986). Children of Byzantium. On *Pawpaws*. Snake Hollow Records. © 1986. Snake Hollow Publishing.

Anne Hills (2008). Fired Up © 2008 Anne Hills (ASCAP), Raven Heart Music

Rod MacDonald. (1997). Timothy. On *And Then He Woke Up*. Gadfly Records. © 1997, Blue Flute Music (ASCAP).

Susan Martin, Jim Daniel, Bill Ward, and Allen Damron, (1991). Cease Fire. On *Family of Friends*. Purple Martin Productions. Independent Release. © 1991 (BMI).

Susan Martin. (1997). Shadow of the blues © 1997, Susan Martin (BMI), Purple Martin Music.

Bill Muse. (1996). Guy's song. On *2 Muses, Head First*. Independent release, and on *2 Muses, Reunite the Heart*. Independent Release. © 2 Muses Music, 1996 (ASCAP).

David Roth. (1993). Don't Should on Me. On *Rising in Love*. Folk Era Productions. Independent Release. © 1986, David Roth/Maythelight Music (ASCAP).

Hans Theessink. (1993). Rock the boat. On *Hans Theessink: Call Me*. Deluge Records. © Marvidic Music (BMI).

Bill Ward and Allen Damron (1992). Tears of the Lakota. On *Allen Damron, Silver*. Quahadi Records. © Bill Ward and Allen Damron, Post No Bills Music (BMI).

# NAME INDEX

# SUBJECT INDEX